MEDIEVAL TRADE

IN THE MEDITERRANEAN WORLD

RECORDS OF CIVILIZATION, SOURCES AND STUDIES

EDITED UNDER THE AUSPICES
OF THE DEPARTMENT OF HISTORY, COLUMBIA UNIVERSITY

GENERAL EDITOR

W. T. H. Jackson
Professor of German and History

PAST EDITORS

1915-1926
James T. Shotwell
*Bryce Professor Emeritus of the History
of International Relations*

1926-1953
Austin P. Evans
Late Professor of History

1953-1962
Jacques Barzun
Seth Low Professor of History

ROBERT S. LOPEZ was born in Genoa and received his education at the University of Milan and the University of Wisconsin. He has held Guggenheim and Fulbright fellowships and has taught at a number of universities in Italy and the United States. In 1946 he joined the history department at Yale, where he is now Durfee Professor of History and Chairman of Medieval Studies.

IRVING W. RAYMOND was educated at Columbia University, and taught ancient and medieval history there from 1920 to 1937. He then joined the faculty of Brooklyn College as Professor of Medieval History, where he remained until his death in 1964.

RECORDS OF CIVILIZATION
IN NORTON PAPERBACK EDITIONS

MEDIEVAL TRADE
IN THE
MEDITERRANEAN WORLD

Illustrative Documents
Translated with Introductions and Notes

by ROBERT S. LOPEZ

and IRVING W. RAYMOND

W · W · NORTON & COMPANY · INC · *New York*

CONTENTS

PART FIVE: TOOLS AND IDEAS

CONTENTS

MEDIEVAL TRADE
IN THE MEDITERRANEAN WORLD

INTRODUCTION

THIS IS THE first collection of documents dealing with all aspects of Mediterranean commerce in the Middle Ages to appear in translation in a modern language. That such a gap should have existed to this moment may be surprising. The feudal system is gone, and the Holy Roman Empire has perished. The quarrel between nominalists and realists has died out, and the word Crusade survives chiefly to label enterprises that have nothing to do with the Crusades. But it is easy for the layman to get firsthand information about these and other themes of the Middle Ages in translations of fundamental sources and even of minor documents. On the other hand, the corporate organization of modern business has its roots in the medieval partnerships, our bill of exchange is a direct descendant of the exchange contracts of the Middle Ages, and our accounting stems from ways contrived by early fourteenth-century Genoese merchant bankers. Yet commercial documents available in translation are exceedingly few and scattered. Of the greatest classic in the history of medieval trade—*La pratica della mercatura* by Francesco di Balduccio Pegolotti, a work which holds in its field as important a place as Bede, Villehardouin, or Machiavelli in other branches of history— no translation has ever been printed. Even the family name of the author is frequently confused with the name of his father.[1] If we turn to legal documents, we cannot find a single *collegantia* contract in English translation, although this type of contract is a milestone comparable in importance to the Magna Charta or the Concordat of Worms.

Even in the original there is no printed collection of documents dealing with all aspects of Mediterranean trade. If countless thousands have been

[1] Balducci is not Pegolotti's family name, as it would appear from call cards in many libraries, but the name of his father, Balduccio, stated in the genitive case. To be sure, many Tuscan family names have the same origin, witness Dante *Alighieri* (son of Alighiero). But ultimately one patronymic emerged as the permanent family name, and in the case of Pegolotti this had already happened before Francesco was born. His father already was known as Balduccio Pegolotti. The true title of the book also is not *La pratica della mercatura*, which was adopted by Pagnini, the scholar who first published Pegolotti's work, and by Allan Evans, who published a second, excellent edition. It is *Libro di divisamenti di pesi e di misure di mercatantie . . .*, the title continuing over four or five lines. The shorter title, however, may be regarded as fitting and is more convenient than the leisurely description originally used by the author. Allan Evans promised to publish a translation of the work but he has not, unfortunately, made good his promise.

published by scholars in all parts of the world, no scholar has hitherto attempted to cover all phases of commerce through a selection of significant examples drawn from a wide range of places and archives. Some two hundred documents have been selected and translated here for the first time. Some of them came from unpublished manuscript records. We hope that our book will be welcome notwithstanding its defects, and we bid for the indulgence usually bestowed upon pioneer works.

Our task was not easy. We had to pick a mere few out of an immense number of records in medieval Latin and Greek, in Italian (including its dialects), in Provençal (including its different shades from east to west), in Catalan, and in old French. Arabic sources we translated into English from German, French, Italian, or Spanish, for we are abashed to admit that we do not know that language. The special vocabulary and style of commercial documents presented problems which do not exist in literary Latin, Italian, or French of the Middle Ages. The larger part of our selections consists of matter-of-fact records such as notarial instruments, judicial acts, promissory notes, and samples of accounting. These, even today, though they may be more respectful of grammar or less redundant than many of their medieval predecessors, are reckless of stylistic beauty. So far as possible we have translated them fairly literally; it seemed more important to reproduce legal formulae faithfully than to make them palatable to the reader.[2] Savory, but informal and sometimes ungrammatical letters of businessmen called for colloquial English in the translation. The literary quality of some documents —the impassioned eloquence in the petition of the tottering Bonsignore company of merchant bankers, the poetical candor in Bonvesin della Riva's encomium of his city, the charm of far-away travel and adventure in Antoniotto Usodimare's letter to his creditors—demanded particular care. We have done our best, but we are aware of our shortcomings. Some documents, especially those of the earlier period, are riddles no scholar has yet been able to understand in every detail.

The two authors of this source book have worked in the manner of a medieval *societas ad dimidium*, an equal partnership of capital and work for an equal sharing of profit and losses. The original selection of the documents,

---

[2] We have, however, made a few exceptions to this rule. Modern punctuation and paragraphs have been adopted, and Roman numerals have been changed into Arabic figures except where it seemed interesting to show the promiscuous use of Roman and Arabic numerals in a period of transition and where both systems of numerals were used to insure accuracy of the figure, such as in orders of payment. For the sake of clarity and uniformity, the better-known names of moneys have usually been abbreviated, and figures often have been placed before instead of after the names of coins as they usually are in the text. In the Note on Coinage, Weights, and Other Technical Terms we give further details on the main principles followed in the translation.

including those hitherto unprinted, and the drafting of prefaces was made by Robert S. Lopez, whereas Irving W. Raymond has been responsible for the editing. Everything else has been a common venture, for which they bear joint and unlimited liability. In the short introductions and footnotes to the sources they have drawn freely from the works of those who first edited the original texts and from other books and articles, most of which are listed in the Bibliography. It was impossible to give full acknowledgments in each of the footnotes, but it is fitting that this introduction bear witness to the great debt owed those who have opened the field and first tilled its soil. The history of trade in the medieval Mediterranean has for the last hundred years or so been explored by an international team. The industry, if not always the insight, of German scholars was predominant at first. Then the Italians jumped to first place, closely followed by French scholars. Soon historians from other countries brought their contributions. It is comforting to see that the American contribution has grown very rapidly and is still growing. In the compilation of this work the authors have received generous assistance from a number of scholars, both in America and in Italy. Of the seventeen documents which have been translated from unprinted originals, three were contributed by Frederic C. Lane, Gino Luzzatto, and Florence de Roover. William H. Dunham, Robert L. Reynolds, Raymond de Roover, Armando Sapori, and Vito A. Vitale have given invaluable advice on a number of obscure documents. Mario E. Cosenza has helped straighten out certain involved Latin passages, Carl A. Boyer has made clearer the mathematics of Leonardo Fibonacci, and Adolf Berger has elucidated difficult points of Roman law. Nor must we forget to thank the staffs of the Yale and Columbia libraries, of the New York Public Library, and of the state archives at Genoa, Lucca, Milan, and Pisa for their helpfulness.

After completion of the work it is pleasant to think of the director of the collection, Austin Evans, and of the editor in charge, Christopher Herold, with gratitude unruffled by memory of past battles. They have been, as editors ought to be, in turn patient and wrathful, encouraging and intolerable. They have a share in the merits of the book and they are not to be blamed for the defects.

One of the problems we had to face was the classification of the material. Putting the documents side by side in chronological order would have been the easiest solution for us, but not for the reader. Very often we have not given the earliest example of a specific class of documents, but one which for some reason seemed more characteristic, clearer, or richer in detail. The date of the earliest extant document, at any rate, is not always significant.

'Law is born old,' Nino Tamassia, the late Italian legal historian, used to say. Maitland in England and Marc Bloch in France have issued similar warnings. When a formula or expression first appears in a notarial instrument, it usually means that it has long been used in unwritten custom. Furthermore, the preservation of commercial documents has been subject to special hazards. Their value in most cases did not outlast the transaction for long; indeed, the proof that an obligation was ended was usually signalized by destroying the original instrument. It was only gradually that the state, the municipality, or the gild ordered notarial minutes, commercial ledgers, and bankers' books to be preserved. Their efforts were often thwarted by fire, mice, bookworms, plunderers, and those other accidents which, happily or unhappily, lighten the burden of historians by reducing the amount of material in the archives. Formal documents, of course, had a better chance of survival than informal papers. Preservation was most likely in towns which fully recognized the importance of business, such as Genoa, Florence, or Marseilles. Finally, let us add that a litigation, a bankruptcy, or a protest often helped to bring to light secrets hitherto jealously guarded, and to transfer to permanent files records which otherwise would have been destroyed after the transaction was completed. This, incidentally, is why the present book may reflect a gloomier picture of medieval business than is warranted, just as modern newspapers give their headlines to the exceptional murderous husbands and forget the long-suffering and the loving ones.

The only rough chronological division we have thought convenient to make was between the early and later Middle Ages, that is, before or after the beginning of the Commercial Revolution which in some places began as early as the tenth century or perhaps earlier, but in others was not noticeable until the twelfth or the thirteenth.[3] We have grouped in the first section all documents relating to the earlier period. They are few, not because we believe that trade all but ceased in the early Middle Ages, but because most of the evidence consists of incidental references, too short or too indirect to

---

[3] Should any reader who is not familiar with periodization in economic history wonder why the term Commercial Revolution has been adopted, and why it is extended to cover such a long period, let him read the opening pages of *Cambridge Economic History*, Vol. II, Chap. IV, Sect. 2: 'The Commercial Revolution.' It is generally recognized that the far-reaching transformations in the volume of trade, in the methods of business, and in the spirit of merchants which took place during the later Middle Ages, as well as the political, social, and intellectual changes which were connected with them, deserve to be called a commercial revolution even as economic changes and their effects since the mid-eighteenth century have been called an industrial revolution. All economic revolutions are by definition slow and gradual—so are political revolutions if one takes into account the gathering of the storm as well as the violent explosion—and the medieval revolution, which traveled at the pace of mules, barges, and freighters, was perforce slower than the revolution of railroads, steamboats, and planes.

warrant inclusion in a source book of this kind. Broad topics, rather than any specific period, give unity to the other sections of this book. It must be borne in mind, however, that no classification would suit all readers. The legal historian will find business contracts elsewhere than in the section especially devoted to them; the historian of commercial techniques will find accounting materials outside the section on accounting; descriptions of merchandise and details of transportation are scattered throughout the book. In fact, most documents have been chosen from those which illustrate more than one point. Only a perusal of the Index can give a fair idea of the contents.

Division by broad topics made it easier for us to give some continuity to a story told by documents drawn from more than a hundred different publications and from originals in four or five archives. To fill some gaps and to make the text clearer to the layman we have written short introductions in addition to the footnotes. Longer commentaries would certainly have been useful, but they would have transformed the book into a general history of Mediterranean commerce. This we did not wish to do. Our views in this field have been expressed elsewhere, especially in R. S. Lopez's chapter in the *Cambridge Economic History*, Volume II, and in I. W. Raymond's chapters in his and R. D. Skinner's forthcoming *Traditions of European History*. These views obviously have influenced the selection and inspired the introductions and footnotes. However, we have endeavored to avoid pronouncements in controversial matters, since we could not support our views except in long discussions. Pointing out that an issue was controversial often seemed all that was needed in the way of a warning. Let the reader form his own judgment with the assistance of the books we have indicated in each disputed case.[4]

It was obviously impossible to present a complete picture of the world of medieval business in two hundred documents and excerpts, no matter how carefully selected. The reader, it is hoped, will not look for what is missing but for what is included, keeping in mind that the perspective of a scholar in commercial law and that of a specialist in history of gilds are different; a compromise had to be adopted to leave each of them at least partially satisfied. We have tried to give a comprehensive idea not only of the principal aspects and problems connected with the history of commerce but also of the different kinds of sources from which information can be drawn. We have neglected no representative town or area in the Western Mediterranean

---

[4] These references do not pretend to be complete. The extensive bibliographies of the *Cambridge Economic History*, Vol. II, should be consulted.

and its hinterland (that is, all of Italy, Provence, Languedoc, Catalonia, Dalmatia, and, to a slighter extent, regions further inland), and we have followed the citizens of these areas wherever they went for trade.[5] We have also explored, so far as the scanty documentation permitted, the non-Romance countries of the Eastern and Southern Mediterranean.[6]

We had to make a number of deliberate omissions. These were determined primarily by the availability of translations and analyses in English, for we wanted no duplications in a field where so little has been done so far. To our knowledge, all but four of our documents have never appeared in English before.[7] We were only too happy when the work of one of our predecessors saved us the trouble of translating other records of the same kind. Thus, to give only a few instances, we have included no excerpts from the Soranzo or the Medici account books, no sea loans from the books of Amalric of Marseilles, comparatively few documents on Catalan banking and commercial papers, little on shipping, and nothing on the popes and on the Spanish and Byzantine Jews. Nor have we translated any of the English Rolls or any of the writings of medieval travelers in the Near and Far East. The works of Richard Brown, Florence de Roover, Cave and Coulson, Abbott Usher, William Lunt, Lionel Isaacs, and Joshua Starr as well as the analyses and translations of Ashburner, Byrne, Reynolds, Lane, and Gras, the Rolls Series, and the Hakluyt and Pilgrims' Societies give sufficient material in English. To fill, at least in part, what otherwise would have been gaps, we have included, whenever possible, sources dealing with like subjects, which had not yet been made available in our language.

Certain omissions[8] we deeply regret, but we had no other choice. We have excluded official documents such as commercial treaties, royal and

---

[5] The number of documents from each town, however, is not always in proportion to the importance of the town. For instance, Piacenza, Bologna, Ragusa (Dubrovnik), Ibiza, and Almeria do not receive adequate representation because few private commercial documents from these cities have so far appeared in print.

[6] There is ample evidence that private commercial documents were made in profusion in Byzantine and Muslim territory, but very few have survived and have been published.

[7] One is the Byzantine *Book of the Prefect*, which was too important to be omitted. Our translation was freshly made from the original and differs in several points from those already published. Another document, an interesting Genoese freight contract, was published in Vol. I of Columbia's *Introduction to Contemporary Civilization in the West* (New York, 1946), pp. 79–82, in a translation by R. S. Lopez (the name of the translator does not appear in that volume). The new translation follows the original more closely than would have been advisable in a book destined primarily for college freshmen. We also have made a new translation of an excerpt of Ibn Khurradadhbah on the Rhadanite Jews and of one of Pegolotti on travel to China because both were particularly interesting and each was unique in its field.

[8] Some omissions, however, are justified by other considerations. For instance, accounts written by pilgrims are seldom reliable as sources of information on trade. Moreover, Catalan private banks were far less important than similar banks in Italy, despite the impression which less

municipal decrees, gild statutes and the like,[9] and we have offered no selections on economic and legal theories, either religious or secular. These groups of sources present characteristics of their own which distinguish them from writings by merchants and for merchants. Their number and bulk are such that, had we included them, they would have taken up half of the book and caused the other half to be grossly inadequate. We had to decide whether we should present the business world as rulers and doctrinaires wanted it to be or whether we should show it as it actually was in its daily routine. We chose the second projection, not only because it is closer to reality, but also because official documents and economic theories have been analyzed and expounded in many works in English.

For another peculiarity of this source book we have no apologies to offer. Italian documents greatly outnumber those of other areas. This is as it should be. Italy north of the Tiber was so far ahead of the other nations in all fields of commercial activity that it would have been possible to give a panorama by using Genoese or Florentine documents exclusively. Moreover, a larger number of records from Italian cities has been preserved in the archives and published in scholarly editions. Materials from other regions have not been selected to show activities absent in northern and central Italy, but most frequently to indicate to what extent 'commercialization' affected these regions as the Commercial Revolution reached them. One of the purposes of our book is to bring home this fundamental point: all investigations of medieval commerce must have as their focus the leading towns of Italy, even as all research on the origins of the Industrial Revolution must center on England. So much has been said about the military and legal exploits of the Italians in the days of Rome and about their literary and artistic production during the Renaissance and after that the man in the street is led to forget another gift of that gifted nation to the modern world— the creation, in the later Middle Ages, of the prototype of the modern commercial economy.

---

careful readers may have gotten from A. P. Usher's *The Early History of Deposit Banking in Mediterranean Europe*, Vol. I, in which, even when dealing with deposit banking in general, he uses Spanish illustrations more often than Italian ones.

[9] This rule, too, has its exceptions. We have published a few semiofficial documents when they embodied petitions and other utterances by merchants, or when there was no other way to show an important aspect of business.

NOTE ON COINAGE, WEIGHTS, AND OTHER TECHNICAL TERMS

IN THE GENERAL INTRODUCTION we have outlined the main principles followed in the translation. Introductory notes to individual sections or selections and footnotes are aimed at clarifying points of detail and at giving explanations of words and sentences which do not seem to have a good equivalent in English. It remains for us here to state briefly how we have dealt with a number of technical problems that recurred throughout the book.

We have retranslated Latinized family and place names into the vernacular of the country of their origin, and we have reconverted into the original vernacular names which had been translated into foreign vernaculars. However, when there was doubt as to how a name may have sounded originally, we have kept the form of the document. Likewise, we have rendered the Latin titles *dominus* and *domina* by 'lord,' 'signore,' or 'sire' and by 'lady,' 'signora,' or 'dame' when they referred to persons of princely blood or to government officials, but by 'Mr.,' 'ser' (or 'messer'), or 'sieur' and by 'Mrs.,' 'monna,' or 'madame' when they seemed to refer to commoners. It was difficult, however, to be consistent throughout the book because the documents themselves are not always consistent and the distinction between commoners and noblemen, private citizens and public officials, is not always sharply defined. We have translated legal terms whenever a reasonably close English equivalent existed, but we have refrained from translating such terms as *commenda* and *compagnia* which designate contracts peculiar to the Middle Ages or to the Mediterranean world. For the same reason we have sometimes used certain words in obsolete meanings (for example, 'companion' or 'messenger'), which transliterated rather than translated Latin or Romance words, in preference to more familiar modern words which would have conveyed the wrong impression that the legal meaning of the term was the same as today. For discussion of quaint legal terms and unusual commodities we refer specifically to the introductory notes, to the footnotes, and, especially, to the documents of Part Three.

Coins, weights, and measures are virtually untranslatable because they have varied according to places and times, and none of them has remained

unchanged down to our days. Our original plan to give between brackets a
comparison with modern American monetary and metrological standards
proved unfeasible. Medieval metrology, notwithstanding the efforts of a
few pioneers, is largely an unexplored field. Medieval numismatics has
been investigated more fully, but the problems connected with coinage,
moneys of account, and credit money are particularly complex and controversial.[1]

In regard to weights and measures we are not in a position to make any
safe generalizations. Many years ago a French scholar, Guilhiermoz, advanced the theory that all metrological systems down to the metric decimal
system—which unfortunately has not been adopted in the United States as it
has been in nearly all other civilized nations—stem from the system of
ancient Mesopotamia. It is a challenging idea, but it has not been tested with
a sufficient number of detailed studies. To be sure, we observe that in every
country the parts of the human body (inches, feet, cubits, and arms) have
supplied the basis for measures of length, and that their multiples often have
borrowed the names of familiar objects (such as the rod or cane) or have
coincided with units of agricultural exploitation (such as the furlong) and
with numbers of footsteps (such as the mile, originally a thousand paces).
But the foot (*pes, piede, pied*) as a unit of length has varied from about 25 to
more than 50 centimeters; the ell and the cubit (*ulna, alla,* or *aune; cubito* or
coudée) also have varied; their multiples have been still more diverse from
country to country. Likewise, practically every container, bundle, pack, and
cartload has been a basis for measures of capacity, but the absolute size of
the 'sack' or the 'cart,' taken as a standard, has varied.

Nearly all systems of weights have been derived from the Roman pound or
libra (of about 327 grams at the time of Constantine I, but of other weights at

---

[1] The best general work on medieval metrology still is P. Guilhiermoz, 'Note sur les poids du
moyen âge,' *Bibliothèque de l'Ecole des Chartes*, LXVII (1906), 161-233, 402-50, and Bibliography. See also his later article, 'Remarques diverses sur les poids et mesures du moyen âge,'
ibid., LXXX (1919), 5-100.

Works on medieval numismatics—that is, external descriptions of coins—are too numerous
for listing. The following can be used for first reference: A. Luschin von Ebengreuth, *Allgemeine
Münzkunde und Geldgeschichte des Mittelalters und der neueren Zeit;* A. Engel and R. Serrure,
Traité de numismatique du moyen âge; E. Martinori, *La moneta;* F. Friedensburg, *Münzkunde und
Geldgeschichte der Einzelstaaten des Mittelalters und der neueren Zeit.*

There are no general works on the economic history of coinage and moneys of account. The
following monographs may be of help on specific points and include bibliographical references:
A. Evans, 'Some Coinage Systems of the Fourteenth Century,' *Journal of Economic and Business
History*, III (1931), 481-96; H. van Werveke, 'Monnaie de compte et monnaie réelle,' *Revue Belge
de Philologie et d'Histoire*, XIII (1934), 123-52; C. M. Cipolla, *Studi di storia della moneta*, Vol. I;
R. S. Lopez, 'The Dollar of the Middle Ages,' *Journal of Economic History*, XI (1951), 209-34;
P. Grierson, *Numismatics and History;* R. S. Lopez, *Il ritorno all'oro nell'Occidente du ecentesco.*

other periods), which was divided into ounces, scruples, and grains. However, both the weight of the pound and the number of its subdivisions have continuously varied. Guilhiermoz, who insists on the fact that 'the prime basis for all weights used in [medieval] Europe was the Roman ounce,' lists both pounds and marks (a smaller unit than the pound), varying from 186 to 550 grams and containing from 6 to 18 ounces each. Every government, that of the emperor as well as that of the smallest town, endeavored to enforce common standards according to models which were preserved in public buildings. Some of these standards have come down to us and can be actually measured. But there would be no end to the listing of the local varieties. In the case of nearly every medieval measure either we do not know its equivalent in modern terms, or scholars disagree about it, or the same name was applied to several units of different value. Let those who regard the anarchy of medieval metrology as an intolerable handicap to commerce consider that we still have the avoirdupois pound and the troy pound, both of medieval origin, besides the metric decimal system; and let them also consider that the American geographical or nautical mile is slightly different from the British geographical mile and considerably different from the statute mile and the kilometer.

The same basic standards of weight which have been used in weighing merchandise have also supplied a base for the monetary system. Medieval currencies and monetary problems, which have seemed hopelessly confused to scholars in the late nineteenth and early twentieth centuries, should not be too confusing to us. Before the First World War most modern states had stable monetary standards, permitted their citizens to convert bullion into coin and banknotes into gold and silver, and allowed all persons to transfer precious metals and coins, banknotes, and money orders from one country to another. Today, however, practices reminding one of the Middle Ages have emerged in the larger part of the world. Most states have repeatedly devalued their currency, forbidden their citizens to hoard or to export precious metals and foreign currencies, and required all persons to accept the national currency at an official rate which seldom corresponds to the quotation in the free market. Modern inflation, of course, differs from medieval debasement—first of all, because the layman now cannot detect overissue of banknotes as easily as he then could notice alterations of the coined metal. Governmental controls are perhaps wiser and probably more efficient than they were in the Middle Ages, but inefficiency, to some extent, made even an unwise control less oppressive.

Nearly all of the innumerable monetary systems of account in medieval

Western Europe were based upon the following theoretic equivalence: £1 = s. 20 = d. 240— where '£' stands for 'pound' (*libra, lira, livre,* etc.), 's.' for 'shillings' (*solidi, soldi, sols,* etc.), and 'd.' for 'pence' (*denarii, denari,* etc.). This equivalence was established by Charlemagne for reasons which need not be explained here. It is still the basis of the English monetary system. In the time of Charlemagne and long thereafter the series did not consist exclusively of real coins but was based upon one real coin, the denier of fine silver, and upon its imaginary multiples (moneys of account). Just as today we speak of hundreds, thousands, millions, and billions, although all our coins are smaller than a hundred dollars and none of our banknotes is valued at one million or one billion dollars, even so in the tenth century a merchant spoke of shillings and pounds although the largest coin was the denier and there were usually other coins worth half a denier (*obolus,* medal, etc.) and a quarter of a denier (*pogesa,* farthing, etc.). To pay one pound, a merchant gave 240 deniers in coin or 480 obols in coin, just as today a businessman would pay a hundred dollars by giving a number of bills or coin of smaller denominations. The breakup of the Carolingian Empire permitted each of the states that succeeded it to establish its own standards for the denier, but this did not alter the theoretic equivalence of the denier to moneys of account. Today a Swiss franc, a Belgian franc, and a French franc have different values, but a million francs in each of these countries means the same number of basic units. Likewise, the Venetian denier and the Milanese denier differed in value, but there were twelve deniers to a shilling and 240 deniers to a pound, the shilling and the pound being moneys of account.

What complicated the problem was not so much the existence of many states with their different standards, but the fact that each state simultaneously used different coins of different weights and alloys. The old denier gradually became a black coin, containing little silver and a large proportion of base metals. At the side of this petty denier, the groat denier of finer silver and, later, the gold denier were issued. There are indications that originally each state wanted the better coins to pass as multiples of the petty denier. If that had been possible, the new coins would have fitted snugly into the old system of accounting pegged to the petty denier. But no fixed ratio between different coins could long endure, however much the governments endeavored to maintain it. First of all, the ratio between gold, silver, and billon (the alloy of silver and of base metals which was used for the petty denier) was subject to the fluctuations in value of precious metals in the free market. Moreover, debasement continued in all types of coins, and it did not proceed at the same rate in each type. While each government endeavored to hold stable the weight and purity of the gold coin, it debased rapidly the silver coin and still more rapidly the billon coin.

Therefore it became necessary to build independent systems of account based on each coin. One system was pegged to the petty denier or *piccolo:* £1 petty (imaginary) = s. 20 petty (imaginary) = d. 240 petty (real coins). Another system was pegged to the groat or *grosso:* £1 groat (imaginary) = s. 20 groat (imaginary) = d. 240 groat (real coins). A third system was pegged to the gold coin, but because of its high value that coin was reckoned as a pound and not as a denier, and it received different names in different places: 1 gold florin (or ducat, *genovina* or genoin, ambrosin, etc.) = s. 20 gold (imaginary) = d. 240 gold (imaginary). Merchants chose one or another system according to custom or convenience. In addition, merchants were sometimes driven to adopt entirely artificial systems of accounting by the fact that governments often attempted to freeze the ratio between one coin and another. Thus, for instance, the Florentine government in 1271 decreed that a florin (real coin) should be exchanged for £1 s. 9 petty (imaginary), that is to say, for d. 348 petty (real coins). The ratio soon became untenable because the denier petty continued to sink, but merchants continued to use a system of accounting in pound, shillings, and deniers by the florin (*a fiorino*), none of which corresponded to a real coin but all of which were pegged to the florin through the legal ratio of 1 florin = £29/20 *a fiorino*. Similar causes gave rise to the Venetian system of accounting by the groat, and to many other systems.

Not all countries and cities adopted all of these systems of accounting. Genoese merchants, for instance, found it simpler to use a single system pegged to the groat, all other coins being reckoned according to their worth in groats. On the other hand, the equivalence £1 = s. 20 = d. 240 was used only for systems of account and for coins stemming from the Carolingian Empire. The Byzantine Empire had its own system, based upon the equivalence of 1 gold bezant (or hyperper, as the coin was later called) = 12 silver *miliarisia* = 24 silver *keratia* (karats), an equivalence which also influenced the Venetian system in which the ratio between the gold ducat and the silver denier groat was for a long time 1/24. The Muslim states had their own systems, usually based on the equivalence of 1 gold dinar (denier) = 10 silver dirhams (drachmas), an equivalence which influenced the Genoese system in which the ratio between the gold genoin and the silver shilling (imaginary) originally was 1/10. Byzantine and Muslim coinages underwent much the same developments as did those in the West. Coins were debased, the ratio between gold and silver fluctuated, and many independent systems of accounting pegged to one or another coin arose. Detailed description of these systems would take more space than we can afford here.

Moreover, we must take into consideration the fact that when a coin was debased, older coins having the same denomination but a higher weight and alloy did not disappear from circulation. Some governments, such as the Byzantine, made no attempt to withdraw older coins; other governments, such as the French, endeavored to do so but met with only partial success. Furthermore, not all coins of the same type and issue had identical weight because medieval techniques of striking coins were not efficient enough to produce uniform specimens and because wear made a coin thinner. Therefore it was often necessary for a merchant to specify the issue and the condition of the coins he intended to receive in payment. For instance, in the early fourteenth century twelve different types of hyperpers circulated simultaneously. Merchants either demanded payment in coins of one specified type (e.g., 'hyperpers kneeling,' coins of an issue which portrayed a kneeling emperor, and 'hyperpers Palaeologate,' issued by Michael VIII Palaeologus) or they accepted all types by the weight and alloy according to specified standards (e.g., 'hyperpers by the assay of Pera,' that is, according to the standard which assayers in Pera would regard as regular, and 'hyperpers by the weight of Chios,' that is, according to the weight which was approved in Chios). To simplify the operation of checking coins, especially when a merchant wanted the best coins available in the market, bankers and governments eventually resorted to the system of enclosing florins and other valuable coins in sealed bags. The color of the sealing wax indicated the standard of the coins in the bag, and that standard was rigorously controlled to guarantee uniformity.

This leads us to the functions of banks and other agents of credit. No long discussion of this subject is necessary here, because credit and credit money will be described in special sections of this book, and because the history of finance as such is not within the scope of the book. Let us only point out that credit money played a very important role at the side of hard coinage. It enabled merchants to carry on an ever-increasing amount of business in an age that possessed an inadequate stock of coins. While any person might occasionally extend credit, three classes of businessmen became specialized dealers in money.[2] Pawnbrokers and other petty usurers often lent to

---

[2] R. de Roover, *Money, Banking and Credit in Mediaeval Bruges,* though dealing chiefly with Flanders, gives a good picture which largely applies to the Mediterranean world as well and contains full bibliographical information. Inasmuch as the development of credit in northern Europe was later than in southern Europe, the book ought to be supplemented with G. Luzzatte, *Storia economica d'Italia,* Vol. I, Chap. VIII, and its Bibliography.

merchants, but their main field of activity was consumers' credit. More important were the money changers (*campsores, cambiatori, changeurs,* etc.) and the merchant-bankers (the partners and agents of merchant companies). The latter will be given due attention in this book because they were concerned with commerce as well as with banking and, in fact, they were seldom described as bankers (*bancherii, banchieri, trapeʒitai*) in medieval documents. Their methods in extending credit did not differ from those of the other merchants. The changers, on the other hand, often engaged in commerce, but their main business consisted in changing money and in keeping deposit banks, variously described as *bancum, tabula, mensa nummularia, banco di scritta,* etc. We shall meet changers and deposit banks in many sections of this book, but we cannot devote to them the same attention as we have to merchants in a stricter sense.

We have little hope that this lengthy note has wholly eliminated the confusion which many readers will feel when coming across monetary terms, but we hope that at least the reasons for the confusion have been clarified.[3]

---

[3] Someone may wish to know the *original* weight of the principal gold coins mentioned in this note. That of the bezant was approximately 4·55 grams of fine gold, that of the dinar was almost the same, and that of the florin was approximately 3·53 grams of fine gold. The American gold dollar weighs 1·6718 grams. But it would be very incautious indeed to draw comparisons based upon metallic weights. The purchasing power of gold has changed very greatly, and it is now a small fraction of what it was in the Middle Ages.

PART ONE

At the Origins of the Commercial Revolution

THE SOURCES OF medieval trade before the tenth century are poverty itself. Indeed, there are practically no commercial documents of the eighth and ninth centuries. Nor do the chroniclers and historians of that period pay much attention to economic developments. Legal sources reflect the spirit of a civilization based upon agriculture. Occasional mention of traders in agrarian documents, scattered remarks of chroniclers and of hagiographers, and incidental references to commerce in law books whet our appetite for knowledge but do not satisfy it. In the absence of adequate sources, widely different evaluations of the importance, amount, and character of trade have developed, ranging from the extreme pessimism of Henri Pirenne to the extreme optimism of Alfons Dopsch.[1] Historians today have tended to avoid either extremity, but there is little hope of a definitive solution ever being reached.[2]

The selections that follow show some specimens of surviving materials, but obviously they do not present a well-balanced picture of the period.[3] It seemed improper to include in this source book those fleeting and obscure references which are of great help to the specialist, but which have little meaning for the general reader.

[1] See especially H. Pirenne, *Mohammed and Charlemagne;* A. Dopsch, *Wirtschaftliche und soziale Grundlagen der europäischen Kulturentwicklung.*

[2] A middle-of-the-road solution has been advocated. Among others, consult R. S. Lopez, 'Lights and Shadows in Early Medieval Trade,' in the *Cambridge Economic History,* II, 257ff. The Bibliography at the end of that volume lists the most important works on the subject.

[3] We have omitted all Carolingian capitularies dealing with trade, both because it has been doubted whether they had practical enforcement in the Mediterranean regions and because many of them have been translated in full or in part in R. C. Cave and H. H. Coulson, *A Source Book for Medieval Economic History.*

CHAPTER I

COMMERCE IN THE BYZANTINE EMPIRE, THE MUSLIM EAST, AND THE CATHOLIC WEST

Commercial Gilds and Control of Trade in Constantinople

It seems fitting to begin our collection with the Byzantine Empire, which transmitted an unbroken commercial tradition from the old classical world to the doorstep of the modern ages. Yet it must be pointed out that written sources of Byzantine trade in the eighth and ninth centuries are even more inadequate than the sources of Western trade. To be sure, the commercial prosperity of East Rome is forcefully, if indirectly, demonstrated by objects in museums and by writings describing the political, military, and economic might of the Empire. But except for a few passages in legal sources and for scattered information in political histories and literary works, documents of Byzantine trade of that period have not come down to us. One of the few sources is the famous *Book of the Prefect* promulgated by Leo VI in 911 or 912 but including later interpolations undoubtedly based upon customs or laws of preceding centuries.

The *Book of the Prefect* (Documents 1 and 2) is a collection of regulations governing essential private gilds in Constantinople. It has been translated twice into English and twice into other languages.[1] We believe, however, that there is still need of a new translation taking into account recent studies in Byzantine administration and trade. The passages selected do not cover the entire field—the *Book of the Prefect* itself is far from furnishing a panorama—but they give illustrations of one of the gilds connected with the famed Byzantine silk industry, and of the control over imports and exports exercised by imperial officials. The Prefect of the City was the highest official in charge of economic affairs in the Byzantine capital.[2]

[1] Namely, the English translations by A. E. R. Boak, 'The Book of the Prefect,' *Journal of Economic and Business History*, I (1929), 597–619, and by E. H. Freshfield, *Roman Law in the Later Roman Empire*. Then there are Latin and French translations by Jules Nicole in 'Le Livre du préfet ou L'Edit de l'empereur Léon le Sage sur les corporations de Constantinople,' *Mémoires de l'Institut National Genevois*, XVIII (1893), 1–100; this volume also contains the Greek text on which our translation is based.

[2] Modern commentaries on the *Book of the Prefect* are too numerous to list in full. Consult

I

Book of the Prefect vi. 31–33
From the Greek[3]

[Constantinople, 911 or 912]

CONCERNING RAW-SILK DEALERS[4]

1. The raw-silk dealers are not to exercise another craft [in addition to their own], but they are to practice their own publicly in the place established for them. And whoever does not do so is to be beaten, shaved, and banished.

2. A raw-silk dealer who engages a journeyman[5] is not to make a contract for a duration longer than one month, nor is he to pay salary in advance for longer than thirty working days, but [he is to pay] only for what the journeyman can accomplish by working the whole month. Whoever pays a salary for more than the appointed period is to lose this [extra amount].

3. A raw-silk dealer is not to engage the journeyman of another before the journeyman has accomplished the work he undertook for his [previous] salary. Whoever does otherwise is to be fined the amount of the [unearned] salary.

4. [The raw-silk dealers] are to pay only one *keration*[6] in each hundred-weight to the exarchs [of the gild].[7] Whoever possesses scales or weights[?][8] not marked with the seal of the Prefect is to be beaten and shaved.

5. Those who come to the *mitata* from outside[9] with raw silk are not to

---

bibliographies in G. Ostrogorsky's review of C. Zoras's 'Le corporazioni bizantine,' *Byzantin-ische Zeitschrift*, XXXIII (1933), 389–95, and in G. I. Bratianu, 'Les Etudes byzantines d'histoire économique et sociale,' *Byzantion*, XIV, 2 (1939), 497–511. Additional references are found in R. S. Lopez, 'Silk Industry in the Byzantine Empire,' *Speculum*, XX (1945), *passim*. On the date of the extant manuscript of the *Book of the Prefect* see now R. S. Lopez, 'La Crise du besant au X° siècle et la date du Livre du Préfet,' in *Mélanges Henri Grégoire*, II, 403–18.

[3] See note 1.   [4] *Metaxopratai*, from *metaxa*, 'raw silk.'

[5] *Misthotos*, literally, 'salaried men.'

[6] We accept Nicole's emendation of *kagkelarion* to *keration*. It is borne out by the testimony of Pegolotti, *La pratica della mercatura*, ed. Evans, p. 44: 'And each party pays a karat per hundredweight of every merchandise which is weighed by the hundredweight.' The passage escaped Nicole's attention. A *keration* or karat was a silver coin, equal to half a silver *miliarision* or to one twenty-fourth of a gold nomisma. A nomisma, later called *hyperperon*, 'hyper-pure,' contained a little more than 4½ grams of pure gold if it was not debased.

[7] One of the titles borne by provosts of Byzantine gilds was exarch; there were others. See R. Lopez, 'Silk Industry,' p. 21, note 1.

[8] *Bolia*, a term which recalls *boulle*, 'bull,' 'seal,' coming immediately after in the text. But the meaning 'wrappings,' may also be suggested if *bolia* can be related to *volia* or *vogia*, often used in this meaning in later Western sources.

[9] On the meaning of *apo ton exothen* and of the expression *exotikoi*, 'outsiders,' see Lopez, 'Silk Industry,' p. 21ff. It may refer to foreign lands only, or it may include the Byzantine provinces as opposed to the capital. The *mitata* were special lodgings for outside merchants.

pay duties[10] except for rent and lodgings.[11] Likewise, those who buy [from them] are not to be asked to pay duties.

6. Whoever is going to be admitted to [the gild of] the raw-silk dealers must obtain the testimony of honorable and reliable men in regard to his good reputation. Then, upon giving two nomismata to the gild,[12] he is to be enrolled.

7. If a raw-silk dealer wants to put his slave in his place in his business, he is to be jointly [liable] with him, assuming the risk if [the slave] should do something wrong.

8. The entire community of the gild at the time of the market[13] is to make a deposit, each member according to his means. And the apportionment is to be effected acccording to the deposit of each member.[14]

9. If a rich [raw-silk dealer] who has bought from outsiders must sell [silk] to others who are poorer, he is to take a profit of only one ounce per nomisma.[15]

10. If a raw-silk dealer deals in silk under his own name for a powerful or rich man or even a cloth maker,[16] and does so for a salary, he is to be beaten and shaved and expelled from the gild.

11. Whoever embezzles the earnest given him for the purchase of silk and raises its price is to be fined the amount of that earnest.

12. If a raw-silk dealer is caught traveling[17] to buy silk, he is to be expelled from the gild.

---

[10] *Pratikia* are probably the ten-percent customs duty usually paid on all imports and exports. The duty was lifted in this particular case in order to stimulate imports.

[11] *Enoikia* and *mone* are practically synonymous, but here they must refer to two different fees specifically collected in the *mitata*.

[12] *Systema* is the term ordinarily used in the *Book of the Prefect*. It usually translates the Latin word *collegium* in Byzantine sources stemming from the *Corpus Juris Civilis*. Another word often used in Byzantine sources is *soma*, translating literally the Latin term *corpus*, 'body,' in the meaning of 'gild.'

[13] *Agora* is the general term indicating any kind of market. It has been in use ever since the classical period. Sometimes Byzantine texts use the word *panegyrion*, 'general market,' with special reference to international fairs.

[14] In other terms, gild members are to pool their resources and to make purchases as a cartel. Whatever amount of silk is bought shall then be apportioned according to the size of individual contributions. For a similar practice in Venice, see Document 54.

[15] That is, 8½ percent. This measure enabled silk dealers who were too poor to contribute to the pool to obtain at a moderate premium whatever silk the members of the pool could spare.

[16] *Dunatos*, 'powerful,' is a technical term describing members of that class of great landowners who at that time were endeavoring to make the small farmers dependent upon them. The 'powerful' were not noblemen by right of birth, but they tended to form a special class endowed with legal and fiscal privileges. The term 'rich man' on the other hand does not seem to have a technical meaning. As for the cloth makers (*serikarioi*), they were members of another gild. Many of them were trying to place the whole silk industry under their control. See Lopez, 'Silk Industry,' p. 19.

[17] The word *taxeideuon*, which we translate by 'traveling,' in classical Greek meant 'making a

13. The raw-silk dealers must not sell unworked silk in their homes but in the market,[18] so that the silk may not be forwarded secretly to those who are forbidden to buy it. Whoever does so is to pay 15 nomismata to the gild.[19]

14. The raw-silk dealers are not to have a license to spin silk, but only to buy and to sell it. Whoever is caught [transgressing this provision] is to be punished by the penalty of being flogged and shaved.[20]

15. The so-called *melathrarioi* are not to buy pure silk either secretly or openly.[21] Whoever does so is to be subject to the aforesaid penalty.

16. The raw-silk dealers are not to sell silk to Jews or to [other] merchants[22] for resale outside the city. Whoever does so is to be beaten and shaved.

2

Book of the Prefect xx. 56–57
From the Greek[23]

[Constantinople, 911 or 912]

CONCERNING THE DEPUTY

1. The Prefect of the City is to nominate a Deputy,[24] presenting him to the Emperor [for appointment]. The Deputy shall take charge of reporting to the Prefect those who come to the City-Guarded-by-God from outside and who import any kind of merchandise, no matter from what locality or region they are. [The Prefect] is to inspect[25] the merchandise which they have imported and to establish for them the manner of the sale, giving them

---

military expedition.' Byzantine Greek, significantly enough, used it with the meaning of 'traveling,' and Venetian documents of the eleventh century adopted the word *taxedion* specifically for business ventures of the *collegantia* type. Hence the expression in the *Book of the Prefect* probably means not only 'traveling' but more specifically 'entering into a business venture as the traveling party.' See Documents 82 and 83 and the introduction to them.

[18] *Phoros*, the permanent market or shopping district as opposed to temporary markets or fairs.

[19] See also Article 16.

[20] Compare with Articles 1 and 13. The regulation of the gild of silk spinners (*Book of the Prefect* vii) shows that the entire gild had fallen under the control of the raw-silk dealers, to whom all silk spinners had to sell the processed raw material. For further details, see Lopez, 'Silk Industry,' pp. 18–19.

[21] On these men, see *ibid.*, p. 16. That article assumes that Nicole and other translators of the *Book of the Prefect* were right in translating *katharan . . . metaxan* 'clean silk.' One could also suggest, however, that the meaning was 'pure silk,' as opposed to silk mixed with cotton or linen thread.

[22] Compare the words *Iudaei et alii negotiatores* in certain Carolingian sources. The Jews, it would seem, were the great export merchants *par excellence*.

[23] See note 1.   [24] *Legatarios* is from an identical word in Latin.

[25] The manuscript has '*ephoronti ta eide aper eisegagon kai par'auton diorizomeno opos opheilousi pipaskesthai, didous. . . .*' This sentence can be translated without difficulty if we assume that *didous* does not refer to the Deputy but to the Prefect. It is quite logical that the Prefect rather

a limited period for the sale of their merchandise. Thus, when that period has elapsed, the Deputy is to bring them before the Prefect with a list of the merchandise which has been purchased by them, so that nothing forbidden may go out of the Imperial City.

2. The Prefect of the City is not to allow those who come in from outside with any kind of merchandise to spend more than three months in the Imperial City,[26] but he is to order that they sell what they have imported and that they purchase what they want and that they leave. Anyone found to overstay the established period is to be beaten, shaved, punished by confiscation [of goods], and banished from the City.[27]

3. Should the Deputy detect any persons hoarding merchandise imported in times of dearth and profiteering [to the detriment] of the community, he must report them to the Prefect, so that they may be beaten and shaved and their hoardings confiscated.

Merchants and Commerce in Muslim Syria

THE THOUSAND AND ONE NIGHTS and other literary masterpieces have made the wealth and thriftiness of the medieval Muslim merchant familiar even to the small child. The economic history of the Muslim world, however, has been neglected by modern Arabists, and non-Arabists do not have ready access to the larger part of the sources.[28] Hence we know little more of the commercial life of western Muslim regions during the eighth and ninth centuries than we do of the trade of the Byzantine

than the Deputy should decide how long a foreign merchant was to be allowed to stay, while the Deputy who was merely a police officer had only to see to it that the order was carried out. Nicole, however, assumed that the passage must necessarily refer to the Deputy and, in order to make it fit his assumption, suggested a whole series of corrections to the text, which were accepted by both Boak and Freshfield. We think no correction is necessary. The word *didous* is slightly ungrammatical, but it would not be more grammatical if Nicole's emendations were accepted. Mistakes in grammar and awkward constructions are very frequent in the *Book of the Prefect*.

[26] Russian merchants a little later were allowed a longer stay, six months. See S. H. Cross, tr., *The Russian Primary Chronicle*, pp. 150ff.

[27] For the punishment, see also Liudprand of Cremona, 'Relatio de legatione Constantinopolitana,' in F. A. Wright's translation of Liudprand's works, p. 268.

[28] The only attempt at giving an outline of Muslim trade in the early Middle Ages is M. J. de Goeje, 'International Handelsverkeer in de Middeleeuwen,' *Verslagen en Mededeelingen der Koninklijke Akademie van Wetenschappen*, Afdeeling Letterkunde, 4th ser., IX (1909), 245–69. In spite of the outstanding reputation of the author as an Islamist, the outline can hardly be called successful. Much valuable information is stored in A. Mez, *Die Renaissance des Islams*, Chaps. XXV and XXVI; a very poor English translation appeared in London in 1937, surprisingly enough under the name of the translator, Khuda Bukhsh! Mez died before he had time to organize the material and to assess it critically. A brilliant article by M. Lombard, 'L'Or musulman du VIIe au XIe siècle,' *Annales: Economies, Sociétés, Civilisations*, II (1947), 143–60, points out some basic trends in one specific sector of Muslim economic history. Further bibliographical information is found in *Cambridge Economic History*, Vol. II; the section on 'The Muslim World,' pp. 281–89, is a brief sketch, but it is the only general outline that has appeared recently.

Empire. Nor are the sources for this period really better than they are for the rest of Europe. Almost no commercial documents have been preserved. The few surviving historical, geographic, and legal works written earlier than the tenth century are often unreliable or uninteresting descriptions of trade. Usually they were written by eastern Muslims who had only indirect knowledge of the 'Western Sea,' as they called the Mediterranean.

One notable exception would be *The Beauties of Commerce*, by Abu al-Fadl Ja'far ibn 'Ali of Damascus, if it could be established that this was written before the tenth century. To place this work we have only a *terminus post quem* (the latest writers quoted in it are al-Jahiz—d. 864 or 869—and al-Kindi, who flourished at about the same time) and a *terminus ante quem* (a manuscript of the work copied in 1174). Hans Ritter, who made a study and a partial translation of the book, tentatively suggests the eleventh or early twelfth century because in his opinion the Muslim world before that period had not reached the commercial development indicated in the book. We believe that nothing in *The Beauties of Commerce* is incompatible with other sources on Muslim trade in the late ninth century, and we think that the lack of any mention of authorities later than that period is a decisive element of judgment.

The selection that follows (Document 3) is taken from the first part of the book, containing general considerations of business ethics and practice. We have omitted some of the leisurely sentences with which Abu al-Fadl embroiders his account. The book also has a very valuable catalogue which describes different wares.[29]

3
Abu al-Fadl Ja'far ibn 'Ali al-Dimishqi, *The Beauties of Commerce*[30]

[Damascus(?), late ninth century(?)]

There are three kinds of merchants: he who travels, he who stocks, he who exports. Their trade is carried out in three ways: cash sale with a time limit for delivery, purchase on credit with payment by installments, and *muqarada*.[31] But the *mutadammin*[32] is not regarded as a merchant because he

[29] See the German translation by H. Ritter, 'Ein arabisches Handbuch der Handelswissenschaft,' *Der Islam*, VII (1917), 17–26. Note that another passage of Abu al-Fadl has been included in our Part V.

[30] The full title of the work is *The Book of Knowledge of the Beauties of Commerce and of Cognizance of Good and Bad Merchandise and of Falsifications*. The present translation is from the German version by H. Ritter (see note 29), 58–59, 66–71, and *passim*.

[31] The *muqarada*, according to the *Khalil*, a Muslim lawbook of the Malikite rite, is 'a contract whereby one entrusts capital to a merchant for investment in trade in order to receive a share of the profits.' The investor bears all risks on the capital; the managing party risks his labor only. For its affinities to the *commenda*, see below, Chap. V. The only monograph on the *muqarada* is J. Kohler, *Die Commenda im islamitischen Rechte*. This work has been criticized—not without reason—but never superseded. It is worth noting that the lawbooks known to Kohler did not include the *muqarada* under the same heading as the *shirka* (partnership), but Ibn Qudama, whose manual has recently been translated, lists the *muqarada* or *mudaraba* among partnership contracts: Ibn Qudama, *Le Précis de droit*, tr. by H. Laoust, p. 109.

[32] *Mutadammin* may mean tax farmer, leaser, contractor, and the like. In the context tax farmer seems the best translation, but the other words are possible.

is nothing but a hired man of the proprietor, and the earnings upon which he relies are the payment for services rendered by him in the management and in the collection of rents. The difference between him and the managing party of a *muqarada* is the following: the managing party[33] is not bound to indemnify [the investor] for accidental loss of the investment so long as he does not go beyond the localities agreed upon. . . .

A combination of craft and commerce occurs, for instance, in the textile and spice trades because both trades consist of two kinds of activity. They belong to the crafts because the cloth merchant must know the standards of the wares, the good and bad qualities, and the fraudulent practices which go with them. Likewise, the spice merchant must know the different drugs, remedies, potions, and perfumes, their good and bad sorts as well as the counterfeits. He must know what commodities are subject to rapid change and spoil and which ones are not, and what means ought to be used to preserve and to restore them, and lastly he also must understand the blends of electuaries and potions, of powders and drugs. The textile merchant must also understand the folding and display of the wares and what means are used to store them. But both the spice merchants and the cloth merchants belong to the class of merchants because they buy and sell and draw their profit therefrom, and so forth. . . .

Know, my brother—may God guide you to what is dear and agreeable to Him—that the rule of the operations of the merchant who stocks consists in buying the wares in the time of their season and whenever the importation is uninterrupted, the supply large, and the demand small. . . .

This type of merchant above all needs early information on the relative situation of wares in their places of origin and native lands, whether the quantity on hand is great or small, cheap or dear, whether business has prospered abundantly and is in a good state or whether it has turned out poorly and has deteriorated, whether the import routes are cut off or are safe. He must try to obtain the knowledge of all this through inquiries and precise questioning of the caravans. . . .

When the merchant who stocks has made up his mind and is resolved to buy a ware, for instance, at 200 dinars cash, he ought not to buy all at once but to divide the purchase into four different times separated by intervals of fifteen days, so that the entire purchase is concluded within two months, the reason being that the price of the purchased ware either ceaselessly rises

[33] For other restrictions which may be imposed upon the manager, see Kohler, *Die Commenda*, pp. 10ff.

and falls or else remains steady. Now if after the purchase of one part the price goes up, he knows that this promises him profit and makes gain possible; and he should be happy about it, if indeed he is a moderate man and values a profit made through foresighted consideration more highly than a dangerous speculation. If, however, the ware becomes cheaper, he can then be happy in two respects, first, because he has remained protected against the fall in price which would have hit him if he had purchased the whole and, second, because he now has the opportunity to buy good wares cheaply. Should, however, the price remain unchanged at the same level, his eye is sharpened to seize the right moment for buying and stocking wares. But if he buys everything in great haste at one time, then something that he has not considered is sure to happen to him, and now he seeks to make up the loss. From this, then, arise the controversies and lawsuits which are so frequent in this profession. . . .[34]

The merchant who travels must, above all, pay attention to what kinds of wares he buys, and here he must exercise great caution. He also ought not to lull himself into the belief that his hopes must necessarily be fulfilled on arrival at the desired destination, because the journey may very easily be delayed or become impossible through some obstacle, perhaps because the route is dangerous or the winds unfavorable to a sea voyage, or because some unforeseen event takes place in the locality to which he wishes to travel. Such things may easily happen to a merchant. He must then sell the ware, for better or for worse, where he has bought it; and if he has not prepared himself in advance for such a contingency, he will suffer a great loss in its price. . . .

Further, it is worthy of note that he should carry with him a price list of all the wares of the locality to which he will return. . . . When he wants to buy an article, he establishes by this record the difference in price of the ware in the two places, takes into account the provisions he will need up to the time of his return, adds to the price list a list of the different tolls in that country, and calculates the profit. . . .

The merchant who arrives in a locality unknown to him must also carefully arrange in advance to secure a reliable representative, a safe lodging house, and whatever besides is necessary, so that he is not taken in by a slow payer or by a cheat. . . .

Know, my brother—may God guide you—that the operations of the merchant who exports consist in employing in the locality to which he

---

[34] Among the omitted material is an interesting, if verbose, bit of advice on how a merchant should take into consideration the power and disposition of the ruler in the conduct of his business.

exports some one who takes care of the wares sent to him. The latter is then entrusted with selling the wares and with buying others in exchange, and he ought to be a trustworthy, reliable, and well-to-do man who has devoted himself fully to commerce and who is also well experienced in it. The goods are shipped to him, and the entire selling is placed in his hands. He receives a share of the gain of all that he buys or sells.[35] If a ware is low in supply, he may stock it, if he thinks it wise. The wares which are sent him must correspondingly be bought with care and shipped prior to the time of the fair in the best quality and in the best condition possible. Therefore one must endeavor to buy the wares with the possibility of extending the term of payment, with easy conditions of payment, and with rights of option. If this is not possible with one ware, one should try to obtain it with another; for the profit, with the assistance of God, depends on suitable purchase.

Lastly, one must send a ware only with reliable carriers who keep it under their protection until it is received by the appointed representative.

The Flow of Merchandise to the Heart of the Muslim World

SYRIA WAS STILL a thriving province when Abu al-Fadl wrote his book, but it was no longer the heart of the Muslim world. The capital of the Caliphate had been moved from Damascus to Baghdad in 750. There is no lack of source material, translated or analyzed, in English, dealing with Baghdad.[36] Hence we present here a passage referring not to the city alone but to the entire province, Iraq or Mesopotamia. The natural maritime outlet of this region was the Persian Gulf, but the Mediterranean was close enough to be accessible to caravans coming from Iraq. Muslim writers often stress the influence and activity of Iraqi merchants in Egypt and in other Mediterranean countries.

Document 4 lists wares coming from all parts of the world. It is taken from *The Investigation of Commerce,* a pamphlet ascribed to a famous writer, Amr ibn Bahr of Basra, surnamed al-Jahiz (d. 864 or 869).[37] The attribution has been challenged, even though his name appears in the manuscript. But certainly the picture given in the pamphlet reflects the commercial currents of the ninth century as we know them in other sources. Mediterranean countries appear less important in trade than does the Asiatic East. Although 'the borders of the Maghrib' (i.e., the westernmost

[35] A. E. Sayous, 'Un Manuel arabe du parfait commerçant,' *Annales d'Histoire Économique et Sociale,* III (1931), 579, interprets this arrangement as a commission contract slightly influenced by the *muqarada.*

[36] See G. Le Strange, *Baghdad during the Abbasid Caliphate;* R. Levy, *A Baghdad Chronicle;* H. Amedroz and D. Margoliouth, eds., *The Eclipse of the Abbasid Caliphate;* and, of course, *The Thousand and One Nights.*

[37] Cf. J. M. Abd el-Jalil, *Brève Histoire de la littérature arabe,* pp. 109ff., which surveys the life and work of al-Jahiz. It is interesting to note that al-Jahiz is one of the authorities quoted by Abu al-Fadl.

part of North Africa), Barbary, and Egypt are mentioned among regions exporting wares to Mesopotamia, the larger part comes from the eastern Muslim world, India, and China. Non-Muslim countries in the list include Armenia and the Khazar state of the lower Volga. The former carried on much of the border trade between the Muslim states and the Byzantine Empire. The latter was an important channel of trade of Muslim merchants with the Slavs and other European peoples.[38]

4

Al-Jahiz(?), *The Investigation of Commerce*[39]

[Iraq, mid-ninth century]

IMPORTS OF IRAQ

From India are imported tigers(?),[40] panthers, elephants, panther skins, rubies, white sandal, ebony, and coconuts.

From China are imported silk stuffs, silk, chinaware, paper, ink, peacocks, racing horses, saddles, felts, cinnamon, Greek unblended rhubarb. [Also] are imported utensils of gold and silver, *qaysarani*[41] dinars of pure gold, drugs, brocades, racing horses, female slaves, knicknacks with human figures, fast locks . . .[42] hydraulic engineers, expert agronomists, marble workers, and eunuchs.

From Arabia: Arab horses, ostriches, pedigreed she-camels, *qan* wood,[43] and tanned skins.

From Barbary and the borders of Maghrib: panthers, *salam* leaves,[44] felts, and black hawks.

From Yemen: collyrium, tanned skins, giraffes, cuirasses, colored gems, incense, *khitr* leaves, and curcuma.[45]

From Egypt: trotting donkeys, suits of fine cloth, papyrus, balsam, and— from its mines—topazes of superior quality.

From the land of the Khazars: slaves of both sexes, coats of mail, helmets, and camails of [chain] mail.[46]

From the land of Khwarizm: musk; ermine, marten, miniver, and fox furs; and very sweet sugar cane.

[38] See Document 5.
[39] This excerpt from *The Investigation of Commerce*, ascribed to al-Jahiz, is translated from its French version, in J. Sauvaget, *Historiens arabes*, pp. 10–12.
[40] The question mark is Sauvaget's. One would assume that wild animals were imported for exhibition in cages.
[41] Probably this expression is derived from the Roman imperial title, 'Caesar,' and describes 'imperial' coins, or coins of the best quality.
[42] The dots are Sauvaget's.   [43] Used to make bows.   [44] Used in tanning.
[45] Used as condiment, dye, and medicine. *Khitr* leaves were used in tanning.
[46] Guards for the neck.

From Samarkand: paper.

From Balkh and its region: sweet grapes and *ghawshana* truffles.

From Bushanj: candied capers.

From Merv: zither players, valuable zithers, carpets, and Merv suits.

From Gurgan: grapes of various sorts, pheasants, excellent pomegranate grains, cloaks of soft wool, excellent raw silk.

From Amid: brocaded suits, scarfs, fine curtains, and woolen veils for the head.

From Damawand: arrow heads.

From Rayy: prunes, mercury, woolen cloaks, weapons, fine suits, combs, 'royal' bonnets, *qussiyat* linen cloth, and pomegranates.

From Ispahan: refined and raw honey, quinces, China pears, apples, salt, saffron, soda, white-lead, antimony sulphide, beds of several decks, extra fine suits, and fruit syrups.

From Qumis: axes, saddle felts, parasols, and woolen veils for the head.

From Kirman: indigo and cumin.

From Ghur: cuirasses and psyllium.

From Barda'a: fast mules.

From Nisibin: lead.

From Fars: *tawwazi* and *saburi* linen suits, rose water, water-lily ointment, jasmine ointment, and syrups.

From Fasa: pistachios, various sorts of fruit, rare fruit, and glass ware.

From Oman and the seacoast: pearls.

From Ahwaz and the surrounding region: sugar and silk brocades ... castanets, dancing girls...[47] extract of grapes, various sorts of dates, and sugar candy.

From Sus:[48] citrons, violet ointment, basil,[49] horsecloth, and packsaddles.

From Mosul: curtains, striped cloth, francolins,[50] and quail.

From Hulwan: pomegranates, figs, and vinegar sauces.

From Armenia and Azerbaijan: felts ...[51] packsaddles, carpets, fine mats, cordons for drawers, and wool.

The Jewish Role in World Trade

JEWISH MERCHANTS had a very large share of the meager trade of the early Middle Ages. In the more backward regions of Western Europe, such as the interior

---

[47] Gap in the manuscript.

[48] Susiana, ancient Elam, is not to be confused with Sus al-Aqsa in Morocco.

[49] A lamiaceous plant, used in cookery.   [50] Birds, closely related to partridges.

[51] Gap in the manuscript.

provinces of France and Germany, they seem to have held almost a monopoly of international commerce. They were less prominent in the highly developed Byzantine and Muslim territories, but even there they were second to none in the scope of their travels.[52]

Our first selection (Document 5), taken from the geographical work of Ibn Khurradadhbah describes Western Europe as it was hazily known to a scholar living in Persia in the ninth century. The second selection (Document 6), from the same source, outlines the itineraries of the Jewish merchants called al-Radhaniyya.[53] It will be noted that Western European place names and articles of trade mentioned in the first selection are almost exactly the same as those mentioned in the second selection describing the scope of trade of Jewish merchants.

5

Abu al-Qasim 'Ubayd Allah ibn Khurradadhbah, *The Book of the Routes and the Kingdoms*[54]

[Between 846 and 886]

. . . Rome, Bulgaria,[55] the countries of the Slavs and the Avars are to the north of Spain.

Through the Sea of the Maghrib,[56] are exported Slavic, Roman,[57] Frankish, and Lombard slaves; Roman and Spanish girls; beaver skins and other furs; among the perfumes, may'a; and among the drugs, mastic. From the bottom of that sea, close to Frankish territory, comes bussadh, a material usually known by the name of marjan.[58]

---

[52] The probable causes of the Jewish commercial ascendancy in the early Middle Ages are discussed in R. S. Lopez, 'Du marché temporaire à la colonie permanente,' *Annales: Economies, Sociétés, Civilisations,* IV (1949), 389–405. See also the stimulating essay by W. Roscher, 'Die Stellung der Juden im Mittelalter,' *Zeitschrift für die Gesamte Staatswissenschaft,* XXXI (1875), 503–26; there is an English translation, by S. Grayzel, of this article: 'The Status of the Jews in the Middle Ages Considered from the Standpoint of Commercial Policy,' *Historia Judaica,* VI (1944), 13–26. Abundant bibliography on the western Jews in medieval trade is found in the good book by G. Kisch, *The Jews in Medieval Germany,* pp. 535ff. Another good book is J. Starr, *The Jews in the Byzantine Empire,* with full bibliographies. On the Jews in the Muslim world, however, there is no general work. Some useful data and excerpts from sources, chiefly for the tenth century and later, are found in W. J. Fischel, *The Jews in the Economic and Political Life of Mediaeval Islam.* See also W. Heffening, *Das islamische Fremdenrecht bis zu den islamisch-fränkischen Staatsverträgen;* L. I. Rabinowitz, *Jewish Merchant Adventurers,* stimulating but over-enthusiastic.

[53] The name has not been satisfactorily explained. The suggestion of D. Simonsen, 'Les Marchands juifs appelés "Radanites",' *Revue des Etudes Juives,* LIV (1907), 141–42, that it is a transcription of Rhodanians, from the Rhone river, finds no support in the sources. De Goeje's tentative suggestion in 'International Handelsverkeer,' p. 256, that it may come from Persian *rah dan,* meaning 'knowing the way,' seems more acceptable.

[54] Ibn Khordadhbeh [Khurradadhbah], *Le Livre des routes et des royaumes,* tr. into French by M. J. de Goeje, pp. 66–67.

[55] Burjan or Great Bulgaria on the middle Volga river.

[56] That is, the Mediterranean, or Western Sea, as contrasted with the Indian Ocean, or Eastern Sea.

[57] That is, Byzantine (including the Byzantine possessions in southern Italy).

[58] May'a, mentioned above, is storax resin or balsam. Notice of this product as a Muslim import

The sea which stretches beyond the country of the Slavs and on the shore of which is the city of Tulia[59] is not frequented by any ship or boat, and no products are exported from it. Likewise, the Western Ocean, where the Fortunate·Islands are situated, has not been explored by navigators and does not supply any object for consumption.[60]

6

Abu al-Qasim 'Ubayd Allah ibn Khurradadhbah, *The Book of the Routes and the Kingdoms*[61]

[Between 846 and 886]

ROUTES OF THE JEWISH MERCHANTS CALLED AL-RADHANIYYA

These merchants speak Arabic, Persian, Roman,[62] Frankish, Spanish, and Slavonic. They travel from the East to the West and from the West to the East by land as well as by sea. They bring from the West eunuchs, slave girls, boys, brocade,[63] beaver skins, marten furs and other varieties of fur, and swords. They embark in the land of the Franks on the Western Sea, and they sail toward al-Farama. There they load their merchandise on the backs of camels and proceed by land to al-Qulzum,[64] twenty-five parasangs

---

from Western Europe is somewhat surprising if one considers that in the eighth century Saint Willibald is quoted as smuggling balsam from Muslim Syria on his return from a pilgrimage. The main center of production seems to have been the Byzantine Empire. Marjan is a coral obtained on the southern seacoast of France.

[59] The name indicated the westernmost island in the Atlantic Ocean and was used, according to the geographic knowledge of the time, for England, Ireland, Iceland, Greenland, or a mysterious country farther west. In 982–83 an anonymous geographical work mentions not only *Thuli* but also the islands of *Britaniya* or *Baritiniya*, 'the last land of the Romans on the coast of the Ocean . . . a mart of the Romans and of the Andalusians.' *Hudud al-'Alam: the Regions of the World,* tr. by V. Minorsky, pp. 59, 158. See also R. S. Lopez, 'Still Another Renaissance?,' *American Historical Review,* LVII (1951), 4ff. Byzantine writers, however, even at a later period often called England 'Tule.' Ibn Khurradadhbah is probably thinking of England. See R. S. Lopez, 'Le Problème des relations anglo-byzantines du septième au dixième siècle,' *Byzantion,* XVIII (1946–1948), 149–50.

[60] Tall tales, mixed perhaps with some truth, about travel to the islands of the 'Pitchy Sea' (the Atlantic west of Portugal and Morocco) are told by some Muslim writers. See Mez, *Renaissance des Islams.*

[61] From De Goeje's translation, pp. 114–16 (see note 54). A few sentences have also been translated by Starr in *Jews in the Byzantine Empire,* pp. 11–12. Rabinowitz, *Jewish Merchant Adventurers,* pp. 9–10, reproduces the translation of J. Jacobs, *Jewish Contributions to Civilization,* pp. 194–96, which in turn is based on De Goeje.

[62] Probably the Greek language and perhaps the Latin language as well.

[63] Jacobs and Rabinowitz translate 'silk.' But it would be hard to believe that the Jews exported silk from the West and took it to the East, as Rabinowitz, pp. 166–67, points out. His suggestion that the word is a mistake or a mistranslation for woolen cloth seems far-fetched. It is more likely that special tissues of silk, of Spanish or Byzantine manufacture, were exported.

[64] Al-Farama, now in ruins, was built on the site of ancient Pelusium, on the Nile delta.

distant. They embark on the Eastern Sea and proceed from al-Qulzum to al-Jar and to Jidda;[65] then they go to Sind, Hind, and China. On their return from China they load musk, aloe wood, camphor, cinnamon, and other products of the eastern countries and they come back to al-Qulzum, then to al-Farama, and from there they embark again on the Western Sea. Some of them sail for Constantinople in order to sell their merchandise to the Romans. Others proceed to the residence of the king of the Franks to dispose of their articles.

Sometimes the Jewish merchants, embarking in the country of the Franks on the Western Sea, sail toward Antioch. From there they proceed by land to al-Jabiya,[66] where they arrive after three days' journey. There they take a boat on the Euphrates and they reach Baghdad, from where they go down the Tigris to al-Ubullah.[67] From al-Ubullah they sail for, successively, Oman, Sind, Hind, and China. . . .[68]

These different journeys may likewise be made by land. Merchants leaving from Spain or France proceed to Sus al-Aqsa[69] and then to Tangier, and from there they set out for Africa[70] and to the capital of Egypt. From there they turn toward al-Ramla;[71] visit Damascus, Kufa, Baghdad, and Basra; cross al-Ahwaz, Fars, Kirman,[72] Sind, and Hind; and reach China. Sometimes also they take the route back of Rome,[73] and, crossing the country of the Slavs, proceed to Khamlij,[74] the capital of the Khazars. They embark on the Caspian

---

Al-Qulzum, on the Red Sea, was in ruins by the seventeenth century, but it has been succeeded by modern Suez. The two towns were linked by a waterway (which was, however, destroyed before the time of Ibn Khurradadhbah) and by a caravan route which is described by Rabinowitz, pp. 114–16.

[65] Al-Jar was the port of Medina before it was displaced by Yanbu. Jidda was and still is the port of Mecca.

[66] The reading is uncertain; De Goeje suggests that perhaps one ought to read al-Hanaya on the Euphrates. Rabinowitz tentatively identifies the locality with Jubba, also on the Euphrates, where after the sixteenth century there was a camel ford. A network of canals links the Euphrates with the Tigris.

[67] Al-Ubullah, now a suburb of Basra, is on the northern shore of the Persian Gulf.

[68] At this point Ibn Khurradadhbah turns his attention to the Russians before resuming, without any transition, his description of the travels of the Jews. Perhaps the order of his account was inadvertently modified by copyists.

[69] Atlantic Morocco. This, of course, implies a short voyage across the strait from Europe to Africa.

[70] Roughly corresponding to modern Tunisia. De Goeje suggests Kairouan.

[71] In Palestine, east of Jaffa.

[72] The three southernmost regions of Persia; Fars refers to a region of central Persia or to Persia as a country.

[73] That is, Byzantium.

[74] Itil, on the lower Volga. On the Khazars consult the abundant bibliographical information of G. Vernadsky and M. Karpovich, *A History of Russia*, II, 378–86, and especially Vol. I, Chap. VI.

Sea, then reach Balkh[75] and Transoxiana,[76] then continue the journey toward the camp[77] of the Tughuzghur, and from there to China.

The Meeting of East and West in Southern Italy

AS EARLY AS the eighth and ninth centuries certain maritime towns of Italy began to vie with the Jews as intermediaries between the advanced Muslim and Byzantine economies and the backward Romano-Germanic Europe.[78] Ever since the Lombard invasion had overrun the larger part of Italy, these towns had remained Byzantine islands in the Western world. They maintained political and commercial ties with the Byzantine Empire, but they had won sufficient autonomy to deal with their Lombard-dominated hinterland and later with the Carolingian and Ottonian empires. At the same time, they managed to keep up good commercial relations with the Muslim world.

Keeping a balance between these three powers—the Caliphate, the Byzantine Empire, and the Western Empire—was not always easy. Sometimes Naples, Gaeta, Amalfi, or Venice had to take sides or was attacked by one of its neighbors, but there were peaceful intervals, and trade continued even in the midst of hostilities. We present here a treaty between Italo-Byzantine Naples and the Lombard prince Sicardo. The treaty concluded a war from which the Byzantine government in Constantinople stood aloof. Sicardo agreed to remove certain obstacles to trade and navigation. The abolition of the *lex naufragii,* the law of shipwreck, was a step far in advance of the times, and there were other favorable measures. On the other hand, the Lombard prince preserved his rights to punish illegal trade in slaves and stolen goods. Some clauses of the treaty recall conditions existing in the Byzantine Empire, but others disclose a less advanced commercial world.

7

The *Pactum Sicardi*

From the Vulgar Latin[79]

[Southern Italy, July 4, 836]

In the name of the Lord God and of our Savior, Jesus Christ, and of the

---

[75] Balkh, in modern Afghanistan, near the Amu Darya [Oxus], is far distant from the Caspian Sea. In the description of the route beyond this sea to the Uighur Empire in Central Asia and to China, Ibn Khurradadhbah is very sketchy, probably because he describes these regions in detail in another section of his book.

[76] The country between two rivers, the Amu Darya and the Syr Darya; Transoxiana in classical sources.

[77] That is, the administrative center. The Tughuzghur were a dominant Central Asiatic people of the time.

[78] On the early development of the Italo-Byzantine cities, see M. Schipa, *Il mezzogiorno d'Italia anteriormente alla monarchia;* L. M. Hartmann, *Zur Wirtschaftsgeschichte Italiens im frühen Mittelalter;* R. Cessi, 'Il "Pactum Lotharii" del 840,' *Atti del Reale Istituto Veneto di Scienze,* 'Lettere ed Arti,* XCIX, 2 (1939–1940), 1111–49; M. Merores, *Gaeta im frühen Mittelalter;* Lopez, Silk Industry,' *passim.*

[79] This treaty has been published in many editions. For our translation we have used the text published in G. Padelletti, *Fontes iuris italici medii aevi,* pp. 318–24, *passim.*

blessed and glorious Mary, Mother of God and Ever Virgin. As long as the parties obey the commandments of God, then His orders are fulfilled and are shown to have led to concord of peace for the salvation of Christian souls. Wherefore we, the lord, the most glorious man, Sicardo, prince of the Lombard people, promise to you, Giovanni, [bishop] elect of the holy Neapolitan Church, and to Andrea, *magister militum*, and to your subject people of the Neapolitan duchy, Sorrento, Amalfi, and the other fortified places or localities which are under your rule, that we shall give you our true peace and grace by land and sea from this fourth day of July, fourteenth indiction, that is, for five full years. . . .

3. It is agreed that you shall not by any means buy Lombard [subjects] nor shall you sell them overseas. And if this is done, the person himself who bought, together with the one who bought [from him], shall be delivered to us, so that both—the one who bought and the one who sold—shall at the same time be delivered to us. And if not, and if there is a delay, [the guilty party] shall pay 100 solidi and the abovesaid persons shall be delivered; and if the sale has been made overseas, the one who committed this evil deed shall pay 200 solidi. . . .

5. In regard to the merchants of both parties, then, it is agreed that they are to be allowed to conduct their business within the borders of our Beneventan principality, and no matter by what way they may have entered the territory they are not to be injured or arrested or made to put up pledges, but shall return to their own country uninjured and without any loss. But if for any reason they are made to put up a pledge, that pledge is to be returned to them in its entirety; and whoever presumes to act contrary shall pay 24 solidi to the one he injured. . . .

13. Also, it is agreed in regard to the rivers which are on the Capuan borders, that is, the Patria, the Volturno, and the Minturno, that permission to cross their fords be given to merchants as well as to *responsales* or *milites* or to other persons of your Neapolitan duchy; our customs being preserved, they are to cross uninjured. The boats, indeed, which have remained there [moored] by cable[80] or have taken refuge from a storm, or have landed anywhere on that entire coast, or have come anywhere within the borders of our principality, are to be secure and uninjured, as is stated above. If however, they also want to do business there, they shall pay according to the old customs. This much [will be granted], that if a ship is wrecked because of the fault [of the men aboard][81] the goods found in it are to be returned to

---

[80] *Ad hora canseverint.* We read *ad oram consederint.*
[81] *Peccato faciente*: literally, 'committing a sin.'

the one to whom they belonged and still belong; the men, however, are to return to their own country sound and uninjured. And it is agreed that from this time forward your ships are not to be detained for any reason in the territory of Lucania or anywhere else within our borders. . . .

15. Also, it is agreed that no one from the territories outside a city is to have permission to buy a horse or an ox except within the city or in the market in the presence of the judges, and the seller himself should be known to them; and if the seller is not known to the judges, he is by no means to have permission to buy. If, however, he bought outside the city, or in the market or in the city and also in the presence of the judges, as is stated above, but the seller not being known, the buyer himself is to be regarded as a thief. . . . [82]

Traces of International Trade in Southern France

WHILE THE SURVIVAL—or the revival—of some long-distance and local trade in certain regions of Italy is conceded even by the most pessimistic historians, it is debated whether any such trade existed in southern France in the eighth and ninth centuries.[83] Among the extremely rare sources revealing trade, the most comprehensive is probably the poem 'Contra judices' by Theodulf, bishop of Orléans in the time of Charlemagne. The excerpts we give (Document 8) come from a list of gifts said to be offered to judges in Arles in order to corrupt them. Granted that Theodulf may have been given to exaggeration and had in mind classic models, nevertheless the poem cannot be entirely discounted. To quote only one instance, Theodulf's emphasis on Arabic gold coins as opposed to Latin silver coins is not an antiquarian note but reflects the gradual disappearance of gold coinage in the West and the predominance of the Muslim dinar as the medium of international exchanges and of large local payments. These phenomena are amply documented in other sources.[84]

[82] We omit the detailed statement of penalties. This passage recalls others in Frankish and Anglo-Saxon laws which also express suspicion of the merchant unless he is well known. See, for instance, Charlemagne's prohibition of transactions at night in R. C. Cave and H. H. Coulson, *A Source Book for Medieval Economic History*, p. 97, note 6.

[83] See the general preface to Part One. Indications of trade in southern France are listed in E. Sabbe, 'L'Importation des tissus orientaux en Europe occidentale au haut moyen âge,' *Revue Belge de Philologie et d'Histoire*, XIV (1935), 811–48, 1261–88; F. L. Ganshof, 'Notes sur les ports de Provence du VIIIᵉ au Xᵉ siècle,' *Revue Historique*, CLXXXIII (1938), 28–37; R. S. Lopez, 'Mohammed and Charlemagne: a Revision,' *Speculum*, XVIII (1943), 14–38; A. Dupont, *Les Cités de la Narbonnaise première depuis les invasions germaniques*.

[84] The fundamental work, not only for Italy but for all of Western Europe, is the essay of U. Monneret de Villard, 'La monetazione nell'Italia barbarica,' *Rivista Italiana di Numismatica*, XXXII (1919), 22–38, 73–112, 125–38; XXXIII (1920), 169–232; XXXIV (1921), 191–218. See also P. Le Gentilhomme, 'Le Monnayage et la circulation monétaire dans les royaumes barbares en Occident (Vᵉ–VIIIᵉ siècle),' *Revue Numismatique*, ser. 5, VII (1943), 45–112, VIII (1945), 13–64.

8

Theodulf, *The Bribery of Judges*
From the Latin[85]

[Arles, 798(?)]

This man, if I so act that he gains possession of the fields of another man, promises crystal and Oriental gems. That man, if only he may acquire farms, fields, and houses, brings a heavy load of coins of precious gold, on which Arabic words or characters are cut in grooves, or coins of white silver, on which words in Latin script are impressed. . . .[86] Another says, 'I have palls dyed in various colors, which, I believe, the grim-faced Arab has sent. . . .' A certain man, if only I give him what he asks but which ought not be given him, promises that he will give beautiful cups. . . . One, that he may win the case, is ready to give a sword and helmet; the other, that he may not lose, is ready to give shields. One brother has the estate of his father; the other wants to have it. The former wishes to give me mules [in order to retain it], the other, horses [in order to gain it]. . . . This man carries hither snow-white skins called after the name Cordoba; that man carries from that place red ones. One man, who can afford it, brings linen gifts; another, who can not, woolen. And this one offers something to cover the head, this one the foot, and that one the hand. There is one who for a gift has a fabric with which we are wont to wipe moisture from our face and hands. Others prepare caskets as gifts, nor is that man lacking who would be delighted to give round cakes of wax.[87]

Merchants, Passports, and Customs in the Lombard Hinterland

COMMERCIAL ACTIVITY and a native merchant class survived not only in the maritime fringe of Italy and, perhaps, in Mediterranean France but also in certain regions of the interior. Indeed, there are reasons to believe that whatever trade was still carried on in France centered in cities of the interior such as Lyons and Verdun rather than in Mediterranean towns. Some scholars have maintained that the larger part of the merchants in France were Jews rather than Gallo-Romans or Franks.[88]

[85] From 'Versus Teudulfi episcopi contra judices,' ll. 171–252, in *Monumenta Germaniae historica, Poetae Latini aevi Carolini*, Vol. I, Part 2, pp. 498–500. The editor of the text is E. Duemmler.

[86] Here and hereafter we have omitted verses which are irrelevant to the history of trade.

[87] *Caereolas rotulas.*

[88] See, however, R. Doehaerd, 'Au temps de Charlemagne et des Normands: ce qu'on vendait et comment on le vendait dans le bassin parisien,' *Annales: Economies, Sociétés, Civilisations*, II (1947), 268–80.

In the Lombard kingdom, however, native merchants (*negotiatores*) are often mentioned. Their wealth is demonstrated by the fact that for fiscal purposes King Aistulf divided them into three classes parallel to the three classes of landowners or *possessores*. The upper class (*negotiantes maiores et potentes*) was held to the same contribution for the army as that class of *possessores* which held at least seven country homesteads.[89] The edict of Aistulf, of which we are translating passages relevant to commercial history, envisaged measures to restrict trade with Byzantine citizens and provided for the restoration of the customs offices at the borders (*clusae*) and for control of commerce by land and sea. We catch glimpses of an organization which to some extent seems to resemble the organization of Byzantine trade in Constantinople. Hints in the edict would be more significant if, as some scholars suggest, the economic and administrative system described in the *Honorantie civitatis Papie* (see Document 20) went back in its main lines to the Lombard kingdom.[90]

9

Edict of Aistulf
From the Latin[91]

[Pavia, 750]

3. Also concerning those men who are merchants and have no cash[?],[92] let the greater and powerful[93] [among them] have breastplate as well as horses, shield, and lance; let the followers[94] have horses, shield, and lance; and let the lesser[95] have quivers with arrows and bow.

4. And this also concerns any man who does business with a Roman without the authorization of the king: if he who has the presumption to do this is a judge, he shall pay his wergild and lose his office; if he is a man-at-arms,[96] he shall lose his property and go about shorn, shouting: 'May he so suffer who contrary to the will of the king does business with a Roman when we have litigation.' Similarly, the judge who shows negligence in investigating shall pay; if it previously came to his notice that his man-at-arms, or any other man in his jurisdiction, has done this, he shall pay his own wergild.

[89] Abundant bibliography on this and other Lombard laws is given in E. Besta, *Storia del diritto italiano: le fonti*, Vol. I.

[90] On the revival of Lombard economy in the eighth and ninth centuries, see F. Carli, *Storia del commercio italiano*, Vol. I, with Bibliography.

[91] The best editions are those of G. Pertz in *Monumenta Germaniae historica, Leges*, IV, 196–97, and G. Padelletti, *Fontes iuris italici medii aevi*, I, 296. We have used Padelletti's edition.

[92] *Pecunias*. Padelletti suggests the reading *peculium*. At any rate, the meaning seems to be that merchants have the alternative of paying money for the army or furnishing the above equipment. See also paragraph 2 in the same edict, which describes the obligations of landed proprietors.

[93] *Maiores et potentes*.   [94] *Sequentes*.   [95] *Minores*.

[96] *Arimannus homo*, 'man disciplined in the use of arms' or 'soldier.' The term is equivalent to *exercitalis*. It is almost equivalent to free man, but the identification of free man and soldier is not yet complete at this early period.

He shall not, [however], lose his office. And if the judge himself says that [the transgression] had not come to his notice, he shall purify himself on the Holy Gospels of God, [swearing] that [notice of the fact] had not reached him.

5. Concerning the customs houses[97] which have fallen into disrepair, let them be restored and let guards be stationed there, so that neither our men may pass without authorization of the king nor similarly may strangers enter into our territory without the authorization or order of the king. And in any customs house where [a transgressor] is discovered, the inspector[98] of the customs house who has neglected to maintain guard shall incur from his [own] judge the same penalty as [is incurred by] the judge himself whom the king placed in charge [of the customs house]. [Nobody may pass without authorization of the king] unless the judge sends his own messenger on service useful to the king or receives [someone coming] on the king's affairs.

6. Concerning shipping and business by land: no one is to wander around in order to transact business, or for any reason whatsoever, without a written permit[99] of the king or without authorization of his judge; and if anyone does so, he shall pay his wergild.

Commercial Investments and Real Estate
of a Venetian Doge

THE ILLUSTRATIONS which we have so far selected are mostly drawn from legal texts and narrative sources, which, in the Preface, we stated we would shun whenever possible. Private charters and commercial records, of course, would supply more direct information on trade. Unfortunately, these are not available. Nor, as we have already noted, are there commercial records from the Byzantine Empire or from the Muslim world. The fuller records of Venice, Gaeta, and other Italo-Byzantine cities begin after the year 1000. We have, however, a few private charters from Venice earlier than that year. One of them is a choice item (Document 10). It is the will of a Venetian doge, Giustiniano Partecipazio or Particiaco, drafted in 829. It discloses a conspicuous fortune made up of real estate, mobile objects, precious metals, cash, and investments in overseas trade.[100]

The comparative importance of real estate in the patrimony of the merchant ruler of a city of merchants may, at first sight, lend support to the theory of Werner Sombart, according to which commercial capital and capitalism owed their origin

---

[97] *Clusae.*   [98] *Clusarius.*

[99] *Epistola,* that is, roughly speaking, 'safe conduct.' See the exhaustive treatment in G. P. Bognetti, *Note per la storia del passaporto e del salvacondotto.*

[100] See G. Luzzatto, 'Les Activités économiques du patriciat vénitien (X^e–XIVe siècles),' *Annales d'Histoire Economique et Sociale,* IX (1937), 25–26, in which the earlier bibliography on this document and its background is given.

chiefly to investments in trade made out of surplus income derived from agricultural possessions. It remains to be decided, however, whether landowners became merchants by investing agrarian profits in trade or whether merchants became landowners by investing commercial profits in real estate. The latter phenomenon is abundantly documented in sources of this and the later period; but so is the former.

The mention of *laboratorii solidi* which may or may not return safely from a voyage is very important for the history of commercial law. The expression certainly refers to commercial contracts—*laborare* in later Venetian documents is the technical word for managing an investment in trade—but it is too vague for us to determine what specific contracts are meant.

10

From the Vulgar Latin[101]

[Venice(?), 829]

In the name of the Lord God, our Savior, Jesus Christ. In the imperial rule of our lords most pious, forever august, Michael and Theophilus, crowned by God, peace-loving, great emperors; in the ninth year of Michael [II], himself senior emperor, and in the eighth year[102] of Theophilus, crowned by God and beloved son of the same, seventh indiction. Under [the guidance] of divine inspiration and of foreseeing mind let every man, so far as possible, so order his will that after death, when he is free from all fear,[103] his wishes may stand out clear and be respected as though he were alive.[104] Wherefore I, Giustiniano, imperial *hypatos*[105] and duke of the province of Venice, having fallen ill but [still] walking and sitting down, and possessing a sound and whole mind and judgment, and considering the weakness of human nature to provide for the future,[106] have drawn up this my last testament and will, and I have directed Deusdedit, priest, to sign it, and I have confirmed it by my own hand below, and I have offered witnesses, invited by me, the number

---

[101] A. Gloria, ed., *Codice diplomatico padovano dal secolo sesto a tutto l'undecimo*, pp. 12–16. The copy from which this document was published was made from an earlier copy, now lost, of the fourteenth century. The usual obscurity of the ungrammatical Latin of the ninth century is here aggravated by mistakes and gaps accumulated in the successive transcriptions.

[102] The text has 'eighteenth.' This is obviously an error since Partecipazio died in 829, the ninth year of Michael II, who began his reign on December 25, 820. His son, Theophilus, had shared the throne only since May 12, 821. We have corrected the text to read 'eighth.'

[103] *Post fata omni terrore moto.* The interpretation is not certain. Most likely the old doge is referring to his impending death, which will cause him no fear if his will is properly made. Of course, there is room for other interpretations.

[104] We prefer the variant *viventis* found in other manuscripts, to Gloria's *juvenis*.

[105] A *hypatos* was a high Byzantine dignitary. The rulers of Venice and of other Italian cities which retained some form of allegiance to the Byzantine Empire, even if they enjoyed almost unrestricted self-government, often were granted titles of this kind and bore them with pride.

[106] *Considerans humane fragilitatis improvidus.* Here and elsewhere the text has had to be corrected if it is to make any sense at all.

being competent . . .[107] so that for all that through this testament I shall give, donate, and bind or order to be given, or command to be done, there shall be a warrant so that it will be given.[108]

You, then, Felicita, my wife, and Romana, my daughter-in-law, I constitute my heirs and will to be my heirs, for my son [as well],[109] in this heritage of mine for three principal shares[110] in their entirety, that is, land, house, gold, silver or spices,[111] adornment, money put to work . . .[112] iron, instruments, beds, tools, and mobile or immobile and self-moving goods from everything that I am known to have from the succession of my lord and father or from what I have obtained from money put to work or from what I have been able to acquire. The other six shares of all that I appear to have, as stated above, I reserve in my own power to dispense according as I shall provide justly and conformably to [the will of] God for the health of my soul, giving by my own hand and word or by whomever I shall commission to dispense them. But in regard to the monastery of the Blessed Zacharias and to the monastery of the Most Holy Hilary I so will and direct that each forever remain in true liberty and privilege, with [possession of] everything that with the help of God I have built, enlarged, and cared for, or that I have donated or shall donate. . . .[113]

Indeed, we make this short list[114] of the vineyards or lands or the rest of the spices which we offer to the said holy monastery [of the Blessed Zacharias] so that through this list it may become the duty of him whom it may concern to see to it that they may not be lost at the hands of any human being, man or woman. First of all, the lands and vineyards and fields which are located in the place named Prato. . . .[115] All this, as well as we are able, God willing, we have donated to the aforesaid monastery. Besides, that the will may be fuller . . .[116] we shall add [two hundred pounds] from money put to work to

---

[107] We omit the words *quo testamentum meum sic caus sue civile nequi*. Apparently the testator is explaining that the witnesses were summoned in conformity with the prescriptions of the *jus civile*. *Sue* may easily be a misreading for *jure*. The exact context, however, cannot be surmised.

[108] *Id ut detur fiat prestitor fidei*. Here, too, our translation is tentative.

[109] Agnello, the son of the doge, had died while on a mission to Constantinople.

[110] *In ternas uncias principales.*

[111] *Species* may mean 'spices,' 'coins,' or 'assorted wares.' We have thought 'spices' to be the most likely meaning.

[112] The dots in the text are Gloria's.

[113] We omit a list of privileges as well as dispositions in regard to the right of Felicita and Romana to live in the monastery 'with all their property.'

[114] *Breviarium.*

[115] The dots in the translation are ours. The section omitted contains a list of specific properties evidenced *per documenti cartas*.

[116] The dots in the text are Gloria's.

the [share of the] aforesaid monastery of the Blessed Zacharias by word of our own mouth or by brief declaration.[117]

In fact, all my property, complete and listed here briefly, in addition to those two hundred pounds just mentioned which [I have given] to the monastery . . .[118] spices and ornaments and money put to work, will amount to 1200 pounds if [that money] returns safely from [commercial] voyages.[119] And of them I have reserved six hundred [pounds] to be distributed for my soul to whomever I shall designate in any place whatsoever by brief declaration. And whatever may remain after my death I entrust to Felicita, my wife, and to Giusto and Deusdedit, priests, to distribute as servants of God would provide for the health of my soul. The remaining six hundred pounds, then, in addition to those two hundred which we have given to the monastery, we bequeath to my wife and daughter-in-law, as we have specified above. . . .[120]

And in regard to the monastery of Saint Hilary I so will and direct as shall be established in this order which is now being made by Deusdedit, priest. I will that a hundred and sixty pounds of silver be given to the said monastery. . . .

Private Documents of Lombard Italy

STRANGELY ENOUGH, the number of extant private documents from Lombard, Frankish, and German territory in the eighth and ninth centuries is far larger than that of private documents from the Italo-Byzantine trading cities.[121] Frankish private records, however, seem to reflect exclusively an agrarian civilization. The same can be said of the rich series of documents from Saint Gall, Switzerland, although Saint Gall was an important station along the route of international East-West trade via Italy. Lombard documents, too, are mainly concerned with agrarian life and economy, but indirectly they illumine trade by showing *negotiatores* buying and selling land or traveling through the country. A very small number is directly concerned with commerce, credit, and navigation.

The first of the documents (Document 11) brings out the prevalence of exchanges in kind over exchanges transacted in cash, a universal phenomenon in early medieval Western Europe, although in Italy money economy fared better than elsewhere.[122]

---

[117] *Breve*, a short document which served as evidence to a previously accomplished legal act.

[118] The dots in the text are Gloria's.

[119] *Cum speciebus et ornamentis et laborantis solidis si salva de navigatione fuerint libras mille ducentas.*

[120] There follows a list of bequests, chiefly lands, to the monastery of Saint Hilary and personal bequests in money to individuals, ending with the usual curses against anyone trying to act contrary to the testament and with a list of witnesses.

[121] The survival may partly be ascribed to the fact that in these regions durable parchment replaced brittle papyrus earlier than in the Italo-Byzantine cities.

[122] On the early medieval moneyers, see R. S. Lopez, 'Continuità e adattamento nel medio evo:

The document, however, also indicates that the underlying reason for barter was not necessarily the unavailability of currency, but the preference of the parties for a means of payment other than money. We have to assume that a moneyer—the man who is mentioned in the first document—had access to sufficient money to pay cash for the full price of a piece of land costing 28 solidi. Yet he paid 15 solidi in coin and a horse, which he probably bought in the market.

Document 12 describes the activity of boatmen transporting grain and salt— these were among the principal articles of trade in Western Europe—on behalf of an ecclesiastical institution to which they pledged quasi-feudal allegiance. The role of the Church and of 'abbey merchants' in early medieval economy was very important, but there is little agreement among scholars as to whether their activity was genuinely commercial or whether it was merely a matter of insuring the necessary supply of consumption goods for the clergy and poor of the Church.[123]

Document 13 is a contract of sale. The 'article' sold is one we already have met in international trade—a slave. Probably in this specific instance neither the seller nor the buyer was a merchant, but the contract would hardly have been different if both parties had been *negotiatores*. The slave boy sold for less than the value of the horse in the first document; this is not an uncommon scale of values at that period.[124]

Documents 14 and 15 are examples of the *mutuum* or loan contract. One of them comes from the Alpine region and the other from Salerno, on the southern seacoast close to the Italo-Byzantine cities. A *mutuum* was essentially a commercial contract, but these instances bear marks of a civilization based upon agriculture. In the Alpine document the borrower gives the lender a piece of land as security and yields the fruit of the land as interest on the loan, in spite of the canonical prohibitions of taking interest on loans. In the second document the borrower gives no land but his own labor. He agrees to share the fruit of his labor with the lender.

II

From the Vulgar Latin[125]

[Lucca, July 2, 768]

In the name of God. In the reign of our lord Desiderius and of Adelchis, kings, in the year of their reign [respectively] twelfth and ninth, the second day after the Kalends of July, sixth indiction; good fortune. It is [hereby] stated that I, Rodingo, son of Teodorico of blessed memory, have sold and through this record delivered to you, Grasolfo, moneyer, one *modilocus* of

un millennio di storia delle associazioni di monetieri nel' Europa meridionale,' in *Studi in onore di Gino Luzzatto*, II, 74–117.

[123] See the opposite views of H. Laurent, 'Marchands du palais et marchands d'abbayes,' *Revue Historique*, CLXXXIII (1938), 281–97, and of R. S. Lopez in *Cambridge Economic History*, II, 265.

[124] See, for instance, C. Sánchez-Albornoz, 'El precio de la vida en el reino astur-leonés hace mil años,' *Logos: Revista de la Facultad de Filosofía y Letras, Universidad de Buenos Aires*, III (1944), 225–64.

[125] L. Schiaparelli, *Codice diplomatico longobardo*, II, 254–55.

my land by measure, which I am known to have near the Church of Saint Columban and near the wall of this city of Lucca. And this same land comes to an end at the land of Peredeo, bishop; the other end touches the land of Pietro; one side borders on the land of Pellegrino, and the other side borders on the land of Pietro. The piece of land in the described location, which is by measure 1 *modilocus*, I deliver to you in its entirety; and if it should be larger, that [additional] land shall be in your power, Grasolfo, just as also is the other. And I, the above Rodingo, have received as the price for that aforesaid land which I gave you, Grasolfo, 15 gold solidi in cash[126] and 1 horse in place of 13 solidi for the completion [of the payment] of that land, so that henceforth that land, as is stated above, shall be in the power of you and your heirs. I, the above Rodingo, together with my heirs, now promise you, Grasolfo, or your heirs, that if at any time we should interfere in regard to that land mentioned above, and if at present we were unable to protect it for you in any way against all men, we promise to pay a fine to you for that aforesaid land in the double, with the improvements, in whatever place [made], at the estimated [price] such as it then is. And I asked Prandulo to write [this record]. Done in Lucca.

The sign of the hand of Rodingo, a devout man, seller and author.

The sign of the hand of Deusdedit, son of the late Baroncello, witness.

The sign of the hand of Prandulo, cleric, son of the late Aspert, witness.

The sign of the hand of Wallerino, cleric, son of Gente, witness.

I, Fortunato, cleric, invited by Rodingo, undersigned as a witness to this record.

I, Prandulo, after delivery completed and gave [this record].

12

From the Vulgar Latin[127]

Lucca, August 26, 768.

In the name of God. In the reign of our lord Desiderius, king, and of his son our lord Adelchis, likewise king, in the year of their reign [respectively] the twelfth and tenth, on the seventh day before the Kalends of September,

---

[126] Or, more probably, 45 *tremisses*. It is doubtful whether the Lombard mints struck gold solidi; the highest denomination was the gold *tremissis* (one third of a solidus), the solidus being a money of account.

[127] Schiaparelli, *Codice diplomatico longobardo*, II, 261–62. The document raises many problems in legal history, which do not have to be discussed here. See the Bibliography in Schiaparelli, II, 261. It is clear that Autperto and Liutperto, who formerly had transported goods in behalf of the duke of Lucca (a lay government official), are now promising to fulfill the same tasks in behalf of the bishop of the same city. Their personal status and the significance of this change of service or allegiance can be interpreted in more than one way.

the sixth indiction. It is clear that we, Autperto and Liutperto, brothers-german, sons of the late Barbula, residents of Oliveto, and our parents have been wont to do duty and service because of [our] status[128] to Duke Walperto of blessed memory and to his sons by transporting both grain and salt by ship. But now, at the present time, for the purpose of security, we deliver and confirm by this record all our property[129] to the household of the holy church of Lucca, so that from this day forever we confirm all our property, movable as well as immovable or self-moving—[that is, ours] both by right of our parents and by our own acquisition—to be wholly in the power (*potestas*) of the Church of Saint Martin, so that we never are to have authority to withdraw anything which we had from the domain (*dominium*) of that church or of its rectors. And the aforesaid duty we promise [to fulfill], that is, to transport grain and salt from the boundaries of the Maremma all the way to that port where it is customary for the produce[130] and salt of that household of the church to be offered for sale[?],[131] our rights (*iustitia*) being preserved just as was previously the custom. And if we or our heirs presume to act in any way contrary to all these provisions promised by us, and if we do not fulfill them in all regards, we, together with our heirs, promise that we shall pay a fine amounting to 50 gold solidi to you, Lord Peredeo, bishop in the name of God, and to your successors. And for confirmation we invited Austriperto, cleric, to write [this record]. Done in Lucca.

The sign of the hand of Autperto, who asked that this record be made.

The sign of the hand of Liutperto, who likewise asked that this record be made.

The sign of the hand of Ratchis, cleric, son of Soldulo, priest, witness.

The sign of the hand of Austriperto, cleric, son of Auchi, witness.

The sign of the hand of Alpulo, cleric, son of the late Lucio, witness.

[128] *Scuvias facere solemus et servitium per condicionem.* The latter term, in our opinion, expresses the fact that the brothers were personally obligated to do labor service for the civil government; this obligation apparently was one of many survivals of the *munera* of the later Roman Empire. *Scuviae,* from classic Latin *excubiae,* originally meant watch or guard duty, but in Lombard times it apparently became another term for personal *munera.* See E. Besta, *Storia del diritto italiano: diritto pubblico,* I, 276. *Servitium,* a generic term, applies to services of a free man or of a serf, whether they are performed as a public duty or in fulfillment of contractual (non-feudal or feudal) obligations.

[129] *Res,* in Roman usage, refers to anything that can form part of the property of a person, whether corporeal (our 'things') or incorporeal (rights of inheritance, etc.). Roman law, however, was no longer the only relevant factor in 768; there also was Lombard law, and what the document calls *consuetudo,* 'custom.' Moreover, the document is a private agreement between the parties, consisting of a number of provisions or articles (*capitula*).

[130] *Laborem,* the product of work in general. Interest on loans also is called *labor* in documents of the period.

[131] *Venire:* from *veneo,* 'I am sold,' or from *venio,* 'I come'? The former seems more grammatical in this context, but the latter is a more popular form. The document is not a literary one.

I, Rachiprando, priest, invited by Autperto and Liutperto, undersigned as witness to this record.

I, Agiprando, cleric, invited by Autperto and Liutperto, undersigned as witness to this record.

I, Austriperto, cleric, after delivery completed and gave [this record].

13
From the Vulgar Latin[132]

Milan, June 6, 725

In the thirteenth year of the reign of our lord, most excellent man, King Liutprand, on the eighth day before the Ides of June, eighth indiction; good fortune. I, Faustino, notary by royal authority, wrote this document of sale, invited by Ermedruda,[133] honorable woman, daughter of Lorenzo, acting jointly with consent and will of that parent of hers, and being the seller. And she acknowledges that she has received, as indeed she at the present time is receiving from Totone, most distinguished man, 12 new gold solidi as the full price for a boy of the Gallic people named Satrelano, or by whatever other name the boy may be called. And she declared that it[134] had come to her from her father's patrimony. And she, acting jointly with her aforesaid father, promises from this day to protect that boy against all men in behalf of the buyer. And if the boy is injured or taken away and they [Ermedruda and Lorenzo] are in any way unable to protect it against all men, they shall return the solidi in the double to the buyer, [including all] improvements in the object.[135] Done in Milan, in the day, reign, and in the eighth indiction mentioned above.

The sign of the hand of Ermedruda, honorable woman, seller, who declared that she sold the aforesaid Frankish boy of her own good will with the consent of her parent; and she asked this sale to be made.

The sign of the hand of Lorenzo, honorable man, her father, consenting to this sale.

The sign of the hand of Theoperto, honorable man, maker of cuirasses, son of the late Giovannace, relative of the same seller,[136] in whose presence she proclaimed that she was under no constraint, giving consent.

[132] Schiaparelli, *Codice diplomatico longobardo*, I, 126–28.

[133] Note the alternation of Lombard and Roman names in persons belonging to the same family.

[134] A slave in Lombard as well as in Roman law was not considered as a person but as a thing (*res*); hence the document uses the neuter pronoun when referring to him.

[135] *Rem vero meliorata*. Again, the boy is considered as a thing. He may learn some skill and hence become more valuable.

[136] *Parenti ipseius uinditrici*. Here the word *parens* has the meaning of 'relative' or 'kinsman,' as frequently in medieval Latin and in Italian *parente*.

The sign of the hand of Ratchis, honorable man, Frank, witness.

Antonino, devout man, invited by Ermedruda, honorable woman, and by her father giving his consent, undersigned as a witness to this record of sale.

I, the above Faustino, writer of this [record] of sale, after delivery gave [this record].

14
From the Vulgar Latin[137]

Trevano [Como], April 9 or 10, 748

In the fourth year of the reign of our lord King Ratchis, most excellent man, on the fourth [or fifth][138] day before the Ides of April, first indiction. It is [hereby] stated that I, Alessandro de Sporticiana, have received and I did receive from you, Arechis of Campione, 1 gold solidus to be put to work for my advantage[139] up to the end of the year. And on account of the 1 solidus I have set aside for you as security, that is, to be held in trust, the following: a small piece of meadowland in the locality which is called Farsiole, bounded on one side by the meadow of Ursone, and on the other side by the meadow of St. Victor, having at one end the river and at the other end the meadow of St. Victor. Let him[140] hold this small piece [of land] in its entirety for the charge[141] of the aforesaid solidus for the period agreed. At the end of the year, then, I promise to return the 1 solidus without charge to the one mentioned above, and I am to receive back my meadow. And I promise to protect the said meadow, to give protection [to it] against all men, so long as I have the said solidus. And if I do not fulfill all that is stated above, I am to pay as a fine to you, the above creditor of mine, the said solidus in the double. And if you grant a postponement beyond [the term], you are to hold that meadow until I can lawfully make [the solidus] good to you. Done in Trevano, the day, the reign, and the indiction aforesaid; good fortune.

The sign of the hand of Alessandro, who asked this memorandum (*cautio*) to be made.

The sign of the hand of Ursone de Sporticiana, witness.

The sign of the hand of Radoaldo de Sporticiana, witness.

I, Cunimondo, invited by Alessandro, undersigned as a witness to this memorandum.

I, Austrolf, notary, after delivery, completed and gave [this memorandum].

[137] Schiaparelli, *Codice diplomatico longobardo*, I, 274-75.
[138] *Q . . . to*, which can be restored either as *quarto* or as *quinto*.   [139] *Meis utilitatibus peragendo*.
[140] That is, Arechis of Campione. The document continuously shifts from the second to the third person and back.
[141] *Onus*, 'charge,' in legal documents of the period means 'interest.'

15
From the Vulgar Latin[142]

[Salerno], February 9, 872

In the name of the Lord. In the eleventh year of the rule of our lord Guaiferio, the ninth day from the beginning of February, fifth indiction.

Whereas I, Ademaro, son of Aceprando, resident of the locality of Iovi in the Salernitan territory, promise[143] by this writing to you, Gaidemaro, son of Tancomaro, that from now on and for four full years I shall make my residence on your property and in your house which you have in the locality of Iovi; and [whereas] I shall preserve all your property that you have in the aforesaid locality and any other thing of yours that you may consign to me there; and [whereas] I shall never leave you while you are absent to gather the vintage or to work, but shall work there for you; and [whereas] you are to take two shares[144] and I one share of the fruit that you shall obtain there from the aforesaid property;[145] and [whereas] I am doing everything mentioned in this writing by permission and grant of Ermetanco, son of Ermenando;[146]

Therefore, [in return] for what is written above, you have lent[147] me 1 tremissis of Lord Arechis[148] on this condition, that when I, being alive at the end of the aforesaid years, leave your aforesaid property, I shall return to you from my own [funds]—since I am not to obtain it from another man—the aforesaid tremissis of good quality, or [as many] deniers as shall be worth a tremissis of good quality at the [rate] current at that period. And if [I die and] after my death the Ermetanco mentioned above or his heirs wish to return the aforesaid sum[149] to you or to your heirs, you are not to take the value of 1 tremissis from my property. But if [neither] I myself, nor the aforesaid Ermetanco, nor his heirs return to you or to your heirs the price of that

---

[142] M. Morcaldi, M. Schiani, and S. de Stefano, eds., *Codex diplomaticus Cavensis,* I, 95–96.

[143] Here and in many places throughout the document, each of the parties shifts from the singular to the plural in referring to their obligations—as if to indicate that they pledge their families as well as themselves.

[144] *Sorti due.* Usually *sors* is the capital, but here obviously it indicates shares of the profits.

[145] *Poma que ibi in suprascripta rebus tua habueri:* certainly 'fruit' in general and not 'apples' only.

[146] Apparently a man who had some rights upon the person or the labor of Ademaro. In the document, however, he seems to act as a *fidejussor* rather than as a master or lord. There is no hint of the existence of any restriction on Ademaro's ability to contract an obligation as a free man.

[147] *Prestasti.*

[148] Two persons bearing this name were princes of Benevento at the time when the principality included Salerno. The *tremissis* was a gold coin worth one third of a solidus.

[149] *Pretio.*

aforesaid *tremissis* after the completion of the years mentioned above, you and your heirs are to be allowed to take from my property the value of 1 *tremissis*. . . .[150]

[150] *Per adpretiatum uno tremisse.* We omit the rest of the document which contains the usual pledges of keeping the document 'as settled as if it were a record of sale.' The penalty of 20 solidi is extraordinarily high. The document also contains the list of witnesses. The record was written by Wiso, notary, in Salerno.

PART TWO

*Markets, Merchants, Merchandise, and Means of Exchange
During the Commercial Revolution*

THE TENTH CENTURY marks the beginning of a long period of almost unbroken economic expansion of the Mediterranean peoples, an expansion of production and consumption in the home market, of overseas trade to the commercially advanced regions, of land commerce over formerly stagnant areas. This startling surge does not slacken its pace until the onset of the great depression of the mid-fourteenth century. Even then it is only temporarily slowed and not stopped. It moves forward again to form the basis for that further period of expansion which culminates in the Industrial Revolution of modern and contemporary times.

At first the Byzantine and Muslim worlds seem to have profited as much as Western Europe did from this quickening of the economic pulse. But Europe, with Italy at its head, advanced much faster and took the leadership from the Eastern Mediterranean, which had dominated trade since antiquity. The Commercial Revolution caused tremendous changes in the political, social, religious, and artistic life of Europe and was, in turn, stimulated and influenced by these changes.[1]

Our documents aim at showing certain aspects of the economic growth of the Mediterranean people—such as the development of markets, the emergence of new merchants, the diversification of merchandise, and the evolution of means of exchange. For this purpose we can now draw not only from narrative sources but also from the increasingly abundant series of private commercial documents.

[1] Some scholars apply the term 'Commercial Revolution' only to the last stage in the medieval commercial expansion from the thirteenth century onward. But it seems clear that the advances in the last centuries of the Middle Ages were the continuation of trends and forces the first traces of which we can easily discern in the tenth century, at least in the leading regions of Italy.

CHAPTER II

THE DEVELOPMENT OF MARKETS

Towns in North Africa and Southern Italy in the Tenth Century

MANY ECONOMIC historians have regarded and still regard grants of market rights as the first significant signs of the commercial awakening of a region. Other historians, including the writers of this book, ascribe far greater significance to the development of towns. As a matter of fact, a market may channel existing trade, but it does not create the flow of goods. Charters granting markets were particularly numerous in the ninth century not because trade was then picking up, but because each market catered almost exclusively to the needs of its surrounding area. A town, however, by its very existence stimulates trade and manufacture. It brings together a number of consumers who need food and other necessities that they cannot produce. So long as a town is merely an administrative, religious, or military center, its commercial importance cannot be very great. Many Roman towns never developed beyond the stage of consumption centers. Medieval towns, however, played a greater role in commercial development because an ever-growing proportion of the population was made up of craftsmen—that is, of producers—as well as of merchants.[1]

During the early Middle Ages a few towns in Western Europe[2] included some merchants and craftsmen besides the kernel of military, religious, and administrative officials and personnel, but large trading cities existed only in Byzantine and Muslim territory. By the tenth century, however, the most advanced towns in Italy were rivaling in size and economic importance all but the larger Byzantine and Muslim cities. The comparison is made clearer when we read Ibn Hawqal's description of three African and two Italian centers in the late tenth century[3] (Documents 16, 17, 18). North Africa at that time had reached its commercial and political zenith, while southern Italy was still far short of its fullest development. It is worth noting that Ajadabiya, where the Muslim geographer found a solid if modest

[1] See especially the forceful discussion of the problem in H. Pirenne, *Economic and Social History of Medieval Europe*, Chap. I.

[2] We should prefer the term 'Catholic Europe,' which is historically and geographically more correct—'Catholic' is a shortened form of 'Roman Catholic,' that is, peoples who acknowledge the jurisdiction of the pope—but we yield to popular usage and use 'Western.'

[3] Ibn Hawqal was not always an original writer. He borrowed from Istakhri (fl. *c.* 950) who in turn borrowed from al-Balkhi (*c.* 931). But he generally brought former accounts up to date, and he knew Africa well because he was born there. See M. J. de Goeje, 'Die Istakhri-Balkhi Frage,' *Zeitschrift der Deutschen Morgenländischen Gesellschaft*, XXV (1871), 42–58.

commercial and agricultural prosperity, began to decline shortly afterwards. Its name was twice in the headlines of the newspapers when the British advances in Mussolini's Libya were checked there; but Ajadabiya had become a squalid oasis in the desert.[4] Sijilmasa, once the medieval queen of the Sahara and the terminus of caravans from the gold-bearing regions of Senegal, today even lacks ruins to witness its greatness.[5] Kairouan has preserved some importance only as a religious center. While these Muslim cities declined, Naples and Amalfi were rising to higher and higher commercial peaks.[6]

16

Abu al-Qasim Muhammad ibn Hawqal, *The Book of the Routes and the Kingdoms*[7]

[North Africa, c. 977]

AJADABIYA

Ajadabiya, a town adjacent to the country of Barca, is situated in a stony plain. It has some buildings of stone, but the larger part is constructed of clay or bricks. It also has a very clean mosque. In the neighborhood there are many Berber camps. Their cultivated fields are not watered, water being lacking as it is in Barca. Date trees are sufficient for the needs of the population. The emir who presides over the public prayer collects the taxes. He collects from the Berbers dwelling in the neighborhood of the town the tithe, the *kharaj*, and the tax on their vegetables and fruits; he also levies tolls on the caravans leaving for the country of the Negroes and those arriving from it. This town is situated close to the sea. Ships call there with merchandise and carry away other wares. The largest exports are inexpensive suits and woolen cloth by the piece. People there drink rain water.

17

Abu al-Qasim Muhammad ibn Hawqal, *The Book of the Routes and the Kingdoms*[8]

[North Africa, c. 977]

KAIROUAN AND SIJILMASA

Kairouan, the largest town of the Maghrib, surpasses all others in its

[4] On the decadence of the coastal towns of North Africa, see the brilliant though one-sided reconstruction of E. F. Gautier, *L'Islamisation de l'Afrique du Nord; les siècles obscurs du Maghreb.*

[5] There is no adequate work on Sijilmasa, but some information may be found in G. Marçais, *Les Arabes en Berberie, du XIe au XIVe siècle,* and in R. S. Lopez, *Studi sull'economia genovese nel medio evo.*

[6] On Naples see G. Doria, *Storia di una capitale,* and on Amalfi see G. M. Monti, *L'espansione mediterranea del mezzogiorno d'Italia e della Sicilia,* with Bibliography.

[7] This excerpt is translated from the French version by M. G. de Slane, 'Ibn Haucal, Description de l'Afrique,' *Journal Asiatique,* ser. 3, XIII (1842), 162–63.

[8] *Ibid.,* pp. 249–53.

commerce, its riches, and the beauty of its buildings and bazars.[9] It is the seat of government of the whole Maghrib, the center to which flows the wealth of the land, and the residence of the sultan of that country. I heard from Abu al-Hasan . . .[10] head of the [public] treasury in A.H. 336 (A.D. 947-48), that the income of all provinces and localities of the Maghrib . . . was between seven hundred and eight hundred million dinars. . . .[11]

The exports from the Maghrib to the East are fair mulatto girls, who become concubines of the 'Abbasid princes and of other [great persons]; many sultans were born of these women. . . . Other exports are young and handsome European slaves, amber, silk, suits of very fine woolen, fineries, woolen skirts, carpets, iron, lead, mercury, eunuchs from the countries of the Negroes and of the Slavs. People there possess excellent draft horses and camels inured to fatigue, which they procure from the Berbers. Prices of foodstuffs, edibles, drinks, and meats are extremely low because [the Maghrib is] so distant from large towns and villages. Fruits and vegetables are of good quality, and the number of camels owned by the Berbers and the peoples of the deserts far surpasses that belonging to the Arabs. . . .[12]

Kairouan and Sijilmasa are similar in salubrity of climate and in their nearness to the desert. Rich caravans constantly leave Sijilmasa for the Sudan and bring great profits to the inhabitants of that town. . . . The inhabitants of other towns in that country [Maghrib] perhaps resemble those of Sijilmasa in their characteristics and the conditions of their existence, but they are inferior to the latter in wealth and comforts. I myself have seen at Adughast a record in which a man of Sijilmasa acknowledged that he owed a person of the same town 40,000 dinars, and when I spoke about this later in Khurasan and in Iraq, the fact was regarded as unique.[13] Throughout his reign, al-Mu'izz levied a tax on the caravans going to the Sudan. He also collected the tithe, the *kharaj*, dues on the sales of camels, oxen, and sheep, taxes on all

[9] A bazar is an exchange or market place.

[10] Here and hereafter dots indicate omission of passages not concerned with the commercial economy of North Africa.

[11] This figure is certainly exaggerated. De Slane suggests that we read 'thousand' for 'million' or at least that we substitute 'dirhams' for 'dinars.' But 800,000 dinars, compared with figures quoted by other Muslim writers for the income of the 'Abbasid caliphs, seems to be too little for the income of the Fatimid caliphs; 800,000,000 dirhams seems still too high. A dinar was a Muslim coin equivalent to the Byzantine nomisma, a gold piece weighing about four grams and a half; unlike the nomisma it was steadily, though not recklessly, debased both in weight and alloy. The dirham was a silver coin originally worth one tenth of a dinar, but hardly worth more than one twelfth of a dinar at the time of Ibn Hawqal.

[12] The Arabs of Arabia proper.

[13] It is indeed the highest figure of this kind ever quoted in Muslim private records, and it has few parallels in figures quoted for Western European trade in the prime of the medieval commercial revolution.

wares sent from there to the province of Africa, Fez, Sus, and Aghmat. All this, plus the farming of the mint, amounted to 400,000 dinars.

18

Abu al-Qasim Muhammad ibn Hawqal, *The Book of the Routes and the Kingdoms*[14]

[North Africa, *c.* 977]

NAPLES AND AMALFI

The territory of Calabria borders on that of Lombardy,[15] the first state of which is Salerno. Then there is Amalfi, the most prosperous town in Lombardy, the most noble, the most illustrious on account of its conditions, the most affluent and opulent. The territory of Amalfi borders on that of Naples. This is a fair city, but less important than Amalfi. The main wealth of Naples is linen and linen cloth. I have seen there pieces the like of which I found in no other country, and there is no craftsman in any other workshop[16] in the world who is able to manufacture it. They are woven 100 *dhira'*[17] [in length] by 15 or 10 [in width], and they sell for 150 *ruba'i*[18] a piece, more or less.

The Permanent Market in Milan in the Tenth Century

TRADE IN MEDIEVAL cities was carried on from the windows of residential houses, in the homes of merchants, in front of craftsmen's workshops, on docks of seas and rivers, and in many other places. The busiest center, however, was the public market. This usually was a square occupied by carts, removable stalls, benches (*banchi, tabulae,* etc.), or by semipermanent stands (*stationes*), and surrounded by buildings with the shops and the vaulted storage rooms of the more important merchants (*apothecae, voltae, fundaci*). As time went by, permanent structures tended to displace removable stalls, the single market branched out into many specialized markets and into district markets, and the shopping center spread over one street after another. In the tenth century, however, the public market still was the commercial core in the more advanced cities of Western Europe. We can form some idea of a public market by studying the market in Milan through the charter whereby Otto I granted certain plots of land to the Church of Saint Ambrose

[14] This excerpt is translated from the Italian version by M. Amari in *Biblioteca arabo-sicula*, I, 24–25.

[15] 'Lombardy,' of course, here means primarily the Lombard principalities of Salerno, Benevento, and Capua, but it was also used to indicate the surrounding area. Cf. the Byzantine theme or province of Longobardia.

[16] *Tiraz* originally meant embroidery, then robe from the embroidery on it, and finally a workshop in which robes were manufactured. *Tiraz* very frequently refers to workshops under supervision of the government.

[17] The *dhira'* is the length from the elbow to the tip of the middle finger.

[18] The *ruba'i* was a coin worth one fourth of a dinar.

(Document 19). Milan, it must be noted, was one of the most thriving commercial centers in Lombard Italy, although it had not yet surpassed Pavia, the political capital.[19]

19

From the Latin[20]

[Como, February, 952]

In the name of the Holy and Indivisible Trinity, Otto, king ruling by divine clemency. Be it known to the diligence of all the faithful of the Holy Church of God and of our present and future [subjects], that by intervention and petition of our beloved wife Adelgida and of our dearest brother Bruno we concede, give, and bestow by this order, so far as we justly and legally may, to the monastery of the blessed confessor of Christ, Ambrose, where his venerable body lies buried, five plots of land appertaining to our crown inside the city of Milan and lying in the locality where is the public market: One plot, where there are stands[21] which Giovanni, son of the late Ambrogio, and also Giovanni, who is surnamed Grasso, and Prando, son of Magnone, are known to hold, borders on two sides the roads, on the third side [the property] of Saint Ambrose and of Annone, brother of Walzone, merchant,[22] on the fourth side likewise [the property] of Saint Ambrose. Another plot where there are also stands, borders on the one side the sewer, on another side [the property] of the heirs of the late Adoaldo, on the third side the road. Also, the third plot borders on three sides [the property] of Saint Ambrose, on the fourth the road. Also, the fourth plot nearby, where the well of the king is, borders on the one side [the property] of Saint Ambrose, on the other side [the property] of the heirs of the late Gisprando, on the third side the road, on the fourth side the entrance. The fifth plot, indeed, borders on the one side the road, on another the entrance to the house of Arduino, on the third side the land and house of the aforesaid Arduino, on the fourth side [the property] of Domenico, who is surnamed Carlo. In addition we concede to the said monastery a hall[23] together with the plot on which it is situated—likewise appertaining to our kingship—being inside the aforesaid city in the market mentioned above, with the stands therein having before

---

[19] On the Milanese commercial economy of that period, see A. Visconti, 'Ricerche sul diritto pubblico milanese nell'alto medio evo,' *Annali della R. Università di Macerata*, III (1928), 101–229; VII (1931), 205–45; and, by the same author, 'Negotiatores de Mediolano,' *Annali della R. Università di Macerata*, V (1929), 177–96. See also A. Bosisio, *Origini del Comune di Milano*.

[20] *Monumenta Germaniae historica, Diplomata regum et imperatorum Germaniae*, I, 226.

[21] Here and henceforth, 'stand' translates *statio*.   [22] *Negotiatoris*. The word refers to Walzone.

[23] *Salam*, a building with a large hall; it sometimes but not always has other rooms of smaller size.

them small benches,[24] where the aforesaid sewer is the border on the one end, on another side our public property, on the two remaining sides the roads. And the above-mentioned five plots with the aforesaid [buildings], taken together, are by correct measure 24 *tabulae*. . . .

Trade in Lombardy Before the Rise of the Communes

WE HAVE CAUGHT a glimpse of a small section of a market place. Let us now enlarge our perspective to watch the entire picture of commercial activity in Pavia and along the political frontiers of the Lombard kingdom of Italy in the tenth century. Wrathful Anglo-Saxons and other transalpine merchants clear their wares through the border customs houses, already mentioned in the law of Aistulf, and make ready to buy in Pavia the precious Eastern merchandise which Italo-Byzantine merchants carry on Lombard rivers and roads. The city itself bustles with the activity of merchants and craftsmen grouped in mysteries under the leadership of appointed masters.[25] Royal officials seem to supervise the entire economic life in a way reminiscent of Constantinople.

They will not do so for long. Control by royal authority in Italy does not survive the dawn of the Commercial Revolution. The new economic forces help the bishops undermine the power of the emperor and king, but at the same time they also prepare the future downfall of both bishops and imperial officials and the victory of the free Commune. Document 20 is a nostalgic list of the rights and incomes lost by the royal treasury (*camera*) in Pavia. Compiled in the early eleventh century, it commemorates a regime which was already doomed even as the document was drafted.

20

Regulations of the Royal Court at Pavia
From the Vulgar Latin[26]

[Pavia, between *c.* 1010 and *c.* 1020, based upon tenth-century sources]

2. . . . Merchants entering the kingdom [of Italy] were wont to pay the

[24] *Banculas.*

[25] See especially the masterly work by A. Solmi, *L'amministrazione finanziaria del regno italico nell'alto medio evo,* and the other monographs quoted in it. On the *ministerium* (mystery) of the moneyers, see R. S. Lopez, 'Continuità e adattamento nel medio evo: un millennio di storia delle associazioni di monetieri nell'Europa meridionale' in *Studi in onore di Gino Luzzatto,* II, 74–117, and R. S. Lopez, 'Byzantine Law in the Seventh Century and its Reception by the Germans and the Arabs,' *Byzantion,* XVII (1942–1943), 445–61. On the *clusae* (customs houses), see R. S. Lopez, 'Du marché temporaire à la colonie permanente,' *Annales: Economies, Sociétés, Civilisations,* IV (1949), 389–405.

[26] A. Solmi, ed., *Instituta regalia et ministeria camere regum Lomgobardorum* [*seu*] *honorantie civitatis Papie,* in *L'amministrazione finanziaria del regno italico,* pp. 21–24. The document is also published by A. Hofmeister in *Monumenta Germaniae historica, Scriptores,* Vol. XXX, Part 2, pp. 1450–57. The text of the eleventh-century document has come down to us as the central part of a fourteenth-century pamphlet. The later writer by his own mistakes in copying has made still more confused and ungrammatical a text which even in its original form must have been hard to interpret.

decima[27] on all merchandise[28] at the customs houses and at [the beginning of] the roads appertaining to the king.[29] And the [customs houses] are these: the first is Susa, the second Bard, the third Bellinzona, the fourth Chiavenna, the fifth Bolzano, the sixth Volargne, the seventh Trevile, the eighth San Pietro di Zuglio on the Monte Croce road, the ninth near Aquileia, the tenth Cividale del Friuli.[30] All persons coming from beyond the mountains into Lombardy are obligated to pay the *decima* on horses, male and female slaves,[31] woolen, linen, and hemp cloth, tin, and swords. And here at the gate they are obligated to pay the *decima* on all merchandise to the delegate of the treasurer.[32] But everything that [pilgrims] bound for Rome to Saint Peter's take with them for expenses is to be passed without payment of the *decima*. No one ought to exact the *decima* from the pilgrims themselves bound for Rome or to hinder them in any way.[33] And if anyone does so, let him be anathema.

3. As for the nation[34] of the Angles and Saxons, they have come and were wont to come with their merchandise and wares. And [formerly], when they saw their trunks and sacks[35] being emptied at the gates, they grew angry and started rows with the employees (*ministrales*) of the treasury. The [parties] were wont to hurl abusive words and in addition very often inflicted wounds upon one another. But in order to cut short such great evils and to remove danger [of conflicts], the king of the Angles and Saxons and the king of the Lombards agreed together as follows: The nation of the Angles and Saxons is no longer to be subject to the *decima*. And in return for this the king of the

---

[27] A ten-percent tax.

[28] *Negocium* usually means 'business transaction,' at least in later documents. Here, however, it clearly means 'merchandise,' even as *negociator* here means 'merchant.'

[29] *Vias … Regi pertinentes*, i.e., roads subject to the jurisdiction of the king as parts of the royal demesne; public highways under royal administration as opposed to private roads maintained and exploited by vassals.

[30] The list includes both those customs houses which Italy had recently lost—when part of its territory was transferred to the German kingdom—and the new customs houses established along the new borders. Each *clusa* or fortified customs house was situated in the first town inside Italy along a road from one of the Alpine passes. The list mentions the *clusae* in their geographical order from west to east, but it mentions no customs house along some of the most important roads crossing the Alps. Solmi believes that these omissions are accidental, but one might suggest that the roads for which no *clusae* are mentioned had ceased to 'appertain' to the king, that is, were no longer under his jurisdiction.

[31] *Servis, ancillis.* The fact that they are mentioned as taxable 'merchandise' after horses and before textiles makes it clear that they were slaves and not serfs.

[32] *Camerarius.* A synonymous expression used in this document is *Magister Camerae*, which we translate by 'master of the treasury.' As for *missus*, in this specific instance he is a delegate of the treasurer rather than a messenger or agent; cf. the *Legatarios* of the Byzantine Prefect.

[33] The exemption of pilgrims was both rooted in custom and guaranteed in certain cases by law. The same conditions prevailed in the Muslim countries.

[34] *Gens.*   [35] *Males et bulges.*

Angles and Saxons and their nation are bound and are obligated to send to
the [king's] palace in Pavia and to the king's treasury,[36] every third year,
fifty pounds of refined silver, two large, handsome greyhounds, hairy or
furred, in chains, with collars covered with gilded plates sealed or enameled
with the arms of the king, two excellent embossed shields, two excellent
lances, and two excellent swords wrought and tested. And to the master of
the treasury they are obligated to give two large coats of miniver and two
pounds of refined silver. And they are to receive a safe-conduct[37] from the
master of the treasury that they may not suffer any annoyance as they come
and go.

4. As for the duke of the Venetians with his Venetians, he is obligated to
give every year in the [king's] palace in Pavia fifty pounds of Venetian
deniers. These deniers are of one ounce each, equally good as the Pavian
deniers in regard to weight and silver [content]. And to the master of the
treasury [he is obligated to give] one excellent pall[38] on account of [the
rights] that appertain to the king of the Lombards. And that nation does
not plow, sow, or gather vintage. This tribute is called pact[39] because
[by it] the nation of the Venetians is allowed to buy grain and wine in every
port[40] and to make their purchases in Pavia, and they are not to suffer any
annoyance.

5. Many wealthy Venetian merchants were wont to come to Pavia with
their merchandise. And they were wont to pay to the Monastery of Saint
Martin, which is called Outgate, the fortieth solidus on all merchandise.
When the Venetians [or rather] the maiores [among them] come to Pavia,
each of them is obligated to give to the master of the treasury every year
one pound of pepper, one pound of cinnamon, one pound of galanga, and
one pound of ginger. And to the wife of the master of the treasury [they are
obligated to give] an ivory comb and a mirror and a set of accessories,[41]
or else twenty solidi of good Pavian [deniers].

6. Likewise the men of Salerno, Gaeta, and Amalfi were accustomed to

[36] Cameram Regis.   [37] Sigillum.

[38] The word palium is almost exclusively used for silk cloaks of Byzantine manufacture. The
tribute of a palium was remitted in 1001 by Otto III.

[39] Istud censsum [sic] appellatur pactum: the word censum was a technical term for tribute in
Western Europe, whereas pactum was not the name of the tribute, as the writer seems to believe,
but the name of the agreement (pakton in Greek; the word was of Latin origin, but in the early
medieval West it appears only in treaties concluded by Italo-Byzantine cities).

[40] Portus in the early Middle Ages does not necessarily mean 'port' in the modern sense, but
any center to which commodities are carried or any legitimate mart under the control of public
authorities.

[41] Paraturam unam, apparently meaning any object besides the comb and mirror that is
required for the dressing table of the treasurer's wife.

come to Pavia with abundant merchandise. And they were wont to give to the treasury in the king's palace the fortieth solidus. And to the wife of the treasurer [they gave] individually spices and accessories just as did the Venetians.[42]

7. As for the great and honorable and very wealthy *ministri*[43] of the merchants of Pavia, they have always received from the emperor's hand credentials with every honor,[44] so that they suffer no harm or annoyance in any way, wherever they may be, whether in the market or [traveling] by water or by land. And whoever acts contrary to this is obliged to pay a thousand gold *mancusi*[45] into the king's treasury.

8. As for the *ministerium* of the mint of Pavia, there are to be nine noble and wealthy masters above all the other moneyers, who are to supervise and to direct all other moneyers jointly with the master of the treasury, so that they never strike deniers inferior to those they always have struck in regard to weight and silver [content], to wit, ten out of twelve.[46] And those nine masters are obligated to pay for the rent[47] of the mint twelve pounds of Pavian deniers into the king's treasury every year and four pounds of the same to the count [palatine] of Pavia. If a mint master discover a forger, [they are to act] in this wise: They, together with the count of Pavia and the master of the treasury, are under obligation to have the right hand of that forger cut off. And [they must see to it] that all the property of the forger is turned over to the king's treasury.

9. As for the moneyers of Milan, they are to have four noble and wealthy masters, and with the advice of the treasurer in Pavia are to strike Milanese deniers, equally good as Pavian deniers in regard to silver [content] and weight. And they are obligated to pay rent to the master of the treasury in Pavia twelve pounds of good Milanese deniers every year. And if they dis-

[42] Solmi suggests, probably with reason, that the lack of a mention of tributes to the treasurer himself is an accidental omission of the manuscript. The entire paragraph is particularly ungrammatical and obscure.

[43] *Ministri* simply means members of a *ministerium* ('mystery' or 'craft'; usually, but not necessarily, a craft gild). There may be some doubt as to whether one ought to read instead *magistri*, 'masters,' since the expression *ministri negociatorum* is redundant (*negociatores*, 'merchants,' would have been sufficient). We know that the Pavian merchants had masters at their head.

[44] *Preceptum cum omni honore*. This *preceptum* must have been a charter promising imperial protection to the Pavian merchants throughout the territory of the Empire. Similar charters were issued in behalf of the *negociatores* of many other cities. The word *honor* is much more ambiguous. It may mean specific privileges of a fiscal character (exemption from some tribute?) or merely 'honor' in its modern meaning of esteem or token of esteem.

[45] All Muslim (nonfigured) gold coins and all imitations of these coins that were struck in Western Europe were most commonly called *mancusi*.

[46] This seems to mean that the moneyers retained two deniers out of twelve as their fee.

[47] *Fictum*.

cover a forger, they are under obligation to cut off his right hand and to turn over his entire property to the king's treasury. . . .[48]

13. There are other *ministeria*. All shipmen and boatmen[49] are obligated to furnish two good men as masters under the authority of the treasurer in Pavia. Whenever the king is in Pavia, they themselves are obligated to go with the ships and these two masters are obligated to outfit two large vessels, one for the king and one for the queen, and to build a house with planks, and to cover it well. As for the pilots,[50] they are to have one vessel, so that [people] may be safe on the water. And they, together with their juniors, are to receive every day their expenses from the king's court. . . .

17. And in regard to all these *ministeria* you should know this: that no man is to perform [his functions] unless he is one of the *ministri*.[51] And if another man does, he is obligated to pay the *bannum*[52] into the king's treasury and to swear that he will no longer do so. Nor ought any merchant to conclude his business[53] in any market before the merchants of Pavia do, unless he is one of the merchants of Pavia. And whoever acts contrary to this, let him pay the *bannum*. . . .

The Final Product of the Commercial Revolution: Milan in 1288

IT WOULD BE highly interesting to follow step by step the growth of the city as a permanent market. But this would require more space than we have at our disposal. It will suffice to compare the pictures of Milan and Pavia in the tenth century with a long description of Milan (Documents 21, 22, 23) by Friar Bonvesin della Riva, a thirteenth-century author who wrote in Latin, in Italian, and in Milanese dialect and won for himself by his literary work a modest but respectable renown. The reliability of his data and figures formerly was strongly challenged, especially because his praise of his native city had been known only through excerpts inserted in a very unreliable compilation by another friar, Galvano Fiamma. Discovery of a manuscript of his work and careful checking of his data against other sources have gone a long way towards restoring his reputation.[54] To be sure, some of his figures may have been wrongly transcribed by the copyist of the only extant manuscript;

---

[48] We omit here the description of a number of *ministeria* carrying out various crafts—gold washers, fishermen, leathermakers, soapmakers.

[49] *Naute et nauterii.* The two words are practically synonymous, but there must have been a difference.

[50] *Gubernatores.*   [51] *Nullus homo debet illorum ministerium facere, nisi illi qui ministri sunt.*

[52] *Bannum* was the fine due from one incurring the ban.

[53] *Dissolvere eorum negocium.* Here *negocium* does not seem to mean 'merchandise' but 'transaction.' The Pavian merchants are given priority rights.

[54] On Bonvesin della Riva as a literary figure, see G. Bertoni, *Il Duecento*, pp. 188ff. On his value as a historical source, see C. Barbagallo, *Storia universale: il medioevo*, pp. 925–31.

his love for his fatherland has led to some exaggeration; accurate statistics were not available at his time. But it is now generally believed that Bonvesino did his best to obtain trustworthy data from well informed sources, and that he used some discernment in weighing the evidence.[55]

21

Bonvesin della Riva, *On the Marvels of the City of Milan*
From the Latin[56]

Milan, [1288]

IN PRAISE OF MILAN'S HOUSING

In regard to housing . . .[57] the truth is there before the eyes of those who see. The streets in this city are quite wide, the palaces quite beautiful, the houses packed in, not scattered but continuous, stately, adorned in a stately manner.

1. Dwellings with doors giving access to the public streets have been found to number about 12,500, and in their number are very many in which many families live together with crowds of dependents. And this indicates the astonishing density of population of citizens.

2. The roofed commons [open to all] neighbors in those squares which are popularly called *coperti*[58] almost reach the record number of sixty.

3. The court of the Commune, befitting such a great city, spreads over an area of ten *pertiche* or thereabouts. And in order to make this more easily understandable perchance to some people, [I shall specify that it] measures 130 cubits from east to west and 136 from north to south. In the midst of it stands a wonderful palace, and in the court itself there is a tower, in which are the four bells of the Commune. On the eastern side is a palace in which are the rooms of the podestà and of the judges, and at its end on the northern side is the chapel of the podestà, built in honor of our patron, the Blessed Ambrose. And another palace prolongs the court on the north; so, similarly, on the

[55] There is no general history of the Milanese economy in the high Middle Ages, but information on various aspects and periods can be found in T. Zerbi, *Aspetti economico-tecnici del mercato di Milano nel Trecento;* G. Barbieri, *Economia e politica nel ducato di Milano;* G. Biscaro, 'Gli estimi del Comune di Milano,' *Archivio Storico Lombardo,* LV (1928), 345–495.

[56] Bonvicinus de Rippa [Bonvesin della Riva], 'De magnalibus urbis Mediolani,' ed. by F. Novati, in *Bullettino dell'Istituto Storico Italiano,* XX (1898), 67–114. There also is a free Italian translation, with useful comment, by E. Verga: Fra Bonvesino dalla Riva, *Le meraviglie di Milano.*

[57] The only extant manuscript of the entire work has a gap here; this cannot be filled by using other incomplete manuscripts and excerpts.

[58] The *coperti*, the Milanese version of what elsewhere was the portico or arcade, finally disappeared during the nineteenth century. Glass-roofed galleries have to some extent taken their place in affording citizens promenades and meeting places sheltered from sun and rain and adorned with shop windows; but the portico still plays an important part in the life of Italian towns.

west. To the south there is also the hall where the sentences of condemnation
are publicly proclaimed.[59]

4. The city itself is ringed as a circle, and its wonderful rounded shape is a
mark of its perfection. . . .[60]

5. . . . Outside the wall of the moat there are so many suburban houses that
they alone would be enough to constitute a city. . . .

6. The main gates of the city are also very strong, and they reach the
number of six. The secondary gates, named *pusterle*, are ten. . . .

7. The sanctuaries of the saints . . . are about two hundred in the city
alone, having 480 altars. . . .

8. [In honor of the Virgin Mary] thirty-six churches have been built in the
city, and undoubtedly there are more than 260 in the county (*comitatus*). . . .

9. The steeples, built in the manner of towers, are about 120 in the city. . . .

10. In the county there are pleasant and delightful localities, even stately
towns, fifty in number; and among them is Monza, ten miles distant from
the city, worthier to be named a city than a town.[61] Indeed, 150 villages with
castles are subject to the jurisdiction of our Commune, and among them
there are a great many, each of which has more than five hundred inhabitants
able to bear arms. And in these very towns as well as in the villages not only
farmers and craftsmen live but also very many magnates of high nobility.
And there also are other isolated buildings, some of which are called mills
and others, popularly, *cassine*[62]—the infinite number of which I can hardly
estimate. . . .

22

Bonvesin della Riva, On the Marvels of the City of Milan
From the Latin[63]

Milan, [1288]

IN PRAISE OF MILAN'S POPULATION

When considered in regard to population, it seems to me that it outshines
all the other cities in the world.

[59] The central building, built between 1228 and 1233, is still extant (Palazzo della Ragione).
The entire square has been preserved much as Bonvesino describes it, although the buildings underwent partial modifications or total reconstruction at various periods ranging from 1316 to 1654.

[60] There follows a description of the walls and moats; the figures, however, are not certain
because slight differences appear in the various manuscripts. According to Novati, the most
probable figure is 10,141 cubits for the outer wall, which enclosed the moat. A. Mazzi, 'Nota
metrologica,' *Archivio Storico Lombardo*, ser. 3, X (1901), 351–69, tentatively gives the length of
the cubit as 0.44820 meters.

[61] In fact, Monza was an important center of the woolen industry and of other trades.

[62] *Cassine* are farm houses in a not too precise sense. The word is still alive in Italian.

[63] See note 56.

1. In fact, its natives of both sexes have the peculiarity of being rather tall, jovial in appearance, and quite friendly, not deceitful, still less malicious in dealing with people from outside their town, and because of this they also are more highly considered abroad than are others. . . . They live decently, orderly, and magnificently; they use clothing that does them honor; wherever they may be, at home or elsewhere, they are quite free in spending, esteemed, honorable, good-humored[64] in customs and way of life. . . .

2. The population, as numerous in the city as in the county or in its district, increases every day, and the city spreads out with the [erection of new] buildings. How could the people not thrive where it is so glorious to live? For this reason, if citizens are counted together with strangers of all kinds they are found in all to be many more than 200,000 men [in the entire county]—each of them to be regarded as an able man at war. And we have not counted in their number men of different kinds exempted [from military service]—monks, canons, and other clerics and religious, both those professed and those living in their own homes with their servants. . . .

3. In the city, indeed, there are ten canonries, excluding from this number the house of canons [located] where the cathedral church is. But in the county there are seventy, not including seven canonries of the Order of the Humiliati,[65] and the canons regular complete the number with twenty-one.

4. Then there are in the city ninety-four chapels. . . .

5. In the city there are six convents of monks, and the nunneries are eight. . . .

6. Again, in the city, including the suburbs, which are always to be regarded as included whenever the city is mentioned, there are ten hospitals for the sick, all properly endowed with sufficient temporal resources. The principal one of these is the Hospital of the Brolo, very rich in precious possessions; it was founded in 1145 by Goffredo de Bussero. In it, as its friars and deacons testify, at times and particularly in the days of dearth[?],[66] when count is made, there are found more than five hundred poor bed patients and just as many more not lying down. All of these receive food at the expense of the hospital itself. Besides them, also, no less than 350 babies and more, placed with individual nurses after their birth, are under the

[64] *Faceti* is almost as close to 'having a sense of humor' as to 'good-humored.'

[65] Bonvesino, according to reliable traditions, was himself a member of the Third Order of Humiliati. These religious were active in the woolen industry, and a special kind of coarse cloth was named after them. Their importance, however, must not be exaggerated; see L. Zanoni, *Gli Umiliati nei loro rapporti con l'eresia, l'industria della lana e i Comuni.*

[66] *Carastii* is a word which neither Novati nor Verga explains. They suggest that the day must have been during Lent, inasmuch as the hospital was also named 'of the Holy Lent.' The modern Italian word *carestia*, dearth, seems more plausible.

hospital's care.[67] Every sort of the poor people mentioned below,[68] except the lepers, for whom another hospital is reserved, are received there; and they are kindly and bountifully restored to health, bed as well as food being provided. Also, all the poor needing surgical care are diligently cared for by three surgeons especially assigned to this task; the latter receive a salary from the Commune. In conclusion, the misery of no man who is in want meets refusal or rejection here. In the county, indeed, there are fifteen hospitals or thereabouts.

7. There are also houses of the Second Order of the Humiliati of each sex which in the city and the county reach the number of 220; inside them there is a copious number of persons leading the religious life while working with their own hands. . . .

8. The houses of the Order of St. Augustine of each sex undoubtedly are sixty. . . .[69]

11. This, however, I affirm with certainty, that inside as well as outside the city, counting priests and other clerics of all orders . . . more than ten thousand religious are eating Ambrosian bread. . . .[70]

12. What else can be said of the huge number of the multitude living in Milan and in the county? Silence; whoever can grasp it, let him grasp it. This, however, will be forgiven me: that I am by no means silent. For, as I roughly estimate—and many definitely assert the same—more than 700,000 mouths of the two sexes, including all infants as well as adults, obtain their sustenance from the surface of the Ambrosian earth. Every day—and it is wonderful in what manner—they receive, from the hand of God, Ambrosian food.

13. Why not, even if their number is so great, since in the city alone, with its dense population, there undoubtedly are 115 parishes, among which there certainly are some in each of which indeed more than five hundred families live, while in a few others about one thousand live?

14. Let therefore anyone who can count how many persons live in such a city. And if he is able to do it accurately, he will count up to the number of about 200,000, as I firmly believe. For it is certainly proved and supported

---

[67] In 1168 the different foundations already existing for the relief of the poor and the foundlings were grouped into a unit by Archbishop Galdino.

[68] *Sic*—but in fact 'mentioned above.' The lepers' hospital mentioned immediately after probably is that of Saint Lazarus, although a little earlier we also hear of another hospital for lepers, Saint Materno's.

[69] There follows a very long list of other religious orders with the number of their convents and houses.

[70] *Ambrosian* means Milanese, from Saint Ambrose, the patron of the city; but here, when speaking of religious orders, Bonvesino must be thinking particularly of the patron saint.

by serious, careful investigation, that every day, taking into account the different seasons, 1,200 *modii* of grain and more are consumed in the city alone. That this is the truth of the matter, those who are wont to collect the tribute of the grain ground in the mills can certify.

15. Whoever wishes to know how many warriors there are in time of war should know that more than forty thousand—that is, counting each and all—live in this city who are able to fight the enemy with sword or lance or other weapon. . . .

16. In it and in its county more than ten thousand could easily maintain war horses [if] ordered by the Commune. . . .

17. There are in this city alone 120 doctors of both laws, and their college is believed to have no equal in the entire world, either in number or in learning. All these, ready to give [judicial] sentences, gladly take the money of the litigants.

18. The notaries are more than 1,500, among whom there are a great many who are excellent in drawing contracts.

19. The messengers of the Commune, popularly named *servitori*, undoubtedly are six hundred.

20. Six, indeed, are the principal trumpeters of the Commune, honorable and distinguished men. . . .

21. The experts in medicine, who are popularly named physicians, are twenty-eight.

22. The surgeons of different specialties, indeed, are more than 150, among whom are a great many who, obviously being excellent physicians, have derived from the ancestors of their family the ancient traditions of surgery. They are believed to have no equals in the other cities of Lombardy.

23. The professors of grammatical art are eight. They supervise crowds of pupils, each professor with his rod, and teach grammar with great industry and diligence, surpassing the doctors of other cities, as I have clearly determined after careful examination.

24. There are fourteen doctors in the Ambrosian chant, of so excellent renown that because of them this city is noted for its crowds of clerics.

25. The teachers of the elements of reading and writing indeed number more than seventy.

26. The copyists, although there is no university (*Studium generale*) in the city, surpass the number of forty, and by writing books with their hands every day they earn their bread and other expenses.

27. Indeed, there are three hundred bakeries in the city (as one learns from

the books of the Commune) which bake bread for the use of the citizens. There are also very many other bakeries exempt [from taxation] which serve monks or religious of each sex; of these I think there are more than a hundred.

28. The shopkeepers,[71] who sell at retail an amazing amount of goods or all kinds, doubtlessly are more than a thousand.

29. The butchers number more than 440, and excellent meat of quadrupeds of all kinds, as suits our customs, is sold in great quantity in their shops.

30. There are more than eighteen fishermen [who catch] all kinds of fish—trout, carp, large eels, tench, grayling, eels, lampreys, crabs—and who every day bring a supply of large and small fish of every species from the lakes of our county. Those who bring fish from the rivers number more than sixty, and those who bring fish from the numberless mountain streams state that they are far more than four hundred.

31. The hostelries giving hospitality to strangers for profit number about 150.[72]

32. The smiths who outfit quadrupeds with iron shoes number about eighty, and this indicates the multitude of horsemen and horses. How many are the saddlers, how many the smiths of bridles and spurs and stirrups, I pass over in silence.

33. The makers of the sweet-sounding brass bells which are attached to the breasts of horses—and which we do not know are made anywhere else—are more than thirty, and each of them has under him many assistants in his craft. . . .

23

Bonvesin della Riva, *On the Marvels of the City of Milan*
From the Latin[73]

Milan, [1288]

IN PRAISE OF MILAN'S FERTILITY AND ABUNDANCE OF ALL
GOODS

When considered in regard to the fertility of territory and the abundance of all goods useful for human consumption, [its excellence] already is evident, but I shall explain it more plainly.

[71] *Tabernarii* evidently stems from classic Latin, *taberna*, 'shop,' and not from medieval Latin, *taberna*, 'inn.'

[72] Unlike many other cities, Milan allowed innkeepers to buy and to sell wares in their inns, as appears from the statutes of 1216.

[73] See note 56.

1. In fact,[74] in our territories, fertile, fortunate, fruitful,[75] all kinds of cereals are produced: wheat, rye, millet, panic from which bread is made, and all kinds of vegetables which can be cooked and are excellent to eat—beans, chickpeas, navy beans, small chick peas, lentils—in such an amazing quantity that after being distributed in different places they not only make good the deficiency of foodstuffs in the city of Como but also are transported and distributed to feed peoples beyond the Alps. Why not, since ... more than thirty thousand yoke of oxen cultivate our territory? ... Also, in our fields an infinite and unbelievable quantity of flax is produced. ...

3. Sour and sweet cherries of all kinds, both cultivated and wild, grow in such great quantity that sometimes it happens that more than sixty carts of them are in one day brought through the gates of the city, and they are available for sale in the city at any hour from mid-May until almost mid-July. Plums, too, white, yellow, dark, damascene, likewise in almost infinite quantity, are distributed ripe from shortly before the Kalends of July until the month of October.

At the same time plums begin to appear, pears, summer apples, black-berries, and the figs named 'flowers' appear in abundance; then follow culti-vated filberts; afterwards the cornel-berries, particularly appropriate for ladies;[76] also jujubes and peaches amazingly abundant; likewise, figs and grapes of various kinds; also almonds, although few of them; wild filberts, nuts in unbelievable quantity, which all citizens who like them enjoy all the year round after all meals. Nuts can also be mixed, ground, with eggs and cheese and pepper to stuff meat in winter. Also an oil is obtained from them which is liberally consumed among us. Then again, winter pears and apples and crabapples grow, all of which abundantly supply our citizens throughout winter and beyond. Also pomegranates appear, most useful to the sick. Grapes of many kinds are abundant, and they appear ripe about the middle of July and are available for sale until the Kalends of December or there-abouts.

4. Also the common and the noble chestnuts—the latter named *marroni*— grow in infinite quantity and they are distributed all the year round in abundance to both citizens and foreigners. These, served in different ways, abundantly refresh our families. In fact, they may be cooked green in the open fire, and may be consumed after the other foods instead of dates and,

---

[74] *Etiam* is probably a mistake for *enim*.

[75] *Felici fetu fertilibus.* Bonvesino delighted in this pun, and we have tried to keep it in the translation.

[76] *Corna mulieribus aptiora*, in those days, was one of the customary jokes about the unfaithful-ness of women.

in my opinion, they taste better than dates. Often they are boiled, and many eat them, cooked like this, with a spoon; then, very often, the water in which they were cooked is poured out and they are chewed without bread, indeed instead of bread. Also, when dried out by the slow heat of the sun, they are then recommended for the sick. Very many medlars, so displeasing to bankrupt gamblers,[77] appear in the month of November. Olives grow in some parts of our county, although they are not very abundant, and laurel berries, which should be eaten with warm wine to cure pains in the stomach. Other kinds of fruit also grow, but what was said above about them will be enough for the present. No dates, pepper, or any of the very many spices from overseas are grown here—and I am not sorry for this, since they do not grow anywhere except in arid and extremely hot climates. . . .[78]

6. . . . The monastery of Chiaravalle alone gathers in its own fields every year more than three thousand cartloads of hay, as the monks of that house tell me. . . .

8. . . . More than 150,000 cartloads [of firewood] are certainly burned every year in the city alone. . . .

11. . . . It is worth noting that in the city alone about seventy oxen are slaughtered every day—counting only the days in which the consumption of meat is permitted to Christians—as I investigated carefully from a few butchers.

12. . . . As the sellers of fish themselves, having investigated carefully the truth of the matter, plainly declare, counting all days from Quinquagesima Sunday to the feast of Saint Martin [November 12], more than seven *modii* of crabs are eaten every day in the city alone. And in order that no one may remain in doubt as to what quantity is understood by *modius*, let him know that the size of the *modius* with us is eight *sextaria*, and it weighs [as much] as a heavy man. . . .

16. . . . It was learned after careful examination of those who collect the tribute of the salt for the Commune that 65,830 *sextaria* of salt or thereabouts are brought every year through the gates of the city. . . .[79] But how much pepper is likely to be consumed within the city . . . I could not learn in any way.

[77] That this fruit was as loved by the rich as hateful to the poor was a recurrent saying in popular poetry of that time, but the reason is not clear. Was it because it contains little pulp and very large seeds?

[78] The description of foodstuffs produced in the district and consumed by the inhabitants of the city goes on at great length, beginning with a list of vegetables and ending with an evaluation of the production of the more than nine hundred water mills existing in the rivers of the district. Imports of foodstuffs are also mentioned. We give only some of the most significant figures.

[79] The figure cited in the main manuscript is 55,830, but we prefer the figure above (which is

17. Four general fairs[80] are held in the city every year, that is, on the day of the ordination of the Blessed Ambrose, on the feast of the Blessed Lawrence, on the Ascension of the Blessed Mother of God, and on the feast of the Blessed Bartholomew. It is amazing to see almost innumerable merchants with their variety of wares and buyers flocking to all these fairs. Furthermore, ordinary markets[81] are held in different parts of the city two days a week, that is, on Fridays and Saturdays. Indeed—and this is more [amazing] —practically anything that man may need is brought daily not only into special places but even into the [open] squares, and all that can be sold is loudly advertised for sale. Also, there are many fairs in the towns and villages of our county, being held every year on certain days. In many of them, indeed, there is a market[82] every week, and merchants and buyers hasten to all of them in large numbers. It is evident, after [all] that has been said, that in our city it is a wonderful life for those who have money enough. Every convenience for human pleasure is known to be at hand here.

18. Also it is obvious that here any man, if he is healthy and not a good-for-nothing, may earn his living expenses and esteem according to his station. And it is worth noting that here the fecundity in offspring is just as prolific as the abundance of temporal goods. In fact, when on festive days one looks at the merry crowds of dignified men, both of the nobility and of the people, also at the bustling throngs of children incessantly scurrying here and there, and at the comely gatherings, comely groups of ladies and virgins going back and forth or standing on the doorsteps [of their homes], as dignified as if they were daughters of kings, who would say that he has ever met such a wonderful show of people this side or the other side of the sea?...[83]

Florence, a Masterpiece of the Commercial Revolution

THE FOUR ITALIAN cities of Milan, Venice, Genoa, and Florence far outstripped all other European business centers during the Commercial Revolution.[84] Milan's

---

given in the 'Ambrosian Excerpts' of the same work) for reasons pointed out by Novati, p. 113, note 1. Note that Bonvesino after citing the figure in regard to salt, which he can obtain from a reliable source, declines to evaluate the figure of pepper imports, which cannot be calculated with any precision.

[80] *Generales nundine.*   [81] *Forum comune.*   [82] *Fera.*

[83] The writer goes on to say that 'spiritual goods' are as plentiful as temporal, and lists saints, good archbishops, relics, and other blessings of Milan.

[84] In Western Europe only Paris had a larger population—probably well above 200,000—but it could not compare with the four great Italian cities in economic importance, political autonomy, or size of the bourgeois class. In these respects Ghent, Bruges, and other Flemish towns came closer to Italian business centers.

greatness was connected to some extent with its tradition as an ancient metropolis of the Roman Empire and as a leading archbishopric in the early Middle Ages. In the twelfth century the city already was both the political and economic head of Lombardy. Venice began its career after the collapse of the Roman government in the West, but it had already left behind all other maritime powers in Western Europe before the tenth century. At this period Genoa was barely lifting its head after a long period of decline and distress, but the First Crusade found the city advancing by leaps and bounds. Florence, on the other hand, did not stand out among Tuscan towns before the twelfth century. The city grew from mediocrity to splendor in many fields—artistic, political, economic—in barely more than a century and a half. Milan, Venice, and Genoa surpassed Florence in one or another aspect of commercial life, but probably none of them witnessed so complete a triumph of the bourgeoisie over the nobility. Thus the description of Florence by Giovanni Villani, a famous chronicler and a merchant by profession, is particularly valuable (Document 27). The reliability of Villani's figures, challenged more than once, can now be regarded as definitely established.[85]

Genoese and Venetian chroniclers also give detailed information on economic matters, but they supply no general picture comparable to those of Bonvesino and Villani. One has to wait until the fifteenth century to find a statistical survey of Venetian economy set forth in a speech of the doge Tommaso Mocenigo.[86] Of Genoa we have only the lively but hardly accurate description of a vernacular poet, but we can measure the commercial growth of the city in the later thirteenth century, its richest period, by comparing figures of the taxes derived from maritime trade. According to extant data, the value of wares imported and exported by sea and subject to tax increased more than four-fold from 1274 to 1293. It has been calculated that the peak figure of 1293 represents a value almost ten times as high as the exports by sea from Lübeck, the leading Hanseatic port, in 1368, the year in which the trade of Lübeck reached its highest figure.[87]

[85] See especially A. Sapori, 'L'attendibilità di alcune testimonianze cronistiche dell'economia medievale,' *Archivio Storico Italiano*, ser. 7, XII (1929), 19–30, republished in his *Studi di storia economica medievale*, 2d ed., pp. 127–35. Excerpts from Villani were published in translation by R. E. Selfe, *Selections from the First Nine Books of the Croniche Fiorentine* (London, 1896). The passage we have selected was not translated by Selfe. E. Mehl, *Die Weltanschauung des Giovanni Villani*, is of slight value. The very recent essay of E. Fiumi, 'La demografia fiorentina nelle pagine di Giovanni Villani,' *Archivio Storico Italiano*, CVIII (1950), 78–158, does not substantially impair the validity of Villani's figures.

[86] There is an excerpt from Mocenigo's speech in English under the title, 'Resources of Venice,' in *Translations and Reprints from the Original Sources of European History* (University of Pennsylvania, Department of History, Philadelphia, 1896), Vol. III, Part 2, pp. 11–14. See also G. Luzzatto, 'Sull'attendibilità di alcune statistiche economiche medievali,' *Giornale degli Economisti*, ser. 4, LXIX (1929), 122–34.

[87] See Lopez in *Cambridge Economic History*, II, 314–15. Consult also Document 207, which is an excerpt from a poem written in the Genoese vernacular.

24

Giovanni Villani, *The Chronicle of Giovanni Villani*, Book XI, Chap. xciv
From the Italian[88]

Florence [with reference to the years 1336–1338]

MORE ON THE GREATNESS AND STATE AND MAGNIFICENCE OF THE COMMUNE OF FLORENCE

Since we have spoken about the income and expenditure of the Commune of Florence in this period, I think it is fitting to mention this and other great features of our city, so that our descendants in days to come may be aware of any rise, stability,[89] and decline in condition and power that our city may undergo, and also so that, through the wise and able citizens who at the time shall be in charge of its government, [our descendants] may endeavor to advance it in condition and power, seeing our record and example in this chronicle. We find after careful investigation that in this period there were in Florence about 25,000 men from the ages of fifteen to seventy fit to bear arms, all citizens. And among them were 1,500 noble and powerful citizens who as magnates[90] gave security to the Commune. There were in Florence also some seventy-five full-dress knights. To be sure, we find that before the second popular government now in power was formed there were more than 250 knights; but from the time that the people began to rule,[91] the magnates no longer had the status and authority enjoyed earlier, and hence few persons were knighted. From the amount of bread constantly needed for the city, it was estimated that in Florence there were some 90,000 mouths divided among men, women, and children, as can readily be grasped [from what we shall say] later;[92] and it was reckoned that in the city there were always about 1,500 foreigners, transients, and soldiers, not including in the total the citizens who were clerics and cloistered monks and nuns, of whom we shall speak later. It was reckoned that in this period there were some 80,000 men

---

[88] *Cronica di Giovanni Villani*, ed. Magheri, VI, 183–87. This is the most recent edition of the chronicle, but it is far from satisfactory. Another edition, *Istorie fiorentine di Giovanni Villani*, ed. 'Classici Italiani,' VII, 201–06, has also been helpful in places. A critical edition of Villani is still an unsatisfied want.

[89] The word *stare*, which we have translated 'stability,' is found only in the Classici Italiani edition.

[90] The legislation against the nobility required magnates to put up bail with the Commune.

[91] *Poichè 'l popolo fu*, literally, 'after the people was.' 'People,' of course, means commoners or bourgeoisie as opposed to magnates or patriciate (*grandi*).

[92] Classici Italiani: *come si potrà comprendere appresso*. The Magheri edition has *come si potrà comprendere*, which has little meaning in this context.

in the territory and district of Florence. From the rector who baptized the infants—since he deposited a black bean for every male baptized in San Giovanni and a white bean for every female in order to ascertain their number—we find that at this period there were from 5,500 to 6,000 baptisms every year, the males usually outnumbering the females by 300 to 500. We find that the boys and girls learning to read [numbered] from 8,000 to 10,000, the children learning the abacus and algorism from 1,000 to 1,200, and those learning grammar and logic in four large schools from 550 to 600.

We find that the churches then in Florence and in the suburbs, including the abbeys and the churches of friars, were 110, among which were 57 parishes with congregations, 5 abbeys with two priors and some 80 monks each, 24 nunneries with some 500 women, 10 orders of friars, 30 hospitals with more than 1,000 beds to receive the poor and the sick, and from 250 to 300 chaplain priests.

The workshops of the *Arte della Lana*[93] were 200 or more, and they made from 70,000 to 80,000 pieces of cloth, which were worth more than 1,200,000 gold florins. And a good third [of this sum] remained in the land as [the reward] of labor, without counting the profit of the entrepreneurs. And more than 30,000 persons lived by it. [To be sure,] we find that some thirty years earlier there were 300 workshops or thereabouts, and they made more than 100,000 pieces of cloth yearly; but these cloths were coarser and one half less valuable, because at that time English wool was not imported and they did not know, as they did later, how to work it.

The *fondachi* of the *Arte di Calimala*,[94] dealing in French and Transalpine cloth, were some twenty, and they imported yearly more than 10,000 pieces of cloth, worth 300,000 gold florins. And all these were sold in Florence, without counting those which were reexported from Florence.

The banks of money-changers were about eighty. The gold coins which were struck amounted to some 350,000 gold florins and at times 400,000 [yearly]. And as for deniers of four petty each, about 20,000 pounds of them were struck yearly.

The association[95] of judges was composed of some eighty members; the notaries were some six hundred; physicians and surgical doctors, some sixty; shops of dealers in spices, some hundred.

Merchants and mercers were a large number; the shops of shoemakers, slipper makers, and wooden-shoe makers were so numerous they could not be

---

[93] The gild of wool merchants and entrepreneurs in the woolen industry.

[94] The gild of importers, refinishers, and sellers of Transalpine cloth. Their name is derived from Calle Mala, the 'bad street,' where their shops were located.

[95] *Collegio* was similar to but not quite identical with an *arte* or gild.

counted. There were some three hundred persons and more who went to do business out of Florence,[96] and [so did] many other masters in many crafts, and stone and carpentry masters.

There were then in Florence 146 bakeries. And from the [amount of the] tax on grinding and through [information furnished by] the bakers we find that the city within the walls needed 140 *moggia*[97] of grain every day. By this one can estimate how much was needed yearly, not to mention the fact that the larger part of the rich, noble, and well-to-do citizens with their families spent four months a year in the country, and some of them a still longer period.

We also find that in the year 1280, when the city was in a good and happy condition, it needed some 800 *moggia* of grain a week.[98]

Through [the amount of] the tax at the gates we find that some 55,000 *cogna* of wine entered Florence yearly, and in times of plenty about 10,000 *cogna* more.

Every year the city consumed about 4,000 oxen and calves, 60,000 mutton and sheep, 20,000 she-goats and he-goats, 30,000 pigs.

During the month of July 4,000 *some* of melons came through Porta San Friano, and they were all distributed in the city. . . .[99]

[Florence] within the walls was well built, with many beautiful houses, and at that period people kept building with improved techniques to obtain comfort and richness by importing designs of every kind of improvement. [They built] parish churches and churches of friars of every order, and splendid monasteries. And besides this, there was no citizen, whether commoner or magnate, who had not built or was not building in the country a large and rich estate with a very costly mansion and with fine buildings, much better than those in the city—and in this they all were committing sin, and they were called crazy on account of their wild expenses. And yet, this was such a wonderful sight that when foreigners, not accustomed to [cities like] Florence, came from abroad, they usually believed that all of the costly buildings and beautiful palaces which surrounded the city for three miles were part of the city in the manner of Rome[100]—not to mention the costly

[96] These were the factors or agents of the companies of merchant bankers which had branches abroad.

[97] *Gabella della macinatura.* The *moggio* was a dry measure equal to 16·59 + bushels.

[98] Here Villani refers to an earlier period, when Florence was not as large as it was in 1336–1338, the period to which the other figures refer.

[99] We omit here a description of the different magistracies having jurisdiction in the city. Their large number seemed to Villani another proof of the greatness of Florence.

[100] It would seem that Villani compares the suburbs of Florence with those of Rome. Elsewhere (III, 52, Magheri edition) he says that 'Florence, the daughter and creature of Rome, was on the

palaces with towers, courts, and walled gardens farther distant, which would have been called castles in any other country. To sum up, it was estimated that within a six-mile radius around the city there were more than twice as many rich and noble mansions as in Florence.

A North African City at Its Medieval Zenith

To CONCLUDE our contrast we ought to compare an African city at its zenith with the Italian centers we have just observed. The period will have to be about one century earlier because the Muslim world as a whole seems to have reached its fullest economic development in or before the twelfth century. Fez, founded in the ninth century and therefore having a cycle of development about as long as that of the Commercial Revolution in Western Europe, will furnish a fair comparison if we view it in the best years of the Almohad domination, that is, the reigns of al-Mansur (1184–1199) and of al-Nasir (1199–1213).

Unfortunately, the description of Fez that follows is unreliable as regards statistical data. To be sure, the fact that it was inserted in a work of the fourteenth century does not alter its value as a contemporary document, since the author, probably one Ibn Abi Zar' of Fez, is known to have written his book by juxtaposing notes he had taken from earlier writers without the slightest attempt at correcting even obvious contradictions among his authorities.[101] But Muslim writers with a very few exceptions are utterly heedless of statistical accuracy. In this particular case exaggeration is manifest; probably the figures ought to be cut by one half or even three fourths. Nevertheless, the description of districts, shops, and markets in Fez is a valuable document.

25

Ibn Abi Zar'(?), *The Pleasant Garden of Cards and Information about the Kings of the Maghrib and the History of the City of Fez*[102]

Fez [fourteenth century, after earlier sources]

In the time of the Almoravids and of the Almohads the city of Fez attained a degree of prosperity, happiness, comfort, and peace such as no other town in the Maghrib has ever enjoyed. The number of mosques in the time of al-Mansur, the Almohad [1184–1199], and of his son al-Nasir

---

increase and destined to do great things, even as Rome was in her decline. . . '. Rome was the standard term of comparison for many ambitious medieval cities: see W. Hammer, 'The Concept of the New or Second Rome in the Middle Ages,' *Speculum*, XIX (1944), 50–62.

[101] Gautier, *L'Islamisation de l'Afrique du Nord*, pp. 37–52, gives a colorful, if slightly over-critical, characterization of the work. Its title, literally 'The Garden of Cards,' probably means merely 'the collection of filing cards.' See also the description of Cordoba by al-Maqqari in P. de Gayangos y Arce, *The History of the Mohammedan Dynasties in Spain*, I, 207ff.; but al-Maqqari was a seventeenth-century writer and his description of a tenth-century town can hardly be regarded as a contemporary document.

[102] We have used the Spanish translation by A. Huici: Ali ibn Abd Allah ibn Abi Zar al Fast, *El Cartás; noticias de los reyes del Mogreb e historia de la ciudad de Fez*, pp. 44–45.

[1199–1213], rose to 785. There were 122 canals and pools for ablutions, 42 of the latter, [80] of the former being the balance, some of spring water and others of stream water. Public bathing houses were counted at that time and were found to number 93. The mills situated within the city walls were 472, not counting those outside. In the time of al-Nasir, houses numbered 89,236; masriyya[103] 19,041; fanadiq[104] reserved for merchants, travelers, and foreigners, 467; shops 9,082.[105] There were two silk markets, one in the borough of al-Qarawiyin and the other in the borough of the Andalusians on the Masmuda river. The places fitted out with looms were 3,064; the houses used for the manufacture of soap were 47; those used for tanneries, 86; the dye houses, 116. There were 12 copper foundries, 135 ovens where bread was made and sold, and 11 places where crystal was made. Outside the walls there were 188 potteries. Along the two banks of the large river which divides the city into two parts from its entrance into the city to its exit in Ramila were the houses of the dyers and their shops, the houses of the tanners and their shops, those of the soap makers and sellers of grain, those of the butchers, the bakers' ovens, [those] used for drying hemp, and the others which need water, and, in the upper part, the weavers' looms.

In the city there is no river that can be seen except the large river; the others have been covered by houses and masriyya and shops. There are no gardens or orchards inside the walls save the olive grove of Ibn 'Atiya. There were in the city 400 workshops manufacturing paper. All this was ruined in the period of famine and revolts occurring during the reign of al-'Adil and of his brother al-Ma'mun and of al-Rashid, from A.H. 618 to 637 [A.D. 1221–1239]. The period of desolation lasted twenty years, until the dynasty of the Marinids appeared and the country was restored and the roads became safe.

Rural Markets and Urban Shopping Centers

WHILE THE permanent market or shopping center catered to the daily needs of larger towns and fed the normal exporting channels, temporary markets were better

[103] Masriyya were small houses or single rooms with separate exits, usually connected with larger houses. The word is also used for apartments or rooms to accomodate guests or apprentices.

[104] Note the distinction between the fanadiq, which were special warehouses reserved for use of those who were not citizens or residents, and the shops run by the merchants of Fez.

[105] It may be interesting to compare this statement with that of Nasir-I Khusraw, a Persian traveler who visited Cairo in the middle of the eleventh century. 'I estimate that there are no less than 20,000 shops there, all of which are owned by the sultan. Many of them are rented at 10 dinars of Maghrib a month and a few at less than 2 dinars.' We translate from the French translation of C. Schefer, Sefer Nameh: relation du voyage de Nassiri Khosrau . . . , p. 127.

suited to the needs of smaller centers and rural districts. They also fulfilled an important function in the larger towns since these, too, had lively economic relations with the surrounding countryside. Many descriptions of both permanent and rural markets are found in the remarkably alert travel diary of Ibn Jubayr, an inhabitant of Spain, who visited all the Muslim countries of the Mediterranean basin as well as Christian communities of Sicily, Sardinia, and the Holy Land.[106] The rural market described in the passage we have chosen (Document 26) is that of Dunaysar, a small town of strongly agrarian character. The permanent market is that of Aleppo, one of the most important trading centers in Syria.[107] Aleppo most probably also had temporary markets.

Ibn Jubayr made his journey in northern Syria at a period in which travel was particularly unsafe. Trade, however, was not entirely disrupted. The merchants traveled in comparative safety if they went in caravans.[108] The examples chosen happen to be taken from Muslim lands, but much the same types of markets prevailed in Christian territories.

26

Abu al-Hasan Muhammad ibn Jubayr, *Journey*[109]

Dunaysar, June 13–15 [1184]

Next morning, Wednesday, 2 Rabi' al-awwal [June 13], we left with a large caravan of mules and donkeys, together with men from Harran and Aleppo and others from the Bilad Bakr and the neighboring countries.... We kept on the lookout for an attack from the Kurds infesting these regions from Mosul to Nisibin and the town of Dunaysar and raiding the roads and trying to bring disorder into the land. They live among inaccessible mountains in the neighborhood of these countries, the sultans of which have never been assisted by God in subduing them.... There is nobody who can drive them out and keep them away but God, the Great and Powerful....

[Dunaysar] lies in a broad plain and is surrounded by fragrant plants and irrigated vegetable gardens. It is rather agrarian in aspect and has no walls; it is crowded with people; it has well-attended and well-supplied markets; and it is the supply center of the people of Syria and Diyarbakr,[110] of the

---

[106] On the attractive personality of the writer, see the preface of the translator, C. Schiaparelli, to Ibn Jubayr (Ibn Giobeir), *Viaggio in Ispagna, Sicilia, Siria e Palestina, Arabia, Egitto, compiuto nel secolo XII.*

[107] See J. Sauvaget, *Alep: essai sur le développement d'une grande ville syrienne.*

[108] Ibn Jubayr himself, remarking that trade between Muslims and Christians in Palestine went on in the midst of war, noted: 'The military men are busy in their wars, the peoples trade in peace, and the world belongs to whoever takes it.'

[109] We have used the Italian translation of C. Schiaparelli: Ibn Jubayr (Ibn Giobeir), *Viaggio in Ispagna, Sicilia, Siria e Palestina,* pp. 230–31, 242–43.

[110] The text has also Amid, but this is an old Armenian form for Diyarbakr and hence redundant.

countries of the Romans subject to Emir Mas'ud,[111] and of the neighboring
countries. It has broad fields and abundant foodstuffs. We camped outside
the city with the caravan and in the morning of Thursday, 3 Rabi' al-awwal,
we rested in the city. . . . We remained in Dunaysar until after prayer on
Friday, 4 Rabi' al-awwal. The caravan postponed its departure from this
locality in order to be present at the market, because on Thursdays, Fridays,
Saturdays, and the following Sundays they hold here a well-attended market.
In it congregate the peoples of the neighboring places and of the nearby
villages, since the entire road to the right and to the left is an unbroken series
of villages and inns.[112] This market, to which people come from various
places, they call the bazar.[113] All these markets are held on fixed days.

· · · ·

As for the city [of Aleppo], it is built upon an immense area; it is excellently
laid out, of extraordinary beauty, with large and monumental markets
regularly arranged in long adjacent rows. You go from [the row reserved
for] one craft to that of another, until you have gone through all the crafts in
the city. All these markets are covered with wooden [roofs] so that whoever
is inside enjoys plenty of shade, and everybody keeps gazing [at them]
because of their beauty, and [even] those in a hurry to leave stop there in
admiration. Its *qaysariyya* market,[114] then, [looks like] an enclosed garden
because of its gracefulness and beauty. It surrounds the venerated cathedral
mosque. Whoever sits there does not wish to see anything else, not even if
he could see [real] gardens. Its shops are mostly stores constructed of wood
and of an original style, and every row looks like one shop. They are divided
by wooden gates artistically wrought, all of which lead to the shops, so that
it is the most wonderful thing to be seen. Each of these rows leads to a door
of the venerated cathedral mosque.

Markets and Peddlers in Underdeveloped Areas

EVEN AS CERTAIN regions today are hardly affected by the Industrial Revolution
and others have not been completely 'industrialized,' so in the Middle Ages certain
regions were almost untouched by the Commercial Revolution and others were

---

[111] The Saljuq ruler, Qilij Arslan II.

[112] The *khan* was an inn for traveling merchants and pilgrims.

[113] On the difference between temporary markets (*suq*, plur. *aswaq*) and groups of shops,
usually but not always situated together in one part of the town (also called *suq* or, more specifically, *bazar*), see M. Gaudefroy-Demombynes, *Muslim Institutions*, pp. 184-85.

[114] The main ('imperial'; the term is derived from the Greek) market. Usually it was a great
rectangular building with stables and storehouses and an upper floor, containing rooms opening
only on the courtyard.

not fully 'commercialized.' In these regions trade was still largely carried on by
peddlers, and temporary markets preserved their local importance. Therefore it
was very important for a center to be granted the right to establish a market or a
fair. The difference between a market and a fair in the Mediterranean basin was by
no means as clear-cut as many modern historians have assumed, the words *mercatum,
feria, forum, nundinae* being often interchangeable.

So many grants of markets have been published in translation that we feel we
would add nothing by supplying another example. Instead, we shall give an example
(Document 27) of a rejection of a petition to the French king to obtain a market.
The town in question, Riom, is situated in the mountainous region of Auvergne,
which was not unaffected by the Commercial Revolution but which did not blossom
as fully as did other parts of southern France. It should be noted that a charter was
necessary only for towns subject to a territorial monarch. Communes enjoying ful
independence or a very large degree of self-government were the arbiters of their
own fairs. They established a fair if and when they wanted one, and they made
provisions to render it especially attractive by granting special concessions to
patrons and by ensuring safety to visitors through treaties with the neighboring
towns.

Document 28 shows the curious means by which a small town in the heart of the
Alps secured the cooperation of the gild of Provençal mercers. That all this occurred
only a few miles distant from Marseilles and other great centers of international
trade makes the rural character of the document still more interesting.[115]

27

From the Latin[116]

Paris, June 3, 1306

On supplication or request by the men of the town of Riom in Auvergne,
we then had inquiries made through our *bailli* of Auvergne whether it
would be beneficial to the community and to ourselves to have two new fairs
established in said town at the specified times and under the specified conditions that said men were requesting from us. After an inquest had been
made in regard to this by said *bailli* or by men deputed by him, the evidence
was seen and carefully examined. Since it was found sufficiently proved that if
we should concede said request, it would be harmful to us and to the community of the country, our *curia* finally pronounced judgment that the aforesaid
request is not to be conceded to them.

Friday after Trinity [Sunday].

[115] See also our Document 32, referring to the same district. Rural and semi-rural markets
in the Byzantine Empire at the same period are mentioned in our Document 155. An excellent
picture of economic life in Provence is found in the pertinent chapters of Paul Masson, ed.,
Encyclopédie départementale: les Bouches-du-Rhône, II, 261–302, 714–52.

[116] G. Fagniez, ed., *Documents relatifs à l'histoire de l'industrie et du commerce en France*, II, 7.

28

From the Latin[117]

Sisteron [Provence], September 12, 1392

... Petition was recently made ... to the Lords Syndics and to the Council of this present city of Sisteron in behalf of His Benignity Giles Dupont, mercer, residing in Forcalquier in Provence, Viceroy of the Mercers of Provence. This same Viceroy, by God's guidance, arranged to come in person with a not inconsiderable group[118] of mercers to this present city of Sisteron in order to decorate the fairs of Saint Domnin with various wares or merchandise and to do there what is customary to do in new fairs out of respect and honor for the city itself and the citizens of the same, provided, however, that this should be carried out with the permission and will of the Lords Syndics and Councilors themselves, and that they be willing to welcome there the Viceroy himself with his company[119] and graciously and benevolently to offer the customary gifts, bearable and not burdensome to the city itself.

The said Lords Councilors, whose names appear below, ordered that an epistolary answer[120] be made to the said Viceroy of the Mercers, [requesting] that he should come here at the said next feast of Saint Domnin, inasmuch as the said community intends to welcome him with his company, as is customary in the new fairs, and they promised to give and to allot to him for the performances promised [by him] ... 10 gold florins only.

Mediterranean Merchants at the International Fairs

INTERNATIONAL fairs enabled merchants coming from distant regions to meet one another in easily accessible places and to enjoy special protection from the local authorities. The latter usually exempted visitors to fairs from the ordinary restrictions placed upon foreigners and from some aspects of local legislation. At the same time, international fairs enabled the authority which organized them to attract, to tax, and to control more easily foreign traders and trade. They were particularly useful when long-distance trade began to pick up in regions previously isolated. They tended to decline whenever and wherever this trade became too large to be fully carried on in the short time allotted to the fair. At this stage of development individual merchants and merchant companies had to entrust their

---

[117] J. Billioud, 'Le Roi des merciers du comté de Provence aux XIVe et XVe siècles,' *Bulletin Philologique et Historique du Comité des Travaux Historiques et Scientifiques* (1922–1923), p. 60.

[118] *Societas:* but the word here does not appear to have a strictly technical meaning.

[119] *Comitiva* seems related to *comitatus,* a personal following.

[120] *Litteratoria responsio.* We have retained this gem of pompousness. Both the Viceroy of the Mercers and the Lords Councilors of tiny Sisteron took themselves very seriously.

foreign trade to partners, agents, and correspondents permanently established in foreign towns.

In the Mediterranean regions long-distance trade was so developed even at the beginning of the Commercial Revolution that very few international fairs of any importance were held.[121] But in the inland regions of Europe international fairs played an important role, and they survived as meeting grounds for exchange and financial operations after their function as markets of merchandise had ceased. Up to the early fourteenth century the fairs of Champagne far surpassed all others. Since six fairs were held successively in four towns of the region—Troyes, Provins, Lagny, and Bar-sur-Aube—their combined duration covered almost the entire year. Furthermore, the presence of merchants from all parts of the Western world enabled them to become a sort of clearing house for merchandise and currency exchanges between the Mediterranean and the North Sea basin. Many documents referring to trade and exchange in the Champagne fairs will be found in other sections of this volume.[122]

Eventually even the fairs of Champagne lost their importance. During the later part of the Middle Ages the fairs of Frankfort-on-Main, Lyons, and Geneva were prominent, although none of them equaled those of Champagne as they had been in their heyday. Geneva was controlled by the dukes of Savoy, whereas the fairs of Lyons were organized by the kings of France, who endeavored to channel through them most of the external trade of the kingdom.[123] Louis XI, however, decided to shift the dates of his fairs in order to reduce competition with those of Geneva and to improve his relations with the duke of Savoy. The selection that follows (Document 29) is a report of negotiations held with the prospective patrons of the fairs, mostly Mediterranean merchants, in order to choose dates suitable to them. The report was made by Guillaume de Varye, who represented the French king in the negotiations.

[121] Giovanni Villani, the Florentine chronicler, points out that an attempt at creating fairs in his town in the fourteenth century failed because 'there always is a market in Florence,' that is, international trade is a daily occurrence in the city. Nevertheless, certain fairs in Italy played a fairly significant part in the first centuries of the Commercial Revolution; see our Document 74 on the Florentines at the fairs of Bologna. In southern France, which was economically less advanced than Italy, Beaucaire attracted many merchants from a wide area; see G. de Gourcy, *La Foire de Beaucaire*. In the Byzantine Empire, the fairs of Salonika, which went back to the early Middle Ages, continued to be the meeting ground of merchants from the advanced Mediterranean regions with traders from the underdeveloped Balkan countries; see the description (in English translation) published by H. F. Tozer, 'Byzantine Satire,' *Journal of Hellenic Studies*, II (1881), 244–45, and P. Charanis, 'Internal Strife in Byzantium during the Fourteenth Century,' *Byzantion*, XV (1940–1941), 208–30. On Spanish fairs, see L. G. de Valdeavellano, 'El mercado, apuntes para su estudio en León y Castilla durante la edad media,' *Anuario de Historia del Derecho Español*, VIII (1931), 201–405.

[122] See Documents 75, 76, 77, 129, 192, and 193. The Lendit fairs at Saint Denis near Paris also were very important; on them, see our Document 93. The charter of foundation by Dagobert, published in translation by Cave and Coulson, *A Source Book for Medieval Economic History*, pp. 114–15, is a tenth-century forgery partly based upon authentic material. The very abundant bibliography on the Champagne fairs is listed in E. Chapin, *Les Villes des foires de Champagne des origines au début du XIVe siècle;* later works are listed in R. H. Bautier, 'Marchands siennois et draps d'outremont aux foires de Champagne,' *Annuaire-Bulletin de la Société de l'Histoire de France* (1945), pp. 87–107.

[123] Earlier Philip III had made a similar attempt in behalf of the fairs of Nîmes.

29

From the French[124]

Lyons, April [1467]

... The aforesaid [inhabitants of Lyons],[125] speaking by the mouth of said Messire Varinier, after he had pointed out and stated how the maintenance of said four fairs in Lyons would be to the great good and profit of said city, of the king, and of his kingdom, for several reasons that he alleged and stated, pointed out with several other remarks the damage that the breaking off or the separate maintenance of said fairs will or would cause to the king and to his kingdom, and most particularly to said city of Lyons. These reasons, remarks, and remonstrances we have dispensed with putting down in writing because for the present they can be of no particular service in the matter. But in regard to the relative value of the said fairs the aforesaid men asked our advice, which we gave them, to wit: of the said four fairs the two better ones are Easter and All Saints' Day. But because we are afraid that we cannot obtain by negotiation with the said [House] of Savoy that the said two better fairs remain in the city of Lyons, and because the king wants to retain for said city the better of said two better and desires the better of the two less good ones, which are August and Epiphany, to remain in said Lyons, it seemed to us, in conscience, that for the profit of said city of Lyons and for the good of the commerce of the kingdom it would be preferable to retain for said city of Lyons the fair of All Saints' Day rather than that of Easter, because of spices and cloth as well as of skins, these being the largest items of said fairs. And also the fair of August is more valuable than that of Epiphany. Whereupon the aforesaid men answered us that they preferred the fair of Easter to that of All Saints' Day, and that if it is the king's pleasure for them to lose two, they would prefer Easter and August to the other two. However, if it is the king's pleasure that they may hold four fairs in said Lyons, just as they were wont from antiquity to hold them there—and that those of Geneva may similarly hold four others, provided that the subjects of the king should be permitted to attend only two of the said fairs of Geneva, this would contribute to the maintenance and advantage of the said city of Lyons and to the profit of the commerce of the king and of the kingdom. . . .[126]

[124] F. Borel, Les Foires de Genève au quinzième siècle, pièces justificatives, pp. 161–64, 167–68.

[125] That is, Pierre Varinier, Pierre Balarin, and Jehan Grand, doctors in law—the latter was also lieutenant général of the bailli of Lyons—Master Pierre Fornier, licensed at law, and Pierre Brunier, Ymbaud de Varey, Anthoyne Bailli, Clément Mulat, Jehan Buatier, and Denys Loup.

[126] We omit a passage from which it appears that the procureur of the city of Lyons, Jacques Mathieu, attempted to challenge the legality of De Varye's mission. He was quickly brushed aside, and De Varye turned his attention to the foreign merchants.

And on this same day of Thursday [April 9] we gave orders to invite to a meeting the following day in our said lodging some of the ablest and richest merchants of all and each of the foreign nations attending said fairs, and who already were in said city [of Lyons] in order to hold the fair which is now being held, namely, the fair of Easter.

On the following day, which was a Friday, the tenth of said month of April [the following persons] assembled in our said lodging: Giuliano Zaccaria, Francesco Capponi, Angelo della Luna, Bindaccio da Pensano[?],[127] Giovanni Perrini, and Luca Doni, all Florentines; Ottobono Marino, Giovanni Vignoso[?],[128] and Gerolamo Gallo[?],[129] Genoese; Ambrogio Giannantoni, factor of Bevacqua, Milanese; Geronimo Comello, Venetian; Francesco di Magrino, Filippo di Lucca, Lucchese; Heinz Wackenel, Lukas and . . .[130] of the Great Company, Germans; Onofrio di Fabriano of the March of Ancona; Guiot le Pelé and Jehan la Molu of Troyes in Champagne; and Jehan le Roy of Rouen. And to these we stated and pointed out the good pleasure and will of the king about the lifting of said edict concerning two of the said fairs of Geneva, to which he wants all his subjects to be allowed and permitted to go if they choose. [He acts in this manner] in order to maintain the love and alliance which from ancient times has existed between the kings of France, his predecessors, and the lords of the House of Savoy, and especially on account of the close [family] ties which exist at present between the the king and said [lords] of Savoy, and to show approval of the very urgent prayer and request of my lord the count of Bresse, his brother,[131] who had asked him very urgently for it and had many times prayed and made request. We also told them how the king did not want to terminate [the edict] without informing them, and we pointed out very clearly to them the reasons which had prompted and were prompting him to do so, just as we had previously stated and pointed out to those among them whom we had brought together in said city of Lyons, in the month of March recently passed. We asked them to give us their advice about the allotment of the said four fairs and to point out which two it would be more convenient and profitable to hold in said Lyons and which two in Geneva. Whereupon the aforesaid merchants, by the mouth of said Giuliano Zaccaria, replied and asked us to be willing to

[127] Dappensain.

[128] De Vigoles. The name closest to this is that of an important Genoese merchant family, Vignoso.

[129] Coq. It may be a popular etymology for Cocco, which was the name of a Venetian family—the name does not appear in Genoa—or a translation of Gallo, a well-known Genoese name.

[130] The dots are Borel's. The 'Great Company' is that of Ravensburg.

[131] Louis XI's wife was the sister of Duke Amadeus IX of Savoy and of Philip, count of Bresse. Amadeus IX himself was married to Yolande, sister of the king of France.

give them a little time to talk together, and [they said] that soon thereafter they would give us their answer. And this we freely granted them and we went out of our room where we were assembled and left them there for about a half hour, after which they asked us to return in order to hear the answer. And in order to give it, the said merchants gave the floor to the said Giuliano Zaccaria, who jointly with the others warmly and particularly thanked the king, [exhibiting] great reverence, for the honor he paid them in causing his pleasure concerning said fairs to be thus communicated and stated to them. He stated and pointed out to us that for the good of themselves and of the merchandise it was neither expedient nor profitable that said fairs should be maintained separately or divided; and that, should it please the king to maintain them separately, it would entail for them and the other merchants attending said fairs a very great crowding, burden, and loss, both because of the transportation which they would have to provide and of the rebinding[?][132] of their merchandise, and because of the renting of houses and other charges and expenses that they would be forced to undergo on account of said separate maintenance and allotment of said fairs. He also told us that it seemed to them that the most useful and profitable thing for them and for the entire problem of said merchandise would be to hold said four fairs either in said city of Lyons or in said city of Geneva or in both of said localities, and that his [the king's] subjects should be at liberty to go to two of said fairs [in Geneva], if it seemed good to them, and that it should please the king furthermore to order that no one be allowed to appeal the sentences pronounced by the keeper (*conservateur*) of the fairs or his lieutenant concerning the transactions and the debts [contracted] in said fairs—at least, up to such an amount as it would please the king to determine—without first complying with and carrying out the terms of the judgment or directions of the said keeper or of his said lieutenant. And as regards the advice we were asking them in order to learn which two of the said four fairs—viz., one of the better ones and one of the others, less good—would be more useful and profitable to said city of Lyons, they had decided not to tell us anything further about it in addition to what has been said above, because they perforce had decided not to say anything concerning said fairs that would be displeasing either to the king or to my lord of Savoy. And upon this they left. . . .[133]

---

[132] *Rebray* is not registered in the leading dictionaries of old French. Perhaps from *braie,* 'breeches,' and hence any kind of wrapping or binding.

[133] We omit the description of a new attempt by a delegation of jurists to retain the four fairs in Lyons. Then a delegation of churchmen was heard. Both delegations, when asked their opinion in regard to the comparative importance of the fairs, refused to commit themselves. Jurists and

[On Saturday, the eleventh day of said month], immediately after dinner, since we were informed that some merchants of the Spanish nation had come to said city of Lyons, we sent for them. And soon afterwards Martin de Soria and Juan de San Martín, merchants of the city of Burgos in Spain, appeared before us. And to them we related and explained in effect and substance the good pleasure, will, and intention that the king had touching the matter of the said fairs in the very same way and manner as we had stated and pointed out in the month of March, and later in this present month of April, to several prominent merchants, [both] foreigners and of this kingdom, who were mentioned above. And the said De Soria and De San Martín thanked the king and us very humbly, and in answer they told us in effect that in their opinion and in their conscience the breaking off and separate maintenance of said fairs of Lyons would be very harmful to them and to the other merchants who are wont to attend the said fairs. [They thought so] both because of the rent of the houses which they would have to keep and to pay for, and because of the deterioration and damage that their merchandise would and could suffer in being carried back and forth from Lyons to Geneva and from Geneva to Lyons, and also because of the loss that they would have on account of the carrying and transportation for which they would have to pay in order to do it. For in these transport [operations] part of their said merchandise would be expended and consumed since they have many of their said wares that they cannot sell in any of the five or six fairs after they have had them brought from their country to the places where the said fairs are held; and they have to store them in houses which they keep under lease, well and neatly arranged, without rebinding them,[134] in order to wait one year or two for their sale. . . .[135]

Special Buildings for Foreign Traders

DURING THE EARLY Middle Ages special buildings permanently reserved for foreign traders filled much the same function in the Mediterranean region as did international fairs in the European hinterland. They afforded protection and privileges to merchants and made it easier for governments to keep the merchants under surveillance.[136] The first document in this volume describes the Byzantine *mitata*, which supplied the

churchmen again challenged the validity of the commission of De Varye who took new steps to prove it.

[134] *Sans les rebrayer.*

[135] The last part of the document is a report of discussions that took place in Montluel between De Varye and his staff on the one side and delegates from Geneva on the other. No definite conclusion was reached. Both parties decided to report to their respective governments and to meet again in the following June.

[136] See Bibliography in R. S. Lopez, 'Du marché temporaire à la colonie permanente.'

model for all establishments of this kind throughout and beyond the Mediterranean world. As we have seen, foreign merchants were not allowed to spend more than three months in the *mitata*. Time limitations, however, are no longer found in such special buildings for foreign traders as were still maintained in the Mediterranean region after the tenth century, but often there were other restrictions. The *funduq* of many Muslim towns and the Venetian *fondaco* of the Germans resembled the *mitata* in many respects. Considerations of the same kind also have prompted the regulations of the special buildings for foreign merchants (*Hof, Halle, Lonja*) in many German, French, and Spanish towns. Notwithstanding, it is worth noting that in the larger number of Italian towns and in many centers of Mediterranean France and Catalonia foreign merchants lived and traded freely in the same places as did the natives.

Document 30 indicates some of the restrictions placed upon foreign merchants in the Venetian *fondaco*. It gives an example of the lifting of restrictions in a special case because the town found this to its advantage.

30
From the Latin[137]

Venice, [June 19, 1383]

... As Philip Gross of Nuremberg, merchant in our *fondaco* of the Teutons, relates, he is wont to transport and to have transported large quantities of wool to the territory of Lombardy, [acting] for himself and for his *societas*. For these he obtains by way of barter[138] Lombard cloth which he has transported to Venice. And this would result in great profit to the tolls of our Commune and to the advantage of our merchant citizens and of Philip himself if only he were assisted by this special privilege—that whenever he brings or causes to be brought [to Venice] the cloth which he has obtained [in exchange] for the said wool, and after [the cloth] has been duly presented and marked and registered item by item by our *vicedomini*,[139] he be permitted to remove that cloth from the *fondaco* and to put it in a store[140] in Rialto, which has a window,[141] with the purpose of exhibiting the cloth and of selling it as best he can, paying to our Commune the tolls established for the said cloth. And our Commune itself would obtain great advantage from this, since in our *fondaco* there is no place with a window to exhibit the cloth, and furthermore the merchants do not believe that fine cloth should be brought

---

[137] H. Simonsfeld, *Der Fondaco dei Tedeschi in Venedig und die deutsch-venetianischen Handels-beziehungen*, I, 113–14.

[138] *Ad baratum.* As F. Edler, *Glossary of Mediaeval Terms of Business: Italian Series, 1200–1600,* p. 43, points out, transactions of this kind were mainly exchanges of goods valued in terms of money, sometimes with an additional cash payment on the part of that party whose goods might be of slightly less value.

[139] Government officials in charge of the *fondaco*.   [140] *Volta.*

to the *fondaco*. And therefore [Philip] respectfully has supplicated our government that, considering the aforesaid facts, we should be good enough to
concede to him as a special favor that after he brings or causes to be brought
to Venice to our *fondaco* some of the said cloth and after [the cloth] has been
presented to and registered by our *vicedomini* and marked by them, and the
established toll has been paid, he be allowed to remove it from the *fondaco*
and to put it in a store in Rialto, which has a window, with the purpose of
exhibiting and of selling the cloth just as he would do in the *fondaco*. And
for the present, in order that your[142] government may see clearly that the
request of said Philip is just and useful to our Commune and merchants,
he would be content to have this favor granted to him for one year, more or
less, just as it pleases our government. . . .[143]

[142] *Sic.*   [143] The request was granted.

CHAPTER III

THE GROWTH OF THE MERCHANT CLASS

War Spoils and New Types of Traders

THE GROWTH OF THE merchant class in numbers and wealth is one of the main themes of this book. In this particular selection and in those immediately following we do not try to illustrate the general theme so much as to sample some changes brought about by the Commercial Revolution. New recruits coming from all walks of life enriched the merchant class. New types of traders appeared in regions where very little commerce had heretofore existed. New problems challenged old merchants such as the Jews and old institutions such as the Catholic Church. These are only some of the elements which deserve attention. The omission of others does not mean that they are less important but only that it was not possible to present them without using a larger number of documents than space allowed. Indeed, the more important a merchant, the more complex his activity. Materials on the careers of the great men in the business world are not presented in biographies but can be found only by using the whole body of information gathered in this book.[1]

[1] There is a good number of monographs dealing with individual merchants, groups of merchants, or the entire merchant class of specific towns in the Mediterranean basin. Some of the more important are R. Aubenas, 'La Famille dans l'ancienne Provence,' *Annales d'Histoire Economique et Sociale*, VIII (1936), 523–41; E. Bensa, *Francesco di Marco da Prato;* R. Brun, 'A Fourteenth Century Merchant of Italy,' *Journal of Economic and Business History*, II (1930), 451–66; E. H. Byrne, 'Genoese Trade with Syria in the Twelfth Century,' *American Historical Review*, XXV (1920), 191–219; M. Chiaudano, 'I Rotschild del Duecento: la Gran Tavola di Orlando Bonsignori,' *Bullettino Senese di Storia Patria*, new ser., VI (1935), 103–27 and Appendices, 139–42; A. Fanfani, *Un mercante del Trecento;* R. Heynen, *Zur Entstehung des Kapitalismus, in Venedig;* F. C. Lane, *Andrea Barbarigo, Merchant of Venice;* R. S. Lopez, *Genova marinara nel Ducento, Benedetto Zaccaria;* G. Luzzatto (under the pseudonym, G. Padovan), 'Capitale e lavoro nel commercio veneziano dei secoli XI e XII,' *Rivista di Storia Economica*, VI (1941), 1–24; M. Merores, 'Der venezianische Adel,' *Vierteljahrschrift für Sozial- und Wirtschaftsgeschichte*, XIX (1926), 193–237; L. Mirot, 'Etudes lucquoises,' *Bibliothèque de l'Ecole des Chartes*, LXXXVIII (1927), 50–86, LXXXIX (1928), 299–389; XCI (1930), 100–168; Y. Renouard, *Les Hommes d'affaires italiens du moyen âge;* R. L. Reynolds, 'Merchants of Arras and the Overland Trade with Genoa,' *Revue Belge de Philologie et d'Histoire*, IX (1930), 495–533; R. L. Reynolds, 'In Search of a Business Class in Thirteenth-Century Genoa,' *Journal of Economic History*, Suppl. V (1945), 1–19; Florence de Roover, 'Francesco Sassetti and the Downfall of the Medici Banking House,' *Bulletin of the Business Historical Society*, XVII (1943), 65–80; R. de Roover, *The Medici Bank;* A. A. Ruddock, *Italian Merchants and Shipping in Southampton*, 1270–1600; A. Sapori, *Mercatores;* A. E. Sayous, 'L'Activité de deux capitalistes-commerçants marseillais,'

Document 31 presents the story of men who found military campaigns an invitation to commercial ventures. Their success in wars waged in distant countries acquainted them with unknown riches, apprenticed them to travel by sea and land, won for them privileges in important business centers, and gave them much needed capital with which to start a business. To be sure, we do not know how many of the Genoese officers and sailors who obtained a share in the booty divided at Caesarea, Palestine's famed seaport, returned to the Holy Land as merchants and settlers. There is no doubt, however, that many did. The earliest Genoese notarial registers show that a few decades after the capture of Caesarea the larger part of the population directly or indirectly took part in Eastern trade. Among the leading figures we meet descendants of the Genoese leaders of the First Crusade and the new rich whose names had recently emerged from obscurity. The former probably had some capital and commercial experience before the Crusade, but they gained more during the Crusade. The latter no doubt included descendants of the ordinary sailors and soldiers who had profitably reinvested in commerce the pepper and the coins first gained through war at Caesarea and other Muslim cities.

31

Caffaro, *Annals of Genoa*
From the Latin[2]

[Genoa, 1101]

The Genoese, wearing the cross on their right shoulders, climbed a palm tree leaning against the wall of the city and, calling Christ to their aid, at once crossed swords with the Saracens. The Saracens, however, dropped their swords and other weapons on the spot and began to flee to their mosque. But before the Saracens could reach the mosque, the Genoese struck dead all men fighting on the walls, in the city [streets], and at every corner. And all the Christian [inhabitants of the city] in company with the patriarch[3] rushed without delay to the mosque. And a thousand wealthy merchants, who had gone up into the tower of the mosque, began to cry out to the patriarch: 'Sir, sir, give us a safe conduct[4] so that we shall not die, because we hold to

---

Revue d'Histoire Economique et Sociale, XVII (1929), 137–55; A. Terroine, 'Etudes sur la bourgeoisie parisienne: Gandoufle d'Arcelles et les compagnies placentines à Paris,' *Annales d'Histoire Sociale*, VII (1945), 54–71; R. di Tucci, *Il genovese Antonio Malfante;* L. Vergano, 'Il mercante astigiano nel medio evo,' *Rivista di Storia, Arte, e Archeologia per la Provincia di Alessandria,* XLVII (1938), 305–79; P. Wolff, 'Une Famille du XIIIe siècle au XVIe siècle: les Ysalguier de Toulouse,' *Mélanges d'Histoire Sociale,* I (1942), 35–58.

[2] L. T. Belgrano, ed., *Annali genovesi di Caffaro e de' suoi continuatori dal MXCIX al MCCXCIII,* pp. 12–13.

[3] Daiberto, archbishop of Pisa.

[4] *Fiducia,* a Latin word which probably translates the Arab word *aman,* the safe-conduct which every Muslim had the right to give on the battlefield to a surrendering adversary. The legal basis for the survival of Christian communities in Muslim lands was the *aman.* The Christians of Caesarea probably asked for the same grant from their fellow believers. The *aman* guaranteed the life but not necessarily the property of those who received it.

the rule of Christ, your God, and we shall give you everything we have.'
And the patriarch asked permission from the Genoese to grant the safe
conduct. The Genoese then granted this permission to the patriarch. And
immediately after the permission was granted [the Genoese] went through
the city, seizing men and women and much money, and they took possession
of everything that was inside. . . .

Later the Genoese with their galleys and the entire expeditionary force
went to the beach of San Parlerio near Solino[5] and encamped there. First,
they set aside from the money [pooled together] in the encampment one
tenth and one fifth [which was due] to the galleys.[6] But all the remaining
money they divided among the eight thousand men. And they gave 48 solidi
Poitevin and 2 pounds of pepper to each as his share, [all this] apart from the
honorarium of the consuls, the ship-masters, and the better men, which was
a great sum.[7] Later, on the eve of the feast day of Saint James the Apostle,
they began the return voyage to Genoa with the galleys. And in the month
of October they were back in triumph and covered with glory.

The Increasing Importance of the Itinerant Merchant

THE PEDDLER WAS not a new figure in the trade of the period of the Commercial
Revolution, but his activity found new scope as commercial opportunities expanded.
According to Henri Pirenne, peddlers were almost the only native merchants in
Western Europe during the early Middle Ages, and they played an important role
in bringing about the revival of trade in the tenth century and after. These views,
however, have been challenged in the last few years.[8]

At any rate, itinerant merchants contributed to the growth of trade during the
Commercial Revolution by bringing the 'novelties' of the larger cities to smaller
centers and even to the tiniest villages. France remained for a long time a particularly
good area for these traveling salesmen because French towns were numerous and
fairly prosperous, as were most rural areas, but few centers had achieved a high
commercial development. Document 32 shows how various and significant were
the wares carried in the bags of members of the mercers' gild in Provence.[9]

[5] Probably al-Suwaydiyya, harbor of the ancient city of Antioch.

[6] That is, to the owners of the galleys.

[7] The booty seems to have included the famous cup, Sacro Catino, which was believed to be of
emerald but actually was of crystal. It is still preserved in the treasury of the Genoese cathedral.
See sources and bibliography in Belgrano's footnote to *Annali genovesi di Caffaro*, p. 117.

[8] See J. Lestocquoy, 'The Tenth Century,' *Economic History Review*, XVII (1947), 1–14, with
bibliographical references.

[9] Besides the preface by Billioud to his documents on the Provençal mercers, see L. Lempereur,
Les Chevaliers merciers du Rouergue. In Germany the *Krämer* (mercers) also exercised an important function, but as a rule they were not itinerant; see E. Köhler, *Einzelhandel in Mittelalter*. In
Italy peddlers and mercers were overshadowed by the great merchants who usually did not consider it below their dignity to engage in retail trade as well as in large-scale commerce; see G.

32

From the Latin[10]

Aix [-en-Provence, April 26, 1343]

[The charge:]

'In the city of Aix, at a certain hour of the night that [in itself] arouses suspicion, [Peire Cambafort of Alès, mercer, resident of Aix, and Peire Gilles of Montpellier] had loaded on certain animals four tied bales of mercery [obtained] from the neighborhood, and they had them carried and directed toward the road by which one goes from said locality to the fairs of Saint Maximin. . . .' [The bales were seized by the toll collectors of Aix.]

A. [Deposition of Peire Cambafort . . . :]

'He stated and deposed that it was true that [he], the deponent, who had [maintained] his domicile and his residence in the city of Aix ever since the feast of Saint Michael recently past, went this year to Paris from said city of Aix eight days before the feast of Quinquagesima Sunday just past. And in that locality of Paris, he bought certain mercery or merchandise for the sake of commerce and profit; and on the third day after Mid-Lent recently past he transported it from said locality of Paris to his place of residence within said city of Aix; and in the latter he sold a certain amount of it. Afterwards, having left the remainder in that house, he, the deponent, went to Montpellier in the week before the feast of Palm Sunday recently past with the money received from those goods which he had sold, as has been related above. And there he bought with the same money certain other mercery or merchandise, with which, leaving the locality of Montpellier on the Wednesday immediately following the feast of Easter, he returned to Provence. And he journeyed through Arles, where he sold some part of it, and transported the remaining part to his house within said city of Aix, which he entered on the Saturday recently past, this being the nineteenth day of the said month of April. And on that day, in the same city of Aix, he sold at wholesale a part of the remaining part of the merchandise thus imported from Montpellier to Quentin, Henri, and Jehan de Brinds, mercers, residents of the same city, and to other foreign mercers whose names he does not remember. And after doing this, he, the deponent, bound up within said house of his a portion of that merchandise which remained to be sold and another portion of the other

Luzzatto 'Piccoli e grandi mercanti nelle città italiane del Rinascimento,' in *In onore e ricordo di Giuseppe Prato, saggi di storia e teoria economica,* pp. 27-49.

[10] J. Billioud, 'Le Roi des merciers du comté de Provence aux XIVe et XVe siècles,' *Bulletin Philologique et Historique du Comité des Travaux Historiques et Scientifiques* (1922-1923), pp. 56-59. Part of the document is given only in summary.

lot transported from Paris, as has been related above; and he made two bales with it. These he handed over and delivered, on the Sunday recently past, within the said house, to Guillem Pons of Aix to be carried from there by pack animals to the fairs of Saint Maximin. . . .

'Asked from whom he rented the aforesaid house in the said city of Aix, he, the deponent, said from Jehan du Puy, mercer, and for one year at the price of five florins. . . .'

B. [Deposition of Peire Gilles:]

'On the same day the aforesaid Peire Gilles of Montpellier, journeyman,[11] as he states, of Peire Dinand, mercer of the same locality . . . interrogated on his oath about this, said that it was true that he, the deponent, was a mercer and that for the four years recently past without interruption he has been a journeyman and servant in the art of mercery, selling in many localities and in special fairs of Provence the mercery of said master of his, as is usually done, and for that purpose therefore traveling by land and going from place to place, from castle to castle, from village to village. . . .'

C. [Inventory of merchandise seized:]

[Content of the bales of Peire Cambafort]

'Six large dozen woolen cords for hats; 6 large dozen cotton ribbons; 12 large dozen woolen belts; a certain small basket full of iron trumpets; 1 petty dozen writing tablets;[12] 6 petty dozen children's bags; 10 petty dozen imitation gold; 1 petty dozen girls' garlands; 1 dozen gold veils; 3 pounds of black silk; 1 pound of *botea*(?)[13] silk; 6 pieces of green or grayish linen; 7 fleeces of red and black wool; a certain box full of combs; $17\frac{1}{2}$ dozen small silk belts without silver studs; 15 dozen woolen belts; 1 dozen belts of red leather; 2 dozen ladies' bonnets with gold ribbon; 6 dozen bags of golden silk, made in Paris; 4 large dozen woolen cords for hats.'

[Content of the bales of Peire Gilles]

'18 dozen woolen belts; 10 dozen silk belts without silver studs; 7 dozen Catalan linen bonnets for men; 11 dozen linen bonnets for ladies; 3 large dozen brass rings; 8 dozen bags of golden silk, made in Paris; 1 dozen small bags of golden silk, made in Paris; 6 Parisian girdles adorned with brass; 300 brass thimbles for cobblers; 4 dozen writing tablets; 18 dozen woolen

---

[11] *Familiaris.*

[12] *Pugillaria,* which Billioud translates by 'plumes à écrire.' But in classic Latin the word meant writing tablets. They must have been a specialty of Montpellier, since a Genoese document of the thirteenth century shows a man from Montpellier contracting a partnership with an Englishman for the manufacture of writing tablets of wax; see R. S. Lopez, 'The English and the Manufacturing of Writing Materials in Genoa,' *The Economic History Review,* X (1940), 132–37.

[13] The question mark is Billioud's. It is difficult to identify this kind of silk, unless *botea* means 'shop.'

belts with adornments, of Montpellier; 6 dozen linen bonnets for men; $13\frac{1}{2}$ dozen woolen belts for ladies, 3 dozen girdles of Rouen; 2 dozen silk belts with brass; 3 dozen bags of golden silk, made in Paris; and 1 large dozen brass rings.'

[After the decision of the court, the four bales were restored to the merchants.]

Commercial Investments of Noblemen

WHILE PIRENNE traced the origins of merchants and commercial capital to enriched peddlers of the early Middle Ages, Werner Sombart suggested that capital was formed by the accumulation of land rents. The noblemen, or at least the landowners, would thus be the original kernel of the capitalistic classes. This thesis seems to be as oversimplified as Pirenne's.

There is little doubt, however, that many noblemen invested capital in trade and gradually fused with the rich bourgeois families to form a new urban patriciate. This was especially common in the leading Italian cities.[14] Document 33 is an inventory of assets after the death of a scion of the higher Genoese nobility, a descendant of the town's viscounts. Except for the house which was his residence, he held no property in land. All of his capital was invested in *commenda* contracts and in other commercial speculations.

33
From the Latin[15]

Genoa, June 20, 1240

I, Simone Malfiliastro, legal administrator for Guglielmino, my son, nephew of the late Guglielmo de Castro and his heir, wishing in the name of my said son to take advantage of the benefit of the constitution of the most sacred emperor Lord Justinian and to avoid the penalties set for those who do not make an inventory . . .[16] acknowledge that I have found in the estate of said late Guglielmo the following: first of all, the share which Guglielmo himself had in the house in which he was living during his life, this house being in the section of San Damiano and bounded on two sides by the street

---

[14] A brief discussion of this subject is found in A. Sapori, *Studi di storia economica medievale*, 2d ed., pp. 705ff. See the stimulating book of J. Lestocquoy, *Les Villes de Flandre et d'Italie sous le gouvernement des patriciens.* See also *Cambridge Economic History*, II, 267–68, 294–97.

[15] R. S. Lopez, *Studi sull'economia genovese nel medio evo*, pp. 247–49; the background of the document is discussed at pp. 210–11. As will be clear to those who have read our introductory Note on Coinage, both the Genoese pound and the bezant mentioned in the document were moneys of account. The former corresponded to 240 Genoese deniers, the latter to 12 silver *miliarisia* or *miliarenses*. On the *commenda* or *accomendacio* see Chap. IX.

[16] We omit here part of the involved legal formulae given prior to the listing of the inventory.

and on another by the house of Opizzo de Castro. . .;[17] also, one instrument done by the hand of Guglielmo di Chiavica, notary, April 3, 1236, by which it is stated that Guglielmo Figallo acknowledged that he has received in *accomendacio* from Aimellina, wife of the late said Guglielmo, from the money of her husband £ 26 s.13 d.9; also another instrument made by the hand of Andrea, notary, September 15, 1236, by which it is stated that Pietro di Negro acknowledged that he has received in *accomendacio* from said Guglielmo £ 50; also, another instrument done by the hand of Guglielmo di Chiavica, notary, May 16, 1236, by which it is stated that Giacomo Suppa acknowledged that he has received in *accomendacio* from the said Aimellina £ 100; also, another instrument done by the hand of Ansaldo of Piazzalunga, notary, September 12, 1237, in which it is stated that Simone Marcone acknowledged that he has received in *accomendacio* from said Guglielmo £25; also, another instrument done by the hand of Ansaldo of Piazzalunga, notary, August 15, 1237, by which it is stated that Adelardo, son of Opizzo di Castro, acknowledged that he has received in *accomendacio* from said Aimellina, from the money of the husband, £ 42; also, another instrument done by the hand of Matteo Fagiolo, March 31, 1236, by which it is stated that Simone Balico acknowledged that he has received in *accomendacio* from said Guglielmo 100 bezants of *miliarenses;* also, another instrument done by the hand of Ansaldo di Piazzalunga, notary, May 15, 1237, by which it is stated that Ansaldo Stralleria acknowledged that he has received in *accomendacio* from said Aimellina, from the goods of the husband, £ 50; also, another instrument done by the hand of Matteo Fagiolo in 1236, by which it is stated that Pasquale Porco acknowledged that he has received as a free loan from said Guglielmo 100 bezants of *miliarenses;* also, another instrument done by the hand of said Matteo, September 11, 1236, by which it is stated that Berfoglio Berfogli acknowledged that he has received in *accomendacio* from said Guglielmo 200 bezants of *miliarenses;* also, another instrument done by the hand of Bonifacio of Noli, on the sixth day before the end of August, 1236, by which it is stated that Guglielmo Calderario acknowledged that he owes Guidotto Zurlo in place of said Aimellina, wife of said Guglielmo, £ 23; also, another instrument done by the hand of said Ansaldo, April 20, 1238, by which it is stated that Anselmo of Pegli acknowledged that he has received in *accomendacio* from said Aimellina, from the goods of her husband, £ 35; also, another instrument done by the hand of said Ansaldo on the day before the last of July, 1236, by which it is stated that Guglielmo Visconte acknowledged that he has received in *accomendacio* from the late Guglielmo £ 100;

[17] We omit here a long list of household goods.

also, another instrument done by the hand of Andrea, September 15, 1236, by which it is stated that Ugo Fornario acknowledged that he has received in *accomendacio* from said Guglielmo £ 59 s.12 d.7; also, another instrument done by the hand of said Ansaldo, August 13, 1236, by which it is stated that Giovanni Zaccaria acknowledged that he has received in *accomendacio* from said Guglielmo de Castro, son of the late Pietro de Castro, from the money of said Guglielmo, £ 50; also, another instrument done by the hand of Ansaldo of Piazzalunga, May 16, 1237, by which it is stated that Pietro Stralleria acknowledged that he has received in *accomendacio* from said Aimellina, from the money of her husband, £ 103; also, another instrument done by the hand of Bartolomeo, notary, August 28, 1236, by which it is stated that Enrico Suppa acknowledged that he has received in *accomendacio* from said Guglielmo £ 100; also, another instrument of *accomendacio* of £ 50, made to Pietro di Negro by Guglielmo de Castro, done by the hand of Andrea, notary, September 15, 1236; also, another instrument done by the hand of Matteo Fagiolo, March 31, 1236, of an *accomendacio* of £ 50, made to Berfoglio by the said late Guglielmo; also, another instrument done by the hand of said Matteo, March 31, 1236, of *accomendacio* of £ 29, made to Simone Balico by said late Guglielmo; also, another instrument done by the hand of Riccobono Merlone, the last day of February, 1234, of *accomendacio* of 40 bezants of *miliarenses*, made to Guglielmino, son of Opizzo de Castro, by Riccio Marzocco in the name of Guglielmo de Castro; also, another instrument done by the hand of Ansaldo of Piazzalunga, May 15, 1237, of *accomendacio* of £ 50, made to Ansaldo Stralleria by Aimellina, wife of Guglielmo de Castro, from the goods of her husband; also, another instrument of *accomendacio* done by the hand of said Ansaldo, September 16, 1236, of *accomendacio* of £ 53 s.6, made to Riccio Marzocco by said Guglielmo; also, another instrument done by the hand of Andrea, notary, September 15, 1236, of *accomendacio* of £ 53 s.6, made to Riccio Marzocco by said Guglielmo; also, another instrument done by the hand of Andrea, notary, September 15, 1236, of *accomendacio* of £ 59 s.12 d.7, made to Ugo Fornario by said late Guglielmo.

The space above has been left open so that if something comes to mind later it may be written down. Done in Genoa in the portico of the Genoese archiepiscopal palace. In the year of the Nativity of the Lord 1240, indiction twelfth, June 20, between nones and vespers. Witnesses: the aforesaid and Enrico, son of Rosso della Volta, and Folco, son of Corrado de Castro.

Merchants in Frontier Towns

THE INVENTORY of the estate of Armano, the skinner (Document 34), and the accounts of the Bonis brothers (Documents 35 and 36) illumine the rapidly growing stature of merchants in towns of recent formation along the expanding frontier of the 'commercialized' world.

Bonifacio was founded by Genoese settlers in 1195. They chose for its location a rock overlooking the strait between Corsica and Sardinia. The countryside furnished salt, skins, and cheese—products common to rugged and underdeveloped lands. But its position on trade routes held the promise of a brighter future. Ships carrying freight from Liguria to Africa and the Levant found it convenient to stop there. Its location, moreover, was ideal as a home port of piratical expeditions. Less than fifty years after its foundation the town was buying all kinds of cloth from northern France and Flanders, except those of the most expensive quality. It also purchased spices and imported other wares. Its trade was lively enough to enable the proprietor of a general store, Armano, to buy houses and shares in ships with the profits of his business. Armano's credit was good. He had obtained no less than £1,601 Genoese in *commenda* and *societas* agreements from twenty-seven small investors.[18]

Montauban in Languedoc also grew rapidly from the year of its foundation (1144). Its development, however, was not as brilliant as that of Bonifacio. It owed its prosperity not so much to trade as to the progress of agriculture in its district. The accounting books of the Bonis brothers—bankers, pharmacists, merchants of cloth, and sellers of spices—show the kinds of business that could be carried on in a modest but thriving provincial city of the mid-fourteenth century.[19]

34
From the Latin[20]

Bonifacio, December 28, 1239.

We, Orenga and Riccafina, mother and daughter, wishing to undertake, with the benefit of inventory, the administration of the goods which belonged to the late Armano, skinner, husband of Orenga and father of Riccafina . . .[21] desired to make an inventory or repertory of said inheritance.

---

[18] See V. Vitale, 'La vita economica di Bonifacio nel secolo XIII,' in *Studi in onore di Gino Luzzatto*, I, 129–51; F. Borlandi, *Per la storia della popolazione della Corsica*, pp. 43ff.

[19] Besides Forestié's thorough preface to his edition of the accounting books, *Les Livres de comptes des frères Bonis, marchands montalbanais du XIVe siècle*, see R. de Roover, 'Aux origines d'une technique intellectuelle: la formation et l'expansion de la comptabilité à partie double,' *Annales d'Histoire Economique et Sociale*, IX (1937), 186–87. On urbanization in Languedoc see P. Ourliac, 'Les Villages de la région toulousaine' and O. de Saint-Blanquat, 'Comment se sont créées les bastides du sud-ouest de la France,' *Annales: Economies, Sociétés, Civilisations*, IV (1949), 268–77; 278–89.

[20] V. Vitale, 'Documenti sul Castello di Bonifacio nel secolo XIII,' *Atti della Società Ligure di Storia Patria*, new ser. LXV (1936), 57–59. Riccafina, daughter and heiress of Armano, was the wife of Gregorio de Bargono.

[21] We omit part of the involved legal formulary preceding the listing of the goods.

First of all, we found in said inheritance 4 uncut pieces of green cloth; 1 piece of vermilion cloth; 2 uncut pieces of cloth of *gaboxium;*[22] [1 remnant], 7 *cannae* and 1 *palmum* of green cloth; 11 *cannae* of rosy [cloth]; 5 *cannae* of *gaboxium;* 10 dyed covers; 1 blanket of *bagadellum;*[23] 2 wrappings of fustian; 2 bundles[24] of cloth; 25 pieces of canvas; 14 pieces of fustian; 1 package[25] of fustian; 1 bundle of Sardinian ware; 10 *cannae* and 2 *brachii* of Albenga [cloth]; and in another remnant 10 *cannae* of Albenga [cloth]; and in another remnant 1 *canna* and 2 half *brachii* of Albenga [cloth]; and in another remnant 11 *cannae* of the same cloth; 3 *cannae* of black lace. Also, another small bundle of Sardinian ware; 1 cover of foxskin; 1 package of fustian which is torn; 1 sack of cotton; 4 *tortae* of linen. Also another cover of foxskin for the legs, a yellow jupe and another, white; a lady's green tunic; 1 purple cloth; 34 pieces of light canvas; 3 pieces of corded [cloth]; 2 pieces of purple [cloth]; 2½ pieces of sendal; 4 *palmi* of green; 1 *palucellum*[26] of heavy cotton; 5 cuts of canvas; 1 white belt adorned with silver; 6 pieces of heavy canvas; 44 pieces of *vintenae;*[27] 2½ *palmi* of blue. We [also found] 34 utensils, which were in a certain closet; 1 sign with a cross;[28] 1 chartulary; 1 *capitulum;*[29] 1 chartulary of debts; 21 *cannae* of stamins; 1 piece of Pontremoli fustian; 3 *cannae* of green [cloth]; 3 *cannae* and 2 *brachii* of kermes cloth; 2 sacks of wax, which was 3 *cantaria* and 12 *rotuli;* also 1 loaf of wax, which was 86 pounds; also, 2 skins of rabbits; also, a barrel in which there was 1 stomach guard with handles and another without handles; 1 sack in which there is 1 iron breastplate; 1 barrel in which there is a bassinet with brassarts; 1 basket in which is 1 hauberk with *infula* of iron and with three brassarts; 1 breast-plate; 3 *cannae* of canvas; 2 *turellae* full of grain; 7 casks full of grain; 2 cauldrons of copper and 2 others broken; 2 swords; 1 mantle of brown [cloth]; 1 ax; 1 large ax; 75 packages[30] of Corsican cheese; 5 *rubii* of pepper; 2 saddles; 4 casks full of wine; 2 closets; 1 chest; 1 arbalest of horn with hook; 2 large scales of copper, and others small; a small chest in which there are 2

[22] We cannot identify this cloth.

[23] Imitation Baghdad blanket? Or from the Italian *bagatella*, trifle, that is, light blanket?

[24] *Fardellos.* Cf. the modern Italian, *fardello.*

[25] *Volia*, like *vogia*, is probably a dialectical form close to the Italian *involto*, 'wrapping,' package.'

[26] *Palucellum* or *palutellum* would seem a diminutive of *pallium*, 'pall,' but the latter usually was an expensive cloth of silk, whereas those mentioned here are coarse textiles.

[27] A textile, the web of which is made of twenty times a hundred threads. Cf. G. Fagniez, ed., *Documents relatifs à l'histoire de l'industrie et du commerce en France*, II, 336.

[28] *Ensegnam unam cruciatam*, probably a shop's signboard, cf. modern Italian, *insegna.*

[29] No doubt this was one of the books of accounting, which must have contained the posting of credits; a chartulary of debts is mentioned almost immediately after.

[30] *Ligatos*, literally 'tied.' The expression always occurs in documents concerning shippings of Corsican and Sardinian cheese.

belts of silver, and another silver belt bound in a certain piece [of cloth] with 65 *miliarenses;* also 1 neck scarf of silk; and 1 Sardinian silver belt; and another silver belt with 2 breast straps. Also [we found] elsewhere 150 instruments; 1 ring in the form of a star; 1 jupe of yellow sendal with 1 *palutellum;* 1 silver cup; 26 ounces of sterling and *miliarenses;* 2 *cantarii* with 2 *romani;*[31] irons for horses; 1 flask of wine . . . 2 bridles; 1 cask of barley; 1 green and vermilion blanket; 2 *rubii* and 8 pounds of tin; £ 10 Tournois; 202 goatskins; 52 buckskins; 364 skins of she-goats; 280 lambskins; 63 tanned hides; 34 deer skins; 20 kid skins; 3 fox skins; 2 marten skins. Also . . .[32] [we found] 1 house situated in Bonifacio, [owned] jointly with Gregorio de Bargono; 3 houses near the gate of the castle of Bonifacio; and another house which is in front of the house of Simone de Bargono; and another house which is by the small tower; 1 orchard which is in the locality called *ad Lungonum;* 2 donkeys, 1 horse, 1 saddle, 2 pack-saddles; 1 orchard in the Cape of Bonifacio, and another house which is in Castelletto; 1 blanket; three-legged tables and bed tables; one eighth [share] in a certain *galiota*[33] and another eighth in the galley of Milano of Portovenere and partners; 1 grotto by the sea on the shore of Bonifacio, [owned] jointly with Gandolfo, skinner, in which there are 200 *minae* of salt. Also we found that said Armano had in *accommendacio* from Pietro of Vedereto £ 70; also, from Ambrogio Bonaventura, £ 35; also, from Ottone, draper, £ 60 Genoese; also, from Guglielmo of San Siro, draper, £47; also, from Baldovino di Celsa, £ 36; also, from Enrico de Guiberto, £ 20; also, from Guglielmo of San Siro, box maker, £ 37; also, from Giovanni Pignatario, £ 139; also, from Guglielmo, cleric, £ 229; also, from Lady Secca, £ 6; also from Ogerio of Prè, £ 24 s.2 d.9; also, from Bartolomeo Arduino, £ 10; also, from Gandolfo, skinner, £ 50; also, from Gherardo Archerio, £ 10; also, from Oberto Balbo, £ 29; also, from Montanaro, draper, £ 35 s.4; also, from Altadonna Peluca, £ 50; also, from Talia, £ 12; also, from Guglielmo de Porta, £ 20; also from Baldizone Japacassa, £ 46; also, from Guglielmo Rubeo, £ 50; also, from Simone Morello, £ 19; also, from Ogerio, draper, £ 41; also, from Nicola Beccorubeo, £ 122; also, from Armannino, nephew of the said Armano, £ 10; also, from Gregorio de Bargono, in *societas*, £ 400. Also we found his last will, in which he had bequeathed and distributed [his estate] according as it is stated in the last will written by the hand of me, Tealdo, notary.

---

[31] The *cantarium* is a unit of weight; here it doubtlessly designates the weight itself, used with a scale with two arms. The *romanum* (Italian: *romano*) is the weighing counter used in a scale with one arm.

[32] We omit here mention of a few more household goods.

[33] A ship; see the description in R. di Tucci, *Il genovese Antonio Malfanta*, pp. 17–18.

Witnesses: Gherardo Barberio, Ranficotto, Calvo of Levanto, Vivaldo Sparviere, Recupero. Done in Bonifacio, in the house which belonged to the said Armano, on Tuesday, December 28, between nones and vespers, 1239, eleventh indiction.

35
From the Provençal[34]

[Montauban, 1339–1369]

1. *Bernat Brunet, merchant of Montauban,* owes on account of the cash which I lent to Na Ramonda, his sister in Albi, to buy grain, witness En Bernat de Vitrac: 1 gold florin.

Item, he owes for one ounce of loaf sugar which Franses, his nephew, took on October 10, for the said Bernat was ill: s.1.

Item, he owes for one syrup and for one electuary which Maestre Felip Sudre[35] ordered for him, on October 12, at [the exchange of] 23 sols the écu: s.17 Tournois.

Item, he owes for spices which Franses took on October 19:

d.4 Tournois.

Item, he owes for three twisted candles, which weighed five pounds less one piece of tallow, which he had on November 20 when he went to visit his wife, at [the exchange of] 23 sols the écu: s.22 d.6 Tournois.

Item, he owes for one ounce of pimento, which he had on the day above mentioned: s.1 d.[1] Tournois.

Item, he owes for one gilded coffer of Paris, and for one silver necklace of the latest style, and for one silk pin cushion, and for four thick nets, and one *sentenar*[36] of amber, and for one piece of large German veil, and for two *doblos*[37] of Paris linen, and for one plain gold wedding ring, which he had as a jewel for his wife, witnesses W. del Casanh and Guiraut Bonis,[38] at [the exchange of] 23 sols the écu, amounting to: £ 25 s.18.

Item, he owes for spices for the wedding, and for three ounces of pimento, and for one twisted candle of one pound: £ 1 s.1 Tournois.

[34] Forestié, *Les Livres de comptes des frères Bonis*, II, 310–12. Entries are recorded in pounds, shillings, and deniers Tournois *of account*. The coinage consisted of French royal coins of different weights and alloys such as silver deniers Tournois of various issues, gold écus, and gold florins. According to Forestié such expressions as 'a xxii s. l'escut,' which we translate 'at [the exchange of] 22 sols the écu,' are evaluations of the coins actually paid in terms of gold écus. But the customers did not pay in cash; that is why their debts were inscribed in the ledgers. We suggest that the rate of exchange may include the interest charged by the seller.

[35] Felip Sudre was a physician, a lawyer, and a member of a distinguished family of Quercy.

[36] Probably a hundred beads.   [37] Modern French *doublet*, a textile of thick linen.

[38] Guiraut was a brother of Berthomio Bonis, who lived with him and who was entrusted with the direction of the laboratory (*obrador*) of drugs and with the making of candles.

Item, he owes for two ounces of a draught, which Maestre Felip Sudre ordered for him on November 27:   s.1.

And we [owe] him for one coffer which we recovered from him, which we sold to the lord of Folcaut: s.34 Tournois.

Item, he owes for seven and a half eighths [of a pound] of silk, and for six palms of silk trimmings on December 4, for the dress of the lady, at [the exchange of] 22 sols the écu: £ 1 d.9.

Item, he owes for almonds, and for starch, and for sugar which was taken on four occasions on December 12:   s.2 d.8.

Item, he owes for three eighths [of a pound] of silk, for the short dress of his wife, on December 16:   s.7 d.6.

Item, he owes for one silver clasp with pearls, which he had for his wife on the aforesaid day, witness W. del Casanh: 2 écus.

Item, he owes for spices which Franses Grifol, his nephew, took on Christmas Eve: s.3 d.8.

Item, he owes for two palms of stamin to make a sleeve, and for three ounces of pimento which Maestre Felip Sudre ordered on January 15, which Franses took: s.6 d.6.

And we [owe] him what the lady, his wife, delivered to us, counting in this sum four sestiers of barley which we had from her, at [the exchange of] 23 sols the écu, amounting to: £ 21 s.8.

Item, he owes for two *aunae* of wide silk trimmings, and for a quarter of silk for a twofold cape for his wife, which Dona de Nozias took, on July 22:
s.8 d.6 Tournois.

There remain 10 écus 3 sols which he owes.

And we [owe] him for the remainder [of the price] of the millstone which En B. Guasbert de Gros sold: 2 écus.

[The account] was settled with him on September 2, the year [13]50.

2. *Maestre Johan Delbosc, notary of Montauban,* owes for nine twisted candles of one pound each; and for eight small candles[39] of a half quarter each, and for one twisted candle of one pound for the Mass of the day follow-ing decease, which Guiraut Delbosc, his brother, and Maestre Jacme Apcheta, notary, took on June 4 for the funeral of the aforesaid Maestre Johan Delbosc, witnesses Guiraut Bonis and Tozet Guasc, at [the rate of] 22 sols the écu, amounting to: 66s. Tournois.

And we have from him £ 2 in deposit.[40]

[39] *Tersos.* Forestié notes that *tersos onsals* were candles of three ounces; one may assume that *terso* was any candle of small size.

[40] *Comanda,* which in this instance is not the *commenda* venture of maritime trade but 'deposit.'

3. *Maestre Guilhem de Lauriac, commendator of Saint Antonin of the monastery of Montauban,* owes by one account in the ledger F[41] in fol. 57— and it was for spices and for the trimmings of a robe which he had in [several] pieces, witnesses his squire and Guiraut Bonis—at [the exchange of] 23 sols the écu, amounting to: £ 3 d.3 Tournois.

4. *Friar W. Gui, reader of the Preacher Friars of Montauban,* owes for one draught which he had: s.2 d.6[42]

Sum: £ 6 s.8 d.9 Tournois.[43]

36
From the Provençal[44]

[Montauban, 1347–69]

2. *To Na Guilhalma, shepherdess of Montauban,* we owe for everything she had delivered to us in different coins at different times, counted with her, with the knowledge of W. Gaubert, in the year [13]66 at vintage [time]:

24 florins 6 groats.

Item, in addition we owe her, for what she delivered on January 8, [13]67,[45] in four *moutons* and two *nobles terses:*[46]   9 florins 1 groat.

She was paid on October 26, the year [13]69.

To Arnaut-W. de Roseu, our servant, we owe for what he delivered to us at vintage [time] in the year [13]66, with the knowledge of W. Gaubert, four *nobles* old and one *mouton,* which are worth: 8 1/2 florins.

The said Arnaut-W. owes us for what we delivered to him to pay his fine,[47] which he took to Moissac for the lord of Lagraulet: 8 1/2 francs.

Sum £ 8 s.1 d.6, which we owe.

[41] We do not know of a ledger marked F, but the above accounts are from what was called ledger C, and they contain frequent references to a ledger B.

[42] The text has 's.2 s.6,' but the second 's' evidently is a lapsus for 'd.'

[43] Most of the folios of the ledger contain sums of accounts previously itemized. This particular sum does not seem to correspond to the accounts of the folio. Perhaps other items were omitted in the accounts but included in the sum.

[44] Forestié, *Les Livres de comptes des frères Bonis*, II, 543–44.

[45] Style of the Incarnation; 1368, our style.

[46] The *mouton* or *agnels* were French gold coins, and the *nobles* were English gold coins.

[47] *Finansa.* 'Fine' seems a more proper translation than 'finance,' suggested by Forestié in his glossary.

The Church and the Merchants

IN ANCIENT MESOPOTAMIA temples played a prominent part in commerce and banking,[48] and some Greek temples also displayed considerable activity in money lending. The medieval Church, however, does not seem to have had the same interest in trade that it took in exploiting the land. One of the reasons, though not the only one, is that trade and moneylending were looked upon as sinful, or, at best, suspect activities.[49] One ecclesiastical institution, however, displayed extensive activity in moneylending—the Order of the Knights Templars. The Order was powerful in northern France and England, but it had much less influence in the development of Mediterranean trade.[50] Nevertheless it has seemed worth while to include one document concerning a loan granted by a Templar on the security of a cargo of grain shipped from Catalonia to Cyprus (Document 37).[51]

Probably the most significant indication of the small importance of ecclesiastical institutions in medieval finance is the fact that the popes did not use the Templars for their financial operations but preferred to rely upon lay merchants and bankers of Italy. The relations between the popes and the bankers have been fully illustrated in another volume of this series and it has seemed useless to offer additional evidence here.[52] The only document in this field that has been included (Document 38) is a mere token of the awareness of the translators that transactions by and for the popes certainly deserve attention.

37
From the Latin[53]

Famagusta, December 13, [1300]

In the name of the Lord, amen. I, Master Thomas, physician, resident of Famagusta, acknowledge and publicly recognize to you, Sanç Pérez of Sant Martí, receiving this acknowledgment and stipulation in behalf of the noble count, Lord Bernat Guillem of Emprença, that I have had and have

---

[48] The latest article on this subject, with bibliographical references, is B. Bromberg, 'The Origin of Banking: Religious Finances in Babylonia,' *Journal of Economic History*, II (1942), 77–88.

[49] Many relevant texts have appeared in English translation. See B. Jarrett, *Social Theories of the Middle Ages*; B. N. Nelson, *The Idea of Usury*; and A. E. Monroe, *Early Economic Thought*.

[50] The Templars are often mentioned in connection with loans extended by Genoese and other Mediterranean capitalists to Louis IX, but only as keepers of the French treasury.

[51] A recent monograph on the Templars as traders is Jules Piquet, *Les Banquiers au moyen âge: les Templiers*; also still of use is L. Delisle, 'Mémoire sur les opérations financières des Templiers,' *Mémoires de l'Institut National de France, Académie des Inscriptions et Belles-Lettres*, XXXIII, 2 (1889), 1–246.

[52] W. E. Lunt, *Papal Revenues in the Middle Ages*. See also Y. Renouard's monumental work *Les Relations des papes d'Avignon et des compagnies commerciales et bancaires de 1316 à 1378*, from which our selection is taken.

[53] C. Desimoni, 'Actes passés à Famagouste de 1299 à 1301 par devant le notaire génois Lamberto di Sambuceto,' *Revue de l'Orient Latin*, I (1893), 333–34.

received from you and Bernat Marquet, captain of the ship named Saint Nicholas, which is in the port of Famagusta, 8,000 *modii* of grain, according to the *modius* of Cyprus, belonging to the said noble count, and that you, jointly with the said Bernat, have consigned them to me as a security for those 16,350 silver [deniers] Tournois of France which we state that the aforementioned noble count has received in loan from Master Theodore, my brother, physician of the Temple; waiving. . . .[54] And this grain I promise you, in the said name, to sell and to send the [proceeds] wherever it pleases the aforementioned noble count or his accredited messenger, with the exception, however, that I or my said brother are to be allowed to obtain full payment concerning the said amount of money out of the bezants which will be collected from the said grain, according as it is sold. And in regard to that grain we state that it is registered with the customs office[55] of Famagusta. Also, on the other hand, I acknowledge that I have had and have received from you, said Sanç, and from said Bernat Marquet, in the said name of the aforementioned noble count, in my keeping and trust[56] 3,006 *modii* of grain according to the said *modius*, and in addition thirty jars of Catalonian oil belonging to the aforementioned noble count; waiving. . . . And out of that oil, then, I am to be allowed to obtain full payment of 229½ white bezants for the expenses incurred by me. And of all these aforesaid goods I promise you, in the said name, that I shall always make full account to the afore-mentioned noble count or to his accredited messenger. . . . Under penalty. . . . Waiving. . . . And the said parties ordered that. . . .

Done in the said place[57] on December 13, around terce. Witnesses called and invited: Pere Cambaceres of Tarragona, Anthony Faber, John of Acre, and Gratian of Acre.

38

From the Italian[58]

Naples, May 5, 1324

In the name of the Lord, amen. May 5, 1324.

We, Matteo Villani and companions, of the Bonaccorsi *compangnia* of Florence, resident in Naples, acknowledge and recognize by this present receipt (*polizza*) that we have received in Naples, May 5, 1324, from Messer

---

[54] The dots here and hereafter are the editor's.   [55] *Comerzium*, from the Greek.
[56] *In mea custodia et recommendacione*; that is, on deposit.
[57] Probably the *stacio* of Pietro, furrier, of Genoa, which is mentioned two acts before, and not the *logia* of the Venetians, which is mentioned in the instrument preceding this one in the notarial book from which our document is taken.
[58] Renouard, *Relations des papes d'Avignon et des compagnies commerciales*, pp. 631–32.

Raymond of Toulouse, treasurer of Benevento, 408 ounces of silver carlins [marked] with the lily,[59] at [the rate of] 60 to the ounce, for which we promise to have paid in court[60] to the chamberlain[61] and treasurer of our Lord the Pope and his Camera 400 ounces of the aforesaid[62] [carlins marked] with the lily, at [the rate of] 60 to the ounce, in consideration of a 2 percent [commision] for the transfer.[63] And we promise that we shall hand over to him the receipt of the said chamberlain and treasurer as soon as we have[64] received it, or sufficient guarantee[65] of this payment. And for further confirmation of this matter and guarantee to the said Messer Raymond, I, the aforesaid Matteo Villani, have written this receipt and sealed it with the seal of the said *compagnia* by my own hand. And we are to deliver to him the said receipt or guarantee in Naples or in Benevento as he wishes.

Jews and Christians in Trade and Money Lending

FROM THE BEGINNING of the Crusades the Jews lost their predominant position in international trade and tended gradually to confine their financial activities to petty money lending. Even in the latter field they faced the competition of Christian pawnbrokers and usurers such as the so-called Lombards, who were mostly from Chieri in Piedmont but also from other Italian towns, the Cahorsins from Cahors in southern France, and the Catalans, one of whom we present here (Document 41).[66]

When we consider that the Jews were almost the only merchants whose lot became worse during the Commercial Revolution, we are led to ascribe their declining fortunes chiefly to the tightening of discriminatory measures against them. To be sure, restrictive laws and anti-Jewish pronouncements by bishops and kings are found in the early Middle Ages. But there was no sustained persecution by the governments, and, above all, Jews were performing an indispensable function at a time when there was no sizable non-Jewish merchant and banking group in the larger part of Western Europe. In the later Middle Ages, when native merchants felt strong enough to do without the services of the Jews, they grouped

[59] The ounce was a money of account, whereas the carlins marked with the lily, or gigliats, were silver coins issued in the kingdom of Naples.

[60] In *corte*, that is, at the Curia.

[61] *Camarlingho* is the chamberlain or treasurer. The title *camerlengus* still exists in the papal hierarchy. *Camera* (chamber) is the treasury, or a branch of it.

[62] Read *predetti* for *pro e detti*.

[63] *Portagio*, the carrying or transfer. But the money did not have to be transported; a letter of payment or of exchange could replace it.

[64] *Abiano*, but we read *abiamo*.

[65] *Cautela* may mean any written evidence, notarial or chirographic.

[66] Other examples of 'usury' by non-Jewish lenders are found in Documents 66–71 and 143–44. On the Cahorsins, see N. Denholm-Young, 'The Merchants of Cahors,' *Medievalia et Humanistica*, IV (1946), 37–44; P. Wolff, 'Le Problème des Cahorsins,' *Annales du Midi*, LXII (1950), 229–38.

together and excluded them from many areas of business (Document 39). Henceforth Jews in business survived by exception and privilege rather than by permanent right.[67] Their settlement in a town was often the result of an agreement with the municipal government, which established the rates of interest that they could charge (Document 40).

39
From the Latin[68]

[Venice, October 27, 1412]

... As we learn from letters of the nobleman Ser Lorenzo Donato, our rector[69] at Retimo, some noble citizens and vassals of our locality of Retimo are making complaints to him. They have explained that the Jews of the said locality, not content with the interest and the incalculable profit that they obtain from usuries and *colleganze*,[70] capture all profit and proceeds that are obtained from the art and profession of commerce in that locality, so much so that one could say that these very Jews are lords of the money and of the men of that locality and district; and further, that these very Jews occupy nearly all the stalls, shops, and stores,[71] both those located on the square of Retimo and those around and near that square; and this brings very great harm upon our faithful and their utter destitution, because only these very Jews sell and dispose of their merchandise, and our citizens, being unable to have the said shops, are not able to sell anything or have any proceeds. And since our rector, considering that nowhere in our cities and localities of the island is it seen that the said Jews have stalls allotted to them outside the Jewish quarter,[72] and being aware of the damage and injury which our said subjects are suffering on account of the aforesaid facts, wishing to make provision for this, discovered a certain privilege concerning a concession made by the late Ser Marco Marcello, when he was rector of Retimo, to a certain Salomon, son of the late Lazarus, son of Meir, Jew, and to his sons, heirs, heirs of heirs, and descendants, by which [permission] is granted to

---

[67] F. Gabrieli, *Italia Judaica*, lists nearly all of the bibliography on Italian Jews. Some more recent publications are quoted in C. Roth, *History of the Jews in Italy*. There is no general work on the Jews of Mediterranean France in the later Middle Ages; see, however, G. Saige, *Les Juifs du Languedoc*, and A. Messé, *Histoire des Juifs d'Avignon*. On Spanish Mediterranean Jews in the same period, see F. Baer, *Die Juden im christlichen Spanien: Aragonien und Navarra*. For the Levantine Jews, see J. Starr, *Romania: the Jewries of the Levant after the Fourth Crusade*. On the medieval conception of the Jew as a usurer, see G. Kisch, *The Jews in Medieval Germany*, pp. 327ff. and Bibliography.

[68] H. Noiret, ed., *Documents inédits pour servir à l'histoire de la domination vénitienne en Crète de 1380 à 1485*, p. 213.

[69] The Venetian governor of the town.

[70] *Colleganze* is another term for *commenda*. See Chap. IX.

[71] *Stationes, appothecas et magacena.*

[72] *Judaicam.*

them and to any one of them to keep stalls and shops in the square and places
of Retimo outside the limits of the quarter. . . .[73]

40
From the Latin[74]

Siena, July 16, [1309]

Mosè [son] of Diodato, Salomone [son] of Ser Manuele, and Rosso Levi,
Jews residing in the city of Siena, to the men of great nobility and wisdom,
their lordships . . . the Twelve Defenders of the Commune of San Gimignano:
Greetings and increase of desired happiness!

In regard to taking up residence in your territory and in regard to the pacts
and negotiations undertaken between us and you, just as we had suggested
to you, we made it our concern to answer you briefly by the present letter
that it is our intention as best we can to please you and every individual
person in everything, but that we suggest as a pact that we should be allowed
to receive six deniers per pound as interest[75] and no more from anyone; for
you know well that on a small amount it would not be convenient to receive
less than six deniers [per pound]. In regard to large sums everyone could make
a pact with us, and it is our intention to receive [interest] up to the said
amount in accordance with the pact. And [we request] that all the articles,
pacts, and conditions included in our petition be accepted by you in their
entirety. And if it be your pleasure to have the aforesaid carried out, be
pleased to give orders in regard to the aforesaid to the Syndic of your
Commune, and let the Syndic himself come to us with a legal mandate, and
on our side we shall have everything carried out in the name of God. And
we transmit to you that petition enclosed in the present letter, and the petition
itself is of the same tenor as the other petition consigned to you at another
time, although at that time we were divided among ourselves because we
were not yet in mutual agreement, but at present we are unanimous in the
aforesaid.

Done in Siena, Wednesday, the sixteenth of the month of July.

[73] The Venetian senate, in whose records this petition is inserted, granted the request of the
'noble citizens and vassals' and revoked the privilege of Marcello. See also J. Starr, 'Jewish Life in
Crete under the Rule of Venice,' *Proceedings of the American Academy for Jewish Research*, XII
(1942), 89ff.

[74] R. Davidsohn, *Forschungen zur älteren Geschichte von Florenz*, II, 328.

[75] Six deniers per pound a month, that is, 30 percent a year. Let us recall in passing that at about
the same period the legal rate of interest in Nuremberg was 43 percent, but the Holzschuher firm
lent money to the Jews of that city at the average rate of 94 percent. See A. Chroust and H.
Proesler, *Das Handlungsbuch der Holzschuher in Nürnberg von 1304–1307*. In many states of the
United States today the maximum legal rate on small loans is higher than that demanded by the
Jews in San Gimignano. Five states allow as much as 42 percent a year.

41
From the Latin[76]

Pera [Constantinople], July 17, 1281

I, Nicolau de Palacio, Catalan, being sick of body and of sound mind, fearing the judgment of God if I die intestate, in contemplation of my last will make the following disposition of my person and goods: First, if I am to die, I elect that my body be buried at the Church of Saint Mary in Constantinople, and to this church I bequeath for my burial and for my funeral rites, for [the salvation of] my soul, 10 assayed gold hyperpers.[77] Also, I bequeath for my soul to the *bailo*[78] of Venice 1 hyperper; also, I bequeath for my soul to the hospital of Pera 2 assayed gold hyperpers; also, I bequeath for my soul to the hospital of the [Knights of] Jerusalem in Acre 5 assayed gold hyperpers; also, I bequeath for the souls of those from whom I believe I have taken [interest] unjustly 20 hyperpers, to be distributed by my executors (*fideicommissarii*);[79] also, I bequeath for my soul all my personal clothing to be distributed by my executors. And I also bequeath to Irene, my woman and the one who is serving me during my present illness, for my soul, 5 assayed gold hyperpers, one old cover, two sheets, one interwoven blanket, and the other utensils and furniture of my house which are not put down in writing below. I also declare that I am to recover from the persons mentioned below the sums of money written below under the pledges written below: First, from Bernardo Trincia, Pisan, 10 hyperpers, in regard to which I affirm that there is a [notarial] instrument; also, from Pere Goxabis, Spaniard, 9 hyperpers; also, from Ximen, Spaniard, 1 hyperper; also, from Guido of Bologna, my partner and godfather, 60 hyperpers which he had in *accomendacio*[80] from me and of which I affirm that there is a public instrument; also, from a certain woman of Pera, under pledge of two scarlet

[76] G. I. Bratianu, *Actes des notaires génois de Péra et de Caffa de la fin du treizième siècle* (1281-1290), pp. 103-4.

[77] On the meaning of 'assayed gold hyperpers' (*iperperi auri de sagio*), see our Note on Coinage. Evidently in this context the expression means coins of the standard which assayers in Pera would regard as regular.

[78] The head of the Venetian colony. The hospital of Pera, mentioned immediately after, was in the Genoese quarter. The legacy to the hospital of the Knights of Jerusalem probably can be explained by the fact that the Catalans had not yet a quarter of their own in Constantinople and depended upon the assistance of the Knights Hospitalers. Inasmuch as he was a usurer, Nicolau needed the protection of all Western authorities in Constantinople. Another safeguard against possible ecclesiastic action against his testament was the proviso that 20 hyperpers should be given for the souls of those from whom interest had been taken. On the problem of restitution, see our ntroduction to Chap. VI.

[79] A *fideicommissum*, in contrast to the formal *legatum*, was an informal type of bequest in which the deceased imposes a purely conscientious obligation upon others to confer benefits upon the heirs. In this context, however, the distinction seems to have faded. Bequests are called *legata*.

[80] *Acommendacio* or *commenda* is the commercial contract discussed in Chap. IX.

mantles which I have, 10 gold hyperpers; also, from Domingo, Spaniard, under pledge of one cape and one sword, 6 hyperpers and 12 keratia; also, from a certain Valeros Megadoukas, under pledge of one tunic of half. . . .[81] I cannot remember the name, under pledge of one tunic with lace . . . also, from a certain Spaniard, whose name I do not know, under pledge of one [piece of] green cloth . . . to give 4 hyperpers and 3½ keratia; also, from Guido of Pera, under pledge of twelve [pieces of] blue cloth, 7 hyperpers and 11 keratia; also, from Pedro Navarra, under pledge of one tunic, one fustian, and breeches, and two hoses, 20 keratia; also, from someone named Manzo, under pledge of one iron breastplate,[82] two shoes, two *arotetis*,[83] and one necklace, 4 hyperpers; also, from Conrad, taverner, under pledge of one lace, 10 keratia; also from Battifucina, under pledge of one piece of fustian, 22 keratia; also, from Antonio of Pera, under pledge of one white blanket, 3 hyperpers; also, from the same Antonio, under pledge of one old cover, one *sclavina*,[84] one bonnet, and one purse, 2 assayed gold hyperpers. Also, I declare that I have as my own the goods written below: First, one carpet. . . .[85] Also, I will that Bernardo da Ponte, furrier, Bernat of Montpellier, and Lord Martí be the distributors of the said legacies and goods of mine and my executors in regard to my aforesaid goods. And I charge them upon their souls to give and to dispense my aforesaid legacies as has been written above. My other remaining goods which I have in these regions of Constantinople and the Black Sea, and which may remain after my aforesaid legacies, I bequeath for my soul to my son Joan, son of Maria, if he is alive. And if he is not alive, I will that the said Maria, his mother, shall have from my afore-said goods 10 assayed gold hyperpers and no more, and I will that my remaining goods, which I have in these parts and the Black Sea, shall be given and distributed for my soul by my said executors wherever it shall seem best to them that they be distributed. This is my last will; and if it has not the legality of a testament, let it at least possess the strength and validity of codicils. All other testaments and last wills, if I made any, I void and invali-date, and I order them to be voided and invalidated and of no value. Done in Pera, in the house in which said Nicolau lives, in the year of the Nativity of the Lord 1281, eighth indiction, July 17, after vespers. Witnesses called and invited: Leonardo de Morleo, Venetian, and Giacomo, Lucchese; Guido of Vicenza; Enrico Zenno, citizen of Messina; Guglielmo, Genoese; and Jaume, tailor.

[81] These and the following dots are Bratianu's. [82] *Coirello feni*, no doubt a misprint for *coirello ferri*. [83] Perhaps a misprint for *archetis*, small bows? [84] The word means 'Slavic' or 'Slavonian,' but we do not know what object of Slavic origin or fashion is meant in this context. [85] We omit here a short list of modest household furniture and objects.

CHAPTER IV

THE DIVERSIFICATION OF MERCHANDISE

Two Hundred and Eighty-eight 'Spices'

SPICES, THAT IS, seasonings, perfumes, dyestuffs, and medicinals of Oriental and African origin, were of paramount importance in early medieval Mediterranean trade, and they still held a very prominent place in the commercial life of the later Middle Ages. During the Commercial Revolution Western merchants grew more exact and expert in distinguishing kinds and grades. They used the term 'spices' in a more and more general sense, so that it covered practically all types of dyestuffs, textile fibers, and other raw materials from the Orient and Africa. Furthermore, in the loose speech of many merchants, 'spices' included many other wares which did not come from either the Orient or Africa and which had nothing in common with the original group of aromatics described by that name. Then another term, 'minute spices,' was adopted to indicate specifically those wares which sold in small quantities at high prices. The list in Pegolotti's manual of commercial practice (Document 42) shows both the increasing diversification of spices proper as they were sold in Western markets and the growth of the term to encompass a much wider variety of goods than is today known as 'spices.'[1]

[1] The special section on the articles of Levant trade in W. Heyd, *Histoire du commerce du Levant au moyen-âge*, is still the best introduction to the study of medieval 'spices.' Other valuable works are quoted by A. Evans in his edition of Pegolotti; Evans's glossary of commodities, pp. 411–35, explains in detail the characteristics of the 288 spices and their uses in industry, pharmaceutics, and cookery. In addition, one may mention L. Bardenhewer, *Der Safranhandel im Mittelalter*; F. Borlandi, 'Note per la storia della produzione e del commercio di una materia prima: il guado nel medio evo,' in *Studi in onore di Gino Luzzatto*, I, 297–326; A. Castro, 'Unos aranceles de aduanas del siglo XIII,' *Revista de Filología Española*, VIII (1921), 1–29, 325–56; IX (1922), 266–76; X (1923), 113–36; C. J. Singer, *The Earliest Chemical Industry*.

42

Francesco di Balduccio Pegolotti, *The Practice of Commerce*
From the Italian[2]

[Florence, between 1310 and 1340]

SPICES

*That is, names of spices; and all those having a dot before
should be understood to be minute spices*

Quicksilver

Corrosive sublimate

●Hepatic aloes

●Socotra aloes

●Caballine [black] aloes

Rock alum of Karahissar

Choice alum of good alum works

Phocaea alum

Kutahieh and Ayassolük alum

Ulubad alum

Cyzican alum, Cord alum, Diaschilo alum; these three are the worst brands and the worst qualities

Processed alum in scales

Castile alum

Sugar alum

Vulcano alum

'Alum' from wine lees [tartar]

●Ammoniacum gum

●Asphalt

●Asafetida

●Anise

●Fine ambergris

Fine agaric

Armenium

Sheet silver[3]

Ultramarine blue

German blue [azurite]

Starch

Fresh oranges

Stavesacre

Sarcocolla

Litharge

●Rose water

Alcohol

Belliric [myrobalans]

Cotton of Syria

Cotton of the Byzantine Empire

Cotton of Apulia

Cotton of Calabria

Sicilian cotton

Malta cotton

[2] Pegolotti, *La pratica della mercatura*, ed. A. Evans, pp. 293–97. Inasmuch as nearly all of the commodities are discussed in detail in Evans's excellent glossary, we have explained only those terms which we have translated differently from Evans, and terms which Evans does not explain. Pegolotti's list follows the order of the Italian alphabet. There seem to be two duplications. *Chebuli* and *cetrini*, listed under C, probably are the same as *mirabolani chieboli* and *mirabollani cetrini* (chebulic and citron myrobalans), listed under M. Both *aghetta* and *litargiro* we have translated 'litharge,' but it is possible that the two terms indicated different grades of silver-bearing lead ore.

[3] *Argento battuto*, literally 'beaten silver,' can hardly be 'crushed silver,' as Evans suggests. Metal beaters, who hammered the metal into thin leaves or sheets, were found in all towns of any importance.

White cotton thread

Dyed cotton thread

●Balsam

White lead, medium quality

White lead, with the braiding[4]

Fresh bitumen[?][5]

●Borax, stone and paste

Biono da maestri[6]

●Barberry

Balaustine—these are pomegranate flowers

Wax of Montenegro[7]

Wax of Ragusa (Dubrovnik)

Wax of the Byzantine Empire

Bulgarian Wax[8]

Wax of Spain

Wax of Poland

Wax of Riga

Cronco wax—that is, as it is extracted from honey without being refined

White wax

Red wax

Green wax

●Cinnamon of the *sporta*[9]

●Cinnamon of the *gabbia*

●Cultivated cardamoms

Cassia

Cummin of Apulia

Cummin of Cerrinchan

Cummin of Spain

Cinnabar

●Chebulic [myrobalans]

●Wild cardamoms

●Citron [myrobalans]

Rock candy

●Camphor

●Castor

●Carpobalsam

Paper from the Marche[10]

Royal paper

Paper of Damascus

Waste paper[11]

Florentine glue

Bolognese glue

Fish glue

●Caraway

Sweet flag

●Costus

Sinoper

[4] *Biacca della treccia.* Evans suggests that the 'braiding' or plait may have been a symbol stamped on the molded cakes of white lead as an indication of quality or brand.

[5] *Bituro,* which Evans translates 'butter.' The word is occasionally found with this meaning, but it seems unlikely that butter alone among dairy products was included in the list. Perhaps one ought to read *bitume,* 'bitumen.'

[6] Evans offers no definite suggestion but recalls *buono da maestri* (literally, 'good for masters'), which appears in another source of the same period. *Maestri* apparently refers to master painters or master architects.

[7] Evans prints *Cera di getto* and adds in a footnote: 'Manuscript: *gette?* the script is not clear.' Inasmuch as other qualities of wax from Balkan regions are mentioned in the list, the reading *Ceta* (Montenegro) seems far more plausible.

[8] *Cera zavorra* (no suggestion in Evans) literally means 'ballast wax.' But it is undoubtedly a popular etymology for *Zagora,* the medieval name for Bulgaria, which was one of the great producers of wax.

[9] *Sporta* was a container used in Egypt for pepper and other spices. *Gabbia* (in Italian, 'cage,' but perhaps a transliteration of an Arabic term) suggests another container. Inasmuch as towards the end of the list Pegolotti speaks of *zucchero caffotino* (basket sugar, from Arabic *guffa,* 'basket'), one is led to think that grades of cinnamon also were distinguished according to their containers.

[10] Fabriano, in the Marche region, was famous for its paper.

[11] That is, most probably, paper stock which was remade into paper.

●Colocynth
Glue of leather
Citrons
Contre of Montieri[12]
Cantharides
Cassia bark
Copperas
Capers
●Cultivated cubebs
●Wild cubebs
Red corals
White corals
Black coral
Cheponico[13]
Elephant tusks
Dates
Tragacanth of the Byzantine Empire
Tragacanth of Turkey
Dionvici[14]
Emblic [myrobalans]
Euphorbium
Bougie bark
●Clove stalks
Pistachioes
Domestic fennels
Fennels of Tunis
Crushed ultramarine blue
●Lac in grains [seed-lac]
●Cinnamon flowers

Fenugreek
Native [India] ginger
Quilon ginger
Wrinkled [black] ginger
Peeled ginger
Malabar ginger[15]
Gallnuts of the Byzantine Empire
Gallnuts of Turkey of the Old Man[16]
Cloves
Heavy [minor] galangal
Light [major] galangal
Gum Arabic
Galbanum
Squinanth
Storax
Spikenard
Celtic nard
Baghdad indigo
Indigo of the 'Gulf' [Adriatic Sea]
Indigo of Cyprus
Indigo of Rif[?][17]
Frankincense
Tin of Venice
Tin of Provence
Tin sheet
Sumac
Skink
Scammony
Istamigne[18]

[12] Perhaps one ought to read *cenere*, 'ash' or 'dust.' Montieri was a well-known mining center.

[13] No suggestion in Evans, and we have none to offer.

[14] No suggestion in Evans, and we have none to offer.

[15] *Gengiovo ma a beri*, 'a strange name, surely a corruption' (Evans). But it is certainly Malabar. Quilon ginger, mentioned shortly before, also came from Malabar.

[16] No doubt the 'Old Man of the Mountain,' that is, the leader of the Assassins.

[17] *Rifanti*. No suggestion in Evans; Heyd, *Histoire du commerce du Levant*, also is unable to explain the meaning of the term. Italian sources, however, often mention 'Ceuta indigo,' and Ceuta is the seaport of the Rif region.

[18] *Stamigne* or 'stamins,' as Evans suggests, was the name of a coarse cloth. But no other textiles are mentioned in the list. The word may also mean 'stalks' in general, and it may have been used for the stalk of some particular plant.

Tabasheer
Burnt ivory
Bougie bark[19]
Ladanum
Litharge
Lign aloe
Lynx stone[20]
Shellac
Raw lac
Grains of Paradise
Manna
Melilot
Mastic, first [quality]
Mastic, second [quality]
Mastic, third [quality]
Mummy[21]
Mandrake
Raw honey
Musk with its sac
Musk without sacs
Myrobalan preserves
Mace
Myrrh
Wild brazilwood peelings
Chebulic myrobalans
Citron myrobalans
Cultivated brazilwood peelings
Almonds
Minium

Nutmegs
Nitre
Nenuphar
Fennel seed
Coconut
Nux vomica
Pontic opium[?][22]
Red orpiment
Yellow orpiment
Theban opium
Trani opium
Thin gold sheet
Gold of *Meta*[23]
Laurel oil
Linseed oil
Olive oil
Fine ochre
Hartshorn bone
Round [black] pepper
Long pepper
Powdered sugar of Cyprus
Powdered sugar of Alexandria
Powdered sugar of Cairo
Powdered sugar of Kerak
Powdered sugar of Syria
Sugar lumps
Colophony
Pitch for ships
White tar[?][24]

[19] Both *iscorȝa di Buggiea*, mentioned here, and *erba Buggiea*, mentioned above, seem to be a tannic bark (Evans). The two terms probably designate two different parts of the same plant or two varieties of the plant.

[20] Probably fossil belemnite (Evans).

[21] Either mummy dust, or a sort of natural asphalt; both were believed to have great pharmaceutical value.

[22] As Evans points out, *opopotico* may stand for *oppio pontico*, or it may be a mistake for *opoponaco*, 'opopanax.'

[23] Evans offers no suggestion. Perhaps Meta stands for Mesa, the southernmost port of Atlantic Morocco, from where gold dust of the Senegalese rivers was exported. Cf. V. M. Godinho, *História económica e social da expansão portuguesa*, pp. 123ff. Though the sources do not mention Italian traders in that port before the fifteenth century, Genoese merchants visited southern Morocco as early as the thirteenth century.

[24] See the discussion in Evans, pp. 426–27, under *pegola*.

Pearls

Fresh pellitory roots

Pine nuts

White pepper

Poppies

Lead

Sugar lozenges

Pine resin

Fine realgar

Spanish realgar

Rice from Syria

Rice of Spain

Fine rhubarb

Venetian copper with one bull[25]

Venetian copper with two bulls

Granulated copper

Old copper

Hard copper in large plates

Liquorice

Compact madder of Romagna

Ground madder of Romagna

Madder of Alexandria

Madder of the Byzantine Empire

Madder of Cyprus

Rhapontic

Silkworms' eggs

Sagapenum

Sarcocolla

Fresh senna

Nitre salt

Sal gem

Salammoniac

Soda ash

White sandalwood

Red sandalwood

Hard soap

Soft soap

Dragon's blood[26]

Mustard

Yellow sulphur

Black sulphur

Santonica

Silobalsam

Sinoper

Sermountain [laserworth]

Ordinary vine shoots

Wild brazilwood

Cultivated brazilwood

Quilon brazilwood

Vitriol of Cyprus

Granular sandarac

Refined sandarac

Fine verdigris

Red *vernicanti* [varnish?]

Turpentine

Turbith

Tamarind

Fine theriac

Great *trefola*[27]

Turquoises of Tyre

Sealed earth

Terra di Canmello[28]

Tutty of Alexandria

Tratto[29]

Raisins

Dried grapes of the Byzantine Empire

Verditer

---

[25] Metals were frequently marked with bulls or seals to indicate the quality.

[26] A ruby-red gum resin, used in pharmaceutics and as a color.

[27] An electuary (Evans).

[28] Hardly 'camel dung,' as Evans suggests. Perhaps one should read *terra di cannella*, 'cinnamon dust.'

[29] No suggestion in Evans, and we have nothing to suggest.

Vescovo[30]

Vermicelli, that is, *tria*[31]

Quince wine

Dried grapes of Armenia

Pomegranate wine

Fine zedoary

Basket sugar

Refined sugar

Sugar of Cairo

Muscat[?] sugar, which is in large loaves[32]

Damascus sugar

Tuscan safran

Rock candy sugar

Rose sugar

Violet sugar

India gingerbread

Buying and Selling Works of Art

THE HIGHER STANDARD of living and the more refined taste of the upper and middle classes during the Commercial Revolution made it possible for works of art to be included among articles of ordinary trade. Besides fine furniture and ornamental tapestries, paintings were offered in the market and attracted the attention of great Tuscan companies of merchant-bankers such as the company of Francesco Datini of Prato. The merchant was not always aware of the artistic value of the painting; to him any artist was a master craftsman and any painting was just another 'article.' The rather ungrammatical letter which we present here (Document 43), without disguising in translation the shortcomings in its style, was written by Buoninsegna di Matteo, a partner of Datini in Avignon, to his correspondents in Florence.[33]

43
From the Italian[34]

[Avignon, March 27, 1387]

... You say that you do not find paintings at the price at which we want them because there is none at such a low price. And therefore we tell you this, that if you do not find good articles[35] and at a good price, pass them by, since there is no great demand for them here. They are articles one ought to take

[30] The word appears elsewhere (see Evans, p. 433), but it is hard to explain it. The only well-known meaning is 'bishop,' but it can hardly fit among spices!

[31] From Arabic *atriya* meaning a flour paste fashioned into threads (Evans).

[32] *Musciatto* seems to be the same as *muscato*, musk-flavored. Evans tentatively suggests another explanation, which does not, however, seem convincing either to him or to us.

[33] Besides the article of R. Brun, 'Notes sur le commerce des objets d'art en France et principalement à Avignon à la fin du XIVe siècle,' *Bibliothèque de l'Ecole des Chartes*, XCV (1934), 327–46, see also J. Lestocquoy, 'Le Commerce des œuvres d'art au moyen-âge,' *Annales d'Histoire Sociale*, III (1943), 19–26, a provocative, if sketchy, essay in a field thus far little cultivated. On the Datini firm see also Documents 101, 125, 138, and 195.

[34] Brun, *ibid.*, p. 343.

[35] *Cose*, literally 'things.' Elsewhere, the paintings are called *pezzi*, 'pieces' or 'items.' It is clear that works of art were just another ware to our merchant.

when the master[36] who makes them needs money. And so it is up to you, since we do not have to engage in trade in these articles, because they are not articles that can be sold every day or for which there are many buyers. And if, therefore, some day while you are searching for them, you find a good and fine article and the master needs money, then you ought to take it.

We have sold three of the five pieces that Andrea bought, and for them we got 10 gold florins cash apiece, and we made a very good profit on them. Should the master from whom he got them have any small paintings that are fine and good, of a value of 4 to 5 or 6 florins cash, if fine and cheap, you may take one or two of them and no more; or [you may buy paintings] from another [artist] who might be a better master because if they are good drawings they will sell well. Here inferior ones will not do. . . .

Slave Trade

SLAVES WERE one of the most important articles of trade during the first centuries of the Middle Ages, and they continued to be the object of active transactions throughout and beyond the medieval period. Their number, however, tended to diminish after the tenth century. On the one hand, the spread of labor-saving devices made it less profitable to use slave manpower; on the other hand, the sources of supply in the extensive pagan countries in Eastern Europe were gradually closed as Slavs, Lithuanians, and other peoples were converted to Christianity. The Ukraine, the Crimean region, and the highlands of the Caucasus continued to export a good number of slaves, often children sold by their own parents. Others were captured and enslaved as a result of wars, especially during the Tatar invasions. By the thirteenth century, however, a slave had become a luxury in Western Europe.[37]

Selling children of Christian parents was a widespread practice in early medieval Europe, but in time the notion prevailed that only children of pagan or infidel nations could legally be sold. Whether or not these children or their parents had been baptized made no difference. This may account for certain unusual expressions in the contract we present here (Document 44). The slave girl mentioned comes from Malta, long a Christian island, although her name seems to indicate Muslim origin. The fact that she gives her consent to her own sale is exceptional; everything else in the contract is normal practice.[38]

---

[36] *Maestro* here means master of a craft, not master in the sense of a genius.

[37] See Document 195. In the Muslim world the situation was slightly different. Slaves were sought not only as inmates of harems and servants in luxurious homes but also as recruits for the army and to some extent as agricultural and industrial laborers. Christian merchants of the Western colonies in the Levant were among those who kept the Muslim markets well supplied with Russian and Caucasian slaves.

[38] Ample bibliographical information may be found in C. Verlinden, 'L'Origine de Sclavus–Esclave,' *Bulletin Ducange: Archivum Latinitatis Medii Aevi*, XVII (1942), 37–128.

44

From the Latin[39]

Genoa, May 11, 1248

I, Giunta, son of the late Bonaccorso of Florence, sell, give, and deliver to you, Raimondo Barbiere, a certain white slave[40] of mine, called Maimona, formerly from Malta, for the price of £ 5 s.10 Genoese, which I acknowledge that I have received for her from you. . . . And I call myself fully paid and quit from you, waiving the exception that the money has not been counted and received. I acknowledge that I have given you power and physical dominion [over the slave], promising you that I shall not interfere nor take away the aforesaid slave in any way, but rather I shall protect [her] for you and keep her out [of the power] of any person [under penalty] of £ 20 Genoese which I promise you, making the stipulation, the promise remaining as settled. And I pledge for that.[41] Waiving the privilege of [selecting] the tribunal.[42] And I, said Maimona, acknowledge that I am a slave, and I wish to be delivered and sold to you, Raimondo. And I acknowledge that I am more than ten [years old]. Witnesses called: Oberto de Cerredo, notary, and Antonio of Piacenza, notary. Done in Genoa behind the Church of Saint Laurent, 1248, fifth indiction, on May 11, before terce.

Trade in Foodstuffs and Its Impact on Agriculture

THE GLITTER and glamour of trade in luxuries ought not to overshadow the heavy trade in cheap bulky goods that went on at the same time. Besides Oriental 'spices' and fine textiles of the West, Venice exported leather goods, furs, salt, grain, oil, iron, copper, tin, mercury, timber, fruit, soap, animals, and meat. Genoese merchants brought Russian grain to Italy and Moroccan grain to England. Agricultural staples were exchanged in still larger quantities over shorter stretches of sea and land.

Out of thousands of examples that might have been chosen we have selected two contracts which show the impact of trade upon agricultural enterprises in comparatively underdeveloped regions. Merchants from Trent speculated in future prices of grain grown in the rugged valleys of the Alps (Document 45). Florentine traders bought up the production of cheese in Apulia and introduced into that

---

[39] R. S. Lopez, 'La vendita d'una schiava di Malta a Genova nel 1248,' *Archivio storico di Malta*, VII (1936), 391.

[40] *Sclavam a[n]cillam.* The two words have the same meaning. *Ancilla* is the technical word in Roman law while *sclavus* becomes more and more popular from the tenth century, replacing *servus*. See Verlinden, 'L'Origine de Sclavus–Esclave.'

[41] The notary, writing quickly, evidently forgot to complete this and the preceding sentence.

[42] This privilege could be invoked if there should be litigation. The transaction took place in Genoa, but the seller is a Florentine.

region the feverish rhythm and the business spirit familiar to their own highly developed commercial circles (Document 46).[43]

45
From the Latin[44]

[Trent, June 12, 1236]

On the same day, in the house of Ser Ottone Grasso, in the presence of the same Ottone and of Ezzelino of Egna, Giovanni of Tuenno, Olderico of Terlago, Gislemberto of Denno, and others. And there Ser Ottonino of Denno, in consideration of the full price of £ 200 Veronese, which he acknowledged having received from Ser Corrado of Ora, waiving, etc., promised to give in payment by reason of sale to the latter 500 *modii* of cereals according to the *modius* of Fiemme, [to be delivered] yearly as follows: in the octave of the feast of Saint Vigilius[45] coming next, 100 *modii* of rye, 50 *modii* [divided] among grain and beans or potherbs, 90 *modii* of barley, and 10 *modii* of millet or panic; and then later, in the octave of the feast of the following year, just as many. [The cereals are to be] given and delivered in Tesero to said Ser Corrado or to his messengers—indeed, fine grain and winnowed and dry, [accepting] the judgment of Mengo and Giannesino if there should be disagreement about it. Otherwise, indemnification and expenses. Security, his goods. Guarantor for him, Ser Roperto, his brother. And thus both swore.

46
Francesco di Balduccio Pegolotti, *The Practice of Commerce*
From the Italian[46]

[Florence, between 1310 and 1340]

APULIA. CONCERNING THE MAKING OF CHEESE

First of all, for making [cheese], 2 *tarì* per *migliaio*.[47]

[43] On Apulian commerce and agricultural exports, see F. Carabellese, *Saggio di storia del commercio delle Puglie*, and M. de Boüard, 'Problèmes des subsistances dans un état médiéval: le marché et le prix des céréales au royaume angevin de Sicile (1266–1282),' *Annales d'Histoire Economique et Sociale*, X (1938), 483–501. But there is no satisfactory history of southern Italian agriculture in the Middle Ages; nor is there any competent treatment of agriculture in the Trentino region.

[44] H. von Voltelini, *Die südtiroler Notariats-Imbreviaturen des dreizehnten Jahrhunderts*, Part 1, p. 155. The parties are from villages in the hills and mountains near Trent, which lies in the center of the Adige valley. Tesero is one of the highest villages in the Fiemme valley, formed by the Avisio river, a tributary of the Adige. Its height is 991 meters above sea level.

[45] The feast of Saint Vigilius is on November 18; hence the octave is November 25.

[46] Pegolotti, *Pratica*, pp. 164–65.

[47] A *migliaio*, in this context, does not mean 'a thousand pieces' but an Apulian unit of weight.

And for taking it from the yard and placing it in a storage room . . .[48] *tarì* and 1 *grano* per *migliaio*.

And for salt, [to be added in the proportion of] 3 *tomboli* per *migliaio*, 2 *tarì* and 5 *grani* per *migliaio*.

And for having the said salt pounded, 1 *grano* per *migliaio*.

And for water and earth and boys who help in the salting, 1 *grano* per *migliaio*.

And for storage room and custody, according to size [of the room?], 15 *grani* per *migliaio*.

And for the master who salts [the cheese], 9 *grani* per *migliaio*.

And for waste about 11 percent, amounting to . . . *tarì* per *migliaio*.

And for the toll[49] of the country, 4 *grani* per ounce, which amounts to . . . *tarì* per *migliaio*.

And for the local sales tax, without making a special bargain,[50] 18 *grani* per ounce, which amounts to . . . *tarì* per *migliaio*.

And if you sell by the steelyard,[51] you pay the local sales tax for reselling, except that if you have previously made a special bargain you would pay according to the bargain. When one makes the special bargain of 1 *tarì* per *migliaio*, [it covers] buying and reselling as well as buying without reselling. When one makes the special bargain of 4 to 4½ *tarì* per *migliaio*, [it covers] exporting from the kingdom as well as not exporting. And one makes these special bargains because when [cheese] has been sold it is exported in the name of the seller and not in the name of the buyer. In this way there is no other tax[52] except in Bari. Here there is another tax, the seller paying a duty[53] which is called half weighing, and which is 15 *grani* per *migliaio*. And if you sell [cheese] in a privileged fair[54] and [the cheese] is exported, it pays no tax except the said half weighing, which is never waived.

One *migliaio* = 4 *cantara* = 400 *rotoli* = 1,000 *libbre grosse* = 12,000 *once grosse*. One *oncia grossa*, weighs as much as 33⅓ *tarì*, whereas one *oncia sottile* is 30 *tarì*. The *tarì* is both a monetary unit and a unit of weight, but in this context it is always a monetary unit. The *tombolo* is a dry measure.

[48] The dots here and throughout the document indicate a blank in the manuscript.

[49] *Datio*, from *dare*, 'to give.' Italians today say *dazio*. It is a generic name for taxes, especially those collected on foodstuffs.

[50] *Piazza sanza fare patto. Piazza* is 'place' or (market) 'square;' but the name in this context indicates a special local tax. As Pegolotti explains (*Pratica*, p. 162), it was convenient to make an agreement with the customs officers for the payment of a lump sum instead of the regular tax.

[51] *Alla stadera;* that is, 'wholesale.'   [52] *Avaria.*

[53] *Dogana*. Both *avaria* and *dogana* usually were paid in ports, whereas *datio* and *piazza* were inland tolls.

[54] *Fiera franca*. Apulia had a series of such fairs, which were held successively in different towns through almost the entire year.

Raw Materials

THE COMMERCIAL REVOLUTION stimulated trade in the raw materials of industry and the search for them. The documents which follow are instances of these kinds of activity, which deserve greater attention than has been paid them so far. We watch the great Alpine forests being felled to supply timber for the cities of the plains (Document 47). We see the manufacturers of mirrors in the larger towns importing glass from underdeveloped regions (Document 48). We catch glimpses of prospectors from distant parts of Italy converging on the rugged country south of Siena with the hope of finding new mines (Document 49).[55]

47
From the Latin[56]

Cavalese, April 22, 1358

In the name of Christ, amen. In the year of the Lord, 1358, eleventh indiction, Sunday, April 22, in the town of Cavalese, Fiemme valley, in the dwelling house of the undersigned Altomo, in the presence of Ser Engelmardo Riccaino, of Trentino, son of Domenico, of Sémito di Castello, and [in the presence] of Bertoldo, son of the late Martino, all of them of Cavalese, witnesses, and of others. And there Francesco nicknamed Tosco, son of the late Bartolomuccio, of said village of Cavalese, [appeared] as principal debtor for the price and lump sum of £ 20 petty of the good deniers now current in Merano. With this money and price the aforesaid Francesco was satisfied, and he acknowledged, declared, and agreed that he has had and has received it from Altomo, notary, son of the late Ser Bennassu of Cavalese,[57] paying in the place, stead, and name of the noble knight Francesco Bevilacqua of Verona and as [the latter's] attorney, and from me, [Gerardino Pasquale of Vicenza], undersigned notary, as a public official, making the stipulation in the name of the same person. [Francesco] waived the exception that said money has not been given, delivered, and counted by him, and yielded every right of appeal. . . . And for this money and price the aforesaid Francesco, by stipulation and under pledge of all his property, movable and unmovable,

[55] Besides the works from which the documents were drawn one may consult F. C. Lane, *Venetian Ships and Shipbuilding of the Renaissance*; R. Cessi and A. Alberti, *La politica mineraria veneziana*; G. Volpe, 'Montieri,' *Vierteljahrschrift für Sozial- und Wirtschaftsgeschichte*, VI (1908), 315–423; A. Schulte, *Geschichte des mittelalterlichen Handels und Verkehrs zwischen Westdeutschland und Italien mit Ausschluss von Venedig*—all of them with bibliographies. But the history of the exploitation of natural resources in the Mediterranean basin has not yet been written.

[56] G. Sandri, 'I Bevilacqua e il commercio del legname tra la val di Fiemme e Verona nel secolo XIV,' *Archivio Veneto*, ser. 5, XXVI (1940), 178–80. We have omitted some of the involved legal formulae. Cavalese (999 meters above sea level) is less than four miles distant from Tesero, mentioned in Document 45.

[57] Bennassù or Bennassudo of Cavalese, like his son, had been a lumber merchant.

existing and future, as security, promised to give, to pay, to transport, and to present to said Altomo, receiving in the aforesaid capacity as attorney, or to me, undersigned notary, making the stipulation as a public official and receiving in the same capacity, twenty timbers of fir, of four *passus* each in length, of one and a half feet in breadth[?],[58] [and] of one foot in thickness each, [to be delivered] on the bank of the Avisio at the head of the bridge or beyond it by the middle of the month of April coming next. This pact was made and endorsed with solemn stipulation between them, so that if said debtor should not give or present the said twenty timbers at the said place and time limit as has been stated, he will incur and is to incur . . . the penalty of the double of said amount of money, to be collected by said creditor whenever he wishes. This double of the said amount of money the aforesaid Francesco [of Cavalese], the debtor mentioned above, promised to give and to pay to the same Altomo and to the undersigned notary, receiving and making the stipulation as public official, in the place, stead, and name of the above mentioned Ser Francesco [Bevilacqua], and he agreed [to this] by express pact; waiving the exception that said pact and promise has not been made and any other legal aid to which he is now and in the future entitled. And on request and demand of the aforesaid Francesco [of Cavalese], principal debtor mentioned above, for the firm undertaking and observing of all that was written above and is written below, the persons [whose names are] written below constituted themselves guarantors for him and principal debtors for the quantities written below . . . to wit: First, Domenico, son of the late Matteo of the said village of Cavalese, constituted himself guarantor and principal debtor for the same Francesco to the extent of seven timbers of fir, by the measures, kinds, pacts, and conditions written above and below. Paolo, son of the late Ottonello of the said town, made himself guarantor and principal debtor for the said Francesco to the extent of seven timbers of fir, by the measures, kinds, pacts, and conditions named above and below. And Altomo, notary, son of the late aforesaid Ser Bennassù, constituted himself guarantor and principal debtor for the other six timbers of fir, of the aforesaid measures, by the pacts and conditions already written and to be written below.

[58] *Per bancham et stroʒiam.* The editor is unable to explain these words and so are we. Since the length and thickness are also indicated, it would seem that they indicate the breadth at a certain point. The Italian word *stroʒʒare*, 'to choke,' seems to us more appropriate than the word *stroʒegare*, 'to drag' (in Trentino dialect), which Sandri tentatively suggests. *Stroʒia*, then, would mean the place where the plank was at its narrowest, or 'choked.' Another suggested explanation is that the *viginti planchonos* were undressed logs, each to be four *passus* long by one and a half foot through at the stump (*per bancham et stroʒiam*, i.e., the spot where the bole of the tree spreads as it joins the root system) and one foot through at the top (*per altitudinem*).

Said guarantors waiving [the benefits] of the Epistle of the divine Hadrian. . . .[59] The aforesaid debtors and guarantors waiving in regard to these [the benefit of] all [legislation of] fairs, statutes, articles, proclaimed and to be proclaimed, laws, reforms of the council of the city of Trent and of any other city and locality, existing and future, and the customs of the said valley of Fiemme. . . . Promising further to said debtors and guarantors not to bring forth anything against the aforesaid or anything of the aforesaid, and not to demand a copy of this record, a petition (*libellum*), a payment, a time limit, a moratorium, or anything else that may be useful to them and harmful to said creditor, except the record torn by him or [records] written for the parties[60] by the hand of a notary at the request of [both] parties.

And I, Gerardino Pasquale of Vicenza, notary public by imperial authority, was present to all the aforesaid and, invited by the aforesaid debtor and guarantors, wrote this.

48
From the Latin[61]

Genoa, July 24, [1215]

I, Arnulf of Basel, promise you, Enrico Medico, to import for you into Genoa four *centenaria*[62] of good and fine glass, of the best and finest for making mirrors that I can find in Germany and from the best furnace; and I promise to deliver and consign it to your possession or to that of your accredited messenger by the next [feast of] All Saints, under penalty of the double, all my goods being pledged, etc. And I am doing this for you in consideration of £ 3 Genoese which you are obligated to give me for each *centenarium*. Furthermore, I, the aforesaid Enrico, promise you at that time to accept said glass personally or through my messenger and to give said price to you or your accredited messenger peacefully and without causing trouble. Otherwise, I promise you, making the stipulation, the penalty of the double, all my goods being pledged, etc. Witnesses: Guglielmo Provenzale,

[59] We have omitted here a series of long-winded reservations, which differ in no manner from the usual and add nothing to the understanding of the transaction. The Epistle of the Emperor Hadrian settled the order of suit of codebtors.

[60] *Per eum cartam incisam, vel arcibus* [sic] *scriptam.* We emendate *arcibus* in *partibus.* The words describe the two methods by which the debtor usually proved his fulfilment of the contract. He might ask for the contract and tear it to pieces in the presence of the creditor, or he might ask the creditor to give him a notarial statement that he had fulfilled the contract.

[61] R. Doehaerd, *Les Relations commerciales entre Gênes, la Belgique et l'Outremont d'après les archives notariales génoises aux XIIIe et XIVe siècles,* II, 173.

[62] Doehaerd reads *centum.* But the abbreviation *cent* in this context probably ought to read *centenaria,* a measure of weight.

dealer in spices; Giovanni d'Usignolo; and Nicoloso, dealer in spices. Done in Genoa in the home of Enrico di Negro and his kin, July 24, between terce and nones.

49

From the Italian[63]

[Siena, April, 1445]

Before you, magnificent and powerful lords, our most particular lords, premising the humble recommendations, etc.

It is related with due reverence by your most faithful servants, Vitale, son of Maestro Allegro of Imola, Jew, and Stefano di Giovanni of Ragusa, that they have heard through report that in some parts of your district there are certain mountains which have veins of every kind of metal; and for that reason they have come to your city and wish to mine in said mountains. They would like to ask by singular grace[64] to be allowed to mine in the territory of Montieri, that is, in the village of Boccheggiano and in the village of Roccastrada, with these pacts, conditions, and procedures: that where they begin to mine no other person be allowed to mine within a mile from them for a period of twenty-five years; and if it should happen that two years pass without their mining anything, then this grace is to be understood to be null and void; and they offer forever to give your Commune out of anything they mine or find one part out of twelve. Also, in regard to everything they mine —that is, gold, silver, and any other metal—they promise your Commune that they will have it melted and refined by artisans living in your town, that is, by goldsmiths; and if [the goldsmiths] themselves wish to do this, they promise not to send [the metal] to others, that is, outside your city. Also, [they promise] that they will have it all struck in the mint of your Commune.

Also we wish to be allowed to use any water in the said localities and to erect there any building [needed] to work the said metal, and to be allowed to cut wood without detriment or damage to any of your communities or to private persons, [since] this grace is not to be understood to be detrimental in any part to them.

And this they would like to ask by grace of your lordships, to whom they ever recommend themselves, whom may God preserve as they wish. Praise be to God.[65]

---

[63] A. Lisini, 'Notizie delle miniere della Maremma Toscana e leggi per l'estrazione dei metalli nel medioevo,' *Bullettino Senese di Storia Patria*, new ser., VI (1935), 255–56.

[64] That is, by a grant reserved exclusively to them.

[65] In Latin, *Laus Deo*. The petition was approved on April 6, 1445.

Trade in Manufactured Goods

THE INDUSTRIAL growth of Western Europe provided a great stimulus to the Commercial Revolution and was, in turn, greatly stimulated by it. The variety of goods offered for sale defies summary description. Wholesale trade in cloth probably surpassed in volume and value all other branches of specialized commerce even though much cloth was sold retail by the handworker himself. The trade in arms also attained considerable proportions. There was no article so unusual or so humble that it could not interest a dealer. But any detailed discussion of trade in manufactured goods would require a long excursus into the history of industry, labor, and the related fields. We have no room here for such a venture or for bibliographical data upon it.

Our documents aim only at giving examples of some commercial practices especially connected with the sale of industrial products. A merchant who wanted to purchase cloth manufactured in distant places needed to know exactly its quality and length. Gilds in each city required all members to standardize their products, so that a man who bought 'rays of Ypres,' for instance, knew in advance that they would be 42 ells long and that they would have characteristics different from those of the rays woven in other towns (Document 50).[66]

On the other hand, masters in every craft imparted a personal touch to the products of their shops. This is true even for industries producing for mass consumption. Coarse cloth such as the so-called fustians was sold cheaply and could easily be standardized, yet the brand of one master became better known than that of another, and the cloth marked by that brand sold at a slightly higher price, just as today 'brand names' bring a small premium. Hence a certified trademark was a valuable property; it could be sold when a master retired from business.[67] In industries where the personal touch of a skilled master added much to the value of a product, a brand could become internationally famous (Document 51). The medieval gilds forbade their members to advertise their products, but merchants could enter into agreements to promote the sale of blades made by a great foreign swordmaker (Document 52).

50

Francesco di Balduccio Pegolotti, *The Practice of Commerce*
From the Italian[68]

[Florence, between 1310 and 1340]

CLOTH OF YPRES, FLANDERS

All covertures of any sort are [in length] 21 ells apiece.

[66] A town could, however, imitate the products of another town. Thus Ypres manufactured imitation 'Malines' cloth, and 'Ypres' cloth was made in several towns besides Ypres.

[67] Trademarks were also used for metals. See the list of brands of steel manufactured in the valleys near Brescia in Giovanni di Antonio da Uzzano, *La pratica della mercatura*, pp. 105–6. On the whole subject of trademarks, see F. I. Schechter, *The Historical Foundations of the Law Relating to Trademarks*.

[68] Pegolotti, *Pratica*, p. 285.

All rays of any color are 42 ells apiece.

White *tiree*[69] of any sort are 36 ells apiece.

Dyed cloth and imitation Malines medleys, 36 ells apiece.

Quality[70] white cloth of Ypres is weighed and not measured by the ell....[71]

And an ell is ... *braccia*[72] in Florence.

And all [cloth of Ypres] is sold there at so many gold *royaux* apiece, [according] to the quality, a *royal* being s.2 Tournois groat. And it is tagged in Florence in pounds Parisian [according] as the *royal* is worth in Parisian deniers.[73]

And covertures and rays and other [cloth] are tagged in marks, the mark being s.31 d.4 Parisian.

51

From the Latin[74]

[Milan, June 10, 1383]

On Wednesday, June 10, Ser Pietro Preda, son of the late Ser Gaspare, [citizen] of the city of Milan [and resident in the quarter] of Porta Comacina, parish of San Simpliciano Outside the Walls, has sold and sells and gives the [trade]marks[75] written below, free and unencumbered by any rent, payment, condition, servitude, or charge [that may be] owing, due, or payable to any one, to Ser Petrolo Tanzio, son of the late Ser Nicola, [citizen] of the said city of Milan [and resident in the quarter] of Porta Comacina, parish of San Cipriano, present, buying, stipulating, and receiving. [The trademarks have been recorded] in a certain book or copybook [kept] by the provosts (*abati*) of the society and community of the Art of Fustian in Milan, and they are sketched and designed below. [They are] suitable for marking, and Ser

[69] No satisfactory explanation has yet been found for this term. One would feel inclined, however, to connect the term with French *tirer* and Italian *tirare*, 'to pull' or 'to draw.'

[70] *Di sorta*. This term has baffled Evans (see his Glossary to his edition of Pegolotti, p. 425), but it evidently means 'of [good] quality.'

[71] In the only extant manuscript these words are followed by the expression *e sono di bianchi così*, which means nothing at all, even if one inserts *alle ... il panno*, as Evans suggests. Evidently the text is badly corrupted here.

[72] At this point Pegolotti probably gave the equivalence of the Ypres measure of length (ells) with the Florentine measure (*braccia*), but the extant manuscript quotes no figure. See Evans's note 5 to p. 278.

[73] The *royal* is Flemish currency whereas the pound Parisian is a money of account used in Florence to indicate the cost to the seller of a piece of cloth offered for sale. See Document 180.

[74] Unprinted. Archivio di Stato, Milan, *Notaio Marcolo Golasecca*, n. 404; transcribed and translated from a microfilm copy in the Yale University Library, n. 2164 roll 1. Some excerpts from the document were published by E. Motta, 'Per la storia dell'Arte dei Fustagni nel secolo XIV,' *Archivio Storico Lombardo*, ser. 2, VII (1890), 143-45.

[75] *Signa*.

Pietro himself has used them for marking fustians on top and over the folds of every piece of fustian. [They were] assigned to him, Ser Pietro, by the provosts of the society and community of said Art. And these marks are of the form and designs sketched and designed below, viz.[76]

[The said Ser Pietro sells] the right and permission of using the said marks, or any of them, or similar ones, and marking fustians and anything else of any description with them, at the will of Ser Petrolo Tanzio himself. And likewise [he sells] all rights, suits, and advantages in and from these marks, and on account or by reason of them, which belong and appertain to the seller, Ser Pietro himself. . . .[77]

And for that sale, [that is], for the price and the agreed payment of the price and transaction concerning all and each of the aforesaid [trademarks], the seller has acknowledged and acknowledges, and gives receipt that he has received from the said Ser Petrolo, buyer, 100 florins in silver coins of the Milanese coinage now current, waiving the objection that he has not had and received the said deniers. . . .[78]

Done in the Broletto Nuovo of the Commune of Milan, in the presence of. . . .[79] There were present as witnesses Ser Orsino Tanzio, son of the late Ser Paolo, [resident in the quarter] of Porta Nuova, parish of Sant' Eusebio, notary; Ser Francescotto Dugnani, son of the late Ser Leone, jurist, [resident in the quarter] of Porta Nuova, parish of San Protasio ai Monaci; and Giovannino Malcalzato, son of the late Ser Andreolo, [resident in the quarter] of Porta Orientale, parish of San Giorgio al Pozzo Bianco, all of them [citizens] of the city of Milan, invited and qualified.

52
From the Latin[80]

Genoa, February 3, 1248

We, Giovanni and Rubaldo of Monleone, swordsmiths, promise and make agreement with you, Bartolomeo Bonannato, not to sharpen, grind or work any new blade that may be brought to Genoa for anyone and that

---

[76] There follow the drawings of the trademarks, four of which are crowned heads (one full face and three profiles), the fifth being the top of a helmet with two plumes. See the reproduction in Motta, 'Arte dei Fustagni,' p. 144.

[77] We omit part of the formulary, which is extremely verbose.

[78] Again we omit part of the formulary. Note that the florins were gold coins. What was actually given in payment was silver deniers.

[79] The manuscript is partly unreadable and there is a tear involving two lines at the end of a page. The Broletto Nuovo was one of several municipal buildings.

[80] Unprinted. Archivio di Stato, Genoa. *Cartulario di Bartolomeo de Fornari*, Vol. I, Part 2, fol. 151.

is of the brand[81] of Bonfante of Firenzuola until you have sold the seventy-five blades that you have of said brand of Bonfante; and we also promise you to give and to place at your disposal assistance and counsel in buying and acquiring, so far as we can, all blades of said brand brought to Genoa for sale until the aforesaid seventy-five blades are sold and no longer. Each and all of the aforesaid [stipulations] we promise on oath to undertake and to observe as stated above and not to violate them. Otherwise we promise you, making the stipulation, the penalty of £ 10 Genoese, the aforesaid remaining in force. And for this we pledge to you as security all our goods, existing and future. And I, Rubaldo, acknowledge that I am more than twenty-five years old. On the other side, I, said Bartolomeo, promise and make agreement with you, the aforesaid Giovanni and Rubaldo, not to give to sharpen, to work, or to sell any blade of said brand of Bonfante that I shall buy within said time limit to anyone but you, until the said seventy-five blades have been sold. And I promise you to observe [the agreement] as stated above under the said penalty of £ 10 Genoese promised and stipulated, and under pledge of my goods. Done in Genoa in front of the house where Aimone, seller of spices, lives, in 1248, fifth indiction, February 3, after nones. Witnesses, Guglielmo de Valle and Opizzo, wool maker, and Girardo, *executor*. And they asked two instruments to be made of it.

Monopolies and Cartels

ALTHOUGH MEDIEVAL laws often thundered against traders endeavoring to monopolize wares to the detriment of the general public, monopolies and cartels were not infrequent during the Commercial Revolution. Indeed, some writers describe all merchant and craft gilds as cartels for the establishment and protection of a monopoly. A discussion of gilds is not within the scope of this book, but Document 1 shows that the Byzantine raw-silk dealers in some respects behaved as a cartel. An examination of the statutes of Western gilds would lead to similar conclusions.[82]

The creation of a cartel other than a gild was not always regarded as illegal. It was even fostered when it protected nationals against the competition of foreigners. On the other hand, agreements among a small number of merchants to control

---

[81] *De opera.* This expression in this context means not only 'of the work' but also 'of the shop' or 'of the brand.'

[82] See especially G. Mickwitz, *Die Kartellfunktionen der Zünfte und ihre Bedeutung bei der Entstehung des Zunftwesens,* with Bibliography. Many statutes and regulations of Western gilds have been published in translation. See, for instance, T. Mendenhall, B. Henning, and A. Foord, *Ideas and Institutions in European History,* pp. 88ff.; R. C. Cave and H. H. Coulson, *A Source Book for Medieval Economic History,* pp. 169ff., 193ff.

prices and supplies, and monopolies held by single capitalists, were generally held objectionable.[83] Document 53 presents a tangled web of conflicting monopolies. The Byzantine Empire up to 1204 had forbidden Western ships to cross the Straits into the Black Sea, thus making the entire trade of that region with Europe a virtual monopoly of the Byzantine traders. Then the Latin Empire of Constantinople (1204–61) threw the Straits open to all Western ships; however, since this empire was almost a Venetian protectorate, the Venetians managed to succeed the Byzantines as leading traders in the Black Sea. But when in 1261 the Byzantine Empire was restored at Constantinople with the assistance of the Genoese, the Empire excluded from the Black Sea all the competitors of Genoa, of which Venice was one. The Genoese monopoly proved short-lived. A few years later the Byzantine emperor allowed the Venetians to cross the Straits, but they could not dominate trade because Genoese primacy in the Black Sea was solidly established. It was momentarily threatened by the efforts of a Genoese family, the Zaccarias, to establish a private monopoly in the trade of alum. In 1264 Benedetto and Manuele Zaccaria obtained from the Byzantine emperor the port of Phocaea on the Aegean Sea and the nearby alum mines. A few years later, in order to suppress the competition of alum from the Black Sea region, Manuele persuaded the emperor to close the Straits to Genoese ships coming from the Black Sea and loaded with alum. The incidents that followed brought Genoa to the brink of war with the Byzantine Empire. Eventually the order was revoked, and the Zaccaria brothers vied with other Genoese merchants in exporting alum from the Black Sea as well as their own alum from Phocaea.

Documents 54 and 55 do not require extensive comment. They show two aspects of the Venetian policies in regard to cartels. The government frowned upon them if the result was to prevent Venetian citizens from obtaining a share in a branch of trade, but fostered them if the purpose was to strike collective bargains with foreign merchants.

53

Georgios Pachymeres *Michael Palaeologus* v. xxx
From the Greek[84]

[Byzantine Empire, early fourteenth century; dealing with events of 1275 or thereabouts]

At that time the emperor [Michael VIII Palaeologus] decided to humble

---

[83] See J. Strieder, *Studien zur Geschichte kapitalistischer Organisationsformen: Monopole, Kartelle und Aktiengesellschaften im Mittelalter und zu Beginn der Neuzeit;* G. Luzzatto, 'Sindacati e cartelli nel commercio veneziano nei secoli XIII e XIV,' *Rivista di Storia Economica,* I (1936), 62–66. The field, however, needs further investigation.

[84] *Corpus scriptorum historiae Byzantinae,* Bonn ed., pp. 419–20. P. Possini's seventeenth-century Latin version, included in the edition of Bonn, is a redundant paraphrase. It uses full sentences to render single words, often embellishing the original with elaborations and reflections which are Possini's own and which are hardly consistent with Pachymeres' elliptic, obscure, but vigorous style.

the Genoese, who were full of impudence. In fact, the Venetians and their community[85] formerly greatly surpassed them in wealth, in arms, and in all [kinds of] materials because they made greater use of the [narrow] waters than did the Genoese and because they sailed across the high sea[86] with long ships,[87] and they succeeded in gaining more profit than did the Genoese in transporting and carrying wares. But once the Genoese became masters of the Black Sea by grant of the emperor and with all liberty and franchise, they braved that [sea], and sailing in the midst of winter in ships of reduced length—which they call *taride*[88]—they not only barred the Romans[89] from the lanes and the wares of the sea but also eclipsed the Venetians in wealth and material [goods]. Because of this they came to look down not only upon those of their own kin but also upon the Romans themselves. Now the emperor personally had granted to a certain Genoese nobleman, called Manuele Zaccaria,[90] the mountains to the east of Phocaea which contained alum metal. [These] the latter exploited after having settled down there with his own people. And having collected a good deal [of profit] from these works, he wanted to obtain still more from the benevolence and good disposition of the sovereign toward him. Thus he thought it fitting that the Genoese be not allowed to transport across the Black Sea the alum-bearing metal from the mountainous districts[91]—for they use a large quantity of it in dyeing the woolen textiles in different colors, as one can [easily] see—and the emperor, assenting, made a law [to this effect].[92]

[85] Probably what is meant is not the motherland but the Venetian colony in Constantinople, which had autonomous institutions as a Commune.

[86] *Ta pelage,* as opposed to *thalassa,* which we have rendered by 'narrow waters.' Commercial and navigation treaties of the later Middle Ages often draw a distinction between territorial waters and 'profunda pelagi,' the high seas. Here, however, 'high sea' seems to refer to the broad Black Sea as opposed to the Aegean Sea, which is narrower and studded with islands.

[87] That is, galleys.

[88] The *tarida* represented a compromise between the galley, which was the sturdiest, largest, and fastest ship, relying chiefly upon oar propulsion, and the *nef,* which was sometimes still larger but far less strong, and which relied chiefly upon sails. It is true that sails were a cheaper means of propulsion, but they could not always be depended upon. Winds might fail, and the problem of sailing against the wind was not fully solved before the fourteenth century. Navigating during winter was a specialty of the Genoese and is mentioned as such also by Jacques de Vitry, a Western chronicler of the same period. But the Venetians also did not entirely discontinue their sailings in winter.

[89] That is, the Byzantines.

[90] Actually the grant was made to his brother, Benedetto Zaccaria, but Manuele shared in the benefits.

[91] Namely, the 'Colonna' (Karahissar) alum, which came from the mountains of Pontus and was the only quality better than that of Phocaea. See Document 176.

[92] Pachymeres goes on to tell how some Genoese tried to break the law by exporting alum from the Black Sea and how they were caught in a bitter encounter under the walls of the imperial palace on the Bosphorus. The culprits were blinded, according to Byzantine law.

54
From the Latin[93]

[Venice, July 22, 1283]

Item, a motion was passed in the Great Council[94] to the effect that the following instructions should be added to the commission of the bailiff[95] of Ayas, or should be sent to him and be binding upon him under oath:

That in the Great Council which he shall hold at Ayas[96] he shall move that our merchants present there shall form a *societas* for the [purchase of] cotton, buckrams, and pepper. And if two thirds of that Great Council pass [the motion] regarding the formation of that *societas,* he may and shall order under such penalties as shall seem proper to him that [the merchants] form that *societas* and that nobody may purchase [the aforesaid wares] except those [representatives of the *societas*] appointed for this purpose. And those who will go there later are to be [received] into that *societas* and have such share [of the merchandise] as is due to them pro rata after their arrival. And in regard to the formation of this *societas* it should be understood [that it applies only] to the [merchants] who have [taken along] with them 200 bezants or more.[97]

55
From the Latin[98]

Venice, April 28, [1358]

On April 28 [motion was] passed [in the Senate as follows]:

Whereas our [fellow citizens] frequenting Cyprus have of late engaged in the formation of rings and conspiracies (*conventiculas et conspirationes*) in the business of transporting cotton to Venice, entering upon mutual obligations and pacts to prevent the transport of more than a certain amount [of cotton];

[93] Unprinted. Archivio di Stato, Venice. *Deliberazioni del Maggior Consiglio, Luna,* fol. 17v. This document is followed by one calling for the formation of similar cartels for the purchase of pepper in Alexandria.

[94] The lower house of the Venetian Republic.

[95] The appointed head (*bailo*) of the self-governing Venetian colony in Ayas. Venetian colonial officers received a commission outlining their principal duties.

[96] The colony governed itself through a constitution similar to that of the motherland. Hence the *bailo* summoned the lower house of the colony just as the doge summoned the lower house of the motherland.

[97] A Syrian bezant was roughly equivalent to one third of a Venetian pound. Hence the minimum sum required to be admitted to the cartel was comparatively small. Indeed, it is improbable that many merchants made the long journey to Ayas with a smaller capital than 200 bezants, including, of course, borrowed money as well as their own.

[98] Unprinted. Archivio di Stato, Venice. *Senato Misti,* XXVIII, fol. 44v.

And [whereas] this is against the interest of the Commune, which loses its customs duties upon what would be imported and used to be imported beyond the said amount; and it is also against the welfare of the city because cotton needed in the West is transported to Ancona and elsewhere while it ought to be transported to Venice,[99] and [thus the conspirators] are building up foreign countries while ruining ours; and it is also against the good of the community and of individual persons because such profit as used to be distributed among the whole community is turned over to three or four [persons];

And [whereas] it is useful in view of all above considerations to provide a remedy to this [situation]:

Let a motion be put to vote that three wisemen shall be elected within the assembly of the Senate, who shall make an inquiry in regard to these rings [of dealers] in cotton as well as to [others dealing] in powdered sugar, salt, and other merchandise, and also in regard to those in shipping and to all conspiracies that may be formed in Venice, in Cyprus, and in any other place. And they shall draft provisions and give us their advice in writing. We shall meet here with this [advice at hand], and we shall act as shall seem proper, and any one [of us] shall be entitled to put a motion to vote. And [the wisemen] may be chosen from any post, but each is to accept only one office.

And the first vote is to be for the said proposal and [its individual] articles, and the second for the election [of the wisemen].

And [the wisemen] are to have as a deadline [for the completion of the inquiry] the end of the coming month of May.[100]

The Flow of Merchandise to a Trading City

WE HAVE PRESENTED examples of wares of the four main groups—luxuries, food-stuffs, raw materials, and manufactured goods. For a general picture of all goods available for sale in a city we must resort to custom, excise, or brokerage tariffs. Of these there is so great a number that a choice is difficult. Tariff schedules of a very large city, if they list all items, would tend to give an exaggerated impression of the variety of goods normally available in any town. Tariff schedules of a very small center, on the other hand, would be inadequate to represent the variety.[101] We

[99] Venice claimed the monopoly of long-distance trade on the Adriatic Sea. Ancona was the most dangerous competitor on that sea.

[100] It is worth noting that the wisemen presented a majority and a minority report, and that the Senate did not approve either, so that the monopolists, who had strong support in the Senate itself, practically won the fight. See Luzzatto, 'Sindacati e cartelli.'

[101] Cave and Coulson, *Source Book for Medieval Economic History*, pp. 916ff., contains a translation of tariffs of the Catalan port of Colibre or Collioure (in Roussillon). This town, however, was too unimportant to serve as a representative example.

choose the brokerage tariff of Narbonne in the thirteenth century because Narbonne at that period well represented an average town. It was directly connected with the sea but not situated on the shore. Its commerce chiefly served the needs of the local bourgeoisie and the population of the surrounding agricultural region, but it was to some extent connected with the great international trade channels of the Mediterranean basin and of the European Continent.[102]

56

From the Languedocian[103]

[Narbonne, thirteenth century]

These are the brokerage fees that one must give to brokers for the goods they sell.

[Cloth of] Arras and Bruges, and barracans, and *stamfords*[?][104] of Saint-Omer, and says, and [cloth of] Chartres, and cloth of Reims: for each piece one must give the broker: d.3

Colored cloth and white [cloth] of France, and *stamfords* of Arras and of Paris, and plush *stamfords:* d.6 Narbonnese apiece

Vermilion cloth dyed with kermes: d.12 apiece

A *carga* of kermes, by the *carga:* s.2

Cloth of Figeac, and of Cahors, and of Albi: d.2 apiece

Cloth of Lerida, both brown and scarlet,[105] of twenty *canas:* d.3

Cloth of Narbonne selling at less than s.40 apiece: d.2

Coarse *vintenas*[106] and canvas, by the *corda:* 1 *pogesa*

[102] The old and rather unsatisfactory monograph of C. Port, *Essai sur l'histoire du commerce maritime de Narbonne*, has not yet been superseded. The meager bibliography on the subject is brought up to date in A. Dupont, *Les Relations commerciales entre les cités maritimes du Languedoc et les cités méditerranéennes d'Espagne et d'Italie*. See also R. W. Emery, *Heresy and Inquisition in Narbonne*, Chap. I.

[103] G. Mouynès, *Ville de Narbonne, inventaire des archives communales antérieures à 1790, Annexes de la série AA*, pp. 206–8. The *carga* (load), the *saumada* (packload), the *sporta* (basket) are units of weight. The *sestier* and the *modius* are units of volume. The *cana* (cane or rod) and the *corda* (rope) are units of length. The *pogesa*, originally a very debased denier struck in Le Puy, was used as the smallest fraction of the denier; the *mesala* or medal was a half denier.

[104] *Estans fortz*. This word (Italian *stanforte*, French *estamfort* or *estain fort*, Latin *stamen forte*) has been connected by many with the English market town of Stamford, Lincolnshire, which was known for its cloth. Notwithstanding the good arguments recently brought forward by R. L. Reynolds, 'The Market for Northern Textiles in Genoa, 1179–1200,' *Revue Belge de Philologie et d'Histoire*, VIII (1929), 831–51, the assumption that *stamen forte*, 'strong stamins' or 'strong worsted,' is merely a popular etymology does not seem fully convincing to the writers. Perhaps the two words had an independent fortune and later were associated to designate the same kind of cloth. This would account for the extraordinary diffusion of the term. We find 'stamfords' of Arras, of Genoa, of Como, of Ayas, etc. Although the English 'stamfords' were good, one hesitates to admit that their renown may have spread so far.

[105] E. *sarlaz*; but read, probably, *escarlaz*.

[106] A textile the web of which is made of twenty times a hundred threads.

Vintenas and linen of Champagne selling at s.15 or more: 1 medal per *corda*

Linen of Reims, which is of 7 *canas:* d.1 apiece

Cuts of sendal: d.6 Narbonnese

Stamins of 12 *cordas:* d.2 Narbonnese

White and colored fustians of Lombardy: 1 medal apiece

Variegated fustians of Lombardy and Barcelona: d.1 Narbonnese apiece

Other white and dyed fustian of Barcelona: 1 medal Narbonnese apiece

Any fur made of lambskin: 1 medal Narbonnese

Ox hide: 1 *pogesa* Narbonnese

Goatskins: d.12 Narbonnese for each hundred

Cordovan and sheepskins processed in the Cordovan manner, by the dozen: d.2 Narbonnese

Buckskins: d.15 Narbonnese for each hundred

Vermilion cordovan: d.3 Narbonnese a dozen

Sheep leathers: d.1 Narbonnese

Rabbit and squirrel and lamb [skins]: d.2 Narbonnese for each hundred

Rabbit fur: d.1 Narbonnese per pelt

Furs of lamb, and furs of belly skins of rabbit, and cloaks of dormouse: 1 medal Narbonnese each

Furs of otter: d.1 Narbonnese

Moles[?],[107] and foxes: d.1 Narbonnese a dozen

Kid skins: d.1 Narbonnese for each hundred

Indigo of Baghdad and of Cyprus: s.2 Narbonnese per *carga*

Any other indigo, and brazilwood, and incense, and all other spices: d.12 per *carga*

Wax, and loaf sugar: each d.6 per *carga*

Sugar alum, and [alum] of Castile and of Aleppo, and cumin, and almonds[?],[108] and cassia[?],[109] and gallnuts, and yellow weld, and

---

[107] *Tavarz.* E. Levy, *Provenzalisches Supplement-Wörterbuch*, VIII (Leipzig, 1924), 89, quotes the passage in question as his only example for the word, but offers no translation for it. Although *talpa* is the regular word for mole in other Provençal texts, the P could conceivably have become a V if the liquid had undergone a metathesis.

[108] *Amenlos*, instead of the usual *amenlas*, 'almonds,' appearing a little further in the same text (*amenlas ab closc*, 'almonds with shell'). Probably those mentioned here were bitter almonds, whereas the 'almonds with shell' (cf. Pegolotti's *mandorle col guscio*) were the common domestic almonds.

[109] *Classa*, not listed in the leading Provençal dictionaries.

rice, and wool *de presseʒ*,[110] and flax, and hemp, and copper, and brass, and madder, and tin, and metal, and thread of Burgundy, and other thread: d.6 per *carga*

Iron: 1 *pogesa* Narbonnese per quintal

Steel: d.1 Narbonnese per quintal

Alum of Vulcano, and clavellated ashes: d.3 Narbonnese per *carga*

Waste silk: d.12 Narbonnese per *carga*

Silk and saffron, each, by the pound: d.1 Narbonnese

Bleaching and hard soap: d.6 Narbonnese per *carga*

Soft soap: d.1 Narbonnese per quintal

Pitch of Tortosa: d.1 Narbonnese per *sporta*

Pitch of Le Puy, by the quintal: 1 medal Narbonnese

Flour, by the quintal: d.2 Narbonnese

Lead: d. 1 Narbonnese per *carga*

Figs, and dry raisins, and chestnuts, and honey, and sulphur, and dyewood, and tar, and salted meat, by the quintal: 1 medal Narbonnese

Surcingles, of twelve binders: d.1 Narbonnese

Straps for the back: 1 medal Narbonnese a dozen

Straps, medium: 1 *pogesa* Narbonnese a dozen

Filberts, by the sack: d.2 Narbonnese

Dates, by the quintal: d.2 Narbonnese

Almonds with shell: 1 *pogesa* Narbonnese per *sestier*

Fat, tallow, and cheese, by the quintal: d.1 Narbonnese

Oil, by the *sestier:* d.1 Narbonnese

Wine: d.2 Narbonnese per *modius*

Grain, by the *sestier:* 1 *pogesa* Narbonnese

Horse selling at £20 or more: s.2 Narbonnese

Mule or draft horse: d. 12 Narbonnese

Donkey: d.6 Narbonnese; and, if it is bartered, let each of the sellers pay [the fee]

Carga of washed wool that be not *de presseʒ:* d.3 Narbonnese; and unwashed wool: 3 medals Narbonnese

Ox: d.6 Narbonnese

---

[110] 'Pressed' wool would be the easiest explanation, but we do not know that raw wool was pressed. One may think of *pers* or its plural *perses: pers* is dark blue color and cloth dyed with that color. But it would be hard to see why *pers*-dyed wool should be considered of such exceptional quality as to pay twice the fee of other wool. Persia, as a country of origin, must be excluded, since no other Western document speaks of imports of wool from there. Perhaps the Narbonne tariff understands 'purple' by *pers*; purple was an expensive dyestuff.

Sheep and goats: d.4 Narbonnese a dozen

Irons for lances and knifeblades: d. 3 Narbonnese a gross dozen

Stirrups: d. 3 Narbonnese a petty dozen

Blankets: d. 3 Narbonnese a dozen

Cuttlefish: d. 1 Narbonnese for each hundred

Bowls[?]:[111] d. 1 Narbonnese for each thousand

Wood, worked: d.1 Narbonnese for each thousand [pieces]

Wood, rough: d.1 Narbonnese for each thousand [pieces]

Mirrors: d.1 Narbonnese for each hundred

Spoons: d.3 Narbonnese for each thousand

Silver, by the mark: 1 medal Narbonnese

Gold, by the mark: d.12 Narbonnese

Any *honor*[112] within the town for the pound of deniers: d.1 Narbonnese

Any *honor* outside the town, for the pound of deniers, d.2 Narbonnese

Vintage [grapes?]: 1 medal Narbonnese per *saumada*

Saracen [slave],[113] male or female, by the pound of deniers: d.2. Narbonnese

Hauberk and skirt, by the pound of deniers: d.2 Narbonnese

Spun gold, sample of twelve reels, d.3 Narbonnese

[Spun] gold of Lucca, of twelve straws: d.1 Narbonnese

Paper: d.6 Narbonnese a box

Cabas:[114] 1 medal Narbonnese a bundle

Jars: 1 medal Narbonnese a dozen

Jarful of sage and mustard: 1 *pogesa* Narbonnese per quintal

Flints: 1 medal Narbonnese a dozen

Ploughshares and hoes: 1 medal Narbonnese a dozen

Small glassware: 1 *pogesa* Narbonnese for each hundred

Bottles of medium size: d.1 Narbonnese for each hundred

Anything that male or female peddlers or auctioneers will sell for s.2 or less, let [the broker] have 1 medal Narbonnese. Also, from

---

[111] *Copons.* This word is sometimes used in the meaning of 'cuts' or 'remnants' of cloth; but in this context a derivation from *copa*, 'bowl,' seems more plausible.

[112] The word is found frequently in the meaning of fief, benefice, or any land property, see Ducange *s. v.* 'Honor.' Sometimes, especially in Italian documents of the early Middle Ages, it means interest on a loan. In this context one may tentatively suggest that it meant loans obtained through a broker.

[113] *Sarraʒin* and *Sarraʒina* seemingly mean slaves of Muslim extraction; on slave trade in this period, see Documents 44 and 195. There were wares called 'Saracen' after their origin, but if wares had been meant, there would have been no reason to use both the masculine and the feminine gender.

[114] The typical flat baskets with two handles which are still widely used along the Mediterranean coast of France.

s.2 on, up to s.10: d.1 Narbonnese. Also from s.10 on, up to s.20: 3 medals Narbonnese. Also, for [each] s.20: d.2; and from here up, at the same rate, exception and reserve being made of what was said elsewhere in regard to the cloth of Narbonne.

Statistical Data on the Flow of Merchandise

TARIFFS GIVE a fairly complete description of the wares, but they say nothing about the quantities imported or exported. With the possible exception of the hitherto unpublished records of the port of Aigues-Mortes in the fifteenth century, no detailed descriptions of the amount of incoming and outgoing wares are extant to our knowledge, for any Mediterranean town in the Middle Ages.[115] Statistical data can be found but for certain customs houses along international routes leading from Italy to France. We present some excerpts from the records of tolls in Saint-Jean-de-Losne and in Villeneuve de Chillon. The records show only certain aspects of trade, since not all wares were subject to special tolls and since some merchants were exempted from paying customs. Even so, they come closer than any other record to giving us an absolute idea of the volume of traffic at a determinate place.

57
From the French[116]

[Saint-Jean-de-Losne, July 1341]

[Receipts from the toll on wool:]

... Item, from 'the Cleric'[117] of Cremona, of Milan, on July 6, for 19 *charges* and 13 stones, [carried] in nineteen sacks: £ 19 s.10 d.5

Item, from Nicolino Vettura of Venice, on July 6, for 2 *charges* in two sacks: s.40

---

[115] On the Aigues-Mortes records, see J. Morize, 'Aigues-Mortes au XIIIe siècle,' *Annales du Midi*, XXVI (1914), 313–449. Detailed records have been preserved for the taxes on foreign trade in London and other English harbors. Some of them have been published in translation by N. S. B. Gras, *The Early English Customs System*.

[116] L. Gauthier, *Les Lombards dans les Deux-Bourgognes*, pp. 201–8; see also the partial photographic reproduction of the document, facing p. 1, and, for the background of the document, pp. 67ff. We have translated the entries for July 1341 from the accounts of Jacquot Garnier, collector of customs duties (*conducte* and *menue conducte*) for the duke of Burgundy at Saint-Jean-de-Losne. The *conducte* was collected on wool exported, each *charge* (load) of 25 stones paying 20 sous. The *menue conducte* was collected on imports of 'great horses' (no doubt war horses, as opposed to work horses), each horse paying 3 sous, and on imports of many other wares, among which cloth paid 2 deniers apiece. In the accounts every entry is preceded by the mark with which each merchant or partnership used to mark the sacks or bales. Translations of Frenchified Italian names are tentative. The collector often deformed them beyond recognition; moreover, Gauthier's transcription is not always faultless, as it appears from a comparison with that part of the document of which he gave a photographic reproduction.

[117] *Dou clerc*. Probably it was a nickname, but it might be a deformation of the name Chierici, Clerici, or Cherchi.

Item, from Francesco Grasso of Milan, on July 8, for 9 *charges* and 12 stones in eight sacks: £ 9 s.9 d.7

Item, from Comello[118] of Como, on July 8, for 6 *charges* and 23 stones in seven sacks: £ 6 s.18 d.5

Item, from Giovannino of Monza, of Milan, on July 8, for 22 *charges* and 3 stones in twenty-two sacks: £ 22 s.2 d.5

Item, from Giovannino of Monza, of Milan, on July 9, for 8 *charges* and 10 stones in eight sacks: £ 8 s.8

Item, from Bartolino del Tetto of Milan, on July 10, for 28 *charges* and 9 stones in thirty sacks: £ 28 s.7 d.3

Item, from Germano Campana[?][119] of Milan, on July 17, for 27 *charges* and 22 stones in twenty-eight sacks: £ 27 s.17 d.8

Item, from Bartolino del Tetto of Milan, on July 25, for 12 *charges* and 10 stones in thirteen sacks: £ 12 s.8

Item, from Ambrogino Borromeo[?][120] of Milan, on July 26, for 20 *charges* and 16 stones in nineteen sacks: £ 20 s.12 d.10

Item, from Giovannino of Monza, of Milan, on July 27, for 45 *charges* and 9 stones in forty-four sacks: £ 45 s.7 d.2

Item, from Ambrogino Borromeo of Milan, on July 27, for 1 *charge:*   s.20

Item, from Marco Morigia of Milan, the said day, for 27 *charges* and 15 stones in twenty-eight sacks: £ 27 s.12[121]

Item, from Nicolino Vettura of Venice, on July 31, for 19 *charges* and 9 stones in nineteen sacks: £ 19 s.7 d.2

[Receipts from the petty toll on great horses:]

... Item, from Maso of Bologna, on July 3, for ten horses: s.30

Item, from Azzo of Bologna, on July 3, for four horses: s.12

Item, from Giovannino of Milan, the said day, for one horse: s.3

Item, from Guglielmino of Milan, on July 9, for two horses: s.6

[Receipts from the petty toll on cloth, mercery, spices, and other wares:]

[118] Gauthier transcribes *Conieu,* but a comparison with the photograph shows that it was *Comeu,* in Lombard dialect the equivalent of Italian Comello.

[119] *Cheu Maincloiche,* where *Cheu Main* probably stands for *Germain* and *cloiche* seems to be a translation of the Italian *Campana,* also meaning 'bell.' But a name like Chioccia cannot be ruled out.

[120] *Borron,* which phonetically might correspond to Borrone as well as or better than to Borromeo. But the Borromeo or Borromei were an important family of Milanese merchant-bankers engaged in trade with the countries of Western Europe. See especially G. Biscaro, 'Il banco Filippo Borromei e compagni di Londra,' *Archivio Storico Lombardo,* ser. 4, XIX (1913), 37–126.

[121] At this point the document gives the sum of all items concerning the toll on wool from Christmas 1340 to July 27, 1341. The collections amounted to £334 s.18.

... Item, from 'the Red'[122] of Combreniet, on July 6, for eighteen [pieces of] cloth: s.3

Item, from Nicola Lordone of Venice, on July 6, for forty-six [pieces of] cloth: s.7 d.8

Item, from Andrea of Cassano and Giacomino of Como, on July 8, for 115 [pieces of] cloth: s.19 d.2

Item, from Andrea Brughiera of Milan, on July 8, for eight bales of fustian and mercery: s.20

Item, from Antonio Terino of Pavia, on July 15, for three and one half bales of cloth, of furs of rabbits and of milk-fed lambs:[123] s.11 d.3

Item, from Bettino of Bergamo, on July 15, for thirty-eight [pieces of] cloth: s.6 d.4

Item, from Liebault of Belle Aigue, the said day, for two bales of peltry and mercery: s.5

Item, from Passelin de Felician, on July 21, for one and one half bales of cloth and old garments: s.3 d.10

Item, from Regnault of Changey, on July 22, for nine sheep: s.2 d.3

Item, from Bertolino of Venice, on July 27, for three bales of fustian: s.7 d.6

Item, from Bernat Resteu of Carcassonne, on July 29, for four bales of cloth, peltry, and old clothes:[124] s.10

Item, from Huguemin de Bannans, on July 30, for ten bales of wooden vessels (*fustaille*): s.12 d.6

Item, from Nicolino Vettura of Venice, on July 31, for two small bundles of peltry: d.20

58

From the Latin[125]

[Villeneuve de Chillon, Vaud, April 2, 1423–February 23, 1424]

Export tolls of the merchants of Milan, as [determined] from their slips[126]

[122] *Dou Roux,* probably a nickname, although the name Leroux or Roux cannot be ruled out.

[123] *Avortons,* which literally ought to mean unborn lambs, but which according to Uzzano means 'agnine piccole,' milk-fed or very young lambs, whereas 'agnelline non nate' (unborn lambs) are called 'fulerni.' See Evans's Glossary in Pegolotti, *Pratica*, pp. 413–14, *s. v.* 'Avortoni.'

[124] *Froperie*; but read *freperie* or *friperie*, 'frippery' or old clothes.

[125] F. Borel, *Les Foires de Genève au quinzième siècle*, Documents, pp. 21–26, and, for the background of the document, Text, pp. 195ff. We have translated part of the entries from the accounts of Jaquemet Medici, collector of tolls (*pedagium* or *péage*) for the duke of Savoy at Villeneuve de Chillon, at the northeastern extremity of Lake Geneva. The toll was collected on wares carried by Italian merchants to the fairs of Geneva (on which see Document 29). The moneys mentioned in the document are the Savoy florin and florin petty—both of them gold coins—and the Savoy silver groat. Of the latter there were different standards. Very probably most merchants paid coins of various currencies which the collector reckoned according as they were worth in Savoy coins.

[126] *Bulleta,* which translates the Italian *bolletta* or *bulletta,* a generic word which may mean a

First, on April 2, received from Giannino Rota[127] for 34 large bales[128] of fustian [and] 5 of mercery carried to Geneva and sold there, as he asserts by the slip: 3 florins petty

Also, from the same, as he swore by the slip to send [them] to Geneva, I received for 52 large bales, both of fustian and of spices, and for 12 large bales of mercery: 4 florins petty

From the same, for 24 bales of custom jewelry:[129]   3 florins 3 groats

On April 6, I received from Guidetto Cusano, merchant of Milan, for 116 large bales of fustian and spices which he carried to Geneva and [wants] to sell there, as he asserts by the slip: 6 florins petty

On April 8, from Giorgio Murisino, for 61 large bales of mercery, fustian, and spices which he carried to Geneva and sold there, as he asserts by the slip, I received: 3 florins petty 4 groats

On April 9, from Guachino Cusano, for 45 large bales, both of mercery and of spices, carried to Geneva and sold, as he asserts by the slip:

6 florins petty

On April 9, I received from Matteo Cagnola, merchant of Milan, for 26 large bales both of mercery and of fustian, which he carried to Geneva and [wants] to sell there, as he asserts by the slip: 2 florins 4 groats

The same Matteo, through another slip, [for] 24 bundles[130] and large bales of fustian and mercery carried to Geneva and sold, as he asserts on his oath, I received: 3 florins petty

On April 11, Arrighino Rota carried to Geneva 56 bundles and large bales of fustian, mercery, and spices, which he [wants] to sell in Geneva, as he asserts by his slip: 4 florins petty

On June 23, from Guachino Cusano, merchant of Milan; he carried 48 large bales, both of fustian and of mercery and spices, which he said [he wanted] to sell in Geneva, as he asserts by his slip, for which I received:

32 good groats

On June 25, Giannino Rota carried 17 large bales of fustian [and] mercery, which, as he asserts by the slip, [he wants] to sell in Geneva, for which I received: 12 good groats

---

receipt or almost any other kind of paper used in commerce, shipping, and administration. In this context it probably means customs declaration.

[127] The text uses indifferently the spellings *de Rot* and *de Roc,* both of which correspond to names that existed in that general area and time (Rota and Rocca). We Italianize Rota or Rocca according to the spelling used in each instance by the document.

[128] *Bollionis,* probably derived from *ballis* with the *-one* suffix, which in Italian and its dialects indicates a larger size.

[129] *Lapidum falcium,* 'false stones.'   [130] *Fardellis,* a smaller bundle than a bale.

On June 26, Giacomo Primigola,[131] of Milan, carried 48 bundles and large bales, which he wants to sell in Geneva, as he asserts by the slip [made out] in St. Maurice, for which I received: 56 good groats

On June 27, Bartolomeo Rocca carried 35 large bales of fustian and mercery, which he wants to sell in Geneva, as he asserts on his oath, for which I received: 28 good groats

On the aforesaid day Biagio of Milan carried 12 large bales of fustian and mercery, which he wants to carry and sell in Geneva, as he asserts by the slip, for which I received: 8 good groats

The same Biagio carried 47 bundles and large bales of fustian and mercery, which he wants to sell in Geneva, as he asserts, for which I received:

2 florins 4 groats

On June 28, Arrighino Rocca carried 35 large bales of fustian and spices, which he wants to sell in Geneva, as he asserts, for which I received:

2 florins petty, 3 groats

On the same day Giorgio Murisino, of Milan, carried 35 bundles and large bales of fustian and mercery, which he wants to sell in Geneva, as he asserts, for which I received: 3 florins petty

On August 23, Cristoforo Borsani, merchant of Milan, [carried] 17 large bales of fustian and 8 large bales of mercery, which he wants to sell in Geneva, as he asserts, for which I received: 33 groats

On the aforesaid day Giovanni Destorzi, merchant of Milan, carried 45 bundles of fustian, both small and large, which he wants to sell in Geneva, as he asserts: 3 florins

On the same day Gaspare delle Missioni carried 20 large bales of fustian and mercery, which he wants to sell in Geneva, as he asserts; I received:

16 groats

The same, 30 large bales of fustian and mercery, which he wants to send to Geneva, as he asserts, for which I received: 20 groats

On August 25, Arrighino Rota, for 26 large bales of fustian and spices, which he wants to sell in Geneva, as he asserts; I received: 18 groats

On the same day, from Arrighino, 40 bundles and large bales of fustian, which he wants to send to Geneva, as he asserts; I received: 3 florins petty

On the aforesaid day Giacomo Pinigola carried 15 large bales of fustian and mercery, which he wants to sell in Geneva, as he asserts, for which he paid: 1[?] florin[132]

---

[131] The name is spelled indifferently Primigola, Pinigola, Pinigrolaz, etc., all of which may be transliterations of Panigarola, a well-known Milanese family. We maintain in every instance the spelling used by the document.

[132] The question mark is Borel's.

On the day as above Giacomo Pinigola carried 50 large bales of fustian and spices and mercery, which he wants to sell in Geneva, as he asserts, for which he paid: 3 florins petty

On August 27, Christoforo Donadei, merchant of Milan, and Bartolomeo of Vaprio[133] carried 41 large bales and bundles of fustian and mercery, which they want to sell in Geneva, as they assert by their slip, for which I received: 3 florins 4 good groats

On the day as above Bartolomeo Rota, merchant of Milan, for 8 bundles of fustian and mercery, which he wants to sell in Geneva, as he asserted on oath by the slip [made out] in St. Maurice, I received:

         8 groats of good standard

The same Bartolomeo, on the day as above, for 30 large bales of fustian, spices, and mercery, which he carried to Geneva and wants to sell there, as he asserts on oath, I received: 20 good groats

On August 28, Raffaele of Concorezzo,[134] merchant of Milan, for 30 large bales of fustian, spices, and mercery, which he says [he wants] to sell in Geneva, as he asserts on oath, I received: 20 good groats

On August 28, the aforesaid Raffaele carried 20 large bales of fustian and mercery, which he wants to send to Geneva, as he asserts on oath, for which I received: 16 good groats

On October 20, Achino Cusano, merchant of Milan, carried 46 large bales of fustian and mercery, which he wants to sell in Geneva, as he asserts on oath, for which I received: 32 groats

The same Achino carried 30 large bales of mercery and fustian, which he wants to sell in and to send to Geneva, as he asserts on oath, and I received:

         20 good groats

On October 26, Arrighino Rota, merchant of Milan, carried 44 large bales of fustian, which he wants to send and sell in Geneva, as he asserts; I received: 3 florins petty

On October 28, Gaspare, merchant of Milan, carried 42 large bales of fustian and mercery, which he wants to sell in Geneva, as he asserts, for which I received: 2 florins 8 good groats

On October 29, Giacomo Pinigrolaz carried 39 large bales, both small and large, which he carried to Geneva and [wants] to sell there, as he swore by the slip, for which I received: ....[135]

On the day as above, Giosuè Corsi carried 32 bundles, both large and small,

---

133 *De Vavres*, elsewhere in the document *de Vabres* or *de Vaprio*, is certainly Vaprio d'Adda near Milan.

134 Concorezzo, like Vaprio, is a small town northeast of Milan.   135 Blank in Borel's text.

which he wants to sell in and send to Geneva, as he asserts on oath, for which I received: 2 florins petty 4 groats

On October 30, Martino Cunino, of Milan, carried 21 large bales of fustian, mercery, and spices, which he wants to send to Geneva, as he asserts on his oath, for which I received: 1 florin 2 groats

Giacomino Pinigola, on the first day of November, carried 22 large bales of mercery and fustian, which he wants to send and sell in Geneva, as he asserts on his oath, for which I received: 14 groats of good standard

On the second of November, Cristoforo Borsani, merchant of Milan, carried to Geneva 42 large bales both of mercery and of fustian, which he wants to send and sell in Geneva, as he asserts on his oath, for which he paid:

32 groats of good standard

On the third of January, in the year of the Nativity of the Lord 1424, Giorgio Murisino, of Milan, carried 40 large bales of fustian and mercery, which he wants to sell and send to Geneva, as he asserts, for which I received:

32 groats of good standard

On the fifth of January, Giacomo Pinigrola carried 39 large bales of fustian and mercery, which he wants to send to Geneva, as he asserts, for which I received: 2 florins 4 groats

The same, 10 large bales of mercery and fustian which [he wants] to send there to Geneva, as above: 8 groats

The same, 8 large bales of fustian and mercery which [he wants] to send to Geneva, for which I received: 8 good groats

On January 5, Gaspare of Milan carried 62 large bales of spices, which he wants to send to Geneva, as he asserts, for which I received:

3 florins 4 groats

On January 8, Giacomo Pinigrolaz, merchant of Milan, carried 63 large bales of fustian and spices and mercery, which he wants to send to Geneva, as he asserts on his oath, for which I received: 4 florins

On January 9, Gaspare of Milan carried 24 large bales of fustian and mercery, which he wants to send to Geneva, as he asserts, for which I received: 16 groats

On the aforesaid day Arrighino Rota carried 40 large bales, which he wants to send to Geneva, as he asserts, for which he paid: 3 florins 4 groats

On January 10, Gherardino of Vaprio, merchant of Milan, carried 3 bundles and 3 large bales of fustian, which he wants to send to Geneva, as he asserts on oath; I received: 8 groats

The same, 3 *centinaia* of tallow,[136] for which I received: 10 groats

On January 12, Achino Cusano, merchant of Milan, carried 42 large bales of fustian and spices, which he wants to send to Geneva, as he asserts, for which I received: 2 florins

Also, on the aforesaid day, 48 large bales of fustian and spices and mercery, which he wants to send to Geneva, as he asserts on his oath, for which were received: 27 groats

On February 20, Cristoforo Borsani, merchant of Milan, carried 28 bundles and large bales of mercery, fustian, and iron lances,[137] which he wants to send to Geneva, as he asserts; and for this, including 3 *centinaia* of tallow, I received: 3 florins petty 4 groats

On February 23, Gaspare of Milan carried 17 large bales of fustian and paper, which he wants to send to Geneva, as he asserts, for which I received:
                    1 florin petty

[136] Here Borel's text reads *currus suppi* and, a little below, *centum suppi*. In both cases one ought to emendate into *cent.*, i.e. *centenaria* or *centinaia* (hundredweight). Note that *El libro di mercatantie et usanze de' paesi*, ed. F. Borlandi, in its description of Milan states 'Everything there is sold by the *centinaio*.'

[137] *Telarum ferri*; but read *telorum ferri*.

CHAPTER V

THE EVOLUTION OF THE MEANS OF EXCHANGE

Survivals of Loans in Kind

MONEY ECONOMY, which had never entirely disappeared during the early Middle Ages, gained a complete victory at the beginning of the Commercial Revolution. Payments in kind were now exceptional in commercial transactions; merchants used them only in underdeveloped regions of southern Russia and darkest Africa.[1] Nearly all business operations in Western Europe as well as in the Byzantine and Muslim countries were settled by payments in cash or in credit money. In loan contracts, however, payments in kind continued, especially when the loan was extended by merchants to persons belonging to other classes.

The first selection shows the simultaneous existence of loans in cash and loans in kind at the dawn of the Commercial Revolution. It is worth noting that the interest rate is higher on the former than on the latter, and that a distinction is implicitly made between consumption loans and commercial loans. The document is a legal text, based upon Roman Law, which in its present form comes from southern France. Recent studies tend to see the text as an adaptation of an earlier compilation made in Upper Italy.

The second selection (Document 60) is a loan in kind combined with the fictitious sale of a horse. The latter is obviously security for the loan. The document dates from the very end of the Middle Ages and comes from an underdeveloped region of France. The large quantity of salt loaned makes it very unlikely that the borrower employed the loan for his personal use, but it is more probable that he distributed the salt to his dependents rather than that he sold it in the village market.

59

From the Latin[2]

[Ravenna, c. 1050: revised in southern France, c. 1120]

Those who give money in loan under usury to a farmer (*rusticus*) are not

[1] See Document 124, where a payment in buckrams (a textile) in southern Russia is mentioned. Buckrams were used as a medium of exchange in that country, and therefore it would not be entirely proper to call it a barter transaction.

[2] This document has been published in three editions. The best and most recent is C. G. Mor, *Scritti giuridici preirneriani*, II, 117–18. The editor gives full references to sources, both in Roman Law and in earlier medieval works.

to take land from him as security. But if they have given the farmer goods that are measured, let them receive as usury only as much every year as amounts to one eighth part of the capital, that is, one *sextarium* for eight, and thus [altogether] nine shall be [owing]. If, however, they have given coins that can be counted or gold or silver that can be weighed, let them receive from the farmer every year one sixth part of the capital, and thus they are to receive seven in the place of six solidi, marks, or bezants. A 'farmer' you will understand to be anyone who does not carry on any profession for his living except agriculture.

In regard to this reckoning, however, you will understand that it holds only when the loan is made to a farmer. If, however, it is made to another, [who is] not a farmer, [and] if the giver is of illustrious rank, such as one who is called *contorius*,[3] or of [still] higher rank, such as a count, he may lend [at the rate of] three for two. And if he is a merchant (*negotiator*), he may lend [at the rate of] five for three. If, however, the loan is given in order that it be carried overseas or to any distant region, he may lend [at the rate of] three for two. But other men, that is, those whom we in vulgar language call *renovarii*,[4] may lend [at the rate] of three for two, as we said above in regard to the nobleman. Let these usuries be reckoned for a full year. If the debtor pays before the year [has expired], usuries shall be reduced according to the aforesaid rate.

This you ought to know for sure, that if anyone makes stipulation for usuries over and above this rate, he cannot exact them under any law nor shall he even retain a security for illicit usuries. The usury of usuries[5] we forbid by all means.

60
From the Provençal[6]

[Beaulieu, Limousin, 1482]

Olmo, son of Sir Aymeric, of the village of La Viatela, in the parish of Lhiordre, has sold to me his bay draft horse, and the price was £ 4 s.5. And these £ 4 s.5 I have paid to him in 17 *emynals*[7] of salt, which I gave to his servant. I made agreement with said Olmo that in case he gives me the said

---

[3] *Contorius*, *comptorius*, or *comitorius*, in Catalan and Provençal use, is a member of a class of noblemen intermediate between viscounts and vavasors.

[4] One of the several terms describing professional usurers.   [5] That is, compound interest.

[6] A. Tournafond, *Les Marchés et foires de Limoges au moyen âge et à la renaissance*, p. 182.

[7] The *emynal*, *hemina*, or *mina*, derived from the mina of Near Eastern and classical antiquity, was still used in France, Italy, and Spain as a dry measure for grain and salt. Its value varied according to places.

£4 s.5 [any time] up to the day of Easter, I must not take the said draft horse.

Spices Used to Supplement Coins

DURING THE FIRST centuries of the Commercial Revolution, trade expanded so rapidly that the output of coins was often unable to keep pace with the growing demand. In time, credit money was used sufficiently to supplement coins whenever there was a shortage, but in the twelfth century merchants often resorted to another makeshift. They made payments in pepper or other spices instead of coins. These commodities are almost as durable as gold, and they were almost as valuable. Therefore it would be wrong to consider these payments as survivals of natural economy. Pepper was merely a temporary substitute for silver and gold.[8]

61
From the Latin[9]

[Genoa], January 14, 1156

I, Rinaldo Gauxone, promise you, Lamberto Grillo, or your accredited messenger, £ 6½ in pepper or in coin [to be delivered any time] up to next Easter; otherwise [I will pay] the penalty of the double, under pledge of my orchard in Sozziglia. And you may enter into [possession] of it for the principal and the penalty on your own authority and without order by the consuls. Done in the chapter house, 1156, on the fourteenth day from the beginning of January, third indiction. Witnesses: Sismondo Muscula, B. Papa Canticula Macobrio, notary, Baldo Rubeo, watchman.

The Return to the Gold Standard in the West

THE SILVER STANDARD was predominant in Western Europe from the Carolingian period to the mid-thirteenth century. The silver denier was the largest denomination actually struck; shillings and pounds were merely moneys of account. One said 'one pound of Genoese deniers' (£1 Genoese) as one today would say 'one million Canadian dollars.' Eastern gold coins such as the Byzantine hyperper or bezant, the various Muslim dinars and fourths of dinars, and imitations of these coins struck in Western mints were often used for larger payments. Their supply, however, was limited.

The first centuries of the Commercial Revolution witnessed the precipitous

[8] See M. Bloch, 'Economie-nature ou économie-argent: un pseudo-dilemme,' *Annales d'Histoire Sociale*, I (1939), 7–16.

[9] M. Chiaudano and M. Moresco, *Il cartolare di Giovanni Scriba*, I, 20. Sozziglia is a section of Genoa. The consuls mentioned in the document are not the chief executives of the Commune but very probably the chief judges, also called consuls.

debasement of the silver denier in weight and alloy. Whatever the reasons for this process—there is no full agreement among scholars about them—prices rose very fast. Soon the need was felt for a heavier and purer silver coin. The solution seemed to be found when a larger denomination, the silver groat or large denier (*denaro grosso*) was adopted. The old, smaller deniers (deniers petty, *denari piccoli*) continued to be used as fractions of the groats. But the steady debasement of the petty denier dragged the groat with it. The groat also fell in value, but it did not sink as fast as did the petty denier.

A more radical step was the resumption of gold coinage. Genoa struck its first gold deniers in 1252. Florence followed in a few months by making gold florins. Eventually all other countries of Western Europe adopted gold currencies, which circulated simultaneously with groat and petty silver currencies and resisted much longer the inflationary trends.[10]

Document 62 presents an early instance of the investment of gold deniers in Eastern trade. The sum was paid in gold, but it was reckoned according to the old money of account based upon the silver standard (pounds Genoese).[11]

62

From the Latin[12]

Genoa, February 23, 1259

In the name of the Lord, amen. I, Anselmo Bufferio, acknowledge to you, Enrico Nepitella, that I have had and have received in *accomendacio* from you £ 50 Genoese. And I acknowledge that I have had them from you in Genoese gold deniers, waiving the exceptions that the money has not been counted, and that said *accomendacio* has not been accepted, that there has been fraud in the act, that the contract is groundless, and any [other] legal right. And with the aid of God I am to carry them on my voyage Overseas[13] for the purpose of trading, and I am to keep expenses and profits from them apart from my other accounts. And I have authority from you to send to you in Genoa their proceeds before me, and not after [me], and to do with them as I shall do with the other goods which I am carrying with me. Then, on my return to Genoa, I promise to place and to deliver the capital and the

---

[10] The masterly article by M. Bloch, 'Le Problème de l'or au moyen âge,' *Annales d'Histoire Economique et Sociale*, V (1933), 1–34, is still the best reference on this general subject. Some additional data are found in R. S. Lopez, 'Mohammed and Charlemagne: a Revision,' *Speculum*, XVIII (1943), 14–38. A few texts on coinage have been translated in R. C. Cave and H. H. Coulson, *A Source Book of Medieval Economic History*, pp. 126ff.

[11] The earliest document mentioning Genoese gold deniers was published by R. S. Lopez, 'Un consilium di giuristi torinese nel Dugento,' *Bollettino Storico-Bibliografico Subalpino*, XXXVIII (1936), 143–50. Further details on the Genoese gold coin and its relation to the silver coinage are given in our introductory Note on Coinage; a full discussion of the problem is found in R. S. Lopez, *Il ritorno all'oro nell' Occidente duecentesco*.

[12] Unprinted. Archivio de Stato, Genoa. *Cartulario di Vivaldo di Sarzano*, IV, fol. 89v. and 90r.

[13] That is, to Syria and the surrounding regions.

profit of said *accomendacio* in your power or in [that] of your accredited messenger, keeping one fourth of the profit. . . .[14] Done in Genoa, in the Piazzalunga, near the house where said Enrico lives, the year of the Nativity of the Lord 1259, first indiction, February 23, after terce. Witnesses: Giovanni Guecio and Andrea Bonacia.

Hard Currencies, Moneys of Account, and Credit Money

THE EXPANSION of trade resulted in greater complexity of the money and credit market. To show the variety of means of payments available to a merchant, we have selected two passages of a manual of commercial practice by Giovanni da Uzzano. The book was not written for the general public but for the professional merchant, to whom many terms and practices which are strange to us were everyday routine. Its elliptic sentences can hardly be intelligible to the layman without some explanation of currencies, moneys of account, and credit money in the later Middle Ages. This we have attempted to supply in our long introductory note (pp. 10–16).

It may also help to understand Giovanni da Uzzano if we summarize the main points of the passages. The first paragraph on Venice deals with the relation of coinage to the money of account used by Venetian bankers and merchants. Coinage included gold ducats, silver *grossi* (deniers groat), and copper *bagattini*. The money of account consisted of pounds, shillings, and deniers groat and of deniers petty.

The second paragraph deals with payments by *scritta in banco*, which we translate, with only a degree of approximation, by 'transfers.' Merchants made deposits in *banche di scritta* run by money-changers. They drew on their deposits (sometimes making overdrafts with the knowledge and consent of the changer) by word of mouth, by sending a written order of payment, or by sending a letter of exchange. Inasmuch as most of their business correspondents also had deposits in the same banks, most payments could be carried out merely by transferring the sum from one account to another in the ledgers of the bank. Nor was it necessary for the payer and the payee to be the clients of the same bank, for money-changers had accounts with one another and with money-changers of other towns. On the other hand, money-changers operated on a fractional reserve principle. Too many demands for payment in cash were likely to embarass them. There was no charge for transfers from one account to another, but when the payment was in cash a commission was charged.

The third paragraph deals with quotations in the letters of exchange. Not any unit of the monetary system of a town or state was used, but almost always one specific unit; for instance, the Venetian ducat was used in letters of exchange drawn on Barcelona, Bruges, and London, but the Venetian pound groat was used in letters drawn on Paris and Florence. With the exchange business we deal at greater length in Chapter VII.

The first paragraph on Lucca lists briefly the means of payment available in that

[14] We omit part of the formulary, which has no importance in connection with the problems in gold currency. Fuller formularies of *commenda* or *accomendacio* contracts will be found in Chap. IX.

place. There, as in Venice, merchants could use letters of exchange, transfers in *banche di scritta*, or currency.

The remaining paragraphs concern currency. To save the merchants the trouble of weighing and testing every coin in large transactions, gold coins of the same standard were tested by experts and placed in sealed purses or boxes. The color of the wax used in the seal indicated the standard. *Scudi* or *écus* were the heaviest; then came Genoese florins (sometimes called *genovine*), especially when freshly issued from the mint; then other florins and ducats of accredited mints, provided they had not grown too thin by wear. Small change consisted not only of Lucchese coins but of coins from many other cities or states. These coins, of course, were not placed under seal.[15]

63

Giovanni di Antonio da Uzzano, *The Practice of Commerce*
From the Italian[16]

[Florence, 1442]

VENICE

Payments are made in Venetian ducats, which are [of the same standard as florins] according to Pisan weight. And accounts are kept in pounds groat, that is, in pounds [groat], shillings [groat], deniers [groat], [deniers] petty. The pound groat is worth 10 ducats [in coin]. The ducat is worth 2 shillings [groat], that is, 24 [deniers] groat. And each shilling [groat] is 12 [deniers] groat [in coin]. And each [denier] groat is worth thirty-two [deniers] petty. These petty are not [coins], but [as a money of account] each is worth one *bagattino* and a half [in coin].

And payments are [also] made by transfer in bank. And whoever wants to withdraw [cash] from the bank may [do so], but the changers resent this very much and do not feel inclined to make transfer [operations] for persons who would withdraw [cash] from the bank. And, therefore, changers do not care to deal with persons who do not make reliable transfers.[17] And if nonetheless you have to remit ducats [in coin] without the assent of the bank, [consider that] most people in order not to displease the bank buy ducats in coin elsewhere and bring them to the bank.[18] And for that reason coins are

---

[15] For bibliography, see p. 11, note 1, and our footnotes to Chap. VII.

[16] Uzzano, *La pratica della mercatura* (Vol. IV of G. F. Pagnini della Ventura, ed., *Della decima e di varie altre gravezze imposte dal Comune di Firenze*), pp. 151–52.

[17] *Che non faccino buona scritta*, i.e., with persons who are likely to demand payment in hard coin of the funds they have deposited in the bank.

[18] In other terms, if you want to make a payment in hard coin through a bank without forcing the money-changer to draw from the reserve, bring to the bank the coins needed for the transaction.

always evaluated from one to two percent more than [the same amount] by transfer. Therefore when you draw on [your bank account], take care that the sum be paid to a person who will not withdraw it from the bank, that is, to a changer. For other people would have no consideration for the bank. And if nonetheless you have to make a payment to a person who would withdraw [the funds] from the bank, charge such [commission] as will be [collected by the bank] for the exchange [operation]. Otherwise you will add [to your debit resulting from the payment] the expense for the [commission], and the letter [of exchange] might be protested.[19]

Exchanges on Barcelona are quoted in [so many] shillings Barcelonese per [Venetian] ducat; on Bruges, in so many [Flemish] groats per ducat; on London, in so many sterlings per ducat; on Paris, in so many Venetian groats against francs; on Florence, in so many [Venetian] pounds, shillings, and deniers [groat] per [Florentine] pounds groat *a fiorini;* on Bologna, in so many [units] per hundred [Venetian] units]. Similarly, exchanges on many other places are quoted in so much [foreign currency] per ducat or so much per pound, or in so much [Venetian currency] per silver of the standard [of the place] where the payment is made. . . .

LUCCA

Payments by letter of exchange from all places are quoted in florins under seal and [most frequently in florins sealed] with red wax. And payments are [also] made by transfer in bank. Or [else], whoever wants payment in cash may obtain it.

And there are several [standards of florins under] seal, coming [in purses] sealed with different waxes. And firstly, [florins] may be sealed with red wax; and the florins of the currencies which are put under the said wax ought to weigh 70 grains. And the 'red' ones are [evaluated] 1 percent more [than loose florins]. And all good florins of Italian [mints], the Papal ducats, and the Hungarian florins 'of the gallows' having no gold tare, provided they are of the said weight, are placed under the said seals. And the new florins of Florence [and] the Venetian ducats are placed under that [seal] more [frequently] than any [other gold coins].

Genoese florins are evaluated $3\frac{1}{2}$ percent more than those under red wax, and they come sealed under yellow wax. And [when] new or almost new, the said coins, provided they weigh according to the Pisan weight, come sealed

---

[19] The whole passage is obscure, but it seems to mean that a protest might come if your balance is sufficient to cover the payment but not the commission.

under black wax and are [evaluated] 2 percent more [than those under yellow seal].

Scudi, too, come sealed. And they ought to weigh 3 carats[20] 7 grains, and they are evaluated $12\frac{1}{2}$ percent more than the Florentine florins under seal.

And every account is settled according as has been [previously] agreed.[21]

And furthermore the coins of Bologna, Lucca, Bologna,[22] Perugia, Ferrara, Ancona, and the Pisan *sestini* and *quattrini* are accepted in Lucca. And *sestini* are accepted [at the rate of] four per Bolognese denier, and *quattrini* [at the rate of] 6 per Bolognese denier, and they circulate [in coin] at this rate in the [Lucchese] territory. In banks, however, [they are evaluated] slightly more.

Seasonal Fluctuations in the Money Market

THE EXISTENCE of business cycles and of periodical fluctuations during the Commercial Revolution has been postulated by some scholars. It has been possible to describe and sometimes to chart secular trends, long waves, and short waves in the economic development of a town or in special sectors of the medieval economy. Research in this field, however, is hampered by the poverty of statistical data and by the fact that medieval writers show little if any awareness of the cyclical alternation of prosperity and depression.[23]

Medieval writers, on the other hand, frequently mention seasonal fluctuations in specific fields and most particularly in the money market. Annual fairs, harvests, sailings, and governmental expenditures at regular intervals cause money to be 'dear,' that is, provoke rises in the premiums on letters of exchange, interest on loans, and any other rewards that may be demanded for the extension of credit. A good description of phenomena of this kind is offered in a manual of commercial practice which was compiled in the mid-fifteenth century, partly from earlier sources. The manual has been ascribed to Giorgio di Lorenzo Chiarini, factor of a Florentine partnership in Ragusa (Dubrovnik), but the attribution has not been conclusively proved.[24]

[20] *Denari 3;* but read *carati 3.* This will make the weight of a *scudo* 79 grains, approximately $12\frac{1}{2}$ percent more than the 70 grains of the florins under seal with red wax.

[21] In other words, coins under one or another seal will be used according to the pacts made when the transaction has been concluded.

[22] *Sic.*

[23] See, for instance, C. M. Cipolla, *Studi di storia della moneta,* Vol. I; H. C. Krueger, 'Post-War Collapse and Rehabilitation in Genoa, 1149–1162,' in *Studi in onore di Gino Luzzatto,* I, 117–28; R. S. Lopez, 'The Dollar of the Middle Ages,' *Journal of Economic History,* XI (1951), 209–34.

[24] See also Document 203.

64

From the compilation entitled, *The Book of the Wares and Usages of Diverse Countries*
From the Italian[25]

[Ragusa (Dubrovnik), 1458]

In Genoa money is dear in September, January, and April on account of
the sailing of their ships.[26]

In Venice it is dear from July to September on account of the many dead-
lines [for the payment] of goods sold [to Venetians who] ship them in the
galleys going to Romania,[27] to Syria, and to Alexandria. And it is also dear in
April—but [just] a little—on account of the galleys [sailing] to Flanders; and
also in January, that is, from mid-January to February 10, on account of the
ships going to Syria to [load] cotton.

In Rome or wherever the pope may be, money is dear off and on according
to the [number] of vacant benefices, and [according to the time] when the
pope leaves and when he arrives. Wherever he is, he causes money to be
dear.

In Naples and Gaeta money is dear from the Kalends of August to mid-
September on account of the fair of Saint Michael, and also on account of the
ships that sail from there, built for the Venetians[?].[28] And it is also dear in
November on account of earnest money [given] for oil, and in March and
April on account of the harvesting of oil and fruit.

In Barcelona it is dear from June continuously up to August—in June on
account of the wool and in July on account of the grain and rice harvested
in Valencia. And it is dear throughout October also, because of the
saffron.

In Valencia it is dear in July and August because of the grain and the rice.

In Montpellier there are three fairs which cause great dearth [of money]
there; and in Avignon likewise. The fair of Pentecost lasts from eight days
before [the feast] to eight days after, and this is the best [fair]. The fair of

---

[25] F. Borlandi, ed., *El libro di mercatantie et usanze de' paesi*, pp. 167–68. There is a description
of the same kind in the slightly earlier manual of Uzzano, *Pratica della mercatura*, pp. 155–58.

[26] These are the sailing dates of the regular convoys (*caravane*) under state supervision, which
every year left Genoa for the Black Sea, the Levant, and the North Sea.

[27] The former Byzantine territory in the Balkan peninsula. The dates mentioned are the sailing
dates of the regular convoys (*mude*), owned and controlled by the state, which every year left
Venice for the destinations indicated in the document. The winter convoy bound to Syria
differed from the other Venetian or Genoese convoys in that it consisted of cogs especially
equipped for the transportation of cotton. Other convoys consisted of heavy galleys.

[28] *Per li navili che si spacciano là construtte pelle vinitiane*; the text is probably corrupt and certainly ungrammatical. Uzzano, *Pratica*, p. 157, mentions a seasonal dearth of money in Naples at
the same period.

Our Lady of September lasts eight days. The fair of All Saints. . . .[29] These three fairs always cause a great dearth of money there. The dearth begins fifteen days before and lasts eight days after. . . .

Weights and Measures

THE DIFFERENT systems of money were not the only difficulty in medieval accounts and exchanges. Units of weights and measures were just as various.[30] The manuals of commercial practice devote the larger part of their space to describing these units in each market and giving their relation to units in other markets. Even within one city spices and bulkier materials were not usually measured by the same standard, nor was the unit of measure for cloth the same as that for other wares.

We give only one example drawn from a manual compiled some time after 1345 but including earlier material. The author of the manual was a Venetian; his name is unknown. The short chapter we have chosen deals with weights and measures of the principal wares bought or sold by Venetians in Astrakhan and in Sarai on the lower Volga, the capital of the Mongolian khanate of the Golden Horde, or Kipchak khanate. It also describes the money of account and the coins used there.

65

From the Italian (Venetian dialect)[31]

[Venice, after 1345]

In Sarai all linen is sold by *picho*. And 100 *pichi* are equal to 118 *braʒa* in Venice.

Also, all silks are sold by *mena*. And the said *mena* is equal to 6 lbs. 2 oz. minute[32] in Venice. And [silks] are sold at [so many] pounds in cash the *mena,* and all other wares [are sold] the same way. One pound [in cash] they reckon as 6 *tamgha*. And usually £ 20 circulate and are paid [in exchange] for one *sumo*.[33]

[29] The blank is in the original. Uzzano, *ibid.,* p. 155, mentions two other fairs, which are held at nearby 'Monte Sacco' (Moissac?), but adds that 'they are poor, and there is almost no other cloth but that of the region; yet money gets a little tighter.'

[30] For bibliography, see p. 11, note 1.

[31] *Tarifa ʒoe noticia dy pexi e mexure di luoghi e tere che s'adovra mercadantia per el mondo,* pp. 49–50.

[32] 'In Venice there are two [standards of] weight; one is the gross weight and the other is the minute weight . . . By the gross weight iron, copper, tin, lead, wood, gold, meat, cheese, honey, all [kinds of] fruit, and pitch are sold. And by the minute weight all wares imported from the Levant are sold, that is, cotton, pepper, incense, sugar, ginger, cinnamon, indigo, brazilwood, silk, kermes, all [kinds of] gum, wax, saffron, cloves, rock alum, raisins, flax, and all minute spices, and also amber rosaries. And 100 lbs. gross are [equal to] 158 lbs. minute' (*Tarifa,* p. 11). Note that the list of wares sold by the minute weight includes some which were not imported from the Levant. Amber rosaries usually came from France.

[33] As a monetary unit the pound was a money of account corresponding to 240 deniers. As has been pointed out in the introductory Note on Coinage, the cash value of the pound depended on

Also, all spices, coral, and other wares are sold by another [kind of] *mena*. And 20 *mene* they reckon as 1 *kanter*. And the said *mena* is equal to 8 lbs. minute in Venice, so that the *kanter* [of this standard] corresponds to 160 lbs. minute in Venice.[34]

Spun gold is sold at the rate of [so many] pounds in cash per bundle, which [bundle] weighs ½ lb. in Venice. It also is sold at the rate of [so many] *sumi* in cash per ten bundles.

Gauzes and camlets are sold by the piece [of cloth].

And [actual] payments are made in silver *tamgha*, which is their coinage. And for one *sumo* [of account] 120 *tamgha* [in cash] are counted.

Paper is sold by ream and paid[35] in *sumi*, and also at [so many] pounds in cash per ream.

Leather is sold by hundred [piece] lots.

And horsehides are sold at [so many] *tamgha* in cash a piece.

It should be noted that the weights and measures of Astrakhan are like those of Sarai.

---

the real coin to which it was pegged; probably in this context the coin was the Venetian groat. Likewise, the Kipchak *sommo* or *sumo* was a money of account corresponding to 120 Kipchak *tamgha*. The *mena* was a Kipchak unit of weight.

[34] Evidently there were two standards of weight in the Kipchak khanate as there were in Venice. Both the gross and the minute *mena* were Kipchak units of weight. Twenty of them were equal to a *kanter* or *cantaro*.

[35] *Che constante a sumo:* the text is certainly corrupt. A ream was 25 *quaderni* of 25 sheets each (*Tarifa*, p. 70).

PART THREE

Commercial Contracts and Commercial Investments

THE IMPORTANCE of contracts in medieval commerce can hardly be overestimated. They were, then as now, the basic framework in which transactions and investments were undertaken. The spirit of the medieval man, as has been often remarked, was highly legalistic. Legal techniques not only reflected but also influenced his economic practices. The progress of commercial law was thus interwoven with the expansion of commerce.

Unfortunately, there is probably no aspect of economic history which is as controversial as commercial law. Legal historians do not agree with one another or with economic historians in regard to the nature and definition of some of the most important contracts. Historians who are not specialists often use a very loose terminology which is objectionable to both economists and lawyers. What is worse, the sources themselves are not always consistent in their terminology. The same word often designates different contracts and the same contract often is designated by different words. Yet there is no doubt that the medieval merchant and the notary who drafted the contract knew precisely what kind of agreement was being made.

In a source book it would not be proper for the editors to discuss this controversial topic at great length. Hence they have limited introductory remarks to a minimum. It is their hope that the many examples presented will speak for themselves.[1]

[1] The following general works are helpful in gaining an acquaintance with commercial law of the medieval trade.

With a legalistic approach: E. Besta, *Le obbligazioni nella storia del diritto italiano*, probably the best treatise now available, but very concise and strictly legalistic; L. Goldschmidt, *Universalgeschichte des Handelsrechts* (1891), now outdated in many parts, but still a classic and a most useful work; P. Huvelin, 'L'Histoire du droit commercial,' *Revue de Synthèse Historique*, VII (1903), 60-85, VIII (1904), 198-243, with a sociological slant; W. Mitchell, *An Essay on the Early History of the Law Merchant*, especially concerned with England but covering also the other countries; F. Schupfer, *Il diritto delle obbligazioni in Italia nell'età del Risorgimento* (3 vols.), particularly interested in relations between Roman and German legal traditions.

With an economic approach: A. Lattes, *Il diritto commerciale nella legislazione statutaria delle città italiane* (1884), now outdated in many parts but still a classic; A. Schaube, *Handelsgeschichte der romanischen Völker des Mittelmeergebiets bis zum Ende der Kreuzzüge* (1906), dealing with practices as well as with formulae; A. E. Sayous, 'Les Transformations des méthodes commerciales dans l'Italie médiévale,' *Annales d'Histoire Economique et Sociale*, I (1929), 161-76, one-sided but original and forceful; R. L. Reynolds, 'Gli studi americani sulla storia genovese,' *Giornale Storico e Letterario della Liguria*, ser. 3, XIV (1938), 1-24, challenging many statements of Sayous and outlining work done in the United States.

Dealing most particularly with maritime contracts: A. Lattes, *Il diritto marittimo privato nelle*

CHAPTER VI

LOANS AND THE PROBLEM OF INTEREST

NEXT TO THE contract of sale (*emptio-venditio*), of which it has seemed unnecessary to include examples—their provisions are not radically different from those in the modern contract of sale—the loan contract (*mutuum, mutuo, prestito, prêt*) was the most widespread in medieval commerce. It goes back to remotest antiquity. Interest-bearing loans are found in Babylonian, Greek, and Roman records. In the Middle Ages, however, the influence of the Church made the taking of interest a serious problem. Because the Church did not distinguish between a charitable loan made to a brother in need and a commercial loan to a businessman, all taking of interest tended to be regarded as illegitimate interest or 'usury.' It must be added that in the Byzantine Empire this viewpoint never prevailed, so that interest on loans continued to be regarded as legitimate. In the Catholic West, the Church in time came to a series of compromises involving exceptions, but the legitimacy of interest as such was not recognized.[1]

The first selection (Document 66) is a loan contract openly mentioning interest. It can be compared with the loan contracts included in our chapter on early medieval trade. Contracts of this kind, however, were often in litigation. The lender might be forced to return the interest either because the ecclesiastic authorities intervened or merely because his conscience felt pangs of remorse. Two cases dealing with restitution of 'usury' are shown in the second and third selections (Documents 67 and 68). The other selections (Documents 69–71) present some of the innumerable types of loan contract in which interest was driven underground. The contract may not mention interest, but the sum said to have been lent undoubtedly included both capital and interest. Furthermore, the interest might be disguised as a penalty for

---

carte liguri dei secoli XII e XIII, of a wider scope than the title would suggest since it summarizes earlier work by the same author in the commercial history of the entire Mediterranean; R. Zeno, *Storia del diritto marittimo italiano nel Mediterraneo,* particularly useful for its bibliography.

Dealing most particularly with contracts in overland trade: M. Chiaudano, *Studi e documenti per la storia del diritto commerciale nel secolo XIII;* A. Sapori, *Studi di storia economica medievale,* 2d ed. There is a further bibliography in Y. Renouard, *Les Relations des papes d'Avignon et des compagnies commerciales et bancaires de 1316 à 1378.*

Dealing with notarial instruments and commercial papers: R. Doehaerd, *Les Relations commerciales entre Gênes, la Belgique et l'Outremont d'après les archives notariales génoises aux XIIIe et XIVe siècles* (3 vols.); A. P. Usher, *The Early History of Deposit Banking in Mediterranean Europe,* Vol. I. Both works supply abundant bibliographic information.

[1] The latest work is B. N. Nelson, *The Idea of Usury,* with an excellent Bibliography, pp. 165–220. Also, T. P. McLaughlin, 'The Teaching of the Canonists on Usury (XII, XIII and XIV Centuries),' *Mediaeval Studies,* I (1939), 81–147, II (1940), 1–22.

late payment. The contract may even specifically state that no interest is to be paid; nevertheless, we can be sure that interest was paid, since loans made by one merchant to another customarily drew interest. There are many other varieties of loan contracts, but we lack space to give examples of most of them.[2]

A Contract Openly Mentioning Interest

66

From the Latin[3]

[Genoa,] July 16, 1161

Witnesses: Oberto de Insula, Ansaldo Cintraco, Gozzo and Oberto de Chiberra, Atto Scuvalo. I, Embrone, have taken in loan (*mutuum*) from you, Salvo of Piacenza, £ 100 Genoese, for which I shall pay you or your messenger, personally or by my messenger, £ 120 within one year; but if I wish to pay you the aforesaid £ 100 and accrued interest[4] before the next feast of the Purification, you must accept them and for that purpose have your messenger in Genoa. If I do not so observe [these conditions], I promise you, making the stipulation, the penalty of the double. And on account of this I place in your power all my goods as security, so that if I do not so observe [these conditions], you may then enter [into possession] of whatever of my goods you want in consideration of the capital and the penalty, and you may have estimates made for yourself of an equivalent amount, and this estimated [amount] you may possess by title of sale and you may do with it whatever you please—this, indeed, without decree of the consuls and without objection on my part or of anyone [acting] in my behalf, by your authority alone. I also swear to pay, personally or by my messenger, to you or your messenger, that debt as written above, and [I swear] not on any account to do anything to prevent its being paid except by just impediment or by your permission or by that of your accredited agent—if by impediment, up to its removal, if by permission, up to the expiration of the granted delay or delays. [And I promise] not to deduct anything [from the debt], and I shall not claim release from its payment on account of the emperor[5] or of [any] discord which may exist between our city and yours,

---

[2] There is no general work on the medieval *mutuum* nor adequate discussion of the means used to circumvent the prohibition of usury. Articles such as A. Lattes, 'Di una singolare formula genovese nei contratti di mutuo,' *Rivista del Diritto Commerciale*, XXII (1924), 542–50, and general works such as we have mentioned, contain useful information.

[3] M. Chiaudano and M. Moresco, *Il cartolare di Giovanni Scriba*, II, 24–25.

[4] *Cum parte augmenti secundum racionem temporis*. Literally, we should translate 'together with the part of the increase according to the reckoning of time.' Today we say 'accrued interest.'

[5] At that time Emperor Frederick Barbarossa was besieging Milan, and Piacenza was Milan's

or of [interference from] any person. And for so long a time from then as you leave that money with me, I shall protect it in your behalf against all men and I shall pay you whenever you ask.

I, Simone d'Oria, constitute myself as the proper and principal debtor to you, the said creditor, in regard to this debt, so that unless this is so [observed] I shall then pay within eight days the penalty of the double, etc.—waiving [the exception] under the law according to which the first debtor is sued before the second.

Done in the chapter house, July 16, 1161, eighth indiction.

Restitution of Interest

67

From the Latin[6]

Lucca, March 13, 1220

Ugolino and Arduino, brothers, [sons] of the late Ildebrandino, feeling weighed down by usuries which Genovese, [recently] deceased, had extracted from them, therefore appealed to the Supreme Pontiff, [asking] that Filippo, priest [and] rector of the Church of S. Pietro Somaldi, must not bury him before they are satisfied in regard to the usuries which they had asked him to return. This was done in Lucca, in the court of S. Pietro Somaldi, in the portico, in the presence of Gaiascone, [son] of the late Orlando Guasone, and of Guido, [son] of the late Orlandino. 1220, the third [day] before the Ides of March.

[I], Benedetto, judge and notary of the lord emperor, took part in this entire [transaction], and I wrote this as a record.

68

From the Latin[7]

[Siena, September 27, 1221]

On the same day. I, Aringhiero d'Altavilla, promise you, Magister Pietro,

---

ally. Genoa, while not waging war against the emperor, had hurriedly raised new walls to ward him off.

[6] R. S. Lopez, 'The Unexplored Wealth of the Notarial Archives in Pisa and Lucca,' in *Mélanges d'histoire du moyen âge dédiés à la mémoire de Louis Halphen*, p. 425. See also B. N. Nelson, 'The Usurer and the Merchant Prince: Italian Businessmen and the Ecclesiastical Law of Restitution,' *Journal of Economic History, Supplement*, VII (1947), p. 106: 'By its own admission . . . the church was finding itself increasingly unable to stem the march of the usurer during his life. It was therefore led to redouble its energies in checking him at the point of last confession, the preparation of his will, and the completion of his arrangements for consecrated burial.'

[7] D. Bizzarri, *Imbreviature notarili*, I, 56, and, for the background of the document, *ibid.*, pp. xxxivff.

rector of the Church of S. Pietro delle Scale, and I swear on the holy Gospels of God that if I escape from this illness I shall be and remain [obedient] to the order of the lord bishop of Siena in regard to the usuries which I have collected up to this day, satisfying whoever proves to me his legal [claims] in regard to them and making restitution of these [usuries] as he [the bishop] shall charge me. And in regard to the excommunication laid upon me in the case of the money of Boncompagno, late of the monastery, I shall likewise be [obedient] to his order, so far as it concerns my part.

And I, Mezzolombardo d'Altavilla, in his behalf promise you and swear that if said Aringhiero dies from this illness, I shall remain [obedient] to and shall observe, in regard to the aforesaid, the order of the lord bishop, according to the form and content mentioned above. In the presence of Tornampuglia, [son] of Salsidone, Rustichino, [son] of Sinibaldo, Bartolo of Leonessa, and many others invited.

Interest Driven Underground

69

From the Latin[8]

[Siena,] May 19, 1223

On the fourteenth day before the Kalends of June. We, Ugolino and Ranieri di Albertino, cutlers, for ourselves and [both of us liable] for the whole amount, acknowledge [that we owe] you, Bonaventura di Piero, £8 Sienese, which we have received from you in loan and which [we promise to return] by the Kalends of November, and thereafter the [penalty of the] double and damages, obligating our heirs and goods, etc. In the presence of Durellino di Ugolino and Bonaparte di Corcivaldo, witnesses invited.

70

From the French[9]

Dijon, [September 23, 1381]

Jehan le Joliet, burgher of Dijon, draper, acknowledges that in addition to all other letters [obligatory], etc., he owes Giovanni Bernieri of Chieri, his brother Francesco, and Tommaso della Rocchetta, [all] Lombards,[10] residing

---

[8] *Ibid.*, I, 215.

[9] L. Gauthier, *Les Lombards dans les Deux-Bourgognes*, p. 262, and, for the background of the document, *ibid.*, p. 60–61.

[10] Lombard is used here both in the proper geographical meaning and in the meaning of professional pawnbroker and moneylender.

in Dijon, 312½ gold francs, etc., by virtue of a loan (*prest*) actually made, etc. For this loan, etc., and for these 312½ gold francs, Philippe Griffon, burgher of Dijon, has constituted himself security and principal debtor, etc., personally in the hands of the said Lombards, etc., [The debt] is to be paid within the next six months, etc. And in addition to this, once the said six months have passed, for each of the said francs not paid 2 [deniers] Tournois petty [will be due] as increment (*montes*) each week, so long as, etc., together with all expenses, etc. And wishing, etc., pledging their goods, etc., waiving all graces, etc. Witnesses: Jeoffroy Cathelainche of Dijon, cleric, and Monnot Huice, residing in Dijon.

71
From the Latin[11]

Pisa, March 19, 1302

Bruno, nicknamed Ciantellino, of the parish of Sant' Jacopo di Mercato, son of the late Donato, has received as a free loan (*mutuum gratis*) from Soldo, son of the late Ser Mula of Pistoia, s.30 Pisan petty, which he promised to return by the next Kalends of February. Done in Pisa in the shop[12] of the Church of San Nicola, in the presence of Bindo Chiari, notary, and Matteo, notary, son of Francesco, notary, witnesses. 1302, fifteenth indiction, fourteenth [day] before the Kalends of April.

[11] R. Piattoli, 'Documenti intorno ai banchieri pistoiesi nel medioevo,' *Bullettino Storico Pistoiese*, XXXV (1933), 132, and, for the background of the document, *ibid.*, p. 130–31. Note that Soldo, although here he appears as a petty moneylender, was a member of one of the wealthiest and most powerful families of Pistoia.

[12] *Apotheca*. Probably the church owned the building where the shop was located and rented it to merchants.

CHAPTER VII

THE CONTRACT OF EXCHANGE
AND ITS DOUBLE FUNCTION

THE PRIME AND original function of exchange operations was to convert one currency into another. Since different moneys circulated simultaneously in different countries, and even in one town, professional money-changers (*campsores*) and often ordinary merchants engaged in the business of paying out one currency in exchange for an equivalent amount of another, charging a commission for the service rendered. So long as the exchange was carried out in one place and from hand to hand, the transaction could be completed at one time and there was no need for a contract. But the very fact that the specialized changer needed a large stock of money to cope with demands for exchange tended to transform him into a professional moneylender who accepted deposits and extended loans. Thus the *campsor* became a *trapezita* or *bancherius*—both words being derived from the table (*trapeza*, in Greek) or bench (*bancum*, in Latin) upon which the changer placed the piles of coins. This development is noticeable in antiquity as well as in the Middle Ages. The history of deposit banking, however, is not included in the plan of the present book.

If payment in a different money had to be made in other places, a contract of exchange (*cambium* or, less frequently, *venditio*) had to be drafted and the character of the exchange operation changed. The changer had to secure correspondents in other towns who would honor exchange contracts drawn on them and who in turn would draw exchange contracts against him. It was an advantage for the customer to eliminate the actual transportation of coins since this involved both risk and expense. Moreover, it gave opportunity for the money changer to forecast and to speculate on fluctuations in the rates of exchange from one place to another and from one time to another. Furthermore, it took some time before the exchange contract reached the correspondent on whom the contract was drawn and before he in turn drew on the drawer to recover the money he paid out. Thus long-distance exchange transactions always involved a credit operation, the giver of local money being actually a lender and the giver of foreign money being a borrower. An exchange contract thus became an instrument of credit, which took the place of hard coin and to some extent served as a sort of 'paper' money, even though it was not payable 'to the bearer' but only to designated persons and to their agents. This development, too, can be observed in antiquity as well as in the Middle Ages.

The extraordinary popularity of the contract of exchange as an instrument of credit in the Middle Ages seems to have been connected primarily, if not exclusively, with the fact that it could be used instead of a loan contract, which by the law of the Church must be made without interest. Exchange contracts included interest charges concealed in the figures of the exchange rates. The rate of interest, however, could not be exactly foreseen. Unexpected fluctuations in the rates of exchange could increase or decrease the premium which the lender expected, and in some extreme cases—these must have been rare—the lender might even suffer a loss.

The parties to an exchange contract might wish to make the profit certain. In the case of *cambium et recambium* or exchange and reexchange, they could do so by stipulating in advance the rate of the *recambium* or reexchange, thus eliminating all speculative risks due to unexpected fluctuations in exchange rates. Such a contract was known as *ricorsa* or dry exchange. It contained the provision that the borrower was not bound to repay the lender in another place and in a foreign currency but had the option to settle the debt in an equivalent amount of local currency computed on the basis of a predetermined rate of exchange. This clause was often pure fiction, because it was understood from the very first that the borrower would avail himself of the option to repay the debt in local currency, so that the contract became a straight loan with interest disguised under another name. There could be, however, *bona fide* arrangements of this kind. But 'dry exchange' contracts frequently quote different rates of exchange for the conversion of the local money into foreign currency and the reconversion of the foreign currency into local money. At other times they do not state the sum originally paid before the merchant began his travels but quote only the amount of foreign currency to be paid abroad and the amount of domestic currency to be paid at home as an alternative. The attempt to circumvent the law of interest in these cases was transparent enough for the Church to condemn 'dry exchange,' but the practice continued nevertheless.

Our six selections show various types of the contracts mentioned above. The first two (Documents 72 and 73) are early exchanges. It is not even clear whether they are true exchange contracts or merely interest-bearing loans in disguise. The money to be paid out is foreign currency, but apparently it is to be paid in the place where the contract was made. The third selection (Document 74) is an excerpt of an account book recording exchange at a far-distant place. Interest is disclosed by the fact that the original sum is not quoted and also by the fact that additional interest is quoted as a penalty in case of late payment. The fourth selection (Document 75) contains the clause of adjustment in relation to fluctuations in the value of foreign currency. Document 76 is a typical 'dry exchange' contract. Document 77 also is 'dry exchange,' but it might be a *bona fide* exchange contract since the reason given for alternative payment at home is that the merchant might be physically unable to reach the foreign place for which he had set out. Even there, however, the rate of exchange for the reconversion of foreign money into local currency is different from the·rate of exchange in the place of origin.[1]

---

[1] The latest work on contracts of exchange is R. de Roover, *L'Evolution de la lettre de change* (Paris, 1953), which contains a very valuable bibliography.

Contracts of Exchange or Loans in Disguise?

72

From the Latin[2]

Genoa, January 31 [1182]

Witnesses: Coenna of Lucca, Girardo Encina, Giovanni Corrigia. I, Alcherio, banker,[3] have received from you, Martina Corrigia, a number of deniers for which I promise to pay, personally or through my messenger to you or to your accredited messenger, £ 9 s.13½ Pavese[4] before the next feast of Saint Andrew [November 30]. Otherwise I promise you, making the stipulation, the penalty of the double, etc. Done in Genoa, in front of the house of Barucio, in the bank[5] of Alcherio, the last day of January.

73

From the Latin[6]

Genoa [February 12, 1190]

Witnesses: Giovanni Patrio, Quilego, and Ugo Caniverga. We, Guglielmo Riccuomo and Egidio de Uxel, have received from you, Rufo, banker, and Bernardo, banker, an amount of exchange[7] for which we promise to pay to you or to your accredited messenger £ 69 Pavese by mid-Lent. Otherwise we promise you the penalty of the double, [both of us liable] for the whole amount, etc. Done in Genoa, in the bank of Rufo, in the shop[8] of Ogerio Vento, on the same day.

[2] R. di Tucci, *Studi sull' economia genovese del secolo decimosecondo*, p. 91.

[3] *Bancherius.* This name, derived from the *bancum* or bench at which the money-changer conducted his operations, by the thirteenth century, or perhaps even by the twelfth century, had also become in certain cases a Genoese family name. But it would be nonsense to infer, as did A. E. Sayous ('Les Travaux des Américains sur le commerce de Gênes aux XIIe et XIIIe siècles,' *Giornale Storico e Letterario della Liguria*, ser. 3, XIII [1937], 88–89), that every mention of the word *bancherius* in Genoese records of the twelfth century designated only members of the Bancheri family, and that the word *bancum* designated nearly always butchers' benches. See the reply of R. L. Reynolds, 'Gli studi americani sulla storia genovese,' *Giornale Storico e Letterario della Liguria*, ser. 3, XIV (1938), 1–24.

[4] No rate of exchange is given here so that we do not know how much the lender received against a promise to pay in another currency later.

[5] *In banco.*

[6] M. Chiaudano and R. Morozzo della Rocca, eds., *Oberto Scriba de Mercato (1190)*, pp. 49–50.

[7] *Cambium*, and not *mutuum*, as in ordinary loans.

[8] *Stacio*, a permanent shop or a counter in a shop, as opposed to *stallum*, a movable stand or booth.

An Exchange Transaction Posted in a Ledger

74

From the Italian[9]

[Florence, 1211]

Orlandino, shoemaker,[10] of Santa Trinita, owes us £ 26 [Florentine] by mid-May in consideration of Bolognese [money] that we gave him in Bologna for the market of San Procolo. If they remain longer [with him, they are to be] at [the rate of] 4 deniers a month [per pound]. And if he does not pay, Angiolino Bolognini, shoemaker, promised to pay us in his stead. Witnesses: Compagno Avanelle and Bellacalza.

A Standard Contract of Exchange

75

From the Latin[11]

[Genoa] September 12 [1191]

Oberto Falzone acknowledges that he shall give to Ricerio Caviglia £ 50 Genoese by the next octave of Saint Andrew [December 7]. And if he does not pay then, he promises to give Provisine [currency at the rate of] 12 [deniers] Provisine for every 15 [deniers] Genoese at the next fair of Lagny. And if [the coins] be deteriorated by alloy or by weight or be debased, he promises to give a mark of good silver for [every] 48 shillings up to the total of the entire debt. And [he promises to accept] the word of the creditor without oath in regard to expenses, losses, and [capital of the] loan (*mutuum*), and he pledges his goods as security.

And Ottolino of San Martino and Rufino Belardengo [constitute themselves] as debtors and payers, and pledge, [both liable] for the whole amount, their goods as security, waiving [exemptions] under the legislation on joint

[9] P. Santini, 'Frammenti di un libro di banchieri fiorentini scritto in volgare nel 1211,' *Giornale Storico della Letteratura Italiana*, X (1887), 170. Published also in A. Schiaffini, *Testi fiorentini del Dugento e dei primi del Trecento*. Note that the document is not a notarial instrument but an entry in the ledger of a partnership of merchant-bankers. The market or fair of San Procolo, in Bologna, had international renown.

[10] *Galigaio* (medieval Latin, *callegarius*) is 'shoemaker,' and not 'tanner,' as stated in F. Edler, *Glossary of Mediaeval Terms of Business: Italian Series, 1200–1600*, p. 132. Santa Trinita was a parish church and a ward of Florence.

[11] M. W. Hall, H. C. Krueger, and R. L. Reynolds, eds., *Guglielmo Cassinese (1190–1192)*, I, 390–91. Provisine deniers, of course, were deniers of Provins, Champagne. Note the word 'loan' peeping through an 'exchange' contract!

liability and the legislation by which it is provided that the principal debtor be sued first.

Witnesses: Gandolfo of Acqui; Firmino, draper. Under the *volta*[12] of the Fornari, on September 12.

'Dry Exchange' Contracts

76

From the Latin[13]

[Genoa] April 19 [1188]

We, Girardo de Valle and Tommaso de Valle, acknowledge that we have received from you, Beltrame Bertaldo, banker, a number of [deniers] Genoese for which [we promise to pay] £ 4 Provisine to you or your accredited messenger at the next May fair of Provins. And if we do not do this, we promise to pay you on our next return from the same fair for every 12 [deniers] Provisine 16 [deniers] Genoese until you are fully paid. Otherwise we promise you, making the stipulation, the penalty of the double, and in addition [we promise] to restore to you the entire expense you may have incurred through it, [trusting] in regard to the debt your word without oath. And for this we pledge to you all our goods as security, waiving, etc. Witnesses: Thibaud Abortateur of Troyes; Bertramo, son of Arduino of Comazzo. In the new shop of the Malocelli,[14] on April 19, between prime and terce.

77

From the Latin[15]

Genoa, July 1, 1292

I, Bonifacino Malocello, acknowledge to you, Guglielmo of Augusta, that I have had and have received from you £ 72 Genoese, waiving the exception that the money has not been had and received in cash, and every legal right. And in consideration of these [goods], which are well worth that amount,[16] I promise to give and to pay you or your messenger, personally or through my messenger, whenever you wish, by reason of exchange (*nomine cambii*),

---

[12] *Volta* was a shop or warehouse, the ceiling of which was vaulted or domed.

[13] Di Tucci, *Studi*, p. 113.

[14] The *stacio* (shop) owned by the powerful Malocelli family was the main center of the banking business in Genoa.

[15] G. I. Bratianu, *Recherches sur le commerce génois dans la Mer Noire au XIIIe siècle*, p. 322. On the gold deniers mentioned in this document see our Document 62 and its introduction.

[16] *Bene tacitum valentibus*; but read *bene tantum valentibus*. Obviously the loan was not in cash but in merchandise.

150 gold deniers Genoese of good and lawful weight in Tabriz—namely,
those [coins] which are worth 10 [silver] shillings Genoese apiece—in hard
coins,[17] current and acceptable in said place. And to that place we are now
about to go, I and you, God willing. And if perchance we are not able to go
to the aforesaid place because the caravans[18] are not going to Tabriz at the
time you disembark at Trebizond, I promise and agree to give and pay you
said debt at Trebizond whenever you wish.[19] And if I do not pay as [stated]
above, I promise and agree to give and pay you in the city of Genoa, by
reason of exchange, for every gold denier Genoese of said sum [remaining]
unpaid 12 shillings Genoese within the next eight months. Otherwise. . . .[20]

Done in Genoa in front of the shop of the Malocelli, July 1, 1292, before
terce, fourth indiction. Witnesses: Nicola Lercari and Leonardo Pessiario,
shoemaker.

[17] *In pecunia numerata:* in hard coins or in counted coins? The expression *numerare pecuniam*
means both to count and to pay cash.

[18] *Caterva.* The term usually designates the convoys of ships sailing to Trebizond and other
seaports (see W. Miller, *Trebizond: the Last Greek Empire*); but here, it must mean 'caravans'
since Tabriz is not on the sea shore.

[19] *Ad meam voluntatem;* no doubt a slip of the notary for *ad tuam voluntatem,* 'whenever you
wish.'

[20] Blank in the original.

CHAPTER VIII

THE SEA LOAN AND THE
SEA EXCHANGE

LIKE THE STRAIGHT loan, the sea loan (*mutuum* or, less frequently, *venditio*) goes back to Greek and Roman antiquity. Its main peculiarity is that the borrower pledges the return of the loan only on condition that the ship carrying the borrowed money or goods bought with it safely completes its voyage. A sea loan may be extended for a voyage one way or for both an outward and a return voyage.[1]

Inasmuch as the sea loan involves a definite risk for the lender, the medieval Church at first recognized the legitimacy of taking a premium, not as interest on the loan, but as compensation for the risk. In our first selection (Document 78) the premium is openly quoted. In the thirteenth century, however, the canonistic legislation against 'usury' was extended to include sea loans as well as ordinary loans. Some modern writers compare the premium of sea loans to insurance premiums, and regard the clause of safe arrival as a primitive form of insurance. Real insurance contracts, however, developed at a later period, independently of the sea loan. They will be described in Chapter XVI.

Many sea loan contracts include a clause whereby part of the ship's cargo, generally the goods bought with the loan, is to be considered a security for the return of the loan. This clause is mentioned in our second selection (Document 79).

Inasmuch as sea loans, when made for the outbound voyage only, involved transfer of capital to another country, they were at times represented as sea exchange contracts (*cambium*), and the money to be returned was quoted in a different currency from that originally lent. Our third selection (Document 80) is an example of this. Such a contract had much the same advantages as ordinary exchange contracts. Any objection which ecclesiastical authorities might raise was circumvented by the fact that no interest or premium was openly mentioned but rather a rate of exchange

---

[1] The only monograph specifically concerned with this contract is C. Hoover, 'The Sea Loan in Genoa in the Twelfth Century,' *Quarterly Journal of Economics*, XL (1925–1926), 495–529; it is not satisfactory. There are good descriptions of the sea loan in the many articles of A. E. Sayous (see the list in M. Glansdorff, 'Les Travaux d'André-E. Sayous sur l'histoire économique,' *Revue Economique Internationale*, VI, 2 [1935], 393–412); in E. H. Byrne, 'Commercial Contracts of the Genoese in the Syrian Trade of the Twelfth Century,' *Quarterly Journal of Economics*, XXXI (1916), 128–70; and in many of the general works quoted in the introduction to Part Three of the present book. G. Ferrari delle Spade, 'Registro vaticano di atti bizantini di diritto privato,' *Studi Bizantini e Neoellenici*, IV (1935), 249–67, has published what seems to be a notarial minute, in Greek, of a Byzantine sea loan contract. Here it is, in translation: 'Kolevas has borrowed from Sgoropoulos 12 hyperpers in the month of February [1363?], second indiction. If the ship returns safely, he will give back 14 hyperpers. Witnesses: Argyropoulos and Alexios.'

which could not be condemned even if it was set in advance to insure a suitable reward for the lender. The actual reward realized was uncertain because it depended on fluctuations in the rates of exchange and these fluctuations could not always be accurately forecast.[2]

The sea exchange, like the land exchange, could insure stability in the rate of interest by adopting the same optional clause as in the 'dry exchange.' Our fourth selection is an example (Document 81).

The Straight Sea Loan

78

From the Latin[3]

Constantinople, December, 1158

In the name of the Lord God and our Savior, Jesus Christ. In the year of the Lord 1158, in the month of December, seventh indiction, in Constantinople. I, Pietro Cornaro of the section of Sant' Apollinare, together with my heirs, openly declare to you, Sebastiano Ziani of the section of Santa Giustina, and to your heirs that I have received from Stefano Ziani, your brother, 100 gold hyperpers of the old weight belonging to you. And with these I am to go and to do business wherever it seems good to me. And I am to carry with me the aforesaid goods (*habere*)[4] by the convoy[5] of ships which will come to Venice from Constantinople or from Alexandria in this first coming September, or [I am] to send the same goods from the aforesaid territories to Venice by a reliable man in the witness of good men. And then, within thirty days after that convoy of ships from the aforesaid territories enters [the waters of] Venice, I am to give and to deliver, personally or through my messenger, to you or your messenger in Venice, 125 gold

---

[2] The most recent work on this type of contract is L. A. Senigallia, 'Il prestito a cambio marittimo medioevale,' in *Atti del Convegno Internazionale di studi storici del diritto marittimo medioevale in Amalfi*, pp. 187–206, with bibliography.

[3] A. Baracchi, 'Le carte del mille e del millecento che si conservano nel R. Archivio Notarile di Venezia,' *Archivio Veneto*, VIII (1874), 365–66; the document is reprinted in R. Morozzo della Rocca and A. Lombardo, *Documenti del commercio veneziano nei secoli XI–XIII*, I, 133–34. It is an original document and not, like the majority of the documents included in this section, a minute in a notarial chartulary; hence the signatures of the witnesses appear in full. Sebastiano Ziani, like Pietro Cornaro, was a member of the merchant patriciate of Venice; he was doge of Venice from 1172 to 1178. See G. Luzzatto, 'Les Activités économiques du patriciat vénitien (Xe–XIVe siècles),' *Annales d'Histoire Economique et Sociale*, IX (1937), 23ff.

[4] It would seem that the loan was not in cash but invested in merchandise. *Habere*, however, may also apply to cash. On the hyperpers (the Byzantine gold coin) see our introductory Note on Coinage.

[5] *Mudua*. At a later period this term was reserved for the regular convoys organized and controlled by the state, but in the twelfth century it probably applied to any group of ships voyaging together.

hyperpers of the old weight. The aforesaid goods, however, are to remain at your risk from sea and [hostile] people, provided [the risk] is proved. If I do not observe all these [conditions] for you as written above, then I, together with my heirs, am to restore to you and to your heirs all the aforesaid hyperpers in the double out of my lands and houses and of all that I am known to own in this world. And let the same capital and [the penalty of] the double bear interest of six per five[6] every year from that time forward.

I, Pietro Cornaro, signed by my own hand.

I, Pietro Lambardo, witness, signed.

I, Marco Signorello, witness, signed.

I, Marco Bembo, witness, signed.

I, Giovanni da Noale, subdeacon and notary, completed and certified [this instrument].

79

From the Latin[7]

Marseilles, April 2, 1227

In the name of the Lord. In the year of the Incarnation of the Same 1227, fifteenth indiction, the fourth [day] before the Nones of April. Be it known to all that I, al-Hakim, Saracen of Alexandria, acknowledge and recognize that I have had and have received, by virtue of a purchase from you, Bernard Manduel, 2 quintals of Socotran aloes and 1 quintal 80 pounds of cassia bark, and 2 *centenaria* of coral, for all of which I owe you 135 bezants of good *miliarisia*, old [and] of correct weight, waiving, with my full knowledge, the exception that the goods have not been delivered to me. And these 135 bezants of good *miliarisia*, old [and] of correct weight, net of duty and of all customs,[8] I promise by stipulation to pay fully and to deliver peacefully to you, said Bernard, or to your accredited messenger, in Ceuta within a space of twenty days after the ship 'The Falcon' arrives there. And for these I pledge to you as security all the aforesaid goods which I bought from you, and these goods are to go and remain at your risk for the said value of 135

---

[6] That is, 20 percent.

[7] L. Blancard, *Documents inédits sur le commerce de Marseille au moyen-âge*, I, 18–19. The Westerners used the terms *beȝant* and *miliarision* or *miliarensis*, borrowed from the Byzantine monetary system, to designate various types of dinars and dirhams struck in Muslim states and in the Christian states of the Holy Land. In this document the bezant (or dinar) is a money of account pegged to the *miliarision* (or dirham), a silver coin.

[8] *De duana et de omnibus avariis.* The first term indicates the main customs duty and the second indicates all kinds of special duties, especially those levied upon ships and sea trade. Both terms are of Arabic origin and are still used in Romance languages (French *douane, avarie*; Italian *dogana, avaria*; etc.).

bezants and any surplus value [to be] at my [risk]. [This is to be] so done that if I do not pay you the said 135 bezants by the established time limit, you are then to be permitted on your own authority to sell all said security or to pledge [it] as security, and to do what you want with it, until you have been fully paid of the aforesaid 135 bezants of good *miliarisia*, old, just as has been stated above. And I [also] promise in good faith, under pledge of all my goods, to restore to you the whole of what [may] be lacking.[9] And I waive in regard to all this the period of grace [10] of twenty days and four months and any other delay and any legal [rights]. This was done in a certain house of the late Anselme, in which Januaire, notary, lives. Witnesses called and invited for this [purpose] were Guy of Aix, Peire de Cardeilhac, Guillem de Conchis,[11] Hermengaud of Narbonne, Guirard Beguin; and I, Januaire, public notary of Marseilles, by commission of both parties, wrote this.

The Mating of the Sea Loan with Exchange

80

From the Latin[12]

Ayas, February 27, 1274

In the name of the Lord, amen. I, Riccomanno, [son] of the late Camissario, Pisan, acknowledge to you, Bandenaco, [son] of the late Bandenaco of Casa Orlandi, Pisan, that I have had and have received from you a number of your new dirhams of Armenia, waiving the exception that the dirhams have not been had and received, [the exception] that there has been fraud in the act, and the claim [that may be made for] a thing given without any ground,[13] and [waiving] every other legal right. Wherefore and for which I promise to give and to pay by reason of correct and true exchange, personally or through my messenger, to you or to your accredited messenger, 300 gold bezants, old of Cairo, good and lawful and of correct weight at the common weight

---

[9] *Restituere totum minus fallimentum*: that is, to make good whatever might still be due after the pledge is sold for the unpaid debt.

[10] *Induciis*.

[11] The De Conchis family was one of the most prominent in trade and politics in Montpellier. The Manduel family was equally prominent in Marseilles.

[12] C. Desimoni, 'Actes passés en 1271, 1274 et 1279 à L'Aïas [Petite Arménie] et à Beyrouth par devant des notaires génois,' *Archives de l'Orient Latin*, I (1881), 450–51, and, for the coins mentioned in the document, *ibid.*, pp. 437ff. Some specimens of the good 'bezants' (or rather dinars) of Egypt at that period still weighed more than 4½ grams of gold, as did the earliest dinars struck by the caliphs. The silver dirhams which the Christian kingdom of Cilician Armenia struck in imitation of Muslim coins were very debased.

[13] *Condicioni sine causa*; but read *condictioni sine causa*, an exception in Roman Law.

of the country of Egypt, net and cleared of all duties and customs[14] of sea and land, within twenty days after the arrival at Damietta of the ship which is named 'Saint Nicholas,' [belonging] to me and to my partner, without any change in the route. This, however, [is to be done] provided that the said ship arrives safely at the risk and fortune of God, the sea, and [hostile] people, and [at the risk] of the security written below. Otherwise the penalty of the double. . . .[15]

And for this penalty and for the observing of this I pledge to you as security in particular 420 chests of iron, which weigh 38 *cantaria* according to the *cantarium* of Acre, loaded in the said ship [belonging] to me and to my partner. And I acknowledge that this security was bought with your own dirhams, which I have had and have received from you, as I have acknowledged above. And if perchance I do not pay the said 300 bezants to you or to your accredited messenger within the aforesaid time limit, I give and concede to you [the power] of selling and obligating the said security, so that you may obtain payment of the said bezants out of the same security and out of my goods if [the security] be insufficient, without objection by me nor by any magistrate in my behalf; and this under the said penalty and pledge of all my goods, existing and future.

Done in Ayas, under the portico of the house of the late Giovanni Clarea, in the year of the Nativity of the Lord, 1274, first indiction, February 27, between prime and terce. Witnesses: Guglielmo, [son] of Pietro; Pietro Riccio, Pisan, resident of Ayas; and Paolo Dedi, Pisan.

'Dry' Sea Exchange

81

From the Latin[16]

Genoa, June 23, 1271

In the name of the Lord, amen. We—[namely, I], Guglielmo Streiaporco, and [I], Porchetto Streiaporco, his emancipated son [acting] in the presence of my said father and by his order and will—both of us [liable] for the whole

---

[14] *Dacitis et avariis.* The first term indicates any kind of import tax (compare Italian *dazio*); for the second, see Document 79.

[15] Desimoni omits a few words or sentences—no doubt the usual legal formulae of contracts of this kind—and replaces them by an 'etc.'

[16] Unprinted. Archivio di Stato, Genoa. *Notari Ignoti,* busta VII, cart. 5. The Streiaporco family belonged to the Genoese merchant aristocracy. In 1289 Benedetto Zaccaria, acting as a representative of the Commune, concluded an agreement with the king of Cilician Armenia whereby a warehouse, formerly belonging to 'the late Guglielmo Streiaporco,' probably the same who is a party to our contract, was transferred to the Commune. On Benedetto Zaccaira, see our Document 53.

amount, acknowledge to you, Benedetto Zaccaria, that we have had and have received from you a number of Genoese deniers,[17] waiving the exception that the Genoese [deniers] have not been received and every legal right and exception. Wherefore and for which we promise, both of us [liable] for the whole amount, to give and to pay to you or to your accredited messenger 53 gold hyperpers, good and of correct weight, in the Byzantine Empire (*Romania*) by the Kalends of September. If, however, we do not give you these [hyperpers] within the said time limit, [we promise] for each of the said hyperpers 11 shillings Genoese in Genoa whenever you wish. Otherwise we promise, both of us [liable] for the whole amount, to give you, making the stipulation, the penalty of the double of the said amount,[18] the aforesaid [conditions] remaining as settled. And we pledge to you as security for the aforesaid [promises] all our goods, existing and future; and we promise the return of the expenses, waiving the legislation on joint liability, the Epistle of the divine Hadrian, and every legal right.

And the said Porchetto acknowledges that he is eighteen years old, and swears that he will undertake, fulfill, and observe everything as above. And the said Porchetto does all this in the presence and by order, will, and authorization of the said father, and by advice of Pietro Streiaporco and Vivaldo Bello, whom he chose and declared [to be] his relatives and advisors.

Done in Genoa, in the street of the Nepitella, in front of the house where Giovanni Guercio lives. Witnesses: the said Pietro Streiaporco and Vivaldo Bello and Federico, servant of the said Benedetto. In the year of the Nativity of the Lord 1271, thirteenth indiction, June 23, after vespers.

[17] *Tot denarios Januinos.* On this formula see A. Lattes, 'Di una singolare formula genovese nei contratti di mutuo,' *Rivista del Diritto Commerciale*, XXII (1924), 542–50.

[18] The notary carelessly repeated here 'both of us liable for the whole amount,' *quilibet nostrum in solidum.*

CHAPTER IX

THE COMMENDA CONTRACT

WHILE SALES, LOANS, and exchange contracts were essential elements of medieval trade, the expansion of trade was made possible chiefly by the *commenda* and *compagnia* contracts. These were the basic legal instruments to pool capital and to bring together investors and managers. Leaving the *compagnia* for the following chapter, let us now turn to the *commenda*.

The name of the contract is virtually untranslatable, although such loose translations as 'sleeping partnership' or 'business venture' have sometimes been used. Nor was the medieval name, *commenda*, universally identified with that contract. Contracts of deposit, of commission, and many others were sometimes called *commenda*. On the other hand, the contract which we call *commenda* was known in different places under the different names of *accomendatio*, *collegantia*, *societas* [*maris*], *entica*, and many others. But *commenda* was the most widespread term for it, and it has won general acceptance among modern legal scholars. This is perhaps the only point of agreement among them; no aspect of commercial law has been the subject of so much heated controversy as the origin, legal character, and economic function of the *commenda*. The controversy still rages. Without trying to reconcile irreconcilable views or to adopt a strictly neutral attitude, we shall concentrate on points upon which agreement is wide, though not unanimous.[1]

Precedents to the *commenda* have been found in the Babylonian *tapputum* contract, in the Muslim *muqarada*,[2] in the Byzantine *chreokoinonia*, and, less convincingly or less directly, in the Greek and Roman sea loan and other contracts of the Hellenistic-Roman world, or even in certain Germanic agrarian contracts. Nevertheless, the *commenda* as it appears in the Western Mediterranean from the tenth century on seems to have peculiarities of its own. It was not the creation of legal scholars but the fruit of a slow evolution in customary law. Although it has sometimes been called a partnership, it seems to hold a position closer to ordinary loans than to partnerships. Profits and risks are shared by the parties as in a partnership, but otherwise the relation between the parties resembles that of lender and borrower. The former does not become jointly liable with the latter in transactions with third parties; indeed, third parties do not need to be aware of the lender's existence. Like

---

[1] A rich, though not exhaustive, list of early work on the *commenda* is found in G. Astuti, *Origini e svolgimento storico della commenda fino al secolo XIII*. This is probably the best monograph on the subject, although some of its statements are open to challenge and its approach tends to slight economic factors. Many of the later works are quoted in R. Zeno, *Documenti per la storia del diritto marittimo nei secoli XIII e XIV*.

[2] See Document 3.

the sea loan, the *commenda* contract is drafted only for the duration of a sea voyage; it is ended when the borrower returns the capital plus the profits or minus the losses.

To describe the *commenda* is easier than to define it. In the unilateral *collegantia* (as it is called in Venice) or *commenda* proper (as it is called almost everywhere else), one party entrusts capital to another party, who is to use it in an overseas commercial venture and to return it together with a previously established share of the profit. Usually the investor who remains at home receives three fourths of the profits and the travelling party receives one fourth. Any loss on the capital is borne exclusively by the investor; the traveling party, in turn, loses the reward for his labor if no profit is made.

In the bilateral *collegantia* or *commenda*, usually called *societas* in Genoa, the investing party who remains at home contributes two thirds of the capital whereas the traveling party contributes one third in addition to his labor. Profits usually are divided by the half according to original investments; losses are borne by both investors according to their respective contributions to the capital. This means that the rules governing the unilateral *commenda* also apply here. As a matter of fact, the traveling party receives one fourth of the profit on the two thirds of the capital contributed by the other party plus all of the profit of the one third of the capital which he himself contributed. The sum is one half of the total profits. If there is a loss, the investor loses twice the amount of the traveling party, but the latter also loses the reward for his labor.

Our first two selections (Documents 82 and 83) are the two earliest extant documents of *commenda*. The contracts are called *collegantia* according to the Venetian use. One is an agreement of bilateral *collegantia* and the other is a settlement after the return of the traveling party. Document 84 is a bilateral *commenda* from Genoa; in this instance this kind of contract is called *societas*, whereas the term *commenda* is reserved for the unilateral contract, of which Document 85 is an example. In Pisa, however, the term *societas* is used not only for the bilateral *commenda* but also for the unilateral contract, of which Document 86 is an example. Document 87, a Barcelonese *commenda*, is a further illustration of the fact that in spite of different names the contract was virtually the same from one end to the other of the Western Mediterranean.[3]

On the other hand, each contract differs from the others in the details. Some contracts, for instance, are of the type usually called *implicita*—that is, 'invested'—because they specifically mention the goods which have been purchased with the capital given in *commenda*. The capital itself is often referred to by the same name as the contract; it is called *commenda, collegantia, entica,* and the like. Sometimes the investment is a share in a ship. These shares (*sortes, partes, loca,* etc.) could be sold, lent, given in *commenda*, or included in the common capital of a partnership. The practice of evaluating ships in shares and dividing the ownership and the management of a ship into shares implies a measure of capitalistic organization; among its advantages is the spreading of risks. Moreover, any object could be divided into shares; we even come across slaves who are owned or given in *commenda* by shares.

---

[3] On the purported spread of the *commenda* to northern Germany see, for instance, F. G. A. Schmidt, *Handelsgesellschaften in den deutschen Stadtrechtsquellen des Mittelalters*, p. 89ff.

The legal definition of, and the difference between *sortes, partes,* and *loca* have formed the object of heated polemics, which need not be reviewed here.[4] But it seemed worth while to give another example of *commenda* contracts concerning shares in a ship, besides Document 82, which briefly refers to them. Document 88 gives further details.

The unilateral *commenda* has been frequently described as an agreement between a sedentary capitalist and an enterprising young man who had no capital but was willing to travel and to risk his life with the hope of gaining a fortune. Documents 89 and 90 indicate that this was not always true. Poor men could invest their meager funds with a rich traveling merchant who was agreeable to accept any contribution that would increase the capital to be carried overseas. The 'sedentary' investor and the 'traveling' manager at times were so equal in wealth and commercial experience that they often reversed their roles. Actually, merchants found it advantageous to alternate the roles of sedentary and traveling party. Furthermore, it often happened that a traveling merchant took along only part of his own capital in addition to capital given in *commenda* by other merchants, and entrusted the remainder of his capital to merchants traveling to different places.[5]

Other features of the *commenda* ought to become clearer through perusal of our selections. Early *commenda* agreements, for instance, usually left to the investor the right of deciding the destination, choice of ship, and other essentials of the commercial venture undertaken by the traveling party. They also insisted on meticulous accounting and often specified that the goods should go and return in the custody of the traveling party. In time, however, greater and greater latitude was left to the traveling merchant. Evidently it was impossible for the sedentary investor to control adequately the management of the venture without hampering the initiative of the traveling party; nor were all merchants willing to accept limitations from investors.[6]

The Venetian Commenda or Collegantia

82

From the Latin[7]

Venice, August, 1073

In the name of the Lord God and of our Savior, Jesus Christ. In the year of the Incarnation of the same Redeemer 1073, in the month of August,

---

[4] The latest work is A. Scialoja, *Partes navis—loca navis.* It is very onesided, but it quotes earlier bibliography which must also be used to obtain a more balanced idea of the state of the question. See also our documents in Chapters XII and XIII and the introductory remarks to them.

[5] This point is fully discussed in G. Luzzatto, 'La commenda nella vita economica dei secoli XIII e XIV con particolare riguardo a Venezia,' in *Atti del Convegno Internazionale di studi storici del diritto marittimo medioevale in Amalfi,* pp. 139–64.

[6] On the inconvenience resulting from this system, see Document 148 and the introductory remarks.

[7] R. Morozzo della Rocca and A. Lombardo, *Documenti del commercio veneziano nei secoli XI–XIII,* I, 12–13.

eleventh indiction, at Rialto,[8] I, Giovanni Lissado of Luprio, together with
my heirs, have received in *collegantia* from you, Sevasto Orefice, son of Ser
Trudimondo, and from your heirs, this [amount]: £ 200 [Venetian]. And I
myself have invested £100 in it. And with this capital (*habere*) we have
[acquired] two shares (*sortes*) in the ship of which Gosmiro da Molino is
captain.[9] And I am under obligation to bring all of this with me in *taxegio*[10]
to Thebes in the ship in which the aforesaid Gosmiro da Molino sails as
captain. Indeed, by this agreement and understanding of ours I promise to
put to work this entire [capital] and to strive the best way I can. Then, if the
capital is saved,[11] we are to divide whatever profit the Lord may grant us
from it by exact halves, without fraud and evil device. And whatever I can
gain with those goods from any source, I am under obligation to invest all
[of it] in the *collegantia*. And if all these goods are lost because of the sea or of
[hostile] people, and this is proved—may this be averted—neither party
ought to ask any of them from the other; if, however, some of them remain,
in proportion as we invested so shall we share. Let this *collegantia* exist
between us so long as our wills are fully agreed.

But if I do not observe everything just as is stated above, I, together with
my heirs, then promise to give and to return to you and your heirs everything
in the double, both capital and profit (*caput et prode*), out of my land and my
house or out of anything that I am known to have in this world.

Signature of the aforesaid Giovanni who requested this [instrument] to
be made.

I, Pietro, witness, signed.

I, Lorenzo, witness, signed.

I, Gosmiro, witness, signed.

The full names of the witnesses are these: Pietro Gossoni; Lorenzo Scudaio;
Gosmiro da Molino.

I, Domenico, cleric and notary, completed and certified [this instrument].

[8] Rialto ('high creek') is the original name of some of the islands which are now called Venice.
Venice at first was the name of the entire region of which Rialto became the capital in the early
ninth century.

[9] *Nauclerus*. In later documents this word usually means 'pilot' or 'boatswain,' but here it seems
to mean 'captain.'

[10] *Taxegium* is a word of Byzantine origin and means 'commercial voyage' or 'commercial
journey.' The primary meaning of the word in classical Greek was 'military expedition.' It agrees
with the verb *procertare*, 'to strive' or 'to fight,' which is used a few lines below. See also Document 1, note 17.

[11] *Capetanea salva*. See Ducange, *s. v.* 'Capitale' and 'Capitanea.'

83

From the Latin[12]

Venice, May, 1072

In the name of the Lord God Almighty. In the year of the Incarnation of our Lord Jesus Christ 1072, in the month of May, tenth indiction, at Rialto. I, Domenico Zopulo, son of Vitale Zopulo junior, together with my heirs, do make to you, Giovanni Barozzi, son of Giovanni Barozzi, and to your heirs, full and irrevocable release[13] in regard to an instrument of record which you made to me, whereby I myself invested £ 50 in deniers of good alloy and you by the same [instrument] invested £ 25, and [whereby] you went with all these goods in *taxegio* to Thebes in the ship of which Leone Orefice was captain. But now, since you have returned from said *taxegio*, you have rendered me a full, accurate, and true account of it, in regard to both the principal and the profit; under oath you have handed over everything to me and you have settled [accounts]. From now on you shall always remain released in regard to the principal and the profit or to the [penalty of the] double and to all that is stated in the said record, so that on no day and at no time [henceforth] are we to make any further demand or to exert [any more] pressure by any device, whether small or great. I, moreover, have returned to you the record itself. If a copy of it appears in my possession or in that of any man, it shall remain null and void, wholly without validity and force, because there is nothing left in it whereby we should make any further demand upon you. But if we at any time attempt to demand anything in regard to the clauses stated above, I, together with my heirs, promise to pay to you and to your heirs £ 5 in gold [as penalty], and this release shall [nevertheless] remain in force.

I, Domenico, signed by my hand.

I, Giovanni, witness, signed.

I, Domenico, witness, signed.

I, Leone, witness, signed.

The full names of the witnesses are these: Giovanni, son of Pietro Michiel and Domenico, his brother; Leone, son of Domenico Michiel.

I, Giovanni, subdeacon and notary, completed and certified [this instrument].

---

[12] Morozzo della Rocca and Lombardo, *Documenti del commercio veneziano* I, 11–12. The parties and the witnesses belonged to the highest merchant nobility in Venice.

[13] *Securitatem*, literally, 'security.'

The Genoese Commenda and Societas

84

From the Latin[14]

[Genoa,] September 29, 1163

Witnesses: Simone Bucuccio, Ogerio Peloso, Ribaldo di Sauro, and Genoardo Tasca. Stabile and Ansaldo Garraton have formed a *societas* in which, as they mutually declared, Stabile contributed £ 88 [Genoese] and Ansaldo £ 44. Ansaldo carries this *societas*, in order to put it to work, to Tunis or to wherever goes the ship in which he shall go—namely, [the ship] of Baldizzone Grasso and Girardo. On his return [he will place the proceeds] in the power of Stabile or of his messenger for [the purpose of] division. After deducting the capital, they shall divide the profits in half. Done in the chapter house, September 29, 1163, eleventh indiction.

In addition, Stabile gave his permission to send that money to Genoa by whatever ship seems most convenient to him [to Ansaldo].

85

From the Latin[15]

[Genoa,] October 7, 1163

Witnesses: Bernizone Serra, Raimondo, Crispino and Pietro Vinattiere. I, Ingo Bedello, declare publicly that I am carrying £ 41 s.6 [Genoese] of goods belonging to Guglielmotto Ciriolo [invested] in silk and paper to Tunis, and from there to Genoa [where I shall place the proceeds] in the power of Guglielmotto or of his messenger. And he is not under obligation to contribute toward expenses in regard to them except in furnishing the [original] money. [Ingo] on his return [will place the proceeds] in the power of Guglielmotto or of his messenger and, after deducting the capital, he is to have one fourth of the profit. And Guglielmotto himself reserved as his right that there will be no expense for him in it. Done in the chapter house, October 7, 1163, eleventh indiction.

[14] M. Chiaudano and M. Moresco, *Il cartolare di Giovanni Scriba*, II, 162–63.   [15] *Ibid.*, II, 163.

Other Examples of Commenda

86

From the Latin[16]

Pisa, November 11, 1264

In the presence of myself, Jacopo, notary, etc. Ranieri, [son] of the late Ottaviano, of the parish of Sant'Andrea di Chinzica, has received and has had in *societas maris* from Sigieri, [son] of the late Bianco of San Miniato, £ 25 of good Pisan [deniers] petty. [This sum is] to be carried and employed by him as part of his investment (*hentica*) in the present voyage which he is to make, the Lord permitting, from Pisa to the kingdom of Sicily and to wherever else he may go or send [the investment] for the good and advantage of his investment, without fraud, in whatever ship or vessel, at the risk of the sea and [hostile] people, at one fourth of the profit to be had therefrom. And Sigieri himself has granted [permission] to carry, to send, and to employ it in this manner, in the name of the Lord.

And he, Ranieri, then agreed and promised by solemn stipulation to the aforesaid Sigieri—and by solemn stipulation he obligates himself, his heirs, and his goods existing and future to Sigieri and his heirs in regard to the penalty of the double of capital and profit [to be paid in case of nonfulfilment], and of all expenses that may be incurred for it—that he shall go back to the aforesaid Sigieri within one month after he, Ranieri, has returned to Pisa safely and in good health with his investment or the larger part of his invest-ment, or within one month after the same investment or the larger part has been carried back to Pisa. And he shall pay, personally or through someone else, to the aforesaid Sigieri, or the latter's heirs, or the latter's accredited messenger to whom [Sigieri] shall have given instructions, the aforesaid £ 25 together with three parts of the whole profit which he will have from them. [And he promises to observe these conditions] without contention, *malctha*,[17] complaint, or other [claims for] expenses, keeping for himself one fourth of that profit. And he waived, etc.

Done in Pisa, in Chinzica, in the store of the House of S. Sepolcro, of which Master Giovanni, physician, [son] of the late Jacopo, is the tenant, in

[16] R. S. Lopez, 'The Unexplored Wealth of the Notarial Archives in Pisa and Lucca,' in *Mélanges d'histoire du moyen âge dédiés à la mémoire de Louis Halphen*, p. 429. The document was written in Chinzica, the section of Pisa closest to the arsenal and the port. It is dated according to the Pisan style of the Incarnation. Should the reader think that its formulae are too complicated, let him consider that the contracts tended to grow more and more involved as time went by. Genoese notarial contracts of that period are frequently as complicated as this one from Pisa.

[17] *Sic*. Perhaps a corruption of *mulcta*, 'fine.'

the presence of Bonanno, [son] of the aforesaid late Jacopo, and of Fiam-
muccio, son of Ugolino Guelfo, and of Averardo, servant of the aforesaid
Master Giovanni, witnesses called for this purpose. 1265, eighth indiction,
fourth [day] before the Ides of November.

87

From the Latin[18]

[Barcelona], August 9, 1252

Be it known to all that I, Arnau Fabriz, am carrying in *comanda* from you,
Bernat Fuentes, though you are absent, and from your [partners][19] in this
present voyage which I am making in the ship of Ferrer Descoll and partners
to Overseas Territory[20] or wherever the said ship shall make port in this
present voyage for the purpose of commerce, £ 140 s.4 d.5 Barcelonese
invested in five [pieces of] cloth of Saint-Quentin and in six Saracens.[21]
And I promise you to sell all of this well and faithfully there, and to invest
in good faith the proceeds obtained from it in useful merchandise just as I see
and understand best. And after this voyage is made [I promise] to return into
your possession and into that of your [partners] said merchandise, that is, the
capital and the profit, just as God shall have granted to preserve them, so
[acting], however, that after deducting your said capital for you I am to
have one fourth of all the profit that God shall have granted in this *comanda*
of yours. But you are to have the three remaining parts of the said profit in
addition to your said capital, your *comanda* itself, however, going and being
held [there] and returning anywhere at your risk and fortune. This was done
on the fifth [day] before the Ides of August, in the year of the Lord, 1252.

Shares of a Ship Given in Commenda

88

From the Latin[22]

[Genoa, January 24, 1191]

Guglielmo Visconte acknowledges that he has in *accomendatio* from
Guglielmo Malfiliastro four shares (*loca*) less one quarter [of a share] of a

---

[18] Astuti, *Origini e svolgimento storico della commenda*, p. 10, note. The document was first
published by A. E. Sayous in 'Les Méthodes commerciales de Barcelone au XIIIe siècle d'après des
documents inédits des archives de sa cathédrale,' *Estudis Universitaris Catalans*, XVI (1931), 194.

[19] *A te ... et tuis*. We translate 'your [partners],' but it might as well mean 'heirs,' or 'goods.'

[20] *Ad partes ultramarineas*, that is, to Syria, which was Overseas par excellence.

[21] *Sarracenabus:* Saracen female slaves, or Saracen cloth? For a similar case, see Document 56,
note 113.

[22] M. W. Hall, H. C. Krueger, and R. L. Reynolds, eds., *Guglielmo Cassinese (1190–1192)*, I,

nef. And the [entire] nef is reckoned at forty shares, and it is the nef which Ugo de Figar and the same Guglielmo sailed from Gaeta to Marseille. And with these shares he can do business and sell and do whatever will seem best to him for the purpose of business. On his return to Genoa he promises to replace in the power of Malfiliastro or of his accredited messenger the profit which God may grant in addition to the capital. That day, place, and witnesses.

Commenda Contracts of Humble People

89
From the Latin[23]

Genoa, December 22, 1198

We, Embrone of Sozziglia and Master Alberto, acknowledge that we carry in *accomandatio* for the purpose of trading £ 142 Genoese to the port of Bonifacio and through or in Corsica and Sardinia; and from there we are to come [back]. And of this [sum], £ 25 Genoese belong to you, Giordano Clerico; and £ 10 to you, Oberto Croce. And to you, Vassallo Rapallino, [belong] £ 10; and to you, Bonsignore Torre, £ 10. And £ 5 [belong] to Pietro Bonfante; and to you, Michele, tanner, [belong] £ 5; and to you, Giovanni del Pero, £ 5; and to Ara Dolce, £ 6; and to Ansaldo Mirto, £ 5; and to Martino, hemp-seller, £ 5; and to Ansaldo Fanti, £ 8; and to you, Lanfranco of Crosa, £ 20; and to Josbert, nephew of Charles of Besançon, £ 10. And £ 6 belong to me, Embrone; and £ 2 to me, Alberto. And all the pounds mentioned above are to be profitably employed and invested, and they are to draw by the pound.[24] And we promise to send [back] the capital and the profit which God shall have granted from this *accomandatio*, [to be placed] in the power of the aforesaid persons to whom they belong. And after deduction of the capital we are to have one fourth of the profit; but the [entire] profit which comes to our [own] pounds is to be ours.

And Giordano, and Guglielmo, and Oberto, and Vassallo, and Bonsignore, and the mother of Pietro Bonfante, and Michele, tanner, and Giovanni del

---

51–52. The nef (*navis*) was a sailship, usually of large size. The fact that Visconte makes no mention of any share of the profit retained by him does not necessarily mean that he retained none. It had become so customary to give the traveling party one fourth of the profit that many contracts do not mention it.

[23] J. E. Eierman, H. G. Krueger, and R. L. Reynolds, eds., *Bonvillano* (*1198*), pp. 128–29. Note the small size of each investment, the short distance of the place of destination, and the obscurity of all parties—except perhaps 'Master' Alberto, if 'Master' was a professional title rather than a nickname—none of whom belonged to the merchant and landholding upper class.

[24] *Trahere per libram* means that in each transaction each partner contributes expenses and receives profits proportionately to the amount of his investment.

Pero, and Lanfranco of Crosa give [Embrone and Alberto] permission to send [part] of this *accomandatio* to Genoa, [to be placed] in the power of Giordano Clerico and of Bonsignore; and the same Giordano and Bonsignore are to have [permission] to invest it and to send it invested to the port of Bonifacio or to Sardinia. And if [either] Embrone or Alberto comes to Genoa after the Kalends of September . . .[25] in this to them, that they are to have permission to return together[26] with the money of the *accomandatio*. Done in Genoa in the house of Guglielmo Vento. Witnesses: Arduino de Mari; Baldoino, broker of the Campo; Nicola, spinner. 1198, first indiction, ten days from the end of December.

Interchangeability of Investor and Traveling Party

90
From the Latin[27]

Genoa, June 8, 1262

In the name of the Lord, amen. In the presence of the witnesses written below, Benedetto Zaccaria, son of Fulcone Zaccaria, says and affirms that [the following] is his will and proceeds from it: if perchance he, Benedetto, does not sail or go outside Genoa for the purpose of trading or sailing, his brother Manuele, son of the said Fulcone, may and should carry or have with him in *accomendatio* or *societas* for the purpose of trading £ 5,000 Genoese. And with this [sum] is concerned a certain instrument, written by the hand of Guglielmo Vegio, notary, on August 28, 1261, [and dealing] with the agreement proclaimed between the aforesaid Fulcone on the one part and Benedetto, Manuele, and Nicola, brothers, sons of the said Fulcone, on the other part. And he asked that this public instrument be made in regard to the aforesaid [decisions], in the presence of [these] witnesses: Nicola di Negro; Simone Spezia, tailor; and Luchetto di Negro. Done in Genoa, in the house of Pietro di Negro, judge, who dictated this instrument. In the year of the Nativity of the Lord 1262, fourth indiction, June 8, between prime and terce.

Genoa, June 8, 1262

In the name of the Lord, amen. I, Benedetto Zaccaria, son of Fulcone

---

The dots are in the edition by Eierman *et al.*

Adsimus, probably a slip of the notary for *adsimul*.

[27] Unprinted. Archivio di Stato, Genoa. *Cartulario di Vivaldo de Porta*, I, fol. 44 r. and v. The two instruments follow one the other directly. Then come two instruments identical with the above in every word, with the exception that the role of the principals is reversed: Manuele authorizes Benedetto to carry £ 5,000 in *accomendatio* and gives him powers of attorney.

Zaccaria, make, constitute and appoint you, Manuele Zaccaria, my brother, my accredited messenger and attorney, here present and receiving [the power] to ask, collect, and receive in my behalf and in my name whatever I am to have, to demand, and to receive from whatever person for whatever reason, and to arrange compromises and peaceful settlements, and to defend me against any person in any suit, and to transact and conduct my business, and lastly to do everything that will be necessary in regard to and about the aforesaid [transactions] and that I should do myself if I were present. And I promise to you, undersigned notary, making the stipulation in behalf of the person or persons whom it may concern, to hold and keep as settled and lasting whatever the said attorney shall do in regard to and about the aforesaid [affairs], and not to act contrary to it in anything, under pledge of my goods. Witnesses: Nicola di Negro and Luchetto di Negro. Done in Genoa, in the house of Pietro di Negro, judge. In the year of the Nativity of the Lord 1262, fourth indiction, June 8, between prime and terce.

CHAPTER X

PARTNERSHIPS AND OTHER CONTRACTS USED IN LAND TRADE

PARTNERSHIPS WERE to land trade what the *commenda* was to sea trade—the basic instruments for pooling capital and spreading risks. Unlike the *commenda*, which remained substantially unchanged through space and time, partnerships appeared in a large number of varieties. All of them, however, seem to have derived from one of two basic types or from a combination of both. We shall call these basic types the *compagnia* and the *societas terrae*, although these and many other names are used interchangeably in documents. What shall be said hereafter is but an attempt at drawing provisional conclusions from statements, often antithetic, made by modern scholars in regard to specific forms of partnership. The subject is no less controversial than the history of the *commenda*, but research has been less thorough. There is no modern work studying all forms of partnership as a whole.[1]

Of the two basic types, the *compagnia* was by far the more important in size of capital and scope of business. It is the contract which can be most properly called partnership. The word seems to come from medieval Latin *cumpanis*, 'one eating the same bread,' 'companion.' It indicates the original connection of the *compagnia* with the family. The earliest extant documents of this kind are *fraterna compagnia* agreements of Venice, which are not exclusively commercial but also involve common administration of real estate and other property inherited by members of the same family. Inasmuch as these documents come from a maritime city, the contention of some scholars, that radically different contracts were always used for land trade and sea trade respectively, is an overstatement. It contains, however, a good measure of truth. In Venice the *fraterna compagnia* lost ground steadily to the *commenda*, whereas *compagnia* contracts predominate in the records of interior cities of Tuscany and in other inland centers throughout the Middle Ages. That these records are later than those of Venice may be an accident owing to the fact that we have no early notarial registers from Tuscany.

Family partnerships seem to have existed in early Roman times, but they had become obsolete by the Byzantine period.[2] Possibly they owe their rebirth to conditions of the feudal and early communal Middle Ages, which stressed the need for

---

[1] Fairly complete bibliographies regarding the *compagnia* are found in A. Sapori, *Studi di storia economica medievale*, 2d ed., and in M. Chiaudano, *Studi e documenti per la storia del diritto commerciale italiano nel secolo XIII*. There is no systematic monograph on the *societas terrae* and its derivations.

[2] See, for instance, P. Frezza, 'Actio communi dividundo,' *Rivista Italiana per le Scienze Giuridiche*, new ser., VII (1932), 3–142; A. Poggi, *Il contratto di società in diritto romano classico*.

solidarity of the family in the political, military, economic, and social life. When portions of undivided family estates were invested in trade, the *compagnia* became an instrument of business. Gradually its membership ceased to coincide with that of a specific family and its duration ceased to be unlimited. Contracts made for a specific period contained the provision that they could be renewed. They now included only such members of a family as wished to participate and outsiders who were often grafted into the family by intermarriage or clientship. The *compagnia*, however, preserved throughout and beyond the Middle Ages its character of a group in which all full members, both investors and managers, were bound together in joint and unlimited liability. This was probably the main reason why the contract found little favor in sea trade, where risks were higher.

The other type, *societas terrae*, is closer to the *commenda* and in some instances cannot be called a true partnership any more than can the *commenda*. Both in maritime cities and in centers of the interior an investor could entrust capital to a merchant, craftsman, or banker with the understanding that he would use it in trade during a specific period, usually for one, two, or three years, and that at the end of that time he would return the capital with a share of the profits, usually one half. Losses of capital would be borne by the investor, as was the case in the *commenda*; the managing party would lose his hope of reward for his labor if there was no profit. So far, there was no partnership, and the lender was not liable to third parties. Some scholars deny that the *societas terrae* ever developed into forms of true partnership. Others believe that other *societas* contracts, which seem to create a common capital and joint liability, are derived from the *societas terrae*. It is hoped that the reader will form his own opinion by reviewing the evidence at hand.

The first and second selections (Documents 91 and 92) are, respectively, a record of provisions included in a Venetian *fraterna compagnia* and a record of dissolution of a *fraterna compagnia* in a Venetian colony.[3]

The last two selections (Documents 101 and 102) are contracts of *compagnia* drafted by Tuscan merchants. It will be noted that they are not notarial instruments like the others in this section, but *chirografi*, that is, documents written by the merchants themselves and certified only by the merchants' own seals. The *compagnia* between Francesco Datini and Toro di Berto is a partnership between equals, even though Datini surpassed his partner in wealth and ability and was a member of many other partnerships. The *compagnia* entered upon by Angiolo Tani leaves him in a subordinate position; it is an example of arrangements used by great merchant companies such as that of the Medici to create autonomous branches in foreign cities.[4]

---

[3] On the *fraterna compagnia*, see F. C. Lane, 'Family Partnerships and Joint Ventures in the Venetian Republic,' *Journal of Economic History*, IV (1944), 178–96, with bibliography.

[4] The most important work on Francesco Datini is still that of Bensa from which our Document 101 has been taken. In English one may consult R. Brun, 'A Fourteenth Century Merchant of Italy,' *Journal of Economic and Business History*, II (1930), 451–66. Neither work is fully satisfactory, although both have quality, and neither exhausts the huge mass of material available to study this great merchant. A project to publish all the Datini archives—including some 500 books of accounting and some 15,000 letters—was interrupted by the Second World War. It is still hoped that Armando Sapori, who was in charge of the project, may resume the work. In this volume there are other documents from the Datini archives (43, 122, 125, 138, 195). The most recent work on the Medici bank is R. de Roover, *The Medici Bank*; see also the same author's remarks in his *Gresham on Foreign Exchange*.

Documents 93 and 94, on the other hand, are examples of *societas terrae* particularly close to the original form of *commenda* contracts. One of them comes from a maritime city and the other from a town of the interior. All the other selections represent the great variety of intermediate forms which, in our opinion, form a continuous bridge between two extremes—the *commenda* and the *compagnia*. They are found both in maritime and in land trade. Their diversity makes it impossible to describe them without a fuller discussion of legal problems than would be proper in this book.

The Venetian 'Fraterna Compagnia'

91

From the Latin[5]

Venice, January, 1200

In the name of the Lord God and of our Savior, Jesus Christ. In the year of the Lord, 1199,[6] the month of January, third indiction, in Rialto. I, Domenico Ciba, deacon of the Church of Saint Eustace, do testify that at one time in the past I was at the house of Giacomo and Filippo da Molin of the aforesaid district. And there, in the presence of Pietro da Molin, elder [brother] of the aforesaid Giacomo and Filippo, they let me read their records,[7] both the records that they held in common—the *rogadie*[8] as well as the *collegancie* and the *securitates*[9] belonging to them, each [of them] bringing his [own]—and [the records] about the ownership of lands and houses which were [held] in common. And Giacomo da Molin held in common[10] the aforesaid records in regard to the ownership of lands and houses as well as the records of receipt which were [made] between their father [as one party] and his nephews Rizzo and Gusmiro da Molin [as the other party], and the other records which regarded their estate, divisions as well as partition.[11] And he kept them himself at the wish of the aforesaid

---

[5] R. Morozzo della Rocca and A. Lombardo, *Documenti del commercio veneziano nei secoli XI–XIII*, I, 437–38.

[6] Venetian style; that is, 1200.　　　　　　　　　　[7] *Cartulas.*

[8] *Rogadie* is the Venetian term for a type of commission contract.

[9] *Securitas* has a general meaning of 'caution,' 'security,' 'guarantee,' 'release,' 'receipt.' Here it probably means 'receipt.'

[10] *Communaliter*, as above. Here it means that Giacomo will hold the records in trust for himself and his partner in the *fraterna*.

[11] Apparently the father of Giacomo and Filippo da Molin and the father of Rizzo and Gusmiro da Molin were brothers and there had been another *fraterna* between them. When the father of Rizzo and Gusmiro had died, that *fraterna* was dissolved and the records delivered to the surviving partner, the father of Giacomo and Filippo. In turn Giacomo and Filippo formed a *fraterna* after the death of their father. The records of the earlier *fraterna* were part of the estate they inherited and administered in common.

Filippo, his brother, in order that they be [held in] common between them. I say this as true testimony because I know [it].

I, Domenico Ciba, deacon, witness, signed.

I, Giovanni Bono, witness, signed.

I, Giacomo Caroso, witness, signed.

I, Marino Lambardo, priest and notary, completed and certified [this instrument].

92
From the Latin[12]

[Candia (Heraclion), January 23, 1271]

On the ninth day from the end [of January]. Pietro Scandolario, son of the late Nicola Scandolario, resident of Candia, makes a *securitas*[13] in regard to a company of brothers[14] and to any other [obligation] to Stefano Scandolario, his brother, likewise resident of Candia, [made out] as fully as it can be made. And conversely the same Stefano Scandolario makes a similar *securitas* to the same brother of his, [made out] as fully as it can be made. Witnesses: Giacomo Giuliano and others. To be completed and delivered.[15] And [the other witnesses were] Nicola Bonzi and Marco Barastro.

'Societates Terrae' Resembling Commenda Contracts

93
From the Latin[16]

Marseilles, December 23, 1233

In the name of the Lord. In the year of the Incarnation of the Same 1233, seventh indiction, the tenth from the Kalends of January. Be it known to all that I, Guillem Blancard, acknowledge that I have received in *comanda* from you, Bernard de Manduel[17] and Jean de Manduel, brothers, £ 1,120

---

[12] A. Lombardo, *Documenti della colonia veneziana di Creta*, I, 7.

[13] See footnote 9 above. A general receipt, quittance, or release.   [14] *Fraterna compagnia*.

[15] *Complere et dare*. By these words the notary who wrote this minute reminds himself that he ought to write a fuller version of the contract and to deliver it to the parties. The names which follow are those of the other witnesses, added as an afterthought. Fuller documents of dissolution of *fraterne compagnie* can be found in Morozzo della Rocca and Lombardo, *Documenti del commercio veneziano*, I, *passim*.

[16] L. Blancard, *Documents inédits sur le commerce de Marseille au moyen-âge*, I, 58–59. This is a pioneer work in the difficult field of publishing medieval notarial instruments, and therefore the readings at times must be corrected in the light of more recent editions. We have omitted the list of witnesses at the end.

[17] Manduel, the family name of these brothers, is derived from the name of the town from which they probably came.

regalia coronata invested in fourteen loads of small alum and in cordovan, waiving the exception that said *comanda* has not been delivered to me and that it has not been received. With this *comanda* I shall go to do business for your benefit and for my own, and for a profit of every fourth denier in this present journey which I am about to make to the next regular fairs of Lendit and ...[18] to wit, to Lendit. I agree and promise you, aforesaid brothers, through stipulation, that I shall bring back faithfully and in good faith to this land the entire said *comanda*, and the whole profit that I shall make with it, and the investments made with it. And [I promise] to reckon faithfully in your ...[19] the capital and profit the first time I return to this land from the aforesaid journey, said *comanda* going[20] and coming according to the fortune of God and according to the custom of the sea and land and of yours[?],[21] pledging for this all my goods, existing and future, waiving in this regard the period of grace of twenty days and four months and any other legal right by which I might act against [the conditions]. This was done here in Marseilles in the house of Peire of Saint Maximin ... notary public of Marseilles, who, by invitation of the parties, wrote this record.

94
From the Latin[22]

Bolzano, [July 21, 1237]

On the aforesaid day, in Bolzano, in the home of Federico, [husband] of Spezia, in the presence of Ulrico of Verona and of Werner, [both] mercers,[23] of Hermann, and of other witnesses. And there Federico, husband of Spezia of Bolzano, stood content and acknowledged that he had received from Gambarino, tailor of Trento, £ 100 Veronese as capital in a *societas* [to be kept] from the present to the next feast of Saint Martin [November 11] with half of the profit which he himself makes from it, in good faith, without fraud. This money the said Federico promised by stipulation of all his goods to give and to pay to the said Gambarino [some time] from the present up to the aforesaid time limit, and [also] the profit, [deducting] every loss and payments for salaries.[24]

---

[18] Blancard supplied the word *nomine*, but this word makes little sense.

[19] Blancard in the context supplied the word *posse*, 'power,' a possible but not unquestionable choice.

[20] Blancard supplied the word *cum*; obviously the proper word was *eunte*.

[21] Blancard writes *vestram*. Probably one should emendate into *gentium*, 'of peoples,' meaning at the risk of hostile peoples.

[22] H. von Voltelini, *Die südtiroler Notariats-Imbreviaturen des dreizehnten Jahrhunderts*, Part 1, pp. 305–6.

[23] *Chramarii:* the German 'Krämer.'   [24] *Stipendio* here means 'salary' rather than 'living expenses.'

Intermediate Forms of Partnership

95

From the Latin[25]

[Marseilles, May 8, 1248]

The same day and place. Bonenfant, son of the late Jacob, and Bonseigneur, son of Astruc, and Bonafous, son of the late Chaim, wishing to go on a voyage to Valencia in the vessel of Bertram Belpel, which is named 'Leopard,' have formed a *societas* among themselves in the manner written below, to wit, that the profits of all *comandae* made by the three of them or by one of them, no matter how many the *comandae* are, are to be common to them in equal shares in the aforesaid voyage; and all investments of the said *comandae* made by them or by one of them, and the investments of those amounts of money which any one of them shall carry in the aforesaid voyage, are to be common to them: with this reservation, that whoever of them shall have extra money of his own in the said *companhia* is to receive that extra [share] of the profits, according as it is coming to him, by the solidus and by the pound. And all the aforesaid [men] have promised, by stipulation, each of them to the others, to be faithful and law-abiding one to the other, and to tell each other the truth, and to keep faith throughout the voyage mentioned above, pledging to each other, etc., waiving, etc. And for greater security they all swore on the Mosaic Law, touched by them physically with the hand, to undertake and to fulfill all the aforesaid. Witnesses: R. Boneti, Jehan Gauselin, G. Peire Salvi.

96

From the Latin[26]

[Marseilles, May 22, 1248]

The same day and place. I, Bernard Sanvitour, son of Peire Sanvitour, by authorization of my aforesaid father who is present, willing and acknowledging [it], acknowledge to you, Guillem Sansier, and recognize that I have had and have received in *companhia* from you £ 125 *meslée* money[27] now current in Marseilles, waiving, etc., in which *companhia* I am to add of my own [money] £50 of the said currency. And I am to invest said *companhia* in a changer's bank[28] and to undertake risks with it with your advice from the

---

[25] Blancard, *Documents inédits*, II, 153–54.   [26] *Ibid.*, II, 182–83.

[27] *Meslée* means miscellaneous or mingled; the term frequently occurs in French numismatics.

[28] *Tabula cambii*, the desk or bench of a changer-banker. In this instance it was a movable bench and not a permanent shop, as is shown by the document itself.

next Feast of Pentecost for two continuous and complete years. And I am
to have one half of the profit which God may allow me to make with said
companhia and in addition to said half of the profit s.50 for each of the aforesaid years; and you are to have the other half of the profit. This *companhia* I
promise you, through stipulation, to hold and to guard well and faithfully,
and to trade and do business with it as best I can and know how. And [I
promise] to give and to pay to you at the end of said two years the said £ 125
with half of the profit, as has been stated, and to come with you to an accurate
accounting whenever it shall please you, and to tell you the truth about it
and to be honest in everything, and every evening to carry to your home
the said *companhia;* obligating, etc.; waiving, etc. For this, I, said Peire
Sanvitour, father of said Bernard, constitute and obligate myself debtor and
payer to you, said Guillem Sansier, of everything that is to be undertaken
and completed for you by my said son, under pledge of all my goods, existing
and future, waiving, etc. Witnesses: Giraud Civate, Mercadier of Gironde,
Jacob of Puy, Guillem Cougourle.

97
From the Latin[29]

Genoa, January 19, 1308

In the name of the Lord, amen. Percivalle Grillo, son of Andreolo;
Daniele Grillo; Meliano Grillo; Benedetto Contardo and Nicola Contardo,
brothers, sons of the late Luchetto Contardo; Manuele Bonifacio; Antonino
Grillo, son of Andreolo, acknowledge to each other that they have formed
and made a *societas* for the purpose of maintaining a bank[30] in the city of
Genoa and of engaging in commerce and business in Genoa and throughout
other [and] different parts of the world, according to what shall seem [proper]
and shall be the pleasure of the partners themselves, to continue, God willing,
for the next two succeeding years. This *societas* they acknowledge to be of
£ 9,450 Genoese, in which sum they acknowledge to each other that each of
them has or has deposited as below, viz.: said Percivalle, £ 3,500; said
Daniele, £ 2,000; said Meliano, £ 1,000; the aforesaid Benedetto Contardo
and Nicola, his brother, £ 2,000; said Manuele Bonifacio, £ 450; and said
Antonio Grillo, £ 500. This capital they acknowledge to be in the hands of
said Percivalle in money, in credits,[31] in exchange to be received in France,
and in a vein of iron in Elba. And the aforesaid partners have waived the

---

[29] R. Doehaerd, *Les Relations commerciales entre Gênes, la Belgique et l'Outremont d'après les
archives notariales génoises aux XIIIe et XIVe siècles*, III, 966–68.

[30] *Super bancho tenendo.*   [31] *In debitoribus,* literally 'in debtors.'

exception and legal right by which they could speak against or oppose the aforesaid. And said Percivalle is to use this money in business and commerce in Genoa in said bank which he maintains, in the buying and selling of wares, and in exchange both in France and throughout other [and] different parts of the world, by sea and by land, personally and through his factors and messengers, according as God may dispose better for him, up to the time limit mentioned above, at the risk and fortune of the [partners]. And he has promised said partners of his to act in good faith [and] efficiently for the increase and preservation of said *societas*. And the aforesaid partners promised each other to guard and to preserve the goods and wares and money which may come into the hands of any one of them from the aforesaid *societas*, and not to defraud one another in anything. The profit which God may grant in the aforesaid *societas* shall be allocated to each of them pro rata to his capital; and if any accident befall said *societas* or the goods of said *societas*— may God be our help—it shall be allocated similarly to each of them pro rata to his capital. And they have promised each other in good faith to come to the accounting of the capital and profit of said *societas* at the end of the time limit; and each of them is to deduct his capital and to divide among them the profit pro rata to the capital of each one. The aforesaid *societas* and each and all of the above [conditions] the aforesaid partners promised each other, etc. Firm, etc., and for it, etc. And said Benedetto acknowledges that he is more than twenty-four years old, and said Nicola acknowledges that he is more than nineteen years old, and said Antonio acknowledges that he is more than nineteen years old. And they swore by the sacred Gospels of God, putting their hands on the Scriptures, to undertake and to observe [everything] as above stated and not to do anything or to act contrary in any way by reason of their being minors[32] or by any other cause. And they made the aforesaid [agreement] with the counsel of the witnesses written below, whom for this [purpose] they call their relatives, neighbors, and counselors. Done in Genoa in the Church of Santa Maria delle Vigne, in the year of the Nativity of the Lord 1308, fifth indiction, January 19, about nones. Witnesses: Arnaldo of Spigno, dealer in poultry; Manfredo; and Pagano of Moneglia, dealer in poultry.

98

From the Latin[33]

Venice, August, 1179

In the name of our Lord Jesus Christ. In the year of the Lord 1179, in the

---

[32] *Racione minoris.* Probably the notary forgot to write *aetatis.*

[33] A. Sacerdoti, 'Le colleganze nella pratica degli affari e nella legislazione veneta,' *Atti del Reale*

month of August, twelfth indiction, in Rialto, I, Domenico Sisinulo of the section of Santa Giustina, together with my heirs,[34] openly declare to you, Vitale Voltani, my nephew, resident of the section of Santa Maria Zobenigo, and to your heirs, that we both at one time in the past have established and formed a *compagnia* [for business] in the Byzantine Empire, in which we invested, each of us, according to our recollection, either £ 7 gold in hyperpers or 500 gold hyperpers; and if we had more capital, we were to invest it safely on land in the same *compagnia* and to set it to work to the common advantage of this *compagnia*. We were to draw [profit] from it, however, at the rate of one hyperper in each pound every month. I, then, was to remain in Constantinople and you in Thebes; I was to send and to remit that capital from Constantinople to Thebes overland and through those gulfs and passages,[35] and you, similarly, to me from Thebes to Constantinople. We also were to have the power to give and to send [money and goods] from that capital overland and wherever it might seem good to us; and we were to have the power to draw on the capital of the other in the name of and for the profit and risk of the *compagnia* in such a way that in regard to that debt we both were to be equal debtors in paying and discharging it. And this *compagnia* was to be between us from that time for one year and from then on as long as our wills are in full agreement. Wherefore, I, together with my heirs, solemnly promise you and your heirs that I shall render you an accurate and true accounting of the capital which was sent me in the Byzantine Empire in regard to the aforesaid *compagnia* or of whatever I gave of it to anybody or whatever of it remained with me through any way or device. Whenever you request me [for an accounting], you personally or through your messenger, then, within one month from that time I am to pay you in full, without any fraud, all that I have of it at that time. If, therefore, after you have made the request to me, personally or through your messenger, at any time from then on up to a month, I do not do so and do not observe [these conditions], then I, together with my heirs, am to compensate you and your heirs with 200 silver marks from whatever tangible assets I have in this world, this record of declaration remaining in force. . . .[36]

I, Domenico Sisinulo, signed by my own hand.

Istituto Veneto di Scienze, Lettere ed Arti, LIX (1899–1900), 33–35. Reprinted in Morozzo della Rocca and Lombardo, *Documenti del commercio veneziano*, I, 304–5.

[34] Obviously this does not mean that Sisinulo's heirs are personally making the promise, but only that Sisinulo's word is binding on his heirs.

[35] That is, by sea.

[36] We omit a few involved sentences at the end of the document, whereby Sisinulo promises not to make any claims in advance of the final settlement.

I, Enrico Scarto, witness, signed.

I, Pietro Bobizzo, witness, signed.

I, Giuliano Damiano, deacon and notary, completed and certified [this instrument].

99

From the Latin[37]

Genoa, September 7, 1253

In the name of the Lord, amen. Orlando Paglia; Giovanni Puliti; Ranieri of Verona; Giacomo Migliorati; Consolino, son of the late Konrad, German; and Friedrich, German, acknowledge that they have jointly made among themselves a *societas* to last forever for the purpose of buying mines, furnaces, or veins for the production of silver in Sardinia or wherever God may guide them more [wisely]. In this *societas* said Orlando invested £ 100 Genoese; Giovanni Puliti, £ 50; Ranieri of Verona, £ 25; Giacomo Migliorati, £ 25; waiving the exception that the money has not been had or received in cash. According to [the conditions of] this *societas* all are to go to Sardinia or wherever God may guide them more [wisely] to do said work, except Orlando, who is not himself going at present but may go whenever he likes and [may send] whatever messenger he wishes. And they are to share the expenses of said *societas* in food and drink and chartering of boats and renting of houses, both in sickness and in health, while engaged in said work; and they are to buy with [the capital of] said *societas* the equipment needed to do that work. And Consolino and Friedrich are to be in said *societas* with the above-mentioned [investors] and to labor in good faith and without fraud, and to preserve and to protect said *societas*, and to give aid and counsel for the increase of said *societas*. They promise one another to make an accounting of the profit which God may grant to said *societas* every fourth month. And said Consolino and Friedrich are to have for their labor the sixth share of the profit which God may grant in that *societas*. And of the rest, [after deduction] of said sixth share, Orlando is to have a third share, Giovanni Puliti a third share, Ranieri and Giacomo another third share. And

---

[37] R. S. Lopez, 'Contributo alla storia delle miniere argentifere di Sardegna,' *Studi Economico-Giuridici dell'Università di Cagliari*, XXIV (1936), 7–8. This contract has many peculiar features. Its duration is said to be unlimited, *duraturam in perpetuum*. Two of the partners are apparently German (*Toeschi*) expert miners, who contribute no capital but only their skill; on the leadership of Germans in the medieval metallurgy, see *Cambridge Economic History*, Vol. II, Chap. VII and Bibliography, pp. 561ff. One partner contributes capital but is not obligated to contribute any labor; he is Orlando Paglia, a wealthy merchant from Lucca, whose activities in the exchange business are well known through other contracts. Giacomo Migliorati, a dealer in metals from Viterbo, and the other partners contribute both capital and labor.

Consolino and Friedrich promised to the aforesaid not to forsake that
societas in any way nor to leave it unless for the purpose of going to Tuscany.
And if they, or one of them, should leave for said cause, they promised to
return to said *societas* within two or three months from the day they left.
They all swore, placing their hands on the sacred and holy Gospels of God,
to undertake, to complete, and to observe each and all [of the aforesaid
conditions] and not to violate [them] in any [way] under penalty of £ 100
Genoese, the pact remaining as settled among them [as] mutually stipulated
and solemnly promised and under pledge of their goods, [the penalty] being
given by the one who does not observe to those who do observe [it]. And
we may be sued, wherever any of us and any of our goods [may be], waiving
the privilege of [choosing] the tribunal. Done in Genoa in the house where
said Orlando lives. Witnesses: Giacomo of Parma, son of the late Marino,
and Obertino of Reggio [Emilia]. 1253, tenth indiction, on the seventh day
of September, between terce and nones.

Only one [instrument] was made.[38]

100

From the Latin[39]

Lucca, June 4, 1259

Castracane, changer, [son] of the late Ruggero, and Genovese, [son] of the
late Perfettuccio, likewise a changer, and [both] merchants, are together in
agreement to form a *societas* and *compagnia* in the craft (*arte*) of exchange
and such operations as belong to exchange, and in other [activities]. Castracane invested and has £ 700 Lucchese in this *societas* and *compagnia;* the
aforesaid Genovese invested and has £ 500 Lucchese, and thus they agreed
in the [initial] statement of their accounts,[40] and said that it was true, waiving,
etc. And with this [fund] they are to engage in exchange and to earn profits,
[acting] in good faith, without fraud, for the business and advantage of
themselves and of said *compagnia*. And this *societas* or *compagnia* is to last
from the present time one [entire] year or as much more or less as they shall

[38] This is an annotation of the notary, meaning that only one copy of the document was
drafted for the parties.

[39] R. S. Lopez, 'The Unexplored Wealth of the Notarial Archives in Pisa and Lucca,' in
Mélanges d'histoire du moyen âge dédiés à la mémoire de Louis Halphen, p. 428. We have translated both the contract of partnership and the later annotation of the notary, stating that the
partnership had been terminated. Castracane, changer, who is mentioned in the document, was an
ancestor of Castruccio Castracani degli Antelminelli, the lord of Lucca in the early fourteenth
century and the hero of a biography by Niccolò Machiavelli.

[40] 'Accounts' here translates the words *in conto*; elsewhere in this document it translates the
word *ratio* (Italian *ragione*).

be in agreement. And neither of them in regard to the property[41] of said *societas* or in regard to property which may come into their hands by reason of said *societas* is to do or take part in any theft or robbery or in any withdrawal to the damage of the *societas*, [acting] without fraud or evil device. And of the entire benefit or gain that God may grant therefrom, each of them is to have his share or part which should come to him in proportion to his capital which he had there at that accounting. After having made and settled accounts between them, should they want to separate, either of them ought to have and is to have back his capital without any litigation or quarrel [begun] by any one of them, and also the profit as has been stated. And they have promised and agreed and sworn on the holy Gospels of God so to undertake, to do, and to observe, and not to go against the aforesaid or any of the aforesaid [agreements], obligating themselves and their heirs and all their goods, existing and future, by the law of pledge and mortgage, to the [penalty] of the double and of £ 100 Lucchese, with the stipulation advanced above, and to [the judgment] of the consuls *treguani* and of the podestà of Lucca, present and future, and of the *constitutum* of the gates.[42] Done in Lucca near the house of the Sottotinte in the presence of Guglielmino, [son] of the late Neri di Moiana, and of Bonsignore, [son] of the late Paolo, 1259, the day before the Nones of June, second indiction.

[I], Ciabatto, judge and notary, undersigned here.

February 7, 1260[?]

I have cancelled [this] on verbal instructions given me by the aforesaid Castracane and Genovese, the seventh [day] before the Ides of February, third indiction, in the storehouse which they rent, because they said that they had made an accounting.

The 'Compagnia' Contract in Tuscany

101

From the Italian[43]

Avignon, October 25, 1367

In the name of God, amen. Be it known to all who will read or hear this document read to them that we, Toro di Berto of Florence, party of the

---

[41] *Avere.* This means both 'credits' (as in books of accounting) and 'property' in general.

[42] This sentence may sound almost incomprehensible because it is a condensation of many legal formulae mentioning all sorts of laws and legal authorities concerned with contracts.

[43] E. Bensa, *Francesco di Marco da Prato*, pp. 285–94. Note that this document and Document 102 are not notarial but holograph; see Chapter XIII.

first part, and Francesco di Marco of Prato, party of the second part, [being] the two already named, agree with sincere and well-meaning heart to form together a *compagnia* in Avignon, this day, Monday, the twenty-fifth of October, the year 1367, according to the pacts, covenants, and regulations which we shall hereinafter mention, that is to say, that shall be written by our hands. These pacts, covenants, and regulations one promises to the other to observe and to maintain in good faith and not to violate them nor to do anything at all which might be contrary to said pacts, covenants, and regulations that shall be hereinafter written. Each of the parties promises the other to observe and to maintain these for the next coming three years, which they have ordered and willed that said *compagnia* should last, and longer if they agree about it together.

First of all, the said partners agree that Toro di Berto di Tieri, as party of the first part, is to invest and to keep steadily [invested] in said *compagnia* 2,500 gold florins. This money he invests in merchandise and [office] equipment, and [ready] cash he has of his own in Avignon, as can be seen in a [record] book written by hand of said Toro; and they agree that said Toro is to give his personal services to said *compagnia* without asking for any salary from the *compagnia*.

And Francesco di Marco, mentioned above, party of the second part, is to invest in said *compagnia* and keep steadily [invested] 2,500 gold florins. This money he invests in merchandise, [office] equipment, and [ready] cash he has of his own in Avignon, as can be seen in a [record] book written by hand of said Francesco; and they agree that Francesco is to give his personal services to said *compagnia* without asking for any salary from the *compagnia*.

And these moneys, which total 5,000 gold florins, the said partners agree to employ in commercial operations in said *compagnia*, primarily in three shops[44] that they have this twenty-fifth day of October in Avignon, these shops being those hereinafter described. And further, said partners are to trade and to do business in Florence or in all other parts and localities where they may be of the opinion or may think that it is good and advantageous for the company, according as they will in the future come to mutual agreement. Neither of them, however, is allowed to engage in any trade without consent of the other partner.

And they agree, and it is their will, and thus one promises the other, not to engage without each other's consent in any trade outside of the localities they shall mention and about which they shall come to mutual agreement. And should one of them do this, it is their will, and so they agree, that any profit

---

[44] Here and henceforth the word 'shop' translates the Italian *bottega*.

made from it shall be to the advantage of the *compagnia* just as in the other [transactions]; and in the case loss and unrealized profits[45] should result, the said loss and unrealized profits incurred through this [unilateral venture] must be paid by that partner who has undertaken that trade without consent and approval of the other partner.

Further, the said partners agree that every year they are to go over their accounts[46] according to directions that they will give; that is to say, [accounts] in any place where they shall transact [business] and [concerning] the profit and loss which God may give them—from any resulting loss may He ever protect us, amen. The said partners agree that every profit or loss found wherever they may do business—that is, in Avignon, in Florence, and in all other parts and localities wherever they may do business—must be divided by half; that is, to said Toro the one half, the other half to said Francesco.

And the said partners further agree that in case it should happen or might happen that either of the said parties should have or might have additional money in the *sopra corpo* of the said *compagnia*,[47] the money which each party has in addition [to the common capital], this money is to be remunerated yearly at 8 gold florins in the hundred, to wit, from the general profit that is shown at the closing of accounts at the year's end. And in case it should happen—may God ever protect us from it—that a loss should be found, they agree, and it is their will, that said money which either of the partners has in the *sopra corpo* of the *compagnia* should be remunerated at the rate stated above from what each has in common capital of the *compagnia*. It is understood that the partner who has [money] in the *sopra corpo* of the *compagnia* [is to be paid] one half [of this remuneration] by the other partner out of the share of the latter in the common capital of the *compagnia*, to wit, [at the rate of] 4 gold florins in the hundred. At the beginning of the *compagnia* no one is allowed to make withdrawals from whatever he may have in the *sopra corpo* except at the year's end when their accounts have been closed. And it is to be understood [that this is to be done provided they have been closed] with a profit for their *compagnia*.

Further, the said partners agree and it is their will, that neither of them should do or cause to be done any business outside the *compagnia*, but it is to be understood that they are to be partners in everything the said partners

---

[45] *Interesse.*

[46] Here and henceforth the word 'account' translates the Italian *ragione, ragionamenti.*

[47] The *corpo* (literally, 'the body') is the common capital contributed by the partners in forming the *compagnia*. The *sopra corpo* (literally, 'over the body') constitutes capital invested by partners or by others to be used in the business over and above common capital. We translate *corpo* by 'capital,' but we leave *sopra corpo* untranslated because there is no exact English equivalent.

shall trade or cause to be traded. And they agree, and it is their will, that if either of them should do or cause to be done any business transaction secretly and without consent of the other partner, the profit made by the one so acting, this profit in question must be divided in half for the *compagnia*, and the one half must be given to the other partner who did not hear anything about it just as if they both had been partners in that transaction. And even though none of [the other partner's] own money should be [employed] in it, they agree that it should be so done because the said partners have agreed not to engage in any trade outside the *compagnia*. [There is this] exception, that if either of them should have money [to spare], he would be permitted to give it to a friend to employ in trade, provided that he personally does not take part in that trade; and this should be left to his conscience [to decide].

Further, the said partners agree, and it is their will, to observe [the following]: That a shop with house above—this shop and house being Toro's own place—that this place is to be used in the [business of] the said *compagnia* without his demanding any [extra] compensation. And the said partners agree that if they dissolve the *compagnia* and wish no longer to be partners after its expiration, it is their will, and they so agree, that the said shop and house is to remain Toro's free and unencumbered place. Just as free [from restrictions] as it was when he placed it at the disposal of the *compagnia*, so it is to remain free [when the *compagnia* is dissolved]. And it is the will of the said partners that the rent paid for said shop and house above, which is 37 florins a year, should be paid by said partners out of the money of the *compagnia* for the time that said *compagnia* shall make use of them. Further, said Toro has [another] shop with a house above, and this shop is to remain with said *compagnia* under the same pacts and covenants as written above concerning the other shop and house named. And for it 35 florins are paid for rent every year to the chapter of Saint Peter. [The shop] is the one on the road lying to the side of the gate of Carcassonne and of the lodge of the Knights. The other is in front of the aforesaid and to the side of the gate which belonged to the Cardinal of U. . . .[48]

Further, said partners agree, and it is their will, to observe [the following]: That a shop with house above—this shop and house being Francesco's own place—is to be used in [the business of] said *compagnia* without his demanding any [extra] compensation. And the said partners agree that if they dissolve the *compagnia* and wish no longer to be partners after its expiration, it is their will, and they so agree, that the said shop and house is to remain Francesco's free and unencumbered place. Just as free [from restrictions] as

[48] Here and henceforth the dots are Bensa's.

it was when he placed it at the disposal of the *compagnia*, so it is to remain free [when the *compagnia* is dissolved]. And it is the will of the said partners that the rent paid for said shop and house above, which is 30 florins a year should be paid by the said partners out of the money of the *compagnia* for the time that said *compagnia* shall make use of them. . . . The said shop with house above is situated where once was the lodge of the Knights, from the two sides up to the street.

Further, said partners agree that the salaries of their apprentices and servants, retained to conduct their business in Avignon, Florence, and in all other places where they employ them, are to be paid by the *compagnia*. Further, the said partners agree that expenses for eating and drinking which they and their factors and servants may incur in Avignon are to be paid by the *compagnia*. Also they agree that all expenses which said partners, factors, and servants may incur for eating and drinking, when going and returning on trips on the business of their *compagnia*, are to be paid by the *compagnia*. Further, they agree that none of the expenses incurred by the said partner for themselves, for their houses, and for their families in Florence or Prato, is to be paid by the *compagnia*, but it is to be paid by each out of his own money. And further, the said partners agree that if they have to do [business] in any place outside Florence or Prato, the expenses incurred by the partners or factors for eating, drinking, or rental of houses, or of *fondachi*, are to be paid by the *compagnia;* but the expenses which any of the partners or factors may incur for himself are to be paid out of his own money.

Further, the said partners agree that in case they have need to maintain a *fondaco* in Florence to conduct the business of the *compagnia*, the rent is to be paid out of the money of the *compagnia* and likewise the salary of apprentices whenever they may be needed. [This], however, [is to be done] under this [condition], that neither of the partners may act without the consent of the other partner, because they are under obligation not to undertake any enterprise unless they agree about it beforehand.

Further, the said partners agree that each of them is to be allowed to go to Florence and to return to Avignon at the expenses of the *compagnia*, going with the approval of the other partner, and this is understood to be once a year according to the convenience of the *compagnia* and their own agreement.

Further, the said partners agree that whenever one of them has been in Avignon for one year and the other has been in Florence for one year, the one who has been in Florence for one year is to come to Avignon and to remain one year, and that the one who has been in Avignon is to be allowed

to go to Florence or to Prato at the expense of the *compagnia* and likewise
to return to Avignon after the year is ended, as is stated above.

Further, the said partners agree that if either of them stays in Florence
longer than one year through need of his own affairs and through the need
of the company, for this [extra] time he must pay to the one who has been
one year in Avignon 50 gold florins for the extra year. And this [payment]
should be understood as an addition[49] to the benefit of the common profit
or loss which happens to be made in that year. And it is understood that the
one who was in Florence is to come to Avignon at the deadline mentioned,
unless he has a legitimate excuse.

Further, the said partners agree that neither of them is to be allowed to
extend credit to any of his friends or to noblemen; and if he does so and [the
money] is not recovered, then when they come to dissolve the *compagnia*
the partner who has extended [the credit] is to make good the loss to the
compagnia out of his own money. But it is the will of the said partners that
each of them may extend credit to merchants who are or may be customers[50]
or to artisans who may do [business] with them to the amount that seems
[proper] to them, depending on how reliable and good the individuals are.
And this one [partner] to the other and the other to the one promises to observe and maintain in good faith and in accordance with his good conscience.

And it is the will of the said partners that if any factor or apprentice whom
they may employ extends or shall extend any credit without their permission
and fails to collect that credit within the year, the one who has extended the
credit is to pay out of his own money and that debt in question is to remain
for him [to collect]; and it is understood that this shall be done when they
balance their books.

And also it is the will of the said partners that should they both be at . . .[51]
in Avignon, neither of them is to be allowed to make any purchase of merchandise at wholesale without knowledge and consent of the other partner,
or to extend credit without consent of the other partner, with this exception,
that each is to be free to do whatever is useful to the *compagnia* [in extending
credit] to merchants who may be customers.

And it is the will of the said partners that each of them may and has the
right to withdraw [money] each year from the *compagnia* in order to meet
his own expenses up to the sum of 100 gold florins, withdrawing [the money]
month by month as he has need. And the said partners agree that the capital

[49] Bensa has: *in aggiunta* (?); we think his conjecture is satisfactory.
[50] *Mercatanti usati ovvero usevoli*, literally 'used or useful merchants.'
[51] *A . . . ora*. Probably one ought to read *a dimora*, 'in residence.'

that they have invested in the said *compagnia* is not to be diminished at all within three years, but it is their will that in case it should happen that any one of said partners has any money in the *sopra corpo* of the *compagnia* and he has need to withdraw it, it is his right to withdraw it at any time he has need, giving to the other partner a period of time so he can obtain that [money] from merchandise that they have.

And also they agree that once they have settled their yearly accounts whatever profit is coming to each out of the proceeds [of their transactions], deduction having been made of expenses they have incurred of their own, each party may be permitted to withdraw from the *compagnia* whatever profit [they say] is coming to him in the manner mentioned above.

And in case any one of the said partners does not wish to withdraw [his share of profit], let it be invested for him in the *sopra corpo* of the *compagnia* and rewarded at 8 florins in the hundred as any [other investments] which they may have in the *sopra corpo* of the *compagnia;* and this money in question is to be [invested] in the *compagnia* in cash. And should he at any time wish to draw it for his needs, he is to be allowed to draw it in cash as if he had invested it in cash, being [for that purpose] a partner in the same way as if they were carrying out a division to dissolve the *compagnia*.[52] The said partners understand that when they dissolve the *compagnia*, whatever is owed them from the *sopra corpo* of the *compagnia* or from accrued profits [is to be paid out as follows]: each one who has [invested] in the *sopra corpo* is to receive cash; and let this be carried out before any accounting is made of merchandise they may have.

And said partners agree that when three years have passed, if they wish to part from one another, each should have the right to get back the [proceeds of] the division. But it is their will, and they so decide in order to be able to carry out a more orderly dissolution, that the one who wishes to part is to tell the other six months in advance, so that they may carry it out in good order and without damage.

And the said partners agree, and it is their will, that all the merchandise they happen to have in those localities where they may transact [business] are to be estimated in their behalf according as they may be worth in those localities where they are. And in case that said partners or their attorneys are not in agreement about it, it is their will that two mutual friends ascertain what they may be worth; and whatever the latter shall say, it is their will to accept it and not to go against it.

[52] This means that in regard to the drawing of profits left in *sopra corpo* the same rules are to be followed as in the division of the *compagnia*.

And once this is done, the said partners agree to settle their accounts as they are accustomed to do according to the pacts written below. And it is their will that anything that is owed to either of them from the *sopra corpo* of the *compagnia* and from accrued profits is to be paid in cash after they have settled the accounts. And if they happen not to have cash at that point, let as much merchandise then in their possession be sold as will pay what either one of them should receive through the *sopra corpo* of the *compagnia* and through accrued profits.

And once they have so carried this out, it is their will that whatever merchandise is then in their possession be divided in such a way that each is to have one half; and let it be understood that one party is to have just as much as the other. And if the said partners do not agree about it, it is their will that these objects of merchandise in their possession be divided and made [into] equivalent [lots] by two mutual friends who are to make peace between them.

And the said partners agree that the [office] equipment, that is, boxes and vats and smaller boxes and hardware, which was in the two shops and houses of Toro at the beginning of the *compagnia,* is to remain Toro's for such amount as will be estimated and evaluated in the book which they will make for the [final] accounting;[53] and similarly it should be done with whatever shall be found in the shop and house of Francesco, which is to remain his in the shop for the said price, unless it has been sold with their consent. And if they have bought anew other things, let them be divided by half as were the other things.

Of any other furniture—bedstead, stable, and kitchen or other kinds of furniture they may have ordered, which cannot all be mentioned specifically —it is the will of said partners that each should have one half, each object being made [into] equivalent [lots] either by them or by friends who may undertake to do it; and each promises to be satisfied with what said friends shall do.

Once they have carried out these things, each party is to receive just as much as he gave, and it is their will that each regain his [former] status, so that from that very moment each may be allowed freely to transact his own business.

And in regard to all those who may be indebted to them, to the amounts listed in their books, the said partners have agreed [as follows]: that when they come to a dissolution, these debtors in question, who are indebted to

---

[53] Special accounts of *masserizie* (furniture and fixtures) were kept by the *compagnia* even before the adoption of the double-entry bookkeeping. See an excerpt from the account *masserizie del fondaco* of the Del Bene *compagnia* (1318) in A. Sapori, *Una compagnia di Calimala a primi del Trecento,* pp. 353ff.

them, are to be assigned one half to each partner; and that [the debts] are to be collected in common, and what is obtained from them should be put in a common place according to what they shall order, and each month each is to take one half as his share.

And in regard to all those who may have credits from the *compagnia*, to the amounts listed in their books, the said partners agree [as follows]: that when they come to a dissolution, these creditors in question, who have credits from the *compagnia*, are to be paid out of the money of the *compagnia* before the partners draw up any of their accounts. And should the case arise that because of oversight any one [still] has credits in the *compagnia*, each partner, every account of theirs being settled, is to be held to pay one half. And likewise let it be understood that if any one is [still] indebted to the *compagnia*, the division should be by the half.

And let it be understood by the said partners that these 5,000 gold florins they have invested in the capital of the *compagnia* are to be florins of 24 solidi Provençal each, reckoning the florins of the Camera at . . . solidi,[54] as this was their value on the twenty-fifth day of October, when said *compagnia* began. And the said partners intend to reckon this money according to this [rate] in their accountings which they will make from year to year, so that when they come to a dissolution, each of the partners who may have credits through any account is to be understood to be paid in said money on the day in which they dissolve the *compagnia*.

We, Toro di Berto and Francesco di Marco, mentioned above, are forming the said *compagnia*, and thus each of us promises to hold [together] firmly the said *compagnia*, as is stated above, for the next three years which are to come. And from now on may God grant us grace to maintain the *compagnia* together for a long time with profit of soul and body, and with growth of personal status and goods. And each of us so promises and swears on his good faith that he is to maintain and observe the pacts and covenants aforesaid, and that neither is to go against them; and may it so please God to grant the grace to each that he may observe and maintain his promise, amen. And if either of said partners should break up the *compagnia* before the three years, it is their will that there be a penalty for the one who should break it. And this shall be determined by two mutual friends, who are to supply a third [arbiter] for it.[55]

---

[54] Blank space in the original. *Fiorini della Camera* are Papal florins, but here the partners are not using them as real coins but as a money of account pegged to the Provençal silver shilling at the rate of the day when the *compagnia* is formed.

[55] *E che vi debbiano dare il terzo.* This seems to mean that the 'two friends' must supply a third arbiter, if there is disagreement among them, so that a majority rule may be obtained.

And further, it is the will of the said partners that if it should happen, or shall happen at some future time, that it seems well to them to convert into two shops the three shops they now have in Avignon, and they are in agreement about it, this should be done. Furthermore, it is their will that if it should seem well to them to convert the shops even into a single shop, and they are in agreement about it, this should be done. But it is their will that if they, being in agreement together about it, should convert said three shops into one, when they come to the dissolution of the *compagnia*, all [office] equipment they find in their possession in Avignon is to be divided by half and into two equivalent parts. [The division shall be made] by them if they are in agreement about it or by two mutual friends who shall make the division, whichever seems more reasonable to each of the said partners, so that neither partner may disturb the other. And they are to put aside from this [office] equipment [all] vats and hangers which may be at that time in the shop, in such a way, indeed, that that partner with whom the shop remains at that time is to have the [vats and hangers] at the value at which they will be estimated at that time in this division.

And the said Toro di Berto promises to said Francesco that in case any person should make trouble for the *compagnia* in regard to anything that said Toro has had to do in the time past [before the *compagnia* began] with other partners or persons, he is to free Francesco from any loss and any unrealized profit which may have resulted or could result for him on account of it. And likewise said Francesco promises to said Toro to free him without loss, if any trouble were made for the *compagnia* in regard to anything he has had to do with anybody in the time past. If any other trouble should be made for the *compagnia* during the said three years that they are to be partners together, any expense and unrealized profit that should result on account of it, the *compagnia* is to pay it.

I, Toro di Berto, have read and seen this record of pacts of the *compagnia*, which concern Francesco of Prato and me, Toro di Berto; this record is copied in this secret book of ours, which is covered with red paper, in six pages before this and in this, that is, from c. II to c. V, in articles XXXV including this. These pacts and covenants which are written above by Francesco of Prato in his own hand, are written with my consent, and I so promise to observe and maintain them. And for clarity and firmness of this, I am undersigning it by my own hand. And further, I declare that I have in safekeeping an identical record in the hand of said Francesco and sealed with his great seal, as is said above, in the hand of said Francesco. These [identical] records each shall keep to the best of his ability for clear evidence of the *compagnia* which we have together, and therefore for clear evidence to which each [may appeal] we have copied it in this secret book of ours, which we call Red Book, in the hand of the said Francesco and undersigned in the hand of me, Toro.[56]

102
From the Italian[57]

Florence, July 25, 1455

In the name of God, on July 25, 1455, in Florence.

Be it known to all persons who shall see this contract, or hear it read, that on this aforesaid day, in the name of God and of good fortune, Piero and Giovanni, [sons] of Cosimo de' Medici, and Piero Francesco, [son] of Lorenzo de' Medici; Gierozzo, [son] of Jacopo de' Pigli; and Angiolo, [son] of Jacopo Tani, have set up together and formed a *compagnia* to deal in trade and exchange in the city of Bruges in Flanders as seems best to the said Angiolo, [son] of Jacopo Tani, who is to be [entrusted] with the management (*governo*) of the said *compagnia* to last four years—which, in the name of God, are to begin March 25, 1456, and to end March 24, 1459[58]—subject to the pacts, agreements, and conditions mentioned hereinafter.

And first of all, that the said *compagnia* during the aforesaid four years will be known under the title of 'Piero di Cosimo de' Medici e Gierozzo de' Pigli e Compagnia' and will have the following mark,[59] which will remain [the property] of said Piero, Giovanni, and Piero Francesco de' Medici at the said termination of the *compagnia*.

Said Piero de' Medici,[60] Pigli, and Angiolo Tani are to invest and to keep invested as capital (*chorpo*) in the said *compagnia* during the said period of four years £3,000 groat, Flemish currency—that is to say, said Piero, Giovanni, and Piero Francesco de' Medici are to invest £1,900 groat; Gierozzo de' Pigli, £600 groat; and Angiolo Tani, £500 groat, besides his personal [services]. And the latter is bound to conduct [business] and to stay in residence in Bruges and in the neighborhood [in order to attend] faithfully to all [business] that he shall see and understand to be to the honor, advantage, and welfare of said *compagnia* in accordance with good mercantile custom,

---

[56] A paragraph follows in which the two partners declare that on March 11, 1370, the *compagnia* has been renewed with new pacts and that the above pacts are abrogated.

[57] A. Grunzweig, ed., *Correspondance de la filiale de Bruges des Medici*, I, 55–63. Raymond de Roover has kindly collationed the printed text on the original document.

[58] Florentine style; that is, 1460.   [59] The mark of the *compagnia* is here drawn.

[60] The names of Giovanni and Piero Francesco de' Medici, who contributed part of the capital, have been omitted here, probably through an oversight.

and to all orders and instructions of said Medici and Pigli, engaging in legitimate trade [and in] licit and honest contracts and exchange [dealings]. And said sum of £ 3,000 groat, Flemish [currency], is to be invested by each of the said partners as allocated above immediately at the beginning of said *compagnia*. And from this moment it is agreed that the said Angiolo, manager (*ghovernatore*) of said *compagnia* for said time, is to be allowed to make use of the liquid assets that shall be found in possession of the *compagnia* which is now in operation and which is to end on the next March 24, 1455. And if it should happen that said partners or any one of them fails to supply the above-mentioned sum in the capital of the *compagnia*, then such partner or partners would be bound to indemnify the *compagnia* at the rate of 15 percent per annum until the full share has been paid in.

And they agree that the profits which God by His grace will grant are to be divided in the following manner: to Piero, Giovanni, and Piero Francesco de' Medici, 12 soldi in the pound; to Gierozzo de' Pigli, 4 soldi in the pound; and to Angiolo Tani 4 soldi in the pound. And should there be any losses—which God forbid—they must be divided in the same manner. It is understood that the distribution of profits must take place each time that it is so decided and requested by said Medici and Pigli; apart from that, the said partners or anyone of them are not allowed to withdraw any of the capital or profit during the said period of four years. And any one of them who violates [this provision] is bound and is to compensate the *compagnia* at the rate of 15 percent per annum with the reservation that Angiolo is to be allowed to draw £ 20 groat a year for his necessary expenses.

Further, said Angiolo is not to be allowed and must not lend goods or any merchandise in behalf of the said *compagnia*, nor may he lend money or deliver exchange to anyone who is not a merchant or an artisan. And [even] to such merchants and artisans he should lend with discretion, [limiting] the amount in accordance with their character and standing, always considering well to whom, on what terms, and how much. And further he is not to be allowed to sell exchange on credit on the Court of Rome or on any other place to lords temporal or spiritual, prelates, priests, clerics, or officials, without permission of said Medici or Pigli or of any one of them, such permission appearing in writing. And if he violates [the provision], let it be understood that any ensuing loss is to be charged to him and to his account, and besides a penalty of £ 25 groat to be paid to the said *compagnia* for each offense. And if there should be any profit, let it be understood that it will accrue to said *compagnia*, but that [Angiolo] will incur the said penalty nevertheless.

And further, said Angiolo is not to be allowed and must not assume liabilities for any merchant or other person of whatever status, nation, or standing in behalf of the said *compagnia;* nor may he send liquid assets to persons outside of the *compagnia* of said Medici without expressed permission of said Medici and Pigli or of any one of them, such permission appearing in writing. And the said Angiolo ought to communicate with them about this on the [same] day by letter or by a memorandum brought us by him. . . .[61]

Said Angiolo promises and obligates himself not to do business for himself or to have business done in his own name or in the name of others, directly or indirectly, in the city of Bruges nor in any other place, in any trade, commerce, exchange, or *compagnia* through any means under the penalty of £ 50 groat for each instance to be paid to the said *compagnia*. And besides [he will be liable] to hand over to the said *compagnia* any profits that he may make or have made out of it. And if there should be a loss, let it be understood to be his own in addition to the penalty.

Further, said Angiolo promises and obligates himself not to gamble or have [someone else] gamble in any game of *ʒara*[62] or cards, with dice or with anything else during the life of this said *compagnia,* under the penalty of £ 100 groat for each instance, to be paid to said *compagnia*. And besides [he will be liable] to hand over to the said *compagnia* any winnings, and any losses will be his in addition to the penalty of the said £100 groat. And besides this, let it be understood that he would lose his connection with the *compagnia* and be expelled from it. And let it be understood he will incur the same penalty and disgrace any time he keeps any woman at his quarters and at his expense.

Said Angiolo is to send every year on the twenty-fourth day of March to said Medici and Pigli in Florence the closed accounts and the balance sheet, as is customary. And also if they or any one of them should ask for these within the year, he is bound and must send them. And on termination of said *compagnia* he promises and obligates himself to come in person to Florence to render the accounts well, accurately, and faithfully, in case it should be necessary or if he should be asked by letter of said Medici and Pigli or of any one of them.

On termination of said *compagnia* the house and place of business (*fondacho*) where said Angiolo may have lived or is living is to remain the property of said Medici and Pigli, and also the books, letters, and all other written records, with the understanding that they must be shown and allowed to be

---

[61] There follows the usual formula that if Angiolo violates the provision, he suffers the loss while profits go to the *compagnia*.

[62] *Zara* was a game of chance played with three dice.

seen by said Angiolo any time he may require. Likewise all debtor balances that are still open at the termination of said *compagnia* are to be handed over to said Medici and Pigli and withdrawn from the said *compagnia* for their total amount, they [Medici and Pigli] remaining obligated to pay and to satisfy all those creditors.

Said Angiolo is not to be allowed and must not hire any assistant or factor for a salary or otherwise without the permission of said Medici and Pigli or of any one of them, such permission appearing in writing, with the understanding that assistants who should be or will be hired during that time[63] are not to be allowed to withdraw money for their needs beyond the amount of their salary, said Angiolo remaining obligated [for them] in this respect.

And even though the said *compagnia* is established to last four years, as it appears, they [the partners] agree that it may terminate and ought to terminate before the said time at the pleasure and discretion of said Medici and Pigli. And even if it lasts the said period of four years and any one of the aforesaid partners does not desire to continue it further, he must give notice six months before the end of said four years. And said Angiolo will be obligated to stay in person in Bruges, if need be, up to six months after the termination of the said *compagnia* in order to wind up and to liquidate the said *compagnia* at the expense of the latter but without any other salary or bonus.

And during the said period of the said *compagnia* said Angiolo may not and must not leave the territory of Flanders or travel around Flanders except for the needs and business of the said *compagnia* without permission of the same Medici and Pigli or of any one of them, the permission appearing in writing; there is the exception that he is to be allowed to go to the fairs of Antwerp and of Bergen-op-Zoom, to Middleburgh, Calais, and as far as London, if need be. And if he violates [this provision], let it be understood that he is to go and to return wholly at his own expense and risk; and let any harm and damage that his going or leaving brought or could bring to the *compagnia* be charged to him.

Said Angiolo is not to be allowed and must not buy wholesale for the said *compagnia* wool or cloth of the country [of Flanders] or of England [in amounts] in excess of £ 600 groat a year between the two, without permission of said Medici and Pigli or of any one of them, such permission appearing by letter in their own hand.

They also agree with said Angiolo that he insure or cause to be insured fully all wool, cloth, or other merchandise that may be shipped anywhere in behalf of the said *compagnia*, no matter in what ship it be loaded, with the

[63] *Partecipi* in the printed edition, but *per tempo* in the original.

exception that if he should ship by Florentine or Venetian galleys he may take a risk up to £ 60 groat in each galley and no more. And if he violates this [provision] and if a loss results from it, it will be his and the *compagnia* will not suffer. And in regard to what he may send by land it is left to his discretion to insure or not to insure according as seems advisable to him, without risking, however, more than the sum of £ 300 groat on any one trip, this, of course, in value of merchandise.

Further, they agree that said Angiolo is not to be allowed and must not underwrite any insurance by sea or land nor make any wager, nor may he pledge anything in any way, nor may he stand surety in behalf of the *compagnia,* himself or through others, under the penalty of £ 25 groat for each instance. And any resulting loss will be his own, and any profit is to be and must be for the said *compagnia*.

And they agree that whatever gift might be made to said Angiolo from any persons during [the life] of the said *compagnia* which might be worth £ 1 groat or more, this [gift] he must turn over to said *compagnia;* and if he does not do so, [the amount of the gift] is to be and must be charged to his own account: this applies to money as well as to anything else.

And said Angiolo promises not to obligate the said *compagnia* for his own actions, either in his own behalf or in that of any relative or friend of his, without permission of the said Medici and Pigli or any one of them, said permission appearing in writing. . . .[64]

Further, said Angiolo promises not to do anything that is against the laws and statutes of the country [Flanders] by reason of which he might incur penalties, danger, or loss. And should he do this, let it be understood that any damage, penalty, or loss which he might incur or which might be incurred is to be charged to his own account.

And when the said *compagnia* shall be terminated, said Angiolo is not to be allowed nor must he do or undertake any new business for the said *compagnia,* but he is to attend solely to the winding up and clearing of accounts in order to be able to close the balance, to pay whoever should have credits, to return the capital to all the said partners, and then [to distribute] the profits, if any, as allocated in this [contract]—may God grant us good fortune.

All the aforesaid provisions with said pacts, agreements, and covenants the aforesaid partners promise one to the other in turn to observe well and diligently in accordance with the good custom of merchants, pledging themselves and their heirs and goods, existing and future, both movable and real property, submitting to the jurisdiction of any court and ecclesiastical or

[64] There follows the usual formula; see footnote 61 above.

secular office, and especially to the Six of the Mercanzia of Florence; and the said Angiolo will also submit, in whatever part of the world [he may be, to the legal authorities], thus to the jurisdiction of the magistrates of Bruges just as to the courts of London, Venice, Genoa, or of any other town, castle, province, or kingdom in the world where he may be summoned [by the other partners]; waiving every privilege, laws, statutes, or franchise that might be adduced in his favor by him or by them.

For the clarification and in good faith of this, I, Angiolo, [son] of Jacopo Tani aforesaid, with the will and consent of all the partners mentioned above, have written with my own hand the present record, which shall be subscribed by the hand of the other mentioned parties, in Florence, this day, month, and year written above.[65]

[65] There follow the subscriptions of the partners. Notwithstanding what is stated in the last sentence, these signatures were affixed only on August 2.

CHAPTER XI

DEPOSITORS, FACTORS, AND COMMISSION AGENTS

To CONCLUDE the list of basic contracts in medieval Mediterranean trade we still have to consider the position of depositors, factors, and commission agents.

The contract of deposit, *depositum* (sometimes called *accomendatio* or, in Italian, *accomandigia*, but not to be confused with the *accomendatio* or *commenda* used in sea ventures), was a survival or a revival of the Roman *depositum irregulare*. A party deposited money or other movable goods, usually but not necessarily for a specified length of time, with a changer-banker, a *compagnia* of merchant bankers, or any other businessman. The depositary kept and used the goods, but the ownership and therefore the risks remained with the depositor. The latter, of course, was not liable to third parties except for the amount of the deposit. The obligation was extinguished when the deposit was returned with a premium, which usually was not called interest in order to avoid ecclesiastical censure.

Changers-bankers (*bancherii, campsores, nummularii, banchieri di scritta*) drew most of their financial resources from deposits. These could be made through regular contracts or by written transfer in their ledgers. By the beginning of the thirteenth century, if not earlier, bank ledgers were accepted as binding evidence in court. This explains why the number of deposit contracts which has come down to us is comparatively small; an entry in a ledger was enough.

Compagnia partnerships also usually accepted deposits *fuori corpo* or *sopra corpo,* that is, over and above the partnership's capital, from outsiders or from the partners of the *compagnia*. The latter could deposit their share of the profits or any sum which they might own in addition to their investment in the common capital.

Two examples seem sufficient to illustrate a contract which did not present many possibilities of deviation and modification. One is a banker's acknowledgment of a deposit (Document 103) and the other is an acknowledgment of premium paid by a *compagnia* of merchant bankers (Document 104). Interest in the first example is left to the discretion of the depositary, while in the second example it seems to have been fixed in advance at 8 percent.[1]

---

[1] On deposit banking, see the abundant Bibliography in R. de Roover, *Money, Banking and Credit in Mediaeval Bruges,* and A. P. Usher, *The Early History of Deposit Banking in Mediterranean Europe,* Vol. I; the former deals mainly with Flanders, the latter with Spain. For Italy there is no general work, but one may consult the Bibliography of A. Sapori, *Studi di storia economica medievale,* 2d ed., to which one may add, in English, the excellent article of R. L. Reynolds, 'A Business Affair in Genoa in the Year 1200,' in *Studi di storia e diritto in onore di Enrico Besta,* II, 165–81.

A merchant who could not personally attend to a business transaction appointed an agent. The most comprehensive term for agent is *nuncius* or *missus*, which we translate literally by messenger. A messenger might be a business associate—for instance, a partner in the *compagnia* of the merchant who had appointed him, or the other party in a *commenda* venture. He might be a relative or a friend entrusted with conducting a transaction in behalf of the merchant who supplied him with power of attorney (*procuratio*). He might be a man to whom the merchant had ceded a credit through a special contract whereby he was described as 'attorney for his own interest' (*procurator in rem suam*). Examples of this kind are found in a large number of our selections, but it does not seem indispensable to devote a special section to the innumerable forms of representation. We have to pay special attention, however, to two peculiar types of representatives, the factor and the commission agent.

A factor (Italian, *fattore* or *gignore*; Latin, usually, *negociorum gestor*) was an employee of a *compagnia* or of another long-term partnership who was entrusted with managing and conducting business of the *compagnia* in some specified place and for an indefinite number of transactions. The partners sometimes limited the amount of financial obligations he could incur in behalf of the partnership. They briefed the factor as to what branches of business he was to cultivate, and they sent him frequent and detailed instructions, but they usually left him some freedom of action. Usually the factor was not liable for the obligations of the partnership. He received a fixed salary but no share of the profits, and he was accountable to his employers for gross negligence and dishonesty. A successful factor might not only receive a raise in salary, but eventually he might be promoted to junior partnership. In the latter case, of course, he became jointly and unlimitedly liable for the debts of the *compagnia*.

Commenda ventures were not durable enough to warrant the appointment of factors, although sometimes the power of attorney was given to employees whose position closely resembled that of a factor. A relationship in many ways similar to that of partners and factors could be established, however, through the commission contract. A commission agent was entrusted with carrying abroad money or other movable goods to trade with them and to carry or to send back the proceeds much as was done in the ordinary *commenda*. Instead of a share in the profits, he received a fixed commission. The contract is seldom designated by a special name, although the term *rogadia*, from *rogare*, to pray, is found in the earliest extant Venetian documents. Sometimes it is loosely called *commenda*. Commission agents did not always travel with the goods in the outgoing voyage. Some of them took up their residence in foreign places and accepted orders from anyone who wished to avail himself of their services.

The relation between factors, commission agents, and their employers will be outlined more clearly in the business correspondence which is included in Part Five. Here we present an appointment of a factor (Document 105), two examples of

---

On deposits in the *compagnia* partnerships, besides the works of De Roover and Sapori, already cited, see the Bibliography in Y. Renouard, *Les Relations des papes d'Avignon et des compagnies commerciales et bancaires de 1316 à 1378*. For the problem of deposits by partners in *sopra corpo*, see F. de Roover, 'Francesco Sassetti and the Downfall of the Medici Banking House,' *Bulletin of the Business Historical Society*, XVII (1943), 65–80.

Our Document 63 and Chapters VII and X contain additional information.

commission (Documents 106 and 107), and an example of very broad powers of attorney (Document 108).[2]

Deposit Contracts

103

From the Latin[3]

[Genoa,] November 7, 1200

I, Oberto, banker, of Pollanexi, acknowledge that I have received from you, Maria, wife of Rolando Generificio, £ 50 Genoese in *accomendacio,* which belong to your husband, the aforesaid Rolando. I am to keep them in the bank and to employ [them] in trade in Genoa as long as it shall be your pleasure; and I promise to give you the profit according to what seems to me ought to come to you. Moreover, I promise to return and to restore the aforesaid £ 50 or just as much instead of them, myself or through my messenger, to you or to your husband or to your accredited messenger, within eight days after you tell me and make the request, and similarly [to give you] the profit; otherwise the penalty of the double and the seizure of my goods as security. Done in the house of the late Baldovino de Arato. Witnesses: Rufo de Arato and Aimerico, cooper. In the year of the Nativity of the Lord 1200, third indiction, the seventh day of November.

104

From the Latin[4]

Genoa, October 27, 1277

I, Nicolò di Fiesco,[5] count of Lavagna, acknowledge to you, Ferruccio, son of the late Giacomo of Pistoia, making this stipulation in behalf of Giovanni of Pistoia and partners and acting in this regard as manager in their place, that I have had and received from you, paying in said behalf, £ 1,080

[2]The best descriptions of the factors are given in Sapori, *Studi di storia economica medievale,* pp. 435ff. with Bibliography, and, in English, in De Roover, *Money, Banking and Credit in Mediaeval Bruges,* pp. 29ff. On the commission contract and agent, which have not yet received all the attention they deserve, see E. Besta, *Le obbligazioni nella storia del diritto italiano,* pp. 253ff.; G. Luzzatto, 'Les Activités économiques du patriciat vénitien (Xe–XIVe siècles),' *Annales d'Histoire Economique et Sociale,* IX (1937), 25–57; F. C. Lane, *Andrea Barbarigo, Merchant of Venice,* pp. 93ff.

[3] R. di Tucci, *Studi sull' economia genovese del secolo decimosecondo,* Part 2, pp. 88–89.

[4] Unprinted. Archivio di Stato, Genoa. *Cartulario di Leonardo Negrini,* II, fol. 169v. We have omitted a few sentences of the complicated legal formulary, indicating the omission by dots.

[5] The Di Fiesco, or Fieschi di Lavagna, were a very noble merchant family of the Genoese territory. Jointly with the Grimaldi family, they headed the Guelf party for a long time. Two members of the Fieschi family were popes in the thirteenth century, Innocent IV (1243–1254) and Hadrian V (1276).

Genoese. [This payment covers] the whole capital and profit of a certain deposit (*accomendatio*) of £ 1,000 Genoese which the said Giovanni acknowledged in his own behalf and that of his partners to have had and received in deposit from me and to have placed or invested in his partnership (*societas*), as appears from a record done by the hand of Nicola Scarsella, notary, on October 5, 1276. And I waive the exception of not having been satisfied and of not having received the money in cash, and every other legal [right]. I give quittance, discharge, and total release to you, receiving [this quittance] in behalf of said Giovanni and partners and in your own behalf. And I promise not to demand [anything further] from him, Giovanni, and his partners . . . under penalty of the double of as much or as many times as [the promise] may be violated or a lawsuit may be made, [this penalty being] promised to you by solemn stipulation. And for this I pledge to you in said behalf all my goods as security, ordering that said instrument of deposit be abrogated and invalid and of no value. I acknowledge that I have delivered to you this instrument to be soaked[6] and cancelled and disposed of in whatever way said Giovanni may wish. Done in Carignano,[7] in the house of said Niccolò, in 1277, fifth indiction, October 27, between prime and terce. Witnesses: Simone Guercio, Guglielmo Guercio, and Pietro of Quarto, weigher.

Factor and Commission Contracts

105

From the Latin[8]

Siena, October 13, 1282

In the year of the Lord, 1282, eleventh indiction, the third day before the Ides of October. I, Ugo, [son] of the late Ugolino Gigone, entering into a solemn and legal written stipulation for fee and salary, promise and make agreement with you, Alessandro and Ser Giovanni, [son] of the late Salimbene, receiving [the obligation] for yourselves and for the partners and the *societas* of the Salimbeni . . .[9] to stay and to remain . . . as factor and agent of your business in your behalf from the next feast of All Saints' Day up to [the end of] the four years directly following that date. And [I promise] to go and to remain wherever you wish and order me throughout Tuscany and Lombardy and the kingdoms of France, England, and Sicily and elsewhere, wherever

---

[6] The original record was of parchment and it could be destroyed by soaking it in water.

[7] An urban district in Genoa.   [8] Sapori, *Studi di storia economica medievale*, pp. 502–3.

[9] The dots here and hereafter are Sapori's.

you direct and wish [me] to do business and to gain a profit and to carry on your business well and advantageously and lawfully, acting in good faith, without fraud, to your advantage and to that of your *societas*. Also [I promise] to preserve and to guard your property and goods which come into my hands, and what I receive and have from you or from another in your behalf in the future in gold and silver, [notarial] instruments, books, letters, and other things of whatsoever kind, acting in good faith and without fraud. And [I promise] to return and to consign to you or to any one of you or to whomever you wish, direct, and order me by letter, by word of mouth, or by writing, a correct and legal accounting of each and all that ... or I have managed, and in regard to all your goods which come into my hands [I promise] both to consign and to return and to give intact these goods to you whenever and as many times as you ask and express the wish; and [I promise] not to do anything fraudulent with them nor to conceal them nor to retain [any money] except the salary granted to me by you.

And I also promise you that whatever may be donated or given to me in money or gold or silver or anything else by any person or locality or community or baron or prelate in any way, so long as I remain your factor, I shall turn over and give all to you and to your *societas* and I shall send it to your *societas*, keeping back nothing.

And I promise you that as long as I remain your factor, as is stated above, I shall not gamble in any game of dice with pledge or money, nor shall I have carnal relations with any married woman, virgin, or religious, nor shall I make any expenditures on them out of your goods.

I also promise you to observe and to have carried out each and all that you order me by word of mouth or by a messenger or by letter, acting in good faith and without fraud, and that I shall keep every confidence which you shall order me [to hold] and that I shall not disclose any to anyone without your permission.

Furthermore I promise you not to make or to form any *societas* with any person or persons without your permission and will. I assert and acknowledge that I do not have and did not invest in your *societas* or in another *societas* any amount of money or any cash, neither in your behalf nor for the common work of your *societas*, except the said salary of mine, promised me by you, as shall be apparent from another instrument by the hand of Orlando, notary undersigned.

And I promise you to undertake and to observe all these aforesaid conditions, article by article, under penalty of 100 marks of silver, which I promise to give you, just as is stated, if I do not observe or if I act contrary to the conditions: and [I promise] to observe what is stated above, whether the penalty is paid or not. And for these conditions I pledge myself and my heirs to you and your heirs, and I pledge as security my goods; these goods you are to be allowed to sell and use as security, and to receive possession of them by your own authority without requesting [permission of] the court or the judge; and I designate myself to have and to hold them meanwhile in your name.

And I do and I promise [to do] this for you because you have promised and made agreement to give me £ 450 Sienese as my fee and salary for the said four years on account of the said service and because of all the aforesaid, as must be apparent by another instrument by the hand of Orlando, notary undersigned; wherefore I waive the exception that the promise and obligation has not been made, [the exception] that the salary has not been established and promised, [the exception] that the affair has not been carried out in this way, the privilege of tribunal, and every legal right and remedy of law. And of my own free will I swear on the holy Gospels of God, having placed my hand on the book, to observe all the aforesaid, article by article, and not to violate it nor to act contrary to it.

And Orlando, notary undersigned, admonished the abovesaid Ugo, willing and acknowledging the abovesaid agreement, that by reason of the oath and of the guarantee he must observe this instrument, article by article, in regard to the aforesaid Ser Alessandro and Ser Giovanni mentioned above. Done in Siena in the presence of Jacopo, [son] of the late Ser Uguccione Lotteringhi, and Ventura, [son] of the late Accursio, and Giannino Benini, Lombard, witnesses invited.

I, Orlando, notary, son of the late Ottaviano mentioned above, was present, and having been invited, I wrote and published these things.

106

From the Latin[10]

[Genoa,] April 16, 1161

Witnesses: Lamberto Filippi, Guido of Lodi, Oberto Trentavellate, and Musso de Sarega. Buongiovanni Lercari acknowledged that he is carrying to Bougie, from the goods of Guglielmo Mallone, at the risk and fortune of the latter, 94 pounds in weight of silk and 10 pieces of Spanish linen of 43 *cannae*, all of which Guglielmo himself values at £ 32. Buongiovanni himself is carrying these goods to Bougie, and he is not to make any expenditures

---

[10] M. Chiaudano and M. Moresco, *Il cartolare di Giovanni Scriba*, II, 4.

from them, when going, for the vessel or for eating. [He is] to sell as best he can, to invest [the proceeds] in wax or alum, whichever seems better to him, or, if neither seems better, in gold, and to send back those wares as quickly as possible and to deposit them, witnesses being present, under his own name. He is to have and keep 6 *massamutini*[11] out of it. Done in the chapter house, April 16, 1161, eighth indiction.

107

From the Latin[12]

[Montpellier,] August 7, 1387

In the name of the Lord, amen. In the year of His Incarnation 1387, and on the seventh day of the month of August, Charles [VI] reigning. . . .[13] Be it known to all that I, Pierre Solaces, merchant of Montpellier, [liable] for the whole amount both as factor of Raymond Mouton, of Montpellier, dealer in spices, and in my own behalf, acting in good faith and with good mind in this . . . acknowledge and recognize in truth to you, Jacob Jourdan, merchant of Montpellier, being present, that I have from you in *commanda* and by reason and cause of *commanda* the value of 420 gold francs of good weight, of the coin of France, and of s.10 d.6 Tournois,[14] invested in 37 containers of oil, 5 casks of tartar, 4 bales of violet, 3 bales of *roȝa*,[15] and 11 casks and 5 containers of honey. And these goods are loaded at your direction on the ship called 'Saint Mary and Saint John,' whose captain is Ramon Pons of Barcelona. This aforesaid ship on the nineteenth day of July just past departed from the port of Aigues-Mortes in order to sail toward Rhodes and Alexandria, and is to go and to sail to said countries at your peril and risk . . . at the fortune of God. And I, or another whom said Raymond may wish, am to trade said *commanda* in said regions and do business [with it] well and faithfully, by selling and reinvesting in goods and merchandise listed and expressed in a certain memorandum delivered to you, written by the hand of Bernard Salamon and also by the hand of said Raymond Mouton. And I am to bring back the said reinvestment to this country on said ship or on another, just as I will do with the goods of said Raymond Mouton, at the peril and risk mentioned above, under the following agreement entered into

---

[11] Gold coins of the Almohad rulers of North Africa and southern Spain.

[12] L. Guiraud, *Recherches et conclusions nouvelles sur le prétendu rôle de Jacques Cœur*, pp. 135–36.

[13] The dots here and hereafter are Guiraud's.

[14] The *commanda* consisted of merchandise bought with the coins mentioned here, that is, 420 francs of gold and 126 deniers Tournois of silver, the latter being equivalent to s.10 d.6 of account.

[15] *Roȝa* or *ruȝa*, a dyestuff, probably of red color; see R. S. Lopez, *Studi sull'economia genovese nel medio evo*, p. 100, and note 2, pp. 174–75. As for *violarum*, they certainly are not flowers but another dyestuff.

between me and you: that I should have and am to have 2 in the 100 from
the goods to be sold and also from those to be bought with the [proceeds of]
said *commanda* or with the money which is to be had from the same *commanda;*
on this condition, however, that I or the other who shall be there in behalf
of said Raymond, if [another] engages in the said transaction, should not and
shall not borrow[16] on account of expenses for nourishment, that is, for food
and drink, anything chargeable to said *commanda*. And I promise that I, said
Pierre, or the one who shall sell said *commanda* and shall engage in transactions with it, shall be faithful . . . and we shall return a good accounting
concerning said *commanda* and the profits. And said *commanda,* together
with the profits . . . we shall give back, once said voyage has been made, or
when we are requested from one day to another. For which, etc.

June 22, 1388

And later, in the year of the Incarnation of the Lord 1388, and on the
twenty-second of the month of June, Charles [VI] reigning . . . said Jacob
Jourdan acknowledged to said Raymond Mouton, being present, that he had
received from him 2 *pous* of pepper, weighing 8 *quintalia* 23¾ pounds net, [and]
2 *pous* of ginger of Mecca, weighing 8 *quintalia* 2¼ pounds net, [reckoned] by
the weight of Montpellier, to be deducted from said *commanda*. Concerning
which, etc.

108

From the Latin[17]

Genoa, July 8, 1268

I, Benedetto Zaccaria, make, constitute, and appoint you, Daniele de Mari,
present and receiving [the power], my accredited messenger and attorney to
ship and to sell 201 sacks of alum and 1 *pondus* of mastic.[18] Of this alum 49
sacks are with you in Genoa together with the aforesaid *pondus* of mastic,
while the remaining alum, that is, the [other] sacks, are with Parente Ghisolfi
at Aigues-Mortes. Said alum weighs in total about 350 *cantaria*. And I give
you free permission and full and complete authority to sell, to ship, to
exchange, to barter, and to send [the goods] wherever you wish, by sea and
by land, along the coast of Provence and France, at my risk and fortune,

---

[16] *Nichil mutare habeat seu debeat,* which makes little sense. Read *mutuare,* 'to borrow,' instead
of *mutare,* 'to change.'

[17] Unprinted. Archivio di Stato, Genoa. *Cartulario di Guglielmo di San Giorgio,* III, fol. 21v.

[18] Here and below the notary wrote *castiga*; but read *mastiga*. Mastic was the principal product
of the island of Chios. Benedetto Zaccaria later occupied the island by a sudden move. He
certainly had already established business connections with it in 1268.

and to give them in *accomendatio*, and to invest them. [This is all to be done] in such a way, however, that you are not to be bound at any time to make an accounting to me in regard to said alum or to the money collected from it, except in the manner you wish; and whatever you wish to report in regard to and about the aforesaid is to be believed. And I promise you, notary undersigned, making the stipulation in behalf of the person or persons whom it may concern, to have and to hold these conditions as settled and lasting, and not to violate in any way anything you do and regard as suitable to be done in regard to and about the aforesaid, under hypothecation and pledge of my goods. Witnesses: Faziolo de Castello, son of Oberto Roerigo of Rapallo; Guglielmo Basso. Done in Genoa in the house of the late Pietro Stralleria, July 8, 1268, tenth indiction.

CHAPTER XII

SOME OTHER FORMS OF AGREEMENT

THE TYPES of contract which we have illustrated so far were the most important and most widespread in medieval Mediterranean trade, but they were not by any means the only ones. We now present a few samples of contracts which differed from those already mentioned either in their legal character or in the peculiar kind of business activities they served.

The first selection reminds us of the enduring importance of privateering as a form of business activity. Romantic notions about the life of the buccaneer ought not to make us forget that piracy was a form of economic enterprise and that the pirates had to be businessmen as well as fighters. Most of them, in fact, alternated privateering and ordinary trade. The contract which we have chosen is described as a loan, but it actually differs in many ways from the ordinary loan. It shows how a piratical expedition could be financed and how the investors were rewarded (Document 109).[1]

Document 110 takes us to southern France during the Hundred Years War.[2] It shows one of the many ways through which war could stimulate commerce. An ordinary merchant associates himself with an officer who will 'buy faithfully and legally' booty captured from the English. The adverbs, of course, refer to the behavior which the officer was expected to show towards his associate; it is by no means certain that the purchases themselves were legal. The contract, described as a *societas* or a *compagnia*, seems to be of the *societas terrae* type which we have illustrated in Chapter X. The type of business, however, is peculiar.

The third and fourth selections (Documents 111 and 112) show the influence of practices foreign to the Western Mediterranean. The *iatenum,* as the contract itself clearly states, belongs to the commercial customs of Muslim Syria. The other contract, which has no name, seems to stem from south German commercial practice.

The last two selections (Documents 113 and 114) are not unusual in themselves,

[1] Besides the article from which our selection has been taken, see F. Sassi, 'La guerra in corsa e il diritto di preda seconda il diritto veneziano,' *Rivista di Storia del Diritto Italiano*, II (1929), 99–128, 261–96; A. Lattes, 'Sui prestiti in pane per la corsa marittima nelle carte liguri,' *Bollettino Storico-Bibliografico Subalpino*, XXXVIII (1936), 160–62; G. Falco, 'Appunti di diritto marittimo medievale,' *Il Diritto Marittimo*, XXIX (1927), 123–41. In English there is no monograph on this subject, but references can be found in W. Ashburner, *The Rhodian Sea-Law*, and in E. Byrne, *Genoese Shipping in the Twelfth and Thirteenth Centuries*.

[2] Almost all books dealing with the Hundred Years War refer to profiteering, but there is no special book on this subject. *Cambridge Economic History*, Vol. II, Chap. V, contains a few general remarks and bibliographical references.

one being an ordinary sale (*emptio-venditio*) and the other an acknowledgment that an obligation resulting from a loan has been extinguished; but they indicate how shares in the funded public debt could be objects of trade. We have chosen Genoese examples because Genoa seems to have led other Italian communes in this field, but practices of this kind gradually spread to all of Italy and to other European towns and monarchies.[3] The Genoese Commune floated many loans which were described as purchases of rent and which actually were secured by and rewarded from the proceeds of a tax—hence, in our selection, the use of the term *compera salis* (literally, 'purchase of salt,' but actually a loan on the security of the salt tax). The method was gradually perfected through division of the loan into shares of a fixed value (£100 Genoese), through the adoption of improved systems of accounting, and through the organization of an autonomous administration of the public debt. Shares of the public debt were actively traded in the Genoese market as early as the first half of the thirteenth century.

Piracy and War Booty

109

From the Latin[4]

Genoa, May 23, 1251

We, Guglielmo Mallone and Simonetto, brothers, sons of Ansaldo Mallone, [son] of the late Guglielmo, both of us [being liable] for the whole amount, acknowledge that we have received and have had from you, Pietro Polpo de Mari, £ 250 Genoese in loan at the risk and fortune of the sea for the voyage in which we are prepared to sail as privateers in our ship, which is called 'The Lion,' in order to win profit from the enemies of Holy Church,[5] waiving the exception that the money has not been loaned and that the loan has not been accepted, that there has been fraud in the act, and that claim [be made for something given] without cause. We promise to give and to pay to you or to your accredited messenger these £ 250 as follows: to wit, that if we make with said ship a profit up to the amount of £ 3,000, we shall give back to you said loan and in addition £ 50 in every 100 of said loan in virtue of profit and gain from them; and if we make a profit up to the amount of £ 5,000 or more with said ship, we promise to give and to pay to you for the profit and gain of said loan £ 100 in every 100. We shall give and pay

[3] See especially H. Sieveking, 'Studio sulle finanze genovesi nel medioevo e in particolare sulla casa di S. Giorgio,' *Atti della Società Ligure di Storia Patria*, XXXV (1906), 1–393; G. Luzzatto, *I prestiti della republica di Venezia*; A. E. Sayous, 'Les Valeurs nominatives et leur trafic à Gênes pendant le XIIIe siècle,' *Giornale Storico e Letterario della Liguria*, ser. 3, IX (1933), 73–84.

[4] R. S. Lopez, *Dieci documenti sulla storia della guerra di corsa*, pp. 11–12.

[5] Most likely this refers to the Pisans, who at that time were fighting against the Genoese, who were allies of Pope Innocent IV.

to you this money and its profit within one month after we beach said ship[6] in any place whatever. And for the personal expenses you will incur in said ship in which you are about to embark, we shall give you £ 10 Genoese; and for your personal hire or salary, 25 shares of the profit and gain we make with said ship [to be taken] out of those shares that are made and distributed among the privateers. We promise to undertake, to fulfill, and to observe each and all of the aforesaid, and not to go against [these conditions] in any way. Otherwise we promise you, making the stipulation, the penalty of the double of said quantity, each and all of the aforesaid remaining in full force. And for the observing of all of the aforesaid we pledge to you as security all our goods, and especially the eighth share [of the ship], together with the cordage of that ship belonging to said eighth; in regard to that eighth share of the ship, together with the cordage, we acknowledge that we have turned over to you, bodily, possession and ownership, acknowledging and constituting ourselves to possess it in your name and in *precarium*[7] so long as we possess it; giving to you permission of taking the aforesaid possession by your authority whenever it pleases you; and also we pledge to you as security for said amount the profit of that eighth share, if God may supply any from it. This is expressly established between us in the present contract, [namely], that if by chance no profit be made with that ship, as is stated above, we are not obligated to you except in regard to the payment of the £ 250; and that within eight days after said ship sails from the port of Terone we shall swear, and shall exact oaths from any members of the crew you designate, up to the number of twenty-five, to the effect that we shall undertake all of the aforesaid. We promise to dispatch this ship from said port before the eighth of July next and to sail, God permitting, in order to win a profit, under penalty of the double of said amount and pledge of our goods. And any one of us is to be held [liable] for the whole amount in regard to the aforesaid, waiving the legislation on joint liability, the legislation on the principal [debtor], the Epistle of the divine Hadrian, and every legal [right]. Witnesses, Filippo Safrano, scribe, and Guglielmo Guigino de Castello, scribe. Done in Genoa in the orchard of the Holy Cross, in the year of the Lord 1251, eighth indiction, May 23, before terce.

---

[6] *Cum dicta navi campum fecerimus.* Warships when not at sea were often beached, and a protecting wall was built around them, so that the whole formed a sort of fortified camp.

[7] *Precarium:* that is, subject to revocation.

110

From the Latin[8]

Toulouse, July 23, [1446]

In the year as above, on the twenty-third of the month of July, Arnaut de Fagols, holding position as captain of Castelculier, for himself as the one party, and Jehan Amici, merchant of Toulouse, for himself as the other party, have made and formed with one another a *societas* or *companhia* in such wise that for the sake of said *societas* said Jehan Amici delivered free to said Fagols, being present there and receiving, the sum of 50 gold écus, new, of fine gold, of the coinage, alloy, and weight of our lord the king, to be placed and spent or invested in goods seized as booty by the armed men of our lord the king, conquered or acquired from the English and [in the war] against the English. The same Fagols promised to buy faithfuly and legally these goods with the said sum for the advantage of both parties, and to bring them or cause them to be brought and have them carried to this city of Toulouse, at any time during the next month of August, to the house inhabited by the said Amici. And there, once the said sum has been recovered by said Amici, the profit which God may grant in said goods shall be divided by the half between the two, and so likewise shall be borne the loss, if there is any—may this be far from us. And thus it was agreed, and the same Fagols promised in regard to the aforesaid that, using no deceit and fraud, he will keep a good and legal accounting of everything . . .[9] and, if he happened not to buy any of the goods mentioned above, he [Fagols] promised to return the same sum in Toulouse during the said period, etc.... Witnesses: Jehan Becudech, changer of Toulouse; Antoine del Royre and Bernard of Aigues-Vives, sergeants of the king in Toulouse.

Special Contracts: Syria and Southern Germany

111

From the Latin[10]

Ayas, March 7, 1274

In the name of the Lord, amen. I, Marino Sazo, acknowledge to you, Opicino di Santa Fede, that I have had and have received from you in

[8] G. Fagniez, ed., *Documents relatifs à l'histoire de l'industrie et du commerce en France*, II, 237–38.

[9] The dots here and hereafter are Fagniez's.

[10] C. Desimoni, 'Actes passés en 1271, 1274 et 1279 à l'Aïas [Petite Arménie] et à Beyrouth par devant des notaires génois,' *Archives de l'Orient Latin*, I (1881), 453. *Iatenum*, according to

iatenum, according to the use and custom of Syria, 500 new dirhams of
Armenia, waiving. . . .[11] And this *iatenum,* according to the said use and
custom, I am to carry along the coast of Armenia, and from there to go to
Acre or Tyre, without any change in the route, and having the authority
to send ahead of me said *iatenum* to you only, provided it is accompanied
by an instrument or by witnesses, and to make out of said *iatenum* according
as that *iatenum* has fared.[12] Then, on the return which I shall make to Acre
or Tyre, I promise to place and to consign to your possession or to that of
your accredited messenger the capital and profit which God may grant to me
in the said *iatenum,* after retaining for myself [a share] according as that
iatenum has fared in the region of Syria. Otherwise I promise you, making
the stipulation, the penalty of the double, and I pledge to you as security for
it all my goods existing and future.

Done in Ayas in the lodge of the Genoese where the court of the consuls
is held.[13] In the year of the Nativity of the Lord, 1274, first indiction, March
7, between prime and terce. Witnesses, Oberto of Gavi and Bertolino
Pinello.[14]

112

From the Latin[15]

[Ravensburg,] 1390

Let all those who shall see the present letters know that I, Konrad Segelbach,
citizen of the town of Ravensburg, in the diocese of Constance, as well as
Anna, my legitimate wife, and our legitimate sons born of us, and all our
coheirs, compelled neither by force nor by fear, but sound of body and mind
and after mature deliberation, acknowledge and by the tenor of the present
instrument freely recognize that we shall be obligated to the extent of 1,100

Desimoni, is a word of Turkish origin meaning 'deposited' or 'placed.' Desimoni also gives
details about the new dirhams, which were silver coins of the kingdom of Cilician Armenia.

[11] The dots are Desimoni's, who omitted here one or more clauses which he doubtless regarded
as uninteresting because they were the usual formulae of Genoese commercial contracts.

[12] *Gererit.*

[13] The *logia* was the headquarters of the Genoese semi-autonomous colony in Ayas, where the
curia consulatus (court and tribunal of the colonial consuls, given jurisdiction over the Genoese by
the home Commune) was located.

[14] The Pinelli were an influential Genoese family of merchant-bankers. Gavi is a town in the
Genoese hinterland. The nationality of the parties to the contract cannot be ascertained, but they
certainly were Westerners.

[15] H. Simonsfeld, *Der Fondaco dei Tedeschi in Venedig und die deutsch-venetianischen Handels-
beziehungen,* I, 119. The document, included in a formulary but probably derived from a contract
which was actually made, is not notarial but holograph (see Chapter XIII). It has some peculiarities
not found in the usual Mediterranean contracts.

gold florins, of good and satisfactory weight, namely ducats,[16] to the discreet
and noble men the Messeri Nicola Morosini, [son] of the late Ser Paolo, and
Francesco Amadio, and to their heirs, all citizens of the city of Venice. And
we are bound and obligated [to give] this amount of the aforesaid florins to
these aforesaid men and to their heirs by reason of merchandise equal in
value to the aforesaid amount of the aforesaid florins and wholly converted
to our own use. . . .[17] Therefore we are bound, we will, and we must pay
this amount of the said florins to the same aforesaid Messeri N.[18] and to all
their heirs, without loss to them, [as follows]: in the [first] half of one year
50 florins in good, legal ducats in the aforesaid city of Venice, and in the
other half of the same year similarly 50 florins of the same gold and weight,
and so in all the following years successively, until full payment has been
made to the said Messeri and to their heirs in the said amount of florins or in
other merchandise—that is, in linen or other merchandise acceptable to said
Messeri and equal in value to the said amount of florins—without any damage
that might ordinarily be incurred by the aforesaid [merchandise]. . . . Each
and all of these [conditions we promise] by our aforesaid given pledge, to
hold as settled, agreed, and inviolable, without fraud and deceit. In witness
thereof I, Konrad Segelbach, the aforesaid, in my own behalf and [in behalf]
of my wife and of my sons and of all our heirs, have affixed my own seal to
the present [instrument]; and for even greater security I have urgently
besought T.,[19] magistrate of the citizens of our aforesaid town, to be good
enough to affix his seal to the present [instrument], as witness, without
[becoming liable to] any loss to himself.

Given and done in the year [13]90, etc.

Trade in Shares of the Funded Public Debt

113
From the Latin[20]

Genoa, April 2, 1264

I, Giacomino de Gauterio, sell, give, and deliver to you, Bonaccorso of
Montoggio, one share which I have in the *comperae salis* of the Commune
of Genoa, from the *comperae salis* made and imposed by the Commune at the
time of Alberto Malavolta and Ranieri, then podestà of Genoa, with all the

---

[16] *Florin*, originally the name of the Florentine gold coins, later was often used to designate
any gold coin. The ducats, of course, are Venetian gold coins.

[17] The dots are Simonsfeld's.   [18] *Sic.*   [19] *Sic:* T for *Talis* ('So-and-so'), says Simonsfeld.

[20] Sayous, 'Les Valeurs nominatives et leur trafic à Gênes,' pp. 79–80. We have omitted an
accessory clause, the meaning of which is obscure.

legal rights to receive and to collect which I possess or which belong to me, for the price of £ 107 Genoese, for which I call myself fully quit and paid, waiving any exception that the money has not been received and counted and that the price has not been paid, that there has been fraud in the act, and that claim [be made for something given] without cause, and [waiving] all [other] exceptions. And if it be worth more, I give and forego that surplus as [if it were] a genuine and pure donation among living persons, waiving the right of those who have been deceived by half of the price. Therefore, I sell and deliver to you said share for said price, so that you may henceforth do with it whatever you please and collect in the capacity of owner and by reason of purchase, you and your heirs or anyone to whom you shall give or whom you let have [the share], without any opposition from me or from anyone in my behalf. I acknowledge that I have delivered to you possession and ownership of it, and I promise to yield it to you, not to hinder you nor to take it away from you, but to defend legally its possession from any person, and to give you authority, constituting you attorney in regard to your property. . . . Otherwise I promise you, making the stipulation, the penalty of the double of said amount, the aforesaid [conditions] remaining as settled. And I pledge as security for it all my goods, existing and future, waiving the [special] rights about mortgages, [the privileges of] the Velleian *Senatus Consultus,* and the Julian Law on the appraisal of prices, and all benefits of law, so that you may sue me and my property anywhere. I am so doing by advice of Daniele and Giacomino de Galterio, whom I name my relatives and advisers. Witnesses: the aforesaid advisers and Franceschino de Castro. Done in Genoa in the house of the heirs of the late Rubaldo Alberico, on on April 2, sixth indiction, 1264.

114

From the Latin[21]

Genoa, November 8, 1281

In the name of the Lord, amen. I, Caccianemico Barca de Volta, judge, acknowledge to you, Tommaso de Murta, attorney of Benedetto and Manuele Zaccaria, brothers, that I have had and have received from you, [acting] in behalf of the aforesaid Benedetto and Manuele Zaccaria, four *loca* of salt in

---

[21] Unprinted. Archivio di Stato, Genoa. *Cartulario di Simone Vataccio,* Vol. III, Part 1, fol. 135r. of the modern numeration (old numeration: fol. 125r.). Caccianemico Barca de Volta belonged to the old merchant patriciate and to a family which later became related to the Zaccarias. In 1289 he was sent by his Commune to Tripoli, Syria, to become the first Genoese podestà of the city, but Tripoli fell to the Egyptians before he could assume his office. The De Murta were a prominent popular family, who gave Genoa its second doge.

the *comparae salis* of the Commune of Genoa, and that [the *loca*] have been returned in full and restored to me. And they are those four *loca* which the said Manuele has acknowledged that he has had and has received from me in loan, as appears from an instrument written by the hand of Castellino of Portovenere, notary, in 1280, the second day of July. [I make this statement], waiving the exception that I have not had the *loca* and that their delivery and restitution have not been made, and [waiving] any other exception and legal [right]. Wherefore I promise you and agree, [you] receiving and stipulating in behalf of the aforesaid Benedetto and Manuele, that I shall not make any further demand, interference, or request, in law or in act, in any way, in regard to the aforesaid *loca*, or by reason of the same *loca*, or of any evaluation or income of the same *loca*, or [by reason] of anything of which mention may be made in the said instrument, under the penalty of the double of the said amounts and of that [amount] which might be demanded, and under hypothe-cation and pledge of my goods. And I will and order that said instrument be canceled and void and of no value.

Done in Genoa in the portico of the palace of the podestà of Genoa. Witnesses: Giorgio of Camogli, notary; Giovanni de Rovegno de Castro; and Gianuino Vataccio. In the year of the Nativity of the Lord 1281, eighth indiction, November 8, after nones.

CHAPTER XIII

INFORMAL COMMERCIAL PAPERS

NOTARIAL instruments have so far supplied nearly all of the evidence on commercial contracts. This reflects the peculiar importance of the notary public and the extraordinary value of notarial records for the reconstruction of the economic, legal, and social history of medieval trade in the Mediterranean world. The meticulous exactitude of notaries in listing accessory clauses and anticipating possible objections throws full light upon all facets of an obligation.[1] But we must now turn to holograph records—that is, obligatory documents wholly in the handwriting of the parties or one of the parties—for certain aspects of trade which are not covered by notarial contracts.

Holograph records were used in antiquity and in the medieval Muslim world. In early medieval Italy, Lombard legal practice, supported by religious principles which upheld any obligation regardless of legal forms, accepted records written by anyone who was learned enough to draft them. Notarial instruments, however, gradually became the favorite means to prove the existence of an obligation and, through the introduction of certain formulae of Roman Law, they were regarded as equivalent to an obligation. In the later Middle Ages, Tuscan merchants relied upon holograph records to a larger extent than did merchants of other Mediterranean regions; but this tradition can hardly be connected with any greater diffusion of literacy in Tuscany, as some scholars have suggested. Genoese, Venetian, or Marseillais merchants also were literate and sometimes quite learned; but they usually preferred notarial instruments, probably because they wanted the legal form of the record to be impeccable and irrefutable. Yet even in Genoa and Venice certain records which were not notarized, such as bank ledgers and chartularies of ships, had the same legal authority as notarial records. Moreover, there are indications that for some obligations a notarial instrument and one or several holograph records were written at the same time. Some transactions were recorded both by a notarial instrument and by an entry in a bank ledger. In exchange transactions, according to many scholars, besides the notarial contract an informal 'letter of exchange' was usually written and sent to the payor or the drawee. Finally, it must be noted that the popularity of notarial instruments was virtually confined to the Mediterranean area. In northern Europe records certified by municipal or gild

---

[1] General bibliography on notarial instruments and their significance is found in R. S. Lopez, 'The Unexplored Wealth of the Notarial Archives in Pisa and Lucca,' in *Mélanges d'histoire du moyen âge dédiés à la mémoire de Louis Halphen*, pp. 417–32. For a summary description of other records of obligation one may read W. Mitchell, *The Law Merchant*.

authorities enjoyed much the same authority as notarial records in the south. Holograph records also were widely used.

In most cases the fact that a record is holograph instead of being notarized has some interest for the history of law and of diplomatics but does not affect greatly the economic character of an obligation. Except for the fact that they omit many legal formulae which would have been present in a formal notarial instrument, the holograph documents we have so far encountered do not substantially differ from the others. To this general class belong the holograph *compagnia* agreements of Tuscan merchants (Documents 101 and 102), the agreement entered into at Toulouse and written in the personal book of a merchant (Document 110), and the obligation which a Ravensburg merchant certified with his own seal and the seal of a town official (Document 112). The greater simplicity and informality of holograph documents, however, permitted some types of them to evolve more rapidly than notarial instruments and to play a significant role in the development of commercial practices. The most important among these are the bills of exchange, checks and other kinds of promissory notes, orders of payment, and the like. Obviously the informal bill of exchange descended from the notarial contracts of exchange which we have encountered before; checks and promissory notes descended from notarized promises to pay and from orders of payment, one of which we have presented here. But the informal papers profoundly differed from their parents in their greater simplicity and flexibility. A similar development took place in the field of transportation; the formal and informal records connected with it will be discussed in Part Four.

The first three selections are bills of exchange; the others are various kinds of checks and orders of payment, the first of them (Document 118) being a formal ancestor of informal papers. We have endeavored to choose and to arrange the documents in such order as may give some idea of the evolution from formal to informal and of the emergence of standard formulae. It should be noted that no endorsed papers are included. Endorsement was a later development of the informal paper, but we have no instances of it in the Middle Ages. Yet it cannot be said with certainty that it was unknown. Inasmuch as the odds against preservation of informal papers are much greater than those against notarial instruments, it is quite possible that there are earlier developments in the evolution of bills of exchange and promissory notes than the extant documents would show.

The history of informal commercial papers is a battlefield of historians, economists, and lawyers. We cannot tell it briefly, and space forbids discussing it at length. Let the reader who may wish to know more peruse the bulky and controversial literature of the subject.[2]

[2] In English the most detailed survey of informal papers is A. P. Usher, *The Early History of Deposit Banking in Mediterranean Europe*, Vol. I, Chap. III. Its abundant bibliographic references ought to be complemented with those in E. Besta, *Le obbligazioni nella storia del diritto italiano*, pp. 227, 260, 262, 265, itself a masterly short survey of the subject. Usher gives a number of informal papers in English translation; other translations are found in R. de Roover, 'Early Accounting Problems of Foreign Exchange,' *The Accounting Review*, XIX (1944), 381–407.

Bills of Exchange

115

From the Italian[3]

Avignon, October 5, 1339

In the name of God, amen. To Bartolo and partners [*compagni*], Barna of Lucca and partners [send] greetings from Avignon.

You shall pay by this letter on November 20, [1]339, to Landuccio Busdraghi and partners, of Lucca, gold florins three hundred twelve and three fourths for the exchange [*per cambio*] of gold florins three hundred, because I have received such money today from Tancredi Bonagiunta and partners at the rate [*raxione*] of 4¼ per 100 to their advantage. And charge [it] to our account.[4] Done on October 5, [1]339.

Francesco Falconetti has ordered us to pay in your behalf 230 gold *scudi* to the Acciajuoli [*compagnia*].[5]

[*Address on the outside;*]

To Bartolo Casini and partners, in Pisa.

[*Mark of Barna of Lucca*]   First.[6]

116

From the Italian[7]

Palermo, July 4, 1390; Genoa, July 26, 1390

In the name of God, amen.

Done on July 4, 1390.

Pay by this first letter at usance[8] to Mess. Vieri and Francesco de' Medici eight hundred and fifty florins, that is, fl. 850, for which I have been satisfied

---

[3] First published in F. Bonaini, *Statuti inediti della città di Pisa dal XII al XIV secolo*, III 202–3, and reprinted several times—last in G. Mondaini, *Moneta, credito e banche attraverso i tempi*, 2d ed., p. 113, with useful comments. The document is the earliest extant bill of exchange and includes some information not relating to the exchange operation. We do not have the original but only a copy of the letter and its address, which was included in a notarial instrument.

[4] *Conto e ragione:* the two words are practically synonyms, but there is a possibility that *ragione* was used in the sense of 'rate of interest,' as it was in the preceding sentence.

[5] This was one of the greatest companies of Florentine merchant-bankers.

[6] That is, 'original.' Usually several copies were made of every bill of exchange to avoid accidental loss; the document presented here was the original.

[7] E. Bensa, *Francesco di Marco da Prato*, pp. 327–28. This protested bill comes from the archives of the Francesco Datini company. On the meaning of 'first' (original) letter, see the preceding footnote.

[8] *A usanȝa*. We still call usance the time customarily allowed for the payment of a bill of exchange.

here by Ser Nino Lancia. At maturity, make good payment and charge to our account.

May God protect you.

By Tommaso di Messer Guccio in Palermo,
to oblige you.

[*Written in another hand:*]

We do not pay them because we do not have the funds in your [account]. On July 26.

By Ambrogio and Andrea in Genoa.

[*Address on the outside:*]

Ambrogio di Meo and Andrea di Bonanno and Co. in Genoa.

117

From the Provençal[9]

[Drawn on Marseilles], September 26, 1381

To Madonna Thomasa Lhatauba, greetings and good love from me, Barthoumieu Guibert.

Donna, by this first [letter] give to Sen Antoni Pomier 32 florins of 12 groats [each] and 3 groats, because I have received them here. Therefore make good payment to him in eight days after seeing the letter.[10]

The year 1381, on September 26.

F. XXXVII[11] G. III

A Notarial Letter of Payment

118

From the Latin[12]

Cagliari, August 8, 1213

To his friend and very dear father, the most cherished Gerardo Enrigi, physician, Bonaventura, [son] of the late Neri, [sends] greetings and the constance of an intimate affection.

[9] A.-E. Sayous, 'Les Transferts de risques, les associations commerciales et la lettre de change à Marseille pendant le XIVe siècle,' *Revue Historique de Droit Français et Etranger*, 4th ser., XIV (1935), 488. This bill, which shows the spread of Italian commercial techniques to Mediterranean France, was first published in F. Portal, *Lettres de change et quittances du XIVe siècle*, which was not accessible to us. For the bill of exchange in Catalan territory, see L. Tramoyeres Blasco, 'Letras de cambio valencianas,' *Revista de Archivos, Bibliotecas y Museos*, IV (1900), 489–96.

[10] Today we would say 'on sight.' The florin was used in this instance as a money of account equivalent to 12 silver deniers groat.

[11] *Sic*; but it is probably a misprint for XXXII, as in the text of the letter.

[12] Bonaini, *Statuti inediti della città di Pisa*, III, 200. Although this letter was notarized, its context indicates that similar letters written by the party were sometimes sent.

I am appealing as warmly as I can to your affection that you be good enough to give and to pay for me, for all the reasons set forth below, to Ranieri Pellegrino £ 24 [Pisan] new, within fifteen days after the arrival of the new ship in Porto Pisano; for this is my wish and pleasure and such is my will. And I shall always consider and hold as firm and settled their delivery and payment which you will make to him, and I shall not act against [this], either personally or through another, in any way or by any legal [privilege], nor am I going to make to you any further demand or petition in any way. [You should] know that if you do not give and do not pay him the aforesaid £ 24 [Pisan] new, I am going to incur great loss and inconvenience. And in order that greater credence be given and that no doubt arise about this, I have invited Bonagiunta, judge and notary, to write this in such wise.

Done in Cagliari, in the village of Santa Cecilia, under the portico of the house of Marino Piccini, in the presence of Migliore, son of Lamberto Rossi, and Riccomo, [son] of the late Dolcetto, and Bonaccorso, [son] of the late Gerardo Grassi, witnesses invited for this [purpose]. In the year of the Incarnation of the Lord 1213, indiction fifteenth, the eighth [day before] the Ides of August.

I, Bonagiunta, son of the late Allone, notary of the Imperial Majesty, and ordinary judge of Lord Otto, Most Serene Emperor of the Romans, on invitation wrote and signed this which was asked of me.

A Letter of Credit

119

From the Italian[13]

Buda, March 19, 1390

In the name of God, amen. On March 19, 1389.[14]

You shall pay by this letter to Matole, admiral, of Zara, or to [any] attendant[15] of his who may bring you this letter, 200 gold florins Hungarian or their equivalent at his will. And if it happens that you do not have

[13] A. Teja, *Aspetti della vita economica di Zara dal 1289 al 1409*, I, 85. Both the letter and the address were reproduced in a notarial instrument drafted in Zara, April 11, 1390. The instrument stated that the letter was presented in Zara to Ser Andrea, son of Jacopo, a Florentine merchant living in Zara, and that Andrea made the payment of the 200 florins to the payee and bearer of the letter. The latter was Matteo (Matole is a Venetian diminutive of the name) de Cesamis, admiral of the Hungarian king, Sigismund, and citizen of Zara.

[14] Style of the Incarnation; that is, 1390.

[15] *Famiglio*, literally 'servant' or 'attendant;' in this context the term is equivalent to the *missus* or *nuncius* of other documents, which we have translated 'messenger.'

[enough] to be able to pay them there in Ancona, I am to have them paid to him in Rome. But try to satisfy him in whole or in part; and if you give him part, write in this letter what you give him, so that the people in Rome may be advised of it and pay as much less as he may have already received in Ancona. And whoever of you pays the money should draw it on Guido di Messer Tommaso in Florence. [The payment] is for my account in consideration of 200 florins which I have received from Francesco di Bernardo.

May Christ protect you.

Giovanni Tosinghi. Greetings from Buda.

[*Address on the outside:*]

To Dimari Cavalcanti in Ancona [or] Guido di Jacobo and Jacopo di Zanobi in Rome.

A Promissory Note

120

From the Italian (Sicilian dialect)[16]

[Palermo,] August 24, 1486

On August 24, fourth indiction, 1486.

Antonio Doria must have ounces one hundred forty four, which I [Giacomo de Salvo] hereby promise to pay in [deniers] petty[17] through [the bank of] Pietro Aglata by May 26 coming next. They said [it was] in behalf of Niccolò Chilla for the price and payment of grain bought by the latter, as appears by a contract by Pietro Jardinella, notary. And [Doria] obligated himself to deliver said grain to said Aglata at the will of said Niccolò, [my] attorney.

CXLIIII [ounces]

---

[16] V. Cusumano, *Storia dei banchi della Sicilia: i banchi privati*, p. 269. This promissory note (*pagherò* or *ditta*) is a transcription of an entry in the books of Giacomo de Salvo, issued by De Salvo himself. It was preserved among the papers of a tangled lawsuit which can be briefly summed up as follows: Giacomo de Salvo had bought from Niccolò Chilla cloth which the latter had received from Bruges. To pay Chilla he bought grain from Antonio Doria (apparently a Genoese, judging from the name) and made Chilla his 'attorney' to receive the grain, that is, he turned the grain over to Chilla. He paid Doria by delivering him the promissory note. Unfortunately, Chilla himself was not the owner of the cloth; he had received it from one Pietro de Caxina, with the understanding that the proceeds would be invested in Messina silk. Through his attorneys De Caxina asked the tribunal to turn over to him the sum which De Salvo had promised Doria in behalf of Chilla. At this point it was found that De Salvo had no balance in the Aglata bank to cover the promissory note, although the bank was willing to allow him to make an overdraft. On request of the tribunal, De Salvo deposited the sum in the bank but asked it to be paid to Doria. After some additional complications De Salvo carried out the payment.

[17] The ounces were a money of account; the deniers petty were coins.

Orders of Payment

121
From the Latin[18]

Savona, September 21, 1392

On September 21, in Savona.

Please pay from my account at the time of the next Kalends of October to Ser Gregorio Squarzafico £ 134 s.17 d.8, that is, one hundred thirty four pounds seventeen solidi eight deniers. And they are for his share of the profit from grain of Sicily, in which he was a participant.

Niccolò Lomellini.

[*Address on the outside:*]

To be given to Ser Federico de Promontorio, Genoa.

[*Mark of Niccolò Lomellini*]

122
From the Italian[19]

[Prato ?] March 16 and 17, 1400

In the name of God, on March 16, 1399.[20]

Nanni di Geppo will be the bearer of this. Give him nine florins under seal[21] and charge to [my] account: fl. 9 *sug.*

Niccolò Piaciti.

[*Written in another hand:*]

Paid on March 17.

[*Address on the outside:*]

Francesco di Marco and Co.

[*Mark of Niccolò Piaciti*]

[18] H. Sieveking, 'Studio sulle finanze genovesi nel medioevo e in particolare sulla casa di S. Giorgio,' *Atti della Società Ligure di Storia Patria*, XXXV, 2, (1906), 284. This order of payment was found between the leaves of a cash ledger of the bank of Benedetti Lomellini and Percivalle Vivaldi. It was addressed to the Genoese banker Federico Promontorio.

[19] Bensa, *Francesco di Marco da Prato*, p. 355. This order of payment comes from the archives of the Francesco Datini company.

[20] Style of the Incarnation; that is, 1400.

[21] *Fiorini in suggello*, or *fiorini di suggello*, were florins of the best standards, placed in sealed bags to guarantee their quality. A special money of account, pegged to such coins, was used by Florentine and other Italian bankers. See our introductory Note on Coinage and Document 63.

PART FOUR

The Route and the Thorns Along It

THE POSITIVE achievements of the late medieval merchant and the stupendous progress accomplished during the Commercial Revolution must not lead us to exaggerate the stature of commerce at that period. Figures of population, consumption, production, and investment, whenever they are available, are but small fractions of the figures of the early nineteenth century, let alone those of our own times. Furthermore, the medieval merchant found more thorns along his path than would a modern trader. His means of transportation were slow and frail; his clients, associates, and competitors often harmed him by harsh or dishonest dealings; foreign governments and peoples treated him with a hard hand. Years of tireless, intelligent, and successful effort might suddenly end in business failure, usually liquidated according to rigorous laws of bankruptcy.

Yet the medieval merchant succeeded in overcoming many obstacles. He covered himself from losses during transportation by insurance contracts, he defended himself vigorously against sharp business practices, and he used the influence of his gild, Commune, or national government to soften the policies of foreign nations discriminating against him. Even bankruptcy found some mitigation in agreements with the creditors. Medieval business, however slow and small it may appear in contrast with the present, must have seemed fast and big when placed in the background of medieval economy.[1]

The organization of this source book does not permit the gathering of available statistical data, but we can try to present some of the problems which confronted the medieval merchant and the solutions which he often found. That our selections represent difficulties more often than solutions is partly owing to the fact that many difficulties were insoluble, but it is also a result of the circumstance, already stressed in our general introduction, that litigations and complaints left wider and more durable traces in the records than did affairs which were brought smoothly to happy conclusions.

[1] If medieval and contemporary figures must be compared absolutely, there is no doubt that a pessimistic view of medieval business ought to prevail. Absolute figures, however, tell only one side of the story, and not necessarily the most important. When the judgment is based upon a general appraisal seen in the background of the time, there is room for great divergence of opinions. For the pessimistic viewpoint see especially W. Sombart, *Der moderne Kapitalismus*, rev. ed., Vol. I; J. Kulischer, *Allgemeine Wirtschaftsgeschichte des Mittelalters und der Neuzeit*, Vol. I; N. S. B. Gras, *Business and Capitalism: an Introduction to Business History*. For a moderate to optimistic viewpoint see especially G. Luzzatto, 'Piccoli e grandi mercanti nelle città italiane del Rinascimento,' in *In onore e ricordo di Giuseppe Prato, saggi di storia e teoria economica*, pp. 27–49. F. Roerig, *Mittelalterliche Weltwirtschaft*; H. Pirenne, *Economic and Social History of Medieval Europe*; A. Sapori, *Il mercante italiano nel medio evo*, 2d ed.; *Cambridge Economic History*, Vol. II, Chap. v. Naturally, the conclusions will tend to greater optimism if a scholar thinks in terms of Italy, which was at this time the most advanced country in business, and to greater pessimism if he considers Germany or England, countries which were backward.

CHAPTER XIV

TRANSPORTATION BY SEA

THROUGHOUT the Middle Ages transportation by water was far more important than transportation and travel by land, especially in long-distance trade. It was cheaper, usually faster, and often safer. Happily, there is no dearth of monographs and of translated sources in English. This relieves us of the task of covering the subject fully. What we present here is not a panorama of transportation by sea and its problems but a small selection of samples.

The two chartering contracts (Documents 123 and 124) give some idea of the infinite variety of clauses which could be included in agreements of this kind and indirectly bring to notice the two basic types of ships used in Mediterranean trade—the rounded nef, propelled mainly by sails, and the thin, swift galley, propelled mainly by oars. Then there is a bill of lading (Document 125), which is not a notarial but a holograph document, showing how merchandise often was entrusted to the ship's captain without any passenger accompanying the wares to watch over them. Another document (126) tells of the frequent necessity of providing a ship with armed escort. The last document is a reminder of shipwreck.[1]

Chartering Contracts

123

From the Latin[2]

Genoa, February 23, 1250

We, Corrado Guarco, Ponzio Riccio, Pietro d'Oria, Guido Spinola, and

---

[1] In English the most valuable works are W. Ashburner, *The Rhodian Sea-Law*; E. H. Byrne, *Genoese Shipping in the Twelfth and Thirteenth Centuries*; F. C. Lane, *Venetian Ships and Shipbuilding of the Renaissance*; E. Bensa, *The Early History of Bills of Lading*. Descriptions of ships and voyages are found in a great number of works by crusaders, explorers, and other persons whose memoirs have been translated into English. See the exhaustive bibliography in C. P. Farrar and A. P. Evans, *Bibliography of English Translations from Medieval Sources*.

[2] Byrne, *Genoese Shipping*, pp. 85–88. The contract concerns the chartering of a large sail vessel (a *navis* or 'nef') for 'Overseas;' as we have previously noted, this expression meant Syria and the neighboring regions. Its interest stems from the fact that it is one of the most complex documents of the kind; indeed some of its features remain obscure even after the excellent comments of its editor, pp. 37–42, 49–58. Byrne rightly states, on the evidence of this and other documents, that 'ship-owners reckoned their profits chiefly on the freight paid for cargoes fetched back to Genoa from ports over seas, and not on the cargoes exported from Genoa.' This is why the contract requires the merchants to promise for the homebound voyage a far larger weight of

Lanfranco Riccio, shareholders[3] in the nef named 'Great Paradise,'[4] each of us [liable] for the whole amount, charter our aforesaid ship for making this present voyage to Overseas, at the freight charge (*naulum*) written below and with the sailors and equipment written below, to you, merchants: Ido Lercari junior, and Ottolino di Negro (in your own behalf and in behalf of Lanfranco Dugo), and Guglielmino Tartaro (in your own behalf and in behalf of Giacomo Spinola and of Benedetto Castagna), and Filippo de Stacione, Bartolomeo de Mari, Giacomino of Verdun, Ughetto Lomello, Giacomo Rubeo, and Diotisalvi Bonaventura.

Therefore we promise and make agreement with you, the aforesaid merchants, in your[5] own behalf and in that of the others mentioned above, to have the aforesaid nef fitted out and made ready with [the following equipment]: six cotton sails, three of which are to be new, a hemp sail, and nine spars good and sound, and twenty-two anchors, and twenty-five anchors for the return [voyage], and twenty coils of new rope besides other soaked ropes, and ten coils [of rope] with buoys,[6] and all other equipment and fittings sufficient for the said nef to make the aforesaid voyage. And [we promise to have her manned] with a hundred sailors, twenty of whom are to be arbalesters and two are to be experienced warrant officers. And in this number no servant and no shareholder is to be counted, except for the pilot personally.

---

cargo than that of the outbound voyage—10 *cantara* of Acre, equal to 7,250 Genoese pounds, per thousand Genoese pound carried outwards. But we are not convinced by Byrne's explanation of the choice allowed to the merchants between the *cantarata Janue* (which we translate 'Genoese tonnage' in the lack of the expression 'Genoese cantarage;' *cantarata* derives from *cantaro* as *tonnellata*, 'tonnage,' derives from ton) and the *cantarata Syrie*. He assumes that the merchants after their arrival in Syria could either supply the homebound cargo and pay for the round trip at reduced rates (if they chose the *cantarata Syrie*) or supply no homebound cargo and pay the regular charges for the outbound voyage (if they chose the *cantarata Janue*). The contract, however, unconditionally requires the merchants to load in the nef all of their cargo, at the seven-fold rate of weight, for the homebound journey; in turn the ship owners unconditionally promise to reserve nearly all of the space in the nef for that cargo. Moreover, as we shall see later, the rates of the *cantarata Janue* and of the *cantarata Syrie* were approximately the same. The difference was that in the first instance the merchants were to pay Genoese money in Genoa, the weight of the cargo being measured by the Genoese system of weight, whereas in the second instance they were to pay Syrian money in Syria, the weight of the cargo being measured by the Syrian tonnage.

[3] *Participes.* The problem of the meaning of the word *pars* ('part,' 'share'), from which *participes* derives, is one of the most hotly debated in legal history. See the bibliography in the introduction to this chapter.

[4] 'Paradise' has reference not to Heaven but to the huge pavilion (*paradisus*) built on deck to furnish luxurious accommodations for the wealthier passengers.

[5] *Pro nobis et aliis supradictis*; but read *pro vobis*. The small *n* is written practically in the same way as the small *u*. There were no shareholders 'mentioned above' in addition to those specifically named in the instrument, whereas the merchants contracted both in their own behalf and in that of others who were not present at the writing of the instrument.

[6] *Mollis de gropialibus.* The buoys indicated the position where the anchor was cast. See L. T. Belgrano, *Documenti inediti riguardanti le due crociate di S. Ludovico IX rè di Francia*, p. 31.

And we promise to you, merchants, in your behalf and in that of those mentioned above, to have this nef fitted out and made ready to leave the port of Genoa, with the sailors and everything as said before, and to begin the said voyage by the middle of March next, and to go with the said nef to Monaco or Antibes to take on the cargo of the said nef, and to resume the aforesaid voyage from there in order to bring it to completion. And we promise that, within ten days after the said nef has arrived at Monaco or Antibes to take on the said cargo, we shall have her fitted out and made ready to hoist sail and to bring to completion the said voyage with the said nef. But if we should hear news that some naval expedition is being organized in the Sicilian territory[7] or in other places—may this not happen—and if because of this we are unable to go safely with the said nef and your merchandise to the territory of Acre, we promise to you to go with the said nef and your merchandise to Tripoli, if you, merchants traveling aboard said nef, or the majority among you shall so wish, [the majority being determined] pro rata of tonnage.[8]

Moreover we promise to you, said merchants, in your[9] own behalf and in that of the others mentioned above, not to allow in the said nef, either going or returning, more than one hundred pilgrims, among whom there is to be no woman—[this] on condition that we allow no pilgrim to stay [in the space] between the middle mast and the stern of the said nef. And once the tonnage [to be loaded] in the said nef has been computed, [we promise] to take aboard the said nef one merchant for every ten *cantara* of Acre of merchandise computed for the nef,[10] and not to allow any merchant to come aboard the aforesaid nef in Genoa on better terms than any one of you without your permission and will, or that of the majority among you. We may take aboard, however, up to two hundred bales between the two decks of the said nef on the voyage to Overseas. But on returning from Oversea territory to Genoa with the aforesaid nef we promise not to take aboard or allow to be taken aboard the said nef any merchandise between the two decks; nor [shall we do so] at any place we may touch with the said nef when returning from Oversea territory to Genoa.

[7] Genoa was at war with Frederick II, king of Sicily and emperor, who also maintained a garrison in Acre to support his claims as king of Jerusalem.

[8] *Pro parte cantarate*, i.e., not the numerical majority of the merchants but merchants representing the majority of the cargo.

[9] See note 5 above.

[10] As Byrne points out, a *miliarium* (a thousand Genoese pounds) was the customary unit of cargo 'every merchant was supposed to carry in order to rank on board the ship as a merchant in distinction from a pilgrim or common passenger.' The contract a few lines below states that the merchants were expected to supply for the homebound voyage 10 *cantara* of Acre per *miliarium* of Genoa carried in the outbound voyage. According to custom, merchants who had a sufficient cargo paid nothing for the carriage of their persons.

In addition we promise and make agreement with you, aforesaid merchants in your[11] behalf and in that of the others mentioned above, to have the said nef fitted out by the middle of September next, and made ready with every-thing as said above, in the territory of Acre or in whatever place she shall take on cargo, in order to hoist sail and to return to Genoa with the cargo of the said nef. Then, if you should choose and be in agreement [to reckon the freight charges] for the said nef by the tonnage of Acre, we promise to you, merchants, in your own behalf and in that of the others mentioned above, to deduct from the payment of freight charges all that you may have paid us in Genoa for the freight charges of your bales and merchandise, at the rate [of exchange] of 3 bezants Saracen of Syria per pound [of Genoese deniers] paid in Genoa for the aforesaid freight charges.[12] [And we promise] to carry in the said nef all your goods and merchandise and luggage [allow-ing] up to twenty bales per thousand Genoese pounds [of weight].[13]

Conversely, we, the aforesaid merchants, in our own behalf and in behalf of the merchants mentioned above, promise and make agreement with you, the shareholders mentioned above, to board said nef with all our merchandise and bales in order to begin and bring to completion within the said time limit the said voyage as [described] above. And [we promise] to deliver to you [to load for the homebound voyage] in the said nef 10 *cantara* of Acre per thousand Genoese pounds of the amount of merchandise, goods, and bales which we shall carry and load in the said nef [for the outbound voyage]. And [we promise] to give you and pay as freight charges 11 bezants Saracen of Syria per *cantaro* of Acre of the amount which we shall load in the said nef.

Then, within four days after we arrive with the said nef in the territory of Syria or wherever we shall make port with the said nef in order to unload, if we, the merchants, should choose and be in agreement that we want to hold [the cargo] by the Genoese tonnage, [we shall proceed as follows:] At that time we, the aforesaid merchants, in our own name and in the aforesaid names, promise to give and to pay to you, the aforesaid shareholders, 10 *soldi* Genoese per *cantaro* [of Genoa] of the amount of bales and merchandise which we shall load in the said nef [in the outbound

---

[11] See note 5 above.

[12] This was the usual rate of exchange in Genoa at that period: see R. S. Lopez, 'L'attività economica di Genova nel marzo 1253 secondo gli atti notarili del tempo,' *Atti della Società Ligure di Storia Patria*, LXIV (1935), 178ff. Obviously it included interest charges.

[13] As in modern ships, units of cargo were reckoned both by weight and by size; thus the *miliarium* was both a thousand pounds and the space occupied by twenty bales. See A. Lattes *Il diritto marittimo privato nelle carte liguri dei secoli XII e XIII*, p. 103.

voyage], according to the use and manner of Genoese tonnage. And [we promise] to pay you in Genoa the entire freight charges for the amount of merchandise and bales which each of us shall have to deliver for the [homebound] cargo at the rate mentioned above.[14] Then, for the amount of freight charges which some of us will still have to pay to you for our bales and merchandise loaded in the said nef as [described] above, we, in the aforesaid behalf, promise you to pay and give 3 bezants Saracen of Syria per pound [of Genoese deniers] of the amount which some of us, merchants, will still have to pay you.[15] [The payment will be due] within fifteen days after we have decided as above that we want to hold [the cargo] by the Genoese tonnage.

But if we should decide that we want to hold [it] by the Syrian tonnage, at that time we, in the said behalf, promise you to give and pay in Acre, or wherever [the nef] may load in order to return to Genoa, the aforesaid freight charges for the cargo of the aforesaid nef according to the provisions of the [pertinent] Genoese article [of law].[16] And [we promise] not to load in the said nef other merchandise and goods except only [those belonging] to us, the aforesaid [merchants], and to any one of us.

In addition we, the said merchants, promise, in our name and in the name of those for whom we have made the promise, that we shall so act and take care that those above-mentioned [merchants] in whose behalf we made our promise shall undertake and observe each and all the aforesaid [pacts] and shall not violate them in any particular.

We, the shareholders, in our name, and we, the said merchants, in our name and in the name of the aforesaid [merchants in whose behalf we promised], promise to undertake and to observe each and all the aforesaid [pacts] and not to violate [them] in any particular. Otherwise we promise a penalty of £ 1,000 Genoese, each party making this stipulation to the others. For the penalty and for thus observing we pledge as security—each party to the others—all our goods existing and future. And let each of us shareholders

[14] A *cantaro* of Genoa (approximately 50 kgs.) was 150 Genoese pounds, or 150/725 of a *cantaro* of Acre. Ten *soldi* of Genoese deniers at the rate of exchange mentioned above were equivalent to 1½ bezants of Syria. Inasmuch as the outbound cargo was 100/725 of the homebound cargo, the first payment of 10 *soldi* per *cantaro* of Genoa carried one way indicates approximately the same rate as the payment of 11 bezants per *cantaro* of Acre for the round trip.

[15] The meaning of this sentence is not quite clear, but it would seem to imply that some merchants might load for the homebound trip some cargo over and above the 10 *cantara* of Acre which they were obligated to supply.

[16] *Secundum formam capituli Janue.* A *capitulum* was an article in a book of statutes or a separate provision. Unfortunately this *capitulum* has not come down to us, but the contract makes it clear that the merchants will be bound to pay 11 bezants per *cantaro* of Acre of the load supplied for the homebound trip.

be bound for the whole amount in regard to the aforesaid [pledge], waiving the benefit of the new constitution concerning two defendants, and that of the Epistle of the divine Hadrian,[17] and the right of the principal [debtor].

Done in Genoa, in the Church of Santa Maria delle Vigne, 1250, seventh indiction, February 23, between terce and none. Witnesses: Marino of Parma, and Nicolino Guarnieri, judge,[18] and Tommasino d'Oria.

124

From the Latin[19]

Caffa, April 28, 1290

In the name of the Lord, amen. We, Baliano de Porta and Nicola Gallo, both of us [liable] for the whole amount, charter and concede by title of charter to you, Nicola Buonuomo, a certain galley of ours, named 'Holy Savior,' which is now in the port of Caffa. This galley we promise you to have ready at once and outfitted with all tackle, equipment, and apparatus, water, breadstuffs, and everything necessary for said ship. And we promise to leave the port of Caffa with this galley thus adequately outfitted any time from now until the first day of the next May, and to go to Locopa, and there, in the said locality of Locopa, to load or have loaded, through our boat and sailors, from 17 to 20 *miliaria* of fish and caviar.[20] And we promise to await you there during the next fifteen days following the opening of the fair[21] in order to have and receive said cargo, provided, however, that you be bound and expected to buy this [amount of] fish at the rate of 12 buckrams [the *miliarium*]. And when said time has past, we promise to leave the said place with said galley thus loaded and to sail to Constantinople, and to await you there during the next fifteen days following the arrival of said ship there in order to unload and sell said cargo, and to give, deliver, and consign said cargo to you at the beach through our boat and sailors, according to what is the use and custom. [This will be done] provided you give and pay us for freight charges and by reason of freight charges of the said *miliaria* of fish as follows: viz., 12 gold hyperpers by the assay[22] of Constantinople in each one of said *miliaria*, to the full payment and satisfaction of those *miliaria*

<hr>

[17] The Epistle of the Emperor Hadrian settled the order of suit of codebtors.

[18] *Iudicis*, probably a slip of the notary for *Judex*.

[19] G. I. Bratianu, *Actes des notaires génois de Péra et de Caffa de la fin du treizième siècle* (*1281–1290*), pp. 276–77. The document has special interest as an example of triangular navigation and trade between Caffa, Constantinople, and the mouth of the Kuban river, where Locopa is located. In the latter region buckrams, that is, shirts or cuts of cloth, were used as currency.

[20] *Cavealium:* 'caviar' or 'sturgeon'? If caviar is meant, this is probably the earliest extant mention of it.

[21] *Fracto baẓali*, that is, literally, 'after the bazaar is broken.'

[22] That is, according to the weight and fineness of the hyperper acceptable to assayers in Constantinople. The larger proportion of gold hyperpers then in circulation was below standard.

loaded on said galley, and this to be done directly after said galley arrives there—waiving in the aforesaid matters the right of joint liability, the privilege of the new and old constitutions in regard to two culprits, the right of the principal [debtor], the Epistle of the divine Hadrian, the right of the principal, and every right, it being stipulated that both of us are [liable] for the whole amount.

Furthermore I, said Nicola, promise you [that I shall regard it] as settled, approving, ratifying, and confirming each and all the aforesaid conditions. And I promise and agree to give and to deliver to you the said cargo to be loaded in the said galley, and to buy this [amount of] fish at the said rate, and also to have you relieved of the said cargo as above, and to render to you full payment and satisfaction in regard to said freight charges in the manner and form as was stated above.

The said parties have promised to undertake, to fulfill, and to observe each and all [of the conditions] and not to act contrary in any way, under penalty of 100 gold hyperpers by the assay of Constantinople solemnly stipulated and promised between us, each and all of the aforesaid conditions remaining [in force] as settled. And the party which does not observe [the conditions] shall owe this penalty to the party which does observe them. For the undertaking and observing of this they have pledged to each other as security all of their goods existing and future. Done in Caffa in the *fondaco* of the Genoese, in the year of the Nativity of the Lord 1290, on April 28, between nones and vespers, in the presence of the witnesses, Oberto Corrigiario, Francesco Taraburla, and Alessandrino di Rivasco.

A Bill of Lading

125

From the Catalan[23]

Valencia, March 17, 1396

In the name of God, so be it. Done in Valencia on March 17, 1395.[24] Gentlemen:[25]

I am transmitting to you, in the name of God and of salvation, by the ship captained by En Lois Frexinet, who is the bearer of the present, 27 large sacks

[23] E. Bensa, *Francesco di Marco da Prato*, p. 379. Note that the shipment was made to the Genoa branch of the Francesco Datini *compagnia* (headed by Andrea Bonanni), in behalf of the Barcelona branch of the same *compagnia* (headed by Luca del Sera). Francesco Datini of Prato, mentioned twice as if he lived in two places, probably was staying in Prato, at the home office.

[24] Here and hereafter, style of the Incarnation (that is, 1396). The date on the back of the document must be that of the arrival of the cargo in Genoa.

[25] *Senyor*, in the singular; but the context and the address show that the plural should have been used.

of wool, of which 23 are white and 3 black, and one of which is one part white and two parts black; and they are marked with my mark.[26]

And therefore, gentlemen, when it pleases our Lord God that the said ship arrive there, be so kind as to receive the said wool and to give him for freight charges s.11 d.6 Genoese for each quintal of Genoa; for I must see to it that the others who have loaded here be paid in this manner. And do as Francesco of Prato and Luca del Sera, your [branch] of Barcelona, shall wish.

And I say nothing else. I remain at your pleasure and orders. May the grace of the Holy Ghost be with you.

Your Andru Lopiz [sends] greetings.

To be given to Francesco of Prato and Andrea Bonanni in Genoa.

[On the back]

27 sacks.

1395. From Valencia, May 14.

Armed Escort for a Merchantman

126

From the Italian[27]

Genoa, September 1, 1408

We, Officers of the Sea or of the Provisions for the Genoese Shipping, make it known and attest to each and all persons who shall see the present letter that in order to protect the ship of the nobleman Megollo Lercari, which is preparing to sail to the Orient, in such a way as to render futile the assaults of any corsairs, we have now increased through the said padron Megollo the usual crew of said ship, which consists of 73 men, by 25 arbalesters for the present voyage as far as Chios. And the scribe of the said ship is to be required to keep a separate account in regard to them. And the expenses of these 25 arbalesters—the usual food and living costs and salary and the other expenses which shall be specified—are to be paid from said ship and [precisely] from the freight charge and from merchandise now loaded or going to be loaded in the said ship for the present voyage and destined for Gaeta, Naples, and other ports beyond Naples in the direction of parts east and south. Wherefore, in order that justice be done everywhere to the same Megollo in regard to

---

[26] Here the *senyal* or mark of the sender is drawn. The same mark appears at the end.

[27] R. di Tucci, *Il genovese Antonio Malfante*, pp. 29–31; and see pp. 27–28 on the legendary background of Megollo Lercari.

the things mentioned, if there should be need, we have ordered that this letter patent of ours be granted him with the certification of our seal.

Done in Genoa, 1408, the first day of September. . . .[28]

Total [expenditure]: £ 413 s.17 d.176.

On September 1, letters were written in due form on the part of the Office of Provisions for the Shipping, etc., to the Genoese consuls and merchants in Naples, containing special [instructions] for the said Megollo to have [the arbalesters] mustered and [for the consuls] to report to us about it.

On the same day, similar letters in regard to the said subject were written to the Genoese consul and merchants in Gaeta. [Also], on the same day, similar letters concerning it [were sent] to the podestà of Chios.

Freight Charge Canceled on Account of Shipwreck

127

From the Latin[29]

[Genoa, December 24, 1182]

I, Guillem of Tarascon of Aste,[30] give you, Arnaut of Avignon of Narbonne, by [title of] donation among the living, the entire freight charge which you owed me personally for my and my partners' *bucium*[31] which was shipwrecked in the *grau*[32] of Narbonne. The aforesaid donation I promise you, etc. Done on the shore, on that day.

[28] We omit the itemized list of the expenses. Salaries formed the larger part of the total—they amounted to £ 351 s.17 d.5; the individual arbalesters were paid different amounts ranging from £ 12 s.10 to £ 15.

[29] R. di Tucci, *Studi sull' economia genovese del secolo decimosecondo*, Part 1, 'La nave e i contratti maritimi,' p. 59.

[30] Asti in Italy? Alès, in the department of Gard? Asté in the department of Hautes-Pyrénées?

[31] On this kind of ship, see Di Tucci, *Studi*, pp. 13–15, 58.   [32] Channel between two sand bars.

CHAPTER XV

TRANSPORTATION BY LAND

DURING THE early Middle Ages the poor condition of the roads and their lack of security forced merchants to rely very heavily upon transportation by river, in spite of the fact that the Mediterranean countries have few rivers suitable for navigation. The Commercial Revolution witnessed great progress in road building and in the techniques of transportation by land. Internal waterways[1], however, still continued to carry an important part of the freight, especially when this consisted of cheap, bulky goods. Our first selection describes transportation of woad by barge on the Po river, which was probably the most intensively exploited waterway in the Mediterranean world. Fairly long, wide, and deep, it also linked some of the most advanced cities and territories.

The other selections illustrate certain aspects of transport by road.[2] A merchant who wished to ship goods by the more frequented roads could avail himself of the services of common carriers, most of whom were members of gilds of muleteers, carters, porters, and the like (Document 129). A merchant also could obtain for his unaccompanied merchandise any preferential treatment which a customs office might grant to other citizens of his town. It was enough for him to certify the ownership of the goods by letters addressed to the customs officers or by other documents of a similar nature. The two last selections (Documents 131 and 132) show how tolls affected the cost of transporting the same merchandise by different routes. English wool, shipped to Italy via the Atlantic Ocean, southern France, and the Tyrrhenian Sea, followed a roundabout way, but this route had the advantage of reducing to a minimum the distance to be covered by land. The same wool, shipped by the Alpine passes, went by a far more direct route, but it incurred great expenses for transportation, transshipments, and tolls.

[1] See also Document 47, for a more unusual case in which lumber was logged without being loaded into a barge. There are no general works on river transport; see, however, G. Biscaro, 'Gli antichi "Navigli" milanesi,' *Archivio Storico Lombardo*, ser. 4, X (1908), 283-326; G. C. Zimolo, 'Cremona nella storia della navigazione interna,' in *Atti e memorie del III Congresso Storico Lombardo* (Milan, 1939), pp. 221-66; P. Vaillant, 'Etude d'histoire urbaine: Grenoble et ses libertés (1226-1349),' *Annales de l'Université de Grenoble*, new ser., section Lettres-Droit, XII (1935), 123-53; XIV (1937), 87-178. For the early Middle Ages, see L. B. Holland, *Traffic Ways about France in the Dark Ages.*

[2] For the very abundant bibliography of the subject, see J. Kulischer, *Allgemeine Wirtschaftsgeschichte des Mittelalters und der Neuzeit*, I, 229ff. In English, consult J. T. Tyler, *The Alpine Passes in the Middle Ages.* This work, however, is not entirely satisfactory. Nor is there any good general work devoted to the problem of transportation by land. Some legal works on the history of contracts in transportation are listed in E. Besta, *Le obbligazioni nella storia del diritto italiano*, p. 329. Comparative costs are discussed in *Cambridge Economic History*, II, 332-33.

Transportation on the River Po

128

From the Latin[3]

Pavia, [February 23, 1459]

In Pavia ... Giovanni Martino Lazzari, son of the late Ser Ghezzo di Castronovo, honorable doctor in both Laws, on the one part, and the nobleman Gabrino de' Pinzoni of Cremona, son of the late Ser Venturino, on the other part, came to the agreements written below ... to wit:

First, as the aforesaid Giovanni Martino has the intention of having 300 *some* of woad transported by ship from the village of Bastida dei Dossi to the city of Venice, that the said Giovanni Martino be bound and obligated to consign said woad to the ship at the bank of the Po river in said village of Dossi or in the neighborhood, wherever it shall be better to load the ship of said Gabrino.

And he, Gabrino, in turn promised and agreed and is promising and is agreeing to transport or have transported said 300 *some* of woad by ship from said bank, said Giovanni Martino only placing it aboard the ship, that is, with his labor and at his expense as [is stated] above, up to and into the city of Venice, said Gabrino paying every toll and all the labor, costs, and expenses of Gabrino himself, except that said Giovanni Martino be bound to pay the toll or export duty on said woad which is paid to our most illustrious lord, the duke of Milan, to his treasury, or to the farmers of said toll.

And for these 300 *some* of woad so transported, said Giovanni Martino promised and agreed with the same Gabrino ... to give and to pay [freight charges] at the rate of £ 5 s.12 imperial for every *soma* of said woad transported up to and into the city of Venice at the shore in said city.

And that there said Gabrino be bound and must consign to the same Giovanni Martino the said quantity of woad in good order and just as it has been consigned to him, Gabrino, according to the usual custom of good carriers; and of said woad said Giovanni Martino is to be bound to pay the usual toll that is paid in said city of Venice.

Also, that said Gabrino be bound to lend to said Giovanni Martino at once 50 gold ducats or their value in money, which, together with the charge for said transportation of said woad, at the rate of the aforesaid £ 5 s.12 for

[3] C. M. Cipolla, 'In tema di transporti medievali,' *Bollettino Storico Pavese*, new ser., V (1944), 35–36. The dots are Cipolla's. The last paragraph of the document apparently is a primitive form of insurance like that of Document 134, but it is impossible to state it definitely since Cipolla has omitted the last sentences.

each *soma*, said Giovanni Martino shall be bound to give and must give, return, and pay to the same Gabrino. And he promised and agreed to do so within one month after [the *some*] are consigned and transported, as is stated above, up to and into said city of Venice, and as soon as said month has passed. . . .

Land Transportation: Carriers and Invoice Letters

129
From the Latin[4]

Marseilles, July 17, 1248

On the sixteenth day before the Kalends of August. I, Surléon of Chalon[?],[5] carrier (*vetturarius*), acknowledge and certify to you, Rinaldo Bracciforti and Raniero Malano, of Piacenza, that I have had and have received from you two *caricae* of pepper to be carried to the next fairs of St. John in Troyes, for the price of hire of £ 7 Viennese, which we[6] acknowledge that we have had and have received from you, waiving, etc. And we promise you, by stipulation, to carry the said *caricae* well and faithfully, with [pack] animals and without carts, and to guard and to return them to you or to Musso Calderario[7] or to your fellow partners within six days after the cry 'hare,'[8] and to undertake and to fulfill for you all that carriers are bound to undertake and to fulfill for merchants, under penalty of £ 10 Viennese. Done in Marseilles, near the tables of the changers. Witnesses: Berenguer Eguezer, Ansaldo Tiba, Arnaut Gache.

130
From the Latin[9]

Genoa, March 19, 1253

To the provident men, customs officers of Tortona, Giovanni Ascherio, citizen of Genoa, greetings.

I am communicating to you by the tenor of the present instrument that I have sent to the house of Lanfranco de Pulvino in the city of Tortona many *saumae* of wool, cotton, ginger, and other wares, according to the tenor of my letter sealed with my seal, and that I previously have sent through

---

[4] L. Blancard, *Documents inédits sur le commerce de Marseille au moyen-âge*, II, 288.

[5] *Surleo de Celano.*   [6] Evidently the carrier is speaking both for himself and for his partners.

[7] *Caldairac;* but read 'Calderario,' a well-known Piacenzan family.

[8] The opening cry of the fair.

[9] R. S. Lopez, 'L'attività economica di Genova nel marzo 1253 secondo gli atti notarili de tempo,' *Atti della Società Ligure di Storia Patria*, LXIV (1935), 196–97, note 118.

Tommaso de Begato and Guglielmo Monticello and Giovanni Auxico 12 *saumae* of wool. Wherefore I advise that you place full confidence in my letters sealed by my seal, which I shall address to you henceforth, and in those which I have sent you in regard to said number of *saumae*, and that you place full confidence in these as well as in my other letters. I swear by the holy Gospels of God that all the *saumae* which I am sending, have sent, and shall henceforth send belong to me and to my Genoese partners.

Done in Genoa in the store (*volta*) of the house of Giacomo de Porta, 1253, tenth indiction, March 19, between terce and nones. Witnesses: Enrico Balbo and Nicoloso Sapana and Giacomo of San Giorgio.

A Case in Comparative Costs

131

From the Latin[10]

[Milan, *c.*1390]

Here below is listed what has to be paid for customs, conveyance,[11] stops, and other [expenses] which are incurred in regard to the conveyance of bales of wool [from Constance to Bellinzona].

	£	s.	d.
First of all, in Constance, for the toll of every bale of wool	–	16	–
Item, for the carrying[12] of every bale from Constance to Rheineck	–	1	8
Item, in Rheineck for the toll of every bale as above	–	2	7
Item, for carrying from Rheineck to Blatten, two German miles distant	–	5	10
Item, for stop in Rheineck	–	–	$2\frac{1}{2}$
Item, for carrying from Blatten to Sankt Peter	–	2	–
Item, for stop in Blatten	–	–	$2\frac{1}{2}$
Item, in Sankt Peter for toll	–	2	7
Item, for stop	–	–	$2\frac{1}{2}$
Item, for conveyance from Sankt Peter to Schaan	–	2	–
Item, for carrying from Schaan to Balzers	–	2	–
Item, for stop in Schaan	–	–	$2\frac{1}{2}$
Item, for toll in Vaduz	–	2	–
Item, for carrying from Balzers to Mayenfeld	–	1	9

[10] A. Schulte, *Geschichte des mittelalterlichen Handels und Verkehrs zwischen Westdeutschland und Italien mit Ausschluss von Venedig*, II, 38–39.

[11] Here and henceforth, 'conveyance' translates *conductus*.

[12] Here and henceforth, 'carrying' translates *victura*.

	£	s.	d.
Item, for toll in Balzers	–	–	8
Item, for stop at Balzers	–	–	2½
Item, in Mayenfeld for toll	–	1	3
Item, for stop at Mayenfeld	–	–	2½
Item, for carrying from Mayenfeld to Zizers	–	1	7
Item, for stop at Zizers	–	–	2½
Item, for carrying from Zizers to Chur	–	1	7
Item, in Chur for toll	–	3	5
Item, for stop and division and weighing	–	–	9
Item, for conveyance from Chur to Trins	–	6	–
Item, for toll in Trins	–	1	6
Item, for stop at Trins	–	–	2½
Item, for carrying from Trins to Laax	–	6	–
Item, for toll in Laax	–	2	7
Item, for stop in Laax	–	–	2½
Item, for carrying from Laax to Ruis	–	7	6
Item, for toll at a certain bridge	–	–	10
Item, for toll of the lady of Sacho at Ilanz	–	1	6
Item, for stop at Ruis	–	–	2
Item, for carrying from Ruis to Truns	–	7	6
Item, for carrying from Truns to Casaccia	1	5	–
Item, for three stops	–	–	6
Item, for carrying from Casaccia to Biasca	1	8	–
Item, for three stops	–	–	6
Item, for carrying from Biasca to Bellinzona	–	12	–
Item, for stop at Biasca and stop at Claro	–	–	4

Sum £ 7 s.10 d.8 the bale.[13]

132

Francesco di Balduccio Pegolotti, *The Practice of Commerce*
From the Latin[14]

[Florence, between 1310 and 1340]

For expenses in transporting wool from London, England, to Aigues-Mortes, Provence, for 1 sack of wool, which is made into 2 bales, which are

---

[13] We make the sum £ 7 s.9 d.5½. Either an error in addition has been made or an item has been omitted.

[14] Pegolotti, *La pratica della mercatura*, ed. A. Evans, pp. 257–58. See also Introduction, p. xx.

1 load, that is, 1 packload of a mule, which ought to be 4 *cantara* of Provence, which are about 500 lbs. of Florence:

First of all, for the freight from London to Libourne in Gascony it comes to d.12 sterling the bale; the packload amounts to s.2 sterling.

For pilot fee, d.½ sterling the bale; the packload amounts to d.1 sterling.

And for hoisting fee to the sailors of the ship when it is unloaded from the ship in Libourne [d.] ½ sterling the bale; the packload amounts to d.1 sterling.

And for the salary of the swain who comes with it from London to Libourne, d.1 sterling the bale; the packload amounts to d.2 sterling.

And for the custom of Royan on the Gironde, d.1 sterling the bale; the packload amounts to d.2 sterling.

The said 5 entries add up to s.2 d.6 sterling the packload, 1 gold florin being equivalent to s.3 sterling.

And for the custom of Bourg in Gascony, s.1 d.8 the bale; the packload amounts to s.3 d.4 Tournois.

And for the custom of Vayres, d.3 of Bordeaux the load.

And for the custom of Fronsac near Libourne, d.3 of Bordeaux the load.

And for the custom of Libourne, d.2 of Bordeaux the load.

And to unload it from the ship at Libourne and to carry it to the inn and weight it and stock it in piles in the inn, in total, d.8 petty Tournois the load.

And for two ropes to tie the two bales, each one by itself, in Libourne, in total, d.8 Tournois.

And for storage[15] and service of the innkeeper in Libourne, who receives them and sends them from Libourne to Montpellier, s.1 the bale; the packload amounts to s.2 Tournois.

And for carrying and toll from Libourne to Montpellier, in total, from s.50 to s.60 Tournois the load; one can estimate the average price at £ 2 s.15 Tournois the load.

And for storage with the innkeeper of Montpellier, who receives them and sends them entirely at his own expense from Montpellier to Aigues-Mortes, s.2 d.1 the bale; it amounts to s.4 d.2 Tournois the load.

And for the duty of the customs house of Aigues-Mortes, s.5 Tournois the load.

And for the export duty of the king of France, s.30 the load of [sheep's] wool, and s.50 the load of lamb's wool; the [sheep's] wool pays s.30 Tournois.

And for storage with the innkeeper of Aigues-Mortes, who receives it in

---

[15] *Ostellaggio:* see A. Sapori, *Studi di storia economica medievale*, 2d ed., pp. 172ff.; also F. Edler, *Glossary of Medieval Terms of Business: Italian Series, 1200–1600*, p. 198.

his home in Aigues-Mortes and then carries and lades it, personally paying all expenses for porters[16] and small boats until it is loaded in a galley in the port of Aigues-Mortes, s.1 d.4 the bale; the packload amounts to s.2 d.8.

Sum for all expenses written above and in the margin[17] up to this point: £ 5 s.3 d.6 petty Tournois (. . . sols petty Tournois being equivalent to 1 gold florin) and d.8 of Bordeaux (16 sols of Bordeaux being equivalent to 1 gold florin).

Sum for all expenses from England to Aigues-Mortes up to this point written above and previously:

£ – s.2 d.6 silver sterling, 3 soldi being equivalent to 1 gold florin.

£ – s.2 d.8 of Bordeaux, 16 soldi being equivalent to 1 gold florin.

£ 5 s.3 d.6 petty Tournois, . . . soldi being equivalent to 1 gold florin.

And this may be estimated to be in total about 9 gold florins the packload.

[16] *Bastagi,* from Greek *bastagarios.* The term was taken over in Latin as early as the fourth century. It survives in some Italian dialects.

[17] *Dallato,* literally, 'to the side.' Perhaps some of the items were written in the margin of the original manuscript, which has not come down to us.

CHAPTER XVI

THE DEVELOPMENT OF INSURANCE CONTRACTS

IN ANTIQUITY the sea loan was the only means of transferring risks in maritime transport from the shipper to another person. In the Middle Ages, however, the insurance contract gradually took its place. It slowly matured from a series of efforts to fit into old legal definitions and devices an agreement which was definitely new. This has caused modern jurists to engage in heated polemics to decide whether or not one or another contract contained the first elements of insurance. Without trying to take sides, we begin by giving two examples of agreements which some scholars would regard as early examples of insurance.[1]

The word *securitas* originally meant security, safety, or safe-conduct. Later it also meant insurance. It has been debated whether certain Genoese documents of 1191 and 1192, in which a shipper promises a premium for the *securitas* of some goods, are safe-conducts or instances of insurance. Our first selection, of a much later period, seems to indicate insurance rather than safe-conduct. In it the shippers are said to 'let' (*locare*) certain goods to a man who in consideration of a sum 'for security' promises to deliver the goods in a certain place.[2]

A number of German and Italian jurists, and lately an American scholar, have regarded as something close to insurance ('insurance loans') certain documents whereby a shipowner promises to transport goods belonging to a merchant and at the same time extends a loan to the merchant. Upon safe arrival of the ship or of the goods the merchant is to return the loan. If the goods do not arrive, the loan (*mutuum*) is not returned. As usual in medieval loan contracts, the interest is not mentioned, but there must have been interest serving as a sort of insurance premium. The second selection (Document 134) is an example of this type of contract in the thirteenth century. It antedates all examples previously known. A similar clause

---

[1] F. Edler de Roover, 'Early Examples of Marine Insurance,' *Journal of Economic History*, V (1945), 172–200, gives a valuable survey of previous opinions and adds much data on the practice of insurance in the later Middle Ages. Further bibliographical information is found in that article and in E. Besta, *Le obbligazioni nella storia del diritto italiano*, pp. 379–80. See also R. Doehaerd 'Chiffres d'assurance à Gênes en 1427–1428,' *Revue Belge de Philologie et d'Histoire*, XXVII (1949), 736–56.

[2] For the polemic on early *securitas* contracts, see V. Vitale, 'Le relazioni commerciali di Genova col regno normanno-svevo,' *Giornale Storico e Letterario della Liguria*, ser. 3, III (1927), 3–29; A. Lattes, 'L'assicurazione marittima e la voce "securare" in documenti genovesi del 1191 e 1192,' *Rivista del Diritto Commerciale*, XXV (1927), 64–73, and 'Note per la storia del diritto commerciale,' *Rivista del Diritto Commerciale*, XXXIII (1935), 185–92; G. P. Bognetti, *Note per la storia del passaporto e del salvacondotto*, pp. 353ff. Our selection is an unprinted document which Mrs. Edler de Roover kindly placed at our disposal. She did not use it in her article.

apparently was included in a contract of the fifteenth century for transport by river which we have included in Chapter XV. The shipowner extended a loan to the shipper, who was to reimburse him upon safe arrival of the goods.[3]

Unmistakable instances of insurance contracts involving underwriters who were not the same persons as the shipowners appear in the fourteenth century. Genoa was and remained for a long time the main center of this business. Insurance contracts in that city continued to borrow names and formulae from older contracts. They were first presented as loans (*mutuum*), then as sales (*emptio-venditio*). The third selection (Document 135) is an insurance contract of the sale type. The underwriters are said to have purchased for a certain price a certain amount of goods from a merchant, but they add that the contract is to be void if the goods arrive safely at a certain port. Neither the quantity and quality of the merchandise nor the amount of the premium is indicated, according to the Genoese practice of omitting mention of anything that might be objectionable on grounds of 'usury.'[4]

While in Genoa itself such roundabout formulae were still used, many Genoese underwriters abroad drafted unconcealed insurance contracts where the technical terms *assecuratio* or *securitas* and the amount of the premium were plainly stated. Document 136 gives an example of this kind.

Document 137 shows how payment of indemnities was made in a complicated case. The case defies summary description, but it is clearly stated in the document.

Document 138 shows the specialization of certain *compagnie* in the insurance business. Although the lack of full statistical information caused medieval insurance to be somewhat of a gamble—and in fact, insurance was often confused with gambling and wagers—accurate information and the underwriting of many insurance contracts tended to reduce the risk of the insurer. It was a very unlucky insurer who had to pay indemnities on the larger part of the contracts he underwrote. Another way of spreading risks was to have many underwriters take part of each insurance contract. Document 135 shows how this was done.

Space forbids giving examples of overland, life, and other types of insurance contracts, which also were developed in the Middle Ages but did not attain the same importance as marine insurance. Many elements contributed to their development, but in the main they were inspired by the same principles which led to the growth of marine insurance.

'Rent' Insurance and 'Loan' Insurance

133
From the Latin[5]

Lucca, March 3, [1334]

Percivalle, [son] of the late Bernardino Manni, citizen and merchant of

[3] See Document 128. Neither that document nor Document 135 in this chapter has been eolled an insurance loan by its editor, but if a type of 'insurance loan' is recognized as a precedent of true insurance, both documents fit within that class.

[4] See our introduction to Chapter VI. Document 145 helps one to understand why the *mutuum* form was superseded by the *emptio-venditio* form of the contract.

[5] Unprinted. Archivio di Stato, Lucca. *Registro 116, Ser Bartolomeo Buonmesi, Archivio*

Lucca, [liable] for the whole amount in person and [also] as general agent in the capacity of manager[6] for his partners—likewise citizens and merchants of Lucca—both for himself and for them, and [each of them liable] for the whole amount, by this instrument has let[7] to Ser Giorgio Marchesi of Genoa,[8] being present and renting, [liable] for the whole amount in person and [also] as general agent in the capacity of manager for Ser Antonio de Marini of Genoa, both in his own behalf and in the latter's and [each of them liable] for the whole amount, 2 bales of merchandise from Lucca, assessed and valued in common agreement between them at 700 florins of good, pure, and legal gold according to the good weight of the florin. And [they declare that Marchesi] has the [bales] in his possession, etc., and that they were loaded on the second day of March at the mouth of the Arno in Pisa[9] in the galley of Ser Gabriele Vento of Genoa. The latter promises to have them transported to Paris and to deliver [them] into the hands of Matteo Manni, who will receive [them] there for the *societas* itself within the next three months from the present time. And [Marchesi] acknowledged that he has received 32 florins of gold for their insurance.[10] And those, etc.,[11] for which, etc., etc. Done in Lucca in the aforesaid store[12] in which I, notary written below, am living, in the aforesaid house of the sons of Ricciardo, in the presence. . . . In the aforesaid year and indiction the third day of March.

After the aforesaid [transaction], in the year and indiction mentioned above, on the twenty-seventh day of May, said instrument was canceled by me, Bartolomeo [Buonmesi, notary], on verbal instruction[13] of the said Percivalle, absent, said Ser Giorgio being present, [to the effect] that the said bales had been delivered as promised. Done in Lucca in the aforesaid locality in the presence, etc.

134

From the Latin[14]

Naples, March 12, 1261

In the name of the Lord, amen. I, Uggeri Mascolino of Florence, acknowledge to you, Gogo, [son] of the late Giacomo de Marino, that I am under

---

Notarile. We are indebted to Mrs. Florence Edler de Roover for this document and the transcription of the text which we present.

[6] *Procuratore gestorio nomine.*   [7] *Locavit.*

[8] Giorgio Marchesi, a partner or a factor of Antonio de Marini, sold silk to merchants of Lucca and spent much time there while his partner remained in Genoa.

[9] *Fauce Areni Pisis.* The mouth of the Arno is a few miles distant from Pisa proper.

[10] *Securitas.*   [11] The *etceteras* are the notary's.   [12] *Apotheca.*   [13] *Parabola,* literally 'word.'

[14] G. Falco, 'Appunti di diritto marittimo medievale,' *Il Diritto Marittimo,* XXIX (1927), 152–53.

obligation to give to you 4 ounces gold tarini according to the ounce of the kingdom [in consideration] and by reason of the freight charge of goods and merchandise which I possess and which I have loaded in your vessel named 'Saint Nicholas.' This I promise to give and to pay, personally or through my messenger, to you or to your accredited messenger, within two days after you arrive with your aforesaid vessel at . . .[15] in the said place, net and clear from all duties and customs.[16] Otherwise, the penalty of the double, etc.; for the penalty and for so observing I pledge to you as security all [my goods], etc. Witnesses: Lapo, Florentine, nicknamed Alnardino; Matteo Aurigemma; Vernaccio de Curia; Pietro of Porta Nuova. Done in Naples, in the Pisan port, 1261, third indiction, on March 12.

In the name of the Lord, amen. I, Uggeri Mascolino of Florence, acknowledge that I have had and have received from you, Gogo, [son] of the late Giacomo de Marino . . .[17] 14 ounces good gold tarini of legal weight according to the correct weight of Naples, and in regard to them I call myself well satisfied and paid, waiving, etc. In consideration of these I promise and agree to give and to pay to you in Rome, viz. at . . .[18] £ 39 s.18 Roman, viz. 57 soldi in every ounce—and this in silver groats Roman worth 12 Pisan[?][19] each, net and clear from all tolls and customs—and this within two days after the said vessel arrives there. And in consideration of these I assign to you as security and in the name of security 3 *centenaria* of wine and one fourth of a *centenarium* of filberts which I have and I declare to have, as we acknowledge, in your vessel, and all and anything I have in the same vessel; [I do so] in such wise that if I do not make the aforesaid payment as [mentioned] above, you are to have full permission and power to sell the aforesaid goods and to receive and to retain the payment for yourself, by your authority, out of their price; and if you lack anything to complete [the payment of] said debt, I promise to make that good to you. Otherwise, the penalty of the double, etc.; and in consideration of the penalty and for so observing all this [my goods], etc. Witnesses: Lapo Alnardino of Florence, Matteo Aurigemma, Vernaccio de Curia, Pietro of Porta Nuova, and Costanza, *canevarius*. Done in Naples, in the locality named Pisan port, 1261, third indiction, on March 12.

---

[15] Dampness has rendered this short space illegible.
[16] *Dacitis et avariis*. The first word indicated the usual taxes (cf. Italian, *dazio*); the second usually indicated some kind of additional charge, whether legal or illegal.
[17] Reading uncertain.   [18] Reading uncertain.
[19] Reading uncertain: *presieu* is perhaps *pisanos*, according to Falco.

More Mature Forms of Insurance Contracts

135

From the Latin[20]

[Genoa,] September 15, 1393

In the name of the Lord, amen. Geri, [son] of the late Ser Lapo of Florence, Simone Guascone, Moroello Cigala, Gerardo Squarciafico, Amigo Imperiale, Pietro Scotto, Adamo Centurione, Antoniotto Cavanna, Antonio Centurione . . .[21] and Lorenzo del Fiore of Florence, each of them [liable] for the amount written below, have acknowledged and in truth have declared to me, notary undersigned, as a public official [holding] a public office, making the stipulation and receiving in the name and stead of Federico Vivaldi, citizen of Genoa, that they have bought, have had, and have received from him a certain amount of goods of the said Federico—waiving the exception that said goods have not been bought, have not been had, and have not been received, that the fact was not as [represented],[22] and every [other] legal [right]. And for these goods and in consideration of their price each of them has promised and agreed to give and to pay to said Federico or to his accredited messenger [the following amount]: the said Geri, 150 gold florins; the said Simone, 50 florins; the said Moroello, 100 gold florins; the said Gerardo, as many; the said Amigo, as many; the said Pietro, as many; the said Adamo, as many; the said Antoniotto, as many; the said Antonio, as many; and the said Lorenzo, as many; [this to be paid] within the next five months from now. Otherwise they have promised to give and to pay to the said Federico the penalty of the double of it and of the entire amount to which and to the extent of which [the agreement] is violated or is not observed as above, together with restitution of all losses, unrealized profits, and expenses which might be incurred because of it in court or outside—the aforesaid remaining as settled, and under hypothecation and pledge of their goods and [the goods] of any one of them, existing and future.

[The above is binding] with the exception and special reservation that if that amount of goods, property, and merchandise which was loaded or is to be loaded by Federico Imperiale or by another in his behalf for the account of the said Federico Vivaldi in Aigues-Mortes—to be transported to Ayas-solük and Rhodes or to either of these two localities in a certain ship, the captain of which formerly was Giovanni Gerardi and now is Giovanni Lippi,

---

[20] E. Bensa, *Il contratto di assicurazione nel medio evo*, pp. 215–16.   [21] The dots are Bensa's.
[22] *Rei sic non esse.*

or another [captain] in his behalf, and which has departed from Aigues-Mortes or is about to depart in order to sail to the aforesaid regions—is brought and unloaded in the said localities of Ayassolük and Rhodes or in either of them, in safety,[23] then and in such a case the present instrument is canceled, void, and of no value and pro rata.[24] And be it understood that such a risk begins when said ship departs and sets sail from Aigues-Mortes, and it remains and lasts, while the captain goes, stays [in port], sails, loads and unloads, from the said locality of Aigues-Mortes up to the said localities of Ayassolük and Rhodes, in whatever manner and way he wishes, until said amount of goods, property, and merchandise has been brought and unloaded in Ayassolük and Rhodes or in either of these two localities in safety, and pro rata. Let the present instrument also be canceled if the said Federico refrains from asking payment of the aforesaid amounts of money for the space of one year after the time or the time limit has elapsed for asking or obtaining their payment. And they waive whatever rules, decrees, statutes, and ordinances of the Commune of Genoa, and of the Office for Trade and for the Crimea of the Commune of Genoa, and all other legal [rights] by which they could violate the aforesaid.

And the said Geri declares that of the aforesaid 150 gold florins he underwrote 100 gold florins in the name of Cino de Franceschi.

Done as above, September 15, around nones.

136
From the Latin[25]

[Palermo, March 24, 1350]

On the twenty-fourth of the same month. Luchino de Mari and Leonardo Cattaneo, of Genoa, of their own free will, each of them for one half, insured (*assecuraverunt*) Filippo Cavegra of Voltri, captain of that *panfilo* called 'Saint Ampelius,' which today departed from the port of Palermo, for 200 gold florins on said *panfilo* and its equipment and the right to the freight charges of the present voyage of the said *panfilo* against every risk, peril, and fortune of God, the sea, and [hostile] people which may happen to come to the aforesaid *panfilo* and its tackle and equipment from the port of Palermo and from that moment at which said *panfilo* departs from there [to the time of its arrival] at the shore of Sciacca, and from that shore as far as the port of Tunis, and from the port of Tunis as far as the port of Mazara or of Trapani—viz., as far as the one of the aforesaid ports to which said *panfilo*

---

[23] *Ad salvamentum.*   [24] *Sic:* that is, according to the sum which each of the insurers underwrote.
[25] R. Zeno, *Documenti per la storia del diritto marittimo nei secoli XIII e XIV*, pp. 233–34.

shall go in order to make port, going, loading, unloading, returning, [each insurer] pro rata, provided the voyage is not altered without a legitimate impediment of God, the sea, and [hostile] people. [The aforesaid is to be done] in such a way that if perchance total disaster happens to overtake the aforesaid *panfilo* and its equipment and the right to the aforesaid freight charges, said Luchino and Leonardo are to be bound to give and to pay said 200 gold florins to the same Filippo in Palermo within one month after receiving positive news; and if a partial [disaster] occurs, [they are bound to give and to pay] by that proportion and part according to which [loss] has occurred. In consideration of this insurance thus made as above the said Luchino and Leonardo, in the presence and on request of the said Filippo, solemnly acknowledged that they have had and have received from the same Filippo 28 gold florins, waiving, etc.

Witnesses: Pellegrino Coccorello, Martino Leccavela, and Giovanni Salvago.

An Insurance Claim

137

From the Latin[26]

Marseilles, March 29, 1438

In the year of the Incarnation of the Lord 1438, the twenty-ninth of the month of March, at the hour of vespers. Be it know to all, present and future, that not many years ago [the following events occurred]:

The honorable man Oddone Raggio[?],[27] merchant of the city of Genoa, underwrote insurance (*sibi assecurari fecit*), after the custom of merchants, in the name of the honorable man Giacomo Venturo, Florentine merchant residing in the city of Avignon, on a certain quantity of wine loaded in a certain ship, the captain of which was Alvaro Ferrandes of Lisbon in the kingdom of Portugal, and called by the name of Saint Mary. And the aforesaid Giacomo Venturo asserted this quantity of wine to be his, as appears from a certain public instrument made in regard to this insurance (*assecuramento*) by the hand of a certain public notary of the aforesaid city of Genoa in the year and day mentioned in it. The truth of the matter, however, is this:

[26] P. Masson, 'L'Origine des assurances maritimes, spécialement en France et à Marseille,' in *Bulletin du Comité des Travaux Historiques et Scientifiques, Sciences Economiques et Sociales, Congrès des sociétés savantes tenu à Paris en 1921 et à Marseille en 1922*, pp. 214–16.

[27] The document has *Rau*, a name which is not found in Genoa and Liguria. The closest Genoese family name is Raggio.

that quantity of wine is the property of the noble and honorable men Mariotto de Nerli, Florentine, and Bertrand Forbin, merchants, citizens of the city of Marseilles,[28] and it belongs to and is owed to each of them for a specified sum—viz., to the said Mariotto for the sum of 300 florins and to the aforesaid Bertrand Forbin for the sum of 500 florins—and it was loaded for them and at their order in the said ship, as appears from a certain record taken by the honorable and provident man, Maître Raymond Bidaud, notary public of the said city of Marseilles, in the year and day mentioned in it, as is asserted. Then, by fortuitous accident, said ship, loaded with said wine and various other wares, having departed from the port of the said city of Marseilles making its voyage by the direct route toward the regions of Flanders, was captured and held in the harbor of Ceuta by the fleet and the men of the king of Portugal.

And therefore said Giacomo Venturo is striving to collect the aforesaid insurance; and he believes that he shall have and collect it provided he makes a promise and pledge to the said Oddone Raggio in the following manner, viz.: in case that after [taking] said insurance the aforesaid Giacomo Venturo has done anything prejudicial to said insurance or has otherwise impaired it, then he is held for the unrealized profits; and if it is found that the same Giacomo has recovered some of the said wine after the said capture of the said ship, then he is held to pay and to return to said Oddone Raggio twice the amount obtained and collected by the same Giacomo. And Giacomo Venturo himself concedes this, and is not willing to obligate himself in this respect unless he first obtains guarantee and security from the aforesaid merchants of Marseilles, to whom said sum belongs and is owed.

And here are now the aforesaid Mariotto de Nerli and Bertrand Forbin, who, having been informed in full about all that was related above, and desiring to grant said Giacomo Venturo guarantee as well as security, have promised and agreed—themselves and for their own associates, each pro rata and just as it affects and may affect each of them in any way in the future in joint liability—to me, notary written below—[acting] as a public and authorized person, being present and making the stipulation in joint liability and receiving in the place, stead, and name of the said Giacomo Venturo, absent, as if he and his [associates] were present—to maintain and to guard him, Giacomo Venturo, and his [associates'] goods, existing and future, free from liability in regard to the aforesaid promises, obligations, expenses, damages, disturbances, and unrealized profit to be borne by him or his [associates] in

---

[28] Biographical data on these two merchants may be found in E. Baratier and F. Reynaud, *Histoire du commerce de Marseille*, II, 672–73, 679ff.

whatever way in obtaining and collecting the insurance of said wine, made out to him as is explained above.

In peace, etc., under penalty, etc., of which, etc., obligated, etc., submitting themselves in regard to persons and goods, etc., waiving etc., swearing, etc., of which, etc. Done in Marseilles in a certain room of the house of Jean de Paul, situated on the shore. Witnesses: Giovanni Tedaldi, Florentine merchant; the provident men Pierre Blanqui and Paulet Vassal, merchants. And I, Palamède Vinatier, notary, etc.

Insurance as a Regular Business

138

From the Italian[29]

Pisa, August 3–September 23, 1384
[*On the cover of the record book:*]

MCCCLXXXIIII

This is a book of Francesco of Prato and partners, residing in Pisa, and we shall write in it all insurances we shall make in behalf of others. May God grant us profit from these and protect us from dangers.

[*Seal of Francesco son of Marco*]

MCCCLXXXIIII on August 3

A memorandum that on above-said day in behalf of Baldo Ridolfi and partners we insured for 100 gold florins wool in the ship of Bartolomeo Vitale [in transit] from Peñiscola to Porto Pisano. And from said 100 florins, which we insured against all risks, we received 4 gold florins in cash, as is evident by a record by the hand of Gherardo d'Ormanno which is undersigned by our hand.

Said ship arrived in Porto Pisano safely on August 4, 1384, and we are free from said risk.

A memorandum that on August 3, 1384, in behalf of Baldo Ridolfi and partners we insured for 50 gold florins wool in the ship of Simon Trio, Catalan, [in transit] from Minorca, to be unloaded in Porto Pisano. And from the said 50 gold florins we received 2 gold florins, and we insured against all risks, as is evident by a record by the hand of Gherardo d'Ormanno and undersigned by our hand.

[29] E. Bensa, *Francesco di Marco da Prato*, pp. 397–99.

Said ship arrived safely in Porto Pisano on . . .[30] September, and we are free from said risk.

MCCCLXXXIIII

A memorandum that on August 3, 1384, in behalf of Messer Anfrone da Guano we insured for 50 gold florins wine, that is, malmsey, in the ship of Francolino Luziano of Genoa, [in transit] from Cadiz to Sluys or to Southampton. And from the said 50 florins we received 4 gold florins, and we insured against all risks, as is evident by a record by the hand of Gherardo d'Ormanno and undersigned by our hand.

Arrived safely.

A memorandum that on August 16, 1384, in behalf of Francesco di Lotto and partners we insured for 100 gold florins a bale of silk in the ship of Bartolomeo da Padule, [in transit] from Porto Pisano to Barcelona. And from the said 100 florins we received 4 gold florins, and we insured against all risks, as is evident by a record by the hand of Gherardo d'Ormanno, and it is undersigned by our hand. And then said ship did not sail, and the said Francesco sent said bale by the ship of Martino Pocoluglio, and we ourselves underwrote [it] and ran said risk in said ship.

Arrived safely.

MCCCLXXXIIII

A memorandum that on September 7, 1384, in behalf of Baldo Ridolfi and partners we insured for 100 gold florins wool in the ship of Guilhem Sale, Catalan, [in transit] from Peñiscola to Porto Pisano. And from the said 100 florins we received 3 gold florins in cash, and we insured against all risks, as is evident by a record by the hand of Gherardo d'Ormanno which is undersigned by our hand.

Said ship arrived safely in Porto Pisano and unloaded on . . . October, 1384, and we are free from the insurance.

A memorandum that on September 10 in behalf of Ambrogio, son of Bino Bini, we insured for 200 gold florins Milanese cloth in the ship of Bartolomeo Vitale, [in transit] from Porto Pisano to Palermo. And from the said 200 florins we received 8 gold florins, charged to the debit account of Ambrogio on c. 174, and no other record appears [written] by the hand of any broker.

Arrived in Palermo safely.

---

[30] The blanks here and hereafter are in the original.

A memorandum that on September 15, 1384, in behalf of Lodovico Stancato and partners we insured for 100 gold florins cloth in the ship of Simone Tuosi, [in transit] from Porto Pisano to Tunis. And from the said [florins] we received 4 gold florins. We insured against all risks, as is evident by a record by the hand of Gherardo d'Ormanno, and it is undersigned by our hand.

Arrived safely.

A memorandum that on September 19 in behalf of Tieri, son of Lamberto di Domenico, we insured for 200 gold florins 5 bales of cloth and 2 . . . bales . . . [in transit] from Porto Pisano to Naples in the ship of Guido di Fazio of Genoa. And from it we received 8 gold florins. We insured against all risks, as is evident by a record by the hand of Gherardo d'Ormanno and undersigned by our hand.

Arrived safely.

A memorandum that on September 23 in behalf of Joan Nerbonesi, Catalan, we insured for 50 gold florins 5 bales of fustian, [in transit] from Porto Pisano to Barcelona in the ship of Antonio Marinelli. We received from it 2 gold florins 10 soldi. We insured against all risks, as is evident by a record by the hand of Gherardo d'Ormanno and undersigned by our hand.

Arrived safely.

A memorandum that on September 23, 1384, in behalf of Jacopo Bocchetto we insured for 100 gold florins two bales of cloth, [in transit] from Porto Pisano to Palermo in the ship of Antonio Jacopi. And from it we received 5 gold florins. We insured against all risks, as is evident by a record by the hand of Gherardo d'Ormanno and undersigned by our hand.

Said ship arrived safely in Palermo on October 10.

CHAPTER XVII

COMMERCIAL LITIGATION AND SHARP BUSINESS PRACTICES

LITIGATION COULD arise for so many reasons, and dishonest practices could be employed in so many connections, that it is difficult to choose the most significant examples from the mass of extant records.[1] Controversies over contracts involving transportation were particularly frequent. A group of merchants and passengers embark in a ship bound for Cyprus and Cilician Armenia, but the ship unexpectedly changes its course and sails toward the Byzantine Empire. A notary who happens to be on board writes out the indignant protest of the passengers (Document 139). Perhaps the captain of the ship had something to say in his report of the voyage, but his reasons are not given in the document.[2] In the next document (140) a ship captain sues a merchant who had refused to pay freight charges in full because part of his cargo had not been carried to its destination. The maritime court of Majorca finds in favor of the plaintiff because the shipper had failed to deliver the entire cargo as agreed.[3]

Complaints concerning the quality of merchandise are also common. Inspectors of the Commune of Montpellier examine certain saffron from Catalonia. They declare that it is adulterated and therefore not salable (Document 141). On the other hand, saffron of Catalonia is inspected in Frankfort-on-the-Main because some merchants claim that it is adulterated. The claim is not upheld. The officials of the Commune of Barcelona thank the officials of Frankfort and they offer fair and considerate treatment to all who deal fairly with the merchants of Barcelona (Document 142).

Some loan sharks are not content with charging interest, which is contrary to the law and ethics of the Church, but they also display their utter disregard of human

---

[1] For the reasons outlined in the Introduction to this volume we have used notarial documents and other unofficial records whenever possible. It has been impossible, however, entirely to exclude court records and official decrees, which often are the best sources for the study of litigation and sharp business practices.

[2] The document says that the captain ought to take the merchants to Cyprus 'and there learn the news.' This seems to imply that the captain had changed his route because of rumors of war and other information which led him to regard a voyage to Armenia as unsafe. As a matter of fact, Genoa at that time was at war with Pisa, but a war did not normally bring all commercial navigation to a standstill. Obviously the presence of a large enemy fleet along the route which the ship had to follow would have been a sufficient reason for a change of route. The merchants, however, did not believe that there was such a serious danger as the captain assumed.

[3] Compare the promises made by Baliano de Porta and Nicola Gallo to Nicola Buonuomo (Document 124). Often merchants who chartered a ship pledged themselves to load a minimum cargo.

decency. An inquiry in Nîmes discloses some of the tricks used by pawnbrokers (Document 143). A petition in Florence shows that a nonprofessional lender, a notary, can outdo professional pawnbrokers and go so far as to suppress evidence in order to ruin completely the widow of a colleague (Document 144).

Sometimes it is the lender, not the borrower, who is cheated. Unscrupulous men bind themselves through loan, exchange, or insurance contracts entailing the payment of interest, but when payment is due they appeal to ecclesiastical courts to be released from what is described as a 'usury' contract. Practices of this kind cannot be tolerated in Genoa, which is one of the world's greatest business centers and a proud commune. The city authorities decree that whoever tries to play the Church against the government in order to evade his obligations must pay a fine and nevertheless honor his promise (Document 145).

Even if the borrower does not choose to ask intervention of the Church, he may fail to honor his debt. A Genoese merchant has contracted in Armenia a debt payable in Persia. His creditor, after failing twice to collect the payment, has a protest drafted by a notary in the lodgings of the debtor in Asia Minor (Document 146). A Lucchese merchant presents for payment a bill of exchange drawn on a Venetian merchant in Bruges (Document 147). The Venetian has left the inn and is traveling back home. The Lucchese has a protest drafted by a notary and has it read both in the inn and at the Venetian consulate.[4]

Failure to repay a loan or an exchange contract is comparatively easy to prove, but how can one prove that a traveling party has not given an accurate accounting of a *commenda* venture? Most contracts specify that the traveling party is to be believed 'upon his word, without oath or witnesses.' Nevertheless the investor frequently is not satisfied with a bare statement and may challenge it. Document 148 presents the initial stage of a dispute of this kind; Document 149 presents the discussion of a most involved case before a municipal court.[5]

Litigation over Transport Contracts

139

From the Latin[6]

At sea, off Cape Spatha, Crete, November 16, 1283

In the presence of myself, the notary, and of the witnesses [whose names] are written below, the lord Oberto Boccanegra, podestà for the Commune of Genoa in the Territories Overseas, Margonino Margone, Pietro Streiaporco, Bertone Pinello, Gabriele de Salario, Baliano Brunengo, Simone

---

[4] For a protest informally noted on a bill, see Document 116.

[5] The background of the cases is summarized in the introductions to these Documents.

[6] G. I. Bratianu, *Recherches sur le commerce génois dans la Mer Noire au XIIIe siècle*, pp. 316–17. The dots in the document are Bratianu's. The podestà in the Territories Overseas had jurisdiction over the Genoese colonies in Syria and Palestine. What we translate as 'Byzantine Empire' is *Romania* in the document; the term applies not only to the actual territory of the empire as it was in 1283 but also to the former Byzantine possessions in the Balkan peninsula as they were in the twelfth century.

Speziale di San Siro, Jacopo Tartaro, Manuele de Camilla, Pietro Misclaioto, Gabriele de Gualterio, Luxiardo of Chiavari, Corrado di San Donato, and Donato of Bisagno—all of the above-mentioned being on the ship of Lanfranco of Savignone—give notice to the same Lanfranco of Savignone, captain of said ship, that by commission of the lords podestà, captains, and *abate* of the Fortunate Government of the People of Genoa, all of the above-mentioned [are to go] with the said ship Overseas to the regions of Cyprus and Armenia, as Lanfranco himself must do and has promised them to do, and as was agreed when the ship itself was made ready in Genoa and proclaimed by the voice of the herald throughout the city of Genoa. And let him not take them to the Byzantine Empire, for they do not want by any means to go to the Byzantine Empire; and if he takes them to the Byzantine Empire, he will be taking them against their will, for they have not the slightest desire to go to the Byzantine Empire but to the Territories Overseas, their destination. And from a voyage to the Byzantine Empire they suffer great loss and unrealized profits through loss of their [trip] and through the fact that they shall have to pay for another passage to go to the Territories Overseas. And they also say that he has no legal right to take them ... rather indeed he must take them to Cyprus and there learn the news, and [then], if this pleases the merchants, he could take them to the Byzantine Empire in accordance with what is contained in the instrument of the chartering of this ship, done by the hand of Pagano Durante, notary. And they also say that they will seek [damages for] all loss and unrealized profits that they shall suffer on account of this from said Lanfranco. And said Oberto, podestà for Overseas, also says that he did not board said ship to go to the Byzantine Empire but to go Overseas if possible. ... Wherefore, and in regard to the matters mentioned above, all the aforesaid persons asked me, notary undersigned, to make out a public instrument about the matters mentioned above. Done in the said ship off Cape Spatha of Crete in the year of the Nativity of the Lord 1283, eleventh indiction, November 16, in the evening. Witnesses: Alamanno Metiffeco and Manuele Merello.

140

From the Catalan[7]

[Palma de Mallorca,] July 31, 1477

Sentence pronounced by the honorable Consuls [of the Sea in Palma].

Whereas there was a litigation and contest before the honorable En Guillem Ortola Ciutada and Iohan Nadal, merchant, consuls in the present

[7] R. S. Smith, *The Spanish Guild Merchant*, pp. 130–32.

year, in regard to the acts and commercial dealings between En Gabriel Bruy, captain or master of a caravel as one party, plaintiff, and the discreet En Anthoni Piris, notary and assigned as attorney by the said honorable consuls in this litigation because of the absence of En Pere Soriano, his brother-in-law, to wit:

Said Gabriel Bruy has demanded the freight charge of forty casks, which were delivered and given him by En Pere Soriano here in Majorca to carry from Murviedro to this place, full of wine, as is stated in a contract produced by him. To the contrary, the said Anthoni Piris in behalf of the aforesaid affirmed that he was not bound to pay anything except the freight charge of thirteen casks full [of wine] which said captain had carried with the said caravel, and that in regard to the empty ones he was not bound to him. And if in anything he were bound in regard to them, he affirmed that he could not be bound in anything else but in the £ 10 which the said Soriano had imposed upon himself as penalty according to the form of the said contract. Nevertheless he affirmed that he was not bound to him, inasmuch as the said captain had not observed what he was bound to do, that is, to deliver the wine to him, said Anthoni Piris; and likewise, that [the captain] had to give him account of certain cloth which had been loaded by the said Soriano here in Majorca on the said caravel. And further he affirmed that he was a creditor in the goods of the said Soriano to a large amount, and for this reason he wanted to keep for himself the price of the said wine. And the said Bruy, replying, affirmed that the said freight charge had to be paid to him in whole for all the said forty casks, since for that reason and in that expectation the said caravel had made the said voyage and not for any other, since it was not his responsibility to load all the said forty casks, but that of the factors of said Soriano. He produced certain protests [he had] made against them—that is, that they ought to give him the remainder of the said cargo. And as for the above-said delivery [of cloth], he answered that he had complied with what had been done by the said factors, and that the said cloth had been delivered to the said factors as was shown in the said protests.

And having heard the said parties in regard to all that they wanted to say and to allege, said honorable consuls, having humbly invoked the name of our Lord God, Jesus Christ, in conformity with the counsel of the honorable En Pere de Veri and Guillam Linas, arbitrators (*promens*) chosen by the will of the said parties, pronounce, sentence, and declare, in unanimous agreement and differing in nothing, that the said captain be paid completely, fully, and wholly the freight charge of the said forty casks at the value and freight charge agreed upon by them, for it was not his responsibility to load and to carry all the said cargo, as he shows through said protests and also through two letters of the said factors directed to the said Soriano. To the payment and discharge of this freight charge they condemn said Piris in the said name; and [they declare also] that the said captain should have priority to the wine of the said thirteen casks,[8] deducting first from it, however, all the commissions which said Piris has paid here for the said wine; absolving and freeing the said captain from the demands made upon him by the said Anthoni Piris, since by the said letters and protest it is shown that he is not at any fault; and condemning no one of the said parties in the expenses.

[Signed:] Guillem Ortola, Johan Nadal, Pere de Veri, Guillem Linas.

The said sentence was read, published, and promulgated by order of the said honorable Consuls of the Sea, in the presence of En Gabriel Bruy, captain of the *fusta*,[9] as one party, and of the said discreet En Anthoni Piris, notary, in the said behalf, as the other, and in the presence of En Pere Cernera and Iohan Solsona Vergues, as witnesses, and of the said honorable consuls, on July 31, 1477, at the hour of vespers.[10]

Litigation over the Quality of Merchandise

141

From the Latin[11]

Montpellier, September 11, 1326

In the year of the Incarnation of the Lord 1326, to wit, the third day before the Ides of September, Lord Charles [IV] reigning as king of the French.

Be it known to all that a certain quantity of saffron has been denounced as spurious and adulterated by Uc Fabri, Berenguer Ferrari, Jacme de Ruthena, and Raymon de Segunzac, sworn custodians of goods of Montpellier, to the discreet men the lords Peire Roca, Jacme Pereri, and Bernart Garussi, consuls of the city of Montpellier. This quantity of said saffron was said to belong to Bernart Maestre and Berenguer Carbonelh, Catalan merchants. [Accordingly,] the above-mentioned lords-consuls had the said saffron brought to the consulate building of Montpellier. And since the examination of said saffron and of other adulterated goods is the prerogative of said custodians, according to their statement, the said custodians wished to

---

[8] This means that the proceeds of the wine are to be earmarked first for the payment of the freight charge.

[9] *Fusta* was a type of ship.

[10] There follows the sentence of Matheu Riera, judge of maritime and mercantile appeals in Majorca, rejecting an appeal of Anthoni Piris against the sentence of the consuls and condemning him to pay the expenses.

[11] A. Germain, *Histoire du commerce de Montpellier*, I, 471–72. We omit the list of witnesses in the body of the document.

proceed to the examination and inspection of said saffron—not with the intention, however, of exercising any jurisdiction in this matter but merely in accordance with ancient usage and long-established prerogative, as they stated, [to wit], that of inspecting and examining. [This being so, they] caused to be called and to come to the said building of the said consulate the witnesses written below . . . all of whom, as has been asserted, also are experienced in recognizing adulterated saffron and adulterated goods, most especially as they are merchants and sellers of pepper.

And forthwith all the previously named merchants and sellers of pepper viewed, felt, and carefully inspected said saffron, that is, a certain bale in which were five *alude*. And when said saffron was viewed, felt, and carefully inspected by the aforesaid merchants and sellers of pepper, at the request of the said custodians, the aforesaid merchants and sellers of pepper swore on the four Holy Gospels of God to tell the truth, whether said saffron was adulterated or not. And, carefully interrogated by said custodians, they said and unanimously deposed under oath, in the presence of the said lords-consuls and of the aforesaid custodians, that said saffron was adulterated, and that said bale was adulterated, and that said saffron contained in said bale and in said five *alude* was spurious and adulterated and was not good, legal, or salable, nor would they sell or buy said saffron as good, legal, or salable.

These depositions of said witnesses having been heard and understood by said custodians, the same custodians returned to the said lords-consuls said bale of said saffron, which contained in it said five *alude*, as spurious and adulterated, asking and requiring that a public instrument be drawn up for them concerning the above.

This was done in Montpellier, in the consulate building, in the aforesaid year and day, in the presence of the witnesses Peire Cardinal, cleric; Peire Fabri, messenger of the lords-consuls; and myself, Guillem de la Deveza, notary public of Montpellier, who was called, requested, and asked [to come] by said custodians [and who] wrote this and signed it with my signet.

142
From the Latin[12]

Barcelona, June 15, 1445

To the honorable and very discreet men, the lords burgomasters of the city of Frankfort in Germany.

Honorable and very discreet men, lords, our very dear friends:

[12] A. de Capmany y de Montpalau, *Memorias históricas sobre la marina, commercio y artes de la antigua ciudad de Barcelona*, II, 265–66. The letter is in very poor Latin and at places the exact meaning can only be surmised.

We were sorry to hear that while up to the present the merchants of this city with their goods and merchandise have been well treated in the territory under Your Discretion by you and by the others gathering there, yet in these days just past, when Berenguer Aguilar and Francisco Artus, merchants and citizens of this city of Barcelona, arrived in that territory with their goods and merchandise—viz., saffron of Orta pure and free of any fraud—[they were ill treated]. Some competitors from outside, who were traveling about your territory, inspired by envy rather than by worthy zeal, and presumably in order to root out our merchants from the territories in your surroundings, strove to defame these merchants by maintaining that that saffron was spurious, and also by carrying further their schemes[?][13] to have said saffron burned by fire. However, when these matters came to the notice of Your Great Discretion, Your Discretion took such notable and just steps that said merchants of our [city] were freed from such unjust accusations. For this Your Discretion deserves fitly to be praised.

Therefore, while thanking you for this, we earnestly beg you as affectionately as we can that you punish those competitors, and any others making similar attempts, in such a manner as shall suppress their wicked audacity and furnish an example to others like them. And thus we and the aforesaid merchants, friends of all people who should be cleared of all [charges of] mercantile fraud and bad repute, shall be satisfied. And they [Aguilar and Artus] shall be satisfied, even though they certainly are suffering loss, inconvenience, and defamation in regard to the above matters. . . . Otherwise we shall be obliged to take steps [to deal] with such matters by appropriate means. Up to the present, indeed, your merchants coming to this city of Barcelona with their goods and merchandise have been treated by us like citizens and inhabitants of this city, as is proper, just as if they were natives of this city.

In this way, indeed, we hope that from now on our citizens and inhabitants with their merchandise will be treated by you, offering ourselves to do likewise and even better in behalf of you and of the inhabitants of said city of yours, if the occasion should arise. And may the Omnipotent Trinity happily and in the way you wish preserve Your Great Discretion; and whatever is your pleasure you will write back to us who are always well disposed and most faithfully ready [to conform to your wishes].

Written in Barcelona, on June 15, in the year of the Nativity of the Lord 1445. Ever ready to your pleasure and honor,

The Councillors of the City of Barcelona.

---

[13] *Etiamque ejus vires prosequendum.* Here we probably have an error in transcription and not merely a mistake of the writers of the letter.

Loan Sharks at Work

143
From the Latin[14]

[Nîmes, October 29, 1289]

Peire Negre of Nîmes, after swearing to tell the truth . . . said that by the next month of January two years will have passed since he, the witness, made out a record [of indebtedness][15] to Buto Bonaiuto and Loco di Migliore and Ugolino, partners, of Florence, residing in Nîmes, for £ 280 Tournois payable to them any time from then up to four months, [purportedly] for the purchase of silver plate and gold cloth, all of which they showed to him. And [of these objects] he did not take possession, but in consideration of all the aforesaid they caused £ 200 to be delivered to him in the bank (tabula) of Lemme del Conte and Bonfiglio of Lucca.[16] Only this, however, was agreed between them at the time of the said contract, as he stated: that he could not be forced to pay the said £ 280 to the aforesaid partners for one year starting from that time, and that if he happened to pay the said amount of money at any time within that year he was bound to pay them 8 deniers in each pound for every month of the [additional] time elapsed.[17] Moreover, he said that he, the witness, when coerced by the court of Nîmes upon instance of the aforesaid partners . . . who had demanded that said Peire be forced to pay the said amount of money and be placed in the house or prison of defaulters as a hostage, sold the larger and better part of all his goods and at a much lower price than he should have because of their importunity and haste. Moreover, he said that he paid them £ 240 Melgorienses[18] toward the said sum of money of £ 280 Tournois, and that in addition he made out a record [of indebtedness] of £ 39 to them.

[14] R. Davidsohn, *Forschungen zur älteren Geschichte von Florenz*, III, 36. Davidsohn gives only excerpts of the document—a record of the investigation by the royal seneschal of Beaucaire and Nîmes into usurious practices by Tuscan and Lombard moneylenders—and of these excerpts we have translated a section. The dots in the body of the document are Davidsohn's.

[15] *Incartavit.*

[16] The record of indebtedness was a fictitious sale; the goods were shown to Peire Negre, no doubt in the presence of witnesses, so that he could not use the 'exception that the goods had not been sold or had not been delivered.' Actually Peire Negre contracted a loan of £200 at the interest of 40 percent for four months, which corresponded to 120 percent by the year.

[17] This means that the loan sharks verbally promised to Peire Negre that he would be given the option of keeping the money for a whole year after the deadline established in the record. For every additional month he was to pay an interest of eight deniers per pound, corresponding to 40 percent by the year.

[18] The pound of Melgueil (Melgoriensis) was a money of account pegged to the Melgueil denier, which had a much lower silver content than the Tournois denier.

144

From the Latin[19]

[Florence, June 7, 1308]

Monna Orrevole, widow, formerly the wife of Ser Bonafede Villanelli of the quarter of Saint Laurent in the city of Florence, in her own behalf and in that of Lorenzo, Francesco, and Mattea, her children, orphans of the said late Bonafede, destitute, weak, and powerless, sets forth and says humbly and respectfully in your presence, Lords Priors of the Arti and Gonfaloniere of Justice of the People and Commune of Florence, that Neri, son of the said late Ser Bonafede, as principal, and said Bonafede, notary, as his surety, promised to return and to pay to Neri Orlandi, notary, 80 gold florins by reason of a loan, as appears from a public document, even though said Neri [son of Bonafede] had not had from said Ser Neri [Orlandi] any more than 60 gold florins.

And when the term of said instrument of loan had expired, Ser Neri forced and charged said Ser Bonafede to return to him the said amount of money. And since Ser Bonafede himself did not have at hand at that time the money with which he could repay the same Ser Neri, he sold to the same Ser Neri a certain house of his, located in the city of Florence at the Porta Rossa [and bounded] on the first side by a street, on the second by [the property of] the Strozzi, for the price of 125 gold florins, even though in fact the same Ser Bonafede had not had from him any more compensation than the said quantity of 60 gold florins, and in another transaction 14 gold florins. This house Ser Neri himself promised to resell to said Ser Bonafede, notary, for the price of 125 gold florins.[20] And, after the sale of said house was made, said Ser Bonafede sought from said Ser Neri the return to him of the said instrument of loan of 80 gold florins, and of the other instrument of loan of 14 gold florins. All this said Ser Neri maliciously and fraudulently refused to do for the aforesaid Ser Bonafede, saying that he wanted first good and suitable guarantors for the protection [of his title] to the said house; and thus he kept the said instruments of loan and also the instrument of sale of said house.

[19] A. Sapori, *Studi di storia economica medievale*, 2d ed., pp. 71–73. The government granted the requests of Monna Orrevole. For an explanation of the monetary terms in the document, see our introductory Note on Coinage and Weights.

[20] Contracts of this type—the sale of real estate with the clause that the seller could repurchase it at the same price as that of the original sale—were frequently used as a cover for usurious loans. What actually happened was that the 'seller' borrowed money on the security of real estate and gave the 'buyer' possession of the estate until the loan was repaid.

This Ser Bonafede, notary, died some ten or more years ago, that is, in that year in which he sold that house to Ser Neri. Then, after the death of the said Ser Bonafede, the said Ser Neri by reason of said instruments of loan and of the said amounts of money mentioned in said instruments of loan entered into and acquired possession of all the goods, mobile and immobile, of the said orphans and of the said Monna Orrevole, to wit: one house located in the quarter of San Lorenzo and belonging to the said lady, half by purchase and the other half by dowry; and a certain farm with buildings located in the country and territory of Mugello near Barberino; and the notarial registers[21] of said Ser Bonafede. And he collected from said houses and farms the rents, returns, and yields for some nine years or more, to wit: from the house located at Borgo San Lorenzo £ 44 by the florin in petty deniers, yearly and every year from said time forward, which appears to add up in sum to £ 396; and from said farm, yearly and every year from said time forward, all produce being evaluated in terms of grain, 10 *moggi* of grain according to the Florentine *staio*, which adds up in sum for the entire said time to 90 *moggi* of grain; and from the house located at the Porta Rossa, yearly and every year from said time forward, £ 27 by the florin in petty deniers, which adds up in sum to £ 245 for the entire said time. This very house located at the Porta Rossa is worth, by common appraisal, £ 700 and more; and the house located at Borgo San Lorenzo is worth, by common appraisal, £ 1,200 and more; and the farm with buildings located near Barberino, £ 2,000. And in this manner, on account of said amounts of money—60 gold florins and 14 florins—he deprived the said lady and the orphans of the aforesaid right which they had in said properties, through violence and by his power, maliciously and fraudently, and against God and justice. And for this reason, the aforesaid lady and the orphans mentioned above are begging and go from door to door for alms throughout the city of Florence; this has been for five years and more. And what is more, said Ser Neri craftily had [an order] of banishment issued against said lady and had her condemned [to pay] £ 100 by the florin in petty deniers, with the intent that she could not pursue her rights and those of the said orphans. And he caused them to flee and endeavored so far as he could to have her and said orphans seized and detained on account of said amounts of money.

Therefore, having thus set forth the facts, said Monna Orrevole in behalf of herself and of said orphans petitions that by the love of God and by considerations of pity and mercy, and since you are legally bound and have the obligation to aid, so far as possible, poor, weak, and deceived persons,

---

[21] *Imbreviaturae*, the chartularies in which the notary wrote the rough copies of his instruments.

you be pleased to compel that diabolical and wicked man, Ser Neri Orlandi, notary, to return and to restore to the said lady and said orphans the aforesaid houses at the Porta Rossa and at Borgo San Lorenzo, and the farm of Barberino with the said rents and grain collected therefrom, at the rate of s.12 for every *sestario* and for whatever more it was worth, from said time onward, provided she compensates and deducts from her [accounting] said amounts of 60 and 14 gold florins, which the same Ser Neri retains in his possession; and that you be good enough to restore to that very lady and said orphans possession of the aforesaid goods, and also to compel Ser Neri himself to return to said orphans said notarial registers and to the lady herself her instrument of dowry, which he wickedly and unjustly withholds from her. She invokes for this purpose all statutes and ordinances of the Commune of Florence, seeking also expenses for the litigation in the aforesaid matters; likewise, that the aforesaid Monna Orrevole be freed and absolved and [her sentence] canceled in regard to all condemnations and banishments to which she may be found condemned or banished, for whatever cause.

Canon Law as a Pretext for Breaking Contracts

145

From the Latin[22]

Genoa, October 22, 1369

Against those alleging that exchange and insurance contracts (*cambia et assecuramenta*), no matter for whom they are made, in or without writing, are illegal or usurious.

The magnificent and powerful lord, Lord Gabriele Adorno, by the grace of God Doge of Genoa and Defender of the People and Imperial Vicar, in the presence, with the will, advice, and consent of his Council of the Twelve Aldermen of the city of Genoa, as well as the said Council. . . .

Calling attention to the fact and considering that indebted persons are often unwilling, because of their malice, to satisfy their creditors in making payment of their debts and introduce many obstacles and hindrances, especially by alleging that the contract or loan in regard to which they are being sued and for which they are being prosecuted was illegal and usurious and that according to the Scriptures such a contract may not canonically be sought or demanded of them; and [considering that such debtors] have recourse, and have had recourse on previous occasions, to ecclesiastical

---

[22] E. Bensa, *Il contratto di assicurazione nel medio evo*, pp. 149–51. We have omitted part of the legal formulae at the beginning and at the end.

courts and magistrates in regard to this in order to interpose delays and dilatory cavils;

Decided and decreed and directed that if there is any person of any condition who has obligated himself or who should obligate himself by an instrument toward any person whatever, in or without writing, in regard to any merchandise and in any commercial contract whatever, especially by way of exchange or insurance; and if he alleges that such a contract is usurious or illegal and because of this has recourse to the vicar of the Lord Archbishop or to another magistrate of the city or of the district, ecclesiastic or lay; if he petitions or objects that the said instrument or contract, be it made in or without writing, and in regard to any merchandise, [is illegal]; and if he alleges that the payment, in whole or in part, of the said debt of the said instrument and contract ought not to be made because of the fact that the said debtor or another in the latter's name says and alleges that the said contract was illegal and usurious or made against the canonical sanctions;

Since they [the doge and the aldermen] consider that if instruments of exchange and other trade contracts, in or without writing, could not be enforced because of impediments of this kind, this would result in great loss and inconvenience to the Genoese citizens and merchants, who ordinarily make such contracts, and that otherwise no trade could be carried on nor ships be sent on their voyages:

Let such a person who brings forward the said exception as mentioned above against the aforesaid instruments and against any contracts made in regard to the aforesaid trade be condemned and be understood to be condemned in true justice [to pay] s.10 Genoese in every pound of the entire amount the payment of which was refused. And let this penalty be applied and be understood to be applied by force of the present decree to the works of the harbor and of the wharf.[23] And the Lord Podestà of Genoa and the *sindicatores* of the Commune now in charge, or who will be in charge at the time, and the other magistrates who will be requested to use remedies of law in regard to this, are bound to collect this [fine], even through personal detention, admitting no exception or defense. . . .

The above was drawn from the public acts of the ducal chancery of the Commune of Genoa.

We, the People.

Antonio de Credenza, notary and chancellor.

---

[23] *Applicetur . . . operi portus et moduli.* The upkeep, repairs, and construction works in the harbor of Genoa were entrusted to an autonomous department, which was supported by regular appropriations in the city budget, by the proceeds of judiciary fines, and by voluntary contributions and gifts, especially in the wills of Genoese citizens.

Protests Concerning Unpaid Debts

146

From the Latin[24]

Sivas, May 18, 1280

In the name of Christ, amen. In the presence of myself, the notary under-signed, and of the witnesses whose names are written below, Luchetto of Recco, son of the late Pasquale, gives notice to Lamba d'Oria [as follows]:

Inasmuch as Lamba himself is bound to give and to pay to him 180 lbs. of good silver at the alloy and weight of Genoa, by tenor of an instrument written about it by the hand of Gabriele di Langasco, notary, on July 13, 1279, and likewise [to pay] 18 lbs. of good silver at the alloy and weight of Genoa, by tenor of an instrument written by the hand of Guglielmo of Promontorio, notary, on September 26, 1279—and [Lamba] was bound to give him this silver or as many aspers as will be obtained from all said silver or might be obtained from all said silver, either in Tabriz or in Sivas, at the choice of Luchetto himself;

And consequently since Luchetto himself had chosen that the aforesaid pay-ment was to be made to him in Tabriz, as is contained in an instrument written by the hand of Giovanni Amici of Sozziglia, notary, on January 17 of this year, in Nakhichevan, and likewise in another instrument written by the hand of the said Giovanni, notary, on February 8, in Arzinjan;

And since [Luchetto] did not receive the aforesaid payment, [Lamba] is therefore bound to give and to pay for each pound of said silver £ 7½ Genoese on the Paschal feast of the Resurrection of the Lord, which time limit has now elapsed, and again [Luchetto] has not received said payment from him;

Therefore said Luchetto, wishing to obtain payment of the aforesaid to him, gives notice and requests the same Lamba to give and to pay to him £ 7½ Genoese in each pound of said silver up to full payment of the aforesaid to him, just as Lamba is bound and ought to do by tenor of the said instru-ments, or [to pay] so much silver or aspers as are worth the said £ 7½ Genoese in each pound. And if [Lamba] does not make this payment to him at once, said Luchetto reckons each asper at d.16 Genoese up to full payment of the aforesaid to him. And he asks and requests this from him with every legal right by which he is entitled to do so, reserving to himself every right deriving from said instruments. And in order that full confidence be placed in each

---

[24] Bratianu, *Recherches sur le commerce génois*, pp. 314-15. Lamba d'Oria, a brother of one of the two chief executives (Captains of the People) of Genoa, later won great fame by defeating the Venetian fleet in the battle of Curzola.

and all the aforesaid [statements] he asked me, notary undersigned, to make the present public instrument about it. Done in Sivas in the house in which Lamba himself lives. Witnesses: Pietro Lercari, Giacomo Embriaco, Percivalle Castagna, and Nicola Zaccaria. In the year of the Nativity of the Lord 1280, eighth indiction, May 18, about vespers.

147
From the Latin and from the Italian (Venetian dialect)[25]

[Bruges, October 23, 1397]; Venice, August 21, 1397

Betto Schiatta [of Lucca] . . . went to the inn which is kept at present by Nicolas Bourguignon, citizen of the city of Bruges, and which is the inn where Antonio Spalatino of Venice used to stay when he was last in Bruges. And the said Betto, having met there the lady of the aforesaid inn, wife of the aforesaid Nicolas, asked her whether the said Antonio used to stay in the said inn when he was in Bruges. And she answered yes, but that at present Antonio himself was not in Bruges.

And the said Betto, having heard this answer, and knowing and considering, as he stated, that he understood that the said Antonio Spalatino had left the town of Bruges and gone toward Venice, [acted] in the absence of the aforesaid Antonio, who [evidently] was not in the aforesaid inn in Bruges, which was the inn where the same Antonio used to stay when he was last in Bruges. He produced a certain letter of payment concerning a certain exchange [transaction], which was addressed to the same Antonio on the part of Antonio Dolfin, and had the letter itself read aloud by me, undersigned notary, orally, there, in the said inn. And the text inside this letter follows word by word, and is this:[26]

In the name of Christ, amen. 1397, in Venice. Antonio Dolfin greets with love Ser Antonio Spalatino. By this original [letter] you shall pay in Bruges on October 21 to Ser Betto Schiatta francs two hundred and twenty-nine groats 23½, that is, francs 229 groats 23½, which are for the value of ducats two hundred and one, that is, ducats 201, which I have received here from Ser Gianni del Voglia and Gaspare da Lavaiano and companions. And you shall post the said money to the account of Ser Gianni da Canal for one half of our share of Quilon ginger; and this order is given you by the said Ser Gianni da Canal. The latter does not write to you because at present he is

---

[25] A. Grunzweig, 'Notes sur le fonds du notariat aux archives d'état de Venise,' *Bulletin de l'Institut Historique Belge de Rome*, XIV (1934), 91–92, footnote. The document is not published in full.

[26] Up to here the text is in Latin. The letter is in Venetian.

in Ferrara in behalf of the government. I have nothing else to say. Ready
to your command. The exchange costs 21 groats in the franc. Closed on
August 21.

A Controversy over the Accounting of a Commenda

A GENOESE MERCHANT, Daniele di Fontanella, has received a sum in *commenda* from
his fellow citizen Paschetto Mallone, who has in turn received another sum in
commenda from him. Paschetto died before the accounting and settlement of profits and losses was made. To the guardian of his heirs Daniele declares that on the
first *commenda* he has lost twenty percent; he is willing to deduct what is left of the
sum from the *commenda* which Paschetto had received from him. The guardian,
however, demands a more satisfactory accounting, for he claims that Daniele has
gained fifty percent. The document stops at this point, but we can assume that the
case will be brought before arbiters chosen by the parties or before the city judges
of common pleas (*consoli dei placiti*), as is the custom in commercial litigations of
this kind.

Who is right? It is impossible for us to decide, since we do not have all of the
facts; but the circumstance that Daniele, challenged to produce a written accounting,
has given no details beyond the mere statement that he lost twenty percent leads us
strongly to suspect his good faith.

148
From the Latin[27]

Genoa, May 26, 1268

Daniele di Fontanella, wishing to give to the heirs of Paschetto Mallone[28]
a written accounting of a certain *accomendatio* of £ 100 Genoese, or of so
many goods as were evaluated at £ 100, about which there is an instrument
written by the hand of Guglielmo of San Giorgio, notary, as they state, gives
a written accounting of the said *accomendatio* to Bonvassallo Nepitella, viz.,
as he states, to the guardian of the heirs of the said late Paschetto.

As said Daniele states against the latter, he invested said money for arming
a galley of said Daniele, which he armed for the sake of making profit. And
he states that he made no profit from the said money but lost from that
money and from other [sums] which he had at the rate of 4 soldi in the pound.
And he states that he thus lost one fifth of the said money. Said Daniele, then,
is ready to deduct the remaining part of said money, as he states, up to an
equivalent amount, from a certain other *accomendatio* which said Paschetto

---

[27] Unprinted. Archivio di Stato, Genoa. *Cartulario di Gioacchino Nepitella*, I, fol. 65v. and 66r.
[28] Paschetto Mallone, a member of a very influential family, had been admiral of the Genoese
fleet in 1257.

had from said Daniele, and of which there is an instrument written by the hand of Andegario of Corniglia, notary, in 1267, September 22.

And said Bonvassallo in behalf of the said minors declared to the said Daniele and proclaimed that he must not go out of Genoa without rendering [a fuller] accounting to the same Bonvassallo as a guardian of said heirs; for he states that the same Daniele has made a profit of £ 50 Genoese from said money.

Done in Genoa in front of the house of said Bonvassallo. 1268, indiction tenth, May 26, between nones and vespers. Witnesses: Guglielmo Elia, Agostino of Nervi, Aveto and Andreolo Caenardo.

A Journey to Delhi and Its Legal Aftermath

A MERCHANT HAS left Venice for Delhi together with five other partners, but he has died en route. His brother, who has taken over his share, brings back the proceeds, which have been increased by a gift of the sultan of Delhi. Capital and profits are then provisionally assigned to the merchant's minor heirs, but another man, the father-in-law, intervenes. He has supplied most of the capital which formed the share of the dead man in the common capital of the *compagnia*. The capital of this share had been supplied through a *collegantia* (*commenda*) contract. After hearing many witnesses, the judges assign to the plaintiff the entire capital and three fourths of the profit, leaving to the minors only one fourth of the profit belonging to their father's share. The judges have acted according to the letter of the law, but one has the impression that the father-in-law was a hard, avaricious man.

149

From the Italian (Venetian dialect) and from the Latin[29]

[Venice, September 23, 1346]

The attorney of Alberto da Calle exhibits in court a note written by Giovanni Loredan, as follows:

1338, July. I, Zanin[30] Loredan, son of the late Giovanni, son of Ser

[29] Unprinted. Archivio di Stato, Venice, *Procuratori di San Marco, Misti*, Busta 122. Excerpts from this document, and comments upon its background, are found in R. S. Lopez, 'European Merchants in the Medieval Indies: the Evidence of Commercial Documents,' *Journal of Economic History*, III (1943), 164–84; the author of that article wishes to renew the expression of his gratitude to Gino Luzzatto, who called the document to his attention and supplied him with a partial transcription. Here we have used italics for passages of the lengthy document which were summarized rather than translated verbatim. Monetary terms in the text include moneys of account and coins of various origin. Both the pound groat and the pound petty are Venetian moneys of account, pegged to the groat and to the petty denier. The bezant was a Byzantine gold coin, but the name also was used for various moneys of account pegged to silver coins of several Near Eastern countries; in this context probably the bezant is a money of account. The *tamgha* was a unit of account, an ingot, or a real coin in the monetary systems of the Mongol states.

[30] Zanin is the diminutive of John (Giovanni, Zane) in the Venetian dialect, which is used

Berto Loredan, of San Canciano, acknowledge that I have received from my father-in-law, Ser Alberto da Calle, £ 80 [Venetian] groat to be carried on the journey that I am about to undertake at your profit and loss by *collegan₃a*, you giving my mother £ 3 s.10 groat.

Proof is given that Berto Loredan, son of the late Giovanni (Zanin) Loredan, is more than 12 years old and less than 18. Then the following statements of witnesses are read:

1343, August 30. I, Marco Soranzo of Sant' Apostolo . . . including what I invested in this country and all expenses that I incurred in Ghazni, [declare the sum to be] between £ 105 and £ 110 groat, and up to the latter place I estimate that said Ser Giovanni Loredan invested as much [as I did]. A few days later Ser Giovanni died. Therefore his brother, Ser Paolo, made the payments for the entire share[31] [of the deceased], which amounted to as much as £ 210 groat. And if said Ser Paolo had not done it, we, the partners, would have made the payments and would have taken the profit from whatever we might have invested. And Ser Paolo received in Urjench, when we left, as many pearls as cost 17,000 bezants. I, Marco Soranzo, believe that I have gained from this journey about 3,500 florins, although I had in Delhi 2,000 bezants more than said Ser Paolo Loredan from this sixth share [of mine]. And I can well and truly say that I have sold my goods at much better advantage than any of them did because I sent them to France.

Asked on oath for whom Ser Paolo made the payments: 'I have said that I do not know in whose behalf.'

Testimony of Marino Contarini:

I, Marino Contarini, son of Ser Dardi Contarini of the quarter of San Salvador . . . including what I invested in this territory and what I spent until we were in Ghazni, [declare that] it was about £ 105 groat, and as far as the latter place I believe that Ser Giovanni Loredan invested as much also. After a few days had elapsed he passed away, so that in regard to all the expenses for which payments had to be made for this sixth [share], his brother, Ser Paolo, was given our consent to make the payments. And including what was invested in the *compagnia* by each man or what was later spent, it was about £ 210 groat. And if he had not made the payments for this sixth, we certainly would have made the payments and taken the profit

---

promiscuously with Latin and some Italian in the document; hereafter, however, Venetian and Latin names will be translated into Italian. The Loredan family, like all others named in the document, belonged to the highest merchant nobility in Venice.

[31] *Colomello*, probably from *colonna*, column; its use in the meaning of share is likely to derive from the use of posting all entries concerning each share in separate upright columns of a large sheet.

from whatever we had invested in it. And on account of this, Ser Paolo had in Urjench as many pearls as cost 17,000 bezants of Delhi. I, Marino Contarini, believe that I have gained from this journey £ 300 groat, although I had in Delhi about 4,000 bezants more than Ser Paolo from this sixth.

Second testimony of Marco Soranzo, in regard to what the sultan of Delhi (Muhammad ibn-Taghlak) gave the merchants:

January 9, 1344. . . . I said that we had 200,000 bezants, of which 20,000 bezants remain in the customs house[32] and 2,000 bezants were given the scribe of said customs house. Also, in Delhi we drew from the *monte*[33] 10,000 bezants each, amounting to 60,000 bezants. Also, from 9,000 to 10,000 bezants were given away to those who had paid us great honor, that is, the barons of the Lord. Some other money was invested in *tamgha*, and what remained, which was about 102,000 bezants, was invested in pearls.

Also, asked by the said lords [the Procuratori] whether Paolo paid in Delhi some debts in behalf of his brother: 'I say yes—to a certain Antonio of Cremona, but I do not know how much. . . .'

On request of Ser Paolo Loredan, both witnesses again repeated testimony already disclosed. Then they gave the following answers, on request of Ser da Calle:

I want these questions to be put: First, whether the money that Ser Paolo said he invested in the share of Vacca[34] was taken as a loan. They answered, 'Yes.'

Also, whether Ser Paolo took the said money as a loan on his own account or jointly with the others. They answered, 'Jointly with the others.'

Also, how much the entire *compagnia* received from the lord of Delhi. They answered, 'Two hundred thousand bezants, of which 20,000 remained in the customs house of the lord.'

Also, how much each of the partners—and Ser Paolo for the share of Vacca—received in Delhi from said gift, besides the 17,000 bezants and *centenara* received in Urjench by each of the partners and by Paolo for the share of Vacca. They answered, 'We do not know.'

Also, whether the decision of the companions was that the shares of the dead men should be brought from Delhi to Famagosta and thence to Marina[35] without any expense. They answered, 'Yes, for the share of Ser Baldovino, but not for the other shares.'

Also, how many days they were distant from Delhi when Ser Paolo made

[32] *Casena*, a Western term, may designate a pawnbroker's shop, an office, or a customs house.
[33] The common capital. Compare *corpo* in the Florentine *compagnia* documents.
[34] A nickname of Giovanni Loredan; it means 'cow' in Italian.   [35] The Venetian seashore.

the payments for the share of Vacca with the money taken as a loan. They answered, 'Fifteen days.'

Also, whether or not the money was taken as a loan only up to Delhi. They answered, 'Yes.'

Also, whether or not they paid the money which was taken as a loan from the whole *monte* of said *societas*. They answered that 'they paid it out of those 200,000 bezants which they received from the lord.'

An earlier decision of the judges of the Procuratori, dated September 22, is read, as follows:

That Paolo Loredan, brother of the late Giovanni Loredan nicknamed Vacca, must give and return to the aforesaid lords Procuratori, guardians of said orphans, £ 230 [Venetian] groat, deduction being made of all borrowings, usuries, loans, provisions, and profits out of the money received by the aforesaid late Ser Giovanni Loredan as well as by the aforesaid Paolo Loredan by reason of said *colomello*, and especially [deducting] the money which said Giovanni received from Antonio of Cremona. . . .

The attorney of Alberto da Calle pleads, as follows:

That the lord judges had seen well that the aforesaid Giovanni Loredan had received from said Alberto da Calle £ 80 groat in *colleganza* at [the latter's] profit and loss for the journey which he was to undertake, said Ser Alberto da Calle giving £ 3½ groat to the mother of said Giovanni. And further said attorney set forth that Ser Giovanni Loredan went on the journey to Delhi when he received said money from said Ser Alberto. . . . He also said that the aforesaid Giovanni Loredan died on said journey to Delhi before he could arrive, and that Ser Paolo Loredan managed and administered the account of said Giovanni, which remained in the *monte* with the other accounts of the other gentlemen who were on said journey, up to the locality of Delhi and thence up to the city of Venice; and that in Venice, since said Giovanni had died without a will, the noblemen Marco Loredan and Francesco Querini, Procuratori of Saint Mark, were appointed guardians of Berto, Nicoletto, and Alessandro, sons of the said late Giovanni; and that said guardians obtained a decision of £ 230 groat against said Paolo after taking the legitimate compensations and deductions of all loans, credits, usuries, profits, and gains obtained, made, and paid on said journey both by said Giovanni and by said Paolo. Therefore, on said journey only the account of said Alberto da Calle remained and was [left]. Said Alberto, however, admitted that on said journey there were £ 3 Venetian groat of the account of Ser Francesco Marcello, of which he did not believe the latter had been fully paid; also that said Giovanni brought from Venice on said journey about £ 20

Venetian groat of the account of Antonio of Cremona, which were not brought back from Delhi to the city of Venice, but that in Delhi the investment of Antonio of Cremona was fully paid in regard to those pounds and their profit and gain out of the *monte* of the share of said Ser Giovanni.

Therefore the attorney demands that all the remainder of the £ 230 groat received by the guardians be given to Alberto da Calle, after deducting the sole account of Francesco Marcello and the share of profit owing to Giovanni Loredan according to the custom of the colleganza, *for which Alberto admits that £ 44 s.8 groat should be assigned. He demands at once one third of the sum owing to Alberto, that is, £ 59 s.12 groat and d.10 Venetian petty, which are the share of Berto Loredan, who had just now ended his wardship.*

The two Procuratori of Saint Mark, guardians of the Loredan minors, order a deposition of Ser Andrea Giustiniano to be read, as follows:

Upon petition of Berto, son of the late Giovanni Loredan nicknamed Vacca, and of the guardians of the orphans of said Giovanni Loredan, on September 20, in Mestre, district of Treviso, the nobleman Lord Andrea Giustiniano, podestà of Mestre, questioned under oath, said that while he was going on the journey to Urjench he arrived in Astrakhan, where he found very many persons, among whom was the nobleman Giovanni Loredan, nicknamed Vacca, with the *società* which was [planning] to go on the journey to Delhi. And because of the ice they were delayed there fifty days, and were not able to leave from there. And during said period many times he chanced to go to the temporary abode of said Ser Giovanni, where Ser Giovanni was living, and he saw that [Giovanni] was cutting and making cuttings out of certain pieces of cloth that he had, and was sending them to Tana to be sold. And [Giustiniano] heard him many times complaining that he was losing [money] on said cloth. *He does not know to whom the cloth belonged nor from where it came, but he believes that it came from Venice. He does not know their number, their value, or the extent of the loss.*

The defense lawyers declare that the claims of the plaintiff are exorbitant:

To prove this they showed the above-mentioned testimonies, saying that according to what appeared from them said Giovanni Loredan had invested up to Ghazni, including all expenses, between £ 105 and £ 110 groat in the *monte* of said *società*. And therefore they affirmed that the said Ser Alberto was not entitled to have as much as he asked from said account, because the account of Ser Alberto had been no more than £ 80 groat; and of these, as they affirmed, said Giovanni had lost a good deal by reason of the cloth which they affirmed that he had received from said Alberto for said £ 80 groat. And in addition, they affirmed, it was found that after the death of said Giovanni said Paolo Loredan, his brother, when he was in Delhi, had made payments for the account of said Giovanni, so that the total account of said Giovanni rose to £ 210 groat. And therefore they affirmed that said Ser Alberto . . . had invested nothing more than what had been said above . . . and that the profit of said account was to be divided between the account of said Ser Alberto, and the other money added and invested in this account.

The lawyer for the plaintiff replies that the defense has proved nothing, and in particular it has not proved that the account of Giovanni has risen in Ghazni to a sum between £ 105 and £ 110 groat. Even if this has been proved, the fact remains that Giovanni had also received, in Venice, between £ 20 and £ 25 groat from Antonio di Cremona, and adding these he could well have reached the sum of £ 110 in Ghazni. But Paolo Loredan had settled in Delhi the account of Antonio de Cremona, and therefore the sum ought not to be taken into account a second time. And he so affirmed that he regarded as irrelevant the first point made by the said lords Procuratori and said Berto about the increase of the money in Ghazni. Also he affirmed that, in order that the said account of the said late Antonio of Cremona be entitled to be treated in the same way as the account of the said Alberto, it would have been indispensable that it be not taken out of the *monte*, but [rather] that it remain in the *monte* itself, [sharing] all expenses and all risks in the trip out and back. And this was not done, since the said account was taken out [of the *monte*] in Delhi, as is explained above.

Also, in regard to the second point made by the said lords Procuratori and by the said Ser Berto, [to wit], that the account of said Giovanni, including the loans, credits, and usuries, was found in Delhi [to be] £ 210 groat or thereabouts, the said attorney affirmed that this accounting was not decisive because all loans were received through the *monte* and by the entire *società* and were returned out of the 200,000 bezants received from the lord of Delhi, and therefore must not be deducted and admitted a second time. Also, the said attorney of the aforesaid Ser Alberto affirmed that not only the entire account of the said late Antonio of Cremona, with which the *monte* of the *società* was found increased in Ghazni, including its profit and including any accounting of gain which might have been coming to that account, was deducted when Paolo was given judgment in regard to the said £ 230 groat, but also all accounts of all moneys received in loan or on credit were deducted and compensated together with the profits and gains which might have been coming to those accounts. And to prove this he cited the second testimony of said Ser Marco Soranzo from which it appears that each partner had in Delhi 10,000 bezants. He also cited the first testimony of the said Ser Marco and the first testimony of Ser Marco Contarini, from which it appears that Paolo Loredan had in Urjench 17,000 bezants from the aforesaid account. Hence he affirmed that it was proved that Paolo had had 27,000 bezants which are worth about £ 500 groat, and out of these a judgment had been given only in regard to £ 230 groat. Thus the deduction had been such and so large that it was clearly evident that all the accounts both of Antonio of Cremona and of moneys received as a loan had been fully deducted, including all gains which might have been coming to the accounts themselves. To prove this he cited the testimony of the lords judges, who had given the judgment against the aforesaid Paolo Loredan.

The Procuratori and Ser Berto reply as follows:

Over and above the aforesaid accounts said Giovanni had carried away money from many persons and particularly from his mother from Venice. And to prove this they exhibited and caused to be read from the book of the court certain testimonies, the tenor of which follows and is this:

On petition of the nobleman Bertone Loredan of San Cancian, having a record of commission from Berto Loredan, son of the late Giovanni Loredan nicknamed Vacca, on February 17, Monna Lucia Davanzago of San Giovanni Decollato, sworn and interrogated, being produced as witness under oath, replied that she knows that Monna Caterina Loredan, mother of the aforesaid Giovanni Loredan, gave to the late Monna Angioliera Davanzago of San Giovanni Decollato £ 13 s.15 Venetian groat in behalf of her said son; and to Monna Nicolina Davanzago, of the aforesaid section, the same Monna Caterina Loredan gave £ 13 s.15 Venetian groat in the aforesaid name of the same Giovanni Loredan. Interrogated about the time, said witness replied that she did not know, but said only that he, Ser Giovanni, was outside of Venice at that time, as she believed, and never came back. Interrogated whether she knows that said Giovanni had money from any person in that journey on which he went . . . she replied that she did not know.

Some other testimonies are read. The noblemen Tommaso Loredan, Giovanni Loredan, and Andrea Loredan, questioned whether to their knowledge Giovanni Loredan, nicknamed Vacca, had on his journey to Delhi money from somebody else or of his own, answer that they do not know; Andrea Loredan adds that he heard from Giovanni himself that he had some account belonging to his father-in-law.

The priest Marco Viviano, of the Church of San Giovanni Decollato, also answers that he does not know, but he adds other details, as follows:

Questioned about what he knows . . . he replied that he had made a certain entry in a certain book by his own hand, which entry begins thus: '1338, in the month of September, on the second day, Monna Angioliera Davanzago received from me, Caterina Loredan, mother of the said Vacca, £ 8 groat in behalf of the said Gianni Vacca. Also, the said Monna Angioliera Davanzago has received from the said Monna Caterina Loredan, mother of the said Vacca, £ 6 groat less s.5 groat. . . . 1339, in the month of December, Nicolina received from her mother in behalf of the said Vacca £ 13 s.15 groat of profit and capital which he took for the journey of Cathay.' Said witness, interrogated as to who had the said book, replied that it was in the hands of Monna Caterina Loredan. Interrogated whether he saw the aforesaid money being given, he replied that he did not know.

Testimony of Leonardo Cagnoli, rector of San Gimignano.

When Ser Giannino Loredan, nicknamed Vacca, my intimate [friend], made preparations to go on the journey to Delhi, from which he did not return, his mother, Monna Caterina, and Ser Bertone Loredan not once but a great many times in my presence were beseeching him to give up this journey entirely. And I myself besought him many times both on my part and on the part of the aforesaid persons, that he please give it up. And he answered me that what he was doing was good, and that with the help of God he would return cheered. Also he complained to me of Ser Bertone, who wanted his mother not to give [Giovanni] any money for this journey. How much [money] and how many times I do not know at all, and I do not even know whether his mother gave it. . . .

The judges of the Procuratori declare that the evidence produced in court fully proves the following facts:

The money received as a loan was received through the *monte* and returned from the *monte* itself, and therefore no deduction is to be made, especially as the usuries paid for said money were furnished by the *monte;* and in addition, that it was clear through the testimonies produced in behalf of the party of said Berto that nothing was proved and exhibited in regard to said Paolo Loredan's carrying outside of Venice on the said journey to Delhi anything over and above the said £ 80 groat [of Alberto da Calle] and over and above the money of Antonio of Cremona and of Ser Francesco Marcello (and this the said Ser Alberto conceded); and in addition, they considered that Paolo Loredan, late brother of the said Giovanni Loredan nicknamed Vacca, had placed in the hands of the aforesaid lords Procuratori £ 230 groat net from the aforesaid journey, deduction being made of all moneys, credits, usuries, loans, profits, and whatever expenses were incurred on said journey and also of the money and account of Antonio of Cremona.

First and before everything else they considered that in the said £230 groat said Ser Alberto had £ 80 groat of capital, and said Ser Francesco Marcello £ 3 groat which Ser Alberto conceded should be deducted together with their profit, so that the profit remaining was £ 147 groat.

From these, deduction was made of £ 44 s.8 groat, given and paid both for the goods promised to the wife of said Giovanni Loredan and for other expenses of said orphans and by reason of them; and, in addition, deduction was made of £ 3 s.14 d.2 groat, which may be coming for the profit of said Ser Francesco Marcello. There remains net, of profit obtained and coming for the account of said Ser Alberto, in his share, £ 98 s.17 d.10 groat.

Of these, for the *colomello* or one-third share of said Berto, son and now one of the three heirs of the said late Giovanni Loredan, £ 32 s.19 groat and d.10 petty for the one-third share of said profit, and £ 26 s.13 d.4 groat for the one-third share of said capital of the said £ 80 groat are coming to [Alberto da Calle].

Before pronouncing their sentence, the judges of the Procuratori require Alberto da Calle to declare under oath that he had never conceded in an interview with Marco Loredan and Francesco Querini that the best figure he could get in an accounting of his investment was £ 90 groat.

And he, Ser Alberto da Calle, swore on the holy Gospels of God that he never admitted to the aforesaid lords Procuratori that he was content and satisfied that he could get no better accounting than £ 90 in connection with the said £ 80 groat; nor did he have or receive anything of them.

The judges of the Procuratori give judgment that Berto Loredan shall be held to pay Alberto da Calle £ 59 s.12 d.7 groat and [d.]10 petty for his one-third share as one of the three heirs of Giovanni Loredan; and they reserve for Alberto da Calle all rights in regard to the other two shares, as well as the right to seize the goods of the late Giovanni Loredan to obtain full payment of his claim.

CHAPTER XVIII

BUSINESS FAILURES AND THEIR SETTLEMENT

ACCORDING TO strict law, a merchant who failed to pay his creditors was to be put in prison while his property was sold to extinguish the debt. If the sale did not yield enough and the creditors were unwilling to declare themselves satisfied with a smaller amount than was owing, the bankrupt merchant served a prison sentence and usually suffered other penalties such as loss of civil rights or expulsion from the gild. Extreme cases, such as that of a money-changer who as late as 1360 was beheaded in Barcelona because he had failed to pay his creditors, were practically unheard of in the more advanced towns.[1]

What usually happened in Italian cities and in many other Mediterranean centers was that a merchant who knew that he would be unable to pay his debts ran away from town. He might never return, in which case he was declared *in absentia* a bankrupt fugitive. His property was sold and his sureties, if any, were liable for any outstanding debt that they had guaranteed. More frequently, however, his friends at once tried to round up his creditors and to obtain from them a temporary safe-conduct. He then came back and endeavored to reach a settlement with the creditors during the time the safe-conduct was in force. He might obtain easier terms of payment and sometimes even a reduction of his debt. In time, the procedure became so simple that it gave ground to complaints that dishonest merchants were encouraged to engage in all sorts of crooked practices, relying upon the safe-conduct to escape the consequences of their actions.[2]

[1] Failures have not been studied as fully as the interest of the subject would warrant. See, however, J. Rezzara, *Il concordato nella storia, nella dottrina, nella giurisprudenza: studio di diritto commerciale*; G. I. Cassandro, *Le rappresaglie e il fallimento a Venezia nei secoli XIII–XVI*; Raymond de Roover, *Money, Banking and Credit in Mediaeval Bruges*, pp. 331ff; A. P. Usher, *The Early History of Deposit Banking in Mediterranean Europe*, pp. 237ff. (all of them with bibliography). A case of merciless enforcement of the law is mentioned in Document 144.

[2] See, for instance, the official statement of the Venetian government in 1489, quoted by Cassandro, *Le rappresaglie*, p. 166: 'Ever growing are the plots of those evil men who forsake every consideration of fear of God and worldly honor and deceive and defraud the citizens who are struggling with toil and industry to live righteously. These wicked men . . . buy the merchandise and the wares of our gentlemen and citizens, and after they have brought the goods into their power . . . they go or send for the safe-conduct from the office of the *sopraconsoli*, where they find the safe-conduct prepared and stamped with the seal of Saint Mark and signed, except for the space to insert the name of the man who gets it . . . This is the cause of the ruin of many of our merchants and their families. And [these evil men] turn to universal injury what was established by our venerated ancestors—for the office was established to assist good merchants or citizens who may have been struck by adverse fortune . . . .'

The first three documents (150–152) show the three main steps in the procedure which we have outlined; Document 153 relates the sale at auction of a house belonging to an insolvent merchant who had not run away. It will also be noted that the first selection introduces both the case of a merchant who ran away and did not return and that of another merchant who died before a sentence of bankruptcy was pronounced and was therefore posthumously discharged. Two of the first four documents come from small towns, Castelfiorentino in Tuscany and Traù in Dalmatia, whereas the other two come from great business centers. The procedure, however, is much the same in all cases.

Problems arising from default were much more complex in the case of banks, *compagnie,* and other such businesses. Enterprises of this kind extended credit on so large a scale that the default of even some of their debtors could easily make them in turn default. We are lucky to have the petition which the Bonsignore *Magna Tabula* (great bank) of Siena, probably the world's greatest *compagnia* of merchant-bankers in its time, presented in an effort to obtain a moratorium and a suspension of joint liability. Demands for extension of the term for payment were nothing unusual, but any deviation from joint liability would have been revolutionary. It is not surprising, then, that this demand was not granted and that the *compagnia* failed. Had the partners of the Bonsignore *compagnia* obtained what they asked, each partner would have become liable only for a percentage of the company's obligations equal to his percentage of the company's capital. 'His indebtedness as a result of the failure could still be unlimitedly higher than the sum he had invested, but he would not have to carry the burdens of his partners in addition to his own. This principle was later adopted, for a short time, in the statutes of Siena, but it eventually had to be dropped .... This clause, conservative as it may seem to us, was partly responsible for the rapid decline of Siena as a leading center of business. The public wanted to nail solidly each and all of the partners to each and all of the partnership's debts.'[3]

Procedures for Settling Bankruptcies

150

From the Latin[4]

[Florence] November 14, 1290–January 29, 1291

In the name of the Lord, amen. Book of the decisions, sanctions, denunciations, abuses presented in the presence of the wise man Giovanni di Bilione, judge and notary of Lord Beccadino degli Artinigi, honorable Captain of the Florentine People, and of the various suits written, aired, and argued in the presence of the said Lord Giovanni, and written by me, Giovanni, son of the

---

[3] R. S. Lopez, 'Italian Leadership in the Medieval Business World,' *Journal of Economic History*, VIII (1948), 66. See A. Sapori, *La crisi delle compagnie dei Bardi e dei Peruzzi* and *Liber tercius Friscombaldorum.*

[4] M. Cioni, 'Un fallimento commerciale a Castelfiorentino sulla fine del secolo XIII,' *Miscellanea Storica della Valdelsa*, X (1902), 152–54.

late Alberigo, notary of the [Holy Roman] Empire and of the Lord Captain, in the year of the Lord 1290, third indiction, in the last six months of the administration of the said Lord Captain and judge over fugitives, defaulters, and absentees.

Ciallo, notary, son of the late Lotteringo, attorney of Piero, son of the late Giacomo of the quarter of San Bartolomeo di Tre Santi, of Roberto di Vitolo of Castelfiorentino, and of Chele di Bonagiunta of the quarter of San Felice in Piazza of Florence, acting as attorney for them, sets forth in the presence of you, Lord Beccadino degli Artinigi, defender of the arts and artisans of the city of Florence and keeper of the peace, and of your judge and assessor, Lord Giovanni, [the following facts]:

Cecco, nicknamed Cescolino, son of the late Gherardo of Castelfiorentino, and Fiorentino di Ugolino di Aguglione, of the same aforesaid Castelfiorentino, were hitherto public merchants and partners in the art or trade of buying and selling wool, saffron, and hides, or leather goods, and many other things and wares. And they maintained together publicly and openly a shop (*apotheca*) and have maintained it for a long time in Castelfiorentino as public merchants and partners and artisans in said professions and trades and in many other types of commerce.[5] And they were accustomed to keep and have publicly a book of accounts just as do partners and merchants, and credit was extended to them by transfers in the books and by instruments, as [is the custom] with public artisans and merchants and partners.[6] And the said Piero, together with Giovanni Guerrieri and Pacino Alberti, was and is to receive from the aforesaid partners and merchants, by virtue of an instrument, £ 50 [Florentine] in consideration of the price of crocus sold and delivered to them. And the said Piero and partners were and are to receive from the aforesaid through transfer in the book, without instrument, £ 8 s.7 in one entry in consideration of the price of crocus sold to them, and 7 gold florins through transfer in the book, without instrument, which he gave them in loan. And the aforesaid Roberto is and was to receive from them through instrument £ 5 by reason of a loan, and 10 gold florins and £ 10 through transfer in the book, without instrument, through loan. And said Chele is and was to receive from them 21 gold florins through a right ceded to him by Fiorenzo Machiavelli as guarantor for the said Cescolino and Fiorentino;

---

[5] *Pluribus aliis mercatoribus*; but the last word is obviously a slip for *mercationibus*.

[6] Obviously the attorney is endeavoring to prove that Cescolino and Fiorentino are merchants and that commercial law applies to them. The tests of belonging to the merchant class, in Ciallo's words, are that Cescolino and Fiorentino used to keep a regular commercial accounting (*liber rationum*), and that credit was extended to them through the usual forms of written transfers in the ledgers of bankers (*ad scripturam libri*) and of notarial or holograph instruments (*ad cartam*).

and the latter were bound for this to the said Fiorenzo by a loan through a public instrument. And the aforesaid Cescolino ran away, to the damage of the same aforesaid creditors, [an offense] for which the statutes and ordinances make provision. And both he, Cescolino, and Fiorentino failed to give satisfaction to them in regard to said sums, and [they failed] to pay and give satisfaction concerning the aforesaid amounts.[7] And later, said Fiorentino having died, his heirs also refused to give satisfaction to them and to any one of them in regard to said sums and amounts, like fugitives and defaulters.

For this reason the said attorney in behalf of the aforesaid [creditors] seeks that said Cescolino as partner of said Fiorentino be declared by you to be and to have been a fugitive and defaulter with the above-said money of those creditors, and both said Cescolino and Fiorentino and the latter's heirs to have defaulted and refused to pay and to give satisfaction in regard to said amounts of money which [the creditors] are to have and to receive from them as was stated above. And he seeks the enforcement of all the statutes, penalty, and penalties issued, ordered, and established against fugitives and defaulters, against them and against their sons and daughters and wives and families and against all others for whom the statutes and ordinances make provision, and also against their persons and their goods; and that the oath of their creditors and of any one of the creditors be accepted against them and any one of them. Also he seeks that in the aforesaid or in the said suits what is set forth in all statutes and ordinances and reformed provisions of the art in favor of the same creditors and to the damage and detriment of the fugitives or defaulters or plunderers of another's money be observed in every particular, in every right, way, and cause by which he can better petition.

Presented on November 14.

On December 8.

On petition of said Ciallo, attorney of Piero, Bandino di Bigallo of the quarter of San Pier Gattolino, messenger of the Commune of Florence, reported that he, acting for said defender and said judge, cited said Cesco and the heirs of the late aforesaid Fiorentino in the name and stead of him [Ciallo], and gave notice publicly and in a loud voice in the square of said Castelfiorentino that whoever wants to defend them, or to contradict said petition, or to say that he has some right in their goods, should appear in the presence of said lord defender and of said judge within three days from now. Otherwise the said lord defender and judge will proceed by law.

---

[7] *Pretii quantitatibus*; the first word is probably a slip for *predictis*.

Presented on December 11.

Giunta, notary, son of the late Manetto, attorney of Monna Paola, daughter of the late Uguccione and wife of the late aforesaid Fiorentino; and Manetto, son of the late Lanfranco of San Felice, acting as attorney for them; and Vermiglio, notary, son of the late Gentile of Passignano, in his name; and Ricciardo, notary, son of the late Liberio, attorney of Monna Giovanna and Druda, daughters of the late aforesaid Fiorentino; and, in addition, the attorney of Tuccio and of the sons of Ghino, brothers, sons of the late Guicciardino of the quarter of Santa Felicita; and the [attorney] of Corsino Corsinelli, son of the late Benintendi of Castelfiorentino, acting as attorney for them—plead to obtain a remittance of the debt and of the claim of restitution concerning the said Fiorentino . . .[8] [for the following reasons]:

Said Fiorentino is deceased and has been dead for several months. They did not fail to meet their obligations to their creditors except by reason of death, as it has pleased God. Sons do not succeed in a *societas* and oath made by the father; and his daughters have waived the inheritance of said Fiorentino. And the statutes making provision against fugitives and defaulters do not apply nor make provision against fugitives or defaulters by reason of death nor against their sons and wives. And other reasons and causes to be stated and alleged in their proper place.

On January 14.

On petition and will of the notary, attorney of the aforesaid Roberto, Piero, and Chele, acting as attorney for them, Oliviero di Piacentino of the quarter of San Pier Gattolino, messenger of the Commune of Florence, reported that he, acting for the said judge, cited said Cescolino, summoned in two places according to the form of the statutes; and he assigned to the same a time limit of three days, according to the form of the statutes.

On January 29.

Braccino di Braccio, herald of the Commune and the People of Florence, reported that he had pronounced the ban against the aforesaid Cescolino of Castelfiorentino, proclaiming it in Florence in the customary places at d. 207[9] unless he comes by the third day to comply with the orders of the lord captain and his judge. . . .[10]

---

[8] The lengthy document at this point has some gaps which make it unclear. We omit what is left of some involved formulae to come to the conclusion.

[9] That is, the ban implied the penalty of 207 deniers.   [10] The end of the document is missing.

151
From the Latin[11]

Genoa, July 29, 1255

In the name of the Lord, amen. We, Rico of Recco in my own behalf and in behalf of Guglielmo Cadora, Ugo Croce, Vivaldo of Sant'Ambrogio, Gennaro Mazolo, and Arnolfo Zapatino, creditors of Domafolio, wool maker, give safe-conduct[12] to the same Domafolio and his wife to come to Genoa, for the sake of coming to a settlement with us in regard to the debt which he owes us, and to remain in Genoa fifteen days after his arrival in Genoa. And we promise you, Oberto, dyer, that we shall not raise impediments against them or cause impediments to be raised against their persons or goods, in coming, staying, or returning, up to the said time limit. Otherwise, if we contravene, we promise you, making the stipulation, the penalty of £ 50—and let him incur this penalty who shall have contravened—under pledge of our goods; and it is well understood that this safe-conduct is not to hold except throughout August.[13] Done in Genoa in front of the house of the late Ugo Fornari. Witnesses Guglielmo de Manica, *executor,*[14] and Ugo, *executor.* In the year of the Nativity of the Lord 1255, twelfth indiction, July 29, before terce.

152
From the Latin[15]

[Venice,] April 12, 1301

Pact and settlement made between Niccolò Pellegrino and his creditors.

In 1301, the month of April, on the twelfth day from the beginning, fourteenth indiction, in the presence of the noblemen, lords Marco Contarini, Niccolò Sanudo, and Pancrazio Barozzi, judges of petitions, Niccolò Pellegrino of the district of Santa Maria Maddalena came to the following settlement and pact[16] with his creditors, [whose names are] written below— viz., Niccolò Tron of San Cassiano . . .[17] Bertuccio Diedo of Santa Lucia, Pietro Diedo of San Giovanni in Bragora, Tommaso Tron of Sant'Agata . . .

---

[11] R. S. Lopez, *Studi sull'economia genovese nel medio evo*, p. 202 and, for the background of the document, pp. 141ff.

[12] *Fidanciam.*

[13] Actually the document says July, but it must be a slip for August, as appears from its date and from other safe-conducts granted by other creditors to Domafolio.

[14] A municipal official whose duty it was to serve notice of judicial and administrative decisions and to enforce them.

[15] Cassandro, *Le rappresaglie*, p. 137.   [16] *Concordium et pactum.*   [17] The dots are Cassandro's.

Trevisano of Santa Marina, Francesco Tron of Santa Maria Formosa[18]—in regard to the debts written below, which he is bound to pay to them. For the aforesaid Niccolò Pellegrino promised to the aforesaid [judges] to give and to pay to the aforesaid creditors what he is bound to give them within the time limits written below—that is, on every feast of Saint Michael and on every Paschal feast of the Resurrection of the Lord s.25 Venetian groat— until these creditors of his have been wholly satisfied by him in regard to all debts which he is bound to pay to them. And to make more certain and firm the observing of all this, the aforesaid Niccolò Pellegrino is under obligation to deposit with Bertuccio Diedo and his bank[19] s.25 Venetian groat—and these he has already deposited, as Bertuccio himself has acknowledged—this being done as follows: If the same Niccolò Pellegrino pays his creditors within the above-written time limits, as has been stated, [all is] well; the aforesaid s.25 groat which said Bertuccio holds must be eventually divided and distributed among all the creditors of Niccolò Pellegrino at that last time limit. And if he, Niccolò Pellegrino, at any time limit does not undertake and observe and pay in full to his aforesaid creditors what is reserved for any one of the aforesaid time limits, then the aforesaid s.25 groat deposited by him, Niccolò, at the bank mentioned above must be turned over wholly to the aforesaid creditors of his to be divided pro rata of what is owed them, as a penalty and by name of a penalty; and still he, Niccolò Pellegrino, is to undertake, to observe, and to pay to his aforesaid creditors, as has been stated, all the aforesaid by the aforesaid time limits, as has been stated.

153
From the Latin[20]

Traù [Trogir, Dalmatia], April 23, 1279

In the name of Christ, amen. In the year of the Same 1279, seventh indiction, Sunday, the eighth day before the end of April, in the time of Lord Ladislaus, most serene king of Hungary, of Lord Giovanni, bishop of Traù, of Lord Giovanni, count of the same city, and of the lords Dessa Amblasio, Luca Matteo, and Duymo Dominche,[21] consuls of Traù. Jula Pluzio came before us, said consuls, and before the court of Traù, and caused

---

[18] All these names belong to the highest ranks of the Venetian merchant nobility. Each of the families furnished doges to the republic.

[19] *Tabulam.*

[20] T. Smiciklas, *Diplomaticki zbornik Kraljevine Hrvatske, Dalmacije i Slavonije,* VI, 292–93.

[21] They all were members of the Traù patriciate. Their names are evidently patronymic, after Ambrogio, Matteo, and Domenico or Dominko. Italian and Yugoslav scholars still dispute whether these Latin names ought to be linked to a Romance or a Slavonic form. As for Jula, who is mentioned a little after, his name seems closest to the Hungarian Gyula.

persons and goods; that, for the upholding and increase of the honor of the Commune of Siena, it bore many burdens in connection with customs duties, public loans, and the maintenance of horses, and indeed it bore a goodly share of said burdens; and, to conclude, it would be a heavy and difficult task to recount how great an advantage and how much honor has accrued to the Commune of Siena from the good standing of the *societas*. But since well-known facts need no proof, [the petitioners] rest content with the facts presented above, confident that your discerning minds know this well.

However, just as the status and government of this world forever remains [as it is], not because of the poor condition of [human] society but because of the sins of [men], and because they have not learned what is good from Him who is the Highest Good, [so likewise] the Enemy, [instigator] of discord, has sown among them discord of such nature, so deep, and continued for so long a time that any *societas* in this world would have been eventually destroyed and stripped of all its strength.[25] Yet, very great and almost incalculable though their loss may be, even now if[26] said discord were removed and harmony were to follow, [the *societas*] would recover its strength and would surpass all other *societates* in power and with honor. And may He who can do all things bring this to pass.

But even if this cannot be, even now the *societas* is in a position to meet its obligations at the proper times and places and within the different time limits, as is its custom, to all its creditors and to those who are to receive anything from it. But because of their own discord and also at the urging and instigation of some citizens of Siena—who are acting ill and have no reason or cause for taking any action whatever—all their creditors are agitating and are demanding what the *societas* and its partners owe them; and they are making [these] demands upon certain partners and not upon all [as a body]. And this does not happen because of the poor condition of the *societas* but because of the envy and instigation of some persons, as has been stated above, and not because the *societas* has thus far refused to meet its obligations to anyone. Indeed from the day that discord arose and up to this day, the *societas* has met its obligations in regard to both capital and interest, as had been its custom before the days of discord, and it has already paid out 200,000 gold florins.

Yet, even if [the partners of] the *societas* were in full and good harmony,

---

[25] Apparently the petitioners attempt to draw a comparison between the sad conditions of human society and those of the Bonsignore partnership. Both are in a position to be thriving, but the devil endeavors to destroy them by instigating internal dissensions. There is a play on words between *societas* (human society in general) and *societas* (partnership).

[26] *Quasi adhuc*; but read, probably, *quod si adhuc*.

and all the creditors were to make a run[27] on the *societas* at the same time and hour, the *societas* would fail to meet its obligations not because it is unable [to pay] but for the reason that whatever it is obligated to give it [first] must recover in different parts of the world from kings, counts, barons, and from other *societates* and individuals. And this was well-known to those who extended credit to said *societas*, since the said *societas* did not conceal that it received from [some] men but lent to all others, as every *societas* does. Therefore the demands should be considerate and moderate, so that even as the partners of the said *societas* cannot in one moment recover from all [who owe them], similarly they should not be forced in one moment to meet all their obligations so long as discord exists among them. But even if there were harmony and the [present] demands for payment were made not upon specifically indicated partners but upon the *societas* as a whole, the *societas* would still be unable to meet its obligations. Therefore the time has come for the city of Siena, which has gathered so many advantages and such great honor from the good standing of the said *societas*, to render [that service] to which it is obligated by nature.

The points which [the petitioners] ask and humbly supplicate to be done are as follows:

First: That those who are instigating the creditors of the *societas* to make such demands [for payment] be all equally ruled out. This can easily be done by a provision to be enacted by you and the General Council of the Bell, [to wit], that no one [partner] of the said *societas* may or should be compelled by the lord podestà, the captain, the consuls of the merchants, or by any ruler or official of the Commune of Siena to pay the debts of the said *societas* to a greater extent than that which falls to him in proportion to his capital. If such provision be enacted, those who are instigating the creditors to present demands, realizing that they cannot hurt those whom they have in mind, would refrain from further instigations; and the creditors would temper their less-than-honest demands and would make reasonable, honest, and ordinary demands, and at a proper time, because they know and will be in a position to know that the *societas* and the partners of the *societas* can fully meet their obligations to their creditors—provided, however, that their creditors stand by the partners, so that these may [in turn] collect [what is owing them]. For there is no *societas* in the world which would not fail if all its creditors made a run [on it]. And thus the said *societas* is not failing and could not fail because of inability [to pay], but because of the discord among its [partners] and because of those who are hoping for the destruction of the said *societas*,

[27] *Confugerent.*

[a fate] that must not be tolerated in the slightest degree by you [gentlemen] and the Commune of Siena.

The second point which is petitioned for with humble supplication and prayer: That a suitable delay be granted to the partners of the said *societas* so that they may collect and thus meet their obligations in accordance with the demands of the creditors. And this is fully warranted by custom and by good business practice, and is furthermore sanctioned by imperial legislation.

The third point which is asked for, ever out of grace and with humble supplication: That it may please you to see to it that two ambassadors of the Commune of Siena go to the lord pope and speak in behalf of the said *societas,* and that he [the pope] use the influence of his holy office with the creditors of the said *societas* and especially with those creditors who reside at the Curia, to the end that, in presenting their demands, these creditors may not burden the partners of the *societas* except in the proportion that falls to each one; that the creditors may grant the partners a suitable delay, so that these may be in a position to collect from their creditors and so meet their obligations to the creditors [of the *societas*]; and that, in requiring that, the said lord pope bring to bear the weight of his holy office. And [you should] appoint an embassy in regard to the matters above-mentioned and anything else that you may deem necessary for the well-being and reorganization of the said *societas.*

And you ought to be led to make provisions regarding said matters by [recollecting] the advantages which have accrued to the city from the good standing of the said *societas,* by your love for the citizens, so that. . . .[28] For, if the provision should not be enacted, the individual partners who are being harassed for the total [debits of the *societas*] and who cannot bear [the burden], would be forced to leave [their posts], and the *societas* would not be able to collect what it has to recover in different parts of the world, and hence the city and the businessmen of the city would be oppressed by the reprisals which would be instituted against the Commune of Siena, and its merchants would no longer have free access to trade.

This petition is therefore just in each item. And it is better that said provision be enacted, so that those meet their obligations who are able and who ought to, as has been stated, rather than that so many citizens of this city—the partners of the said *societas*—should be scattered, and the *societas* be ruined, and the merchants of the city of Siena incur restrictions and losses.

And note that the provision demands haste because, at the instigation of

[28] *Ut litas presens.* This can hardly be a simple mistake in spelling of three words but one has to assume that some words have been dropped.

certain citizens of Siena, the creditors in the city of Rome have caused the seizure of the goods of said *societas* which were in the said city, and the factors [of the *societas*] have fled. Wherefore, lest the disgrace and such a great danger increase, [the partners] humbly petition you to help them aid justice and the advantage of the city. And [the partners] themselves offer to their creditors to assign trustworthy debtors [for the sums owing] to them,[29] if only the creditors be willing to wait so long as [the partners] collect and [in turn] meet their obligations.

The [arguments] presented above embody justice; they embody equity, honor for the city, the preservation of its citizens, and the liberty and security of its merchants; and they avert error and scandal.

May God, who can do all things, make His light to shine upon your hearts in these and all other matters that make or may make for the peace and good standing of the city and its territory; and may He preserve the city and its citizens and grant them beneficent peace. . . .

[The petition was denied.]

[29] This seems to mean that the partners shall earmark for each creditor any specific credit of the *societas* that may seem particularly easy to recover.

CHAPTER XIX

INTERNATIONAL DISPUTES
OVER TRADE

WHEN A MERCHANT felt that he had been wronged in foreign territory, he could lodge a complaint with the local government or he could ask his own government to intervene. Commercial controversies thus became a matter of international action and were often debated through diplomatic channels.

Western envoys to the Byzantine courts and Byzantine envoys to the Western states, for instance, very frequently submitted lists of damages and demanded indemnities. The complaints of the Genoese envoy to Constantinople, Nicolò Spinola (Document 155), are a distressing catalogue of injustices which Genoese merchants are alleged to have suffered from private citizens and even public officials of the Byzantine Empire. One might well feel sorry for the Western merchants—all the more so since some of their grievances go back many years and since answers of the Byzantine government, when quoted, are usually negative—but for the fact that complaints of the Byzantine envoys to the Venetian government (Document 156) vent just as many grievances suffered by Byzantine citizens at the hands of Western merchants. Probably part of the charges from both sides were legitimate, but in many cases the complainants had brought the loss upon themselves in trying to evade laws of foreign governments.[1]

Religious differences and national feelings contributed to strain the relations between Westerners and Easterners, but the situation was not much better in territories of the Levant under Western rule. Document 157 shows how a Venetian subject whose merchandise had been seized in Cyprus by a pirate could not recover his goods although the pirate was captured. Indifference and red tape frustrated all attempts of the victim to be heard by the king.[2]

Even where kings were powerful and the administration efficient, the Mediterranean merchant was not sure of prompt and full justice. When Edward II of England ordered an inquisition to be made in regard to the ship and merchandise of a Genoese merchant which had been carried off in the port of Southampton, the answer was that unknown 'evildoers from Scotland' had committed the deed, and

[1] See the lively comments of G. I. Bratianu, *Recherches sur le commerce génois dans la Mer Noire au XIIIe siècle.*

[2] Incidents of the same kind and other complaints arising from commercial disputes continued to embitter the relations between Cyprus and the Western towns and eventually led to war Genoese occupation, and the final ruin of the kingdom. It is fair to say that the Genoese inflicted upon the kingdom far greater punishment than the wrongs they had received would have warranted.

the local authorities had no remedy to suggest (Document 158). Nor were local representatives of the English king always above committing similar robberies. In the French island of Oléron they captured a ship and the goods of another Genoese merchant, Gherardo di Pezagno, under pretext that the law of shipwreck applied to the case, this in spite of the fact that the ship had not been wrecked and that the law of shipwreck had been abolished in England.[3] All that the merchant could do was to have an accurate report written by the municipal authorities of nearby La Rochelle and to present it to the government of Genoa (Document 159). The latter must have lodged a complaint with the king of England, but it can hardly have been successful since a few months later the pope also intervened in behalf of the merchant.[4] We do not know the conclusion of this affair, but it is worth noting that some fifty years later Anthony Pessagno, a descendant of Gherardo, held important positions at the English court as king's merchant, purveyor of the wardrobe, and seneschal of Gascony.[5]

The interest shown by the Commune of La Rochelle in this matter shows that municipal governments generally were more anxious than kings to treat foreign merchants justly. They knew that their own trade would suffer if foreigners shunned the town as unsafe or if the government of the wronged merchant took retaliatory measures. This explains why the town of Como was so quick in paying indemnity to French merchants who had been robbed while traveling in its territory, although the robbers could not be identified and might well have been citizens of another country (Document 160).

Policies of this kind went a long way towards eliminating the custom of 'reprisal,' according to which the persons and the goods of foreign merchants were held for unpaid debts or unatoned crimes of any of their fellow citizens.[6] Reprisals usually led to counterreprisals, and commerce was thereby seriously hampered. The Italian communes led the way in limiting reprisals through reciprocal trade agreements and through constant vigilance to suppress unfair dealings with foreign

---

[3] The so-called *jus naufragii* was not really a law but an inhuman custom whereby if a ship was wrecked in a river or at sea any goods that were recovered were seized by the inhabitants of the region. Originally, indeed, the shipwrecked sailor or merchant also lost his liberty. But in the ninth century the Lombard prince of Salerno and the Byzantine duke of Naples agreed to abolish this custom (see Document 7), and soon afterward the popes and the Italian communes engaged in a long struggle to obtain universal respect for the goods of unlucky voyagers. When, in 1272, the French king of Sicily enforced the *jus naufragii* in his state, his action shocked Italian public opinion. The custom, however, survived much longer in northern Europe, in spite of many legal pronouncements abrogating the law.

[4] See L. Auvray, ed., *Les Registres de Grégoire IX*, I, 901.

[5] The name of the Pezagno family is more frequently spelled Pessagno. Anthony's brother was the first of a long line of admirals of Portugal, who in time changed their name into Pessanha. See L. T. Belgrano, 'Documenti e genealogia dei Pessagno genovesi,' *Atti della Società Ligure di Storia Patria*, XV (1891), 240–380. Gherardo, it may be noted, was not discouraged by his first misfortune but met once again with bad luck in 1252, when he was imprisoned and lost all his merchandise in Flanders. See R. Doehaerd, *Les Relations commerciales entre Gênes, la Belgique et l'Outremont d'après les archives notariales génoises aux XIIIe et XIVe siècles*, II, 403.

[6] On reprisals see G. I. Cassandro, *Le rappresaglie e il fallimento a Venezia nei secoli XIII–XVI*; A. Del Vecchio and E. Casanova, *Le rappresaglie nei comuni medievali*; J. Eiglier, *Etude historique sur le droit de marque ou de représailles à Marseille aux XIIIe, XIVe et XVe siècles;* W .Mitchell, *The Law Merchant*, with bibliography. There is no monograph on the *devetum*.

merchants. In extreme cases, when all other remedies had been unsuccessfully tried, an Italian commune would resort not so much to reprisal as to the *devetum,* an ordinance prohibiting all citizens from having business dealings with a government which had failed to redress wrongs. Document 161 shows how rigorous the *devetum* could be. A merchant who had gone through the territory of a state with which commercial relations had been broken was set free only when he proved that he had no merchandise and that he had been forced to cross that territory because he was ill.

Strains between East and West

155

From the Latin[7]

[Genoa and Constantinople, 1290–1294]

The following petitions for damages inflicted upon Genoese by Greeks and by men of the Most Excellent Lord Emperor are being made to the Most Sacred Emperor [Andronicus II] by the noble lord Nicola Spinola,[8] ambassador of the Commune of Genoa.

First, the same ambassador, acting on the part of the Commune of Genoa, requests that indemnification be made to Manuele Marino, personally and in behalf of Manfredi and of his other partners, for 2,000 gold hyperpers which the same Marino and partners ought to receive and have in consideration of damages inflicted by the galleys and the officials[9] of the Lord Emperor upon them in their ship, as it was leaving the Black Sea with alum. And this ship of theirs had been seized by those galleys in the time of the Most Excellent

[7] G. Bertolotto, 'Nuova serie di documenti sulle relazioni di Genova coll'impero bizantino,' *Atti della Società Ligure di Storia Patria,* XXVIII, 2 (1897), 531–45. This is the shorter of two versions of the same petition; the longer version was published in the same work, pp. 511–31. In the notes below we shall refer to the shorter version, which we have translated (omitting a few details), as *B*; and to the longer version, which we use occasionally in the notes when it brings further light upon the shorter version, as *A*. Both versions include some notations which refer to the answers which the envoy was able to secure or failed to obtain from the emperor. On the date of the document see also C. Manfroni, 'Le relazioni fra Genova, l'impero bizantino e i Turchi,' *Atti della Società Ligure di Storia Patria,* XXVIII, 3 (1898), 683–84. The larger part of the petition refers to incidents which occurred in 1290–1291 and in preceding years, but there also are complaints, entered in a loose leaflet attached to the petition, which cannot have been written before 1294. On the whole the document is ungrammatical and obscure. Its obscurity, however, may have been willful; the envoy tried to present the incidents in the light most favorable to the Genoese, who probably were not without blame in many instances.

[8] Nicola Spinola belonged to the same family as Oberto Spinola, one of the two Captains of the People of Genoa up to 1291. Another member of the family, Alberto Spinola, was sent in 1290 to Egypt, not to convey complaints of his Commune but to offer apologies and indemnities for hostile acts committed by Benedetto Zaccaria and other Genoese against Egyptian subjects. He succeeded in negotiating a commercial treaty, which was signed on May 13, 1290.

[9] *Nuncii:* this word ordinarily means 'messengers,' but here and elsewhere in the document it seems to be a generic word, designating any employee of the Byzantine government.

Lord and Emperor [Michael] Palaeologus, of good memory, father of our Most Sacred and Most Excellent Lord Emperor. [The claim is made] because the above-mentioned late Lord Emperor had promised to the Friars Minor who had been entrusted [with this negotiation] by the Commune of Genoa that he would make restitution of the said damages to the same Marinos.[10]

Item, the said ambassador, acting on the part of the said Commune, requests that indemnification and restoration be made by the Most Excellent Lord Emperor to Guidetto di Negro for 1,800 gold hyperpers. These he seeks as indemnification in consideration of damage suffered by the same Guidetto on account of 2,000 *modii* of grain from Rodosto for which the same Guidetto had to pay the freight charges of the ship which he had chartered. And he had bought them from the Lord Emperor, out of the new grain, for 4,000 hyperpers which the Lord Emperor had received from the said Guidetto. [The claim is made] because he was not able to carry the said cargo or load it in that ship.[11]

Item, he seeks indemnification and punishment in regard to this: When Bertolino, son of the late Oberto of Camogli, a citizen and merchant of Genoa, was coming from Comediarum Gulf in a certain boat (*barchia*) with some Greeks, two of whom were called by the same name, Manuel, and were residents of Pera—and in consideration of a specific freight charge which they were to receive from said Bertolino [the ship was carrying] the goods of the same Bertolino, including merchandise and hyperpers worth in total 800 gold hyperpers—the said Greeks, driven by diabolical counsel, killed Bertolino himself and carried away his goods, property, and hyperpers in their boat. And two of these Greeks have been captured by Kinnamos, at that time captain of the Lord Emperor, who inflicted no punishment upon them.[12]

[10] In all probability the seizure of the ship of the Marinos, loaded with alum and coming from the Black Sea, was connected with the closing of that sea to all Genoese ships by order of Michael VIII and by suggestion of the Zaccaria brothers (1276?). Diplomatic relations seem to have been broken following that order, and this may be the reason why the affair was entrusted by the Genoese to the friars. See Document 53.

[11] Grain trade was under state control; probably the emperor seized the 'new grain' because the harvest had been insufficient. *A* reports the claim of a certain Simone, who demanded 'restitution' of 500 hyperpers 'because they [the Byzantine customs officials] did not let him sell the grain according to the current price of the country,' which evidently was the price of the black market (p. 526). In a treaty with Venice, concluded in 1285, the emperor permitted the export of grain only if the domestic price of a *kentinarion* did not rise above 100 hyperpers.

[12] Kinnamos, who also bore the titles of *logothetes* and *strategos*, was the head of the port of Constantinople. Other documents concerning him have been published by L. T. Belgrano, 'Prima serie di documenti riguardanti la colonia di Pera,' *Atti della Società Ligure di Storia Patria* XIII (1877), 98–317, and by G. I. Bratianu, *Actes des notaires génois de Péra et de Caffa de la fin du treizième siècle (1281–1290)*. Bratianu himself, in *Recherches sur le commerce génois*, pp. 147ff., traces a vivid portrait of this officer, who may have been a descendant of the Byzantine historian by the same name.

Item, in behalf of the merchants who were robbed in Salonika by the despot[13] of Salonika, he seeks 3,684 gold hyperpers which remain to be received by the said robbed merchants in consideration of the goods, property, and hyperpers taken from them by the lord despot himself. And the names of these merchants who were robbed are these: Giacomo Cigala; Percivalle Marabotto in behalf of Pallavicino Pallavicini; Niccolò Bonromino, messenger of Ser Nicola d'Oria; Lanfranco of San Siro; Andreolo dell'Orto; Contardo Bruseto; Contardo Vivaldi; Gianuino de Promontorio; Bonannato da Bonato.[14]

Item, he seeks that restitution be made to Giacomo Cigala, who was robbed of alum, buckrams, and other merchandise in the ship of the Marinos. And there still remains for him to receive as much as amounts to 3,760 hyperpers, without any duty.[15]

No answer.

Item, he seeks that restitution and satisfaction be made to Ardizzone Rubeo, Genoese, of 906 hyperpers in consideration of those hyperpers which were taken from him out of his coffer by the officials of the Lord Emperor without any reason.

Nothing.

Item, he demands that restitution and satisfaction be made to Opizzino Spinola of 150 hyperpers in consideration of the hyperpers taken from him near Laurium by the men of our Most Excellent Lord Emperor, who captured the said Opizzino in the said place with the vessel of the same Greeks, which was a ship of 100 oars. And the names of those [Greeks] are Karruehas Georgios of Stalimene and Georgios of Monemvasia, who were going as pirates with said ship.

He answered that they were.[16]

Item, he seeks that restitution and satisfaction be made to Protaso Portonario and Guglielmo, brothers, in consideration of damages and unrealized profits which they suffered on account of this: In the month of November or December, 1285, they bought from the officials and factors of the *vestiarios* of our Most Excellent Lord Emperor 1,300 *modii* of grain which they were

[13] Probably Constantine, son of Emperor Andronicus II. *Despotes*, of course, meant 'lord' and was a high title in the Byzantine hierarchy. It was frequently used for sovereign princes.

[14] Pallavicini was a member of a powerful family of the Lombard plain, but most of the others belonged to the merchant aristocracy of Genoa.

[15] *Sine aliqua avaria.* On the Marino ship, see note 10 above.

[16] *Respondit quod erant.* Is this an affirmative answer, or does the Byzantine government merely state that the offenders were pirates over whom the emperor had no control?

to obtain near Selymbria[?][17] from the aforesaid ship. And they could not obtain that grain, but they had to travel away from the sea for ten miles and more, at their own expenses, and to accept what grain they could get, which was not good nor of commercial [grade]. And because they had to stay with the said ship and its armament from the Kalends of March—the time when they were to obtain the said grain—up to the end of May, in consideration of all this the said brothers suffered damages of 1,700 hyperpers and more. And he requests these 1,700 hyperpers in consideration of the said damages of the said brothers.[18]

Nothing.

Item, he seeks that restitution and satisfaction be made [in this]: That the Most Excellent Lord Emperor compel Andronikos and Kavalki, merchants of Monemvasia, to pay and to restore to Franceschino Ursetto and Nicola Cigala, citizens and merchants of Genoa, what they are under obligation to give and to restore—[that is], 1,648 gold hyperpers for the grain that the latter bought from the said merchants of Monemvasia in the month of June, 1292. And they have paid the price for this grain, as it also appears in a certain instrument, and yet they were not able to obtain this grain from the said [merchants] in Monemvasia.[19]

Item, he seeks that restitution and satisfaction be made to Manuele Avogario, citizen of Genoa, of 490 gold hyperpers by the standard of Constantinople,[20] which Kinnamos, at that time captain in Constantinople, compelled him to pay—to Kinnamos—during the month of August or September, 1290. [He exacted that sum] because he did not permit the two galleys of said Manuele to enter the Black Sea, just as they were accustomed to enter. This was also against the convention entered into and concluded between the

[17] *Srimula.* Our identification would be supported by the fact that Selymbria or Silivri, on the European coast of the Sea of Marmora, was one of the main outlets for Thracian grain and a port frequented by Italian merchants. The *vestiarios* was a high official of the treasury.

[18] We have changed the order of the words as they appear in Bertolotto's edition; the text as it stands there would be meaningless.

[19] *Nothing,* says *A.* The word which we translate as 'grain' appears under the form *grana* both in *A* and *B.* Inasmuch as this spelling occasionally appears in the preceding paragraph alongside with *grani,* we assume that it is just another misspelling of the frequently ungrammatical document. *Grana,* however, is also a dyestuff which was produced in Byzantine territory; we cannot exclude that Franceschino Ursetto and Nicola Cigala may have bought the dyestuff rather than grain.

[20] *Sagium* means 'test,' 'assay,' or 'monetary standard.' At this period so many hyperpers of different weights and alloys—all of them debased—were in circulation that they were accepted by the weight of fine metal and reckoned according to different standards in different cities. See D. A. Zakythinos, 'Crise monétaire et crise économique à Byzance du XIIIe au XVe siècle,' *L'Hellenisme Contemporain,* 2d ser., I (1947), 166–92, 259–77, 386–99, 483–97, 564–91.

most excellent late [Palaeologus] of good memory and the Commune of Genoa.[21]

Item, he seeks and requests in behalf of the said Manuele that the Most Excellent Lord Emperor cause Paulos Sophianos and Chakouminen of the castle of Monemvasia to give and to pay to the said Manuele 216 hyperpers which the same Manuele ought to receive from the aforesaid [merchants] of Monemvasia in consideration of the price of cloth which he sold them. The said Manuele was not able to receive or obtain any payment for these.

Item, he seeks and requests that indemnification be made to Ferrando Mallone for 300 hyperpers because, when he arrived at Tenedos through fortune of the sea with his ship loaded with grain and barley, the said ship suffered shipwreck. However, part of the cargo, the cordage of the ship, and the luggage of the captains and sailors escaped. The men of the said locality. . . .[22] And these goods are or were worth 500 hyperpers; these hyperpers or the said indemnification he seeks for the reason stated.

Nothing.

Item, he seeks that restitution and satisfaction be made to Gianuino de Valle in consideration of damage [resulting from] the grain seized from him by violence by the officials of the Lord Emperor, viz., by a certain Greek named Magistros. They took that grain because of the scarcity of food in a certain castle of the Lord Emperor. And that seized grain was worth 150 hyperpers; these [hyperpers] he seeks for the reason stated.

He answered.[23]

Item, he seeks that restitution and satisfaction be made to Nicolas of Verdun[24] because of the robbery perpetrated by Greeks of the Lord Emperor in a certain village named Chinokolion, a village to which he had come as a merchant for the sake of buying carpets. In that place the aforesaid Greeks seized Nicolas himself, threw him to the ground, tied his hands behind his

[21] The extant sources mention no official blockade of the Black Sea in 1290, and therefore this must have been a temporary order given by Kinnamos in regard to some specific ships. The convention with Michael VIII mentioned in the document is the Treaty of Nymphaeum (1261), which opened the Black Sea to the Genoese.

[22] The dots are Bertolotto's. *A* gives further details, namely that the islanders of Tenedos took everything the sailors had been able to salvage and sent Ferrando away 'almost naked in the most bitter cold.'

[23] *R.*, no doubt an abbreviation for *respondit*. This seems an affirmative answer.

[24] There was in Genoa a small group of descendants of a merchant from Verdun, France, who by this time were regarded as Genoese. Lanfranco of Prato (probably Prato Ligure near Genoa and not the better known Tuscan city) also was a Genoese citizen, probably a second- or third-generation immigrant; for recently naturalized merchants, such as Nikolaos of Thebes, the words 'citizen of Genoa' are usually added.

back, placed a wooden stick in his mouth so that he could not speak, stripped him of all garments and goods that he had, sent him away naked, and took from him 350 gold hyperpers. In consideration of this, payment and indeed punishment of the said men, criminals in so acting, is due to the aforesaid Nicolas.

Item, he seeks that restitution and satisfaction be made to Lanfranco of Prato, from whom 45 *modii* of salt were seized by the officials of the Lord Emperor. And earlier the customs inspectors[25] or officials of the latter had taken from him 25 hyperpers on account of 500 *modii* of grain. This damage, both for the salt and for the aforesaid hyperpers, amounts to 100 hyperpers.[26]

Item, he seeks that restitution and satisfaction be made to Nikolaos of Thebes, citizen of Genoa, of 1,300 gold hyperpers in consideration of damage inflicted upon him by the most excellent lord, the late Emperor Michael Palaeologus, of good memory, father of our Most Excellent Lord Emperor, on account of a vessel of 108 oars which the said Nikolaos had with his own armament. And the said late Lord Emperor took it from him and placed it with its armament in the service of his own empire. That vessel with the said armament the said Nikolaos valued at the said amount, and of these [hyperpers] he received thereafter no payment nor satisfaction.

Nothing.

Item, he seeks in behalf of the said Nikolaos from our Most Excellent Lord Emperor 100 hyperpers in consideration of those hyperpers...[27] which Kinnamos, at that time captain in Constantinople, took from him without any reason.

Item, the said ambassador seeks in behalf of the said Nikolaos of Thebes 14 silver cups which the despot Assan[28] took and obtained from him, and in consideration of the hyperpers which the said Nikolaos lent to the same despot, 720 hyperpers.

Item, in consideration of the pay which the said Nikolaos was to receive from the said despot for the time that he was in his service, 450 hyperpers.

Item, he seeks that restitution and satisfaction be made by our Most Excellent Lord Emperor to Guglielmo Corvara, Genoese, of 488 gold

---

[25] *Kommerkiarioi.* On these officials see R. S. Lopez, 'Silk Industry in the Byzantine Empire,' *Speculum*, XX (1945), 12, n. 4.

[26] It is worth noting that salt production and trade, although frequently leased out to private farmers, normally was a state monopoly in the Byzantine Empire. Perhaps Lanfranco of Prato was charged with a violation of the monopoly.

[27] The dots are Bertolotto's.

[28] The brother-in-law of Nogai, khan of Kipchak and former governor of Bulgaria. He was now an illustrious refugee at the Byzantine court.

hyperpers, which were extorted and taken from him violently without any reason—the same Guglielmo had not inflicted or done [any harm] to any person—from a coffer belonging to Guglielmo himself, which he had in the house or shop in which he lives in Constantinople. He was forced to open that coffer for the said officials of the Lord Emperor, who took out the said hyperpers from the said coffer.

Item, he seeks that restitution be made to Filippo, furrier, of Oneglia, Genoese merchant, of 322 hyperpers from his own goods, of which Filippo himself was robbed in a certain boat of Musso di Santo Stefano by Greeks near Pasichia at Trefegetum. Concerning these matters the same Filippo received an order from the Lord Emperor, which profited him nothing in being able to obtain payment.

He answered yes.

Item, he seeks that restitution be made to Sozzardo of Domoculta of 350 hyperpers, of which he was robbed in a certain boat or vessel belonging to him by Greeks of Nicaria. And concerning these matters he received an imperial order, and yet it profited him nothing in being able to obtain payment.[29]

Item, he seeks that restitution be made to Lanfranco Ruistropo, son of the late Ambrogio, of 312 gold hyperpers in consideration of the *scamandrum*[30] taken from the same Lanfranco in the port of Constantinople from the vessel of Guglielmo Trespanes by the officials of the Lord Emperor.

Nothing.

Item, he seeks that indemnification and restitution be made to Simonino Rainerio de Gastaldi of 200 hyperpers in consideration of the *scamandrum* taken from him and from the vessel of Guglielmo Trespanes which had come from Pasichia. And that *scamandrum* was 12,613 *pichae* according to the *picha* of the *scamandrum*.[31]

Nothing.

Item, he seeks that restitution be made to Guglielmo Trespanes or his brothers of 114 gold hyperpers in consideration of goods and merchandise taken from him from his said vessel.

Nothing.

Item, he seeks that restitution be made to Giovanni de Carro, haberdasher,

[29] *Nothing*, comments *A.*
[30] It was evidently some kind of cloth, for it was measured in *pichae* or *picchi*, a measurement for cloth. Perhaps the name went back to the same origin as *skaramangion*, a type of cloak or flowing robe worn by Byzantine noblemen and burghers.
[31] *Sic;* but the figure seems too high to be correct.

of 256 gold hyperpers 7 karats by the standard of Constantinople, in indemnification for mastic, carpets, *scamandrum,* and other goods taken from him from the vessel of Guglielmo Trespanes while coming from Pasichia to Constantinople without any fraud or offense done by him against anyone.

Nothing.

Item, he seeks that restitution be made to Giovanni de Carro, furrier, citizen of Genoa, of 47 hyperpers 8 karats which the same Giovanni had in the boat of the said Guglielmo Trespanes.[32]

Nothing.

Item, he seeks that restitution be made to Francesco of Multedo, tailor, of 55 gold hyperpers taken from him on account of a certain vessel belonging to him which entered the Black Sea in 1290, at the time when Lord Baldovino Avogario was podestà.[33]

Nothing.

Item, he seeks that restitution be made to Luchino de Travi of 250 hyperpers in indemnification for *scamandrum* taken from him in the vessel of Guglielmo Trespanes by the representatives of the Lord Emperor.

Item, he seeks that restitution be made to Lanfranco of Prato, Genoese, of 350 hyperpers in consideration of damage inflicted on him by order of the Most Excellent Lord Emperor through the wrecking and destruction of the houses which he owned in Pera on land of the Commune [of Genoa] near the Church of Saint Michael. And these [houses] were two floors high, and the wrecking was done without any reason.

Item, he seeks that restitution and satisfaction be made to Giacomo of Capriata in consideration of 3 bundles of *scamandrum,* which were 1,500 *pichae,* and in consideration of gallnuts, wine, and cotton taken from him from the vessel of Guglielmo Trespanes, when it came from Pasichia. These goods are worth and amount to 290 hyperpers.

Item, he seeks, in behalf of the Commune, that restitution and satisfaction be made to Manuele de Bonis in consideration of damage inflicted on him and the partners of the same Manuele by the Greeks of Pocchi, in consideration of goods taken from him and his partners by the said Greeks in the said locality when they arrived there with a *tarida.* . . .[34]

[32] Both *A* and *B* mention the first Giovanni de Carro as a haberdasher and the second as a furrier, so they must have been two different persons. A Giovanni de Carro, furrier, is mentioned in an instrument done in Pera, July 5, 1281; eight years later we meet a Giovanni de Carro, tailor, in Caffa (Bratianu, *Actes,* pp. 305, 251–52).

[33] No doubt podestà of the Genoese colony of Pera, the suburb of Constantinople.

[34] From this point forward we give only such passages as seem most likely to interest the reader. Among the omitted details there is a list of merchants who suffered damage because of the closing

Item, he requests and seeks that restitution and satisfaction be made to him in behalf of Ranieri Boccanegra of 500[35] gold hyperpers on account of this: As the said Ranieri was coming from Alexandria with a certain ship belonging to him he took aboard said ship some Greek merchants, who promised to give to him 500 hyperpers for the freight charges. And as he withheld[36] in the aforesaid ship as much of the goods of said Greeks as would pay the said freight charges, as is the custom of captains of ships—who hold the goods that they transport until they have been paid in full the freight charges of the ship—Kinnamos, at that time captain of Constantinople, sent for Ranieri to come to speak with him. And he detained Ranieri corporally in Constantinople, telling him that he could not let him go until he had returned the said goods which were being held for the said freight charges. And the said Ranieri was not able to obtain anything for the said freight charges. And he [the ambassador] seeks these 500 hyperpers in behalf of the said Ranieri. . . .

Item, he seeks and requests that restitution and satisfaction be made to him in behalf of Giovannino Zambone, merchant of Genoa, because as Giovannino himself in the year just past was coming from Rhodes in a galley of our Most Serene Lord Emperor, trusting in God and in the same Most Serene Lord Emperor, when he was in the port of Anaia in the said galley the said Giovannino was robbed and plundered of 802 gold hyperpers by the *sevastos*[37] Sarandinos and by Manuel Pattavaris, Greeks, against justice and against the honor of the imperial dignity. And [he also was robbed] of 206 hyperpers by the *sevastos* Kandamis of Rhodes, although an order to the duke of Anaia in this whole affair had directed that the latter should have the stolen goods returned to him [Giovannino]; and he [the duke] refused to do so. Therefore the said ambassador requests that His Imperial Majesty condescend to cause restitution to be made of the aforesaid. . . .

[Additions in a Detached Leaflet]

. . . Item, he seeks [damages] for Clerico dell'Orto, in consideration of a

---

of the Straits to ships coming from and going to the Black Sea. It includes ninety names of merchants (not counting partners of merchants grouped under one heading), mentions ninety-one ships, and lists damages for 5,392 hyperpers.

[35] Both *A* and *B* have 200, but this figure does not match the 500-hyperper claim made by the envoy.

[36] *Desinerent* (*detinerent* in *A*); but read *detineret*.

[37] Originally one of the highest titles in the Byzantine hierarchy (corresponding to Latin *augustus*), it was later debased and used for dignitaries of less exalted rank; see L. Bréhier, *Les Institutions de l'Empire Byzantin*, pp. 139ff.

robbery perpetrated in the fairs[38] of Mandara[?],[39] June, 1294, by Manuel Samandra by order of the *sevastos* Picherni. From him there were taken 29 pieces of [cloth of] Châlons and 7 pieces of Lombardy, worth 1,200 hyperpers.

Item, [damages] for Andreolo Roistropo in consideration of a robbery perpetrated in the said fairs by the said Manuel by order of the said *sevastos* Picherni to the amount of 150 hyperpers, 2,200 *aspers*, and 6 pieces of [cloth of] Châlons, and 3 pieces of Flanders, and 6 pieces of scarlet of quality,[40] and 4 bundles of white [cloth], and luggage, and gold. And these cloths, with all the aforesaid, were worth 850 hyperpers.

Item, from Giovanni Amorose, [Manuel] took in the said fair 9 pieces of Châlons, worth 410 hyperpers, which [the ambassador] likewise seeks.

Item, in behalf of Gabriele Maleggia, robbed in Smyrna of *scamandrum* by the grand domestic,[41] he seeks 900 hyperpers. . . .

Item, he seeks that restitution be made of 190 hyperpers to Pietro, butcher, son of Oliviero, in consideration of 150 animals taken from him and Giovanni, his brother; [also], for animals and oxen, of 112 hyperpers.

156

From the Latin[42]

[Constantinople and Venice, 1319–1320]

These are the articles of the petition of the ambassadors of the Emperor of Constantinople:

. . . Item, that restitution be made for the damages written below, caused by Venetians to subjects of the Emperor, viz.:

[38] *Paniçerio* (abl. *pannigerio* at another place), the Greek *panegyrion*, which usually applies to great fairs frequented by merchants from all parts of the world, such as those of Trebizond and Salonika. In this particular instance, however, the word seems to apply to one of those local markets, usually called *agora*, which are described by G. Ostrogorsky in *Cambridge Economic History*, I, 200.

[39] The question mark is Bertolotto's. Malgara, in the heart of the grain-producing area of Thrace? Mudania, on the Asiatic shore of the Sea of Marmora? Bertolotto also places a question mark after '*sevastos* Picherni,' but the reading is certainly correct. A few years later we hear of a Ioannes Picherni or Pinkernes, 'captain of an army of the Lord Emperor' near Arta; this time (around 1320) it is the Venetians who have to complain about him. See G. M. Thomas, ed., *Diplomatarium Veneto-Levantinum*, I, 136, 159–60. Arta also had a local market, where a Venetian citizen was robbed of his goods, according to the document mentioned above.

[40] *De quantitate;* but read *de qualitate.*

[41] The general commander of the army; see Bréhier, *Institutions*, pp. 396–97.

[42] Thomas, *Diplomatarium Veneto-Levantinum*, I, 125–27. The petition includes a number of demands of a political character, which we have omitted, and the list of complaints (including two complaints of the ambassadors themselves, Gregorios Klidas and the *sevastos* Andronikos Hierachitas), which we have translated. The answer of the Venetian government (*ibid.*, I, 132) was polite but fairly evasive. Note that the offenders included not only Venetian natives but also Greek natives of the Venetian possessions in the Aegean.

In the month of May, tenth indiction, a certain man named Kanachis and his partner Manoys, of Crete, behaving as pirates, took from a village named Nay, which is near Monemvasia, animals and cloth to the sum of 454 hyperpers; and they also captured two men.

Item, in the month of March, eleventh indiction, a certain man named Aretas, Venetian [citizen] of Crete, behaving as a pirate, took from a village or island named Stadion animals, copper, cheese, cloth, and horses belonging to noblemen of Monemvasia, to the sum of 500 hyperpers; and [he also captured] six men.

Item, in the month of May of the aforesaid eleventh indiction, the said Aretas stole from an island named Esopo four children as well as animals, cloth, and cheese, to the sum of 500 hyperpers.

Item, in the month of December of the aforesaid eleventh indiction, Giovanni Fratello, Venetian, while coming to Crete with a galley, met a vessel of Monemvasia which belonged to a man named Maurosumi, and captured it. And in it were cloth, oil, money, and weapons, of a value of 2,200 hyperpers, as well as thirty men, who were sold for 500 hyperpers.[43]

Item, in the month of August, thirteenth indiction, a certain vessel of Lord Niccolò Sanudo[44] met another Monemvasian vessel near Zea and took from it oil, wine, weapons, honey, and leather ware, and many other goods, of a value of 800 hyperpers. And afterward the said vessel, proceeding on its voyage thus unarmed, came across another vessel of pirates, and because of the lack of arms was captured by that other vessel. And all men were lost, which amounts to a great loss.

Item, in the month of December, twelfth indiction, while a certain man named Sophonias of Athens[?],[45] a subject of the Lord Emperor, was coming from Alexandria to Crete, Nicola Carandove, Venetian, attacked him, and took as much of his goods as was worth 150 hyperpers. And Sophonias himself complained in Crete, and this availed him nothing.

Item, in the month of December of the aforesaid indiction, Nascimbene and Marino Sfatto, Venetians of Crete, behaving as pirates, plundered from an island named Tadius six boats with merchandise and forty men. The value

[43] Note the difference between the low price charged for large lots of captives sold wholesale by pirates and the cost of a single slave regularly purchased, Christophoros 'the Turk' (see note 52 below).

[44] Probably a member of that branch of the Venetian family which ruled over Naxos and other islands as vassals of Venice, with the title of dukes of the Archipelago.

[45] *Atheneas*, which may well be the classic word *Athenaios*, 'Athenian,' pronounced the Byzantine way, but which might also be a family name. Athens at this period was under Latin domination, but some of its inhabitants might still be Byzantine citizens.

of all the goods lost is 3,000 hyperpers, and the aforesaid men thus captured were ransomed for 500 hyperpers.

Item, in the ninth indiction, a certain man named [Ioannes] Kalamas, a subject of the Emperor, was in Venice as a merchant[?];[46] and a certain man, named Dimitri Nancizo, a Venetian [citizen], took from the same Ioannes groats and florins to the value of 1,200 hyperpers, and ran away.

Item, in the month of March, eleventh indiction, Nascimbene, behaving as a pirate, took thirty-six men from a place called Ceconi and sold them in Rhodes.

Item, in the month of December, fourth indiction, when Leo Mualdita of Monemvasia came to Corone, the said [inhabitants] of Corone retained fish and camari[47] [belonging to him], of a value of 300 hyperpers.

Item, in the month of January, fourteenth indiction, Dimitri Kalamathiocho and Nikolaos Hagiapostolidi of Modone retained 300 hyperpers belonging to Ioannes Limbeniti.

Item, in the said indiction, a man named Kalarchos, of Corone, subject of Foscolo,[48] holds hyperpers belonging to the duke of Maina.

Item, Francesco Foscari, Niccolò di Marco, and Giacomo Longo, of Negroponte, Venetians, hold 600 hyperpers belonging to Ioannes Mariati.

Item, in the month of August, fifteenth indiction, as I was going to pay homage to my lord, the Sacred Emperor, I came across Righetto Bruno, Pietro Fauro, and Giovanni d'Armiraia, who captured me and took from me everything I had, and then sold my own person. And because of this, my lord, the Emperor, lost a good castle (as [the ambassadors] set forth orally).[49]

Item, in the month of July, fourteenth indiction, two galleys of Venetians, coming from Constantinople, went to Monemvasia. And there many Monemvasians embarked on the said galleys. And the said galleys went to Cape Malea, where they came upon galleys of the Hospitalers. And they handed over all the Monemvasian men to the said galleys of the Hospitalers, who sold the said men; and the Venetians retained the goods. The latter

[46] The text is probably corrupt here. We have tentatively corrected *Venetus mercator* into *Venetiis mercator*, and we have supplied, between brackets, a Ioannes before Kalamas. But the document says *ipso Ioanne* in the following sentence, without there being any previous mention of that name.

[47] *Sic.* Perhaps one should read *caviari*, 'caviar,' which at that time already was imported from the Black Sea.

[48] The Foscolo, like the Sanudo, were Venetian vassals ruling over Greek territory.

[49] Here one of the Byzantine envoys—probably Gregorios Klidas, for the personal losses of the other envoy are taken up in another passage—has spoken in his own behalf. The words which we italicize are obviously not a part of the petition but a comment of the Venetian officials who received it.

amount to 400 hyperpers, and the said galleys of the Hospitalers sold the said men for 500 hyperpers.

Item, men of Corone and Modone—Venetian subjects—plundered the regions of Maina and took animals and other goods of a value of 4 hyperpers.

Item, they took and carried away four hundred men, whom they themselves sold in Crete, Rhodes, and Cyprus.

Item, said [men] of Corone and Modone forcibly hold 4,000 hyperpers belonging to the men of Misitra, merchants and others.

Item, men of Crete forcibly hold 700 hyperpers belonging to George Sukros of Monemvasia; in the twelfth indiction.

Item, in the thirteenth indiction, said [men] of Crete forcibly hold 1,000 hyperpers belonging to Kyrios Michael.

Item, in the thirteenth indiction, said [men] of Crete hold a boat and cloth and merchandise belonging to Leon Grammatikos, of a value of 300 hyperpers.

Item, Nikolaos Mirstitos, of Corone, forcibly holds 200 hyperpers belonging to Ioannes Diominitis.

Item, in the fourteenth indiction, Venetians from Negroponte, going to Salonika, chartered their own boats to Greek subjects, merchants, to convey them and their merchandise to Negroponte. And they retained goods of a value of 8,000 hyperpers and they sold the men and went to Cyprus.

Item, Venetian subjects hold about 10,000 hyperpers belonging to merchants of Salonika and Constantinople and other places. And in regard to this these ambassadors are seeking an accounting.

Item, in the month of May of the second indiction, the Murtati[50] of Negroponte went to an island named Kuluri and took from there five hundred persons, and they sold them to a certain Marco Lambardo and to other merchants. And that island is wont to pay its *akrostikon* to the Greeks of Monemvasia, [subjects] of the Lord Emperor.[51]

Item, the men of Crete hold a Greek of Turkish [extraction] belonging to me, the *sevastos*.[52] His name is Christophoros, and he cost 70 hyperpers.

---

[50] *Sic.* Who the Murtati were we do not know.

[51] This remark is aimed at stressing that Kuluri (Salamis in antiquity) pays taxes to Byzantine Monemvasia and hence must be regarded as Byzantine territory. Often claims and counterclaims are rejected because the sovereignty of either the emperor or of Venice is challenged.

[52] The *sevastos* obviously is Andronikos Hyerachitas, one of the Byzantine ambassadors. Christophoros is his slave—probably a Muslim by birth, but a Christian at the time of the petition, as is evident from his name.

78

8 INTERNATIONAL DISPUTES OVER TRADE

Seeking Justice in Cyprus

157

From the Italian (Venetian dialect)[53]

[Venice, 1306?]

This is the damage which I, Marco Michel the Tartar, have suffered in Cyprus, and in what manner:

In the month of September, the second day from the beginning, in the year of the Lord 1298, I, Marco Michel, was in Famagusta and was waiting for a *gamella*[54] in which I, Marco, had loaded eighteen sacks of cotton of Aleppo and six *sporte* of *beledi* ginger in Ayas. And while I was waiting for this said *gamella*, Niccolò Zugno informed me that an armed Genoese galley, which had been armed by Franceschino Grimaldi[55]—he is a bad man and would seize the goods of friend and enemy [alike]—and which had been in Limassol, was about to sail toward Famagusta. At once I went to the castellan of Famagusta, whose name is Sieur Guillaume de Mirabel,[56] and asked him [to give me] his word that he would arm a *panfilo*[57] and send it to meet the said *gamella* in order to inform its [crew] about this said galley: in whatever part of the island of Cyprus this *gamella* arrives, it should at once unload ashore the said eighteen sacks of cotton and six *sporte* of ginger.

The said castellan gave me his word that he would arm the *panfilo*. He also gave me a letter which he was sending to the bailiff of the Cape Saint Andrew, whose name is Sieur Gervais, recommending to him these goods of mine, should it happen that this *gamella* of mine unloaded ashore the said goods of mine. He dispatched the said *panfilo* to the captain of the said *gamella*, whose name is Arrigo Bracci, of Pisa, and dispatched a letter to him, which contains what is said above.

The said armed *panfilo* sails and comes across the said *gamella* at sea close

---

[53] Thomas, *Diplomatarium Veneto-Levantinum*, I, 39–42. Excerpts of this document have also been published by L. de Mas Latrie, 'Nouvelles Preuves de l'histoire de Chypre,' *Bibliothèque de l'Ecole des Chartes*, XXXIV (1873), 50–54, and earlier by S. Romanin, *Storia documentata di Venezia*, III, 400. We follow the Thomas edition, but we occasionally make use of remarks made by the other editors. The petition, of which we have endeavored so far as possible to preserve the ungrammatical, direct flavor, also includes a few sentences concerning damages received in Cilician Armenia. The petitioner in spite of his nickname (the Tartar) almost certainly was a member of the prominent Venetian family of the Michel or Michiel. His partner, Paolo Morosini, also belonged to the Venetian merchant nobility.

[54] A rounded sailing ship, similar to the caravel (Thomas).

[55] The Grimaldi and the Fieschi were the two leading Guelf families in Genoa.

[56] The Mirabel were French refugees from the Holy Land.

[57] A ship propelled by oars, similar to the galley but much smaller; cf. C. Manfroni, *Storia della marina italiana dalle invasioni barbariche al trattato di Ninfeo*, p. 457.

to [the Cape] of Pistachios, and gives him my letter. The said captain at once did what he was told in the letter I was sending him by the said *panfilo*, and sailed to the Cape of Pistachios. And he unloads my cotton ashore, eighteen sacks, and of the six *sporte* of ginger he puts ashore five; the sixth *sporta* he puts in the armed *panfilo* and sends it to me at Famagusta. And he informs me that he had unloaded ashore all my goods except the said *sporta;* and that I should come to the cape called The Pistachios to have my goods transported to Famagusta; and that the galley of Franceschino Grimaldi had come to The Pistachios. And [Grimaldi] had seen that this *gamella* had been unloaded in the land of the king; he said nothing to them, and left and went to sea.

The other day—the following—I was going to have these goods of mine transported to Famagusta. On the way I met Messer Nicola Anifini, a Venetian, who told me that the said galley of Franceschino Grimaldi had gone to sea, and had taken many *gamelle* of all kinds of people, friends and enemies alike, and then had turned toward the Cape of the Pistachios, just where my goods were on land, and he went ashore, armed, to seize my goods by force. The bailiff of Cape Saint Andrew was hard by my goods and forbade the said Franceschino, in behalf of the lord king, to rob us on the king's land. But he pays no attention to it and seizes my eighteen sacks of cotton and five *sporte* of ginger, which were on land. And he put them by force in his galley.

I was much grieved by this news, and I went to the king in Nicosia, and I made a petition to him—that I had been robbed in his land, and in what manner. The lord king had Sieur Thomas de la Blanche Guarde answer me thus: that the king did not interfere between Genoese and Venetians. I answered him: 'Monsieur, what does the lord king say of the fact that I am robbed on his land?' He says: 'When it shall be the proper time and place, the lord king shall call the attention of the Genoese to it.' I could obtain no other redress for it.

Coming back from Nicosia with the answer which the lord king had sent me, just as is told here in this paper, on the road back to Famagusta I met a courier who was coming to me in behalf of Pantaleone Scortegacan. And he gave me a letter which related that Monsieur Lancelot, admiral of the lord king of Cyprus, had come from Constantinople with galleys of the king, and that near Famagusta he had come acrosss Franceschino Grimaldi, who had engaged in robbery. And he captured people who were with him, and pursued them.[58] And [the admiral] had captured[59] him. And our goods,

---

[58] The Venetian text of the document does not make clear who captures and pursues whom. Probably the admiral captured stray sailors of Grimaldi's galley and pursued the others until he could capture the captain himself.

[59] In this particular case Mas Latrie's reading, *piiado*, seems better than Thomas's *priuado*.

which the said Franceschino Grimaldi had captured on the king's land, were in Famagusta in custody of the government. And [Scortegacan said] that I should return to the lord king to have released to me my cotton and ginger, which had been recovered by the admiral of the king, for he would at once release it to me.

At once I returned to Nicosia and made a petition to the lord king that my goods mentioned above, which had been robbed in his land, had been recovered by his admiral and were held in the storehouse at Famagusta for the lord king; that the lord king should send instructions to Famagusta to his officers to release them to me. To this petition and to many other petitions I could get no answer from the lord king of Cyprus.

While awaiting in Nicosia an answer from the lord king I fell sick with a very serious disease. After I recuperated, I was told that by order of the lord king Franceschino Grimaldi had been brought as a corsair under heavy guard to Nicosia, and there he had been held many days. And eventually he was freed, and he was given back all my cotton and ginger.

I again made petition to the lord king, in the manner stated above, that he should have my said merchandise, which was in Famagusta, released to me, pretending not to know that he had returned to Franceschino Grimaldi my own goods. He gave me no answer at all, but when Christmastide was approaching, Sieur Thomas de la Blanche Guarde told me that the king would go to Famagusta on the feast of Saint Nicholas, and that I ought to be there, for he would do justice and right to me.

I was in Famagusta on the said feast. Many a time I got close to the king, but I never could get an answer from him when I said that the king should answer whether he was willing to give me my own wares, which had been recovered by his admiral from Franceschino Grimaldi, Genoese, [merchandise] which the said Franceschino had stolen in the king's land. Nor was it of any avail, for he never was willing to return an answer to me. This affair went on well six months.

This is the value of my eighteen sacks of cotton—what they cost me at first purchase: I bought in Ayas the eighteen sacks of cotton of Aleppo at the rate of 13 new dirhams the *rotolo* of Ayas. They weigh 486 *rotoli*. The sum, 6,324½ dirhams.[60] Also, I bought in Ayas *beledi* ginger at the rate of 26 dirhams the *rotolo*. They were six *sporte;* the five *sporte* which were robbed from me weigh net 180 *rotoli* and 9 ounces of Ayas. The sum, 4,700 new

---

[60] Actually thirteen times 486 makes 6,318. It is worth noting that Mas Latrie reads 6,323. At any rate, there seems to be a mistake in the accounting. The new dirhams were Armenian silver coins of a new, debased emission.

dirhams. The sum of all this cotton and ginger, 11,024½ dirhams at first purchase, exported from Ayas. The sum, £ 1,102½ Saracen, [reckoning] 10 dirhams per Saracen pound.[61] All these pounds belong to Ser Paolo Morosini and to me, Marco Michel, jointly in partnership.[62]

At the time when [the Venetian envoy] Messer Ugolino Giustinian went to the lord king of Cyprus, the said Messer Ugolino had this matter among his instruction. And when he carried out his mission before the lord king of Cyprus and related this matter of ours to the lord king, he was answered by the said [king] that this matter of ours was news to him. However, he instructed Monsieur Baudouin de Picquigny to make an inquiry into this matter [to find out] how this matter had [really] been. Meanwhile Messer Ugolino left before Sieur Baudouin de Picquigny had yet made inquiry into the matter.

Ser Paolo Morosini, who is interested in this matter, was in Cyprus. He takes steps to have Monsieur Baudouin make inquiry into this matter. Monsieur Baudouin makes the inquiry and tells Ser Paolo Morosini that if the king asked him about this matter, he would tell him what he ought to, but that the king had not asked said Monsieur Baudouin about this matter through the lords of the royal court. He advised Ser Paolo Morosini to make a petition about this matter to the king and to give it to a Friar Minor, who is the confessor of the king and who would give it to him. The said friar gave him the petition: the lord king answered Ser Paolo that he was not willing to make answer to him, but that he would make answer to whom he ought to.

Moreover, it will be found written in the customs office of Famagusta that these eighteen sacks of cotton of mine, and five *sporte* of ginger, were put in the storehouse of the government. And these wares of mine were returned to Franceschino Grimaldi, corsair. And [you can check] if this is the truth: if these goods of mine had been returned to me, the customs would have made me pay the duty.[63]

[61] The multiplications and additions are correct. The Saracen pound was a money of account, pegged to silver coins such as the Armenian dirham.

[62] *Insembre di compagnia*; but it seems unlikely that the two merchants had formed a *compagnia* in the technical sense of the word.

[63] On June 11, 1302, the senate of Venice showed mild interest in Michel's troubles by the following deliberation: 'Decided: that instruction be given to the ambassador [to Cyprus] to demand satisfaction about the affair of Michel the Tartar, and to do in this matter as well as he can, but not to keep from doing the affairs of the Commune because of this' (Thomas, p. 42).

England: Fruitless Good Will, Efficient Bad Will

158

From the Latin[64]

Windsor, May 9, 1317

Edward [II] by the grace of God king of England, lord of Ireland, duke of Aquitaine, to the mayor and the bailiffs of the town of Great Yarmouth, greetings.

From the serious complaint of our beloved Antonio di Negro, merchant of Genoa, we understand that whereas he had recently freighted at Southampton a certain ship called 'La Mariotte of Amela,' the master of which was Henry of Amela, and had caused it to be loaded with 200 quarters gross of salt, of the price of 200 marks, to be transported from there to Newcastle upon Tyne to promote his business,[65] certain evildoers carried off that ship with the aforesaid goods whither they wished, and still are thus holding that ship and the aforesaid goods. As we wish to do what is just in regard to the above-said, we command you diligently to inquire through the oath of honest and lawful men of the aforesaid town, through whom the truth of the matter may be clearly known in regard to the names of the aforesaid evildoers who committed the aforesaid offense and to the place whither they carried off that ship with the aforesaid goods. And [we command] you to send us without delay that inquisition distinctly and openly taken under your seal and the seals of those through whom it will have been taken, and [to enclose] this writ.

Witness myself, at Windsor, May 9, the tenth year of our reign.

Great Yarmouth, May 17, 1317

Inquisition made before the bailiff of the town of Great Yarmouth on Tuesday after the feast of the Ascension of the Lord, in the tenth year of the reign of King Edward, son of King Edward. . . .

We . . . had a diligent inquisition taken concerning the aforesaid matters. [The jurors] state under oath that the said ship with the said goods . . . was captured at sea near Crowe and carried away by some evildoers from Scotland, whose names they do not know; nor do they know whither said ship was carried off.

In witness thereof . . . said jurors affixed their seals.

[64] Unprinted. Public Record Office, London. *Chancery Inquisitions Miscellaneous*, C 145/77, 23. We have translated the royal writ in full, but we have omitted the names of officials and jurors as well as some formulae from the inquisition.

[65] *Ad commodum suum faciendum:* as a private business operation and not in the service of the king.

159

From the Latin[66]

Genoa, August 24, 1232; La Rochelle [1232?]

In the presence of the witnesses written below, Giovanni di Pezagno, judge, in his own behalf and in that of his sons, namely, Gherardo and Nicoloso, presented to Lord Giovanni, judge and assessor of Lord Pagano of Pietrasanta, podestà[67] of Genoa, a letter sealed with two waxen seals, namely, one on one side and the other on the other side. On one of these seals was the effigy of a horse and the effigy of a man sitting on the said horse and holding in his right hand a small twig behind palm branches and in the other hand— the left—the bridle of the said horse. And on this seal were these words: 'Seal of the mayor of La Rochelle.' And on the other seal was the effigy of a certain ship resembling a cog or *noca*[68] with a mast and an unfurled square sail. On this seal were these words, namely: 'Seal of the Commune of La Rochelle.' The content of this letter was as follows:

'To the venerable and discreet men, the noble podestà of Genoa and the whole Commune of that town, the mayor and the burghers of La Rochelle send greetings and full love. We inform Your Discretion by the present letter that whereas Gherardo di Pezagno, your fellow citizen, had come to La Rochelle and had passed his merchandise and goods through customs there, well and legitimately just as he ought to, the same Gherardo loaded nine bales of cloth on a certain ship from Spain. And after that ship left the port of La Rochelle to sail to Spain, on account of a contrary wind and of a chance turn of weather it entered the territory of the king of England, namely, the island of Oléron. Then the seneschal of the said king of England and the men of the said seneschal took by force and violence that ship and the cloth of the said Gherardo, your fellow citizen. And in the excess of their malignity they unjustly forced the said Gherardo to redeem his cloth for £ 186 s.13 d.8 [Tournois?], and they likewise seized with the cloth his share of that ship, which he had bought for £ 20. And the said redemption [price], which they had from Gherardo . . .[69] [Gherardo] sold the remainder of the cloth and

---

[66] Unprinted. Archivio di Stato, Genoa. *Cartulario di Maestro Salomone*, II, fol. 6v. On the family of Gherardo di Pezagno see the introduction to this chapter, n. 3.

[67] The chief executive of the Genoese Commune.

[68] *Ad similitudinem coche alias noche*. The *cocca*, *coque*, or cog was a large rounded sailing ship widely used in the northern seas. What a *noca* was we do not know. Perhaps the notary transcribed wrongly a foreign word in the letter of the community of La Rochelle. The entire record shows evident traces of hurry, and many other words are obviously misspelled.

[69] There is no gap in the manuscript, but some words must have been inadvertently omitted by the notary who wrote this minute. Probably the name *Guirardus* occurred twice in a short space and all words between the two citations were dropped.

entirely lost his passage[70] to Spain. We, then, give you testimony of this through our neighbors and jurors who saw and heard and were present there in the said ship. He, however—[that is], the seneschal of the king of England and his accomplices—asserted that the said ship had been wrecked there and because of this, according to what they said, they seized the ship and the goods that were inside it. And since there was no shipwreck there, as we testify to you, and the said ship had arrived there safe and intact, they made this up most mendaciously as a lie of their own because they wanted to get the ship with all the wares and goods contained in it. But you, as men of legal foresight and discretion, see to it that you exert your authority [to take] in regard to the aforesaid whatever action should be taken.'

Witnesses: Guglielmo de Langasco, notary, and Buonalbergo, *magister Antelami*,[71] and Castellano de Neo, on August 24 between vespers and compline. Done in Genoa, in the house of the Fornarii, where the said Lord Pagano, podestà of Genoa, lives, in 1232, fourth indiction.

Northern Italy Protects Foreign Merchants

160

From the Latin[72]

Como, March 10, 1222

In the name of God Almighty, in the year of the Incarnation of the Lord 1222, Thursday, the tenth day of March, tenth indiction. Adelard, son of the late Adelard de Prudhomme of Lille, and Robert, son of the late Bernard de Neufmarchés, both of Lille, in the bishopric of Tournai, Hainaut, made a final release and pact not to make further demands upon Lord Nicola d'Andito, son of the late Lord Giulio d'Andito, podestà of Como, receiving [the stipulation] on the part and to the advantage of the Commune of Como and of all men of the entire jurisdiction of Como, to wit: In regard to those cloths, pieces of cloth, boots, and all other goods taken away—cloths and boots which were taken away, stolen, or robbed from them or their carriers or transport agents on the public highway near Monte Sordo in the bishopric of Como—and particularly in regard to $13\frac{1}{2}$ pieces of cloth, to wit, 6 pieces of

---

[70] *Viaticum*, which may mean 'voyage,' 'provisions for the voyage,' or 'traveling expenses.'

[71] This name, derived from the Intelvi Valley in upper Lombardy, was given in Genoa to the gild of sculptors-architects; see G. P. Bognetti, 'I magistri Antelami e la val d'Intelvi,' *Periodico Storico Comense*, new ser., II (1938), 17–54.

[72] A. Schulte, *Geschichte des mittelalterlichen Handels und Verkehrs zwischen Westdeutschland und Italien mit Ausschluss von Venedig*, II, 105–6. The gaps are in Schulte's text. The last line, which we have omitted, refers to the witnesses and the notary who wrote the document.

camelin of Lille and 7 pieces of blue of Ypres, and in regard to 2 pieces of ray of Beauvais and 12 pairs of boots of say of Bruges, and in regard to the whole estimated value of all these goods. . . . Moreover, the already mentioned Adelard and Robert had made transfer, sale, and cession to the aforesaid Lord Nicola, podestà of Como, receiving in the name and on the part of the Commune of Como, of every legal right, ground, and action . . . which they themselves . . . had or might have . . . against the robbers and plunderers of the aforesaid goods. . . .

And for all the aforesaid [goods] the aforesaid Adelard and Robert were satisfied and acknowledged that they have received and have obtained from the lords Pietro Albrici and Ottobono de Turline and Pocobello de Adilla, administrators and storekeepers[73] of the Commune of Como . . . £ 97, less 12 imperials of good imperial deniers.

Done in the new palace of [the Commune of] Como.

Genoa Applies Sanctions Against Persia

161

From the Latin[74]

[Genoa, 1343 or early 1344]

The Office of the Eight Wisemen appointed in regard to the affairs of navigation and of the Black Sea, among whom there was a sufficient and legal number of these officials, and the same officials in agreement;

Having seen the demands of Unfredo Gentile, who demanded that Tommasino, his son, be forgiven notwithstanding the fact that he had gone to Tabriz or had crossed through said territory of Tabriz; for that he went by necessity and without merchandise, having remained in Ormuz overtaken by serious and real illness, abandoned by his partners, who had resumed their journey toward Cathay; and that was why he had to go to Tabriz on the return trip, being eager to return to his home since he had been unable to set out for the territory of Cathay, where he had at first planned to go;

[73] *Ministris et canevariis.* The second term refers to treasurers in general, but more especially to those in charge of government storehouses of cereals and other goods.

[74] Unprinted. Archivio di Stato, Genoa. *Cartulario dei notai Domenico Durante e Oberto Osbergerio,* I, fol. 223v. Excerpts from this document, and comments upon its background, are found in R. S. Lopez, 'European Merchants in the Medieval Indies: the Evidence of Commercial Documents,' *Journal of Economic History,* III (1943), 164–84. Here we have omitted some of the lengthy legal formulae at the end of the document. The Eight Wiseman, who were in charge of maritime and colonial affairs, had proclaimed an embargo against al-Ashraf, the usurper who was in control of Tabriz and a large part of Persia, and who had committed many offenses against foreign merchants as well as against his own subjects.

Also, a diligent inquiry having been made by the ducal commission about this with the purpose that truth may be found and prevail;

Everything possible in this connection having been scrutinized, and after it was found through open letters of reliable men shown and presented to said office, as well as through public report of some citizens expert in this matter, that said Tommasino had not gone or crossed to said parts of Tabriz of his own will but by necessity, as is permitted;

Wishing in this matter to provide a salutary and appropriate remedy so that confidence in truth may not perish;

On the ground of innocence, by the power and authority given to said office and by all law, manner, and form by which it was and is better empowered, considered, decided, and ordered as well as declared its will [as follows]:

Said Tommasino did not incur any penalty in the aforesaid circumstances, notwithstanding the decrees, statutes, or prohibitions of these matters and about these matters which go counter to this, enacted by said office by full power from the doge. One of these, issued in 1340 on June 7, begins: 'The Office of the Eight Wisemen appointed in regard to the affairs of navigation and of the Black Sea, etc.,' and the other, issued in 1342, on April 12, begins: 'The Office of the Eight Wisemen appointed in regard to the affairs of navigation and of the Black Sea, by order and consent of its master the mighty lord Simone Boccanegra, doge of the Genoese, etc.'. . .

CHAPTER XX

LEGAL RESTRICTIONS OF TRADE

DECREES, STATUTES, law books, and international treaties in every country and self-governing town placed a great variety of restrictions on the activity of foreign and native merchants. Historians of the nineteenth century, trained in the golden age of economic liberalism, denounced these restrictions as intolerable hindrances to commerce. In our own times, however, increasing governmental interference in trade has led many historians to reconsider their judgment of medieval economic policies. Whether we approve of controlled economy or not, we can no longer regard it as a peculiar medieval absurdity. Moreover, interference during the Middle Ages was not always greater than in our time, nor was it always effective. The majority of the more prosperous cities were more liberal than commercially retarded towns and states. Individual merchants circumvented the law or obtained exemption from it.

The reader may form his own judgment about the workings of the system through our sampling of some of the most typical restrictions. The French government rejects, with some qualifications, a petition of 'transmontane' (that is, mostly Italian) merchants in Paris to be exempted from local taxation or to be granted the same privileges as citizens (Document 162). The municipal authorities of Barcelona strongly support, against the opposition of Valencia and Ibiza, a royal statute which, like the Navigation Acts so often issued in England, endeavors to reserve trade of their own country to their own bottoms (Document 163). The Venetian authorities grant a resident alien special exemption from the prohibition to engage in maritime trade—an unusual concession in a city so reluctant to grant citizenship even after long residence (Document 164). The queen of Naples and countess of Provence agrees to the request of the people of Tarascon that local wine be protected against competition of imported wines (Document 165). A Pisan exporter buys a license to export from the kingdom of Sicily a cargo of grain; he had to do this because cereals as an essential foodstuff could not be exported until local and governmental needs had been fully satisfied (Document 166). The government and the people of Venice endorse a command of the Byzantine emperors, then overlords of the city, to stop sending war material to the Saracens (Document 167). In Saracen territory certain foreign merchants protest that they are not citizens of an enemy state and therefore their persons and goods should be released (Document 168). Finally, two sentences (Documents 169 and 170) of the courts of Genoa and Narbonne show the difficulties of enforcement of reciprocal trade agreements. Two cities may grant each other exemption from certain duties, but each of them must see to it that no goods belonging to third parties are smuggled under the protection of a friendly flag. When in doubt, the authorities of each city tend to disregard the convention.[1]

162

From the Latin[2]

[Paris, November 11, 1282]

Whereas the transmontane merchants staying in Paris had complained to us [Phillip III] that our citizens of Paris, contrary to justice, had tallaged them and intended to force them to contribute toward the gift (*dono*) recently made to us by the city of Paris even though they do not enjoy the franchises and liberties of the city of Paris like the other citizens of the city of Paris, wherefore they petitioned that [either] they be exempted from the said tallage (*tallia*) or, if they are to be tallaged, they enjoy the aforesaid liberties like the other citizens of Paris; and [whereas] the provost of the Parisian merchants and our citizens of Paris asserted the contrary;

After the proposals of both sides were heard, it was pronounced [by the Parlement of Paris] that the said transmontane merchants shall contribute to the aforesaid tallage according to their share and shall be tallaged by reason of the merchandise belonging to them.

And since they do not live continuously in Paris with the intention of remaining there permanently, but leave whenever they want and belong to many partnerships (*societates*) abroad, which would gain profit from [the liberties], they shall not enjoy the aforesaid liberties—with this reservation, that if any transmontane merchant should make his residence in Paris with his wife, children, and family, and there should be no expectation that he is to leave, and he should not belong to a partnership abroad nor pay tallage or any tax or municipal charge beyond the mountains, he shall enjoy the aforesaid liberties.

163

From the Catalan[3]

Barcelona, June 7, 1454

To His Sacred Majesty [Alfonso V], king of Aragon, Sicily, etc.

Most High and Most Excellent Prince and Mighty Lord:

---

[1] The bibliography is too abundant to cite. A masterly, if sketchy, survey of governmental interference in trade is found in E. F. Heckscher, *Mercantilism*, especially Vol. II, Parts 2 and 3.

[2] G. Fagniez, *Documents relatifs à l'histoire de l'industrie et du commerce en France*, I, 297–98.

[3] A. de Capmany y de Montpalau, *Memorias históricas sobre la marina, comercio y artes de la antigua ciudad de Barcelona*, II, 279–80. On the general background see G. de Reparaz, *Catalunya a les mars*.

By other letters of ours to Your Great Lordship we have written and supplicated that you be willing through your mercy not to revoke or in any way depart from the statute made by Your Majesty, [to wit], that in the kingdoms and territories of Your Great Lordship no ships be allowed to take on cargo except those belonging to vassals of Your Great Excellency; for many ships have been built and are still being built in consideration of said statute, in the present city of yours and along the coast. And shortly in these parts two new nefs (*naus*) will be built in the said city, one of them of the tonnage of 1,400 *botes*, under the captainship of En Ramon Dezplá, and the other of 1,000 *botes*, of which En Melchior Mates is captain (*patró*). And within four or five days another of the capacity of 1,000 *botes* will be launched on the beach of the said city, and one has been launched in San Felíu de Guixols which has just been masted, and three are being built elsewhere, among which there is one of the tonnage of 1,500 *botes*. And in this city others are being built, among which there is one of 1,400 *botes*, and so likewise many other kinds of ships are being built. And here many [others] would be prepared for building some, but they doubt whether the said statute will be enforced in its entirety and context. For it is understood that the Valencians and the men of Ibiza have made representations to Your Great Excellency to have the said statute revoked, if they can, offering some arguments in support of them. And [they claim] that since your vassals do not have as many nefs as business requires, said statute would result in great damage; and they affirm that the goods would not be exported from the kingdom and that freight charges would be dearer.

Now it is certain, Most Victorious Lord, that nothing begun anew in this world can on the first day be so arranged and ordered as it is needed. And it is manifest, Most Excellent Lord, that if the said edict is maintained and enforced, your vassals will have so many ships in a short time that it will be a great event [in the history] of the sea, and they will be in such a great number that the business of your kingdoms and territories will not require so many; for as soon as people see that they have prospects to draw profit from it, everyone will want to build some. And Your Great Lordship should think what a great service it will be to Your Royal Majesty to have the seas full of the shipping of subjects of Your Great Excellency, and what a great advantage will result from it to your kingdoms and territories. We truly believe that this is a benefit as conspicuous as any other could be. And as for the freight charges, Most Victorious Lord, which are causing complaints, our opponents have no reason to complain about them; for if the merchants cannot come to agreement about them with the captains in accordance with said statute, they must abide by the decision of the Consuls of the Sea who will be in that place where the goods and merchandise will be loaded or unloaded; and if no Consuls are there, two merchants, one chosen by each party, will arbitrate. And by the said statute it is so provided for the said freight charges that no one ought to be dissatisfied with them. And this benefit will come not only to this city of yours, but also to all your kingdoms and territories. And just now the Valencians themselves have bought a nef of 700 *botes*. If they begin to have a taste of it, they will understand that it is better for them to have the benefit which up to now foreign shipping has had from them.

Therefore, Most High and Most Excellent Prince and Victorious Lord, we supplicate Your Lordship, as humbly as we can, that it may please your mercy to let it be understood that Your Majesty is showing ardor and interest in having said statute enforced, rather than that Your Majesty is wishing to revoke and to annul it—inasmuch as from the latter [course] great ruin would come to those who have built the ships in view of that [statute], and the service which is hoped to result for Your Great Lordship would be lost, and [so would] the welfare of the subjects and vassals of your kingdoms and territories. And the points we have mentioned, Most Excellent Lord, we shall regard as the singular grace and mercy of Your Great Lordship, whom the Divine Majesty may preserve in the government of his kingdoms and territories for the glorious exaltation of your royal crown.

Written in your city of Barcelona on June 7 in the year of the Nativity of our Lord 1454.

Your humble servants and vassals who, kissing your hands as humbly as possible, recommend themselves to your grace and mercy.

The councilors of the city of Barcelona.

164

From the Latin[4]

[Venice, July 25, 1334]

Adopted [by the Senate]. That grace be extended to Maestro Mondino, goldsmith of Cremona, resident of the section of San Gervasio [in Venice] —who, as he related, has lived in Venice with wife and family for twenty-five years and longer, although not enjoying the privilege of citizenship— that since he has sold for 800 gold ducats a clock manufactured with crafts-manship to the lord king of Cyprus, and on this work he has spent a large part of his days, and he is to receive payment only in the territory of Cyprus,

[4] L. de Mas Latrie, 'Nouvelles Preuves de l'histoire de Chypre,' *Bibliothèque de l'Ecole des Chartes*, XXXIV (1873), 64–65. Compare also Document 30.

in consideration of his praiseworthy reputation and the devotion and loyalty that he always had for the honor of our government, he be allowed to send or to bring [himself] the said ducats to Venice invested. And if advice, etc.

[The vote:] No, 18. Uncertain, 3. All the others for the resolution.

165
From the Latin[5]

A versa, December 14, 1377

We, Joan, by the grace of God queen of Jerusalem and Sicily, of the duchy of Apulia and of the principality of Capua, countess of Provence, Forcalquier, and Piedmont, to the seneschals of our counties of Provence and Forcalquier or to their lieutenants and to the *viguiers* of the castle or locality of Tarascon in the aforesaid counties, [and to all] our faithful present and future, grace and good will. It is our aim and intention unremittingly to protect in a maternal manner the interests of our subjects and as best we can to reduce their expenses through our sovereign love. Now a respectful petition on behalf of the community of the citizens (*universitas hominum*) of the said locality of Tarascon, our faithful, recently made to Our Sublimity by their special ambassadors and messengers sent to our court, stated that although the said locality of Tarascon is so well supplied with vineyards that the wine coming from them is quite sufficient for the use of the petitioners, yet it often happens that some inhabitants of the said locality and others, outsiders, carry and have carried wine to that locality from outside; and they consume it not only for their own use but also by offering it for sale. As a consequence of this, citizens there who have surplus wine cannot sell it, and the foreign wine is sold, from which the mentioned petitioners draw no profit. And because of this Our Majesty was humbly entreated on behalf of the petitioners that we should be good enough, through our sovereign charity, graciously to take action with them in this matter, and to order that the import and sale in the aforesaid locality of wine coming from outside the territory and district of the said locality of Tarascon be forbidden.

We, then, being eager through our sovereign love [to promote] the profit and advantage of our faithful, and wishing as best we can to prevent inconvenience to them, benevolently consented to these supplications presented to us, as follows: We thought it fit, out of our certain knowledge and special grace, to grant by the tenor of the present [charter] to the same community and citizens that so long as it pleases us no wine may be or is permitted to be

5 M. Clavel, 'La Mévente du vin à Tarascon-sur-Rhône,' *Mémoires de l'Académie de Nîmes*, ser. 7, XXXI (1908), 318–19. We have omitted a few unimportant sentences at the end

imported or sent into the said locality of Tarascon by any outsider, of whatever status and condition he be, for sale or merely for his own consumption, exception being made only for citizens and inhabitants of the said locality who own vineyards outside the territory of the aforesaid locality. And this wine coming from vineyards which the latter have and own outside the territory of said castle they may send into the said castle, and sell, or convert to their use at their will, provided that whenever it will seem expedient, fit, or opportune, a certain suitable tax on the sale of wine—especially retail [sale]—may be imposed and ought to be imposed by the aforesaid council. . . .

Issued in Aversa by the magnificent man Ligurio Zurullo of Naples, knight, logothete, and protonotary of the kingdom of Sicily, our relative councilor, and beloved faithful of ours, in the year of the Lord 1377, December 14, first indiction, thirty-fifth year of our reign.

166
From the Latin[6]

[Palermo, January 28, 1299]

On Wednesday, the twenty-eighth of the same [month]. Giovanni de Galgano[7] and Neri Bernardi, citizens of Palermo, business managers (*gestores negociorum*) of the noble lord Corrado d'Oria, admiral of the kingdom of Sicily, of their own free will and in behalf of said admiral, sold and conceded to Bonaccorso Gamba, citizen of Pisa, giving his consent, etc., full permit of exit and [exemption] of customs (*ius exiture et dohane*) for 990 *salme* of grain to be exported from whatever port of Sicily said buyer wishes and to be transported from there to lawful and permitted localities outside the kingdom. [This was] at the price of 145 ounces of gold and 15 *tarini* of the common weight,[8] of which they acknowledge that they have [already] received from the buyer 20 ounces of gold, waiving, etc. The remaining amount of that price said buyer promised to deliver to them by the eighth day of the next month of March of the present indiction, and even before said time limit if said sellers with the agreement of said buyer earlier deliver

---

[6] R. Zeno, *Documenti per la storia del diritto marittimo nei secoli XIII e XIV*, pp. 36–37.

[7] Zeno in his analysis of the document translates de Galgano by 'da Gagliano,' which would make the man a southern Italian (Gagliano is in Lucania). The other seller, however, judging from his name, must have been a Tuscan, as was the buyer. Hence Giovanni de Galgano may well have been from San Galgano near Siena, or one Galgano may have been his father. As for Corrado d'Oria, he belonged to a great Genoese family and had been captain of the people (one of the two chief executives) in his town. Now he was hired by the king of Sicily, Frederick of Aragon, to defend the island against the attacks of the Angevin 'king of Sicily,' who ruled the mainland.

[8] The ounce of gold was a money of account corresponding to 30 gold *tarini* or *tarí* (real coins), or pegged to some other coin.

to him, the buyer, an order of the port officials (*portulani*) of Sicily concerning the exit and customs [permit] for the aforesaid amount of grain. And the said sellers promised and agreed to see to it that the buyer would have the order for the said port officers concerning the said exit and customs [permit] whenever he requests it. Each and all of the aforesaid the parties themselves promised to each other to keep as settled, etc., under penalty of 50 ounces of gold for the benefit of the court and of the party observing the aforesaid, etc.; waiving, etc.

Witnesses undersigned: Gerardo Bonzuli, Rigio di Gennaro, Marzio of San Miniato, Pallamo D'Abate, and Perello di Cesario.

167

From the Latin[9]

Rialto [Venice], July, 971

In the name of God and of our Savior, Jesus Christ. In the imperial rule of Lord John [Tzimiskes], the great emperor, and in the second year of his imperial reign, in the month of July, fourteenth indiction. Rialto.

Whereas earlier in the aforesaid indiction imperial envoys were dispatched to us by John [I], Basil [II], and Constantine [VIII], most sacred emperors, to inquire about the lumber and weapons which our ships were carrying to Saracen territory, and to make terrible threats by order of the most glorious emperor—that if [the Venetians] should lend assistance to the barbarians with this lumber, [an act] which would be [against] the dignity of the empire and [against] the Christian people, they would have [all] the ships they found set afire together with the men and the cargo;[10]

Therefore, on a certain day, while Lord Pietro [Candian IV], most excellent doge, our lord, was sitting with Vitale, most sacred patriarch, his son, as well as with Marino, most reverend bishop of the church of Olivolo, and with the other bishops of his territory, and while a great part of the people—

---

[9] S. Romanin, *Storia documentata di Venezia*, I, 373–75. The document is full of grammatical errors and obscure passages. For its historical background, see R. S. Lopez, 'Silk Industry in the Byzantine Empire,' *Speculum*, XX (1945), 26, 38, with bibliography. Venice in 971 was still nominally a Byzantine dependency, and she had to enforce a decree of John Tzimiskes; but it is worth noting that a few years later (976) Pietro Candian IV, the doge who had the decree enforced, was besieged in his palace and killed by a mob. The Orseolo family, which then obtained the supreme power, was more independent in its foreign policy and less high-handed in its relations with the people. In the later Middle Ages the Western emperors, the popes, and sometimes Venice itself took the initiative in issuing similar decrees. The enforcement was never fully effective.

[10] While it is clear that the envoys had threatened to use Greek fire against the ships, it is not quite certain that the wares and the crews also were to be set afire; but the methods of warfare at that time make such an interpretation very likely.

that is, the higher, the middle, and the lower[11]—was standing in their presence, they undertook to hold a council [to decide] how and in what way they could from now on appease the wrath of the emperor and desist from that evil practice of committing that sin.[12]

And because we know most certainly that it is a great sin to supply such assistance to a pagan people, who through it are able to overcome or to harm Christians, therefore, through inspiration of the Divine Mercy, we all deliberated together and affirmed and by this bond of promise are promising, together with our heirs, to you, Lord Pietro, most eminent doge, our lord, and to your successors, that from now on no one is to be so bold as to carry weapons for sale or for gift to Saracen territory, nor lumber for building ships that may cause damage to the Christian people, nor breastplates, nor shields, nor swords, nor lances, nor other weapons with which [the Saracens] may strike Christians; but one may only carry weapons with which one may defend oneself from enemies, and these [cannot] in any way be sold or given to the barbarians. As for lumber, we concede that we are not to carry elms, maples, broad planks (? *spatulas*), oars, spars, or other lumber that may cause harm to Christians, but we may carry only trimmed logs[13] of ash five feet long and one ax wide, and vases, bowls, and cups, and tree planks likewise five or six feet long. And after we have left your port of Venice we are not to take aboard at any place lumber that may be useful for ships [and] which we might be able on any occasion to sell to the barbarians. And if at any time we should attempt to violate the present promise and presume to carry to Saracen territory weapons or lumber, except only as stated above, whoever presumes to do this and is discovered, let him pay as a fine to you, Lord Pietro, doge, our lord, and to your successors, a hundred pounds of pure gold. And if he does not have these pounds to pay the fine, let him suffer capital punishment. And let this record of promise remain in full force forever.

And we do make known that at the present time, before the envoy of the Holy Empire had come to us, three ships were about to sail, two to Mahdiya and one to Tripoli. Therefore, considering the poverty of those men, we granted [them] license to carry logs and spars and vases and saucers and other small objects; but the other lumber which is mentioned above we do

---

[11] *Maiores, mediocres, et minores*, the same generic distinctions which we find in Lombard documents such as Document 9. But here the three groups are assuming a more definite political and institutional significance. This is probably the earliest verbal account of a municipal popular assembly.

[12] From now on the assembled people of Venice speak in the first person.

[13] *Insublo* (or, a few lines below, *insuglos*), probably a corruption of *insubulum*, which Isidore of Seville uses in the meaning of cylinders used in weavers' looms; compare modern French *ensouple*.

not at all allow them to carry. For the future, then, let no one presume to carry to Saracen territory any lumber except such as is mentioned in this record of promise. And if anyone presumes to do otherwise, breaking the promise, let him incur the above penalty.[14]

168

From the Italian translation of the Arabic[15]

[Alexandria, 1207?]

In the name of God, the clement and the merciful. The slaves [of the sultan of Egypt], the unjustly treated merchants, prostrate themselves to the ground before the high person of the Lord Sultan Malik al-'Adil. May God perpetuate his days, may He cause his flags to wave over all parts of the world, may He send the angels of Heaven to assist his armies, and may He cause the kings of the world to be his slaves! And they relate how unjustly they have been treated.

These merchants, having left Beirut, arrived at Alexandria, the [city] guarded [by God], where they paid duty according to the use of their predecessors, being secured by the safe-conduct (aman)[16] of God and the safe-conduct of this clement government, and they engaged in business according to the custom of merchants. When they asked permission to leave, it was denied them, with the words, 'You are from Cyprus.' Yet none of them [is a native] of that place. They are Pisans, Venetians, one from Beirut, another from Crete, another from Jazirat ibn 'Umar, a valet[?][17] and slave of the lord Mu'izz al-Din.[18] And they have been detained here for one year. They had engaged in business with a large amount of merchandise of their own, that is, of mullets. But since it spoiled, they threw it away and they have nothing left save a very small [remnant] of their goods, and the ship, which is rotting in the sea. Therefore they appeal to the compassionate feelings of the sultan, that he, considering the condition of the suppliants, grant them liberty to leave, inasmuch as, being poor, they would have died of starvation if it had not been for charity. Yet it is unusual for the justice of this victorious dynasty to do wrong to merchants. They all are slaves [of the sultan]—nine men who

---

[14] There follow eighty-one signatures of members of the assembly and the notaries who wrote and certified the document.

[15] M. Amari, I diplomi arabi del R. Archivio Fiorentino, pp. 70–71. On the background of the documents, see ibid., p. 410.

[16] On the aman and its significance, see J. Hatschek, Der Musta'min; W. Heffening, Das islamische Fremdenrecht bis zu den islamisch-fränkischen Staatsverträgen; R. S. Lopez, 'Du marché temporaire à la colonie permanente,' Annales: Economies, Sociétés, Civilisations, IV (1949), 395–97.

[17] The question mark is Amari's.

[18] The ruler of Iraq, where Jazirat ibn 'Umar (on the Tigris near Mosul) is situated.

left Beirut with a little merchandise, went to Cyprus, where they bought the rest of the cargo, and came to Egypt under the protection of the safe-conduct. They do not belong to hostile countries, but all are slaves of this dynasty and entered under its obedience.

The views [of the sultan] are most high. And praise be to God, the only One.

169

From the Latin[19]

Genoa, April 6, 1250

Concerning the fact that Guillem de Ouveilhan, Narbonnese, petitions that a sack of wool seized by the Consuls of the Sea, which he states to be his own, be returned to him, because he says that owing to the [special] convention which the men of Narbonne[20] have with the Commune of Genoa he has not incurred the penalty of the article dealing with contraband merchandise, and inasmuch as already at other times it has been decided that the Consuls of the Sea are not to ask anything of the men of Narbonne by way of penalty from the aforesaid article;

We, Simone de Burciago, judge and assessor of Lord Girardo de Corrigia, podestà of Genoa, having seen the recommendations on the part of the Consuls of the Sea and the said convention as well as the allegations of both parties; having also had the advice of Napoleone of Voltaggio and Ansaldo of Asti, jurists (iudices), on this matter;

State and decide that the said sack is to be returned by the aforesaid Consuls to the aforesaid Guillem since the said Guillem has not incurred the penalty of the aforesaid article, Guillem himself swearing that he does not hold the said sack fraudulently from another, but that it is without fraud his own;

With the reservation that the aforesaid decision should not in any way constitute a precedent against the Commune in the future.

The said Guillem swore as above. And [the decision] was given as above in Genoa in the palace of the Fornari,[21] in the year of the Incarnation of the Lord 1250, seventh indiction, April 6. Witnesses: Bartolomeo, judge, and Pietro de Marino.

---

[19] G. Mouynès, *Ville de Narbonne, inventaire des archives communales antérieures à 1790, Annexes de la série AA*, p. 49. The case is an appeal from the Consuls of the Sea, a municipal authority in charge of sea trade, to the supreme court of Genoa. It was a widespread practice for the court to ask for the advice of jurists.

[20] On the convention (of 1224), see W. Schaube, *Handelsgeschichte der romanischen Völker des Mittelmeergebiets bis zum Ende der Kreuzzüge*, Chap. XL.

[21] A private house which was rented by the Commune of Genoa.

170

From the Latin[22]

[Narbonne], March 15, 1254

In the year of the Lord 1254, on the Ides of March.

Whereas the court of Lord Amalric, by the grace of God viscount and lord of Narbonne, and Peire Boyer, *viguier* of the same court, were trying to exact the *leuda* (toll) on alum of Volcano from certain Genoese, while the Genoese themselves were saying and alleging to the contrary that they were not bound, nor was any Genoese, to pay the aforesaid *leuda;*

The consuls of Narbonne, going with the aforesaid Genoese to the said court before the above-said *viguier*, asked the same *viguier* not to try to exact any illegal *leuda* from the aforesaid Genoese.

And after the said statement was made by the said consuls, the said *viguier* and the consuls with the aforesaid Genoese sent and placed the aforesaid controversy in the hands, power, and arbitration of the prud'hommes of the city and borough of Narbonne, viz., Guillem Fabre, son of the late Peire Ramon Fabre, and Ramon Peire, son of the late like-named Ramon Peire, of the city, and Guillem Bonet and André Ramon, of the borough. And the said prud'hommes, having heard the argument of both parties and having investigated the truth about this matter, pronounced that not only these but also [any] other Genoese do not have to pay any *leuda* on the aforesaid alum.

This was done in the year and day mentioned above, Guiraut Pigeon, knight, Peire Ramon of Montpellier, Guillem Alaros, Arnaut Figueria, Ramon of Moissac being consuls of the city.

[22] Mouynès, *Ville de Narbonne, inventaire des archives*, p. 74. The case parallels the preceding one, but Narbonne was not as fully independent as Genoa. Hence the conflicting judgments of the *viguier* or vicar of the lord and of the consuls (who, like the Genoese podestà, are at the head of the Commune) can be solved only through arbitration, the Narbonnese arbitrators or prud'hommes playing a much more decisive part than the Genoese jurists.

PART FIVE

Tools and Ideas

A DESCRIPTION of the tools and ideas of the medieval merchant ought to be visual as well as written. Photographs of ships and shops as represented in medieval manuscripts, paintings, and sculptures; pictures of the extant medieval gild halls, warehouses, and private homes of merchants; reproductions of coins, weights, pottery, and textiles—all of these would give perhaps more eloquent testimony to the spirit of the merchant than anything that we may gather from the yellowed paper of archives. Medieval literature, especially short stories and books of travel written by such merchants as Giovanni Boccaccio or Marco Polo, is another impressive testimonial. But we cannot provide here a literary anthology or a series of illustrations. We shall, therefore, limit our selections to written documents and to nonfictional sources. An unusually large proportion comes from Florence and the smaller towns of Tuscany. While this bears witness to the genius in expression of the Tuscan medieval merchant, it does not mean that the merchants from Genoa, Venice, Marseilles, or Barcelona never paused to think or were incapable of expressing their thoughts. But they did not put their thoughts on paper, or if they did, their papers have not come down to us.[1]

[1] General bibliography on the merchants and their spirit is found in note 1 to our Chap. III.

CHAPTER XXI

MANUALS

THE EDUCATIONAL and cultural level of the merchant class was no more uniform in the Middle Ages than it is today. Obviously, small traders in backward villages were usually more ignorant than great businessmen in important cities, and the latter were seldom as learned as professional scholars. In Italy, however, few illiterate merchants are found anywhere after the tenth or the eleventh century at the latest. By the thirteenth century special schools taught elementary commercial practice and some merchants went through the regular course in the universities, usually being graduated in law. It is not rare to find a number of books listed among the possessions of a merchant. Some of the books are nontechnical, others are texts and commentaries of law and medicine, but a number are manuals specifically designed for the instruction of the merchant.[1]

Among commercial manuals we could list a large number of treatises on arithmetic. The most famous, by Leonardo Fibonacci—that is, Leonardo son of Bonaccio—of Pisa, was not written for merchants only; but Leonardo was the son of a Pisan colonial official, and he grew up in a circle of businessmen. In furnishing examples of practical problems he kept constantly in mind the daily routine of trade. Therefore excerpts from his book (Documents 171 and 172) seemed more interesting than citations from manuals of elementary arithmetic, although these may have had wider diffusion.[2] The title of the work, *Book of the Abacus*, reminds us of the instruments which helped the merchant in performing his calculations— abacuses, exchequers, and the like, all of them humble ancestors of modern calculating machines.[3]

[1] See H. Pirenne, 'L'Instruction des marchands au moyen âge,' *Annales d'Histoire Economique et Sociale*, I (1929), 13–28; A. Sapori, 'La cultura del mercante medievale italiano,' reprinted in *Studi di storia economica medievale*, 2d ed., pp. 285ff.; V. Vitale, 'Vita e commercio nei notai genovesi dei secoli XII e XIII,' *Atti della Società Ligure di Storia Patria*, Vol. LXXII (1949).

[2] Nevertheless we shall give here a few examples of the 'little rules' found in one of these manuals of elementary arithmetic:

'If you wish to write down [a number of] many figures, make a period at every third figure beginning from the right hand and going towards the left, and then you will have as many thousands as are in front of the periods . . . If you wish to multiply numbers ending with a zero, multiply their figures and put all of the zeros at the end. . . . If you wish to multiply fraction by fraction, multiply the numerators with one another, and the denominators similarly. . . . If you multiply the width of a circle by 22 and divide by 7, you will have the circumference. . . .' Paolo Dagomari of Prato, nicknamed Paolo dell'Abbaco, *Regoluzze*, ed. A. Zambrini (Bologna, 1857), pp. 5, 7, 9, Rules 1, 2, 15, 32. The book was written in 1340.

[3] Further information and bibliography on Leonardo Fibonacci may be found in Sapori, *Studi di storia economica medievale*, pp. 293ff., and in H. C. Krueger and R. L. Reynolds, *Lanfranco*,

No less important were the books which supplied information on travel. Geographic treatises and accounts of explorers were eagerly read by many merchants, but they were not designed especially for them. It is worth noting that Marco Polo was one of the top 'best-sellers' in medieval literature, and that the apocryphal book of travel ascribed to one Sir John Maundeville was almost as popular, although far less reliable. The *portolani* were not as good reading, but their detailed descriptions of ports and maritime routes were invaluable aids for commercial navigation (Document 173). Very often texts accompanied maps. It was always assumed that the user possessed compass, astrolabe, and other instruments for determining direction.[4]

It was not enough to find one's way to a distant country, but one had to talk to the inhabitants. Though interpreters existed in every port and inland center of any commercial importance, the man who knew the language had a definite advantage. We know that most merchants in the Western world could speak French, and that Italian also was understood in the entire Mediterranean basin and beyond it, but no bilingual dictionaries of the Romance languages are known to have been written for and by merchants. We know one Arabic-Latin glossary which probably was compiled for the teaching of Arabic in the Spanish schools but which may have been helpful to merchants. Still more interesting is a trilingual dictionary in Latin, Cumanic (the Turkic language which served as a sort of pidgin language in the larger part of Asia from the Black Sea to the Yellow Sea), and Persian. Judging from the Genoese expressions which frequently tinge its Latin, scholars have suggested that the dictionary probably was compiled in Genoa or in one of the Genoese colonies. Some of the terms seem to be included especially for the use of Christian missionaries, but a larger number unmistakably belongs to the world of business (Document 174).[5]

Still more important are manuals of general commercial practice such as those of Abu al-Fadl, Pegolotti, and Uzzano, the Venetian anonymous 'Tarifa,' and the Florentine-Ragusan *Libro di mercatantie,* from which we have already taken several excerpts.[6] These manuals cover nearly every subject of interest to a merchant— descriptions of wares, measures, moneys, tariffs, itineraries, and sometimes complete *portolani*; arithmetic formulae to calculate compound interest, perpetual calendars; methods to make alloys and to test chemicals; economic theories; and advice on how to dodge customs inspection. It would be worth while to publish the full

Introduction. There is no recent monograph on Leonardo Fibonacci, but every history of mathematics devotes a few pages to him.

[4] The bibliography on *portolani* and maps is extremely abundant. Most of it is quoted in P. Revelli, *Cristoforo Colombo e la scuola cartografica genovese.* More recent are A. Delatte, *Les Portulans grecs*; O. Pastine, 'Se la più antica carta nautica medioevale sia di autore genovese,' *Bollettino Ligustico per la Storia e la Cultura Regionale*, I (1949), pp. 79–82. In English the most recent general sketch is G. H. T. Kimble, *Geography in the Middle Ages.*

[5] The Arabic glossary was published by C. Schiaparelli, *Vocabulista in arabico.* The editor has suggested that it was probably written in Spain for the use of schools where Muslim converts received instruction, but the very large number of commercial terms which were included leads us to think that it was also used by merchants.

[6] See Documents 3, 42, 46, 50, 63, 64, 65, 132. Some scholars have claimed that, in Europe at least, manuals of this kind were not intended for public use but were compiled for specific business firms which kept them under lock and key. There is no evidence to support this assumption, and there is some evidence to the contrary.

translation of some of these manuals, but each manual is a book in itself.[7] Here we present samples of one of the most typical subjects treated in the manuals—the art of knowing genuine commodities and of distinguishing good from inferior quality. One of the selections (Document 175) is a long list of commodities with a cursory description of each. The other (Document 176) is a very detailed and searching description of the different types of one commodity. Lastly, we present a new translation of the description of the route to China in the most famous of these manuals. An earlier translation of that description has been printed several times, but the passage is so interesting that we do not wish to pass it by (Document 177).[8]

Practical Arithmetic

171

Leonardo Fibonacci, *The Book of the Abacus*
From the Latin[9]

[Pisa, 1202]

SECOND PART OF THE EIGHTH CHAPTER ON EXCHANGE OF CURRENCIES

If 1 soldus of imperials, which is 12 deniers [imperial], or [1 soldus] of any other currency is sold for 31 deniers Pisan or for [31 deniers of] any other currency, and it is asked how many deniers Pisan anyone should obtain for 11 [deniers] imperial, you write out the problem [in a diagram]. That is, first, the [currency] sold, namely 12 [deniers] imperial, then on the same line to the other side you write its value, namely, 31 deniers Pisan, and place 11 [deniers] imperial under 12 [deniers] imperial, as is shown here. And you will multiply the numbers on the opposite sides [in the diagram], that is, 11 by 31; it will make 341. And divide this by 12, [the result] will be $\frac{5}{12}$ 28 deniers.[10]

[7] Oddly enough, the only book of this kind of which a full English translation has been printed is a Chinese manual of the twelfth century: Chau Ju-kua, *Chu-fan-chi* [*Chronicle of Various Foreign Lands*], ed. and tr. by F. Hirth and W. Rockhill.

[8] Bibliography on the Western manuals of commercial practice may be found in the excellent prefaces of F. Borlandi to the *Libro di mercatantie et usanʒe de' paesi* and of A. Evans to Pegolotti's *Pratica della mercatura*. R. Bautier in a recent journey to Italy has found some manuscripts of manuals which had been unknown up to now, but he has not yet published a report of his findings. On the book of Benedetto Cotrugli, which cannot be properly included among medieval manuals of commercial practice (although it has many features in common with them), see the introduction to Chapter XXIV and Documents 184, 199, and 200.

[9] Leonardo Fibonacci [Leonardo, son of Bonaccio of Pisa], *Liber abbaci*, ed. by B. Boncompagni, p. 103.

[10] Note that Fibonacci, following the Arabic system of writing from right to left, places the whole number to the right of the fraction. The problem is a simple proportion, which we would write out as follows: $x : 11 = 31 : 12$. $12x = 341$. $x = 28\frac{5}{12}$.

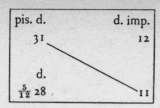

And you should know that whatever number of deniers Pisan a soldus imperial, which is 12 [deniers] imperial, is worth, 12 soldi imperial are worth the same number of soldi Pisan, and 12 pounds imperial are worth the same number of pounds Pisan. Therefore should you have said that the soldus imperial is worth 31 [deniers] Pisan, as we said above, and should it be asked how much 11 soldi imperial are worth, the problem will be as follows: Since 12 soldi imperial are worth 31 soldi Pisan, it is asked how much 11 soldi imperial are worth. Write out the problem [in a diagram] as above, and then multiply 31 by 11, as we have said above, and divide similarly by 12, and the result will be $\frac{5}{12}$ 28 soldi, that is, 28 soldi and 5 deniers Pisan, as is made plain by this second diagram.[11]

172

Leonardo Fibonacci, *The Book of the Abacus*
From the Latin[12]

[Pisa, 1202]

ON THE SOCIETAS OF TWO MEN

If the problem concerns two men who formed a *societas* together, one of whom invested in the above-said *societas* £ 18 of any currency and the other invested in the same £ 25, and they gained from it £ 7, and it is asked how much of these £ 7 should belong to each, you will do thus: Write out [in the diagram] the share of the first partner, that is, £ 18, at the head of the diagram on the right side; then write out to the left on the same line £ 25 [the share of the other partner]; again, place the profit as much as you like to the left, separately from them, as is shown here below. And add together the shares of each partner, that is, 18 with 25; it will make 43. Place this in the [diagram of the] problem under the 18 and extend a small line over that 43, and place another 43 with a small line under the 25, as is shown in the problem. Then multiply the share of the first partner, that is, 18, by the gain, that is, by 7: it will make 126. Divide this by the 43 which was placed under the 18; the

---

[11] Omitted here; the second problem is identical save that soldi are substituted for deniers.

[12] *Liber abbaci*, Boncompagni ed., p. 135.

result will be £ $\frac{40}{43}$ 2. And this much of that profit belongs to the first partner, that is, £ 2 s.18 d. $\frac{11}{43}$7.[13] The remainder of the profit, then, belongs to the other [partner]. That it may be worked out according to this craft,[14] however, multiply the portion of the other partner by the profit, that is, 25 times 7; it will make 175. And divide this by the 43 which was placed under 25; the result will be £ $\frac{5}{43}$ 4. And thus much belongs to the second [partner], that is, £ 4 d. $\frac{32}{43}$ 16. And if you should join with these the £ 2 s.18 d. $\frac{11}{43}$ 7 which belong to the first [partner], you will arrive at the same £ 7. [We omit the diagrams which accompany this problem and which are similar to that reproduced in Document 171.]

Practical Geography

173
From the Italian[15]

[Italy, early fifteenth century]

7. From Plymouth to Falmouth, 50 miles, one fourth of west by south-west.

Falmouth is a good harbor in all weather [for boats coming] from every direction, but beware of a shoal in the middle of the channel which is covered during full tide. Sail in from an easterly direction at one *prodese* and a half.

The way to recognize Falmouth is [to look for] a high mountain inland [and] a flat, irregular cape on the coast, with[16] a very small island hard by the cape; and from an easterly direction there is a black, irregular cape with a broad islet 10 miles from Falmouth.

From Falmouth to Start Point, 70 miles.

From Start Point to the cape of the Lizard, 75 miles, one fourth of west by south.

The way to recognize the cape of the Lizard is [to look for] a rounded mountain with an irregular coastline and with a church on top; and there is a reef hard by the cape.

---

[13] The text in error writes d.11 for d.7, which is correctly stated a few lines below. Let x equate the share belonging to the first partner. Then $x : 7 = 18 : 43$. $x = £ 2\frac{40}{43}$. To change pounds into soldi multiply by 20 the fraction and divide by 43; the result will be s.18$\frac{14}{43}$. To change soldi into deniers multiply by 12 the fraction and divide by 43; the result will be d.7$\frac{11}{43}$. The share belonging to the first partner is £2 s.18 d.7$\frac{11}{43}$. When it is added to the share of the second partner, which is derived in similar fashion, that is £4 s.1 d.4$\frac{32}{43}$, the result will be £7.

[14] *Ut secundum hanc artem operetur*; 'art' is here used in the meaning of 'craft,' 'profession,' 'technique.'

[15] K. Kretschmer, 'Die italienischen Portolane des Mittelalters,' *Veröffentlichungen des Instituts für Meereskunde und des Geographischen Instituts an der Universität Berlin*, XIII (1909), 270–71. The passage we have translated is from the so-called Portolano Parma-Magliabecchi.

[16] *Come*; but read, in all probability, *con*.

8. From the cape of the Lizard to the cape of Lands End, 50 miles west by southwest.

The way to recognize the cape of Lands End is [to look for] a cape not too high, with an irregular coastline and with three islets beyond the cape.

From the cape of Lands End to the Scilly Islands, 30 miles west by south; and beware of certain shoals that are along that route. In the Scillies [there is] good anchorage in all weather.

The way to recognize the Scillies is [to look for] three or four irregular islands, low, at entrance of the harbor and from a southeasterly direction; and when you are close to the island [coming] from the southeast, you will see the castle; go close to the castle, and leave it at your right.

From the Scillies to the cape of the Lizard, 60 miles toward east.

Practical Philology

174

[Genoa(?), 1303][17]

[*Original in Latin*]	[*Persian*]	[*Cumanic*]
I hear	mesnoem	eziturmen
you hear	mesnoy	esitursen
he hears	mesnoet	esitur
And the plural		
we hear	mesnam	esiturbis
you hear	mesnoyt	esitursis
they hear	mesnoent	esiturlar
Past imperfect		
I was hearing	mesindem	esituredim
you were hearing	mesinidi	esitureding
he was hearing	mesinid	esituredi
And the plural		
we were hearing	mesinidim	esitureduc
you were hearing	mesinidit	esituredingis
they were hearing	mesinident	esiturlaredj
Past perfect		
I have heard, or heard	sinide[18]	esitum
you heard	sinidi	esiting

[17] Géza Kuun, ed., *Codex Cumanicus*, pp. 1–2, 90–91, 107–8.
[18] Abbreviation symbol missing. The word should read *sinidem*.

[*Original in Latin*]	[*Persian*]	[*Cumanic*]
he heard	sinid	esitti

And the plural

we heard	sinidim	esittic
you heard	sinidit	esittingis
they heard	sinident	esitilar

Names of professions and what pertains to them

banker	saraf	saraf
scales	taraxu	taraxu
weights	dran	taslar
cartulary	takouî	bitik ul taftar[19]
inkwell	duet	duat
pen	kalam	kalam
table	tacta busmaî	sanar tacta
table cloth	xilu	choux
money	sim[20]	nagt ul acča
scribe	nuisenda	bacsi ul biticči
debtors	mara chi mebahet	borčlurlar
creditors	baarât	
manual	daftar	taftar[21]

. . . . .

linen of Champagne[22]	ketan y jonban	yionban chetan
linen of Reims	ketan y rusi	russi chetan
linen of Germany	ketan alamani	alamani chetanj
linen of Orléans	chetan soltanj	orlens chetan
linen of Novara	sansda chesi	sasda chesi
linen of Cremona	dras chesi	dras ches
linen of Lombardy	chetan lombardi	lonbardi chetanj
linen of Asti	chetan astexâ	astexan chetanj
linen of Ostuni[?]	chetan ostume	ostume chetanj
velvet	catifa	catifa

camocatus[23]

[19] From a Persian word meaning 'book of accounting' or 'book of receipts and expenditures.'

[20] Actually the Persian word means 'silver.'

[21] There follow other lists of names concerning various professions and wares.

[22] *Tella de Cap*. Evidently the abbreviation symbol for the letters *Campania* is missing; read *Campania*. This emendation is borne out by the Persian and Cumanic equivalents (*jonban*, *yionban*), which approximate the sound of 'Champagne.'

[23] The word is untranslated because it is borrowed from the Levant. *Camaca* was a silk cloth, possibly damasked or brocaded, made in Persia, Syria, and Cyprus.

[*Original in Latin*]	[*Persian*]	[*Cumanic*]
tasta[24]		
colors	rangan	ranglar
color	rang	bang[25]
white	sped	ac
black	sia	chara
vermilion	surg	chexel
crimson	cremixi	cremixi
brazil color	bachami	bachami
blue	chabut	coc
yellow	čerd	sari
green	saus	yaxil
camel	boxac	boxag
violet	banaus	ipchin
orange	narangi	narangi
flowered	al	al
linen *de Novo*[26]	ketâ begonia	bergonia katanj
linen of Bergamo	ketâ bgamasce	bgamasce ketanj
linen of Fabriano	aracli	aracli
linen unbleached	chetan can	chetan can

Advice for Buyers

175

From the compilation entitled, *The Book of the Wares and Usages of Diverse Countries*
From the Italian[27]

[Ragusa (Dubrovnik), 1458]

HOW TO KNOW MANY WARES

Hepatic aloe ought to be clear of leathery substance, and it ought to be the

[24] Probably this word also is borrowed from the Levant and therefore is not translated. Perhaps one ought to read *tartan* or *tartaryn*, cloth or robe of Tatar fashion.

[25] *Sic*; but read *rang*.

[26] Judging from the Persian and Cumanic equivalents, *begonia* and *bergonia*, one would think of a place in Burgundy. The best suggestion we can make is Nevers, which is not in Burgundy but very close to it.

[27] *El libro di mercatantie et usanƺe de' paesi* (unwarrantably ascribed to Giorgio di Lorenzo Chiarini), ed. by F. Borlandi, pp. 160–65. The wares are listed alphabetically according to the Italian alphabet. Their characteristics and uses are described in detail in Borlandi's excellent Glossary. Here we have noted only those points which had not been covered in that Glossary, and a few parallelisms with descriptions of wares in other manuals of commercial practice. Further parallelisms have been noted by Borlandi.

color of liver; and there are some who say it ought to be like pitch, black inside, glistening, bitter, and strong. You ought to take a piece of it and pound it, and its powder ought to appear violet.

Dry aloe ought to be clear of leathery substance, black, and glistening, and the more it approaches the color of hepatic aloe, the better it is.[28]

Asafetida ought to be of a mixed reddish and white color.

Ultramarine azure ought to have a deep and delicately warm color.

Ammoniacum ought to be white and granulated and clean.

Borax in stone ought to be white and thick,[29] and [with] little paste.

Boccaccini[30] ought to be white and delicate and well worked; and they should be pleasant to the touch but not be heavy.

Balsam ought to be the color of gold, and [when] in water it should sink to the bottom.

Cannella[31] ought to have a reddish and delicate color and be grooved, and it ought to be strong and sweet, that is, pungent; and [if it is] like that, it is good.

Heads of cloves ought to be rather coarse in powder and delicate inside.

Cubebs ought to be rich in color and clear of stems; they ought to be large and greyish, and they ought to be fully [developed] below the head and hollow within; and the larger part ought to be heads, because the larger part are wild.[32]

---

[28] Pegolotti, *Pratica*, p. 375, mentions three qualities of aloe. One of them, hepatic aloe, corresponds to the first quality described in the *Libro di mercatantie*, but neither of the others— citrine aloe, perhaps the same which Pegolotti himself calls Socotrine aloe (p. 293; 'all good qualities of aloe, however, came from Socotra'), and caballine aloe—corresponds exactly to the second quality mentioned in the *Libro di mercatantia*. The *Tarifa ʒoè noticia*, p. 74, describes hepatic aloe much the same way as do the others, but it says that its powder ought to be yellow.

[29] *Grosso*. This word may mean 'large,' 'coarse,' or 'thick;' apparently our document uses it alternatively in each of the three meanings. We have endeavored every time to translate it in the way that seemed more appropriate in regard to each ware, but slips may have occurred.

[30] The Italian dictionary of the Accademia della Crusca identifies the *boccaccini* with the *bucherami* or buckrams (a kind of fine linen or cotton cloth). Yet it would seem that there was a difference. The *boccaccini* were another variety of linen cloth, manufactured in Egypt and in Cyprus; the name also was improperly used for a coarse cotton cloth made in Western Europe. Cf. W. Heyd, *Histoire du commerce du Levant au moyen-âge*, II, 703.

[31] Inasmuch as the list a few lines below contains another duplication—cubebs are described twice; see notes 32 and 33—it is not impossible that *cannella* and *cienamonno*, listed a few lines below, were the same ware. *Cannella, cioè cennamo*, says Pegolotti, *Pratica*, p. 361; and in modern times, too, the Italian word *cannella* translates the English 'cinnamon.' But the description of *cannella* in our document substantially differs from that of *cienamonno* (which we have translated cinnamon). That the two words were not always regarded as equivalent appears also from G. Dominici, *Trattato della Santissima Carità* (Siena, 1513), fol. 15t.: 'Onde sai che dallo Oriente vengano gherofeni, cannella, cinnamomo, noci moscade, ecc.' Probably the two names indicated two varieties of the same spice.

[32] Here the writer or the copyist must have been in some confusion or dropped a few words. From the description of Pegolotti, *Pratica*, p. 374, we can gather that wild cubebs—which were

Camphor ought to be white and dry, clean and thick, and made like small deep saucers.

Capers ought to be fresh and green and with little salt.

Cassia ought to be thick and heavy, and its seed ought to make no sound [when rubbed], and its stalk ought to be whole, and its bark should not peel off.

Wax ought to have a rich color and be clear to the bottom.

Rock candy ought to be white, glistening, coarse, dry, and clean.

Cinnamon ought to be fine, black, hot, and very pungent.

Cubebs ought to be fresh, thick, and heavy.[33]

Hides of oxen and buffaloes ought to be of thick leather, short-haired, and glistening, and neither moth-eaten nor bald; and likewise any other hide.

Cloves ought to be black and reddish within and tend slightly more to the black than to the red. Their stalks ought to be fuzzy and be thick and dry and clear of [bad] stems.[34]

Tragacanth [gum] ought to be white, large, and clean and it does not matter[?][35] if something in it is reddish.

Dates ought to be fresh, large, and ripe.

Diamonds ought to be well squared, and their color should be rose water mixed with a little greenish [tint], and their surface pale.

Ermine ought to be long, white, and thick.

Gum arabic ought to be white, thick, and clear.

Emeralds ought to be of good color, clear without cracks.

Fine lac, that is, matured [lac], ought to tend to reddish color, and it ought to be thick, contain little powder, and be clear of wood [particles]. [Nor should it be of the kind] which looks within like spongy pitch, that is,

worth only one third as much as cultivated cubebs—had a smaller head, pyramidal rather than rounded (that is, not fully developed below). What the *Libro di Mercatantie* means, then, is that the larger part of the plant should be the head, and those whose heads are smaller are wild and hence less valuable.

[33] This seems to be a partial duplication of the description of cubebs given above. (*Chubebe* the first time, *chubebi* the second—but obviously it is the same word in the singular and in the plural.) Probably the writer, who drew most of his information from earlier books on the same general subject, used materials from two different works and forgot to amalgamate the references under the same heading.

[34] Apparently this ware is the equivalent of what Pegolotti, *Pratica*, **p**. 374, calls *fusti di ghero-fani*, 'stems of cloves,' while his *gherofani* correspond to the 'heads of cloves' listed a few lines above in the *Libro di Mercatantie*. Pegolotti also, while speaking of stems of cloves, points out that the fewer the whitish stems the better the 'stems of cloves.'

[35] *E non forza perchè tenghino alchuna chosa in rossetto*. The sentence is obscure. Still more obscure is the parallel description of tragacanth in the earlier *Tarifa zoè noticia*, p. 73: *non è forza se li tien alguna chosa in loro*. Both works probably drew from a common source and both misinterpreted it.

quite glistening. For [lacs] like that are not matured. And it ought not to have those clots which are [present] only inside but it ought to be grooved.[36]

Rock alum ought to be white, clear, and large, and it should not be in powder, because ground [alum] does not last longer than one year; and when it chances that it tends to green, that kind is better.

Ladanum [resin] ought to be black and perfumed.

Musk ought to be of reddish color and smell like cloves with slight bitterness and strong odor, so that when you put it into the mouth, its odor should go quickly to the brain.

Nutmegs ought to be large and firm and their surface clean; and there are some who say that they ought to be more than one fourth wrinkled. And they ought not to be unripe.

Orpiment ought to be thick, glistening, and clean of stones, and it ought to be gray and gold-colored inside when scaled; and it ought to contain little powder.

[China] rhubarb ought to be heavy, well folded, so that when one breaks it, it should be red and white inside; and there are some who say that it ought to be yellow colored, and glistening, thick, and firm, without holes,[37] and bitter in the mouth.

Rice ought to be white and large, and it should not include those [grains] which have a coating, and it should not be rosy.

Rubies ought to be of a good rosy color, attractive, and clean, and [a ruby] ought to receive leaf of gold.[38]

Rubies of good extraction and perfect in color and condition ought to meet all these specifications: first of all, they ought to have a clear, rosy color that must not tend to dark; their color ought to be fiery red, that is, ardent. And when one meets this specification he can trust it and need not worry about anything else.

Scammony ought to have a minute form [sic], so that when one breaks it, it is effervescent and spongy. It is made from the juice of herbs, and made into a cake; and if it is good it breaks easily. And it ought to be of a rather greasy color inside. And when you break it you ought to put it to your mouth, and wet it with a little saliva, and then place one piece beside the

[36] The whole passage is obscure. In order to clarify certain points we have used the *Tarifa ʒoè noticia*, p. 71, which has a similar discussion of fine lacs.
[37] The early printed editions of the *Libro di Mercatantie* have *fiori* (flowers) instead of *fori* (holes), but a comparison with the *Tarifa ʒoè noticia*, p. 73 (*senʒa buxi*) shows that the version of the manuscripts is the best.
[38] *Che pigli foglia d'oro*: probably a reference to suitableness for use in jewelry with leaf gold.

other, and it will look as if it were welded. And this is fine, and its color should be ashy.

Dragon's blood[39] ought to be red and blood-colored, light, clear, clean, and glistening.

Lahijan silk is a very good silk, and if you want to know it, it ought to be white and coarse and reddish, and it ought to be clear and of a regular thread, but it ought to tend to be reasonably thin rather than thick. And take care that it be not foamy, because it could not [possibly] be good. And it comes from the Levant.

Loaf sugar ought to be white, dry, and a well compact paste; and its powder ought to be large and granulated.

Saffron ought to be new, free of small seeds, and dry.

Sapphires ought to have good and clean colors.

Vairs, when they are crude in the muzzle, are hairy, and they usually tend to reddish; these are not good; and if they tend to be clear and [are] greenish those are good. Also, at the touch of the hand, if you find it well covered with hair underneath those are good.

Zedoary ought to be fresh, coarse, bitter, and firm. The sweet one is not good.

Lambri brazilwood ought to be thick, of good color, and not too dark.[40]

Quilon brazilwood ought to be thick, and vermilion, and of good color, and it ought to have little pith and it should not be holey; and when it contains much pith it is worth less. Its root ought to be firm and the stalk small.

Green ginger ought to be clear, brittle; and it is not like tow, and [it has] little juice, and [it is] made with good sugar.

Ginger of any kind ought to be of large roots, its skin clean and not wrinkled, and it should have good color, and [be] tender to the knife and white inside and firm, that is, not holey, and well filled and not thin.

Note that up to here I have said what many wares should be like if they are good, and why it would be very hard to find articles of such perfection and quality. And therefore a buyer needs discrimination, and he should be quite an experienced man. And if a ware has the said characteristics or perfections to a large extent, and if a thing approaches the aforesaid quality, one may buy it. But always take into consideration the [current] prices of the

[39] A resin used as a medicament and as a color.
[40] According to Pegolotti, *Pratica*, p. 361, Lambri brazilwood ought to be dark red, whereas Quilon brazilwood ought to be bright red. The latter is worth one sixth more than the former, and there is still another variety—China[?] brazilwood, *verzino sieni*—which is worth only one third as much as Quilon brazilwood.

places for which you buy them, and you must take into consideration the quantity which you can buy. For of pepper, of ginger, and of cloves, nutmegs, and other similar things that are easy to sell you can buy any quantity; but of [uncommon wares] such as aromatic aloe, dragon's blood, tutty, and other similar things, one ought to take into consideration to buy only that quantity which it is possible to sell in those places for which you buy them.

176

Francesco di Balduccio Pegolotti, *The Practice of Commerce*
From the Italian[41]

[Florence, between 1310 and 1340]

Alum is of many kinds. And first we shall describe how it is manufactured and then next in what country the best is manufactured and how one kind is graded after another. . . .[42]

And alum is merchandise that never gets spoiled provided you keep it in places where no water can touch it. And if you have to keep it for a long time, take it out of the sacks and keep it out of them, so that the sacks may not become damp and spoiled; but keep it aside and then, if you should return or sell it, you can put it into sacks and make arrangements to move it either from one place to another or from one country to another. And wherever you keep it, whether in or outside sacks, it is good for it to be propped up underneath with planks or any other good propping, raised or removed from the ground, so that the alum may not be spoiled by dampness. And the larger and whiter and clearer alum is, according to its kind, the better it is; and it ought to be clear of stones and dust and earth and sand. And here below we shall describe a few kinds of it.

Rock alum of Karahissar is the best alum that is manufactured. And it is manufactured far from the sea in Turkey and goes to the port of Kerasont in Turkey, on the seashore close to Trebizond; and it takes seven days in coming from the interior. And the said place, according to what is reported, manufactures in total about 14,000 Genoese *cantara*[43] every year. And [Karahissar alum] is of three kinds. One is the said rock of Karahissar, which is the best kind. And another kind is choice alum of the Good Alum Works, which is two fifths the aforesaid rock and three fifths cord alum, that is, pit

[41] Pegolotti, *Pratica*, pp. 367–70. On the use and commercial importance of alum, see Document 53.

[42] We omit a detailed description of the mining and manufacture of alum in Phocaea, which is interesting but not germane to our subject.

[43] According to P. Rocca, *Pesi e misure antiche di Genova e del Genovesato*, a Genoese *cantaro* weighed 57.65 kilograms. Some other scholars give slightly lower estimates.

alum—for 'cord' and 'pit' mean the same thing, and this 'cord' is fine-grained alum. And another kind is cord alum—that is, pit [alum]—which is the finest-grained alum that exists.[44]

And alum of Phocaea is almost like choice alum [of Karahissar], for Phocaea also makes a mixture by mingling together its alum, and it is about two fifths rock and three fifths cord. And [Phocaea] manufactures about 14,000 *cantara* of Genoa every year.

Alum of Ulubad is manufactured in a place in Turkey this side of the Black Sea, [close] to the Sea of Marmora, and it goes to a port on the shore, in a locality named Trilia. And it is a fairly large alum, considerably larger than the large [alum] of Ayassolük or that of Kutahieh. And it takes four days in coming from the interior. And [Ulubad] manufactures 10,000 Genoese *cantara* of it every year.

Alum of Kutahieh, in Turkey, goes to the ports of Ayassolük and of Palatia in Turkey. And it is fairly large and fine-grained mingled together, like that of Ulubad, but [on the whole] it is more finely grained than that of Ulubad. And some people call it Kutahieh and some [call it after] various Turkish places, and some [call it after] Ayassolük; but its correct name is Kutahieh because it comes from the region of Kutahieh in Turkey. And [Kutahieh] manufactures about 12,000 *cantara* of Genoa of it every year.

Cyzican alum comes from and is manufactured on the Sea Island, that is, on an island in the [Sea of] Marmora.[45] And there is little of it, and it is a very poor ware, and it is more [fit] for tanning leather than for anything else. And many alums are named Cyzican because they are very poor and fine-grained, but the one we are speaking of here is the true one. And [the Sea Island] manufactures about . . .[46] *cantara* of it every year.

Diaschilo alum and cord alum—that is, pit [alum]—together with the Cyzican, are the worst kind of alum that come down from the Black Sea of the Byzantine Empire. And as we said, every kind of alum, according to its grade, the more it includes large [lumps] and few fine ones, and the more it is white and clear and glistening and clean of stones and sand, the better it is and the more it is worth.

[44] The meaning of this passage is made clear by Pegolotti's description of alum manufacturing in Phocaea, p. 368: 'Rock alum is attached like ice to the wall of the said vat . . . pit alum is found at the bottom of the said vat.' *Corda* is probably a Greek or Turkish word which we have been unable to identify.

[45] Inasmuch as the extant ruins of Cyzicus are on the mainland, Cyzican alum can hardly have been from Cyzicus itself, as Evans suggests. More probably it came from the nearby Islands of the Princes; cf. Heyd, *Histoire du commerce du Levant*, II, 566ff. Diaschilo, the source of another inferior alum which is mentioned immediately after, is modern Eskel Liman, also on the Sea of Marmora.

[46] The gap is in the manuscript from which the edition was made.

And [note that] about 4,000 *cantara* of alum of Kutahieh also come down to Adalia in Turkey. And it comes from Kutahieh to Adalia by land [in] fourteen carriers' days.

Alum of Castiglione,[47] which in Florence is called feather alum, comes from Barbary. . . .[48] And it has this characteristic, that when alum of this kind is manufactured, the longer it is preserved the better and purer it becomes. And all that [material] that looks like earth, if it remains and is preserved in an earthen place with propping underneath, it becomes white alum, rather elongated and glistening, [so] that to the sight it looks like a feather; and therefore it is called feather alum. And some people say that if it is preserved it grows in weight.

Traveling to China

177

Francesco di Balduccio Pegolotti, *The Practice of Commerce*
From the Italian[49]

[Florence, between 1310 and 1340]

ADVICE ABOUT THE JOURNEY TO CATHAY
BY THE ROAD THROUGH TANA [AZOV],
[FOR MERCHANTS] GOING AND RETURNING WITH WARES

First [of all], from Tana to Astrakhan it is twenty-five days by ox wagon, and from ten to twelve days by horse wagon. Along the road you meet many Mongolians, that is, armed men.[50]

And from Astrakhan to Sarai it is one day by water on a river, and from Sarai to Saraichuk it is eight days by water on a river. And you can travel

---

[47] 'Barbary' alum was well known, sometimes under the names of Tlemcen, Tunis, or Bougie—actually it came from the interior, usually by the way of Sijilmasa—but Evans's tentative identification of Castiglione with Castilia, a Christian settlement in Tunisia, is untenable. There is no indication that Castilia was a trading place. Perhaps Pegolotti confused Barbary alum with alum from Castile. This also was a well-known alum, but definitely inferior to those of the Levant and North Africa.

[48] We omit here a few details on the extraction of this kind of alum.

[49] Pegolotti, *Pratica*, pp. 21–23. A translation of this passage was included in H. Yule, *Cathay and the Way Thither*, II, 287–95, and has been reprinted in many medieval anthologies. Ours is a new translation.

[50] One would think at first that the presence of armed Mongolian guards was an indication of the security of the road. That it was not necessarily so is shown by another short sentence of Pegolotti, p. 29, referring to the road from Ayas to Tabriz: 'And for extortions made along the way by Mongolians, that is, Tatar rangers, you may reckon about 50 *aspri* per packload.' It is true that this road was in the territory of the khan of Persia, whereas the road from the Crimea to China went successively through the territories of the Kipchak khanate, Turkestan, and China.

[both] by land and by water, but people travel by water to spend less [on transportation] of wares.

And from Saraichuk to Urjench it is twenty days by camel wagon—and for those who are carrying wares it is convenient to go through Urjench, because that is a good market for wares—and from Urjench to Utrar it is from thirty-five to forty days by camel wagon. And should you leave Saraichuk and travel straight to Utrar, you would travel fifty days; and for one who has no wares it would be a better way than traveling through Urjench.

And from Utrar to Almaligh it is forty-five days by pack asses. And you meet Mongolians every day.

And from Almaligh to Kan-chow it is seventy days by asses.

And from Kan-chow to a river called . . .[51] it is forty-five days by horses.

And from the river you can travel to Quinsay [Hang-chow] and sell there any silver *sommi*[52] you have, because that is a good market for wares. And from Quinsay on you travel with the money you get for the silver *sommi* you have sold there, that is, with paper money. And said money is called *balisci*;[53] four of these are worth one silver *sommo* throughout the country of Cathay.

And from Quinsay to Khanbaligh [Peking], which is the master city in the country of Cathay, it is thirty days.

THINGS NECESSARY FOR A MERCHANT WISHING TO MAKE THE SAID JOURNEY TO CATHAY

First [of all], it is advisable for him to let his beard grow long and not shave. And at Tana he should furnish himself with dragomans, and he should not try to save by hiring a poor one instead of a good one, since a good one does not cost. . . .[54] And besides dragomans he ought to take along at least two good menservants who know the Cumanic tongue well. And if the merchant wishes to take along from Tana any woman with him, he may do so—and if he does not wish to take one, there is no obligation; yet if he takes one, he will be regarded as a man of higher condition[55] than if

[51] The dots are Evans's. Probably the Yangtze.

[52] A *sommo* was both a silver ingot and the money of account of the Kipchak khanate. It corresponded to the weight of 202 *aspri* (real coins), but the mint in Tana when receiving from private parties an ingot weighing a *sommo* delivered only 190 *aspri*, keeping back the rest for seigniorage. A Genoese statute of 1304 reckoned the Kipchak *aspro* at ten Genoese deniers.

[53] *Balis* or *balish* in Arabic. On Chinese paper money in the Mongol period, see now H. Franke, *Geld und Wirtschaft in China unter der Mongolen-Herrschaft*, with Bibliography.

[54] *Il buono non costa quello d'ingordo che l'uomo non—s'ene megliori via più.* The text is obviously corrupt, but it seems to mean that a poor dragoman would be greedy (*ingordo*), so that a good dragoman, though asking for a higher salary, would actually cost less.

[55] *Sarà tenuto di migliore condizione.* Yule translates: 'he will be kept much more comfortably;' but *tenere* in this context means 'to hold, to esteem.'

he does not take one. If he takes one, however, she ought to know the
Cumanic tongue as well as the manservant. And [for the stretch] from Tana
to Astrakhan he ought to furnish himself with food for twenty-five days—
that is, with flour and salt fish, for you find meat in sufficiency in every
locality along the road. And in like manner, wherever you go in said journey
from one country to another according to the aforesaid [number of] days,
you ought to furnish yourself with flour and salt fish; for other things you
find in sufficiency, and especially meat.

The road leading from Tana to Cathay is quite safe both by day and by
night, according to what the merchants report who have used it—except
that if the merchant should die along the road, when going or returning,
everything would go to the lord of the country where the merchant dies,
and the officers of the lord would take everything—and in like manner if he
should die in Cathay. Actually if he had a brother or a close associate[56] who
could say that he is a brother, the property of the dead man would be given
to him, and in this manner the property would be rescued. And there is still
another danger; that is, should the lord die [and] until the new lord who is to
rule has been sent for,[57] in that interval sometimes a disorder[58] occurs against
the Franks and other foreigners—they call 'Franks' all Christians of countries
from the Byzantine Empire westwards—and the road is not safe until the
new lord is sent for who is to reign after the one who died.

Cathay is a province where there are many towns and many villages.
Among others there is one which is the master city, where merchants con-
vene and where is the bulk of trade. And this city is called Khanbaligh. And
said city has a circuit of one hundred miles and is all full of people and houses,
and of dwellers in the said city.

It is reckoned that a merchant with a dragoman and two menservants and
goods to the value of 25,000 gold florins would spend as far as Cathay, if he
wishes to economize, from 60 to 80 silver *sommi;* and for the entire return
journey from Cathay to Tana, including expenses for food, and salary of
menservants, and all [other] expenses connected with it, 5 *sommi* per packload or [even] less. And the *sommo* may be evaluated at about 5 gold florins.
And it is reckoned that each [ox]wagon will require only one ox, [such] a

---

[56] *Stretto compagno* (Yule: 'intimate friend and comrade') means both a partner (*compagno*) and
a friend. The Venetian merchants en route to Delhi through Mongol territory (see Document
149) adopted the stratagem suggested by Pegolotti.

[57] *Chiamato,* which Yule translates 'proclaimed.' But the rules of Mongol succession to the
throne required all relatives of the dead khan to be summoned from the distant provinces to an
assembly which elected the new khan.

[58] *Novitade,* meaning 'riot,' 'disorder,' and not 'irregularity,' as Yule translates.

wagon carrying 10 Genoese *cantara;* and a camel wagon requires three camels, the wagon carrying 30 Genoese *cantara;* and a horse wagon requires one horse, the wagon usually carrying 6½ Genoese *cantara* of 250 Genoese pounds [each]. And a bundle (*scibetto*) of silk is reckoned at about 110 to 115 Genoese pounds.

It is reckoned that from Tana to Sarai the road is less safe than all the rest of the journey. But should there be sixty men [in the caravan], [even] when the road is in its worst condition you would travel as safely as [if you were] in your own home.

Anyone wishing to leave from Genoa or from Venice in order to travel to the said places and journey to Cathay would do well to carry linen and go to Urjench, and to buy *sommi* in Urjench and proceed with these without investing [them] in any other merchandise, unless he has a few bales of the very finest linens, which are not bulky and require no greater expense [for carriage] than would any coarser linens.

And the merchants on their way may ride a horse or a donkey or whatever animal they like to ride.

All silver which the merchants carry [with them] when going to Cathay, the lord of Cathay causes to be withdrawn and placed in his treasury; and to the merchants who bring it in he gives paper money, that is, yellow paper struck[59] with the seal of said lord, that money being called *balisci*. And with said money you may and can purchase silk and any other merchandise or goods you may wish to buy. And all the people of the country are bound to accept it, and yet people do not pay more for merchandise although it is paper money. And of the said paper money there are three kinds, one being worth more than another according as the lord orders them to be worth.

And it is reckoned that you will get in Cathay from nineteen to twenty pounds of Cathay silk according to Genoese weight for one silver *sommo*, the *sommo* being of the weight of about 8½ Genoese ounces and of the alloy of 11 ounces and 17 deniers fine to the pound. And it [also] is reckoned that you will get in Cathay from three to three and a half pieces of *camaca* silk [cloth] for one *sommo* and from three and a half to five pieces of *na-che-che* silk and gold [cloth] for one silver *sommo*.[60]

[59] *Coniata;* Pegolotti is unfamiliar with a money which is not struck and uses the technical expression for 'striking' metallic money.

[60] It is not sure that *camaca* was damasked silk, as Yule translates. For this term and the term *na-che-che* (Italian *nacchetti*), see Evans's Glossary. On silk prices in Europe, see R. S. Lopez, 'China Silk in Europe in the Yuan Period,' *Journal of the American Oriental Society*, LXXII (1952), 72–76.

CHAPTER XXII

THE PROGRESS OF ACCOUNTING
METHODS

RECENT STUDIES have reversed the unfavorable judgment which some scholars had passed upon medieval bookkeeping. Even the crudest memoranda of the early thirteenth century are clear enough and contain only a fairly small proportion of errors.[1] During that century and the early fourteenth the methods of accounting advanced by leaps and bounds. Credit and debit entries were posted separately, at first in different sections of a ledger, then one above the other, then side by side. A page or a number of pages were reserved for the accounts of each customer, and alphabetic indexes of accounts were provided. Every entry was listed in various ledgers, cross references were included, and in time the principle was adopted that a debit entry should correspond to every credit entry. The addition of impersonal accounts permitted the keeping of records for tangible assets and operating costs. Thus the most advanced techniques of double-entry bookkeeping gradually came into being. Against the prevalent theory that Genoa was their birthplace, it has been recently argued that double-entry bookkeeping originated in thirteenth-century Tuscany. Be that as it may, the earliest extant ledgers in which the new system of accounting is fully developed come from Genoa in the early fourteenth century. The other Italian cities had similar ledgers before the end of the century. Other countries were much slower in adopting the new techniques. Though it would be a gross exaggeration to ascribe to the revolution in accounting a decisive influence in gaining for the Italians a virtual monopoly of foreign trade in Western Europe, it can hardly be doubted that improved tools helped the hands which had shaped them and which employed them skillfully.[2]

[1] The earliest extant fragment of commercial accounting comes from Genoa, 1156–1158; see the excellent edition and comment of G. Astuti, *Rendiconti mercantili inediti del cartolare di Giovanni Scriba*; the book was reviewed by F. Edler de Roover, 'Partnership Accounts in Twelfth Century Genoa,' *Bulletin of the Business Historical Society*, XV (1941), 87–92. But the fragment consists of informal calculations jotted down with a view to dividing the profits of *commenda* operations, and hence it cannot be regarded as regular bookkeeping. An entry from the earliest extant accounting book (1211) has been included in Document 74.

[2] The best works on this subject are R. de Roover, 'Aux origines d'une technique intellectuelle: la formation et l'expansion de la comptabilité à partie double,' *Annales d'Histoire Economique et Sociale*, IX (1937), 171–93, 270–98, and F. Melis, *Storia della ragioneria*. Both contain ample bibliographic information; Melis also has included in his book a great wealth of unprinted source material. The theory of a Tuscan origin of double-entry bookkeeping is propounded by Melis, pp. 425ff. But new arguments in behalf of Genoa have been offered by R. L. Reynolds, 'Bankers' Account in Double-Entry in Genoa, 1313 and 1316,' *Bollettino Ligustico per la Storia e la Cultura Regionale*, III (1951), 33–37. The question cannot be regarded as definitely solved.

A ledger is an integrated whole. Therefore, excerpts can hardly convey an adequate idea of the progress of bookkeeping. Inasmuch as a number of short excerpts from medieval accounting books have already been published in English translation,[3] we shall give only a small number of examples. Document 178 is a very primitive memorandum which reflects practices of a backward town. It is intended not only to enter credit transactions but also to include acknowledgments of debt by the customers, who enter their promises to pay in their own handwriting. There is no attempt at converting the different moneys into one money of account. Document 179 also is a memorandum of credit transactions, but it is all by the same hand, reckons all entries in one money of account, and endeavors to keep separate accounts for each customer. An excerpt from a ledger of a more advanced type, which includes separate accounts for every customer and lists credit and debit separately, has been presented in another section of this book.[4] The third selection (Document 180) is an example of very careful single-entry accounting which refers not to persons but to merchandise. Document 181 is the final balance-sheet of one of the biggest *compagnie* of merchant-bankers in the early fourteenth century. Lastly we present excerpts both from a personal and an impersonal account of a well-kept double-entry ledger of the late fourteenth century (Documents 182 and 183).

Theoretical treatises of double-entry bookkeeping did not appear before the fifteenth century. The earliest extant book that covers the subject in detail is Luca Pacioli's *Summa de arithmetica* (printed 1494), a very impressive work which has, however, been charged with plagiarism by a number of scholars.[5] The section on accounting in that book has been twice translated into English.[6] Therefore we thought it more useful to present the shorter description of bookkeeping methods in Benedetto Cotrugli's *Della mercatura et del mercante perfetto*, written in 1458 but printed only in 1573, almost certainly with some revisions (Document 184). Pacioli was a friar. Cotrugli was a professional merchant; his personality and his book are discussed in the introduction to the last chapter.

[3] By R. Brown, *A History of Accounting and Accountants*; the book is outdated but the translations are still useful.

[4] See Document 36.

[5] Melis, *Storia della ragioneria*, pp. 620ff., has lately championed the thesis of Pacioli's originality. Be that as it may, it is certain that double-entry bookkeeping was taught in schools long before Pacioli wrote his treatise, and it is almost certain that a manual was compiled by one Troilo de Cancellariis in the early fifteenth century.

[6] By J. B. Geijsbeek, *Ancient Double-Entry Bookkeeping: Lucas Pacioli's Treatise, A.D. 1494*, and by P. Crivelli, *An Original Translation of the Treatise on Double-Entry Bookkeeping by Frater Lucas Pacioli*. On the importance of double-entry bookkeeping (or rather, on the necessity of guarding against overstressing it), see B. S. Yamey, 'Scientific Bookkeeping and the Rise of Capitalism,' *Economic History Review*, ser. 2, I (1949), 99ff., interesting in spite of certain factual mistakes.

Early Bookkeeping Methods

178

From the Provençal, the Latin, and the Hebrew[7]

Forcalquier, May 8–25, 1331

... Owes Jacon, son of Astruc[?] of Digne, 30 silver [deniers] Tournois for 1½ *cannas* of *canet*[?][8] of Carcassonne. To pay one half at the fair and the other at the beginning of Lent. And he took it—record by Chabaut[9]—on May 8.

Owes Jacon, in addition, s.4 for some hose of blue [cloth] of Saint-Pons. To pay now. And he took it on the day and year written above.

Owes Chaquon, in addition, 5 Tournois for 2 palms of the same cloth.[10]

In the year of the Lord 1331, on May 9, I, Guillem Ortolani, notary, acknowledge to you, Ugo Teralh, notary [and] merchant of Forcalquier, that I personally have had and have received through purchase from you 1½ *cannas* of checkered [cloth] of Toulouse for the price of s.24 at the rate of s.16 the *canna*.

Also, on the other hand, one third of a *canna* of saffron cloth of Carcassonne, for the price of s.6, to be paid at his request. In witness thereof I wrote this and signed with my signet.[11]

Forcalquier. I, Jacob, owe to Ugo Teralh s.15 for one half *canna* of green cloth and a third of a *canna* of white cloth. And out of it, s.5 are owed by Solomon, my son-in-law.[12]

Owes Jacob of Relhana s.15 cor. for half a *canna* of green and for some

---

[7] P. Mayer, 'Le Livre-journal de Maitre Ugo Teralh, notaire et drapier à Forcalquier,' *Notices et Extraits des Manuscrits de la Bibliothèque Nationale*, XXXVI (1899), 150–51, 152–53. We have translated from this curious book of accounts folios 21 and 23. Originally each entry was preceded by the indication of the place of residence of the buyer, but some of the indications cannot be read because the margins of the folios have been cut. Credit entries are posted in different moneys, with no attempt at reducing every sum to a common money of account. The coins mentioned here are either deniers Tournois, with their multiples of account, or deniers royal crowned strong (royalz coronatz forz), a Provençal coin—abbreviated in the context as r. or cor.—and their multiples of account. *Cannas* and palms are measures of cloth. On the general background of the document, see *Cambridge Economic History*, II, 325–26.

[8] The question marks are Mayer's. *Canet* evidently was some sort of cloth, probably striped (*canna*, the unit of measure, means literally 'rod'), although a derivation from *cain*, 'cinder-colored,' might also be postulated.

[9] Raymon Chabaut, a notary, recorded many sales by his colleague Ugo Teralh.

[10] The entries concerning Jacon or Chaquon were written in Provençal by some assistant of Teralh; see Mayer, pp. 132–33.

[11] The entries concerning Guillem Ortolani were written by Ortolani himself, who also placed his signet at the end.

[12] Written in Hebrew, obviously by Jacob himself.

white hose which he took May 9, 1331; and he has written it above by his hand. To pay on Saint George's day [April 23]. . . .[13]

La Roche-Giron. Owes Mossen P. Richau s.6 cor. for some white hose. To pay on Saint John's day [December 27]. And he took it May 18, 1331.

Caritalles. Owes Biatris Lombarda [with] Guillem Lombart her son s.26 r. [at the rate of] 1 silver [denier] Tournois per d.13 [coronatz strong], for 2 *cannas* of blue of Saint-Pons. To pay at the fair. Record by Pons . . .[14] notary, May 23, 1331.

Peyruis. Owes P. of Limans s.18 r. for 10 palms of medley [cloth] of Toulouse. To pay before it leaves the workshop of Bt. Pelicier, tailor. And he took it May 13, 1331.

Forcalquier. Owes Isnart Barbier and Lumbarda, his wife, s.45 r. for the rest of 4 *cannas* 6 palms of camlet of Montolieu. To pay at the fair. Record of R. Chabaut, May 24, 1331.

Pierrerue. Owes Guillem de Villamus, lord of Pierrerue, s.13 d.4 r. for 2 pairs of hose of *cannet*. To pay on Saint John's day. And he took it May 25, 1331.[15]

179
From the Provençal [Languedocian][16]

Carcassonne, 1340

. . . Na Jacma, wife of En Pons Sabatier, brewer of Carcassonne, owes s.6 d.6 for 2 palms' width of vermilion [cloth] which she took on October 4. Also, she owes a medal.[17] Also, she owes . . . d.7. . . .

Senher Ber.[18] of St. Esteve, nobleman, lord of Lastours, owes s.4 which we lent him. To be paid . . . on October 3.

Mosenher the major judge of Carcassonne owes s.18 for 3 palms of medley French [cloth], which was for the lining of the cape which Maestro Crestiá Rocafort took. Paid s.18. . . .

---

[13] Written in Provençal by Ugo Teralh; it is the same transaction that Jacob certified in his own handwriting.

[14] The dots are Mayer's.   [15] All the entries above are in Provençal.

[16] C. Portal, 'Le Livre-journal de Jean Saval, marchand drapier à Carcassonne,' *Bulletin Historique et Philologique du Comité des Travaux Historiques et Scientifiques* (1901), pp. 440–41. The dots in the document are Portal's. According to him a *cana* of Carcassonne was 178 centimeters and a palm was 22 centimeters.

[17] A *mailha*, *maille*, or medal (a half denier) was the interest charged for the sale on credit. In the present book of accounting, maturing interests are posted immediately after the initial debit entry.

[18] Bernat or Bertram.

Riquart, wife of the late En Adam of Rovenay, of the city of Carcassonne,[19] owes s.10 for 2 palms of vermilion and for 1½ palms of white [cloth], which was for hose with edging for her, which she took on Wednesday, October 4. Also, she owes d.1. Also, she owes d.1. Also, she owes d.1. Also, she owes d.1. Remains [to be paid] s.10 d.4. Also, she owes d.1. Paid s.3 d.11 medal. Paid s.6 d.5 medal.

Senher Uc Garie, £ 11 for 4 canas of cameli.[20] Paid £ 11.

Senher Peyre Fabre of Pomas owes s.4 which we lent to Jacme Rog of Villefranche de Conflent. Also, he owes 15 gold dobles[21] because of what we lent him on Sunday, October 8. Paid in full.

Senher Johan de Layssa, nobleman, lord of Nescas, owes £ 14, which he told us to pay through Peyre Dalmatz, nobleman, of Pezens, for the balance [of the price] of a horse[?].[22] And they must pay in 12 days. Said [transaction] was done on October 7 in the presence of the witnesses Peyre Cortz, of the city, and Miquel Martí . . . Peyre Dalmatz. . . . Also, he owes through two letters[23] s.15 d.8. Also, he owes s.8 through a letter. Paid £ 15. . . . Peyre Sabatier.

On Monday, October 9, year 1340

Na Ramonda, wife of . . . de Cortz, of the city of Carcassonne, owes s.8 for 2¼ palms of palmela,[24] which was for hose, which she took on October 10. Paid at once s.8.

G . . . re, of Bram, owes s.71 d.10 for 3 canas . . . palms of tan [cloth], which was for a cotardia[25] . . . which he took on October 12. Peyre Chacmal made the record.[26] Also, he owes d.6. . . .

---

[19] The old cité and the more recent bourg of Carcassonne still are separate agglomerations. Probably Saval lived in the bourg, and so did his customers 'de Carcassona,' unless it is specified that they lived in the cité.

[20] From Flemish cammelinc, a textile made with wool obtained from combing? Or from Arab khamla, a textile made with mohair or camel's hair?

[21] Portal: deniers d'aur. But deniers were not gold but alloyed silver. Probably Portal misread the abbreviation d., which in this context means doblas.

[22] The question mark is Portal's.

[23] According to Portal, letras means 'messages asking the debtor to give security or to pay.' This explanation is unconvincing. More probably the 'letters' were obligatory notes written by or for the debtor, or perhaps letters of exchange.

[24] Probably a textile made from wool combings: see F. Edler, Glossary of Mediaeval Terms of Business: Italian Series, p. 202; G. De Poerck, La Draperie médiévale en Flandre et en Artois, I, 35.

[25] French cotte-hardie, a garment widely used in Languedoc.

[26] According to Portal, carte means 'pledge' by a third party. Again, the explanation is unconvincing. More probably it means 'notarial record' of the transaction.

180

From the Italian[27]

Florence, 1320

Messer Gualtierotto and Doffo de' Bardi and partners (*compagni*) are owed for cloths which at the fair of Troyes of the year 1319[28] they caused their partners in France, namely in Flanders, to buy for us; and we received these cloths in Florence in the month of April of the year 1320. And here below and thereafter we shall write the price which they cost at original purchase,[29] and how much they are tagged,[30] and the itemized expenses incurred on the said cloths. And we received the said cloths in Florence in eleven bales (*torselli*), and seven [additional pieces of] cloth came to us in the bales of the Bardi [company].[31]

Purchase of Malines cloth, made in Malines[32]

1 white from Jan Delbos, [of] 48 ells, with
white selvage, [purchased] for 19 reals,[33]
short one quarter [ell]. [Price] tagged   £ 22 s.12 Parisian

[27] A. Sapori, *Una compagnia di Calimala ai primi del Trecento*, pp. 307–10, 323–25. The Florentine company of Francesco del Bene, from whose accounting our excerpts are taken, specialized in importing and refinishing Belgian and French cloth; occasionally it also engaged in other business. Inasmuch as Sapori's book is a masterly discussion of all problems connected with the accounting and management of the Del Bene company, we have kept our footnotes down to a minimum except when dealing with details not covered by Sapori.

[28] The Del Bene *compagnia* availed itself of agents of the more powerful Bardi *compagnia* to buy cloth in the place of production. The transaction, however, was linked with one of the Champagne fairs, which served as clearing houses for contracts and bills of exchange.

[29] *Il costo che costarono di primo costo*, literally, 'the cost they cost of first cost'—a colorful tongue-twister, which we did not dare to preserve in English.

[30] *Quello che sono tacchati*. The Arte di Calimala (the gild of importers and refinishers of cloth 'from beyond the Alps') required from its members that they should tag every piece of wool cloth with the indication of the original purchasing price, plus a number of additional cost items which presumably were the same for any gild member regardless of his ability as a businessman. By comparing the price on the tag with the price demanded by the Calimala merchant, the customer in Florence could see what additional charge was made for transporting the cloth, refinishing it, and offering it for sale. The seller was free to set the final price, but the customer could decide whether this price, in his opinion, was 'just,' according to the medieval notion of 'just price.' See R. S. Lopez, 'Italian Leadership in the Mediaeval Business World,' *Journal of Economic History*, VIII (1948), 63–68.

[31] The seven pieces did not fit in the bales of Del Bene, as is stated below.

[32] On the standard measure of imitation Malines cloth, presumably the same as that of Malines cloth, see Document 50.

[33] The gold real was a French coin reckoned here at 24 silver deniers Tournois groat (real coins) or 2 sols Tournois groat (of account). In turn, the price was reckoned on the tags in Parisian money of account, pegged to the Parisian silver denier (a coin). Further complication was involved by the fact that various types of debased Parisian deniers were in circulation. Usually the Parisian deniers used in accounting are 'buoni Parigini' (Parisian deniers of good alloy) but some purchases are reckoned in 'Parigini correnti' (Parisian ordinary deniers, that is, deniers of the usual debased standard). See the tables in Sapori, *Una compagnia di Calimala*, pp. 79ff.

1 white from Pierre of Saint-Omer, [of] 48 ells,
with white selvage, [purchased] for 21 reals.
[Price] tagged   £ 24 s.18 Parisian

2 medleys of three wools,[34] of 38 ells, from
Moulin, [purchased] for 20 reals. [Price]
tagged   £ 12 s.– Parisian apiece

2 medleys of kermes, from Henrik Usina, of 38
ells, [purchased] for 39 reals. [Price] tagged   £ 23 s.3 Parisian apiece

Sum that the above-said cloths cost us, without deducting the
shortage, 99 gold reals of 24 [deniers] Tournois groat a real. And
[the price] is tagged on the cloths at [the rate of] s.23 d.3 Parisian
[for] every 24 [deniers] Tournois groat. And [in addition] s.30
Parisian have been tagged on the aforesaid cloths for 6 *bandinelle*.[35]
And the total sum is £ 117 s.16 d.6 Parisian, without deducting
the shortage.[36] And in total they are tagged £ 117 s.16 Parisian;
d.6 Parisian are deficient in the tagging.[37] The shortage amounts
to d.2½ Tournois groat. The result is that I have paid for them £ 10
d.3 Tournois groat.[38]

And the said cloths cost for God's penny[39] and [for] bringing the cloths
home and flattening and preparing[40] them s.1 Parisian. And they cost for
binding, thread, pourboire, and loading s.1 Parisian. And they cost for customs
at Malines d.6 Parisian apiece, and for customs to the duke [of Brabant] d.3

[34] *Melle* or *mellati*, from French *meslés*; these particular medleys were of three different yarns.

[35] Bands of coarse and heavy canvas used to bind a piece or bolt of cloth for transportation.

[36] *Corteza*, not explained by Sapori; but a comparison with the entry of Jan Delbos leads us to
believe that the tag made a discount because one piece of cloth was one quarter ell shorter (*corta
1 quarto*) than the standard measure.

[37] As we have seen, the cloth was paid for in reals, reckoned at 24 deniers Tournois groat, the
latter in turn being reckoned at 23 sols 3 deniers Parisian on the tags. It was hard to calculate the
equivalence down to the fractions; hence there had to be some discrepancy between the sum
obtained by adding up the tags, each of them representing only an approximation, and the sum
which would have been obtained by translating into Parisian money the total payment in reals.
When the tags indicated figures below the actual purchasing price, the cloth was 'undertagged'
(*sottotaccato*); when they indicated figures above it, the cloth was 'overtagged' (*soprataccato*).
The guild tolerated minor differences but punished overtagging whenever it exceeded the bona-
fide limit.

[38] There seems to be a slight error in this total. As a matter of fact, 99 reals at the rate mentioned
above make £9 s.18 Tournois groat. The other figures quoted—d.2½ Tournois groat for shortage;
s.30 Parisian, roughly equivalent to s.2 d.7 Tournois groat, for the *bandinelle*; d.6 Parisian,
roughly d.1½ Tournois groat, for undertagging—cannot lead to the total mentioned above.

[39] A token offering to a pious foundation, which sealed a contract as earnest money by taking
God as a witness. See C. Paoli, 'Mercato, scritta e danaro di Dio,' *Archivio Storico Italiano*, 5th
ser., XV (1895), 306ff.; Sapori, *Una compagnia di Calimala*, pp. 72ff.

[40] *Apuntarli*, cf. Old French *apointier*, to 'prepare,' and see A. Schiaffini, *Testi fiorentini del
Dugento e dei primi del Trecento*, p. 304, *s.v. appuntarsi*.

apiece; [total] s.3 d.9 Parisian.[41] Thus in total they cost at original purchase, and including all expenses, deducting the shortage, £ 10 d.9¼ Tournois groat.

Purchase of Brussels cloth, made in Brussels

2 medleys of kermes from Engelbert van den
  Noot for £ 64 [Parisian] ordinary, [short]
  1½ quarter [ell]. [Price] tagged   £ 21 s.5 Parisian apiece
2 medleys of three wools in kermes from
  Jacob of Mons for £ 75. [Price] tagged   £ 24 s.12 Parisian apiece
2 medleys from Isabet Hoeskin for £ 52.
  [Price] tagged   £ 17 s.6 Parisian apiece

  Sum that the said six [pieces of] cloth cost us at original purchase, without deducting the shortage, £ 191 [ordinary] at [the rate of] d.18 [ordinary] [for] every [denier] Tournois groat. They are worth, in Tournois groat, £ 10 s.12 d.2⅔ Tournois groat. [The price] is tagged on the cloths at [the rate of] s.23½ [Parisian ordinary for] every real of 24 [deniers] Tournois groat. They amount to £ 124 s.13 d.8 Parisian, without deducting the shortage. And [in addition] s.30 Parisian have been tagged on them for 6 *bandinelle*. Sum, £ 126 s.3 d.8. And they are tagged £ 126 s.6 Parisian, for they are overtagged s.2 d.4 Parisian. We deduct for shortage d.3⅔ Tournois groat. The result is that I have paid for them £ 10 s.14 d.5 Tournois groat.

And they cost for God's penny and [for] bringing the cloths home and refinishing and smoothing [them] s.1 Parisian. And they cost us for customs at Brussels d.2 sterling apiece, and for customs to the duke d.3 Tournois apiece, [in total] s.5 d.2 Parisian. Total sum which the said six cloths cost us £ 10 s.14 d.11⅙ Tournois groat.

Purchase of white Aalst cloth, made in Aalst

2 white from Jan Quaranta[42] for s.44 Tournois
  groat. [Price] tagged   £ 13 s.2 Parisian apiece
1 white from the same for s.22 Tournois groat.
  [Price] tagged   £ 13 s.– Parisian
1 white from Katerijn Serrenaert for s.21 Tour-
  nois groat. [Price] tagged   £ 12 s.11 Parisian

---

[41] Again, the total does not seem correct. Six times d.6 plus six times d.3 makes s.4 d.6.

[42] *Quaranta* means 'forty' in Italian. It is impossible to decide whether the name is a phonetic version of some Flemish name or a translation of the Flemish or French word meaning 'forty.'

1 white from Jean Le Provost for s.22 Tournois
groat. [Price] tagged £ 13 s.5 Parisian
1 white from Levino Golla for s.22 Tournois
groat. [Price] tagged £ 13 s.3 Parisian
2 white from Jan Lerea for s.48 Tournois groat.
[Price] tagged £ 14 s.8 Parisian apiece

Sum that the eight white cost us at first purchase, £ 8 s.19
Tournois groat. [The price] is tagged on the cloth at [the rate
of] s.23½ Parisian [for] every 24 [deniers] Tournois groat. And for
the *maletôte* of the king[43] of d.24 per pound—this was paid by the
partners in Paris, and therefore I do not take it [into account].
[In total, nothing] else but £ 8 s.19 Tournois groat, as I have paid.

Expenses incurred in Brussels on the cloth of Brussels
and Malines and Aalst and 2 whites of Ghent for wrapping

It cost s.4 d.8 Parisian for refinishing the white of Aalst with a stick
and for flattening, folding, and preparing [it]. And it cost s.10 d.8 Parisian
for expenses incurred on the Aalst cloth: that is, s.1 d.4 were for God's penny
and for pourboire which I gave to the broker of Aalst;[44] and s.6 d.8 Parisian
were for carrying the said cloth from Aalst to Brussels, including the crossing of
the Assche;[45] s.2 d.8 Parisian were for customs to the duke at d.3 Parisian apiece
and for bringing the cloth into Brussels, for every cart pays d.12 Parisian.[46]

It cost us s.6½ for its share of s.39 d.2 Parisian, which it cost us [to send]
a bundle (*favoto*) from Ghent to Brussels, including all expenses incurred
in it—and in it were 12 whites of Ghent, and 122 white felts of Ypres and
canvas for making wrapping for the Brabant cloth. For s.6 d.11 were for
bringing the said bundle out of Ghent, and s.2 Parisian for having the said
bundle tied and loaded, and s.4 Parisian for bringing [it] into Brussels with
the toll of the duke, and s.26 Parisian for carrying [it] from Ghent to Brussels.[47]

[43] A levy in exchange for which the French king guaranteed safe transit for the merchandise;
see Sapori, *Una compagnia di Calimala*, pp. 67ff., with bibliography.

[44] On medieval brokers, see J. van Houtte, 'Les Courtiers au moyen-âge,' *Revue Historique de
Droit Français et Etranger*, ser. 4, XV (1936), 105–41, and R. S. Lopez, 'Sensali nel medioevo,'
Nuova Rivista Storica, XXII (1938), 108–12. What we translate, as 'pourboire' is in Italian
danari da vino, 'money for wine.'

[45] The *Esca* cannot possibly be the Escaut, which flows west of both Aalst and Brussels, but the
small Assche River.

[46] Actually the expenses mentioned in this first paragraph are not common to all of the cloth
mentioned in the headline, but they are incurred solely by the Aalst cloth. They parallel the last
paragraphs in the lists of expenses for Malines and Brussels cloth, which we have already encountered.

[47] The four expense items quoted add up to s.38 d.11 and not to s.39 d.2 Perhaps a fifth expense
item of d.3 was inadvertently left out in the recapitulation.

It cost us s.1 d.4 Parisian for carrying the felts and canvas and linen from Brussels to Malines; and it cost s.5 Parisian for two large ropes of *meẓa* with which the said cloth was tied. It cost £1 s.10 Parisian for 40 ells of canvas which were its share for sarplers [to pack] the said cloth.

It cost us £2 s.12 Parisian for four felts of Ypres, and s.4 Parisian for its share of binding and loading and wine and thread and interlining; and it cost us s.1 Parisian for paper to make tags for the said cloth, and thread to stitch them, and indigo; and it cost s.5 Parisian for its share of the expenses and salary of a valet who went from Brussels to Paris with the two packages (*gibbe*) which were made.

It cost us £4 s.3 d.4 Parisian for carrying the said cloths from Brussels to Paris at s.4 d.2 Parisian apiece, which I paid for twenty [pieces of cloth]. And the others went under wrappings (*per invoglie*).

> Sum [of] these expenses, £10 s.3 d.6 Parisian [at the rate] of d.12 [Parisian] a [denier] Tournois groat. They are worth s.16 d.11½ Tournois groat.

> Sum that 6 pieces of Malines and 6 pieces of Brussels and 8 whites of Aalst cost us at original purchase, with all expenses, transported as far as Paris, deducting the shortage, as appears above and to the side, £30 s.11 d.8 Tournois groat.

.   .   .   .   .

> Expenses incurred in Avignon on the said cloth listed below, as will be said hereafter—and these [expenses] Messer Gualtierotto and Doffo de' Bardi and partners incurred in our behalf

It cost £70 s.12 d.4 *a fiorini*[48] paid in Avignon for eleven bales of the said cloth, for the balance of their transportation from Paris to Avignon at [the rate of] s.5 Tournois a bale, and for the key duty of Aigues-Mortes,[49] and for transportation from Avignon to Nice, and any other expense that may have been incurred in their behalf until they were loaded in a galley, according as the said Bardi [company] charged them to us. In total, including the [charge for the] exchange [transaction] from Avignon to Florence, [payment being] due on the Kalends of April of the year 1320, it cost

£72 s.1 d.– *a fiorini*

[48] The pound *a fiorini* ('by the florin') was a money of account; see our introductory Note on Coinage.

[49] A harbor tax (*chiaveria*, from Provençal *clavaria*) paid to the 'keeper of the key,' a port magistrate of Aigues-Mortes. The French kings had made Aigues-Mortes an obligatory calling place for all ships unloading and loading wares to and from French territory on the Mediterranean. A watch was kept in the Tower of Constance (the largest unit in the still extant fortifications of Aigues-Mortes) to discover ships sailing along the coast and force them to enter the port and to pay the toll.

We post the said amount in the black ledger on [folio] 221 to the credit [account] of Messer Gualtierotto and Doffo de' Bardi and partners.[50]

Expenses incurred in Pisa on the aforesaid cloth in eleven bales— and these expenses Messer Gualtierotto and Doffo de' Bardi and partners incurred in our behalf

It cost £ 237 s.4 d.8 *a fiorini*, including the [charge for the] exchange of said money from Florence to Pisa; and for freight and insurance (*rischio*) of the said 11 bales from Nice to Pisa and for unloading in Porto Pisano, and for transportation from Porto [Pisano] to Pisa, and for *gabella*[51] of the said cloth in Pisa, and for all expenses incurred in behalf of said cloth from Nice to Pisa, and for clearing [from all expenses and customs] in Pisa for sending it to Florence, in total, [payment being] due on May 4 of the year 1320— [and] we post the said amount in the black ledger on [folio] 221 to the credit [account] of Messer Gualtierotto and Doffo de' Bardi and partners

£ 237 s.4 d.8 *a fiorini*

Expenses incurred in Florence on the said cloth, that is, 11 bales and 7 [additional pieces] of cloth

For the cost of transportation and all expenses incurred in behalf of the said 7 pieces of cloth from Paris to Florence—and those [pieces] came in the bales of the Bardi [company], for they would not enter into ours—we paid on July 2, 1320, £ 21 s.17 d.– *a fiorini*

For the cost of transportation of 11 bales of the said cloth from Pisa to Florence and for crossings and *gabelle* from Pisa to Florence and for the *gabelle* of Florence—[we paid] on May 10 of the year 1320

£ 20 s.14 d.6 *a fiorini*

Sum, £ 42 s.11 d.6 *a fiorini*, [which] we transferred from the debit [account] of the 11 bales of cloth, in the black ledger, on folio 37. 22 felts of Ypres and Ghent, and 207 ells of canvas, traded in the fair of Troyes of the year 1319, cost us to be transported to Florence, including all expenses, as is shown here by items, between original cost and expenses, from [folio] 27 to this [folio] in [good] order, in total £ 4,660 s.13 d.2 *a fiorini* on February 9 of the year 1319, [all currencies being] converted [into pounds

---

[50] The black ledger (*libro nero*) included the accounts of the partners and dependents of the Del Bene company, the accounts of all those who transacted business with the company, and a number of impersonal accounts of expenses, inventory, and industrial production. The excerpts which we have translated come from the ledger of purchases and sales (*libro delle comprevendite*), which dealt with purchase and sale of whole pieces of cloth. See Sapori, *Una compagnia di Calimala*, pp. 224ff.

[51] A municipal customs duty.

a fiorini]. The said [cloth] came in 11 bales and 7 additional [pieces of] cloth which came in the bales of the Bardi [company]. And we received these cloths in Florence on April 17 and May 24 of the year 1320.

A Final Balance Sheet

181

From the Italian[52]

Florence], 1335

1335. In the name of our Lord Jesus Christ, amen. When we settled our General Accounts[53] of two years on the Kalends of July, 1332—that is, from the Kalends of July, 1330, to the Kalends of July, 1332—we found [that we had] gained more than lost, as appears from the accounting made of what we found is owed us by others and of what we have in merchandise and in other goods—of which we have made the sum here on the side; and as appears from the accounting made of what we found we owe to others—of which we have made the sum further along on folio 421. In totals we find that on the Kalends of July, 1332, we had gained more than lost in the said two years £ 41,285 s.13 *a fiorini*. And breaking [the profit] down as closely as possible, we saw that from the Kalends of July, 1330, to the Kalends of July, 1331, we had gained more than lost about £ 22,492 s.9 *a fiorini* up to said day; and from the Kalends of July, 1331, to the Kalends of July, 1332, we had gained more than lost about £ 18,792 s.4 *a fiorini* up to said day.[54]

Moreover, [for the period] from 1330 to 1332, the said partners are credited as of the Kalends of July, 1332, £ 39,954 s. . . .[55] to which amount Messer

[52] A. Sapori, *La crisi delle compagnie mercantili dei Bardi e dei Peruzzi*, pp. 218–19. It will be noted that the balance sheet is a recapitulation of several separate accountings: 'General Business' (*gienerale ragione*), which includes most of the commercial and banking transactions of the *compagnia*; 'Wool Business' (*ragione della lanagione*), covering all transactions in English wool; 'Cloth Business' (*drapperia*), covering all transactions in manufactured cloth; and some unnamed items, which perhaps included special dividends or the interest owing on the investments of the partners in the *sopracorpo* (over and above the common capital). The director of the wool and cloth businesses, Ridolfo de' Bardi, also was the head of the *compagnia*, and hence of the General Business. Probably the *compagnia*, not unlike that of the Medici at a later period, consisted of a main home office and of autonomous branches for such special activities as the wool import business and the manufacturing of cloth. All entries are reckoned 'by the florin' (*a fiorini*). On the meaning of this money of account—the *lira a fiorini* or 'pound by the florin'—see our Note on Coinage.

[53] *Nostra gienerale ragione*. Henceforth the word *ragione* will be translated as 'account,' and the word *ragionamento* as 'accounting.' The document in dating constantly omits the figure one thousand (330 for 1330, 331 for 1331, etc.), but we have restored it for greater clarity.

[54] The sum of the latter two figures is lower by £1 than the total given above.

[55] The dots are Sapori's. If the breakdown figures for the two years are correct one ought to read £ 39,954 s.11.

Ridolfo de' Bardi and partners were debited to us in the account of the Wool Business. We posted later on folio 422 a debit to him, for profits (*guadagno*) made from many [consignments] of wool brought from several lands and sold in Florence, all expenses and debts deducted. And we saw that from 1330 to 1331 £ 22,491 s.11 *a fiorini* were credited to us on said day; and from 1331 to 1332 £ 17,463 *a fiorini* were credited to us.

Moreover, [for the period] from 1330 to 1332, the said partners are credited, as of that day [July 1, 1332] £ 7,821 s.8, to which amount Messer Ridolfo de' Bardi and partners were debited to us in the account of the Cloth Business. We posted later on the said folio a debit to him, and it is for the gain (*avanzo*) made in Florence in the said Cloth Business during the said two years. And, broken down, it is as much in one year as in the other.

Moreover, [for the period] from 1330 to 1331, the partners are credited, as of that day, £ 856 *a fiorini*, which we transferred from the account on folio 290, in which that [amount] had been credited to the [partners]. And [for the period] from 1331 to 1332 the said partners are credited, as of that day, £ 500 s....[56] *a fiorini*, which we transferred from the account on the said folio, in which that [amount] had been credited to the [partners].

Moreover, [for the period] from 1330 to 1332, the partners are credited, as of that day, £ 2,000 *a fiorini*, which we transferred from the account on folio 283, in which that [amount] had been credited to the [partners].

[The total] sum credited to the [partners] on the Kalends of July, 1332, is £ 92,420 s.10 *a fiorini*,[57] of which there are, as can be seen [from the breakdowns], £ 50,753 s.12 *a fiorini* [for the period] from 1330 to 1331 and 41,666 s.18 *a fiorini* [for the period] from 1331 to 1332.

We have given to the partners on the Kalends of July, 1332, £ 50,753 s.12 *a fiorini* [for the period] from the Kalends of July, 1330, to the Kalends of July, 1331, which we posted further along on folio 322 in their credit account.

We have given to the partners on this day £ 41,666 s.18 [for the period] from the Kalends of July, 1331, to the Kalends of July, 1332, which we posted further along on said folio in their credit account.

The total that we have given them up to the Kalends of July, 1332: £ 92,420 s.14[58] *a fiorini*.[59]

[56] The dots are Sapori's.

[57] The sum of the breakdown figures ought to be £ 92,417 s.1, to which one must add the s.11 of the first lacuna and an unknown figure in soldi (between 1 and 19) of the second lacuna. At any rate, the total ought to be somewhere between £ 92,317 s.13 and £ 92,418 s.11.

[58] *Sic*; but the total is £ 92,420 s.10, as is more correctly stated above.

[59] The document occupies one side of a sheet detached from a book of which only that sheet has been preserved. On the other side there is the beginning of a detailed accounting, preceded by

Double-Entry Bookkeeping

182

From the Latin[60]

[Milan], 1396

1396

Alberico of Meda, maker of spurs, must give—Credited to the account of Marco Serrainerio on folio 6 on March 6—[for money] which he [Marco] paid to him £ 9 s.– d.–

Item—[credited] to said Marco on folio 6 on March 11—[for money] deposited for Filippo, his [Alberico's] brother, in [the bank of] Paolino of Osnago £ 15 s.– d.–

Item—[credited] to Giovanni of Dugnano, on folio 8 on March 24—[for money] which he [Giovannino] ordered to be given him [Alberico or Filippo?] in [the bank of] Andrea Monte £ 18 s.– d.–

Item—[credited] to Marco Serrrainerio, on folio 6 on May 13—[for money] deposited in [the bank of] Mano, [son] of Ser Jacopo

£ 15 s.– d.–

Item—paid in his behalf on the aforesaid day to Pietrino Bazuella—posted in the cash account on folio 23 £ 10 s.– d.–

1396

He [*Alberico*] *must have*—Debited to the account of Merceries on folio 15 on February 24—for 6 dozen fine jeweled spurs, at £ 4 s.10 imperial per dozen, amounting to

£ 27 s.– d.–

Item, posted as above, for 6 dozen small fine jeweled spurs, at s.54 per dozen £ 16 s.4 d.–

Item, posted as above, for 6 dozen Cordovan spurs, at s.48 per dozen, amounting to £ 14 s.8 d.–

Item, posted as above, for 4 dozen spurs with a prick, at s.26 per dozen, amounting to £ 5 s.4 d.–

Item, posted as above, for 4 dozen quality spurs with thick arms, at s.23 per dozen £ 4 s.12 d.–

Item, posted as above, for 4 dozen spurs of medium quality, at s.20 per dozen £ 4 s.– d.–

the interesting remark that the balance sheet for 1330–1332 was prepared as late as January 1, 1334, 'owing to the fact that many accounts were kept back by our factors abroad, who delayed too long their return, and for many other reasons.'

[60] T. Zerbi, *Il mastro a partita doppia di una azienda mercantile del Trecento*, pp. 64–65. The excerpts are from a ledger of the Catalan branch of the Serrainerio and Dugnano company. The home office, headed by Marco Serrainerio, one of the governing partners, was in Milan. The other governing partner, Giovannino Dugnano, usually operated in Lodi. Lanfranco Serrainerio, Marco's brother, headed the Catalan branch. The company also employed another brother, Aliprando Serrainerio. It availed itself of commission agents in Genoa, Pisa, and Venice, and it had accounts in several Milanese banks.

Item—for the [balance] posted to the credit account of the joint profit [of the partnership] on folio 20 on January 3, 1397   £ 4 s.8 d.–[61]

Total £ 71 s.8

Andreolo of Concorezzo must give— Credited to the account of Giovannino of Dugnano on folio 8 on March 17   £ 16 s.– d.–
Item—[credited] to Marco Serrainerio on folio 6 on March 31—[for money] which he [Marco] paid to him   £ 4 s.16 d.–
Item—[credited] to said Marco on folio 6 on April 28—[for money] deposited in [the bank of] Manno, [son] of Ser Jacopo   £ 10 s.– d.–
Item—[credited] to said Marco, on folio 6 on May 6—[for money] deposited in [the bank of] Paolino of Osnago   £ 6 s.8 d.–
Item—[credited] to said Marco on folio 6 on May 16—[for money] deposited in [the bank of] Paolino of Osnago for the remainder   £ 12 s.– d.–
Item—for the balance posted to the common credit, profit, and loss [of the partnership] on folio 20 on aforesaid day   £ – s.7 d.6

Total £ 49 s.11 d.6

He [*Andreolo*] *must have*—Debited to the account of Merceries on folio 18 on March 6—for 12 thousand needles for sacks, marked Antonio   £ 10 s.16 d.–
Item, posted as above on aforesaid day, for 12 thousand long needles, marked Masso, at s.13 [per thousand]   £ 7 s.16 d.–
Item, posted as above, for 24 thousand long needles, marked Stefano, at s.12 d.9 [per thousand]   £ 15 s.6 d.–
Item, posted as above, for 12 thousand old woman's needles . . .[62] marked with a ship, at s.8 [per thousand]   £ 4 s.16 d.–
Item, posted as above, for 12 thousand old woman's needles, large, marked with a ship, at s.12 d.9 [per thousand]   £ 7 s.14 d.–
Item, posted as above, for 3 thousand needles for fine shoes, at s.21 d.6 [per thousand]   £ 3 s.4 d.6

Total £ 49 s.11 d.6

---

[61] The sum is omitted, but the total matches that of the debit. In the following account, however—that of Andreolo of Concorezzo—there are two errors which cancel each other out. The total of the debit column should be £ 49 s.12 d.6; but the amount posted for the next-but-last item should be £ 7 s.13 d.–. If we correct the latter item, we also obtain the correct total—£ 49 s.11 d.6. for the debit column.

[62] *Agugarium de veglia cecit.* . . . The lacuna prevents us from catching the meaning of the last word.

183
From the Latin[63]

[Milan], 1396

Account of the baskets . . .[64] of figs sent from Valencia by
Lanfranco to Genoa to Marco de Negri and Maffio of Mercato

Said baskets . . . of figs must give—
Credited to the account of Lanfranco
on folio 4 on March 1—for the aforesaid figs sent by him from Valencia to
the aforesaid Marco and Maffio in the
ship of Salvatore Orte—they cost
£ 70 s.5 d.7 Barcelonese—sent in the
year 1396—they are worth [in converted currency]　　£ 149 s.18 d.6
Item—credited to the account of
Marco de Negri and Maffio of
Mercato on folio 34 on July 23—
[for money] which they entered as
having been paid for the freight of
132½ baskets which they received
from Valencia in the ship of Salvatore Orte: £ 45 s.18 d.9. And for the
customs [at the rate of] d.3 per
pound: £ 2 s.8 d.11. And for unloading and carrying them to the
warehouse:[65] £ 3 s.13. And for the
ripa.[66] £ 2 s.9 d.6. And for brokerage: £ 1 s.8. And for the rent of the
warehouse engaged for said figs:
£ 3 s.8. And for their commission:
£ 2 s.2. Total £ 61 s.6 d.2 Genoese.
They are worth [in converted
currency]　　　　£ 78 s.9 d.6

They [*the baskets*] *must have*—
Debited to the account of Marco de
Negri and Maffio of Mercato on folio
34 on July 23—for 129 baskets of
figs sold by them [Marco and Maffio]
up to the day . . . at s.30 Genoese per
basket—in all £ 193 s.10 Genoese—
plus 4 small baskets, sold at s.16 [for
the lot of four]. Total, £ 194 s.6
Genoese. They are worth [in converted currency]　　£ 248 s.14 d.–

---

[63] Zerbi, *Il mastro a partito doppia*, pp. 234–35. The credit and debit columns are not balanced.

[64] The dots here and below are Zerbi's. The debit account shows that there were 129 large baskets and 4 small baskets.

[65] *Volta*, the characteristic domed rooms at the ground level or slightly below ground where wares were stored and sometimes business was transacted. Structures of this kind are still visible in the old section of Genoa and other Mediterranean towns.

[66] A tax paid at the shore or in the proximity of it (*ripa* means 'river bank' or 'seashore').

184

Benedetto Cotrugli, *On Commerce and the Perfect Merchant*
From the Italian[67]

[Naples, 1458]

ON THE METHOD[68] OF KEEPING RECORDS IN THE MANNER OF MERCHANTS

The pen is an instrument so noble and excellent that it is absolutely necessary not only to merchants but also in any art, whether liberal, mercantile, or mechanical. And when you see a merchant to whom the pen is a burden or who is inept with the pen, you may say that he is not a merchant. And [a good merchant] not only must be skilled in writing but also must keep his records (*scritture*) methodically. And with these records we plan to deal in the present chapter. For no merchant ought to transact his business by heart, unless he were like King Cyrus, who could call by name every person in his entire army, which was innumerable. And in the same way Lucius Scipio, the Roman, and Cynea, the legate of Pyrrhus, the day after entering Rome, greeted every member of the senate by his name. But since this is not possible for everyone, we shall turn to the practice of [keeping] records. These not only preserve and keep in the memory [all] transactions, but they also are a means to avoid many litigations, quarrels, and scandals. And they also cause literate men to live thousands upon thousands of years. . . .[69]

Mercantile records are the means to remember all that a man does, and from whom he must have, and to whom he must give, and the costs of wares, and the profits, and the losses, and every other transaction on which the merchant is at all dependent. And it should be noted that knowing how to keep good and orderly records teaches one how to draw contracts, how to do business, and how to obtain a profit. And undoubtedly a merchant must not rely upon memory, for such reliance has caused many persons to err. Of this speaks Averroes, the commentator. When he wished to chide Avicenna, who was relying upon his own intelligence, he said: 'Two things cause men to err in natural matters, reliance upon [one's own] intelligence, and ignorance of logic.'

Therefore the merchant ought to keep three books, that is, the ledger

[67] Cotrugli, *Della mercatura et del mercante perfetto*, fol. 36–38.

[68] *Ordine*, used by Cotrugli in the double meaning of 'order' and 'method' or 'system.' Here and hereafter we shall adopt the translation which best fits the context.

[69] We omit here a few flowery sentences in praise of the art of writing and of Carmenta, Evander's mother, 'who first invented the pen.'

(*quaderno*), the journal (*giornale*), and the memorandum (*memoriale*). And the ledger ought to have its alphabetical [index] through which one may quickly find any account written in the said ledger. And it ought to be marked *A;* and on its first sheet [the merchant] ought to invoke the name of God and [to state] what it deals with and of how many sheets it consists. And he also will mark by the said [letter] *A* his journal, alphabetical [index], and memorandum.

In the journal you shall reconstruct methodically all [your] capital, item by item, and you shall carry it forward in the ledger. Then you shall be able, as you please, to begin your management with that capital and to do business with it.[70] And when you have finished writing the said ledger, you shall settle all accounts opened in it, extract from them all balances (*resti*) to the debit or likewise to the credit, [and carry forward the balances] in the last sheet after the last account. Then, when you carry them forward in a new ledger, give every balance its separate account. And you shall mark that ledger by [the letter] *B*, also marking by the same [letter] the new journal, alphabetical [index], and memorandum [corresponding] to it. Always continue like that successively from one book to another, up to the last syllable[71] of the alphabet, always invoking in the first sheet of a ledger the name of God, etc., as above.

In the memorandum you ought to note every evening or morning before you leave your home everything you have traded and transacted on that day because of your commerce or of [any] other necessary and incidental [expense]—such as sales, purchases, payments, receipts, remittances, orders of payment (*assegnamenti*), exchanges, expenses, promises, and any other business—before any account originates from it in the journal. For many things happen while [business] is transacted without making accounts in the journal.

And you should further note that you ought to keep always with you a small notebook (*libriccino piccolo delle ricordanze*) in which you shall note day by day and hour by hour even the minute [detail] of your transactions, so that later you may at your best convenience create accounts in the memorandum book or the journal. And always exert yourself to carry the accounts, or part of them, forward from the said memorandum into the journal the same day or the following one; then carry them forward in the ledger daily.

And at the end of every year you shall check the ledger against the accounts

---

[70] 'These, to our knowledge, are the first words that have been written on double-entry accounting,' says Melis, *Storia della ragioneria*, p. 605. The practice of double-entry accounting, of course, antedated this first theoretical statement by much more than a hundred years.

[71] *Sic*; but read 'letter.'

in the journal, making the trial balance (*bilancione*) of them, and carrying forward all profits or losses (*avanzi overo disavanzi*) in your capital account.[72]

Further, you ought to keep two more books, one to copy the statements (*conti*) which are sent out, the other to copy the letters you sent, [including] even those of the smallest importance.

Also you must keep your writing desk in order, and note on all lett receive where they come from, and of what year, and of what day acc as you have received them daily. And then every month you shall make bundles of those letters, and you shall put away each bundle into the drawer of the proper class in your writing desk, together with all other records— such as contracts, instruments, chirographs, [bills of] exchange, statements, policies, etc.—keeping them there as true merchants are wont to do.

And for the sake of brevity let it be enough to have said this about the method [of keeping] books and records; for if I wanted to tell everything here in detail I would be too long-winded—and it is almost impossible to explain it, since one can hardly learn it from a book without oral instruction. And therefore I warn and encourage any merchant to take pleasure in knowing how to keep his books well and methodically. And whoever does not know [how to do this], let him get instruction, or else let him keep an adequate and expert young bookkeeper (*quaderniero*). Otherwise your commerce will be chaos, a confusion of Babel—of which you must beware if you cherish your honor and your substance.

[72] Obviously the trial balance will be regarded as accurate when the 'profits or losses,' that is, the credit and debit in the capital account, are balanced. We must not confuse it with the final balance sheet (*saldo* or *bilancio saldo*) which is made at the closing of the books when a partnership or a *ragione* is terminated; see Documents 181 and 196.

CHAPTER XXIII

COMMERCIAL CORRESPONDENCE

THERE IS NO better key to the psychology of the merchant than his correspondence. Letters illumine hidden angles of private lives, express frank opinions on politics, religion, and society, and above all discuss business matters more openly than other documents. Their careless handwriting, their slangy style, their frequent reference to matters mentioned in other letters or whispered in secret make them often hard to interpret. But their immediacy and spontaneity are ample compensations and often make them delightful reading.

Two collections of merchants' letters of the sixteenth century have been published in English translation, but for the Middle Ages we have only originals and the larger part of them is still unprinted.[1] The archives of the Datini *compagnia* in Prato contain some 15,000 items of correspondence between the home office and its branches and correspondents abroad. We have a great many letters of certain other Tuscan companies of merchant-bankers, but some companies are not represented at all in the archives. Only a handful of letters from regions other than Tuscany and from business partnerships and associations other than the *compagnie* are known to survive. This uneven distribution of the material is reflected somewhat in our selections, but we have endeavored to give examples from all regions and types of business.[2]

Some of the earliest business letters that have come down to us were included in notarial chartularies. Informal duplicates probably were sent out by mail, but the original was notarized to make it more solemn and binding. These dry, short notarized letters, which usually contain only specific instructions, bear to later holograph letters of the same kind the same relation as notarial contracts of exchange and orders of payment to holograph bills of exchange and promissory notes. Documents 185 and 186 are examples of the notarial and of the informal letter of this type.[3]

Documents 187 and 188 also are matter-of-fact letters aimed at giving specific instructions, but they are richer in interesting details. Antonio Pacheron tells his relative and correspondent, Troilo Pacheron, what transactions he wants to be carried

---

[1] G. R. B. Richards, *Florentine Merchants in the Age of the Medici*; V. von Klarwill, *The Fugger News-Letters*. Richards's translation is not always satisfactory. Short excerpts from the letters of a Venetian merchant of the fifteen century are found in English translation in F. C. Lane, *Andrea Barbarigo, Merchant of Venice*.

[2] A list of published business letters of the Middle Ages is found in A. Sapori, *Studi di storia economica medievale*, 2d ed., p. 287, note 5. See also the bibliography in R. H. Bautier, 'Marchands siennois et draps d'outremont aux foires de Champagne,' *Annuaire-Bulletin de la Société de l'Histoire de France* (1945), pp. 87–107.

[3] It is worth noting that the informal letter of which we give the translation is preserved in two identical copies. Duplication served much the same purposes as notarization.

out, but he gives Troilo great latitude in choosing means and frankly expresses his hopes, fears, and wishes. Likewise, Alvise Ca' da Mosto—who, incidentally, is the author of an engrossing description of exploration in Africa—explains carefully his plans and expectations to the shipmaster and merchant who is about to carry his wares to Flanders.[4]

Document 189 has extraordinary interest, although it is an ordinary business letter aimed at informing and appeasing discontented creditors. Antoniotto Usodimare endeavors to persuade them to be patient in awaiting payment by telling them of the wonders he has seen in tropical Africa. The letter has long been regarded as a valuable record of exploration and geographic lore.[5]

Documents 190 and 191 both take us to Tunis at a moment when a serious incident has caused a sudden break in the relations between Pisa and the Almohad government of the town. The Pisan merchants have been forced to flee, 'leaving both their goods and their debts,' but the incident is not expected to last. Their Arab correspondents send them the latest political news, reports of unfinished business, and claims for money still owing. The letters through their many innuendos reveal the existence of close relations between Christian and Muslim merchants, all of whom join in legal and sometimes illegitimate business.[6]

All of the remaining selections (Documents 192–196) are from the regular correspondence between partners of Tuscan *compagnie*. The letters are so full that their backgrounds cannot be summarized here, but we have endeavored to make them more easily understandable through a large number of footnotes. The correspondents write about market conditions, business prospects, internal management of their partnership, political events, and often their personal problems and feelings.[7]

Notarized Letters and Informal Notes

185

From the Latin[8]

Genoa, May 6, 1205

To his beloved friend Ceso, son of the late Aldobrandino Fattinelli of Lucca, Bonattino Inzuppatoio [sends] greetings and love.

I am sending [word] to you to request your nobility by every means I can, and as I have the strongest confidence in you, that as soon as you have seen this writing you return ... to my brother-in-law in their entirety all those

[4] A translation of the book of Ca' da Mosto is included in R. Kerr, *A General History and Collection of Voyages and Travels*, Vol. II.

[5] On the background of this letter, see the bibliography in R. S. Lopez, 'European Merchants in the Medieval Indies: the Evidence of Commercial Documents,' *Journal of Economic History*, III (1943), 167ff.

[6] On the background of these letters, see the bibliography in G. Rossi-Sabatini, *L'espansione di Pisa nel Mediterraneo fino alla Meloria*.

[7] The editors of these letters usually give the background in their prefaces, from which we have drawn the larger part of the information supplied in our footnotes.

[8] M. W. Hall-Cole, H. G. Krueger, R. G. Reinert, R. L. Reynolds, eds., *Giovanni di Guiberto* (*1200–1211*), I, 477–78. The dots in the document are theirs.

goods which Enrico Antelminelli[9] gave us in *accomendacio* at Palermo and which he sent me through you, just as you were to give them to me. And these goods are 1,000 rabbit skins and 600 less 21 fox [skins], and other goods of mine if you have any.

Witnesses: Ceso Moreno, Ottone Gualfredo, [both] Lucchese. Done in Genoa in the warehouse (*sub volta*) of the Fornari, May 6, about nones.

186

From the French[10]

London, [early fourteenth century]

To his very dear and trusted friend Giacomino of Recco, merchant of Genoa, Sir John Trape, furrier of London, greetings and good love.

Dear friend:

I beg you, as well as I rely upon you, in regard to the 800 furs of powdered miniver[11] and to the 1,000 furs of black budge[12] which you were to have ordered from me on the thirtieth now past—and at that time you did not want to do so because your money was not available as you wished—that you please order them from me now through the bearer of this letter. And the same bearer will make out a good receipt for the money above mentioned. May God protect you.

Issued in London on the eighteenth day of the month of September.

Letters of Instruction

187

From the Italian (Venetian dialect)[13]

[Venice], February 11, 1431

1431, February 11. Copy of a letter with the seal of St. Mark,[14] written to Ser Troilo Pacheron in Fermo, sent by Ser Antonio Pacheron.

[9] Probably an ancestor of Castruccio Castracani degli Antelminelli, lord of Lucca and head of the Ghibelline party in Tuscany in the early fourteenth century.

[10] R. S. Lopez, 'I primi passi della colonia genovese in Inghilterra,' *Bollettino Ligustico per la Storia e la Cultura Regionale*, II (1950), 69–70. The article gives further details on the background of the document.

[11] *Miniver pure*: from old French *menever poudré*, according to the *New English Dictionary* (Oxford). Godefroy, however, does not include the word in his dictionary of medieval French. The usual old French expression was *menu vair*.

[12] *Buge noir*, black budge or lambskin, perhaps from *bouge*, 'bag' or 'purse.'

[13] Unprinted. Archivio di Stato, Venice. *Troillo Pacheron, Account of Fermo*, ledger A. We are indebted to Frederic C. Lane for this document and the transcription of it.

[14] *Bolà di San Marcho:* apparently the original had a mark or an appended bull with St. Mark's image.

Dearest:

The purpose of this letter is just to let you have my opinion concerning the grain, which is the following: if you can get it at the prices you mentioned in your letters or even at 4 soldi more, you should buy 1,000 *staia* for my account (*per mia razon*). . . .[15] If after reading the present letter you deem it best, I shall appreciate your beginning to buy, because I fear that if you delay, money transfers may rise in price. Do me this favor if you can and please, for I shall forward the payment by the ships of Ziotarolo and Andrea da Teia, which will set sail again as soon as they have unloaded, God willing, safely and with profit. I should gladly have made the remittance by bill of exchange but I have not found a taker—and to send the payment by land would not be convenient for me. Once you have made the purchase, if you can send me the grain before the above-mentioned ships arrive, I should appreciate it. And I have nothing further to say in the present letter because the said ships will inform you more fully.

May Christ bless you and keep you and make you prosper.

188

From the Italian (Venetian dialect)[16]

[Venice, 1478?]

In the name of Christ.

I, Alvise da Ca' da Mosto, am making a memorandum for you, Messer Giovanni Saba Contarini, on your going on the voyage to Flanders; and I pray God our Lord to keep you safe through everything and to let you have honor and good profit.

As you know, I have loaded at your order[17] 3 casks of malmsey of the usual sort, of 12 *quarte* each, in your galley for London. They are marked by an iron seal impressed in the front and also marked by your iron seal. These wines are regarded as very good, clean, and clear. Kindly sell them in England for the best price you can get, acting with them as you would with your own.

---

[15] We omit here a sentence which contains obscure references to earlier instructions.

[16] Alvise da Ca' da Mosto, *Le navigazione atlantiche*, ed. by R. Caddeo, 2d ed., pp. 347–48; facsimile of the document, p. 320; general bibliography on Ca' da Mosto, pp. 121–31, to which one may add the English translation cited above, footnote 4. The present document has the form of a letter, but it probably was handed personally by Ca' da Mosto to Saba Contarini as the latter was about to sail in one of the Venetian state galleys of the regular navigation line to Flanders and England. It was a widespread practice of Venetian merchants to entrust wares to captains of galleys or to passengers. On the Venetian navigation line, see J. Sottas, *Les Messageries maritimes de Venise aux XIVe et XVe siècles*; A. A. Ruddock, *Italian Merchants and Shipping in Southampton, 1270–1600*.

[17] *A ordine vostro*, that is, addressed to Contarini as if he had been the owner.

For I shall be satisfied with everything you do, because, since we regard each other as true brothers, I am quite certain that you will do with my things as you would with your own. From the proceeds of these wines you will have to pay the freight just as you do for your own.

Also I have delivered to you a small bundle of handkerchiefs of sheer silk, which are 4 bolts (*maҳi*); they weigh 49 lbs. net by our short pound; they are packed in a stitched wrapper of hemp, and tied; [they are] marked in the front. Since this silk is sheer, as I have said, I am certain you will sell it as Malaga silk. And since it is a small quantity and you will not call at Malaga, as I presume, because of the war of the king of Castile, I expect you will not fail to get a good price. Nevertheless, be free to do with it as if it were your own, for I have great confidence in you, etc.

From the proceeds of these wines and silk, then, I should like you first of all to obtain for me three curtains of fine and fast colored satin, by the yard (*a braҳa*), of the kind and size pictured and noted in a sheet of paper which I gave to you, where the length and width are described. Try to the best of your ability to see that I am well served, as I am certain you will because of the love that is between us. Also I want you to have some fine [pieces of] pewter bought for me in London, of the kind and quality specified in a slip enclosed in this letter. And kindly give me a special report of the progress you have made.

Offering myself ever to do better things for you; may our Lord always be with you.

Memorandum from me, Alvise da Ca' da Mosto,
to you, Messer Giovanni Saba Contarini, for London.

The Lures of Exploration

189

From the Latin[18]

[Lisbon?], December 12, 1455

In the name of Christ. December 12, 1455.

Honorable brothers:

I can well imagine how much you know that has been written ill of

[18] P. Zurla, *Di Marco Polo e degli altri viaggiatori veneziani*, II, 154–56. Later editions of this letter—of which only a very corrupt copy is extant—are listed in *Navigazioni atlantiche*, p. 124. The letter indicates that Usodimare, like Ca' da Mosto, was in close touch with the Portuguese explorers and their leader, Prince Henry the Navigator. But he also was well aware of the older Genoese tradition which went as far back as the attempt of the Vivaldi brothers to find a western route to the Indies in 1291. On Genoese explorations in Africa see, R. S. Lopez, *Studi sull'economia genovese nel medio evo*, pp. 1–60, with bibliographical information.

me; and it is not enough that I keep what is yours but I also have to visit you with bad [news] about your [property]. Still, at a time when I was unable to send you any good news, and when I truly had in mind to come to you and to place myself in your hands and [in those] of the other creditors, that fortune of mine, while I was feeling so much shame that I would rather die than live, dispatched me in a caravel to the territory of Guinea. And I traveled more than eight hundred miles beyond where any Christian had ever gone; and having found the Gambia River in very full tide, I went upstream, knowing that in that country one gathers gold and grains of paradise.[19] Those fishermen launched attacks against me with bows, that is, with poisoned arrows, believing that we were enemies; and I, seeing that they were not willing to receive us, was forced to go back. And then, close to seventy leagues from there, a certain noble Negro lord gave me thirty-one head [of slaves] and some elephant tusks and parrots, with a little bit of civet, [in exchange] for certain objects presented to him. And after learning my intention he sent along with us his secretary with certain slaves to the most serene king of Portugal. And this secretary is undertaking peace negotiations with that king of Gambia. And the most serene king [of Portugal], having seen that secretary, allowed me to go to those regions, but only with [that man].

Therefore I am now taking over[?][20] a caravel, in God's name,[21] and I am going in it, and shall have one of the cargoes [belonging] to the Infante [Prince Henry the Navigator]; and I shall get ready for whatever may come. And within ten days I shall send this ambassador in the caravel to go to negotiate peace. He himself leaves all his [property] with me, so that I may invest it with my own. Therefore, O Lord,[22] it behooves me to see what this fortune of mine decrees this time. Were it not so much against me, I could live with great. . . .[23]

[You ought] to hear what this secretary tells; if I wrote it down for you, you would think it is nonsense. But altogether there remained three hundred leagues overland for us to reach the land of Prester John—I do not say him in person, but rather the beginning of his territory. And if I could have stayed longer, I would have met the captain of [the troops] of my king, who

[19] Pungent seeds of a West African zingiberaceous plant, popularly called wild pepper and used as a substitute for pepper.

[20] *Compello* is certainly a mistake of the copyist.

[21] The expression may be merely a pious invocation or it may be a reference to the religious character of the enterprises carried out under the direction of Henry the Navigator.

[22] *Domine* is perhaps a mistake of the copyist for *Domini*, the creditors to whom the letter is addressed.

[23] Evidently the copyist left out a few words here.

was just six days [distant] from us with a hundred men and with five Christians from Prester John's [territory].[24] And I have spoken with people from his army.

And I met there a man of our own nation—[a descendant], I believe, of [one of the crew of] the galley of the Vivaldi, which was lost 170 years ago.[25] And he told me—and this secretary confirms it—that nobody remained from that stock but he. And the other things he told me—about the elephants, unicorns, civets, and other most strange things, and about men with tails who eat their children—would seem impossible to you.

Believe me, if I had sailed one day further, I should have lost the Polar Star. And the reason why I could not stay longer was that I lacked food—and their food no white man can in any wise eat without falling sick or dying, those Negroes born in these parts being an exception. The air, however, is excellent, and the country the most beautiful under heaven, and almost equinoctial; that is, in the month of July days have twelve and a half hours and nights eleven and a half.

I am reporting to you all this and I am certain that you are going to say that you would sooner get back your goods and those of the others than hear this jumble. You ought to have patience for six months, and then . . .[26] because I am having myself insured, which was quite unnecessary since those seas are as [calm] as our dock.

The present letter should be for all the creditors who believe—and you together with them—that if I had had the means, I would have satisfied them with a payment of 60 percent [and] I would not have thrown myself into such an adventure with one caravel alone. Perhaps [all this] will be for the better. Therefore they should have patience for the love of God.

Yours, Antonio Usodimare

Solidarity of Muslim and Christian Merchants

190

From the Italian translation of the Arabic[27]

Tunis, [1201?]

In the name of God, the Clement and Merciful!

To the most noble and distinguished sheikh, the virtuous and honored

[24] To reach the territory of Prester John (who by the fifteenth century had been identified with the king of Ethiopia) and to join with him in an attack against the Muslims was the constant dream of Henry the Navigator. Moreover, a legend had slowly formed to the effect that one of the two galleys of the Vivaldi brothers in 1291 had reached Ethiopia but that the crew had been detained there by Prester John.

[25] *Sic*; but actually 164 years.   [26] Again the copyist must have left out a few words.

[27] M. Amari, *I diplomi arabi del R. Archivio Fiorentino*, pp. 50–52. The letter is one of several

Pace, Pisan; may it please God to preserve his honor, to decree his salvation, and to help and to assist him in the performance of what is good! Hilal ibn Khalifat al-Jamunsi, your affectionate, well-wishing friend, to him who follows a good path [sends] greetings and the mercy and blessings of God.

After [wishing] that He may give you salvation, my dearest friend, [let me recall how] you departed on the day of the event which took place by decree and will of the Most High God, Whose orders cannot be resisted and against Whose judgment one strives in vain; and you left in Tunis both your goods and your debts.

Through 'Abd-Allah al-Zagag I had sold to the people of the *tarida*[28]— Greco, Tegrimo[?],[29] and Ildebrando—1,031 skins. Total price, at the rate of 16 dinars a hundred, 165 dinars. Then I sold to Tegrimo and Ildebrando 605 skins for the price of 90 dinars 7 dirhams in cash. And I had from Greco his third part of the price of the 1,000 skins, and from Ildebrando the third part of this price and his half of the 90 dinars 6 dirhams,[30] so that I remain the creditor of Tegrimo for 100 dinars $3\frac{1}{2}$ dirhams of the mint. Moreover, Greco had given security to me for Ibn Qasum, and when leaving he did not pay me anything.

Further I am letting you know, my dear friend Pace, that I had credits against the people who smuggled in the steel, among whom Sabi owed me 73 dinars.[31] With this, since it was my own, I bought copper at the auction sale. But after his departure, when I demanded the said sum, I was told that I had no credits against him. Yet it appears from a record that 166 dinars $1\frac{1}{2}$ dirhams in cash are owing to me under the name of Bukir al-Akrash by Sabi and his partners who smuggled in the steel. I have obtained from the

which Tunisian merchants sent Pace, son of Corso, of Pisa, after a serious incident which led to the seizure of all of the goods owned by Pisans in Tunis. The incident had been provoked by the Pisans themselves, who committed acts of piracy against the Genoese and the Tunisians themselves in the waters of Tunis. As one can see from the letters, in spite of this and other incidents the merchants of Pisa and their Muslim correspondents were closely united in all kinds of business. On the general background, see A. Schaube, *Handelsgeschichte der romanischen Völker des Mittel-meergebiets bis zum Ende der Kreuzzüge*, pp. 295ff.

[28] A merchant ship of a type intermediate between the galley and the cog.

[29] Amari transliterates this name as *Al.d.k.r.m* and makes no attempt at finding an Italian equivalent. The most plausible transcription is Tegrimo (a common name in Lucca and not an unusual one in Pisa) preceded by *al*, the Arabic article. Another possible transcription is Aldighierino.

[30] *Sic*: but read 7 dirhams?

[31] This Sabi may have been the same person as one Sabi, dragoman, who appears in another letter as the intermediary in a sale of skins to other Pisan merchants. The steel had to be 'smuggled in,' and the operation had to be carried out through intermediaries and under the cover of fictitious names, because the export of war materials from Christian to Muslim countries was forbidden by law; see Document 167.

sheikh[32] 9 quintals of steel at the rate of 7 dinars the quintal, so that I still am creditor for 20 dinars.[33] The truth is that Ibn Qasum does not pay what he owes us and demands what we owe him.[34]

Therefore we beg you to get information about these men—who is dead and who is alive? For Sabi, to whom I am indebted for the copper, already was my debtor—so that the rest of my credit with him, I mean after [deducting] the copper, is 7 dinars. If he is no longer living, [before his death] he may have entrusted you by letter [to settle] his debt.

Because of the arrest of Greco after your departure from here, I have received nothing of what he guaranteed for Ibn Qasum.

All of your goods here are under seizure. Nobody has taken any of them, and the sultan has forbidden us to touch them until the owners come.

To him who follows a good path [I send] greetings and the mercy and the blessings of God.

[*Address*]

To the most illustrious, most honorable sheikh, the virtuous and dear friend . . . Pace, Pisan, may God decree his salvation and give him plenty of goods!

191
From the Italian translation of the Arabic[35]

Tunis, [1201?]

In the name of God, the Clement and Merciful!

To the illustrious sheikhs, my revered and dear friends Ser Forestano, Ser Viviano,[36] Ser Benenato Cerchi, and Ser Albano; may God grant them salvation and keep them under His guard! Your friend who relies upon your affection, the pilgrim[37] Sadaqa, dealer in leather in Tunis—may God protect that city—sends you the very fullest greetings.

---

[32] Amari thinks that the sheikh in question must be the head of the customs house where the goods of the Pisans were kept under seizure. The letter, however, states that nothing had been released. More probably the sheikh is some one else who did not wish to be mentioned by name in an affair of dubious legality.

[33] The figure seems incorrect. Probably other data, not mentioned in the letter, were taken into account.

[34] Other correspondents of Pace also make complaints against Ibn Qasum, who, as Schaube remarks, was probably a partner or a commission agent of Pace.

[35] Amari, *Diplomi arabi*, pp. 60–62. The letter belongs to the same group and has the same background as Document 190. It is less friendly than the other; yet at the same time it shows greater concern for the interruption of commercial relations. The interruption did not last long.

[36] Arabic *F.f.ian*, which Amari tentatively interprets as Papiano. But this classical name was obsolete in the thirteenth century; Viviano was much more common in Tuscany at that period.

[37] To have completed a pilgrimage to the Holy Places was a title of honor which a Muslim treasured during his whole life.

And he reminds you that you bought from him 1,485 lambskins through 'Uthman ibn 'Ali, dragoman, for the sum of 251 dinars 6 dirhams in cash—of which I did not receive a single dirham! Then, owing to the fact that the *musattah* captured the ship at the mouth of the canal,[38] you left without paying me at all; nor could I take anything of what you left at the customs house.

Therefore your kindness is requested to act as you should as gentlemen and prominent merchants, [that is], to come [back] to satisfy my credit against you. For we asked in the customs house, I and others like me, [that they pay us] from what assets of yours may be kept there; and they answered us that they would pay us nothing unless you first came to take all your goods and to honor our credits.

And if you do not come here now, we hope you will write us letters and send someone entrusted with getting your goods out of the customs house and paying what is owing to us. Let the one you send carry an order of the prince of Pisa, with letters of the latter [to our authorities] and with powers of attorney from you. It would be [still] bettter if you came in person. Commodities here are cheap. Moreover, [there is] security and prosperity as before you left, and [indeed] more of it. And you will be treated with every regard and honor as has been customary in the past.

Ser Forestano, whom may God honor, is requested to go to see Sigiero Barba, Pisan, and to give him special greetings from the sheikh Yusuf, dealer in leather—the man from whom he bought 500 lambskins for 80 dinars through the dragoman whose name, in Frankish language, is Azmat Dafraka[39] —and to beg him to come with you in order to pay [the sheikh Yusuf] this sum, as is your practice and that of honorable merchants. We do not need to press you to do it, nor do we need to insist more urgently because your integrity is well known. [Indeed], we write down [in our records] that you will arrive soon, if it please God; may He safely guide you. And we greet you.

[*Address*]

To the illustrious sheikhs, revered friends, Ser Forestano and partners, Pisans, their admirer, the pilgrim Sadaqa, dealer in leather in Tunis—may God protect it!

[38] The incident had been provoked by a clash between Pisan, Genoese, and Tunisian ships (the *musattah* was a ship) in the canal linking the lagoon of Tunis with the sea.

[39] Apparently a European: Ansaldo or Arnaldo de Franchi?

Reports from the Fairs of Champagne

192
From the Italian[40]

[Siena], July 5, 1260

In the name of the Lord, amen. Reply to the letters from France [brought] by the first messenger of the May fair of Provins, year 1260.

[Dear] Giacomo di Guido Cacciaconti:

Giacomo and Giovanni di [Gregorio, Vincente di Aldobrandino Vincenti?],[41] and the other partners send you greetings. And we are informing you that we have safely received the letters which you sent us by the messenger of the gild merchant from the May fair of Provins of this year. And through these letters we perfectly understand what were your instructions, and we shall get busy on what will be our business here. Therefore we beg you to be on the alert and to make it your concern to work and get busy on what you have to do. And especially we beg you to be careful in investing and in lending what you have in your hands and what you will have in the future to good and reliable payers, so that we can have it back at any time we may need it or we may want it back. And to do this we ask from God our Lord mercy, that He grant you the grace to do it so that honor may come to you personally and that the partnership (*compagnia*) may come out in good standing. Amen.

You ought to know, Giacomo, that we shall write accurately [all] that we have to write, and especially what you will instruct us by your letters, such as your receipts (*auti*), your payments (*renduti*), and the loans you will make. Just as you will instruct us by your letters at each fair, so at each fair shall we write and enter it in our book. The receipts we shall post to your receipts, the payments we shall post to your payments, and the loans we shall write

---

[40] This letter has been printed in four editions, of which the three more recent supply useful information and background: G. Gargani, *Della lingua volgare in Siena nel secolo XIII*, pp. 50ff.; C. Paoli and E. Piccolomini, *Lettere volgari del secolo XIII scritte da Senesi*, pp. 13–24, 124–34; Sapori, *Studi di storia economica medievale*, pp. 320–25. The letter was written by the partners of a *compagnia* of Sienese merchant-bankers to a partner who was at the fairs of Champagne; it was entrusted to one of the employees of the Mercanzia (the merchant gild of Siena), who shuttled between Siena and France to carry the mail of the gild members. The time was highly dramatic because of the war between Siena and Florence. Two months later (September 4) the Sienese army, with the help of a contingent sent by the king of Sicily and of the Florentine Ghibelline exiles commanded by Farinata degli Uberti (Dante, *Inferno*, Canto x), crushed the Florentine army at Monteaperti.

[41] The original document is torn here; for the restoration of the names, see Paoli and Piccomini, pp. 126–27.

to the loans, just as we have always done up to the present time. Therefore, any money which you collect or which comes into your hands, when you have instructed us once by letter about it, do not repeat it any more; for as soon as you have instructed us about it, we post it at once—whatever you tell us are receipts among the receipts, and we post the payments to the payments, and the loans to the loans. And we do so for every letter. Therefore, if you should instruct us through more than one letter, you see that it would not be a good thing to do; for just as many times as you instruct us, so many times we shall post it in the book in our customary way. Therefore do take care. And we mention this in connection with the £ 3 Provisine, which Testa Tebaldi takes and Tederigo Lei gives. For you received out of them 34 soldi less 4 deniers, and you have sent me instructions about this through several letters. For if we had not remembered that we had posted them once to your receipts, we certainly would have posted them a second time. Therefore take care—do not instruct us about it more than once.

And just as we instructed you in the other letter, so we repeat in this that you must not be astonished that we have sold and are selling Provisines; for you ought to know, Giacomo, that we are under great expense and extremely busy because of the war we are having against Florence. And you ought to know that we have to have money to spend and to make war; on account of this, we see that we cannot raise money from any source more advantageous for us than by selling Provisines. And should you say that we ought to obtain a loan here, it would do us no good: for you ought to know that money costs from 5 to 6 deniers a pound from one merchant to another, and it costs those who are not merchants from 10 to 12 deniers a pound in *corsa*,[42] although it is in the same state. Now you see what [the conditions of] lending are here. Therefore do not feel too badly that we are selling Provisines, since we had rather be in debt in France than be in debt here or sell sterling. For it is worth far more to us so long as we can get Provisines at the price they cost you today than it would be to sell the sterling or to borrow here; because we draw greater interest in England than we would in France, and in order to raise a loan here today we should have to pay a price greater than would be any profit that we could get in France. Therefore be satisfied with what we are doing, and do not be astonished at all about it. And you ought to know, Giacomo, that if in the country of France one could profit more than one can profit there today, we should do well, since you would have a great

---

[42] That is, in dry exchange or exchange with *ricorsa* (see Documents 76 and 77). Note the sharp difference in rates between consumption loans ('to those who are not merchants') and commercial loans ('from one merchant to another').

many Provisines, so that you would well get whatever arrangement you may wish, and we would certainly get our share of whatever profit might be made in that land; and about that be of good cheer.[43]

And we understand from you through your letter that you have gone, both without and with Tolomeo Pelacane, to see the dean of Saint Etienne of Troyes about the business of Lyons-on-the-Rhone, and that you spoke and argued a good deal with the procurator of that archbishop of Lyons-on-the-Rhone, and you could not persuade him to come to any conclusion or agreement that was good for us; nor could you persuade him unless we sent you a letter from the papal Curia against him. In this matter you ought to know that we have had and are still having a great deal of trouble, because of the war and making expeditions and cavalry raids, so that we have not been able to devote our attention to obtaining the letter. Therefore you ought to know that as soon as we have a [breathing] spell to devote our attention to it we shall do so, and we shall see to it that you get the said letter against them.[44]

And we also understand from you through that letter of yours that you and Tolomeo Pelacane had been to see Bonico Maniardi and had told him that you wanted to go to Lyons to learn if you could get any agreement at all from that person, and the said Bonico answered that you could go all right but that he would not pay one bit of the expenses unless Mino Pieri instructed him to do so; for he told you that Mino had not sent a word of instruction about the matter. This astonishes us, for we were in agreement about it here with Mino Pieri, and Mino told us he would instruct him to pay us whatever was his share of our expenses. And in this letter we cannot tell you anything further about it, because Mino Pieri is with the army at Montepulciano while we are writing this letter. Through other letters we shall get in touch with him; and if he has not instructed [Tolomeo] about it, we certainly shall tell him to instruct him, and we shall communicate to you what he will answer us.

And we also understand from you through a note of yours that we are expected to beg Orlando Bonsignore[45] that he should instruct his partners over there that whenever you wish to borrow from his partners they should

---

[43] To understand this paragraph one has to bear in mind that the operations designated as 'selling' deniers Provisine or sterling are contracts of exchange.

[44] Very frequently Italian merchants who were unable to recover their credits on ecclesiastic borrowers demanded and obtained papal letters against them.

[45] One of the two Sienese brothers, sons of Bonsignore (the other brother, Bonifazio, died a few years before this letter was written), whose *Magna Tabula* or 'Great Bank' was, until its failure, probably the greatest organization of merchant bankers in the latter part of the century (see Document 154).

consent to it, for that would be a great boon to us. In this regard we tell you that the said Orlando Bonsignore was not in Siena when this letter was written, but he was with the army at Montepulciano. Therefore, when he returns, we shall get in touch with him and remind him about it; and we definitely believe that he will do what we wish about it.

You ought to know, Giacomo, that I, Vincente, will give 60 [sic] to Madonna Pacina, just as you have instructed me. And Niccolò, son of Messer Nicola, wants us to beg you for his love that if you have not sold for him his Kirkoswald[?] biffa,[46] you get it sold. He would have instructed you about this in a letter if he had not been with the army at Montepulciano; for he went there before the letters were written, and he begged me, Vincente, that I should write you about it in this letter.

And also we let you know that we have sold £ 106 Provisine to Giacomo Ubertini, changer, to be paid at the fair of Saint John,[47] year [12]60; and we sold them at the rate of s.33 a dozen, and we have been paid. Therefore you shall pay them at his order to Rimbotto Buonaiuti at the latter's pleasure; and when you make the payment to him, have a record (scritta) made of it in the book of the Officials of the Merchants, as is customary to do.

And also we have sold £ 24 Provisine to Accorso Guarguaglia and his partnership, to be paid at the said fair of Saint John, at the rate of 31 a dozen, and we have been paid. Therefore you shall pay them to Gregorio Rigoli at his pleasure at that fair; and when you pay them, have a record made of it in the book of the Officials of the Merchants, as is customary to do.

On the other hand, we want to let you know about the developments in Tuscany. For you ought to know, Giacomo, that we are today under great expense and extremely busy because of the war we are having against Florence. And you ought to know that it will take plenty out of our pocket; but we shall lick Florence so [badly] that we shall never have to guard ourselves from her any more, if God protects from evil the lord King Manfred, to whom may God grant long life, amen. . . .[48]

You ought to know, Giacomo, that after this letter was written up to this point we had news that Montepulciano had come to terms and had pledged loyalty to the lord king—King Manfred—and to Siena. And she will make

---

[46] *Chrcivaldo de la biffa.* The *biffa* was a light cloth. *Chrcivaldo* is regarded by Paoli and Picco-omini as a hopeless misspelling. But cf. the spellings of Pegolotti, *Pratica della Mercatura*: Chiricchistallo (Kirkstall), Chiricchistede (Kirksted), Condisgualdo (Cotswold), etc.

[47] The first of the two annual fairs of Troyes in Champagne.

[48] We omit here a long and colorful description of the military and political developments in the war, which makes very good reading but which adds nothing to the understanding of the business situation.

expeditions and cavalry raids against whomever we wish, will hold our friends as friends, and our enemies as enemies. And when that was done, lord Count Giordano left Montepulciano with all the expedition he had and went against Arezzo; and we believe that he will have the town at his will. Well, things up to now have been like this; for the future they will be the same and better, if it please God.

Dispatched Monday, the fifth day of July.

[*Address on the outside*]

To Giacomo di Guido Cacciaconti, and let it not be given to anyone else.

193

From the Italian[49]

Troyes, November 29, 1265

In the name of the Lord, amen. Letter [dispatched] through the first messenger of the fair of Troyes, in the year 1265, written on Sunday, the day before the last of November. To be dispatched the following day.

[Dear] Messer Tolomeo and the other partners:

Andrea sends you greetings. And you ought to know that the Sienese people who are here have dispatched [their letters] through a common messenger after the last fair of Saint-Ayoul, as usual. And so I sent you a bundle of letters through Balza, a carrier from Siena. If you did not receive them, do try to get them. . . .

The messenger of the merchant gild (*merchantia*) has not yet come. May God send him to us with good news—for he has [already] taken too long [in coming]. And when he is here, then I shall see the letters which you send us through him; and I shall be on the alert to get busy as well as I can about what they will advise; may this turn out well for you.

[49] Paoli and Piccolomini, *Lettere volgari*, pp. 49–58. Another letter concerning the same partnership of merchant-bankers, and dispatched from another of the Champagne fairs, is published in the same volume, pp. 25ff. The Tolomei were one of the most important families in Siena; their medieval palace is still one of the landmarks of the town. The present letter was sent through the messenger of the Sienese merchant gild from the first of the two annual fairs of Troyes, that of St. John. It followed another letter dispatched through a mail carrier especially hired by the merchants after the first of the two annual fairs of Provins, that of St. Ayoul. Some of the information sent by Andrea de' Tolomei to his second cousin Tolomeo de' Tolomei and the other partners of the *compagnia* concerns unfinished routine business and could be fully understood only if we were in possession of the entire correspondence. We have omitted it. Much more interesting are the listings of current quotations and the allusions to political events and their presumable economic repercussions. The preparations for the campaign of Charles of Anjou, chosen by the pope to wrest the kingdom of Sicily from King Manfred, are followed with mixed feelings. Manfred is the ally of Ghibelline Siena. On the other hand, the Sienese merchant-bankers have close relations with the pope. Military expenditures bring about fluctuations in the exchange market, from which the Sienese may draw some profit.

Lord Simon, the cardinal,[50] is trying as hard as he can to have the tithe collected which is to be paid for the enterprise of King Charles. And I believe they will collect a large sum between now and the coming Candlemas, and I believe the said king will have a good deal of that [money] sold in order to have money in Rome and in Lombardy. And if this is done, it does seem that [deniers] Provisine ought to fall [in price]. And on the other hand, I believe that the people from this country who are going to assist the said king are now in Lombardy; and they have with them a huge stock of money and [letters of] exchange. And I believe they will spend there a good proportion of it, so that [deniers] Tournois and [letters of] exchange ought to be at a great bargain there, as I have advised you by another letter. And if you see a way to draw profit from this, do try to do it right away.

And people say that many more good men of this country are going to take the cross to go to the assistance of the said king. Whether this is true or not I do not know; may God, who is the Lord, see to it that whatever is done in this matter is best for us and for all Christendom.[51]

Here commodities are selling [so] badly that it would seem impossible to sell any here; and there is plenty of them. And pepper is worth here ... ty-six pounds the load, and it does not sell well. Ginger, from 22 to 28 deniers, depending on quality. Saffron has been much in demand here—and it sells here for s.25 per pound—and there is none [in the market]. Wax of Venice, d.23 per pound. Wax of Tunis, d.21½. The partner of Scotto has a lot of commodities and cannot turn them into cash; and he is negotiating to send them to sell in England.

Sterling, [letter of] exchange, s.59 per mark.[52] Good Freiburg silver, s.57 d.6 per mark. Gold *tarì*, £ 19 s.10 per mark. Gold dust (*paliuola*), depending on quality.[53] *Agostari*, s.11 each.[54] Florins at [the fair of] Saint-Ayoul were worth s.8 each and one denier more, because of the Crusade; but now I do not believe they could sell for more than s.8 less three deniers. Money of Le Mans is worth one fifteenth, that is, 15 [sous] of Le Mans are equivalent to 2 sous Tournois. *Meslée* money, one fifteenth and a half.[55]

---

[50] Simon of Brie (later Pope Martin IV) had been entrusted by Pope Clement IV to collect a special tax on the clergy of France to finance the 'Crusade' of Charles against the excommunicated King Manfred.

[51] *Que 'l miliore sia di noi e di tut ... ta*. We supply *tutta la cristianità*, as Paoli and Piccolomini suggest.

[52] The price quoted is not that of coins but that of silver of the same alloy as sterling deniers.

[53] On *paliuola* or *pagliola*, gold dust of Senegalese origin, see Lopez, *Studi sull'economia genovese nel medio evo*, pp. 35–60, 265–66. See also Document 189.

[54] The *agostari* or *augustali* were gold coins issued by Frederick II in Sicily.

[55] *Meslée* means 'medley'; hence the name was given to various types of debased coins.

If you have not paid £ 10 Sienese petty to the wife of Giacomino del Carnaiuolo, as I advised you from the past fair of Saint-Ayoul, pay them, for they are for the £ 3 Provisine which I received from said Giacomino. And post them to my debit (*scriveteli a mia avuta*) for the past fair of Saint-Ayoul, for I have posted them for the said fair and I forgot to write it in the letter I sent you from the said [fair of] Saint-Ayoul. And if you have delivered to the said wife of Giacomino the *camelin* [cloth] about which I advised you, advise me about it, for [then] I would demand payment of whatever amount you mention; and he [Giacomino] keeps on hoping that she has received that *camelin*. Therefore, if you have not had it delivered as yet, do so, if it is all right with you, and tell me the cost.

[*Address*]

To Messer Tolomeo, son of Ser Giacomo, or to be given to the partners.

The Many Troubles of a Moneylender

194

From the Italian[56]

Beaulieu and Bourges, January 26, 1330

Greetings from Beaulieu. As I have written you by other letters, I am surprised that after you left us here we received no letter except the one which you sent from Nice. And were it not that I definitely think the fault is not yours—it is [the fault], I believe, of those to whom you entrusted the delivery —I should say that you have entirely forgotten us. I am not writing anything more about this, except that you should be careful to whom you entrust [letters], so that they be delivered to us.

I was in Paris the day before yesterday, I wrote you the reason and I shall write it once more here from beginning to end. And then I gave Bonagiunta Dondori[57] two letters to send to you. I believe you should have received them, because he gave me his word that he would entrust them to someone who would certainly deliver them to you.

[56] L. Chiappelli, 'Una lettera mercantile del 1330, e la crisi del commercio italiano nella prima metà del Trecento,' *Archivio Storico Italiano*, ser. 7, I (1924), 249–56. His introduction and footnotes are very valuable for the interpretation of the document. Further bibliography on the general subject in A. L. Funk, 'Confiscation of Lombard Debts in France, 1347–1358,' *Medievalia et Humanistica*, VII (1952), 51–55. The letter was written when the 'Lombards,' that is, the Italian moneylenders, were hit by one of the numerous decrees of confiscation issued by French kings; the ordinance mentioned in it is found in *Ordonnances des Roys de France*, II, 59. It was sent to the home office of the Partini *compagnia* in Pistoia by its partners in Touraine. Most of it was written in Beaulieu, a small abbatial town near Tours; the postscript was written in Bourges. Its Italian is full of Gallicisms.

[57] The Dondori also were merchants and moneylenders from Pistoia.

These are the new developments that have occurred here and are still [in progress]. First [of all], on the Thursday after All Saints' Day [November 8], all the Lombards in the kingdom who are in the profession[58] were arrested, with the exception of those in Touraine. And the latter remained [free] because the *bailli* was in his own country [place], so that, thank God, we had the time to put our business in good order. Later the *bailli* returned and had them arrested—[that is], those whom he could catch—with the exception of the sons of Messer Vinciguerra[59] and their factors, because Vanni[60] procured his own liberation and that of his brothers, [together] with Cancellieri. Us he forgot. Yet Giovanni[61] had been in Tours earlier and had asked Vanni to include him in the bond (*finança*) when paying the fine—and we would have paid whatever was our share. Giovanni and I decided that it would be the best course to let one of us be arrested, and that I should be the one, because he knew the ways of Paris better than I did. I was arrested—courteously—and inventory was made of all our goods; and then I was taken to Tours to the *bailli*. When I was in Tours, the *bailli* wanted 600 florins from me as a pledge that I would present myself in Paris 'by a certain day.'[62] Gianni Cibotto and Gramma d'Oro,[63] who had come to Tours with me to attend to business of their own, put up the pledges. I presented myself in Paris in the presence of the officials—'by the day.'[64] The officials at once had me put in Saint-Martin-des-Champs, and they did the same to all those who presented themselves.

A few days after this, the king [Philip VI] had all of them released under pledges, the one [putting up pledges] for the other; and he issued certain ordinances by which commissioners were to go through every *bailliage* and *sénéchaussée*[65] of the kingdom in order to listen to all who wanted to place complaints against us, and to cause the return of all profits anyone had received from [loans to] the said persons who would place the complaints. And

[58] That is, moneylenders. In time the word became a synonym of 'usurer,' but originally it was used for any merchant of Italian origin who made interest-bearing loans.

[59] Vinciguerra Panciatichi, also from Pistoia.

[60] Vanni or Giovanni Panciatichi, son of Vinciguerra. He later became the leader of one of the two parties that struggled for control of Pistoia. The other party was led by the Cancellieri.

[61] This Giovanni also was a Panciatichi; two persons with the same name are mentioned at the same period in other documents. Chiappelli, whose admirable erudition has led to the identification of most persons mentioned in the letter, makes a *lapsus* when he says that the partner of the writer of the letter—the Giovanni mentioned here and later—is the son of Vinciguerra. The sentence before this makes it clear that Vinciguerra's son was the Vanni mentioned in it.

[62] The writer uses the French words of the injunction, in a somewhat Italianized version: *dedens certana giornata.*

[63] Probably a member of the dell'Oro family of Bologna. Another dell'Oro is mentioned a little further on in the letter.

[64] Again in dubious French: *dedens la giornata.*

[65] That is, every province—*bailliages*, under *baillis*, in the north, and *sénéchaussées*, under *seneschals*, in the south.

whoever had extended credit at [a rate of] more than one denier[66] should be subject to forfeit of body and goods at the will of the king. And it should be proclaimed that no one was to pay us, under penalty of body and goods; and that those who owed [money] to us and knew the terms were to disclose them, under the penalty mentioned above. And there are many other articles about which I do not write you fully because that course of action seems to have been abandoned, according to what Vanni has written. And they are following another, about which I am writing to you—and it is this, that one . . .[67] agreed that he must have 80,000 pounds; and we have to give a rebate to all our debtors of one fifth of what they owe us; and we must not extend credits at [a rate of] more than one denier per pound.

Vanni had sent [news] that the king wanted all the Lombards in the king-dom to go to live in Champagne. Now, in the last letter he sent us, he writes us nothing about this. I believe the king was saying this to bend us more to his intention. I pray God that He give us counsel, for we have been and still are in great trouble and conflict, and we have not yet gotten out of it. May God in His compassion free us from this; for the agreement is not yet clear in all details, although Vanni writes that they believe that it has been definitely made.

You ought to know that I have returned to Bartolomeo Dondori[68] the 200 *reali* which were borrowed when you left. Vanni told me that he wants me to pay interest (*merito*) on them throughout the month of August because he kept them [ready] for us from St. Christopher's Day up to the day you took them. We, however, have not yet figured it out; hence, when we figure it out, I shall talk to him about deducting those 4 *reali* from the total of 200;[69] and if I can I shall pay [interest] only from the Kalends of September. Should I see that he does not feel satisfied, I shall do what he wants, so that he may not feel ill-paid by us. At any rate I want you to know what he has in mind.

We have no money here, nor is there anyone who pays us anything, both because the population is poor on account of the total loss of the vintage and because of the prohibition issued [by the king]. [The situation of] our debtors has not been carefully studied because Giovanni went to Paris on

---

[66] One denier per pound a month, or one shilling per pound (5 percent) a year—a much lower rate than those prevailing at the time.

[67] A blot caused by dampness makes the original unreadable at this point.

[68] The son of Bonagiunta Dondori, mentioned earlier in this letter.

[69] Apparently the interest—2 percent a month, or 24 percent a year—was concealed in the figure of the loan. The *reali* were French gold coins. Some French coins also were usually called florins, but the florins mentioned in this letter probably were a money of account pegged to the Florentine florin.

Saturday directly after you had left. And he stayed there up to the vigil of All Saints' Day; and later, as I have written you above, we were arrested on the following Thursday.

As I have written you by other letters, your wine was sold to Jehan de Samson for £ 37. He has not yet fully paid us for it, and [the interest] for the remainder must be figured out with him. If I can help it, none of it will be rebated because he has delayed payment more than he should have.

The two horses were sold for 17 florins. The she-mule was sold in Bourges for fl.10 s.10. Pierrot de Châtillon gave me no more than fl.1 s.15; he told me that through[?] Lancia dell'Oro[70] he would give me as much as he could. I do not want to antagonize him because it is not the [right] moment until contribution is levied upon us and our goods. Then, if I can make him pay by nice words, I shall do it; if not, I certainly shall use the arm of the Church. Should that be of no avail, I shall use the other.[71]

For the present I am sending you no money for the reasons mentioned above; and in regard to this I beg you for God's sake to be willing to consider me excused, since you see that the excuse is good. I am certain that when the contribution is levied upon us, we shall have to pay a great sum of money. Notwithstanding this, as soon as the agreement is made I shall borrow from Bartolomeo Dondori 200 florins and send them to you; and if I can get more I shall send you more. And if in this interval you still need money and if Corrado is willing to be kind enough to lend you some, I would return it to them from here and would pay for it at the rate (*pregio*) at which one borrows here. And he could very well be kind enough to do so, if he wishes, because Vanni sent him a large amount of money after All Saints' Day.

Lapino, son of Cecco del Signore, is here with us and has been [ever] since you left. I told Giovanni that we did not need a factor and that we could easily handle what there was to do, and more if it were necessary. He answered me that it was his intention that Lapino be with us, so that if he wished to leave [at any time] between now and two or three years hence, he would want to have someone remain here in his place; and that I had Ranieri.[72] At last, seeing that I could not do any better, I came to the agreement that so far as I was concerned he would bear nothing else but the expenses. And before coming to this agreement I had spoken about it with Bonagiunta and

---

[70] *Dedens Lancia dell'Oro.* The latter according to Chiappelli was a Bolognese.

[71] Pierrot de Châtillon must have been an ecclesiastic against whom the bankers could invoke the assistance of the Roman Church. It was not uncommon for the pope to excommunicate insolvent or reluctant debtors of Italian moneylenders. The other power that could be used was that of the royal officials—once the agreement between the king and the Lombards had been concluded.

[72] Ranieri Partini, son of Balduccio. Balduccio was the writer of the letter.

Bartolomeo, when we were in Paris, and to them it seemed that what I said was the best [solution]. Nevertheless he wanted [Lapino] to remain, and so he remains. So far as I can see up to the present, he is a good and loyal person. Then, when I spoke to Bonagiunta and to Bartolomeo, I told them that they should indicate politely to Giovanni, in any way that would seem proper to them, that he should not be so hard toward me. They told him this; he at once said that he wanted to leave the partnership, and told Giannotto, son of Messer Vinciguerra, to tell me this.

As I saw the great trouble in which we were, and I saw the great damage that might come to us and to him from this, I spoke to his uncle and to his cousin and showed them that this was his ruin and ours. They had a talk with him, so that matters remained just as they had been before.

His motive for leaving, according to what Vanni told me, was this: that I had complained to his uncle and to his cousin about him. And he made up reasons [such as these]: that I did not trust him and that I had said, 'You are taking the money and leaving me the records.' As a matter of fact, when he went to Paris he had 170 florins, and only 30 florins remained with me; and he came and asked for them, and I gave them to him. Only I told him, 'You are leaving me here without money; neither the records nor the accounts will pay my expenses.' That was all. I do not know whether you knew it. I am telling you that there is no one in the world who can do anything that pleases him. He wants to boss the entire world, and there is no valet nor maid who can put up with him for long. Nevertheless this does not disturb me, and I am looking to the profit which may come to us with the help of God, so that I am indifferent to his bossiness and with the help of God I have hope that my patience will get the better of his shouting and of his bad disposition, so that his conduct will not cause our business to run down. And be confident about it, because I know what benefit and grace have been granted me by God and by you; so that, if it pleases our Lord God, neither the folly of another nor my own folly will make me lose them. I believe that it is in our interest that you act as if you knew nothing at all about it. He told me and Giannotto many times that you have taken away all the furniture from this place, and Giannotto told me the same. I answered both of them that you have taken away what was yours—what you had bought with your own money—and that you had touched nothing that belonged to the business. I am writing you all this with the purpose that you may be informed. And he reproached me about the 20 florins you took away from the business, which we had lent you. I told him that he should take just as much and keep it as long as you had.

In Bourges there is no money, according to what they wrote me, because of these bad conditions. I have not yet gotten around to go there to see; I believe I shall go there now.

[*Postscript*]

After I had written this letter, I decided to go there so that I could better write you the truth, and I am here in Bourges. I have found bad debts.[73] However, so long as one cannot make official prosecutions,[74] one can hardly write the full truth about it. But so far as I can see, I believe we are quite close to the sum I have written to you another time. The horse which was bought in Bourges we have not yet been able to sell except in a way that would bring too great a loss.

The bishop of Noyon has been made archbishop of Bourges; the archbishop of Bourges has been made archbishop of Sens; the archbishop of Sens has been made archbishop of Rouen. So that, thanks be to God, we shall be near to Gaio,[75] and we shall get from him good support and good advice, for we need it. When things have quieted down, we shall then see clearly our position here and in Beaulieu; and then I shall write you from beginning to end how things are and how they are developing.

Give my regards to Monna Lapa, and my greetings to all our friends over there. Giovanni Naldino and all our friends here send you greetings. Basiglia and Cibotto are writing to you. Jeoffroy Raers and his wife, the daughter of the late Giovanni Ribaldo, have died. The prior of Chartreuse and the others have been very kind to us, and they have done great services for us in going and in coming and in guarding our property.

We have done for them what we believed was proper. He told me the day before yesterday that he was surprised that you had not written him after you left. I said that you had written but that [the letters] had not been delivered either to him or to me. I believe it would be well for you to write to him and to the convent to show that you remember them. We are all well. Ranieri is a fine boy.

Done in Bourges, January 26, 1330.

The bearer of these letters is Ranieri, son of Ser Migliore, who has been in Laon[76] with the sons of Messer Vinciguerra.

---

[73] *Male dette*, which Chiappelli on the authority of the Crusca dictionary interprets as 'bad development' or 'bad news.' The frequent use of Gallicisms in this letter, however, leads one to think of French 'males dettes,' bad debts, which fits the context better.

[74] *Sergentare*, from *sergente* (French *sergent*), royal officer entrusted with the enforcement of legal summonses.

[75] Probably Corrado Gai, a merchant of Pistoia.

[76] *Loduno*, which Chiappelli interprets as Laudun, a village in Languedoc. But it is certainly Laon (Latin *Laudunum*.)

[*Address*]

To be given to Gualfredo, son of Messer Dato Partini, in Pistoia, etc.

News from Genoa

195

From the Italian[77]

Genoa, May 23, 1393

In the name of God. On May 23, 1393.

We have written you in these days all that was needed; and the last was on the twenty-first, and in it we told you all that was needed; [we assume] you will have received it and answered it. And then, today, we have three letters of yours, written on the twelfth, fifteenth, and seventeenth, and we answer by this letter what is needed.

And before we tell you anything else, this morning Lorenzo, son of Ser Niccolò, arrived here safely, praise be to God.[78] He looks like a fine lad. We shall give him a good start and treat him as one of our own; and we need say nothing further about it. Neither our people at Pisa nor those at Florence ever told us that he had left from there, and we had no notice from them except from you; and in Pisa he stayed about eight days; and of this, too, they should have informed us.

You will have received the cloth from Pisa, and you and Monna Margherita[79] ought to be very pleased with it. We are awaiting an answer from you to learn how [well] you think we have served you—which we hope we have. We are informed of the arrival of Tieri[80] there, and that in a few days from

---

[77] R. Piattoli, 'Lettere di Piero Benintendi, mercante del Trecento,' *Atti della Società Ligure di Storia Patria*, LX, 1 (1932), 127–31. The letter, written to the home office of the Datini *compagnia* by the head of the semi-autonomous branch of Genoa, Piero Benintendi, is one of thousands preserved in the Datini archives. Letters of this kind were exchanged several times a month, answers being dispatched frequently on the day of reception.

[78] He had been sent to learn the trade in Genoa and had left from Prato on May 2, as we learn from a letter of Datini (*ibid.*, pp. 123ff.). Francesco Datini recommended him to his Genoa agents, adding these words: 'Please teach him because he seems a good boy to me and he will learn willingly. Fellows like him, however, should be watched closely because wisdom and boyhood cannot go together. Therefore, please, teach him everything that is good, so that he may grow into a worthy young man.'

[79] Francesco Datini's wife.

[80] Tieri di Benci, of the Avignon branch. From a document published in E. Bensa, *Francesco di Marco da Prato*, p. 400, we learn that he actually sailed on the ship of the Catalan captain, Steve Miquel, mentioned in the letter. The ship was captured by two galleys from Bonifacio, probably as a consequence of the Genoese-Catalan strife mentioned in the letter; Bonifacio was a Genoese possession in Corsica. Tieri had to pay ransom for himself and his merchandise. Cf. also Bensa, pp. 108, 297ff.

now you will send him away on a journey to Provence. We have told you that the ship of Giovanni Grisolfi is here; he says he will leave on June 4, although we think it will be the middle of June before he leaves. If you think that he [Tieri], the wife of Maestro Naddino, [81] or Priore should sail on that ship, you ought to press them to leave from there as soon as possible, else they will not be able to sail on the ship or on the new *panfano* of Steve Miquel, which is awaited from day to day at Pisa and will return to Provence unless it undertakes the voyage to Catalonia. We shall keep you informed of everything; then you will decide whatever you want to do about it.

We were informed that you have had a test of the woad made. We suppose you had it tested by Niccolò,[82] and you have informed us about results. We have sent to Pisa four sacks of another lot and told them to send two sacks to you; therefore you have this also tested at once and inform us.

You have been told the reason why Luca[83] has not left for Valencia. He will leave as soon as possible. It is very serious that there is no answer as yet from Catalonia about later developments. May God send us the best news, and may the news be peace between the two peoples and likewise among all Christians. Should there be anything new, you will learn it.

In the matter of the papers and other things that are in Savona to be sent to Catalonia, we shall use such means as seem the best to us. We shall send everything by the first ship that leaves. May God keep everything safe. You will learn the later developments in this matter.

Of the wool you have with you, we agree that you should do with it whatever can be done to close it out. Hold it there: it is impossible that it will not receive soon a better offer there.

We are glad you have been informed of what we told you about the lambskins sold out here, ours and those of the people of Pisa. And there is nothing else to add. Everything was done for our and their good.

You received the oranges; we are glad.

We are informed about the little slave girl you say you personally need, and about her features and age, and for what you want her. *We are informed.* We shall see if there is anyone we consider suitable and we shall get her, although at present we are badly supplied here; nevertheless so far as we are able you shall have one.

[81] Naddino from Prato was a physician at the papal court. Priore di Ghino was a merchant from Prato.

[82] Niccolò di Piero Tucciarelli, a relative of Datini and his associate in the dyeing workshop in Prato.

[83] Luca del Sera, the chief collaborator of Datini in Spain.

We sent a letter to Nofri.[84] We heard that he left for Prato a few days ago. About that we have spoken at length in letters of Andrea and our own, and likewise you will be fully informed by him verbally, so that there is nothing further to say about it. As yet the consuls and councillors of the gild (*arte*) have not met to establish what they want him to pay in order to exercise the craft. When they meet, they will do it, and you will know the developments.

From [our] people of Florence you will have been informed of the news that came yesterday from Marseilles, for we told them to inform you because at that time we could not write to you ourselves. As you will have heard from them, the three ships of the corsair of Spain and likewise two Catalan ones were at Marseilles, close to the chain of the harbor, armed and fully ready to defend themselves against anyone. . . .[85]

We have heard later that letters have now arrived from Catalonia. It is said that the Genoese who were in Catalonia have all been seized with their goods. We think that the affair will have a good ending, so that there will be no war. But before a ship goes from here to there or from there to here, we think it will take a long time, because the Catalans will want to see their own people released and what they claim returned, and likewise the Genoese will want their fellow Genoese released; and, as we are telling you, matters will perhaps take a longer time than we should like. When we again receive letters, we shall inform you of what we hear from there and what develops here. These Catalan shipmasters who are here have addressed petitions to the government to have [the other Catalans] released. It is believed that permission will be granted for some ships to leave. If it is granted, Luca will embark; otherwise he will go by land in whatever way he can travel with the most safety. But I should like it much better if he could go by sea on account of safety and also because of the lower cost.

I am informed about the little slave girl you want, and about the age and everything. And it seems to me that for the time being you could not be well served because for a long time none has come from Romania, and at present anyone who has any, keeps them. Despite this I am still trying to find one, and I have others trying so far as possible, so that you may be served. I am telling you what we are doing—but for the time being I have little hope to succeed. Whenever ships come from Romania, they should carry some

<hr/>

[84] Nofri, a Florentine, was a worker in wool. On the objections moved against him by the local craftsmen when he endeavored to get established in Genoa, see another letter in Piattoli, 'Lettere di Piero Benintendi,' p. 142 and note 1.

[85] We omit here a detailed description of these and other developments of sea warfare against pirates.

[slave girls]; but keep in mind that little slave girls are as expensive as the grown ones, and there will be none that does not cost 50 to 60 florins if we want one of any value. If we find one, we shall do our best.

We have nothing further to say in this letter. May God protect you.

[To] Francesco di Marco and Andrea di Bonanno. In Genoa, on the twenty-fourth. And there is no other news.

[*Address*]
Francesco di Marco, in Prato.
[*Annotation on the cover in another hand*]
From Genoa, on May 29, 1393. Answered same day.

News from Bruges

196

From the Italian[86]

Bruges, May 14, 1464

My magnificent and honorable Superior:

After due recommendations, etc., I wrote you last on the fifth of this [month]; then I received yours of the fourteenth past, which I shall answer below.

And first of all I am sending with this letter the final balance (*bilanco saldo*) of this *ragione*[87] with the usual memoranda and accounts, by which you can see the present status of this branch. And I shall take no more time discussing it since I believe I have elucidated everything through this balance. Moreover, as Angiolo[88] happens to be over there [in Florence], he will supplement it

[86] A. Grunzweig, ed., *Correspondance de la filiale de Bruges des Medici*, I, 130–45. The letter is one of the many which were regularly exchanged between the home office of the Medici *compagnia* and its semi-autonomous branches. It was sent by Tommaso Portinari, acting manager of the Bruges branch during the absence of the manager, to Cosimo il Vecchio, head of the *compagnia*. On the background of the letter, see Grunzweig's preface and footnotes. On the relation between the Bruges branch and the home office, see Document 102.

[87] The word *ragione* is used promiscuously in different meanings, two of which are fundamental: (a) accounting; (b) a partnership, a *compagnia*, or a local branch. A third meaning, close to our expression 'fiscal year'—or rather, 'fiscal period,' since it lasted more than a year—stems from a combination of the other two. At determinate intervals every *compagnia* or local branch made a general accounting and was reorganized with a reapportionment of shares and often the inclusion of new partners, the withdrawal of old ones, and changes in the governing board. The reorganized *compagnia* was then called *ragione nuova* (the new partnership, or the new accounting) and the *compagnia* before reorganization was referred to as *ragione vecchia* (old partnership, or old accounting). In our translation we have adopted the expressions 'accounting,' 'branch,' or 'fiscal period,' according as the context seemed to suggest, and we have kept the word *ragione* when the three meanings seemed to be simultaneously present.

[88] Angiolo Tani, the manager of the branch during the *ragione* of 1456–1460 and that of 1460–1465. Tommaso Portinari succeeded him as manager in 1465.

verbally, for he is well informed about everything. You will see how many are the debtors included in the old fiscal period, for we have made a full accounting for all of them except for the account of Bernardo de' Bardi;[89] this we shall add up shortly until it comes to the sum we enter, and then we shall include it in the said account. And you can see how much the new fiscal period is burdened by the old, both because of hopeless debtors and of others whose money will take a long time to collect, as I elucidate by the balance. For I have felt it necessary to give you information on all points.

Our profits, as you will see, are very low this year, and expenditures have been high. To many deposits placed with us I have assigned no interest. Likewise there are a few accounts in which there will be a loss, as I indicate in them. To offset this, I estimate there will be a few [accounts] we are going to collect from the court [of Burgundy]—and let the new year bear the rest of the liabilities. We have made a good start in it and we shall continue in such a way that I hope that, through God's grace, we shall partly recoup the losses of the past. And, besides, we shall make it our care as far as possible to eliminate debtors and to move to a clean slate.

Our foundation rests upon trade, because, as you see, we have a large part of our capital invested [in it]. And therefore we shall have little for exchange operations, and we are forced to exert our ingenuity elsewhere. This, however, in my opinion, does not involve greater risk than one incurs in exchanges today, especially when no risks at sea are run;[90] nor does it bring smaller profits. And [trade operations] are more legal and more honorable. In them we shall so govern ourselves that every day you will have more reason to be content; may God grant us His grace.

About the matter of the old *ragione* of London, I do not think I have anything else to tell you. You will have seen the balance sent to Francesco Sassetti,[91] and how matters stand: that by withdrawing all [their] money from Sicily as well as from Milan, Pisa, and Florence, they will take care of the debt, especially when Simone[92] pays the 700 florins as he promised; and there

---

[89] A member of the same family which in the early fourteenth century controlled the greatest *compagnia* in Florence (see Document 181) but which became bankrupt before the middle of that century. In 1465 Giovanni de' Bardi was made manager of the London branch of the Medici *compagnia*, jointly with Gherardo Canigiani and under the supervision of Tommaso Portinari.

[90] That is, when shipments by sea are insured.

[91] The manager of the Geneva branch and later the trusted advisor of Lorenzo the Magnificent, for whose financial misfortune he was partly responsible. See the excellent article by F. de Roover, 'Francesco Sassetti and the Downfall of the Medici Banking House,' *Bulletin of the Business Historical Society*, XVII (1943), 65–80.

[92] Simone Nori, the manager of the London branch. Other letters of Portinari mention this debt but do not specify its origin. The Bruges branch had some authority over the London branch.

will be no need to make other provisions. You will get their books by the galleys,[93] while [our] people at London retain a list of what remains to be collected. And we shall continuously press the collection; and, should they collect any portion of it, they will remit it to Florence, and we shall inform you of it.

In England they have again adjourned Parliament till St. Michael's Day,[94] and that is why we could do nothing about that matter of Simone; and because of this Lady Hungerford still has to pay what she owes to [our] people in Geneva and to us. About this we must have patience; may God get us out of it soon without loss.[95]

About the business of the alum we spoke at length to you in another [letter], and Angiolo will also supplement it verbally, and therefore I shall not dwell on it any more. As we have said, the buyers have begged us not to press them for the time being to take what we have [in store], because they are well supplied. This does not bother either us or our people at Rome, so long as the present terms remain in force. As for trying to persuade them to include in the agreed transaction 1,000 *cantara* of the alum which is still to arrive—it does not seem wise to me, as I told you, to tell them anything for the present, but to wait until we are closer to the arrival of the ship; and then I have no doubt that I shall persuade them to do what you want, and maybe even more, unless something else occurs. And we shall so conduct the business that we shall deserve praise from you and more gratitude from the people of Rome than they have shown thus far, since they have believed wholly the mere reporting of that Spannocchia[96]—whom, as I am writing them, they would do well to recall from here, because his stay in many respects is bound to be more harmful than anything else.

If you have made any decision in the matter of the nef[97] and if here we ought to do one thing rather than another, we suppose you have said so, and we shall take all measures necessary.

[Our] people of the silk shop[98] should have sent us the accounting for the last cloth they sent us, and they should have adjusted the price in such a way

---

[93] The Florentine galleys of the regular navigation line controlled by the Commune.

[94] September 29; actually, Parliament was adjourned on November 26.

[95] On the unpaid debt of Margaret of Hungerford, see Grunzweig, *Correspondance*, I, 115–16, note 4.

[96] Niccolò Spanocchi, of Siena, had been sent to Bruges by the Apostolic Chamber to promote the sale of the alum of the Tolfa-Ischia cartel under joint control of the pope and the Medici *compagnia*.

[97] A ship which Portinari had suggested to equip for trade with Burgundy via the Catalan ports, and which was to hoist the flag of the duke of Burgundy. See Grunzweig, *Correspondance*, I, 119.

[98] A workshop operated by the Medici in Florence under autonomous management.

that we can continue to do business, and in this way they will not have to incur the risk of extending credit nor any loss of time.[99]

The [Florentine] galleys arrived in Southampton by the first of this month, and they expect they will be finished within the month, and so will the Venetian galleys[100] about that time, because neither these nor the others will load wool. Thus, this time too, we shall have guessed right. We shall advise you of their leaving.

As you can see from the balance, we happen to have some wool in Milan, and presumably we ought to do well on it. And as I told you by my last letter, since no [wool] will go your way by sea, it has come to my mind to send shortly a quantity of it to Milan, with the intention that, if the plague does not cause damage over there,[101] I shall have some forwarded to you, and likewise to the other regions where it is in demand. For there will be little of it anywhere and, in my opinion, we should make good profit from it. And as for expenses, I told you that we have means to send wool your way at the same cost as we would incur with the galleys, or somewhat less. I shall inform you of what we shall do next; may God help us to make the best decision in everything.

The galleys that are being built in Pisa for this lord [the duke of Burgundy],[102] are not to be used in this expedition, as you will have seen, but by him personally whenever he may go. That is why there is no particular hurry to get them. But since Messer Jeoffroy is over there, we have to do about them whatever he wishes; and [presumably] you will have given orders to that effect. . . .[103]

With the Bastard of Burgundy we made an exchange [contract] for 40,000 écus, all of which we have received in cash; and we have ample time to supply [the exchange money], so that although the charge is low, we cannot but make out well.

We have put Tommaso Guidetti in charge of book[keeping], and we shall

[99] An earlier letter (Grunzweig, *Correspondance*, I, 120–21) explains that the Bruges branch wanted to be informed of the prices of the cloth which the Florence shop periodically sent to Bruges, and urged that prices be kept at a lower level, 'for if they want to get all the cream for themselves, nothing would be left for us; and we would rather quit [dealing in that cloth] or try to get a supply through other channels. . . .'

[100] The Venetian state navigation line was older and more powerful than that of Florence.

[101] An epidemic had hit Italy and Provence at that period.

[102] Duke Philip of Burgundy had promised to take part in the Crusade organized by Pope Pius II and had ordered a number of ships to be built for him in Pisa, while others were being prepared in Flanders. Jeoffroy de Thoisy was in charge of the preparations in Pisa. The Bastard of Burgundy was to leave in 1464 with a first contingent from his country; the duke himself was to leave the following year. All plans, however, were brought to nothing by the sudden death of Pius II.

[103] We omit here other details on the preparations for the Crusade.

reorganize our business by freeing me from so much writing. For I need to do this so that I can take better care of other business and also for my own sake, for I could not possibly last much longer at it.

In England one faction has encountered the other and, so far as we know, that of King Edward has had the best. And they say that Sir Ralph Percy died as well as many others of the faction of King Henry, and that the horse of Sir [Robert] de Moleyns was killed under him and that he incurred great danger. . . .[104]

[*Postscript*]

Held over. Last night the duke of Burgundy arrived unexpectedly. He comes to watch the departure of this expedition, which will leave very soon.

In this letter I have nothing further to say. I recommend myself very warmly to you; may God Most High keep you in happiness for a long time.

In Bruges, May 14, 1464.

Your Tommaso Portinari recommends himself to you.

[*Address on the reverse side*]

To the magnificent and noble man, Cosimo de' Medici senior, honorable man, in Florence.

[104] We omit other details on the war in England.

CHAPTER XXIV

MORAL STANDARDS AND PRACTICAL ADVICE

MEDIEVAL MERCHANTS were seldom concerned with abstract economic theory or ethics. They wrote heap upon heap of bills, promissory notes, books of accounting, and other business records besides a small number of manuals of business practice. When they wanted an escape from the daily routine of commerce, they did not philosophize about it but wrote, more often than most persons realize, literary works, or embellished their halls and their private homes. As a consequence, the task of expounding economic doctrines and ideals of the Middle Ages was left mostly to theologians, canonists, or political writers such as St. Thomas Aquinas, St. Antonine of Florence, Nicholas Oresme, and Diomede Carafa. Outstanding though these men were, they were strangers to commerce, and they had a biased approach to the psychology of merchants. Excessive reliance upon their statements has led many modern scholars to draw inaccurate pictures of medieval trade and traders.[1]

Unfortunately, the merchants themselves failed to draw attractive self-portraits. Their rare excursions into the field of generalizations and aphorisms dealing with the ideal behavior for a business man are of no arresting significance. Men who in their own transactions showed the greatest daring and inventiveness became circumspect and orthodox in giving advice to others. They tuned down their passions, their virtues, and their skills to an ideal of golden mediocrity. To be sure, the documents included in this section display a good measure of common sense, orderliness, honesty, patriotism, and piety. But piety is so thoroughly blended with business spirit that a great bank posts its charitable contributions in a special account entitled 'to God.' Patriotism often edges on municipal chauvinism or on supine obedience to whoever happens to be in power. Honesty is marred by mistrust of everybody else. Orderliness borders on pedantry. Common sense without economic theory and a feeling of purpose smacks of flat materialism and abounds in commonplace statements. Yet is it not a characteristic trait of many businessmen, even in our

---

[1] Among the rare works that examine discrepancies between theoretical statements and everyday practice we may list the following: E. Bridrey, *La Théorie de la monnaie au XIVe siècle*; A. Lattes, *Il diritto commerciale nella legislazione statutaria delle città italiane*; B. N. Nelson, 'The Usurer and the Merchant Prince: Italian Businessmen and the Ecclesiastical Law of Restitution,' *Journal of Economic History*, Suppl. VII (1947), 104–22; R. L. Reynolds, 'In Search of a Business Class in Thirteenth-Century Genoa,' *Journal of Economic History*, Suppl. V (1945), 1–19; A. Sapori, 'Il giusto prezzo nella dottrina di San Tommaso e nella pratica del suo tempo,' reprinted in *Studi di storia economica medievale*, 2d ed., pp. 189ff. The list does not aim at exhaustiveness.

own times, that they shy away from heroic or romantic attitudes in order to appear thoroughly reliable, practical, and proper? Few are the books of merchants about merchants, and usually they are not very impressive.[2]

In the Middle Ages the two books which come closest to an apology for merchants by merchants belong to the very beginning and the very end of the Commercial Revolution. One is *The Beauties of Commerce* by our old acquaintance, Abu al-Fadl of Damascus; it was written very probably in the late ninth century.[3] The other— *On Commerce and the Perfect Merchant,* by Benedetto Cotrugli of Ragusa (Dubrovnik)—was written in Naples in the late fifteenth century and bears the trace of alterations made by its sixteenth-century editor.[4] Abu al-Fadl, about whose personality we know very little, was not exclusively a merchant but also a gentleman farmer. Cotrugli, if we may believe his words, turned from 'the sweet activity of learning' to the mercantile profession 'because of necessity.' Both writers are lavish in their praise of the status of merchants, both are prolix and fond of showing off their erudition, and both are at their best when they turn from general panegyric to practical advice on specific business matters.

Apart from these books one may glean a good many significant, wise, and witty statements from memoirs, manuals, poems, books of accounting, and any other records written by merchants. We have collected here a few examples; other interesting hints are contained in some of the documents included in other chapters of this book. We can learn much from them, provided we expect no masterpieces. The masterpiece of the medieval merchant was the medieval town, with its art, its religion, its literature, its atmosphere of free opportunity. The grandeur that was Florence in the time of Giotto and Dante far outshines the words of Dino Compagni, a contemporary of Dante, in praise of the merchants who built that town and made the achievements of Giotto and Dante possible. Yet Dino Compagni was a stimulating historian, a courageous political leader, and a tolerable poet, as well as a merchant of high standing. Though the plain verses which we have translated here preserve no spark of the passion which ignites his chronicle, their quiet realism points out the minimum standard which every merchant, be he ever so humble, was expected to follow. What we may call the Hippocratic Oath of the medieval merchant was not so very different from that of the modern businessman.[5]

The unknown copyist to whom we owe the manuscript of the best medieval manual of business practice—that of Pegolotti—regarded the verses of Dino Compagni as worthy of inclusion at the beginning of the manual, as a reminder that learning the tricks of trade is not enough to make a good merchant. We are satisfied with placing them at the conclusion of our panorama of medieval trade in the Mediterranean world.

<hr/>

[2] See the brilliant, if somewhat paradoxical, introduction of Miriam Beard to her *History of the Business Man.*

[3] See our introduction to Document 3.

[4] See C. P. Kheil, *Benedetto Cotrugli: ein Beitrag zur Geschichte der Buchhaltung*; F. Melis, *Storia della ragioneria*, pp. 604ff.

[5] The only substantial difference is the greater stress on religious duties, including the canonical prohibition of usury. Yet it is worth noting that Dino Compagni does not list these duties among those which are indispensable for a merchant to be worthy; if the merchant observes them 'he will be worthier' but his worth may be great without them.

Rules for Succeeding in Business

197

Abu al-Fadl Ja'far ibn 'Ali al-Dimishqi, *The Beauties of Commerce*[6]

[Damascus(?), late ninth century(?)]

NECESSARY PIECES OF ADVICE FOR MERCHANTS—WITH THE DISPENSATION OF GOD, THE EXALTED AND ALL POWERFUL

If the merchant deals in bulky articles, he must have reliable associates and sufficient assistants to help him with buying, packing, loading, transporting, and selling. For if he has to take care of everything by himself, his mind and body come to grief; moreover the camel drivers, carriers, and boatmen as well as all others whose help he needs in transporting the goods are always eager to steal his property.

The best [solution for] a merchant who is thrown entirely upon his own resources will be to concern himself only with light things which he can handle by himself.

The foundation of all trade in relation to selling and buying consists in buying from a man who does not care for the article or whom need compels to accept the price [offered] and in selling to a man who is eager to acquire the article or who is under necessity to buy. For that is the surest way to fare well with the merchandise bought and to obtain a rich profit.

The merchant must be no more pessimist than optimist, since pessimism induces him to hold back his capital, but optimism induces him to take such risks that he has more to fear than to hope.

And let him also know that disappointment comes easily with too much greed in seeking advantage, and excessive pursuit of gain is the road to loss. The explanation consists in this: that between the purchase of one who has a wild desire to buy and the purchase of another who has a faint desire and who heals his soul of the madness of greed and keeps it free from the slavery of passion, [between these] there is a wide chasm and a great difference. Not otherwise is it in trade. Whoever desires too strongly becomes so blind that he cannot see the right way and loses the right insight, inclines to passion, and strays from the right judgment of reason. The best things are always those which are happy in the present and reach a beautiful ending in the future.

---

[6] We have used the German translation of H. Ritter, 'Ein arabisches Handbuch der Handelswissenschaft,' *Der Islam*, VII (1917), 64–65. For the complete title of Abu al-Fadl's book, see Chap. I, note 30.

And whenever a merchant realizes that a certain branch of trade brings him good fortune, he ought to devote himself to it—with the exception of those enterprises which bring with them obvious dangers and which do not insure him against disappointment, because in that particular branch a man's good fortune is frequently determined by fate. It is told in the tradition of the Prophet that once a man came to him and told him that his way of earning a living was commerce, but that he had no luck in it; he bought no goods that did not become hard to sell or spoil on his hands. Then [the Prophet] said to him, 'Have you ever had profits to your satisfaction on something you have purchased and on which you have taken some risk?' [The man] answered: 'I do not remember that this ever occurred except in the *qard* business.'[7] At that the Prophet said, 'Then throw yourself into the *qard* business.' The man did so and acquired riches and became well-to-do and lived in fine circumstances. When the Prophet learned this, he said, 'Whoever is blessed with fortune in one enterprise should devote himself to it.'

Moreover, the merchant must grant deductions in selling, for this is one of the essential means of the profession by which he earns his daily bread. It consists in this: that a merchant ought to make it definitely clear to himself that out of a profit of a dinar one half goes to deductions, either at the weighing, or at the paying, or as a gift to the middleman, or as rebate if the buyer asks for it. But if the merchant is greedy and thinks, 'I have been too hasty in the bargain so that I contented myself with a profit of one dinar; and had I exerted myself, [the buyer] would have allowed me a profit of one dinar and a quarter, since he was very anxious to buy; therefore the best thing to do now is in the weighing to take over-full measure and through over-weighing to recover the loss, and to exact the currency which I deem best; also I shall give nothing to any broker or middleman'—if he has said that to himself and has acted accordingly, then discord will follow. For a disruptive element thrusts itself between the thoughts of the two; the buyer turns away and [the seller] loses everything. Now the latter would like the former to come back, and he has exchanged the sparrow in the hand for the pigeon on the roof. From the Prophet the saying is transmitted, 'Deductions are profit,' and 'God grants blessings to a man who grants deductions when paying and charging, when buying and selling.' And a popular proverb says, 'The oil sells the cake.'

[7] A branch of business connected with lending, not to be confused with *qirad* or *muqarada*, the Muslim contract resembling the Western *commenda* (see Chap. I, note 31). The story told by Abu al-Fadl is certainly untrue; the Koran condemns interest bearing loans. But it indicates that Muslim merchants like their Christian colleagues, sought for release from religious prohibitions.

198

Abu al-Fadl Ja'far ibn 'Ali al-Dimishqi, *The Beauties of Commerce*[8]

[Damascus(?), late ninth century(?)]

THE CONSERVATION OF WEALTH

To the conservation of wealth five things are essential. First, that you give out no more than you take in; for whenever that happens, then property disappears directly and nothing of it remains. [The story] is told of a man who, possessing a capital of 500 dinars, had a yearly earning of 500 dinars and a yearly expenditure of 500 dinars. Then, one year, he had an expenditure of two dinars more and he had to take this from his capital. Nine years later, because of this, he had become a pauper who had nothing left and indeed he was imprisoned by the kadi on account of unpaid debts. The key to this tale lies in this, that in the first year 2 dinars were lost [to him], in the second 4 dinars, in the third 8, in the fourth 16, in the fifth 32, in the sixth 64, in the seventh 128, in the eighth 256, and in the ninth 512 dinars.

Second, expenditures ought not to be equal to income but must be smaller, so that a surplus may remain for unforeseen emergencies or losses that may occur at sea or, if you are a merchant, for losses incidental to business—such as, for instance, that a commodity does not sell and eventually threatens to spoil so that it must be sold with great loss; or that your grain and the crops of your vineyard and orchard have been struck by some misfortune, and the like. All this does not permit the expenses of another day to be measured by the expenses of one day; but you must take as a standard for reckoning a long period, approximately a year. Evil may follow directly upon good, since receipts which at one time flow in sparingly and are small may at another time within the same period be either smaller or larger. Just so is it with expenditures; they, too, depend upon the change of events. Take this to heart. May God, the Exalted and Almighty, lead you to the good. Amen.

Third, the conservation of wealth requires that you be on your guard against stretching out your hands for things to which you are not adequate and which you cannot keep—as if, for instance, you invest money in a village pasture that you cannot cultivate, or in different estates that you cannot supervise in person and for the management of which you have no suitable

[8] From Ritter's translation, pp. 75–77 (see note 6). The first paragraph of our excerpt seems to anticipate Mr. Micawber's famous dictum: 'Annual income twenty pounds, annual expenditure nineteen nineteen six, result happiness. Annual income twenty pounds, annual expenditure twenty pounds ought and six, result misery.'

help at your disposal; or if you buy so many slaves and cattle that your expenditures outstrip your means. One who does so is like a greedy man who eats what his stomach cannot digest; for an indigestible food not only does not serve to nourish the body but oftentimes involves the elimination of substances the removal of which from the body is harmful. But if he pursues [only] enterprises for which his financial strength is adequate, then he creates the right conditions not to lose any profit, not to mention the capital.

Fourth, you ought not to invest your money in goods of which you can dispose but slowly, that is, in goods for which there is only a small demand because ordinary people do not need them. So it is with precious stones—of which only magnates and princes have need, and which cause you to fear that you may have treated the middlemen with too little consideration or may have not laid out sufficient money for them—and with scientific books, which are bought only by scholars and learned men who usually are poor and, besides, few in number. And this also applies to other goods for which there is little demand.

As for those people whose income consists of a steady salary, such as secretaries and soldiers and whoever [else] belongs to these groups, or such as the mechanics who work with their hands and with their bodies, the right behavior for their profession is persistent, honest, and loyal work. [If they so behave], success is right before them.

Fifth, and last, for the conservation of wealth you must be quick in selling merchandise but slow in selling real estate, even when the gain is small in the former and great in the latter.

199

Benedetto Cotrugli, On Commerce and the Perfect Merchant
From the Italian[9]

[Naples, 1458]

ON THE UNIVERSAL MANNER AND ORDER OF BUSINESS

Inasmuch as all things in the world have been made with a certain order, in like manner they must be managed—and most particularly those which are of the greatest importance, such as the business of merchants, which, as we have said, is ordered for the preservation of the human race. Hence a merchant must manage himself and his merchandise with a certain order tending to his purpose, which is [the attainment of] wealth.

[9] Cotrugli, *Della mercatura et del mercante perfetto*, fol. 25v.–29r. We omit some digressive sentences and some citations from classic and ecclesiastic authorities.

Nonetheless the order must be different according to the different substance and capital which a man happens to have. A very rich man must
manage one way, a rich man another, and a man who has a small capital still
another. This is why some people have knowledge and ability to manage
large sums, others to manage small ones. For those who are rich and have
the management of many weighty matters ought to maintain their intelligence on a high [plane], and to investigate lofty matters in a rational way,
as the saying goes, 'The greater the ship, the greater the labor.' And we
must not undertake great things trusting the advice of sailors or of certain
frivolous men and passers-by. Because a sailor deals with gross things and
has a gross intelligence, when he drinks in a tavern or buys bread in the
[public] square people would believe that he is an important man and that
he brings you valuable advice on wine and bread by saying that whoever
carries it to some place would make out well with it. A moderate merchant,
and especially one who has great things in his care, must not engage in
purchases of grain and wine on the advice of such men. But he must strive
to obtain advice from merchants and to search and probe his own mind,
always remembering that excellent saying of Lactantius. . . .

A great merchant, then, must plan his business and apportion it in a
[certain] order. And he must not keep all money together, but he should
distribute it in various solid businesses. And this method, in my opinion, is
very efficiently followed by the Florentines more than by any other people;
this I say as a generalization, for many others also follow it. That is to say,
[suppose] that I am a great and rich merchant in Florence. I acquire an interest
(*intravengo*) in the Altoviti [partnership], whose management is in Venice,
and I invest 2,000 ducats of my own in that partnership (*compagnia*); and I
draw one fourth of the profit. . . . And I enter into another partnership in
Rome, and invest 1,000 ducats in it; into another in Avignon, and invest
1,000 ducats in it; in a shop of the Art of Silk, 1,000 ducats. And according
to my lot and substance I keep within my own management 6,000 ducats
with which I do business in my own name and in such merchandise as seems
best to me at the moment. And since I have a finger in many places, in solid
and planned [investments], I cannot but make out well, for the one makes up
for the other; whereas if I had all money gathered together I would have
grounds for fear—for I would always have extra money, and I would wish
to catch every bird, and deal with very bad payers; or else, wishing to
embrace [too] much, I would lose [my own] and take a bad fall. But in
this way, if I distribute my own [capital], every partnership has its managers
who are restricted and under orders. And [the managers] do not put out too

much beyond the little capital (*corpo*) that they have, both because they do not always receive a commission and because they do not have too much extra money. Therefore this is a sound, solid, and healthy management for those who are very rich.

Those who have a medium amount of money, such as 4,000 ducats, must manage another way. That is, they must not divide that capital of their own, but keep it solidly tied in one body, except that they may sometimes—yet seldom—make *commenda* contracts of 400 to 500 ducats, and get [them] back, and frequently see the accounting and clear the profits; so that your money may often come back into your hands. And our own people of Ragusa are very skilled in this [kind of] management; I should praise them at leisure in this respect if I did not think that a critic would ascribe this to my love of fatherland. [This happens] both because they employ wares which are quickly [disposed of], such as silver, gold, lead, copper, wax, crimson, leather, and the like, and because of the dexterity of mind which they have —[or rather, which they would have] if they did not blunder. For as they begin to increase their capital they begin to build or to overturn stones in making gardens, vineyards, and in other pursuits outside rather than inside the ground; so that they have made such a great and beautiful show of palaces that it is a wonderful thing to see. To them I shall say with St. Paul, 'I give praise for everything, but I do not give praise for this. . . .'

We shall now speak of those who have little money, up to some 500 ducats. They must get personally busy with said money, and make no *commenda* contracts nor anything else; and [they must] not spread it over several businesses. And they must help the money with personal effort, for if you wish to stand still with so little money you will consume it. For usually the profits which stand still are limited and small; and with little money you cannot save.

Those who do not have anything must strive to engage in any personal exertion without being ashamed of adapting themselves to the circumstances, even as the Tragedian warns when he cries out, 'It is fit to adapt oneself to the circumstance.' One should not be ashamed of being with others and serving—witness the same Seneca: 'Nor do I regard as shameful anything that fortune may command to the unfortunate'—and of making any low and mean exertion, provided it is honest, to enable oneself to begin to have [something]. To be with others we do not regard as mean, indeed we consider it as necessary for a merchant. . . . The experienced Genoese, Florentines, and Venetians are wont to do it today, and our own country also was accustomed to it not long ago, during my early youth. And I saw many gentlemen entrust to their [fellow] citizens their own sons, [to be] trained and placed in some good position, so that from childhood they could learn their art, of which they were much more avid than they are now; wherefore our income has grown and [our] soul has enlarged. I also saw [sons of gentlemen] exert themselves in their profession, not only in the services belonging to their required tasks but even in sweeping the shop; nor were they ashamed. But this custom has been well preserved by the Florentines—both to place [their sons] with others and to engage in any other honest endeavor, mean though it may be.

I have seen great men who, being impoverished, were not ashamed of lending horses to carters, and of engaging in brokerage, innkeeping, and any other business of the kind. And I have seen some of them return rich in a short time, with 10,000 ducats; for the sake of honesty I do not wish to name them or to extol them in praise—I should not wish to make them proud or humiliated in their glory. And it will be noted that usually, when a Genoese is impoverished through some accident of adverse fortune, he becomes a pirate, and [so do] some Catalans; the Florentines [become] brokers or artisans in some craft, and they exert themselves and help themselves with industry. . . .

200

Benedetto Cotrugli, On Commerce and the Perfect Merchant
From the Italian[10]

[Naples, 1458]

ON THE DIGNITY AND OFFICE OF MERCHANTS

The dignity and office of merchants is great and exalted in many respects, and most particularly in four. First, with respect to the common weal. For the advancement of public welfare is a very honorable [purpose], as Cicero states, and one ought [to be willing] even to die [for it]. . . . The advancement, the comfort, and the health of republics to a large extent proceed from merchants; we are always speaking, of course, not of plebeian and vulgar merchants but of the glorious merchant of whom we treat [and who is] lauded in this work of ours. And with respect to mercantile business and activity [we may say] this: Through trade, that ornament and advancement [of republics], sterile countries are provided with food and supplies and also

---

[10] *Ibid.*, fol. 64v.–66v. This chapter is particularly verbose; we have omitted some of the redundant sentences and trimmed a few adjectives.

enjoy many strange things which are imported from places where [other] commodities are lacking. [Merchants] also bring about an abundance of money, jewels, gold, silver, and all kinds of metals. They bring about an abundance of gilds of various crafts. Hence, cities and countries are driven to cultivate the land, to enlarge the herds, and to exploit the incomes and rents. And [merchants] through their activity enable the poor to live; through their initiative in tax farming they promote the activity of administrators; through their exports and imports of merchandise they cause the customs and excises of the lords and republics to expand, and consequently they enlarge the public and common treasury.

Secondly, I exalt the dignity and office of merchants with respect to the useful and honorable management of their private properties and goods. As a matter of fact, a sparing, temperate, solid, and upright merchant increases and augments his wealth. This is why we observe that merchants abound in movable and immovable property, in the wealth of their homes and furniture, in the ornaments and clothing of their families, in the dowering of their sons and daughters, and consequently in the continuous improvement of their condition through intermarriage with ever higher [families]. . . . And quite the reverse happens to those who do not have this glorious initiative. That is why the proverb was popular and commonplace with our elders: Sad is the house which [never] engaged in trade. For [whenever] a farmer or a gentleman lives on his income without supplementing it through commercial initiative, [the income], large though it may be, is worth much less than it would be in the hands of a merchant. . . . If he wants to marry off his daughters, he has to sell real estate and to take bread from his own mouth. As for what is left after the death of a farmer who during his life was unable to enlarge his estate through trade and initiative . . . his goods must be divided among his children according to the share which is going [to each of them]. And if his sons do not end in an almshouse, his grandsons or great-grandsons will, and the house will continue to decline. . . .

Third, the dignity of merchants is to be esteemed and appreciated with respect to association, both private and public. Private [association] means at home, where [the merchant] associates with an honorable family in continuous and virtuous activity. For you have to consider that where silver, gold, money, and other things of similar value are handled, there is no room for rogues, retainers, henchmen of all sorts, partisans, thieves, runaways, and gamblers such as are wont to live at the courts of princes, magnates, and lords. . . . Outside their homes, merchants associate with artisans, gentlemen, lords, princes, and prelates of every rank, all of whom flock [to see] the merchants since they always need them. And very frequently great scholars come to visit merchants in their homes. . . . For no professional [man] understands or has ever understood the monarchies of this world and the states in regard to management of money—upon which all human states depend—as does a good and learned merchant. . . .

We have left for the fourth [place] the dignity of merchants with respect to [good] faith. . . . It is generally said that today [good] faith abides with merchants and men-at-arms. . . . Neither kings nor princes nor any [other] rank of men enjoy as much reputation or credit as a good merchant. Hence, a merchant's [reputation and credit] serve him readily for cash, while those of others do not: and if they [i.e., the credit and reputation of others] are given in payment, they carry a much higher interest [charge than the merchants']. And whereas a simple and plain receipt of a merchant is valid even without witnesses, the rulers and any other people are not believed without an instrument and strong cautions. Hence, and for the reasons [already] given, merchants ought to take pride in their outstanding dignity.

And to proceed according to our design we shall state that in order to maintain this dignity it is necessary for a merchant to remove from himself any undignified ornament both of the soul and of the body. And merchants must not have the fierce manners of husky men-at-arms, nor must they have the soft manners of jesters and comedians, but they must be serious in speaking, in walking, and in all actions, maintaining as much as possible their dignity. . . .

Oath of the Money Changers

201
From the Latin[11]

[Lucca,] 1111

To preserve its memory and to maintain the justice of the court of the Church of St. Martin, we shall write down the oath which was sworn by all [money] changers and dealers in spices of this court, in the time of Bishop Rangerio—so that all men can exchange, sell, and buy with confidence. All changers and dealers in spices swore that from that moment forward they

[11] E. Lazzareschi, 'Fonti d'archivio per lo studio delle corporazioni artigiane di Lucca, *Bollettino Storico Lucchese*, IX (1937), 78. A photograph of this inscription, which can still be read under the porch of the Cathedral of St. Martin in Lucca, is found in F. Carli, *Storia del commercio italiano*, II, 164. The cathedral square was for a long time Lucca's main market place.

would commit no theft nor trick nor falsification within the court of St. Martin nor in those houses in which men are given hospitality. Those who shall wish to dwell here [as dealers] in exchange or spice take this oath. Moreover, there also are [officials] who always guard this court and who see to it that any wrong that may have been done be amended. In the year of the Lord IIII. Let every one coming peruse this inscription, and place trust in it, and fear nothing for himself.

God's Credit Entry

202
From the Italian[12]

[Florence, 1347]

Hereafter we shall write down the properties assigned to the Company of Orsanmichele for the money of the poor, which must be given in behalf of God.

Belonging to Messer Ridolfo:

1 farm (podere) with land and vineyards, situated in the parish of San Lorenzo or San Giorgio in Grignano, locality called 'Alla Casa,' with 5 plots of land. Evaluated at   750 gold florins

1 farm situated in the parish of Santa Maria in Cintoia, locality called 'A Celle di Sopra,' with 9 plots of land. Evaluated at   200 gold florins

1 farm with land, situated in the parish of San Cristoforo in Strada, locality called 'Sabatino.' Evaluated at   160 gold florins

1 farm with houses, situated in the parish of Sant' Ellero in Pitigliolo, locality called 'Alla Corte,' with three plots of land. Evaluated at

350 gold florins

Belonging to Taldo di Valore:

1 farm with a house and a piece of land, situated in Maiano, locality called 'Marmagnole.' Evaluated at   430 gold florins

[12] Sapori, *Studi di storia economica medievale*, pp. 18–19. Charitable contributions of the Bardi company of merchant-bankers were regularly allocated in the books until the company failed. Then the receivers of the estate (*sindachi*) appointed by the Commune of Florence chose the pious Brotherhood of Orsanmichele to take over the credits of the poor. Both in the bookkeeping of the bank and in that of the receivers these credits were designated as an account open to 'the Lord, God' (*messer Domeneddio*), the Lord being regarded as a partner or a depositor who was entitled to a share in the profits or in the liquidation. Ridolfo, Taldo, and Gianni, mentioned in the document, were partners of the Bardi bank.

Belonging to Gianni de' Bardi:

1 farm with house and land, locality called 'Al Poggio.' Evaluated at

400 gold florins

Sum, 2,290 gold florins.

We assign to the captains of the Company of Orsanmichele the aforesaid properties for £ 3,320 s.10 *a fiorini*,[13] [which] we transfer from the debit account [of the properties][14] to the account headed 'We must give in behalf of God,' in the black book of the syndics, fol. 9   2,290 gold florins

Down-to-Earth Advice from Florence

203

Giovanni di Antonio da Uzzano, *The Practice of Commerce*
From the Italian[15]

[Florence, 1442]

The good rule in making exchange [operations] should be as follows: Beware not to find yourself in debt in a certain territory at a time when money can be expected to be high, either because of fairs, or because of ships sailing out, or because of large sales of merchandise, or because of payments which may be due to soldiers, rulers, Communes, or the like, or because of anything [else] of an ordinary or extraordinary nature as a result of which you may hear that money is going to be withdrawn from banks and changers. But you ought to find yourself [well supplied] with money.

And never be eager to remit money where there is dearth, nor to withdraw it from where is abundance. For wherever money is expensive, cash flows in from every place, money is withdrawn from banks, and therefore abundance is bound to come. And where there is great abundance, cash is drawn away, and money is bound to become tight. And in times of great abundance it is more likely that [the rate of interest] will go up one percent than that it will go down one half percent; and in times of dearth in all probability it should go down one percent rather than go up one fourth percent. And therefore

[13] The *lira a fiorino* was a money of account pegged to the florin; see our introductory Note on Coinage.

[14] *Levamo di ragione ove deono dare.* Excerpts from this account also have been published by Sapori, *Studi di storia economica medievale.* pp. 10–15.

[15] *La pratica della mercatura* (Vol. IV of G. F. Pagnini della Ventura, ed., *Della decima e di varie altre gravezze imposte dal Comune di Firenze*), pp. 153–54. We have translated only the most significant passages in a chapter which, like a chapter of the *Libro di mercatantie* included in another section of our book (Document 64), joins some general idea of the cyclical nature of business to practical advice on specific points.

be eager to remit to and not to withdraw from where there is great abundance; but rather withdraw from where there is dearth, and you will be doing better. . . .

Merchandise: the same thing occurs. That is, you ought never to buy in [time of] dearth, for very seldom do you do well with it, and [while] you may do well with it, you [also] may incur great loss from it. And hence, when a commodity is expensive, [barely] touch it with your finger, but when it is underpriced you can let yourself go.

And when I say, 'Do not remit in [time of] dearth,' I am not saying that when there is dearth you should not find yourself [well supplied] with money; but quite the reverse, you ought to have foresight and to be in a position that you [already] have made remittances there, so that you may have [money] at good [price] in the territory where there is dearth and that you [do not][16] have to make remittances in time of dearth. And likewise in regard to merchandise, you ought to have foreseen the dearth and to be in a position that you have bought in time of abundance and that you have [the commodities] later, when they are dear. But do not buy them when they are dear in order to await the abundance. For you must consider that after dearth follows abundance. . . .

Whenever you want money in a certain place or [you transfer it] from one place to another, see to it that you get it there by the fastest way you can— without buying it, [however], at an excessive price—so that you take the least time possible. And often it turns out that you can do it. Let us take the example that you are in Florence and want money in Paris or Bruges. Whereas by letter of exchange from Florence you will have it there in two months, by the way of Venice you will have it there in 40 days. [This is] because one draws from Venice on Bruges at two months' [usance], just as from Florence. Hence by remitting from Venice to Bruges [and from Florence to Venice] you obtain there [in Bruges] in two months money you have to pay [in Venice] in 20 days, and you save these 20 days.[17] And therefore you, [who] are in Florence, have some one in Venice remit money for you to any other place, prices being equal. . . .

---

[16] *E nella carestia avervegli a rimettere*: the addition of a *non* is necessary for the meaning.

[17] In his elliptical way Uzzano suggests that Florentine merchants should not remit money to Bruges directly, but through correspondents in Venice. The correspondents can issue simultaneously letters of exchange on Bruges, at two months' usance, and letters of exchange on Florence, at twenty days' usance. The Florentine merchant will thus have money remitted to Bruges in two months but he will not have to pay before twenty days. Had he remitted directly from Florence, the letter would still have been at two months' usance but he would have had to pay at once.

204

Giovanni Morelli, *Chronicle*
From the Italian[18]

[Florence, 1393]

If you engage in the wool or French-cloth business,[19] do [it] on your own and do not try to grow rich in two days. Manage on your own money and never borrow for profit's sake. Transact your business with trustworthy persons who enjoy good reputation and credit and who have something to show for their name.[20] And if you ever get cheated by them, do not again fall into their clutches. Do not sell your merchandise to persons who may be willing to overpay for it; never be ensnared by greed for [high] prices; always demand flawless records;[21] better go slowly, [but] do go safely.

If you exercise the wool craft (*Arte di Lana*), manage on your own money. Be not eager to send your merchandise abroad unless you have someone to whom it matters as much as to you. If you can do without a partner (*compagno*) do so. If you cannot, get a partner wisely—a good and rich man, and not one higher than you, especially in [social] status or in [connection with] families with overbearing manners.

Do not exercise any trade or business in which you have no experience. Do what you are able to do and beware of everything else, for [otherwise] you would be cheated. And if you want to become experienced in anything, practise it as a child, be in shops (*fondachi*) and in banks with others, go abroad, frequent merchants and merchandise, see with [your own] eyes the places and countries where you have in mind to do business. Try a friend— or rather the man whom you believe to be a friend—a hundred times before you rely upon him a single time, and never rely upon anyone so deeply that he may ruin you. Go cautiously in [placing] your confidence, and do not be gullible,[22] and the more one shows himself loyal to you and wise in words, the less trust him. And do not trust at all one who makes overtures to you in anything. Enjoy listening to tall talkers, braggers, and men lavish of compli-

---

[18] Giovanni Morelli, *Cronica* (Appendix to R. Malespini, *Istoria fiorentina*, pp. 260–61).

[19] That is, in the *arte della lana* or in the *arte di Calimala*, the gilds of cloth manufacturers and of importers and refinishers of French cloth.

[20] *Che del loro si veggia al sole*, literally, 'that something of theirs be visible under the sun.' The expression is still used in idiomatic Italian to indicate persons owning land or houses.

[21] *Iscritte ispecchiate*. Morelli seems to intimate that those who offer too high prices are likely to have crooked intentions and shady records.

[22] *Non t'abbottacciare*. The Italian dictionary of Crusca, quoting this passage, corrects it into *non t'abborracciare*, do not engage in hasty talks. But the dictionary of Tommaseo and Bellini links the word to *botte*, cask, and to the idiom *bere*, to drink, in the sense of swallowing, accepting a lie as if it were the truth. This seems a reasonable suggestion and requires no correction of the text.

ments, and give words [in return] for words; but do not give any credit[23] that may bring harm to you, and do not rely upon them at all. As for Pharisees and hypocrites smiting themselves and covering themselves with the cloak of religion, rely not upon them but sooner [rely] upon a soldier. Have nothing to do with one who has often changed his business, partners, and masters. And with one who gambles, lives in luxury, overdresses, feasts himself, or is a scatterbrain—do not get involved by entrusting your goods or committing your business to him.

If you do business abroad, go often yourself—at least once a year—to see and to settle the accounts. Watch what [kind of] life the man who is abroad in your behalf[24] leads—whether he spends too much. [Make sure] that he extends sound credits, that he does not rush to [start] things or lies down too low[?],[25] that he acts cautiously and never oversteps instructions. Should he cheat you in anything, fire him.

And always behave with wisdom and do not get involved. And never show off your wealth but keep it hidden, and always by words and acts make people believe that you possess one half as much as you have. By following this course you cannot be too badly cheated, neither you nor those who will be left after you.

205

Giovanni Frescobaldi, A Bit of Advice for Those who Cross to England
From the Italian[26]

[Florence, early fourteenth century]

Wear modest colors, be humble, be dull in appearance but in fact be subtle: if the Englishman [tries to] floor you, woe to him!

Flee cares as well as any one who fights you; spend bravely, and do not show yourself mean.[27]

[23] *Credere*, meaning both 'to believe' and 'to lend.' Both meanings are probably implied here.

[24] The *fattore* or another agent or employee.

[25] *Che non s'avventi alle cose nè si metta troppo nel fondo.* The first part of this clause is obviously a warning against rash precipitation; the second may be a warning against the opposite excess—literally it means 'that he does not place himself too much at the bottom'—but it might conceivably be another exhortation to prudence. Inasmuch as *fondo* is sometimes used in the meaning of capital of an enterprise, the sentence might mean 'that he does not draw too much on the capital.'

[26] Sapori, *Studi di storia economica medievale*, p. 642. The 'bit of advice,' in verse, was written by Giovanni Frescobaldi (died 1337), a member of a family of merchant-bankers whose rise and downfall in England is described by Sapori in this work and in 'Italian Companies in England,' *Banca Nazionale del Lavoro Quarterly Review*, no. 15 (October-December 1950). The Frescobaldi were also a family of poets. Bibliography on the many members of the family who wrote poems is found in the article 'Frescobaldi' of the *Enciclopedia Italiana*.

[27] Obviously the poet contrasts bravery on the battlefield, which is not fit for merchants, and bravery in spending, which is more proper to the profession. Yet the Florentines in their own country were fairly good fighters besides being great merchants.

Pay on the day [when payment is due and be] courteous in collecting, showing that need is driving you to the grave. Make no more demands than you are entitled to.

Buy in [good] time if you have good prospects—and do not get involved with people at court. Obey the orders of those who are in authority.

It behooves you to club together with your nation, and see to it that your doors are well bolted early.

206

Paolo di Messer Pace da Certaldo, *The Book of Good Usages*
From the Italian[28]

[Florence, after 1350]

Never engage in any trade that your Commune forbids, for you could not help getting ill fortune from it. And should you once get good fortune from it, you would get ill fortune many times. Cherish the honor and the good and the welfare of your city and of your lord,[29] and to this devote your property and person, and never support any other party but that of your Commune. 'Your Commune' and 'your city' means the one where you live with your family and [have] your property and relatives.

. . . . .

If you have money, do not stand still nor keep it at home dead, for it is better unprofitably to act than unprofitably to stand by. Because if you act, [even] if you gain nothing else, you will not lose your trade contacts. And if you lose nothing of the capital and do not lose your trade contacts, you gain enough.

This above all . . .

207

From the Italian [Genoese dialect][30]

[Genoa, end of the thirteenth century]

If you engage in commerce or [keep] a shop,[31] do not have an unseeing

[28] Paolo di Messer Pace da Certaldo, *Libro di buoni costumi*, ed. by A. Schiaffini, pp. 226–27. While Pace, the father of Paolo, was born in Certaldo, Paolo was born in Florence itself.

[29] *Signore:* not a feudal lord, but the legal or illegal despot of the town, usually of bourgeois or popular extraction. Note that many towns, including Florence, did not have a *signore* at that time.

[30] E. G. Parodi, 'Rime genovesi della fine del secolo XIII e del principio del XIV,' *Archivio Glottologico Italiano*, X (1886–1888), 114–15, verses 77–116. The name of the author is unknown; we know that he was a Genoese patrician, a Guelf, and probably a notary. See F. L. Mannucci, *L'anonimo genovese e la sua raccolta di rime*.

[31] *Se merchantia usi o butega;* that is, 'if you are a merchant or a craftsman.'

mind. Look carefully around you, by night and by day, and weigh your reason[32] well. But be careful of the season, so that you know well when to give and when to take; for the way you buy indicates the way you [will] sell. And when someone comes to your house, open your eyes and watch out. Do not rely upon all [kinds] of people; be wary of the hands![33] Be courteous to everyone, but consider well in what way; while making nice manners and cheerful and pleasant appearance part of yourself, beware, ahead and behind, of men who are too flattering. These, for [all] their sweet tongue, usually have a stinging tail. Much they promise and nothing they give. Nay, always keep this before you, that too great a promise usually turns out to be a small gift. And should you get mixed up with them in commerce or in money [matters], at first they will put up a handsome show for you, but you will lose your feathers in it.

Make your weighing so accurate that you may not be caught [in error],[34] remembering the scales in which you are going to be weighed. Nay, you want always to remember to write down well whatever you do. Do write it at once, so that it may not go out of your mind.[35] Be just and keep measure in giving as well as in receiving. Always follow truth, peace, love, and loyalty. . . .

208

Dino Compagni, *Song on Worthy Conduct*

From the Italian[36]

[Florence, beginning of the fourteenth century]

A merchant wishing that his worth be great

Must always act according as is right;

[32] *Raxon*, which here is probably used in the double meaning of 'reason' and 'business' or 'accounting.'

[33] It is not clear whether 'the hands' are those of the merchant, who is warned to be wary in entrusting or lending his money, or those of the flatterers, who, according to the poem, offer great promises and small gifts.

[34] *Peiso;* but read *preiso. Peiso,* meaning 'weight' or 'weighed,' already occurs in the verse before this; even such a poor rhymester as the anonymous Genoese would hardly have used it again.

[35] This was a favorite idea with the writer, who devoted to the same subject a short poem, 'De tardando ad scribendo facta sua,' where he stated that 'whoever . . . is slow in writing his records cannot live long without damage and error.'

[36] The best edition is that of I. Del Lungo, *Dino Compagni e la sua cronica,* Tome I, Vol. I, p. 389. This stanza is part of a poem, 'Canzone del pregio,' which lists the virtues men in various professions must have in order to deserve poetical and moral praise. Its popularity surpassed that of the whole poem. The stanza alone, without the first verse and with an added title ('What behooves a true and upright merchant'), is included in the only extant manuscript of Pegolotti, *Pratica della Mercatura,* p. 20. Here it appears without the name of the author and with a number of variants. We mention in the footnotes the most significant among them.

And let him be a man of long foresight,
And never fail his promises to keep.

Let him be pleasant,[37] if he can, of looks,
As fits the honor'd calling that he chose;[38]
Open when selling, but when buying close;
Genial in greeting and without complaints.

He will be worthier if he goes to church,
Gives for the love of God, clinches his deals
Without a haggle, and wholly repeals
Usury taking.[39] Further, he must write
Accounts well-kept and free from oversight.[40]

[37] Pegolotti adds: 'and honorable.'

[38] The verse in Pegolotti is as follows: 'according as he attends to the profession or to book-keeping.'

[39] Pegolotti adds: 'and playing dice.'   [40] Pegolotti concludes: 'Amen!'

LIST OF WORKS CITED

Unprinted Sources

ARCHIVIO DI STATO, GENOA

Cartulario dei notai Domenico Durante e Oberto Osbergerio, I, fol. 223v.
Cartulario di Bartolomeo de Fornari, Vol. I, Part 2, fol. 15r.
Cartulario di Gioacchino Nepitella, I, fol. 65v. and 66r.
Cartulario di Guglielmo di San Giorgio, III, fol. 21v.
Cartulario di Leonardo Negrini, II, fol. 169v.
Cartulario di Maestro Salomone, II, fol. 6v.
Cartulario di Simone Vataccio, Vol. III, Part 1, fol. 135r. of the modern numeration
    (old numeration, fol. 125).
Cartulario di Vivaldo de Porta, I, fol. 44r. and v.
Cartulario di Vivaldo di Sarzano, IV, fol. 89v. and 90r.
Notari Ignoti, busta VII, cart. 5.

ARCHIVIO DI STATO, LUCCA

Registro 116, Ser Bartolomeo Buonmesi, Archivio Notarile.

ARCHIVIO DI STATO, MILAN

Notaio Marcolo Golasecca, n. 404; transcribed and translated from a microfilm copy
    in the Yale University Library, n. 2164 roll 1.

ARCHIVIO DI STATO, VENICE

Deliberazioni del Maggior Consiglio, Luna, fol. 17v.
Procuratori di San Marco, Misti, Busta 122.
Senato Misti, XXVIII, fol. 44v.
Troillo Pacheron, Account of Fermo, ledger A (transcribed by Professor F. C.
    Lane).

PUBLIC RECORD OFFICE, LONDON

Chancery Inquisitions Miscellaneous, C 145/77, 23.

Books and Periodicals

Abbaco, Paolo dell'. *See* Dagomari, Paolo.
Abd el-Jalil, J. M. Brève Histoire de la littérature arabe. Paris 1943.

Abu al-Fadl Ja'far ibn'Ali al-Dimishqi. *See* Ritter, H.

Amari, M. I diplomi arabi del R. Archivio Fiorentino. Florence, 1863.

——*See also* Ibn Hawqal.

Amedroz, H., and D. Margoliouth, eds. The Eclipse of the Abbasid Caliphate. 7 vols. Oxford, 1920–1921.

Ashburner, Walter. The Rhodian Sea-Law. Oxford, 1909.

Astuti, G. Origini e svolgimento storico della commenda fino al secolo XIII. Turin, 1933.

——Rendiconti mercantili inediti del cartolare di Giovanni Scriba. Turin, 1933.

Aubenas, R. 'La Famille dans l'ancienne Provence,' *Annales d'Histoire Economique et Sociale*, VIII (1936), 523–41.

Auvray, L., ed. Les Registres de Grégoire IX, Vol. I. Paris, 1896.

Baer, F. Die Juden im christlichen Spanien: Aragonien und Navarra. Berlin, 1929.

Baracchi, A. 'Le carte del mille e del millecento che si conservano nel R. Archivio Notarile di Venezia,' *Archivio Veneto*, VIII (1874), 365–66.

Baratier, E., and F. Reynaud. Histoire du commerce de Marseille, Vol. II. Paris, 1951.

Barbagallo, C. Storia universale: il medioevo. Turin, 1935.

Barbieri, G. Economia e politica nel ducato di Milano. Milan, 1938.

Bardenhewer, L. Der Safranhandel im Mittelalter. Bonn, 1914.

Bautier, R. H. 'Marchands siennois et draps d'outremont aux foires de Champagne,' *Annuaire-Bulletin de la Société de l'Histoire de France* (1945), pp. 87–107.

Beard, Miriam. History of the Business Man. New York, 1938.

Belgrano, L. T., ed. Annali genovesi di Caffaro e de' suoi continuatori dal MXCIX al MCCXCII. Rome, 1890. Fonti per la storia d'Italia, No. 1.

——'Documenti e genealogia dei Pessagno genovesi,' *Atti della Società Ligure di Storia Patria*, XV (1891), 240–380.

——Documenti inediti riguardanti le due crociate di S. Ludovico IX rè di Francia. Genoa, 1859.

——'Prima serie di documenti riguardanti la colonia di Pera,' *Atti della Società Ligure di Storia Patria*, XIII (1877), 98–317.

Bensa, E. Il contratto di assicurazione nel medio evo. Genoa, 1884.

——Francesco di Marco da Prato. Milan, 1928.

——The Early History of Bills of Lading. Genoa, 1925.

Bertolotto, G. 'Nuova serie di documenti sulle relazioni di Genova coll'impero bizantino,' *Atti della Società Ligure di Storia Patria*, XXVIII, 2 (1897), 338–573.

Bertoni, G. Il Duecento. Milan, 1911.

Besta, E. Le obbligazioni nella storia del diritto italiano. Padua, 1937.

——Storia del diritto italiano: diritto publico, Vol. I. Milan, 1941.

——Storia del diritto italiano: le fonti, Vol. I. Milan, 1923.

Billioud, J. 'Le Roi des merciers du comté de Provence aux XIVe et XVe siècles,' *Bulletin Philologique et Historique du Comité des Travaux Historiques et Scientifiques* (1922–1923), pp. 43–73.

Biscaro, G. 'Gli antichi "Navigli" milanesi,' *Archivio Storico Lombardo*, ser. 4, X (1908), 283–326.

Biscaro, G. 'Il banco Filippo Borromei e compagni di Londra,' *Archivio Storico Lombardo*, ser. 4, XIX (1913), 37–126.

———'Gli estimi del Comune di Milano,' *Archivio Storico Lombardo*, LV (1928), 343–495.

Bizzarri, D. Imbreviature notarili. 2 vols. Turin, 1934.

Blancard, L. Documents inédits sur le commerce de Marseille au moyen-âge. 2 vols. Marseilles, 1884–1885.

Bloch, M. 'Economie-nature ou économie-argent: un pseudo-dilemme,' *Annales d'Histoire Sociale*, I (1939), 7–16.

———'Le Problème de l'or au moyen âge,' *Annales d'Histoire Economique et Sociale*, V (1933), 1–34.

Boak, A. E. R., tr. 'The Book of the Prefect,' *Journal of Economic and Business History*, I (1929), 597–619.

Bognetti, G. P. 'I magistri Antelami e la val d'Intelvi,' *Periodico Storico Comense*, new ser., II (1938), 17–54.

———Note per la storia del passaporto e del salvacondotto. Padua, 1933.

Bonaini, F. Statuti inediti della città di Pisa dal XII al XIV secolo. 3 vols. Florence, 1854–1870.

Boncompagni, B., ed. *See* Leonardo Fibonacci.

Bonvesin della Riva [Bonvesino dalla Riva, Fra]. Le meraviglie di Milano. Tr. into Italian by E. Verga, Milan 1922.

———[Bonvicinus de Rippa]. 'De magnalibus urbis Mediolani,' ed. by F. Novati, in *Bullettino dell'Instituto Storico Italiano*, XX (1898), 67–114.

Book of the Prefect, The. *See* Boak, A. E. R.; Nicole, Jules; Freshfield, E. H.

Borel, F. Les Foires de Genève au quinzième siècle. Geneva, 1892.

Borlandi, F. 'Note per la storia della produzione e del commercio di una materia prima: il guado nel medio evo,' in Studi in onore di Gino Luzzatto (Milan, 1950), I, 297–326.

———Per la storia della popolazione della Corsica. Milan, 1943.

———*See also* Libro di mercatantie et usanze de' paesi.

Bosisio, A. Origini del Comune di Milano. Messina, 1933.

Boüard, M. de. 'Problèmes des subsistances dans un état médiéval: le marché et le prix des céréales au royaume angevin de Sicile (1266–1282),' *Annales d'Histoire Economique et Sociale*, X (1938), 483–501.

Bratianu, G. I. Actes des notaires génois de Péra et de Caffa de la fin du treizième siècle (1281–1290). Bucharest, 1927.

———'Les Etudes byzantines d'histoire économique et sociale,' *Byzantion*, XIV, 2 (1939), 497–511.

———Recherches sur le commerce génois dans la Mer Noire au XIIIe siècle. Paris, 1929.

Bréhier, L. Les Institutions de l'Empire Byzantin. Paris, 1949.

Bridrey, E. La Théorie de la monnaie au XIVe siècle. Paris, 1906.

Bromberg, B. 'The Origin of Banking: Religious Finances in Babylonia,' *Journal of Economic History*, II (1942), 77–88.

Brown, Richard. A History of Accounting and Accountants. Edinburgh, 1905.

Brun, R. 'A Fourteenth Century Merchant of Italy,' *Journal of Economic and Business History*, II (1930), 451–66.

——'Notes sur le commerce des objets d'art en France et principalement à Avignon à la fin du XIVe siècle,' *Bibliothèque de l'Ecole des Chartes*, XCV (1934), 327–46.

Byrne, Eugene H. 'Commercial Contracts of the Genoese in the Syrian Trade of the Twelfth Century,' *Quarterly Journal of Economics*, XXXI (1916), 128–70.

——Genoese Shipping in the Twelfth and Thirteenth Centuries. Cambridge, Mass., 1930.

——'Genoese Trade with Syria in the Twelfth Century,' *American Historical Review*, XXV (1920), 191–219.

Ca' da Mosto, Alvise. Le navigazioni atlantiche di Alvise Ca' da Mosto. Ed. by R. Caddeo. 2d. ed. Milan, 1929.

Cambridge Economic History. Vol. I, Cambridge, 1941. Vol. II, Cambridge, 1952.

Capmany y de Montpalau, A. de. Memorias históricas sobre la marina, commercio y artes de la antigua ciudad de Barcelona. 4 vols. in 3. Madrid, 1779–1792.

Carabellese, F. Saggio di storia del commercio delle Puglie. Trani, 1900.

Carli, F. Storia del commercio italiano. Vol. I: Il mercato nell'alto medio evo. Padua, 1934. Vol. II: Il mercato nell'età del Comune. Padua, 1936.

Cassandro, G. I. Le rappresaglie e il fallimento a Venezia nei secoli XIII-XVI. Turin, 1938.

Castro, A. 'Unos aranceles de aduanas del siglo XIII,' *Revista de Filologia Española*, VIII (1921), 1–29, 325–56; IX (1922), 266–76; X (1923), 113–36.

Cave, R. C., and H. H. Coulson. A Source Book for Medieval Economic History. Milwaukee, 1936.

Certaldo, Paolo di Messer Pace da. *See* Paolo di Messer Pace da Certaldo.

Cessi, R. 'Il "Pactum Lotharii" dell' 840,' *Atti del Reale Istituto Veneto di Scienze, Lettere ed Arti*, XCIX, 2 (1939–1940), 1111–49.

Cessi, R., and A. Alberti. La politica mineraria veneziana. Rome, 1924.

Chapin, E. Les Villes des foires de Champagne des origines au début du XIVe siècle. Paris, 1937.

Charanis, P. 'Internal Strife in Byzantium during the Fourteenth Century,' *Byzantion*, XV (1940–1941), 208–30.

Chau Ju-kua. Chu-fan-chi [Chronicle of Various Foreign Lands]. Ed. and tr. by F. Hirth and W. Rockhill. St. Petersburg, 1911.

Chiappelli, L. 'Una lettera mercantile del 1330, e la crisi del commercio italiano nella prima metà del Trecento,' *Archivio Storico Italiano*, ser. 7, I (1924), 229–56.

Chiaudano, M. 'I Rotschild del Duecento: la Gran Tavola di Orlando Bonsignori,' *Bullettino Senese di Storia Patria*, new ser., VI (1935), 103–42.

——Studi e documenti per la storia del diritto commerciale nel secolo XIII. Turin, 1930.

Chiaudano, M., and M. Moresco. Il cartolare di Giovanni Scriba. 2 vols. Turin, 1935.

Chiaudano, M., and R. Morozzo della Rocca, eds. Oberto Scriba de Mercato (1190). Genoa, 1938.

Chroust, A., and H. Proester. Das Handlungsbuch der Holzschuher in Nürnberg von 1304–1307. Erlangen, 1934.

Cioni, M. 'Un fallimento commerciale a Castelfiorentino sulla fine del secolo XIII,' *Miscellanea Storica della Valdelsa*, X (1920), 139–52.

Cipolla, C. M. 'In tema di trasporti medievali,' *Bollettino Storico Pavese*, new ser., V (1944), 21–56.

————Studi di storia della moneta, Vol. I. Pavia, 1948.

Clavel, M. 'La Mévente du vin à Tarascon-sur-Rhône,' *Mémoires de l'Académie de Nîmes*, ser. 7, XXXI (1908), 316–26.

Compagni, Dino. *See* Del Lungo, I.

Cotrugli, Benedetto. Della mercatura et del mercante perfetto. Venice, 1573.

Crivelli, P., tr. *See* Pacioli, Lucas.

Cross, S. H., tr. The Russian Primary Chronicle. Cambridge, Mass., 1930. Harvard Studies and Notes in Philology and Literature, No. 12.

Cusumano, V. Storia dei banchi della Sicilia: i banchi privati. Rome, 1887.

Dagomari, Paolo, of Prato [Paolo dell'Abbaco], Regoluzze. Ed. by A. Zambrini. Bologna, 1857.

Davidsohn, Robert. Forschungen zur älteren Geschichte von Florenz. 4 vols. Berlin, 1896–1908.

Delatte, A. Les Portulans grecs. Liége, 1947.

Delisle, L. 'Mémoire sur les opérations financières des Templiers,' *Mémoires de l'Institut National de France, Académie des Inscriptions et Belles-Lettres*, XXXIII, 2 (1889), 1–246.

Dell'Abbaco, Paolo. *See* Dagomari, Paolo.

Del Lungo, I. Dino Compagni e la sua cronica. 2 tomes in 3 vols. Florence, 1879–1887.

Del Vecchio, A., and E. Casanova. Le rappresaglie nei comuni medievali. Bologna, 1894.

Denholm-Young, N. 'The Merchants of Cahors,' *Medievalia et Humanistica*, IV (1946), 37–44.

De Poerck, G. La Draperie médiévale en Flandre et en Artois, Vol. I. Bruges, 1951.

Desimoni, C. 'Actes passés à Famagouste de 1299 à 1301 par devant le notaire génois Lamberto di Sambuceto,' *Revue de l'Orient Latin*, I (1893), 58–139, 275–312, 321–53.

————'Actes passés en 1271, 1274 et 1279 à L'Aïas [Petite Arménie] et à Beyrouth par devant des notaires génois,' *Archives de l'Orient Latin*, I (1881), 434–534.

Di Tucci, R. *See* Tucci, R. di.

Doehaerd, R. 'Au temps de Charlemagne et des Normands: ce qu'on vendait et comment on le vendait dans le bassin parisien,' *Annales: Economies, Sociétés, Civilisations*, II (1947), 268–80.

————'Chiffres d'assurance à Gênes en 1427–1428,' *Revue Belge de Philologie et d'Histoire*, XXVII (1949), 736–56.

————Les Relations commerciales entre Gênes, la Belgique et l'Outremont d'après les archives notariales génoises aux XIIIe et XIVe siècles. 3 vols. Brussels, 1941.

Dopsch, Alfons. Wirtschaftliche und soziale Grundlagen der europäischen Kulturentwicklung aus der Zeit von Caesar bis auf Karl den Grossen. 2d rev. ed. 2 vols. Vienna, 1923–1924. The English translation, Economic and Social Foundations of European Civilization (London, 1937), is abridged.

Doria, G. Storia d iuna capitale. Naples, 1936.

Dupont, André. Les Cités de la Narbonnaise première depuis les invasions germaniques. Nîmes, 1943.

——Les Relations commerciales entre les cités maritimes du Languedoc et les cités méditerranéennes d'Espagne et d'Italie. Nîmes, 1942.

Ebengreuth, A. Luschin von. *See* Luschin von Ebengreuth, A.

Edler, Florence [Florence Edler de Roover]. Glossary of Medieval Terms of Business: Italian Series. Cambridge, Mass., 1934.

——*See also* Roover, Florence Edler de.

J. E. Eierman, H. G. Krueger, and R. L. Reynolds, eds. Bonvillano (1198). Genoa, 1939.

Eiglier, J. Etude historique sur le droit de marque ou de représailles à Marseille aux XIIIe, XIVe et XVe siècles. Paris, 1888.

Emery, R. W. Heresy and Inquisition in Narbonne. New York, 1941.

Engel, A., and R. Serrure. Traité de numismatique du moyen âge. 3 vols. Paris, 1890–1905.

Evans, Allan. 'Some Coinage Systems of the Fourteenth Century,' *Journal of Economic and Business History*, III (1931), 481–96.

——*See also* Pegolotti.

Evans, Austin P. *See* Farrar, Clarissa P., and Austin P. Evans.

Fagniez, G., ed. Documents relatifs à l'histoire de l'industrie et du commerce en France. 2 vols. Paris, 1898–1900.

Falco, G. 'Appunti di diritto marittimo medievale,' *Il Diritto Marittimo*, XXIX (1927), 123–56.

Fanfani, A. Un mercante del Trecento. Milan, 1935.

Farrar, Clarissa P., and Austin P. Evans. Bibliography of English Translations from Medieval Sources. New York, 1946. Records of Civilization, No. 39.

Ferrari delle Spade, Giannino. 'Registro vaticano di atti bizantini di diritto privato,' *Studi Bizantini e Neoellenici*, IV (1935), 249–67.

Fibonacci, Leonardo. *See* Leonardo Fibonacci.

Fischel, W. J. The Jews in the Economic and Political Life of Mediaeval Islam. London, 1937.

Fiumi, E. 'La demografia fiorentina nelle pagine di Giovanni Villani,' *Archivio Storico Italiano*, CVIII (1950), 78–158.

Forestié, E., ed. Les Livres de comptes des frères Bonis, marchands montalbanais du XIVe siècle. 2 vols. Paris and Auch, 1893.

Franke, H. Geld und Wirtschaft in China unter der Mongolen-Herrschaft. Leipzig, 1949.

Freshfield, E. H. Roman Law in the Later Roman Empire. Cambridge, 1933. Includes English translation of the *Book of the Prefect*.

Frezza, P. 'Actio communi dividundo,' *Rivista Italiana per le Scienze Giuridiche*, new ser., VII (1932), 3–142.

Friedensburg, F. Münzkunde und Geldgeschichte der Einzelstaaten des Mittelalters und der neueren Zeit. Munich, 1926.

Funk, A. L. 'Confiscation of Lombard Debts in France, 1347–1358,' *Medievalia et Humanistica*, VII (1952), 51–55.

Gabrieli, F. Italia Judaica. Rome, 1900.

Ganshof, F. L. 'Notes sur les ports de Provence du VIIIe au Xe siècle,' *Revue Historique*, CLXXXIII (1938), 28–37.

Gargani, G. Della lingua volgare in Siena nel secolo XIII. Siena, 1868.

Gaudefroy-Demombynes, M. Muslim Institutions. London, 1950.

Gauthier, L. Les Lombards dans les Deux-Bourgognes. Paris, 1907.

Gautier, E. F. L'Islamisation de l'Afrique du Nord; les siècles obscurs du Maghreb. Paris, 1927.

Gayangos y Arce, P. de. *See* Maqqari, al-.

Geijsbeek, J. B., tr. *See* Pacioli, Lucas.

Germain, A. Histoire du commerce de Montpellier. 2 vols. Montpellier, 1861.

Glansdorff, M. 'Les Travaux d'André-E. Sayous sur l'histoire économique,' *Revue Economique Internationale*, VI, 2 (1935), 393–412.

Gloria, A. ed. Codice diplomatico padovano dal secolo sesto a tutto l'undecimo. Venice, 1877.

Godinho, V. M. História económica e social da expansão portuguesa, Vol. I. Lisbon, 1947.

Goeje, M. J. de. 'International Handelsverkeer in de Middeleeuwen,' *Verslagen en Mededeelingen der Koninklijke Akademie van Wetenschappen*, Afdeeling Letterkunde, ser. 4, IX (1909), 245–69.

———'Die Istakhri-Balkhi Frage,' *Zeitschrift der Deutschen Morgenländischen Gesellschaft*, XXV (1871), 42–58.

———*See also* Ibn Khurradadhbah.

Goldschmidt, L. Universalgeschichte des Handelsrechts. Stuttgart, 1891.

Gourcy, G. de. La Foire de Beaucaire. Poitiers, 1911.

Gras, N. S. B. Business and Capitalism: an Introduction to Business History. New York, 1939.

———The Early English Customs System. Cambridge, Mass., 1918.

Grierson, Philip. Numismatics and History. London, 1951.

Grunzweig, A. 'Notes sur le fonds du notariat aux archives d'état de Venise,' *Bulletin de l'Institut Historique Belge de Rome*, XIV (1934), 57–95.

Grunzweig, A., ed. Correspondance de la filiale de Bruges des Medici, Vol. I. Brussels, 1931.

Guilhiermoz, P. 'Note sur les poids du moyen âge,' *Bibliothèque de l'Ecole des Chartes*, LXVII (1906), 161–233, 402–50.

———'Remarques diverses sur les poids et mesures du moyen âge,' *Bibliothèque de l'Ecole des Chartes*, LXXX (1919), 5–100.

Guiraud, L. Recherches et conclusions nouvelles sur le prétendu rôle de Jacques Cœur. Paris, 1900.

Hall, M. W., H. C. Krueger, and R. L. Reynolds, eds. Guglielmo Cassinese (1190–1192), Vol. I. Genoa, 1938.

Hall-Cole, M. W., H. C. Krueger, R. G. Reinert, and R. L. Reynolds, eds. Giovanni di Guiberto (1200–1211), Vol. I. Genoa, 1939.

Hammer, W. 'The Concept of the New or Second Rome in the Middle Ages,' *Speculum*, XIX (1944), 50–62.

Hartmann, L. M. Zur Wirtschaftsgeschichte Italiens im frühen Mittelalter. Gotha, 1911.

Hatschek, J. Der Musta'min. Berlin, 1919.

Heckscher, E. F. Mercantilism. 2 vols. London, 1935.

Heffening, W. Das islamische Fremdenrecht bis zu den islamisch-fränkischen Staatsverträgen. Hanover, 1925. Beiträge zum Rechts- und Wirtschaftsleben des islamischen Orients, No. 1.

Heyd, W. Histoire du commerce du Levant au moyen-âge. 2 vols. Leipzig, 1923 (reprint of 1885 edition).

Heynen, R. Zur Entstehung des Kapitalismus in Venedig. Stuttgart, 1905.

Hirth, F., and W. Rockhill, eds. and trs. See Chau Ju-kua.

Holland, L. B. Traffic Ways about France in the Dark Ages. Allentown, 1919.

Hoover, C. 'The Sea Loan in Genoa in the Twelfth Century,' Quarterly Journal of Economics, XL (1925–1926), 495–529.

Houtte, J. van. 'Les Courtiers au moyen-âge,' Revue Historique de Droit Français et Etranger, ser. 4, XV (1936) 105–41.

Hudud al-'Alam: the Regions of the World. Tr. by V. Minorsky. Oxford and London, 1937.

Huici, A., tr. See Ibn Abi Zar' al-Fast.

Huvelin, P. 'L'Histoire du droit commercial,' Revue de Synthèse Historique, VII (1903), 60–85, 328–71; VIII (1904), 198–243.

Ibn Abi Zar' al-Fast, Ali ibn Abd Allah. The Pleasant Garden of Cards and Information about the Kings of the Maghrib and the History of the City of Fez; Spanish tr. by A. Huici, El Cartás; Noticias de los reyes del Mogreb e historia de la ciudad de Fez. Valencia, 1918.

Ibn Giobeir or Ibn Gubayr. See Ibn Jubayr.

Ibn Hawqal, Abu al-Qasim Muhammad. The Book of the Routes and the Kingdoms; Italian tr. by M. Amari, Libro delle vie e dei reami, in Biblioteca arabo-sicula, I (Turin and Rome, 1880), 10–27. French tr. by M. G. de Slane, 'Ibn Haucal, Description de l'Afrique,' Journal Asiatique, ser. 3, XIII (1842), 153–258.

Ibn Jubayr, Abu al-Hasan Muhammad [Ibn Gubayr, Ibn Giobeir]. Journey; Italian tr. by C. Schiaparelli, Viaggio in Ispagna, Sicilia, Siria e Palestina, Arabia, Egitto, compiuto nel secolo XII. Rome, 1906.

Ibn Kurradadhbah, Abu al-Qasim 'Ubayd Allah [Abou'l-Kasim Obaidallah ibn Khordadbeh]. The Book of the Routes and the Kingdoms; French tr. by M. J. de Goeje, Le Livre des routes et des royaumes, in Bibliotheca Geographorum Arabicorum, Vol. VI (Leiden, 1889).

Ibn Qudama. Le Précis de droit. Tr. by H. Laoust. Beyrouth, 1950.

Jacobs, J. Jewish Contributions to Civilization. Philadelphia, 1919.

Jahiz, al- [Amr ibn Bahr of Basra, surnamed al-Jahiz], putative author. The Investigation of Commerce; French tr., 'L'Examen du commerce,' in J. Sauvaget, Historiens arabes (Paris, 1946), pp. 10–12.

Jarrett, Bede. Social Theories of the Middle Ages. London, 1926.

Kerr, Robert. A General History and Collection of Voyages and Travels, Vol. II. Edinburgh, 1811.

Kheil, C. P. Benedetto Cotrugli: ein Beitrag zur Geschichte der Buchhaltung. Vienna, 1906.

Kimble, G. H. T. Geography in the Middle Ages. London, 1938.

Kisch, Guido. The Jews in Medieval Germany. Chicago, 1949.

Klarwill, W. von. The Fugger News-Letters. 2 vols. New York, 1922–1924.

Köhler, E. Einzelhandel im Mittelalter. Stuttgart, 1928.

Kohler, J. Die Commenda im islamitischen Rechte. Würzburg, 1885.

Kretschmer, K. 'Die italienischen Portolane des Mittelalters,' *Veröffentlichungen des Instituts für Meereskunde und des Geographischen Instituts an der Universität Berlin*, Vol. XIII (1909).

Krueger, H. C. 'Post-War Collapse and Rehabilitation in Genoa, 1149–1162,' in Studi in onore di Gino Luzzatto (Milan, 1950), I, 117–28.

Krueger, H. C., and R. L. Reynolds. Lanfranco. 3 vols. Genoa, 1953.

Kulischer, J. Allgemeine Wirtschaftsgeschichte des Mittelalters und der Neuzeit. Vol. I: Das Mittelalter. Munich and Berlin, 1928.

Kuun, Géza, ed. Codex Cumanicus. Budapest, 1880.

Lane, F. C. Andrea Barbarigo, Merchant of Venice. Baltimore, 1944.

——'Family Partnerships and Joint Ventures in the Venetian Republic,' *Journal of Economic History*, Vol. IV (1944).

——Venetian Ships and Shipbuilding of the Renaissance. Baltimore, 1934.

Lattes, A. 'L'assicurazione marittima e la voce "securare" in documenti genovesi del 1191 e 1192,' *Rivista del Diritto Commerciale*, XXV (1927), 64–73.

——Il diritto commerciale nella legislazione statutaria delle città italiane. Milan, 1884.

——Il diritto marittimo privato nelle carte liguri dei secoli XII e XIII. Vatican City, 1939.

——'Di una singolare formula genovese nei contratti di mutuo,' *Rivista del Diritto Commerciale*, XXII (1924), 542–50.

——'Note per la storia del diritto commerciale,' *Rivista del Diritto Commerciale*, XXXIII (1935), 185–92.

——'Sui prestiti in pane per la corsa marittima nelle carte liguri,' *Bollettino Storico-Bibliografico Subalpino*, XXXVIII (1936), 160–62.

Laurent, H. 'Marchands du palais et marchands d'abbayes,' *Revue Historique*, CLXXXIII (1938), 281–97.

Lazzareschi, E. 'Fonti d'archivio per lo studio delle corporazioni artigiane di Lucca,' *Bollettino Storico Lucchese*, IX (1937), 65–81, 141–60.

Le Gentilhomme, P. 'Le Monnayage et la circulation monétaire dans les royaumes barbares en Occident (Ve–VIIIe siècle),' *Revue Numismatique*, ser. 5, VII (1943), 45–112; VIII (1945), 13–64.

Lempereur, L. Les Chevaliers merciers du Rouergue. Rodez, 1928.

Leo VI, Emperor. The Book of the Prefect. *See* Boak, A. E. R.; Nicole, Jules; Freshfield, E. H.

Leonardo Fibonacci. Liber abbaci. Ed. by B. Boncompagni. Rome, 1857.

Lestocquoy, J. 'Le Commerce des œuvres d'art au moyen-âge,' *Annales d'Histoire Sociale*, III (1943), 19–26.

——'The Tenth Century,' *The Economic History Review*, XVII (1947), 1–14.

——Les Villes de Flandre et d'Italie sous le gouvernement des patriciens. Paris, 1952.

Le Strange, G. Baghdad during the Abbasid Caliphate. Oxford, 1900.

Levy, R. A Baghdad Chronicle. Cambridge, 1929.

Libro di mercatantie et usanze de' paesi, El. Ed. by F. Borlandi. Turin, 1936.

Lisini, A. 'Notizie delle miniere della Maremma Toscana e leggi per l'estrazione dei metalli nel medioevo,' Bullettino Senese di Storia Patria, new ser., VI (1935), 185–256.

Liudprandus, bishop of Cremona [Liudprand of Cremona]. Works. Ed. and tr. by F. A. Wright. London, 1930.

Lombard, M. 'L'Or musulman du VIIe au XIe siècle,' Annales: Economies, Sociétés, Civilisations, II (1947), 143–60.

Lombardo, A. Documenti della colonia veneziana di Creta, Vol. I. Turin, 1942.

Lopez, R. S. 'L'attività economica di Genova nel marzo 1253 secondo gli atti notarili del tempo,' Atti della Società Ligure di Storia Patria, LXIV (1935), 163–270.

——— 'Byzantine Law in the Seventh Century and its Reception by the Germans and the Arabs,' Byzantion, XVII (1942–1943), 445–61.

——— 'China Silk in Europe in the Yuan Period,' Journal of the American Oriental Society, LXXII (1952), 72–76.

——— 'Un consilium di giuristi torinesi nel Dugento,' Bollettino Storico-Bibliografico Subalpino, XXXVIII (1936), 143–50.

——— 'Continuità e adattamento nel medio evo: un millennio di storia delle associazioni di monetieri nell'Europa meridionale,' in Studi in onore di Gino Luzzatto (Milan, 1950), II, 74–117.

——— 'Contributo alla storia delle miniere argentifere di Sardegna,' Studi Economico-Giuridici dell' Università di Cagliari, XXIV (1936), 3–18.

——— 'La Crise du besant au Xe siècle et la date du Livre du Préfet,' in Mélanges Henri Grégoire, II (Brussels, 1950), 403–18.

——— Dieci documenti sulla storia della guerra di corsa. Casale Monferrato, 1938.

——— 'The Dollar of the Middle Ages,' Journal of Economic History, XI (1951), 209–34.

——— 'Du marché temporaire à la colonie permanente,' Annales: Economies, Sociétés, Civilisations, IV (1949), 389–405.

——— 'The English and the Manufacturing of Writing Materials in Genoa,' The Economic History Review, X (1940), 132–37.

——— 'European Merchants in the Medieval Indies: the Evidence of Commercial Documents,' Journal of Economic History, III (1943), 164–84.

——— Genova marinara nel Ducento, Benedetto Zaccaria. Messina, 1933.

——— 'Italian Leadership in the Mediaeval Business World,' Journal of Economic History, VIII (1948), 63–68.

——— 'Mohammed and Charlemagne: a Revision', Speculum, XVIII (1943), 14–38.

——— 'I primi passi della colonia genovese in Inghilterra,' Bollettino Ligustico per la Storia e la Cultura Regionale, II (1950), 69–70.

——— 'Le Problème des relations anglo-byzantines du septième au dixième siècle,' Byzantion, XVIII (1946–1948), 139–62.

——— Il ritorno all'oro nell'Occidente duecentesco. Rome, 1953.

——— 'Sensali nel medioevo,' Nuova Rivista Storica, XXII (1938), 108–12.

Lopez, R. S. 'Silk Industry in the Byzantine Empire,' *Speculum*, XX (1945), 1–42.

———'Still Another Renaissance?' *American Historical Review*, LVII (1951), 1–21.

———Studi sull'economia genovese nel medio evo. Turin, 1936.

———'The Unexplored Wealth of the Notarial Archives in Pisa and Lucca,' in Mélanges d'histoire du moyen âge dédiés à la mémoire de Louis Halphen (Paris, 1951), pp. 417–32.

———'La vendita d'una schiava di Malta a Genova nel 1248,' *Archivio Storico di Malta*, VII (1936), 391.

Lunt, W. E. Papal Revenues in the Middle Ages. 2 vols. New York, 1934.

Luschin von Ebengreuth, A. Allgemeine Münzkunde und Geldgeschichte des Mittelalters und der neueren Zeit. 2d ed. Munich, 1926.

Luzzatto, G. 'Les Activités économiques du patriciat vénitien (Xe–XIVe siècles),' *Annales d'Histoire Economique et Sociale*, IX (1937), 25–57.

———(under the pseudonym, G. Padovan). 'Capitale e lavoro nel commercio veneziano dei secoli XI e XII,' *Rivista di Storia Economica*, VI (1941), 1–24.

———'La commenda nella vita economica dei secoli XIII e XIV con particolare riguardo a Venezia,' in Atti del Convegno Internazionale di studi storici del diritto marittimo medioevale in Amalfi (Naples, 1934), pp. 139–64.

———'Piccoli e grandi mercanti nelle città italiane del Rinascimento,' in In onore e ricordo di Giuseppe Prato, saggi di storia e teoria economica (Turin, 1930), pp. 27–49.

———I prestiti della republica di Venezia. Padua, 1929.

———'Sindacati e cartelli nel commercio veneziano nei secoli XIII e XIV,' *Rivista di Storia Economica*, I (1936), 62–66.

———Storia economica d'Italia, Vol. I. Rome, 1949.

———'Sull'attendibilità di alcune statistiche economiche medievali,' *Giornale degli Economisti*, ser. 4, LXIX (1929), 122–34.

McLaughlin, T. D. 'The Teaching of the Canonists on Usury (XII, XIII and XIV Centuries),' *Mediaeval Studies*, I (1939), 81–147; II (1940), 1–22.

Makkari, al-. See Maqqari, al-.

Manfroni, C. 'Le relazioni fra Genova, l'impero bizantino e i Turchi,' *Atti della Società Ligure di Storia Patria*, XXVIII, 3 (1898), 574–858.

———Storia della marina italiana dalle invasioni barbariche al trattato di Ninfeo. Leghorn, 1899.

Manucci, F. L. L'anonimo genovese e la sua raccolta di rime. Genoa, 1904.

Maqqari, al- [al-Makkari]. The History of the Mohammedan Dynasties in Spain. . . . Tr. by P. de Gayangos y Arce. Vol. I. London, 1840.

Marçais, G. Les Arabes en Berberie, du XIe au XIVe siècle. Constantine and Paris, 1913.

Martinori, E. La moneta. Rome, 1915.

Mas Latrie, L. de. 'Nouvelles Preuves de l'histoire de Chypre,' *Bibliothèque de l'Ecole des Chartes*, XXXIV (1873), 47–87.

Masson, P. 'L'Origine des assurances maritimes, spécialement en France et à Marseille,' in Bulletin du Comité des Travaux Historiques et Scientifiques, Sciences Economiques et Sociales, Congrès des sociétés savantes tenu à Paris en 1921 et à Marseille en 1922 (Paris, 1933), pp. 204–18.

Masson, P. ed. Encyclopédie départementale: les Bouches-du-Rhône. 16 vols. in 17. Marseilles, 1913–1937.

Mayer, P. 'Le Livre-journal de Maître Ugo Teralh, notaire et drapier à Forcalquier,' *Notices et Extraits des Manuscrits de la Bibliothèque Nationale*, XXXVI (1899), 129–70.

Mehl, E. Die Weltanschauung des Giovanni Villani. Leipzig, 1927.

Melis, F. Storia della ragioneria. Bologna, 1950.

Mendenhall, Thomas, B. Henning, and A. Foord. Ideas and Institutions in European History. New York, 1948.

Merores, M. Gaeta im frühen Mittelalter. Gotha, 1911.

——'Der venezianische Adel,' *Vierteljahrschrift für Sozial- und Wirtschafts-geschichte*, XIX (1926), 193–237.

Messé, A. Histoire des Juifs d'Avignon. Paris, 1934.

Mez, A. Die Renaissance des Islams. Heidelberg, 1922.

Mickwitz, G. Die Kartellfunktionen der Zünfte und ihre Bedeutung bei der Entstehung des Zunftwesens. Helsinki, 1936.

Miller, William. Trebizond: the Last Greek Empire. London, 1926.

Minorsky, V., tr. *See* Hudud al 'Alam.

Mirot, L. 'Etudes lucquoises,' *Bibliothèque de l'Ecole des Chartes*, LXXXVIII (1927), 50–86; LXXXIX (1928), 299–389; XCI (1930), 100–168.

Mitchell, William. An Essay on the Early History of the Law Merchant. Cambridge, 1904.

Mondaini, G. Moneta, credito e banche attraverso i tempi. 2d ed. Rome, 1942.

Monneret de Villard, U. 'La monetazione nell'Italia barbarica,' *Rivista Italiana di Numismatica*, XXXII (1919), 22–38, 73–112, 125–38; XXXIII (1920), 169–232; XXXIV (1921), 191–218.

Monroe, A. E. Early Economic Thought. Cambridge, Mass., 1924.

Monti, G. M. L'espansione mediterranea del mezzogiorno d'Italia e della Sicilia. Bologna, 1942.

Monumenta Germaniae historica. Diplomata regum et imperatorum Germaniae, I (Hanover, 1879), 226.

——Leges, IV (Hanover, 1868), 196–97.

——Poetae Latini aevi Carolini, I, 2 (Berlin, 1881), 498–500.

——Scriptores, XXX, 2 (Leipzig, 1934), 1450–57.

Mor, C. G. Scritti giuridici preirneriani. 2 vols. Milan, 1935–1938.

Morcaldi, M., M. Schiani, and S. de Stefano, eds. Codex diplomaticus Cavensis. 8 vols. Naples, 1873–1893.

Morelli, Giovanni. Cronica. Appendix to R. Malespini, Istoria fiorentina. Florence, 1718.

Morize, J. 'Aigues-Mortes au XIIIe siècle,' *Annales du Midi*, XXVI (1914), 313–449.

Morozzo della Rocca, R., and A. Lombardo. Documenti del commercio veneziano nei secoli XI–XIII. 2 vols. Turin, 1940.

Motta, E. 'Per la storia dell'Arte dei Fustagni nel secolo XIV,' *Archivio Storico Lombardo*, ser. 2, VII (1890), 140–45.

Mouynès, G., ed. Ville de Narbonne, inventaire des archives communales antérieures à 1790, Annexes de la série AA. Narbonne, 1871.

Nasir-I Khusraw. Sefer Nameh: relation du voyage de Nassiri Khosrau ... Tr. by C. Schefer. Paris, 1881.

Nelson, B. N. The Idea of Usury. Princeton, 1950.

———'The Usurer and the Merchant Prince: Italian Businessmen and the Ecclesiastical Law of Restitution,' *Journal of Economic History*, Suppl. VII (1947), 104–22.

Nicole, Jules, ed. and tr. 'Le Livre du préfet ou L'Edit de l'empereur Léon le Sage sur les corporations de Constantinople,' *Mémoires de l'Institut National Genevois*, XVIII (1893), 1–100.

Noiret, H. Documents inédits pour servir à l'histoire de la domination vénitienne en Crète de 1380 à 1485. Paris, 1892.

Novati, F., ed. *See* Bonvesin della Riva.

Ordonnances des Roys de France, Vol. II. Paris, 1723.

Ostrogorsky, G. Review of C. Zoras's 'Le corporazioni bizantine,' *Byzantinische Zeitschrift*, XXXIII (1933), 389–95.

Ourliac, P. 'Les Villages de la région toulousaine,' *Annales: Economies, Sociétés, Civilisations*, IV (1949), 268–77.

Pachymeres, Georgios. 'Michael Palaeologus,' in Corpus scriptorum historiae Byzantinae, Vol. I. Bonn, 1835.

Pacioli, Lucas. Ancient Double-Entry Bookkeeping: Lucas Pacioli's Treatise, A.D. 1494. Translated by J. B. Geijsbeek. Denver, 1914.

———An Original Translation of the Treatise on Double-Entry Bookkeeping by Frater Lucas Pacioli. Tr. by P. Crivelli. London, 1924.

Padelletti, G. Fontes iuris italici medii aevi. Turin, 1877.

Pagnini della Ventura, G. F., ed. *See* Uzzano, Giovanni di Antonio da.

Paoli, C. 'Mercato, scritta e danaro di Dio,' *Archivio Storico Italiano*, ser. 5, XV (1895), 306ff.

Paoli, C., and E. Piccolomini. Lettere volgari del secolo XIII scritte da Senesi. Bologna, 1871.

Paolo di Messer Pace da Certaldo. Libro di buoni costumi. Ed. by A. Schiaffini. Florence, 1945.

Parodi, E. G. 'Rime genovesi della fine del secolo XIII e del principio del XIV,' *Archivio Glottologico Italiano*, X (1886–1888), 109–40.

Pastine, O. 'Se la più antica carta nautica medioevale sia di autore genovese,' *Bollettino Ligustico per la Storia e la Cultura Regionale*, I (1949), 79–82.

Pegolotti, Francesco di Balduccio [Francesco Balducci Pegolotti]. La pratica della mercatura. Ed. by Allan Evans. Cambridge, Mass., 1936.

Piattoli, R. 'Documenti intorno ai banchieri pistoiesi nel medioevo,' *Bullettino Storico Pistoiese*, XXXV (1933), 55–66, 129–36.

———'Lettere di Piero Benintendi, mercante del Trecento,' *Atti della Società Ligure di Storia Patria*, Vol. LX, No. 1 (1932).

Piquet, Jules. Les Banquiers au moyen âge: les Templiers. Paris, 1939.

Pirenne, H. Economic and Social History of Medieval Europe. London, 1936.

———'L'Instruction des marchands au moyen âge,' *Annales d'Histoire Economique et Sociale*, I (1929), 13–28. Reprinted in H. Pirenne, Histoire économique de l'Occident médiéval (Bruges, 1951), pp. 551–70.

Pirenne, H. Mohammed and Charlemagne. New York, 1939.

Poggi, A. Il contratto di società in diritto romano classico. Turin, 1934.

Port, C. Essai sur l'histoire du commerce maritime de Narbonne. Paris, 1854.

Portal, C. 'Le Livre-journal de Jean Saval, marchand drapier à Carcassonne,' Bulletin Historique et Philologique du Comité des Travaux Historiques et Scientifiques (1901), pp. 440–41.

——Lettres de change et quittances du XIVe siècle. Marseilles, 1901.

Rabinowitz, L. I. Jewish Merchant Adventurers. London, 1948.

Renouard, Y. Les Hommes d'affaires italiens du moyen âge. Paris, 1949.

——Les Relations des papes d'Avignon et des compagnies commerciales et bancaires de 1316 à 1378. Paris, 1941.

Reparaz, G. de. Catalunya a les mars. Barcelona, 1930.

Revelli, P. Cristoforo Colombo e la scuola cartografica genovese. Rome, 1930.

Reynolds, R. L. 'Bankers' Account in Double-Entry in Genoa, 1313 and 1316,' Bollettino Ligustico per la Storia et la Cultura Regionale, III (1951), 33–37.

——'A Business Affair in Genoa in the Year 1200,' in Studi di storia e diritto in onore di Enrico Besta, II (Milan, 1939), 165–81.

——'In Search of a Business Class in Thirteenth-Century Genoa,' Journal of Economic History, Suppl. V (1945), 1–19.

——'The Market for Northern Textiles in Genoa, 1179–1200,' Revue Belge de Philologie et d'Histoire, VIII (1929), 831–51.

——'Merchants of Arras and the Overland Trade with Genoa,' Revue Belge de Philologie et d'Histoire, IX (1930), 495–533.

——'Gli studi americani sulla storia genovese,' Giornale Storico e Letterario della Liguria, ser. 3, XIV (1938), 1–24.

Rezzara, J. Il concordato nella storia, nella dottrina, nella giurisprudenza: studio di diritto commerciale. Turin, 1901.

Richards, G. R. B. Florentine Merchants in the Age of the Medici. Cambridge, Mass., 1932.

Rippa, Bonvicinus de. See Bonvesin della Riva.

Ritter, H., tr. 'Ein arabisches Handbuch der Handelswissenschaft,' Der Islam, Vol. VII (1917); German tr. of Abu al-Fadl Ja'far ibn 'Ali al-Dimishqi, The Book of Knowledge of the Beauties of Commerce and of Cognizance of Good and Bad Merchandise and Falsifications.

Riva, Bonvesino dalla, Fra. See Bonvesin della Riva.

Rocca, P. Pesi e misure antiche di Genova e del Genovesato. Genoa, 1871.

Roerig, F. Mittelalterliche Weltwirtschaft. Jena, 1933.

Romanin, S. Storia documentata di Venezia. 2d ed. 9 vols. Venice, 1912–1921.

Roover, Florence Edler de. 'Early Examples of Marine Insurance,' Journal of Economic History, V (1945), 172–200.

——'Francesco Sassetti and the Downfall of the Medici Banking House,' Bulletin of the Business Historical Society, XVII (1943), 65–80.

——'Partnership Accounts in Twelfth Century Genoa,' Bulletin of the Business Historical Society, XV (1941), 87–92.

——See also Edler, Florence.

Roover, Raymond de. 'Aux origines d'une technique intellectuelle: la formation et l'expansion de la comptabilité à partie double,' *Annales d'Histoire Economique et Sociale*, IX (1937), 171–93, 270–98.

———'Early Accounting Problems of Foreign Exchange,' *The Accounting Review*, XIX (1944), 381–407.

———L'Evolution de la lettre de change. Paris, 1953.

———Gresham on Foreign Exchange. Cambridge, 1949.

———The Medici Bank. New York, 1948.

———Money, Banking and Credit in Mediaeval Bruges. Cambridge, Mass., 1948.

Roscher, W. 'Die Stellung der Juden im Mittelalter,' *Zeitschrift für die Gesamte Staatswissenschaft*, XXXI (1875), 503–26. This article was tr. by S. Grayzel, 'The Status of the Jews in the Middle Ages Considered from the Standpoint of Commercial Policy,' *Historia Judaica*, VI (1944), 13–26.

Rossi-Sabatini, G. L'espansione di Pisa nel Mediterraneo fino alla Meloria. Florence, 1935.

Roth, Cecil. History of the Jews in Italy. Philadelphia, 1946.

Ruddock, A. A. Italian Merchants and Shipping in Southampton, 1270–1600. Southampton, 1951.

Sabbe, E. 'L'Importation des tissus orientaux en Europe occidentale au haut moyen âge,' *Revue Belge de Philologie et d'Histoire*, XIV (1935), 811–48, 1261–88.

Sacerdoti, A. 'Le colleganze nella practica degli affari e nella legislazione veneta,' *Atti del Reale Istituto Veneto di Scienze, Lettere ed Arti*, LIX (1899–1900), 1–45.

Saige, G. Les Juifs du Languedoc. Paris, 1881.

Saint-Blanquat, O. de. 'Comment se sont créées les bastides du sud-ouest de la France,' *Annales: Economies, Sociétés, Civilisations*, IV (1949), 278–89.

Sánchez-Albornoz, C. 'El precio de la vida en el reino astur-leonés hace mil años,' *Logos: Revista de la Facultad de Filosofía y Letras, Universidad de Buenos Aires*, III (1944), 225–64.

Sandri, G. 'I Bevilacqua e il commercio del legname tra la val di Fiemme e Verona nel secolo XIV,' *Archivio Veneto*, ser. 5, XXVI (1940), 170–80.

Santini, P. 'Frammenti di un libro di banchieri fiorentini scritto in volgare nel 1211,' *Giornale Storico della Letteratura Italiana*, X (1887), 161–77.

Sapori, A. 'L'attendibilità di alcune testimonianze cronistiche dell'economia medievale,' *Archivio Storico Italiano*, ser. 7, XII (1929), 19–30. Republished in his Studi di storia economica medievale, 2d ed., pp. 127–35.

———Una compagnia di Calimala ai primi del Trecento. Florence, 1932.

———La crisi delle compagnie dei Bardi e dei Peruzzi. Florence, 1926.

———'Italian Companies in England,' *Banca Nazionale del Lavoro Quarterly Review*, No. 15 (October–December 1950).

———Liber tercius Friscombaldorum. Florence, 1947.

———Il mercante italiano nel medio evo. 2d ed. Florence, [1945?].

———Mercatores. Milan, 1942.

———Studi di storia economica medievale. 2d ed. Florence, 1947.

Sassi, F. 'La guerra in corsa e il diritto di preda secondo il diritto veneziano,' *Rivista di Storia del Diritto Italiano*, II (1929), 99–128, 261–96.

Sauvaget, J. Alep: essai sur le développement d'une grande ville syrienne. Paris, 1941.

————Historiens arabes. Paris, 1946.

Sayous, A. E. 'Un Manuel arabe du parfait commerçant,' *Annales d'Histoire Economique et Sociale*, III (1931), 577–80.

————'L'Activité de deux capitalistes-commerçants marseillais,' *Revue d'Histoire Economique et Sociale*, XVII (1929), 137–55.

————'Les Méthodes commerciales de Barcelone au XIIIe siècle d'après des documents inédits des archives de sa cathédrale,' *Estudis Universitaris Catalans*, XVI (1931), 155–98.

————'Les Transferts de risques, les associations commerciales et la lettre de change à Marseille pendant le XIVe siècle,' *Revue Historique de Droit Français et Etranger*, ser. 4, XIV (1935), 469–94.

————'Les Transformations des méthodes commerciales dans l'Italie médiévale,' *Annales d'Histoire Economique et Sociale*, I (1929), 161–76.

————'Les Travaux des Américains sur le commerce de Gênes aux XIIe et XIIIe siècles,' *Giornale Storico e Letterario della Liguria*, ser. 3, XIII (1937), 81–89.

————'Les Valeurs nominatives et leur trafic à Gênes pendant le XIIIe siècle,' *Giornale Storico e Letterario della Liguria*, ser. 3, IX (1933), 73–84.

Schaube, A. Handelsgeschichte der romanischen Völker des Mittelmeergebiets bis zum Ende der Kreuzzüge. Munich and Berlin, 1906.

Schechter, F. I. The Historical Foundations of the Law Relating to Trademarks. New York, 1925.

Schefer, C., tr. *See* Nasir-I Khusraw.

Schiaffini, A. Testi fiorentini del Dugento e dei primi del Trecento. Florence, 1926.

————*See also* Paolo di Messer Pace da Certaldo.

Schiaparelli, C., ed. Vocabulista in arabico. Florence, 1871.

————*See also* Ibn Jubayr.

Schiaparelli, L. Codice diplomatico longobardo. 2 vols. Rome, 1929–1933.

Schipa, M. Il mezzogiorno d'Italia anteriormente alla monarchia. Bari, 1930.

Schmidt, F. G. A. Handelsgesellschaften in den deutschen Stadtrechtsquellen des Mittelalters. Breslau, 1883.

Schulte A. Geschichte des mittelalterlichen Handels und Verkehrs zwischen Westdeutschland und Italien mit Ausschluss von Venedig. 2 vols. Leipzig, 1900.

Schupfer, F. Il diritto delle obbligazioni in Italia nell'età del Risorgimento, 3 vols. Turin, 1921.

Scialoja, A. Partes navis—loca navis. Rome, 1944.

Senigallia, L. A. 'Il prestito a cambio marittimo medioevale,' in Atti del Convegno Internazionale di studi storici del diritto marittimo medioevale in Amalfi (Naples, 1934), pp. 187–206.

Sieveking, H. 'Studio sulle finanze genovesi nel medioevo e in particolare sulla casa di S. Giorgio,' *Atti della Società Ligure di Storia Patria*, XXXV (1906), 1–393.

Simonsen, D. 'Les Marchands juifs appelés "Radanites",' *Revue des Etudes Juives*, LIV (1907), 141–42.

Simonsfeld, H. Der Fondaco dei Tedeschi in Venedig und die deutsch-venetianischen Handelsbeziehungen. 2 vols. Stuttgart, 1887.

Singer, C. J. The Earliest Chemical Industry. London, 1948.

Slane, M. G. de, tr. See Ibn Hawqal.

Smiciklas, T. Diplomaticki zbornik Kraljevine Hrvatske, Dalmacije i Slavonije, Vol. VI. Zagreb, 1908.

Smith, R. S. The Spanish Guild Merchant. Durham, N. C., 1940.

Solmi, A. L'amministrazione finanziaria del regno italico nell'alto medio evo. Padua, 1932.

Sombart, Werner. Der moderne Kapitalismus, Vol. I. Rev. ed. Munich and Leipzig, 1921.

Sottas, J. Les Messageries maritimes de Venise aux XIVe et XVe siècles. Paris, 1938.

Starr, Joshua. 'Jewish Life in Crete under the Rule of Venice,' Proceedings of the American Academy for Jewish Research, XII (1942), 59–114.

———The Jews in the Byzantine Empire. Athens, 1939.

———Romania: the Jewries of the Levant after the Fourth Crusade. Paris, 1949.

Strieder, J. Studien zur Geschichte kapitalistischer Organisationsformen: Monopole, Kartelle und Aktiengesellschaften im Mittelalter und zu Beginn der Neuzeit. 2d ed. Munich, 1925.

Tarifa zoè noticia dy pexi e mexure di luoghi e tere che s'adovra mercadantia per el mondo. Ed. by the Istituto Superiore di Scienze Economiche e Commerciali di Venezia. Venice, 1925.

Teja, A. Aspetti della vita economica di Zara dal 1289 al 1409. Part I: La pratica bancaria. Zara, 1936.

Terroine, A. 'Etudes sur la bourgeoisie parisienne: Gandoufle d'Arcelles et les compagnies placentines à Paris (fin du XIIe siècle),' Annales d'Histoire Sociale, VII (1945), 54–71.

Thomas, G. M., ed. Diplomatarium Veneto-Levantinum, Vol. I. Venice, 1880. Monumenti storici dalla R. Deputazione Veneta di Storia Patria, No. 5.

Tournafond, A. Les Marchés et foires de Limoges au moyen âge et à la renaissance. Limoges, 1941.

Tozer, H. F. 'Byzantine Satire,' Journal of Hellenic Studies, II (1881), 244–45.

Tramoyeres Blasco, L. 'Letras de cambio valencianas,' Revista de Archivos, Bibliotecas y Museos, IV (1900), 489–96.

Tucci, R. di. Il genovese Antonio Malfante. Bologna, 1935.

———Studi sull'economia genovese del secolo decimosecondo. Turin, 1933.

Tyler, J. T. The Alpine Passes in the Middle Ages. Oxford, 1930.

Usher, A. P. The Early History of Deposit Banking in Mediterranean Europe, Vol. I. Cambridge, Mass., 1943.

Uzzano, Giovanni di Antonio da. La pratica della mercatura scritta da Giovanni di Antonio da Uzzano nel 1442. Lisbon and Lucca, 1766; printed in Florence. This is Vol. IV of G. F. Pagnini della Ventura, ed., Della decima e di varie altre gravezze imposte dal Comune di Firenze, della moneta e della mercatura de' Fiorentini fino al secolo XVI.

Vaillant, P. 'Etude d'histoire urbaine: Grenoble et ses libertés (1226–1349),' Annales de l'Université de Grenoble, new ser., section Lettres-Droit, XII (1935), 123–53; XIV (1937), 87–178.

Valdeavellano, L. G. de. 'El mercado, apuntes para su estudio en León y Castilla durante la edad media,' *Anuario de Historia del Derecho Español*, VIII (1931), 201–405.

Verga, E., tr. *See* Bonvesin della Riva.

Vergano, L. 'Il mercante astigiano nel medio evo,' *Rivista di Storia, Arte, e Archeologia per la Provincia di Alessandria*, XLVII (1938), 305–79.

Verlinden, Charles. 'L'Origine de Sclavus–Esclave,' *Bulletin Ducange: Archivum Latinitatis Medii Aevi* XVII (1942), 97–128.

Vernadsky, G., and M. Karpovich. A History of Russia, Vols. I and II. New Haven, 1943, 1948.

Villani, Giovanni. Cronica di Giovanni Villani. Magheri edition. 8 vols. Florence, 1823.

————Istorie fiorentine di Giovanni Villani. 'Classici Italiani' edition. 8 vols. Milan, 1802–1803.

————Selections from the First Nine Books of the Croniche Fiorentine. Tr. by R. E. Selfe. London, 1896.

Visconti, A. 'Negotiatores de Mediolano,' *Annali della R. Università di Macerata*, V (1929), 117–96.

————'Ricerche sul diritto pubblico milanese nell'alto medio evo,' *Annali della R. Università di Macerata*, III (1928), 101–229; VII (1931), 205–45.

Vitale, V. 'Documenti sul Castello di Bonifacio nel secolo XIII,' *Atti della Società Ligure di Storia Patria*, new ser., LXV (1936), 1–403.

————'Le relazioni commerciali di Genova col regno normanno-svevo,' *Giornale Storico e Letterario della Liguria*, ser. 3, III (1927), 3–29.

————'Vita e commercio nei notai genovesi dei secoli XII e XIII,' *Atti della Società Ligure di Storia Patria*, Vol. LXXII (1949).

————'La vita economica di Bonifacio nel secolo XIII,' in Studi in onore di Gino Luzzatto, I (Milan, 1950), 129–51.

Volpe, G. 'Montieri,' *Vierteljahrschrift für Sozial- und Wirtschaftsgeschichte*, VI (1908), 315–423.

Voltelini, H. von. Die südtiroler Notariats-Imbreviaturen des dreizehnten Jahrhunderts, Part 1. Innsbruck, 1899. Acta Tirolensia: urkundliche Quellen zur Geschichte Tirols, Vol. II.

Werweke, H. van. 'Monnaie de compte et monnaie réelle,' *Revue Belge de Philologie et d'Histoire*, XIII (1934), 123–52.

Wolff, P. 'Une famille du XIIIe siècle au XVIe siècle: les Ysalguier de Toulouse,' *Mélanges d'Histoire Sociale*, I (1942), 35–58.

————'Le Problème des Cahorsins,' *Annales du Midi*, LXII (1950), 229–38.

Wright, F. A., ed. *See* Liudprandus, bishop of Cremona.

Yamey, B. S. 'Scientific Bookkeeping and the Rise of Capitalism,' *Economic History Review*, ser. 2, I (1949), 99ff.

Yule, Henry. Cathay and the Way Thither, Vol. II. London, 1866.

Zakythinos, D. A. 'Crise monétaire et crise économique à Byzance du XIIIe au XVe siècle,' *L'Hellénisme Contemporain*, ser. 2, I (1947), 166–92, 259–77, 386–99, 483–97, 564–91; II (1948), 57–81, 150–67. Also published separately as a volume with the same title (Athens, 1948).

Zambrini, A., ed. *See* Dagomari, Paolo.

Zanoni, L. Gli Umiliati nei loro rapporti con l'eresia, l'industria della lana e i Comuni. Milan, 1911.

Zeno, R. Documenti per la storia del diritto marittimo nei secoli XIII e XIV. Turin, 1936.

————Storia del diritto marittimo italiano nel Mediterraneo. Milan, 1946.

Zerbi, T. Aspetti economico-tecnici del mercato di Milano nel Trecento. Como, 1936.

————Il mastro a partita doppia di una azienda mercantile del Trecento. Como, 1936.

Zimolo, G. C. 'Cremona nella storia della navigazione interna,' in Atti e memorie del III Congresso Storico Lombardo (Milan, 1939), pp. 221–66.

Zurla, P. Di Marco Polo e degli altri viaggiatori veneziani. 2 vols. Venice, 1818.

INDEX

IN THE NORTON LIBRARY

Gosse, Edmund. *Father and Son.* N195

Grantham, Dewey W. *The Democratic South.* N299

Graves, Robert and Alan Hodge. *The Long Week-end: A Social History of Great Britain, 1918-1939.* N217

Green, Fletcher. *Constitutional Development in the South Atlantic States, 1776-1860.* N348

Halperin, S. William. *Germany Tried Democracy.* N280

Hamilton, Edith. *The Echo of Greece.* N231

Hamilton, Edith. *The Greek Way.* N230

Hamilton, Edith. *The Roman Way.* N232

Hamilton, Holman. *Prologue to Conflict.* N345

Hansen, Alvin H. *The Postwar American Economy: Performance and Problems.* N236

Harrod, Roy. *The Dollar.* N191

Haskins, Charles Homer. *The Normans in European History.* N342

Herring, Pendleton. *The Politics of Democracy.* N306

Hill, Christopher. *The Century of Revolution 1603-1714.* N365

Hobsbawm, E. J. *Primitive Rebels.* N328

Holmes, George. *The Later Middle Ages 1272–1485* N363

Huntington, Ellsworth. *The Human Habitat.* N222

Jones, Rufus *The Quakers in the American Colonies* N356

Kendall, Paul Murray (editor). *Richard III: The Great Debate.* N310

Kennan, George. *Realities of American Foreign Policy.* N320

Keynes, John Maynard. *Essays in Biography.* N189

Keynes, John Maynard. *Essays in Persuasion.* N190

Langer, William L. *Our Vichy Gamble* N379

Leach, Douglass E. *Flintlock and Tomahawk: New England in King Philip's War.* N340

Maitland, Frederic William. *Domesday Book and Beyond.* N338

Mason, Alpheus Thomas. *The Supreme Court from Taft to Warren.* N257

Mason, Alpheus Thomas and William M. Beaney. *The Supreme Court in a Free Society.* N352

Mattingly, Harold. *The Man in the Roman Street.* N337

Morgenthau, Hans J. (editor). *The Crossroad Papers.* N284

Neale, J. E. *Elizabeth I and Her Parliaments,* 2 vols. N359a & N359b

Nilsson, Martin P. *A History of Greek Religion.* N287

Nilsson, Martin P. *The Mycenaean Origin of Greek Mythology.* N234

Noggle, Burl. *Teapot Dome: Oil and Politics in the 1920's.* N297

North, Douglass C. *The Economic Growth of the United States 1790-1860.* N346

Ortega y Gasset, José. *Concord and Liberty.* N124

In the Norton Library

Medieval and Early Modern European History Titles in Norton Paperback Editions